Constructing Spanish Womanhood

SUNY series in Gender and Society

Cornelia Butler Flora, Editor

Constructing Spanish Womanhood

Female Identity in Modern Spain

Edited by

Victoria Lorée Enders
and Pamela Beth Radcliff

State University of New York Press

Cover: "Pamplona, San Fermin de 1949."

Published by
State University of New York Press, Albany

Printed in the United States of America

For information, address State University of New York Press,
State University Plaza, Albany, N.Y. 12246

Production by Laurie Searl
Marketing by Fran Keneston

Library of Congress Cataloging-in-Publication Data

Constructing Spanish womanhood : female identity in modern Spain /
Victoria Lorée Enders and Pamela Beth Radcliff, editors
p. cm. — (SUNY series in gender and society)
Includes bibliographical references and index.
ISBN 0–7914–4029–X (alk. paper). — ISBN 0–7914–4030–3 (pbk. : alk. paper)
1. Women—Spain—Identity. 2. Sex role—Spain. 3. Women—Spain—Social conditions. 4. Women—Spain—History—19th century. 5. Women—Spain—History—20th century. I. Enders, Victoria Lorée, 1944– . II. Radcliff, Pamela Beth. III. Series.

HQ1692.C66 1998
305.42'0946—dc21

98–6190
CIP

10 9 8 7 6 5 4 3 2 1

To My Husband
Curtis M. (Kit) Hinsley
who believed

To My Mother
Gladys Mae Radcliff
1931–1997

Contents

Illustrations

Foreword

Spanish women's history has become a burgeoning field of inquiry in Spain since the end of the Franco regime. Gender analysis (which explores the relationship between "masculine/feminine" in all aspects of culture) is also attracting increasing attention. The founding of the Asociación Española de Investigación Histórica de las Mujeres in 1991 and the debut in 1994 of the historical journal, *Arenal* (named after the writer and feminist Concepción Arenal) marked rites of passage for Spanish scholarship by bringing women's history and gender issues into the center of contemporary historiographical concerns. The publication of Mary Nash's landmark study, *Defying Male Civilization: Women in the Spanish Civil War* (1995) made available to English language readers a host of new insights into the recent historical experience of women in Spain, as did her earlier landmark essay, "Two Decades of Women's History in Spain: A Reappraisal,' published in *Writing Women's History: International Perspectives* in 1991.

Apart from these contributions, the new historical scholarship on modern Spain has not been widely disseminated beyond the Spanish-speaking world, and what was available in English was, with only a few exceptions such as the work of Temma Kaplan, due more to the contributions of literary scholars and critics than to historians. In consequence, and until recently, synthetic treatments of European women's history in the English-speaking world have inadvertently neglected (due more to unfamiliarity than ill-will), the important findings of historical research on women and gender in Spain, even as all too few historians outside Spain had embarked on such analyses.

The publication of *Constructing Spanish Womanhood: Female Identity in Modern Spain* assures that such neglect by the English-speaking world will no longer be possible. This is a *wonderful* book, a landmark collection of well-integrated, highly readable scholarly studies by a cross-section of Spanish-based and Anglo-based research scholars, both established and newcomers. Its contents will virtually double the amount of contemporary historical and theoretical scholarship on modern Spanish women and gender issues available in the English language.

This book links the concerns of Spanish women's history to those of women's history elsewhere in Europe and throughout the world. The contributors' articles represent the best of the new historical scholarship. They expand our knowledge of the general field of Spanish history and contribute to the reconfiguring of European history more broadly through inclusion of the Spanish experience.

The editors, Victoria Enders and Pamela Radcliff, are to be congratulated for bringing this book to completion. Their introductions are theoretically sophisticated and eloquently crafted, persuasive and suggestive. They tie empirical inquiries into the history of women in Spain to current feminist theoretical concerns, including debates about identity and agency, and they show how contesting identities also lead to contesting categories and into broad debates about cultural particularism. The book as a whole makes a strong contribution to comparative gender studies; it sparkles with unexpected insights and flashes of recognition. The various articles are harbingers of book-length studies to come, even as their contributions will stimulate new research.

Constructing Spanish Womanhood deserves and will attract a broad audience, encompassing general readers interested in Spain and Europe, as well as students in all areas of modern European history, Iberian studies, and Spanish literature and cultural studies courses. There is no other collection of this range and magnitude currently available in the English-language literature. May it be the harbinger of more such scholarship to come.

KAREN OFFEN

Institute for Research on Women and Gender
Stanford University

Editors' Preface

The need for this volume originated in the dramatic dearth of publications on modern Spanish women and gender topics. For those of us teaching and researching in modern Spanish and European history, the lack of even the most basic information on Spanish women's lives was immensely frustrating. At the same time, however, we also knew that there was a growing interest in gender and women's history among a new generation of Spanish scholars. After an informal survey, we discovered that there was indeed a critical mass of research being done on Spanish women and gender in the modern period, often as a part of larger projects that were not specifically identified as "women's history."

As a result, we felt that the time was ripe to coordinate this research and to propose an anthology that would gather together in one location the work that was being done in isolation by a variety of scholars in different fields. In 1993, Pamela first posed to Victoria the idea to co-edit such an anthology when she was on sabbatical from Northern Arizona University and in residence at the University of California at San Diego. We then sent formal inquiries to elicit specific proposals for original articles, and received an overwhelmingly positive and enthusiastic response. What gratified us even more was that all of the scholars were pursuing similar and related themes that tied into larger debates within women's and gender studies. Over the course of several revisions, we encouraged the authors to read each others' work and to further develop these common themes. Thus, what started out as a "catch-all" solicitation of research on modern Spanish women evolved into a coherent volume of Spanish case studies revolving around the central theme of "constructing Spanish womanhood." While the volume could not be all-inclusive, we hope that it provides both an introduction to Spanish women's experiences and a springboard to further research.

Our biggest debt of gratitude of course goes to our patient authors, who endured several rounds of comments and suggestions as well as the usual delays that ensue in the coordination of such a project. Their encouragement and enthusiasm for the volume has sustained us through the moments when it seemed that it would never come together. Mary Elizabeth Perry and Karen Offen (who meticulously read the manuscript) also offered their support by validating the importance of the project, and we received many helpful suggestions from anonymous readers. We would like to thank Luella Holter and Dan Boone of the Bilby Research Center at Northern Arizona University and Lee Merrick at the University of California at San Diego for their invaluable professional assistance in various stages of developing the manuscript into its final form. Finally, we thank SUNY Press—especially Chris Worden, Priscilla Ross, Jennie Doling and Laurie Searl, and Cornelia Butler Flora as editor of the Gender and Society series—for their enthusiasm and dedication to the project.

General Introduction: Contesting Identities/Contesting Categories

Victoria Lorée Enders and Pamela Beth Radcliff

Constructing Spanish Womanhood: Female Identity in Modern Spain, the first anthology in English on modern Spanish women's history, offers 15 original case studies in the construction of female identities in nineteenth- and twentieth-century Spain.[1] It adds to the ongoing critique of Spain's master historical narrative, which even today remains largely ungendered, while at the same time contributing fresh perspectives, rooted in Spanish evidence, to contemporary international debates about women's history, gender and cultural studies, and feminist theory. At this critical juncture in the study of Spanish women's history, we seek to find a balance between "the drive towards empirical recovery of the lives of women, and the changing and fragmenting possibilities of new explanatory models."[2] Since the relatively new field of Spanish women's history is emerging at a time of profound rethinking of both Spanish history and women's history, these articles, the work of an international group of scholars across a variety of disciplines, are poised to explore the theoretical possibilities of a fluid and flexible moment.

This sense of fluidity is enhanced by a theoretical climate—in our minds beneficial—in which old paradigms are being demolished and new ones are not yet in place. In particular, theorizing about identity has been released from economic or biological essentialism and has embraced the more open concept of social construction. As a social construction, identity is formed in specific historical contexts through a continuous process of contestation.[3] This multivalent and changing nature of identity has excited broad theoretical interest among scholars across disciplines, and we have benefitted from their rethinking of old paradigms.[4] We wholeheartedly concur with Joan W. Scott that the "project of history is not to reify identity but to understand its production as an ongoing process of differentiation, relentless in its repetition, but also . . . subject to redefinition, resistance and change."[5] In that spirit, our project in this collection is to *historicize* the question of Spanish women's identity. Theory itself points us back to the multiple and multivalent experiences of life as the starting point for understanding.[6]

From the work of ethnographers, we also draw a lesson of profound caution towards defining our interpretive framework solely in opposition to other discursive schemas.[7] We are, not surprisingly, unwilling to impose a totalizing explanatory system on new material, to propose new canons to supplant the old. It is our goal to historicize identity by examining the process of production and (re-)definition of identity while remaining theoretically open.[8] We will employ but not reify theory. Accordingly, we seek neither to "present nor represent," but rather to "evoke" women's identities.[9] We use this term to describe our efforts to produce new material without the onerous strictures of a closed interpretive model, which can force unformed knowledge into foreordained categories, usually constructed in binary oppositions. We prefer to rethink—rather than impose—our categories;[10] and in so doing evocation can serve, we hope, as a metaphor for confronting new evidence with open minds. We place this presentation of new historical evidence in what Stephen Tyler (in a different context) calls the "general pattern of cultural dynamics in the late twentieth century . . . ," aiming for more "textured, nuanced, and realistic" studies.[11]

As scholars across the disciplines have been exploring new explanatory models, so women's historians have been reevaluating their frameworks of analysis. Until recently, the dominant model for situating women in the modern period was based on the dichotomy between separate spheres. In applying this approach, scholars have accepted that most women forged their identities within the boundaries of the restricted gender roles defined by the ideological framework of separate spheres. At first, this model relegated the majority of women to the role of passive victim, trapped within the confined space allotted to them. Later, scholars moved beyond this simplistic interpretation to distinguish a "women's culture": the space which women have carved out within significant constraints without challenging them directly.[12] Moving beyond the history of exceptional women who contested the traditional gender system and won, historians of women's culture dignified as historical subjects those women who learned to accommodate to the system. Retrospectively they sought to empower women whose lives were contained in the private sphere, rather than diminish them as victims of male oppression.

While this approach provoked a necessary reevaluation of the categories of agent and victim, it did not question the dualistic model itself and the series of oppositional categories associated with it. For example, the category "public/private" which lies at the heart of the separate spheres model denotes a comprehensive philosophical stance which interprets the world as shaped by mutually exclusive and inescapable opposites: work/home, politics/family, society/nature, reason/emotion, and ultimately male/female. The separate spheres model in women's history does not question this set of binary divides;

rather it accepts women's placement on one side of them. Too often this framework results in the marginalization of women outside "official" history, and the forging of a parallel history of the private sphere in which women can act as protagonists.

The separate spheres approach can, in effect, reproduce these rigid categories within women's history itself—a development which may obfuscate as much as it reveals. Consequently, women's historians have been rethinking the separate spheres framework and challenging its implicit dichotomies.[13] As Karen Offen, Ruth Roach Pierson, and Jane Rendall point out in their introduction to *Writing Women's History: International Perspectives*,

> Some historians are beginning to confront and to deconstruct the earlier representations of their past, recognising the basis of these dualities to lie in a masculinist epistemology. They argue that dichotomies, opposites, contradictions, the whole inheritance of a binary vision, may be unnecessarily confining: the temptations of dualism should be constantly analyzed and where appropriate discarded.[14]

Spain's image as a traditional society gave the appearance of an unchallenged and peculiarly impenetrable world of separate spheres. For this reason, the reassessment of dualistic thinking is especially challenging in the Spanish case. On the surface, Spain has seemed like a casebook study of the historical reality of separate spheres. Spanish women in the nineteenth and twentieth centuries were in fact largely invisible in the classic public arenas of work and politics, and few women openly challenged their exclusion. Their de facto exclusion from public life confirmed women's role as irrelevant to the "big picture" debates about Spain's identity that comprise the official history of modern Spain. In these official narratives, women have lacked not only agency but even identity.

Our investigations into this apparently casebook study of a gender-repressive society have certainly exposed the existence of rigid controls and a victimized female population; however, they have also repeatedly illuminated the infinitely more complex reality of women's lives. Women still struggled to compose their own lives to the degree that they were able and to assert their subjectivity in an often hostile world. It is precisely the balance between constraint and agency, subjugation and subjectivity, that we seek to express in the notion of contesting women's lives.[15]

As the chapters in this volume demonstrate, even without the open confrontation over rigid gender roles, there was constant contestation over female identity, in some cases between (male) institutions and groups of women, and in other cases between women themselves. It was this very contestation that created the space for women's agency. Thus, a common theme of the chapters, whether explicit or implicit, has been the disclosure of the extent of women's conscious action, their decisive purposeful acts within the bounds of traditional gendered limits. But what makes this more than the affirmation of women's culture is that this contestation occurred across opposing categories, such as work/home and political/private. Not only did women cross boundaries from private to public, but public authority crossed boundaries from public to private. Contested identities, in fact, reveal contested categories. "Paradoxically," to quote Judith Butler, "it may be that only through releasing the category women from a fixed referent that something like `agency' becomes possible."[16]

"Spain is different!" Everyone knows this cliché, but how are we to understand what truth remains of it in the late twentieth century? Until recently, Spanish historiography was dominated by a model of Spain's failure to follow the "normal" European path to modernity. Not surprisingly, this interpretation relegated Spain to the margins of European history. Recently, however, revisionists have begun to emphasize similarities with the rest of Europe, arguing that Spain experienced most of the same major trends, from industrialization to urbanization to liberal revolution, that transformed other Western European countries in the nineteenth and twentieth centuries.[17] We call for a more culturally specific interpretive approach[18] that transcends the duality of inclusion or exclusion from the "European model." Consequently, we choose to distance ourselves from the ready assumption that interpretive models derived from Western Europe are not applicable to Spain, as well as from a too-easy application of Anglo-American experience, clothed as the European model.

A case in point is the relevance of the equality versus difference debate to the Spanish context.[19] This conflict—as exemplified by the Sears Case—is too familiar to reprise, but it is markedly pertinent to our concerns. The debate focuses on the core contradiction in feminist theory: the desire to eliminate inequality without eradicating difference.[20] Elizabeth Fox-Genovese argues that the contradiction can be traced to the origin of Western individualism itself, which " . . . has firmly cast women as other, even as it has afforded men models of subjecthood and authority that women have tried to adapt to their own ends."[21] She calls for a critique of individualism that would reveal the extent of each individual's embeddedness in the collectivities that formed them, and " . . . which alone give their identities meaning."[22] Such a critique calls for a rereading of the past focusing not on the contested arena of individual rights, but instead on gender relations which " . . . illuminate[s] the interdependence of men and women in life and consciousness."[23]

This discussion is especially meaningful with regard to Spanish women's (or gender) history. Spain's marginalization from Western Europe occurred partly over differences between Spain's official commitment to communal Catholic values and Western (especially Anglo-American) official commitment to rationalism, individualism, and universalism, a split which bifurcated Spanish society as well. Here the explorations in a more culturally specific interpretive approach are useful to us. For example, Karen Offen has proposed a concept of "relational feminism" to explain a movement to promote female rights on the basis of social relations rather than on individualism.[24] By taking individualism as a universal value, historians have missed the implications of communal-based identity politics. Given the historical importance of communalism among Spanish women—across the political spectrum from Catholic associations, to Anarchist groups, to Falangist organizations—the Spanish case provides an excellent testing ground for new approaches to female mobilization.

More generally, the chapters in this collection demonstrate that the full complexity of women's identities is obscured by established and automatic frameworks for categorizing and recognizing. It is only through dismantling such preestablished classifications that the efforts of women in the past to find voice, assert agency, and establish identity become perceptible. To understand how women formed their identities requires a new historiographical grid, one that acknowledges the permeability of boundaries and categories, rather than reinscribes their rigidity. We thus call for a redefinition, or refined definitions, of such notions as work, politics, agency, and identity. Such an approach reveals the interaction between a powerful gender discourse of separate spheres and the more fluid reality of Spanish women's lives as they struggled to define themselves within the hegemonic culture. In the process, the chapters contribute to the larger agenda of rewriting the "master narrative" of official history that has stubbornly resisted women's historians' efforts to contest it. Thus, we hope that this anthology will provide a contextualized historical setting for exploring the issues raised in the wider discourse of gender history, cultural studies, and comparative women's history, and for discovering further possibilities for rewriting prevailing historical narratives.

The book is divided thematically into three sections, each of which examines a different aspect of the construction of female identity. The first section, entitled "Sociocultural Models: Prescribing Female Identities," explores the institutionalization of the separate spheres model of gender identity that consigned women, regardless of class or status, to a purely domestic role. In contrast to this static vision of prescribed behavior, the other two sections, entitled "Work Identities" and "Political Identities," elaborate the more fluid, contested boundaries of Spanish women's lives. While the official ideology defined women in terms of their domestic roles, the remaining chapters argue that "work" and "politics," although not always in their familiar forms, are also central components of female identity. In the classic separate spheres model, these "public" categories are gendered male in contrast to the feminized private sphere, especially in "traditional" societies like Spain. What the chapters demonstrate is the artificiality of such dichotomies and the categories on which they are based. Thus, on a basic level, the organization of the book is designed to expose the inadequacies of the separate sphere model and to open the door to more fluid conceptions of female identity.

The first section, "Sociocultural Models," deals with various official attempts to impose a static vision of female identity on all Spanish women in the twentieth century. In particular, the four chapters in this section demonstrate how specific cultural discourses and institutions served as the conduit for the ruling gender ideology. Three of the four focus on the Francoist dictatorship (1940s–1975), both because traditional dualistic gender relations were essential to its sense of identity and because it distinguishes Spain from most of northern Europe during these decades. As a group, all the chapters in this section illustrate the degree to which public power was infused with the ideology of separate spheres, well into the 1970s. While this ideology cannot be read as a description of female identity in Spain during these years, it was an important component in the complex process of identity formation.

The first chapter, by Mary Nash, provides an introduction to the dominant separate spheres gender system in the late nineteenth and early twentieth centuries. By analyzing the representation of women in various media, she charts the modernization of gender roles from the "Angel in the House" to the "New Woman," tracing the transformation of the discourse on women from a moral to a scientific basis in modern medicine. Nash focuses on debates over reproduction, sex reform, and birth control, and demonstrates how the new medical discourse aimed not to liberate female sexual identity so much as to reshape it towards modern motherhood. The fact that Spanish women, even those organized in women's groups, had little voice in this debate demonstrates the effectiveness of gender codes in excluding women from public discourse, even on issues that affected them intimately.

Aurora Morcillo, María Escudero, and Clotilde Puertolas each examine the official support of separate spheres ideology in the following decades, as embodied in the cultural institutions of the Franco dictatorship. As an authoritarian state dedicated to the resurrection/invention of a traditional Spain, the Franco regime possessed both the motivation and the tools to impose public gender codes. Aurora Morcillo demonstrates how a gendered model of citizenship shaped the Spanish university and its educational mission during the early decades of the regime. Although middle- and upper-class women attended the university in increasing numbers, their identity as scholars contradicted official notions of the "true Catholic woman." While women were not formally excluded from the university, Francoist educational discourse made it difficult to integrate a university education into female identity without raising problematic tensions among female students. In other words, while the regime did not try to prevent women from pursuing an education, it did try to undermine their identity as scholars. The issue was not the limits of women's behavior, but rather whether they could incorporate this activity into a coherent sense of personal or collective identity as women.

María Escudero also examines the incorporation of gender codes in the Francoist education system, but she focuses on primary school textbooks directed at girls of all classes. What she finds is much more subtle than simplistic messages prescribing female behavior. Instead, she uncovers how gender codes were utilized for naturalizing other hierarchical relationships. In particular, Escudero demonstrates how the textbooks presented a familial but hierarchical relationship between Spain and Latin America through stories about conquistadors and indigenous women during the period of conquest and colonization. In its reimagining of Spain's colonial past, the regime hoped to create a new sense of international stature through its cultural leadership of Latin America. By identifying the masculine conquistadors with Spain and the indigenous women with the "virgin" territory of the new world, the textbooks both justified the conquest and implied a natural hierarchy that never required open articulation. In doing so, the stories both reinforced and demonstrated the rhetorical power of the reigning gender ideology.

Clotilde Puertolas analyzes a different kind of cultural institution, a popular festival known as the San Fermines that, during the Franco period, came to embody the essence of both Navarrese regional identity and traditional Spain. As she argues, the ideal portraits of the male and female festival participants that emerged in local government propaganda, national tourist promotion and the media corresponded to the ideal male and female citizen of Navarre and Francoist Spain. Men were to be brave, virile, and powerful and the exclusive participants in the central rituals of the festival. Women's role was to support their men and applaud from the sidelines as invisible citizens in a masculine world. Even as social roles evolved towards the end of the regime and during the transition, the basic gender protocol remained largely intact, interrupted only by occasional feminist voices. Thus, Puertolas, like the other three authors, amply demonstrates the power of officially imposed gender codes to dominate public discourse and create an apparently seamless web of constraints that dictated women's lives.

The second section, entitled "Work Identities," explores the more complex reality of female identity through analyses of the impact of work in different women's lives. While work has always figured prominently in paradigms of masculine identity formation, the separate spheres model neglected women's work for a number of reasons. First, the tendency to equate "work" with wage work outside the home reduced many female tasks to nonwork. Further, even when women have worked for wages, their relationship to work has always been considered subordinate to their primary identity as wives and mothers. Complicating this subordination is the importance of class categories to work identities. Since the majority of female wage laborers were poor women, they were often viewed as an aberration from normal middle-class standards. Thus, their work experience never challenged the supposedly universal ideal of the domestic woman.

In fact, all women worked, whether they were middle-class housewives or working-class day laborers. If we take Heidi Kelley's definition of work, as "all the activities that women engage in to advance the success of the household," we can begin to focus on what those activities were, what was the context in which they were performed, and how they affected the formation of female identity. At the same time that we acknowledge that work is a central category in women's lives, we must also recognize that it is a problematic and contested category for women. While women did and do work, the reigning ideology created a gendered work culture that shaped what they could do, how their work was perceived by others, and how it was incorporated into their sense of identity. As a result, women's work was less a set of specific tasks than an arena of contestation. Each chapter in this section provides a case study of the contestation over work identity. Two of the chapters focus on female wage workers in urban industrial contexts, and the other two look at groups of women defined by the census as housewives, and who lived in rural, agricultural settings.

Rosa Capel and D.J. O'Connor each examine a particular group of wage workers, the female employees in the tobacco industry, or *cigarreras.* Of the small percentage of Spanish women who entered the formal labor force, these workers made up an elite minority known for their high level of collective identity and their militancy. Rosa Capel focuses on the cigarette makers' identity at the work place. Through a close analysis of the *Regulations Concerning Laborers in Tobacco Factories*, which was approved by royal decree in January 1927, she dissects the official directive on the ordering and disciplining of the female tobacco worker. Capel reveals an identity that is both privileged in its relation to other types of women workers, and strictly hierarchical in its gendered assumptions. While the regulations accept the reality of women workers, they also dictate distinct work for male and female workers, thereby preventing the consolidation of a new, genderless category of worker. The women's work identity is not completely imposed on them, however; their efforts to create and defend their special rights suggest that they were engaged in self-structuring their role as female workers.

D.J. O'Connor looks at the public identity of cigarette makers outside the workplace, especially through the eyes of middle-class observers in the press, popular literature, and theater. She focuses on two events, a strike and a political protest, and analyzes the media's portrayal of these women's presence in confrontational public situations. Rather than admit their reality as militant workers and political actors, the media cast them as picturesque, folkloric stereotypes, i.e. as "Carmen." Thus, they forced the *cigarreras*' anomalous behavior into existing class and gender categories as defined by the traditional religious discourse. By misconstruing their behavior and misrepresenting their activism, the media also helped suppress the emergence of new public roles for working-class women. Despite this suppression, a few cigarette makers' voices did break through, thus providing us with an alternative narrative of their actions. Both Capel and O'Connor have problematized the category of female work: what emerges is an arena of struggle, but one in which different issues are debated than those in the ungendered (male-defined) work world.

Tim Rees and Heidi Kelley also address the problematic category of work, but within the context of rural society. In his piece on the southern region of Andalusia before the Civil War, Rees argues that to define work only in terms of paid employment obscures the varied nature of women's activities in the southern countryside. Rees charts a significant discrepancy between the dominant traditional ideology and the reality of women's lives which included a number of tasks that escaped standard classification. The fact that many women engaged in farm labor, conducted business, and owned land, was not sufficient to classify them—in the official record keeping—as workers or landowners. Rather, official records obscured the multiplicity of women's roles, reinforcing customary perceptions of women's identity, and consequently distorting our understanding of their lives.

In contrast to Rees' overview of rural women's work, teased from between the lines of official records, Heidi Kelley's ethnographic study of a Gallegan fishing village provides an intimate portrait of women's work and identity through the voices of the women she interviewed. Kelley examines how these women "composed their lives," negotiating their way through apparently opposing demands placed on them. While they might appear to be simple, traditional women who followed the roles laid out for them, Kelley demonstrates that they juggled traditional and modern identities and household and community responsibilities in ways that defy simple oppositional categories like work and home. In fact, she argues that women, like men, actively construct public identities/reputations in which work is the central pivot. In Kelley's chapter, as in the others in this section, the point of contestation was not whether women were allowed to work, but whether what they did counted as work and whether they could thus claim identity as workers.

The third section, "Political Identities," shifts the arena of contestation from work to politics. Politics, like work, has been viewed as an almost exclusively masculine realm. The fact that women were denied political citizenship for most of the modern period formalized their exclusion, especially in Spain, where it lasted until 1976, with the brief exception of the Second Republic

(1931–1936). Even when they were granted access to the formal political sphere, women's participation has either been marginalized or denigrated as irrational. In this context, it is easy to assume that women had no opportunity to explore political identities, and that politics was in fact gendered male.

However, this assumption relies on a limited vision of politics rooted in the binary categories of liberalism. That is, it implicitly accepts an orthodox model of politics, built on the acknowledgement of separate spheres, a model from which most women were by definition excluded. The resulting argument is circular. That is, women are nonpolitical according to an a priori definition of politics that marginalizes them. The result is that women have been seen as either nonpolitical or as marginal political actors. Likewise, because women are absent, politics has been defined as a masculine sphere of activity. Thus, politics, like work, has not been treated as central to the formation of female identity.

In fact, as the chapters in this section demonstrate, the relationship between women, gender, and politics was much more complex. Thus, even when women were marginal or nonexistent political actors, gender tensions and images of threatening women still permeated public discourse. In other words, issues defined as private sphere concerns invaded the political realm in ways that diluted the supposed boundaries between the two. The boundaries between the political and the nonpolitical were further weakened by the alternative forms of collective action that existed outside the formal political realm. Thus, women without access to formal politics found other means of collectively expressing their concerns. When women challenged power structures to yield to their collective demands, they pursued political goals that should be recognized as such. As was the case with the category of *work*, women's experiences push us to rethink the category of *politics.* By adopting a broader definition of politics that accounts for a variety of ways of engaging with forms of public power, women emerge much more clearly as political actors.

The chapters in this section are in rough chronological order, but they also fall into two major groups. The first four chapters focus on women, gender, and politics in the years before women were granted formal citizenship; while the last three chapters concentrate on the periods when women had achieved equal political rights. Among the first group, the first chapter examines the centrality of gender in political discourse, even when women were denied formal political agency. The three chapters that follow explore the more informal kinds of political activities that women have pursued to circumvent their exclusion from the formal political sphere. The second group of chapters analyzes the contestation over women's participation in the formal political sphere after the removal of citizenship barriers. While crossing the line between formal and informal politics, all of the chapters explore the ways in which women's participation was denigrated or marginalized because of their gender.

Sarah White's chapter takes the revolutionary period of 1868–1874, when Spain switched from a monarchical regime to a republic and back to a monarchy, to demonstrate the pervading gender distinctions that permeated political life and public discourse. During a period defined by its attempt to democratize liberalism, women's citizenship was a non-issue. Nevertheless, White argues that the political discourse of the period was permeated with gendered images, in particular the feminine political allegories that represented Liberty, the Republic, and the Monarchy. The allegories were twisted and manipulated at crucial moments of political transition; thus, a mythic nurturing Liberty could become, at the next moment, a promiscuous, dishonorable threat to the nation. The power of these allegories lay precisely in the masculine moral order of nineteenth-century Spain, in which codes of honor were inextricably bound up with gender. In exposing these codes, White demonstrates the paradox of a political sphere that dismissed women even as it was obsessed with gender.

The next three chapters, by John Tone, Temma Kaplan, and Pamela Radcliff, all explore women's collective action in the realm of non-institutional politics, where struggles over resources, justice, and collective rights are waged through informal channels. John Tone argues that, beginning with the early nineteenth century, in Spain's war against Napoleon, women participated fully in the "war of independence," even though the vast majority did not become regular combatants. In contrast to the traditional historical narrative, which either ignores women or casts them in the mythic role of Amazons, Tone demonstrates that women joined in the struggle by using the traditionally feminized spaces already open to them. By avoiding the narrow confines of the categories "fought" or "did not fight," Tone reveals their agency as active participants in this political and military struggle.

Temma Kaplan further develops the argument that women's traditional role allowed them to make an important contribution to the larger political realm. Her chapter uncovers the political role of women in a mining community in which their only public identity lay in being wives and mothers of miners. Building on her concept of "female consciousness," she demonstrates how these women could use their role as caregivers to assert broad claims of political justice that authorities could not ignore. In fact, the authorities took them seriously as political actors precisely because they appeared to be nonpolitical representatives of timeless communal interests. Paradoxically, these women challenged the political order, and even existing gender relations, without ever directly attacking either system of authority.

In a similar fashion, Pamela Radcliff demonstrates how poor women used their traditional roles as mothers and housewives to carve out a political role for themselves. She focuses on the consumer riot, one of the most familiar forms of female collective action, in which participants brought private sphere concerns into political confrontation with the authorities. Radcliff argues that, while historians recognize the importance of consumer riots in premodern political structures, most have seen them as displaced by the mass political parties and trade unions of the modern period. She presents evidence that this form continued to thrive as a gendered form of political activity in the twentieth century, and argues that rioting women played a significant role in the political destabilization that forms the central narrative of the official history of early twentieth-century Spain.

The last three chapters focus on women's participation as formal citizens, during the Second Republic of the 1930s, and in the constitutional monarchy inaugurated in 1978. Judith Keene analyzes the first major transition in the formal political sphere, when women were granted suffrage in 1931. She examines the heated debate surrounding the granting of women's suffrage in 1931, and highlights the roles played by three extraordinary women—the first elected female deputies in Spanish history. Despite their individual contributions, Keene demonstrates the general ambivalence towards awarding women the vote and the suspicion with which women political participants were regarded. She argues that women's suffrage was finally granted not out of a concern for women's rights, but out of a desire to fulfill abstract criteria for a democratic state.

Gerard Alexander examines how a much larger group of women entered formal political life—by voting—in the Second Republic and again after the transition in the 1970s. He demonstrates that women's voting behavior, where decipherable, follows closely that of their male counterparts in distribution along the political spectrum. In doing so, he debunks the persistent myth of women's incapacity to carry out the duties of citizenship due to their religiosity and irrational malleability. Instead of acting as destabilizers of the democratic system (as the accusation runs) women behaved as normal democratic citizens. However, the strength of the negative myth, widespread at the time and in subsequent historiography, fostered a hostile environment within which women forged their identities as citizens. The dichotomy between women's actual comportment as citizens and a public portrayal of them that has maligned and marginalized their citizenship potential demands exploration. Again, women's politics, like their work, has been a problematic and contested category.

Contestation is at the center of Victoria Enders' chapter on the women who led the only state-sanctioned women's organization during the Franco regime, the *Sección Femenina*. Enders analyzes their struggle to be acknowledged as patriots and citizens in a post-Francoist world that rejects their values. While they see themselves as model female citizens, as defined by traditional gender discourse and their distinctive political ideology, the dominant voices of the new post-Franco democratic regime condemn them as traitors and dismiss their claims of political agency. Enders shows how these now marginalized women are engaged in a struggle, primarily with women of opposing political views, to legitimize their contributions and reclaim their political agency and, hence, their identity.

All the chapters contribute in their own way to the larger agenda we set forth initially: to pursue the construction of identities in order to question conventional categories and dualisms and reveal unsuspected relationships and complexities in the history of women in modern Spain. Our intention is not to replace the old set of rigid categories with a new set, but to open up a fluid gendered world defined by constraints and agency, by dominant discourses and dissident voices. By uncovering the fluidity of gender roles and ideology, even in a case like Spain which appears to be such a textbook case of rigid dualisms, we hope to contribute to the current exciting project of redefinition being undertaken by a broad spectrum of gender scholars and historians.

Notes

1. In order to make Spanish women and their experiences more visible to the English-speaking world, we draw freely and deeply on a rich body of literature in Spanish, as well as Catalan (as the bibliography of this volume attests), which demonstrates the remarkable vitality of the field of women's history in the past two decades within Spain. For a recent bibliographic essay, see Mary Nash, "Two Decades of Women's History in Spain," in Karen Offen, Ruth Roach Pierson and Jane Rendall, eds., *Writing Women's History: International Perspectives* (Bloomington, IN: Indiana University Press, 1991). Mary Nash and Rosa María Capel Martínez were two of the pioneers of women's history in Spain in the mid-1970s; Capel published *El sufragio femenino en la Segunda República* (Granada, Spain: Universidad de Granada) in 1975, and Nash published *Mujeres Libres: España 1936–1939* (Barcelona: Tusquets) in the same year.

And, of course, we gratefully follow in the footsteps of scholars outside Spain who have pioneered the field of modern Spanish women's history in English. In particular, we would point to the work of Temma Kaplan, who published "Other Scenarios: Women and Spanish Anarchism," in the groundbreaking *Becoming Visible: Women in European History* (Boston: Houghton Mifflin) in 1977, and "Female Consciousness and Collective Action: The Case of Barcelona, 1910–1918," in *Signs* 7, no. 3 (Spring, 1982), among others. Joan Connelly Ullman's excellent overview is still available only in Spanish: "La protagonista ausente: La mujer como objeto y sujeto de la historia de España," in *La mujer en el mundo contemporáneo*, ed. María Angeles Durán (Madrid: Universidad Autónoma de Madrid, 1981).

2. From the Introduction by Karen Offen, Ruth Roach Pierson and Jane Rendall to *Writing Women's History*, p. xxx.

3. See Ruth Behar, "Introduction: Out of Exile," in Behar and Deborah A. Gordon, eds., *Women Writing Culture* (Berkeley, CA: University of California Press, 1995), p. 22. "... identity is always in flux among ethnic, racial, age, professional, and

other markers." And as the Editorial Collective of the journal, *Gender and History*, affirmed: "the creation and preservation of feminine and masculine identities, social roles, images, institutions and belief systems always necessitates negotiation, if not struggle." See "Why Gender and History," *Gender and History* 1 (Spring, 1989): 1.

4. See Sidonie Smith and Julia Watson, eds., Introduction to *De/Colonizing the Subject: The Politics of Gender in Women's Autobiography* (Minneapolis, MN: University of Minnesota Press, 1992); Valentine M. Moghadam, ed., *Identity Politics and Women* (Boulder, CO: Westview Press, 1994); and Carol E. Franz and Abigail J. Stewart, eds., *Women Creating Lives: Identities, Resilience, and Resistance* (Boulder, CO: Westview Press, 1994).

5. Joan W. Scott, "Multiculturalism and the Politics of Identity," in John Rajchman, ed., *The Identity in Question* (New York: Routledge, 1995), p. 11.

6. Anthropologist Michelle Rosaldo, in her last work, and philosopher Linda Nicholson have signalled the need to "historicize our notions of public and private" as quoted in Dorothy O. Helly and Susan M. Reverby, eds., *Gendered Domains: Rethinking Public and Private in Women's History* (Ithaca, NY: Cornell University Press, 1991), p. 7; Sociologist Lise Vogel agrees that "the controversy cannot be settled in the abstract . . . for the issue is largely historical." Helly and Reverby, *Gendered Domains,* p. 11; See also Teresa de Lauretis, "Upping the Anti [sic] in Feminist Theory," in Simon During, *The Cultural Studies Reader* (London: Routledge, 1993), p. 75.

7. See Mary Louise Pratt, "Fieldwork in Common Places," in James Clifford George E. Marcus, eds., *Writing Culture: The Poetics and Politics of Ethnography* (Berkeley, CA: University of California Press, 1986), p. 27.

8. See Chandra Talpade Mohanty, "Under Western Eyes: Feminist Scholarship and Colonial Discourses," in Mohanty, Ann Russo and Lourdes Torres, eds., *Third World Women and the Politics of Feminism* (Bloomington, IN: University of Indiana, 1991), pp. 70, 72, 66.

9. The term and distinctions are borrowed from Stephen A. Tyler, "Post-Modern Ethnography: From Document of the Occult to Occult Document," in Clifford and Marcus, eds., *Writing Culture,* p. 123.

10. "Feminist revision is always about a new way of looking at all categories, not just at 'woman'." See Ruth Behar and Deborah A. Gordon, eds., *Women Writing Culture*, p. 6. See also Helen Graham and Jo Labanyi: "In sum, problematic analytical usage arises from a fundamental failure to historicize the categories in question," from "Culture and Modernity: The Case of Spain," in *Spanish Cultural Studies: An Introduction: The Struggle for Modernity* (Oxford: Oxford University Press, 1995), p. 11.

11. Tyler, p. 223.

12. The separate spheres argument (the universal devaluation of women because they were confined to the domestic world) was introduced by anthropologist Michelle Rosaldo, and the nature/culture dichotomy by Sherry Ortner, in Rosaldo and Louise Lamphere, eds., *Women, Culture and Society*. (Stanford, CA: Stanford University Press, 1974). For studies of women's culture by historians see: Carroll Smith-Rosenberg, "The Female World of Love and Ritual," *Signs* 1 (Autumn, 1975): 1–30; and *Disorderly Conduct: Visions of Gender in Victorian America* (New York: Knopf, 1985); Nancy Cott, *The Bonds of Womanhood: Woman's Sphere in New England. 1790–1835* (New Haven, CT: Yale University Press, 1977); Carol Gilligan, *In a Different Voice* (Cambridge, MA: Harvard University Press, 1982); and Linda Kerber, "Separate Spheres, Female Worlds, Women's Place: The Rhetoric of Women's History," *Journal of American History* 75, no. 1 (June, 1988): 9–39. For a critique of separate spheres see Helly and Reverby, eds., *Gendered Domains*; Michelle Perrot, et. al., "Women's Culture and Women's Power: An Attempt at Historiography," *Journal of Women's History* 1 (Spring 1989): 62–88; and Nancy Jay, "Gender and Dichotomy," *Feminist Studies*, 7, no. 1 (1981).

13. See a growing literature on questioning dichotomies in women's history: Gisela Bock, "Challenging Dichotomies: Perspectives on Women's History," in Offen, Pierson and Rendall, eds., *Writing Women's History*, pp. 1–23; Gisela Bock and Susan James, eds., *Beyond Equality and Difference: Citizenship, Feminist Politics, and Female Subjectivity* (London: Routledge, 1992); Nancy Jay, "Gender and Dichotomy," *Feminist Studies*, 7, no. 1 (1981); Janet Sharistanian, ed., *Beyond the Public/Private Dichotomy* (Westport, CT: Greenwood Press, 1987); and Helly and Reverby, eds., *Gendered Domains*).

14. Karen Offen, Ruth Roach Pierson and Jane Rendall, eds., Introduction to *Writing Women's History*, p. xxxv.

15. On the theoretical problems of defining female agency, especially in the context of postmodern redefinitions of the "subject," see Kathleen Canning, "Feminist History after the Linguistic Turn: Historicizing Discourse and Experience," *Signs* 19, no. 2 (Winter, 1994); Linda Alcoff, "Cultural Feminism vs. Post-Structuralism: The Identity Crisis in Feminist Theory," in Nicholas Dirks, Geoff Eley and Sherry Ortner, eds., *Culture/Power/History: A Reader in Contemporary Social Theory* (Princeton, NJ: Princeton University Press, 1994).

16. Judith Butler, "Contingent Foundations: Feminism and the Question of 'Postmodernism'," in Judith Butler and Joan W. Scott, eds., *Feminists Theorize the Political* (New York: Routledge, 1992), p. 16.

17. See Adrian Shubert, Introduction to *A Social History of Modern Spain* (London: Unwin Hyman, 1990), for a concise presentation of this position. The argument to mainstream modern Spanish history has benefitted from the broader argument against using an ideal British model of development against which to measure other countries' "peculiarities." See David Blackbourn and Geoff Eley, *The Peculiarities of German History* (Oxford: Oxford University Press, 1984). See also Stanley Payne, *Spain's First Democracy: The Second Republic, 1931–1936* (Madison, WI: University

of Wisconsin Press, 1993), and most recently, David Ringrose, *Spain, Europe and the "Spanish Miracle"* (Cambridge: Cambridge University Press, 1996).

18. See Ida Blom, "Global Women's History: Organising Principles and Cross-Cultural Understandings," in Offen, Pierson and Rendall, eds., *Writing Women's History*, pp. 135–149, 140.

19. On equality vs difference see: Joan Scott, "Deconstructing Equality-versus-Difference: Or the Uses of Post-Structuralist Theory for Feminism," *Feminist Studies*, 14, no. 1 (1988): 33–50; Gisela Bock and Susan James, eds., *Beyond Equality and Difference* (New York: Routledge, 1992).

20. See Margot Badran, "Expressing Feminism and Nationalism in Autobiography: The Memoirs of an Egyptian Educator," in Smith and Watson, eds., *De/Colonizing the Subject.*

21. Elizabeth Fox-Genovese, *Feminism without Illusions: A Critique of Individualism* (Chapel Hill: University of North Carolina Press, 1991), p. 225.

22. Elizabeth Fox-Genovese, p. 240.

23. Fox-Genovese, p. 238.

24. See Karen Offen, "Defining Feminism: A Comparative Historical Approach," in Bock and James, eds., *Beyond Equality and Difference*.

Part I

Sociocultural Models: Prescribing Female Identity in Spain

Introduction

We begin with a series of chapters on the social and cultural framework that provided the backdrop for contestations over female identity in Spain during the nineteenth and twentieth centuries. Whether in the field of social relations, work, or politics, women had to confront, adapt, or acquiesce to a web of institutions, laws, values and customs that dictated the "proper" behavior for each sex. As elsewhere in Europe, this web was shaped by the dominant ideology of separate spheres, which posited complementary missions for men and women in the public and private spheres organized in a hierarchical fashion. While the complex reality of gender roles did not conform to the rigidity of separate spheres, as many of the later chapters in this book demonstrate, the ideology and its supporting web of cultural institutions was a necessary point of departure for female identity formation. In this sense, part one sets the stage for the rest of the book and its theme of constructing identities.

Each of the chapters in this section explores how the web of separate spheres was constructed in specific ways and how it supplied a context for the formation of female identity. The first piece by Mary Nash provides a general overview of the evolution of separate spheres ideology in the late nineteenth and early twentieth centuries. The other chapters focus on the reinforcement of separate sphere ideology—in educational policy, in school textbooks, and in community rituals—during the Franco dictatorship, which prided itself on the maintenance or revival of "traditional" culture. This introductory essay will provide a general background on the separate spheres model and its institutional structure in Spain.

As part of Spain's economic and political transformation in the nineteenth century, Spain developed a version of the new gender ideology taking shape in "modernizing" countries, an ideology that attempted deliberately to marginalize women's participation in the social and political transformations taking place. As the new language of liberalism with its rhetoric of individual citizenship and liberty took hold, a parallel language of exceptionalism emerged to explain why certain groups, including women, did not qualify for citizenship. The explanation, in the case of women, was the division of the world into strictly divided public and private spheres. Thus, while the public and political realm got recast as the stage of the modern worker and citizen, women were defined out of that realm and relegated to the private sphere of domesticity.[1] By the mid nineteenth century, the dualistic world of separate spheres constituted the official framework for assigning woman's status and proper function, and its residual impact remains an important constituent of gender roles to the present day.

Within these general parameters, however, the specific contours of separate sphere ideology and its consequences were rooted in the particularities of Spanish history.[2] Because the Spanish context provided an unusually fertile ground for such rigid dualisms, the intensity and durability of separate spheres as a prescriptive model was greater in Spain than in other Western European countries. In simple terms, the binary opposition between domestic and public, female and male, fed into and off of the larger discourse of binary opposition that dominated Spanish political culture from the Napoleonic invasion (1808–1814) to the recent transition to democracy (1975–1978). In other words, the political culture favored and encouraged binary oppositions. Thus, while the ideology of separate spheres took root in many places, it fit particularly well in the Spanish framework.

The black and white world of Spanish political discourse revolved around the opposition between "right" and "left," or traditionalists and modernizers. While this struggle existed to some extent throughout the industrializing world, in Spain it took an especially acute form, summed up in the common image of the "two Spains." Over the course of the nineteenth century, an increasing minority of secular Spaniards set themselves in opposition to the traditional society dominated by the Church, the Bourbon Monarchy, and the large landowners, calling instead for the adoption of "European" ideals of democracy, liberalism, socialism, secularization, and economic modernization. For the modernizers, the old Spain was backward, "African," an antediluvian monster, while for the traditionalists, their opponents were not simply misguided, but anti-Spanish. Eventually, these two mutually exclusive visions of Spain led the country into one of the most brutal civil wars of the twentieth century (1936–1939), followed by the equally brutal attempt by the victors to impose their conception of traditional Spain over the course of General Franco's nearly 40-year dictatorship (1939–1975).

The dominant discursive trope of the "two Spains" reinforced the ideology of separate spheres by investing it with the highest political stakes: those of national identity. The traditionalists who controlled the political and cultural establishment for most of the nineteenth and twentieth centuries viewed women's domesticity as part and parcel of the larger vision of Spain that they would defend literally to the death. In contrast, the image of the "modern" public woman was equated not just with social disorder but with national decadence: the quintessence of anti-Spain. For the secularizers, the image (if not always the reality) of the modern woman embodied the promise of the future, while the traditional (Catholic) woman symbolized religious superstition, the inquisitional black legend of Spain's ignoble past. In this black and white world, there was little room to maneuver between the two extremes and even less incentive to break down polarities of thought.

Furthermore, because the neo-traditionalist forces managed to sustain the upper hand in the hegemonic struggle throughout most of the modern period, their uncompromising version of separate spheres constituted the cultural norm for gender roles until the end of the dictatorship in the mid-1970s. This norm, like most hegemonic systems, did not go uncontested; but its notions dominated the field of gender discourse to a greater degree and over a longer time span than in most other Western countries. Consequently, it created an especially powerful system of constraints within which Spanish women lived their lives.

The impact of this ideology, which emphasized woman's exclusive role as wife, mother, and guardian of the home, is evident in all areas of Spanish life. On the most direct level, the inequalities between men and women were codified in the legal structure, as they were in most European countries in the nineteenth century. In particular, Spain closely followed the oppressive gender prescriptions enshrined in the Napoleonic Code, one of the few legacies of the French occupation. While single women retained a good deal of independence, in terms of the ability to conduct business and manage their public affairs, married women were virtual legal appendages of their husbands, to whom they owed strict obedience. Thus, article 57 of the Civil Code of 1889 stated: "the husband must protect his wife, and she must obey her husband." Wives needed their husbands' permission for everything from selling property to seeking employment or taking a trip, and could be either fined or jailed for disobedience.

In addition to subordination, wives suffered a legal double standard when it came to expectations of fidelity. While any infidelity on the part of the wife was termed adultery and punished by up to six years in prison, a husband's affair did not break the law unless it caused a "public scandal" or occurred in the conjugal bed. Likewise, if a wife killed her husband after discovering him *in flagrante delicto*, she could be condemned to life imprisonment, while for the same crime he received from six months to six years of banishment from his home town.[3]

While this legal situation corresponded to that of most of the other European countries in the mid 1800s, by the end of the century national differences began to appear. Largely in response to feminist activism, some countries, including Great Britain, the Scandinavian nations, and the United States, followed a gradual path towards the equalization of women's legal position, culminating in the vote in the years after the First World War. In other countries, like Russia and Germany, women's legal equality was swept in as part of the post-war revolutionary transformation. And in others, particularly Catholic Italy and France, despite a few small victories legal equality and the vote were resisted until after the Second World War. At this point, a basic legal and political equality between men and women became the norm for most European countries (including the new communist regimes in the east and post-Nazi Germany).

In Spain, there was almost no reform to the gender sections of the oppressive Civil Code until the declaration of the Second Republic in 1931. As in Russia and Germany in 1917–1918, the regime transformation brought basic civil and political equality for women, including suffrage, which was adopted after a hard-fought parliamentary battle. However, the Nationalist forces who overthrew the liberal republic in 1939 revoked all of these changes. In their place, Franco reinstated the old Civil Code that mandated women's unqualified obedience to their husbands, and the portions of the Criminal Code that maintained the double standard on adultery.[4] Not until the 1970s and 1980s did the Spanish legal system again correspond to the European norm of basic gender equality.[5] Thus, for all but a few years in the 1930s, Spanish women as wives lived under one of the most consistently restrictive and hierarchical legal systems in Europe.

This rigidity extended beyond the legal framework into the more informal constraints of cultural and social norms. The most powerful vehicle for the transmission of these norms was the Catholic Church, which acted as the cultural bulwark for the traditionalist forces. As such, it maintained an extraordinary hold on public mores long after secularizing forces began to break that hold in other countries. Although the Church remained strong in other Latin countries, such as France and Italy, only in Spain could the Church work its influence from inside rather than outside the political establishment throughout most of the modern period. Thus, while the Church had to confront secularizing regimes in both Italy and France in the late nineteenth and early twentieth centuries, only the short and tragic Second Republic of the 1930s made a serious attempt to curb the Church's hold on public culture. As a result, the Church's prescription for woman's role, first formulated in a sixteenth century tract by Fray Luis de León entitled "The Perfect Wife," remained the standard frame of reference into the 1970s.[6]

Reinforcing the teachings of the Church, the prevailing Mediterranean discourse of "honor and shame" provided more powerful arguments for women's domestic confinement. Phrased in the language of high moral purpose, women were assigned the heavy responsibility of being moral guardians of the family and home. While guardianship normally implies some sort of authority and action, in this case it translated to a mandate for passivity, for "not doing" rather than "doing." That is, to protect the honor of the household, women were supposed to abstain from any dubious activities that could defile the family name. In obvious terms, this meant the preservation of chastity and purity, but these terms encompassed much more than resisting intimate sexual relations before or outside marriage. For the woman, upholding her purity and thus the honor of the family name required "refraining from actions which are proper to men . . . according to the division of labor, because women are under the tutelage of men."[7]

In other words, the boundaries of gendered spheres were further protected by the onus of family dishonor and ultimately social extinction. While all of these terms—honor, dishonor, chastity, and shame— existed and shaped gender roles in European society in general, anthropologists have noted the higher value attached to these labels and the increased time invested in the Mediterranean countries in distinguishing and defending the barriers between them.[8] Whether or not the honor/shame complex actually dictated the lives of men and women in modern Spain, its common cultural usage necessarily fortified the foundations of a separate sphere ideology. Like the rigid legal structure, then, the gendered discourse of honor and shame put up further barriers to women's range of motion. The result was an impressive bulwark, woven together from overlapping cultural, social, religious and legal texts that, at least in theory, consigned women to a predetermined set of roles. While the reality of female identity was more complex, no Spanish woman could completely ignore this bulwark.

Notes

1. For extended treatments of this topic, see Joan Landes, *Women and the Public Sphere in the Age of the French Revolution* (Ithaca, NY: Cornell University Press, 1988); and Carol Pateman, "The Fraternal Social Contract," in *The Disorder of Women: Democracy, Feminism and Political Theory* (Stanford, CA: Stanford University Press, 1989).

2. We use the word particularity not to indicate Spain's difference from a general model, but in recognition of the specificity of each national context.

3. For more details on women's legal position, see Geraldine Scanlon, *La polémica feminista en la España contemporánea, 1868–1974* (Madrid: Ediciones Akal, 1986), Chap. 3.

4. Adrian Shubert, *A Social History of Spain* (London: Unwin Hyman, 1990), p. 214. The double standard on adultery was finally done away with in 1958 (p. 216).

5. Thus, Article 14 of the 1978 Constitution stated that "all Spaniards are equal before the law, and no discrimination whatsoever may prevail by reason of birth, race, sex, religion or opinion." Cited in Mónica Threlfall, "The Women's Movement in Spain," *New Left Review* 151 (May–June 1985): 49.

6. See Bridget A. Aldaraca, *El ángel del hogar: Galdós y la ideología de la domesticidad en España* (Madrid: Visor, 1992), Chap. 1, for a discussion of de León's book.

7. Julián Pitt-Rivers, "Honor and Social Status," in Jean G. Peristiany, ed., *Honor and Shame: The Values of Mediterranean Society* (Chicago, IL: University of Chicago Press, 1974), p. 69.

8. See, for example, J.G. Peristiany, Introduction to *Honor and Shame: The Values of Mediterranean Society* (1974), p. 10.

1

Un/Contested Identities: Motherhood, Sex Reform and the Modernization of Gender Identity in Early Twentieth-Century Spain

Mary Nash

Gender is one of the defining features of contemporary society and a key category in the cultural construction of human difference. In early twentieth century Europe and North America, gender discourse as an explanatory principle of a stratified sociopolitical order had developed cultural values with wide resonance in social norms and popular collective imagery. The cultural representation of human difference in terms of gender categories crystallized the other—male/female—through the establishment of absolute distinctions based on asserted natural, biological differences. Although many outmoded analytical frameworks have attempted to claim Spain's integral difference from the rest of Europe in its historical development,[1] this chapter argues, in line with current historiography in other fields such as politics, culture or economics, that in modern Spanish society gender issues also followed the parameters of development current in many Western countries. Thus, in contrast to the conventional explanatory framework of Catholicism or political conservatism, this chapter highlights the modernization of gender discourse in Spain in the early twentieth century.

In order to explore the modernization of gender discourse in Spain, this study focuses on cultural ideology with a specific emphasis on modern medical sources in the construction of gender discourse. Political conservatism, the weight of the Roman Catholic Church as a pervasive political institution, and economic underdevelopment have often been argued as the key explanatory factors to the situation of women in contemporary Spain.[2] It is one of the main contentions of this study that biological essentialism rather than religion became a core feature in the construction of gender difference and the modernization of the notion of femininity in early twentieth-century Spain, and, thus, a key feature in the development of women's shared cultural identity and their collective definition of identity politics and a woman's agenda.[3] In order to account for the paths Spanish women took either in the public arena, in a mode of feminism, or in their private life projects relating to motherhood or sexuality, the development of gender discourse and the significance of gender identity in shaping women's agency in society must be addressed.[4]

In line with Wieviorka's analytical framework on the development of the notion of race, this study contends that the "biologization of social thought"[5] through gendered discourse was a core feature in the formulation of cultural norms on sexual difference in contemporary Spain. Biosocial thought converted gender identity and the cultural representation of women into a cultural myth that justified gender hierarchies, discriminatory values, and gendered social roles. In nineteenth- and early twentieth-century Western society, the discourse on race proposed to transmute ethnic differences to stratified social categories of inferior/superior.[6] In a similar way, gender discourse of sexual difference transposed human sexual difference to a cultural and ideological plane that legitimated a hierarchical order based on the subordination of women and social assymetry between the sexes.[7] The cultural representation of gender in Western society presented human distinction in terms of an irrevocable natural, sexual difference that established a hierarchical ordering based on this asserted natural difference.[8] Thus, biological essentialism functioned as a cultural device that asserted the hierarchization of human difference and justified gendered social roles.[9] This chapter suggests that such a conceptualization of sexual difference is also decisive in accounting for the historical development of women in Spanish society in the early twentieth century and is also a critical factor in assessing the difficulties they had in contesting cultural norms and established gender identities. Gender discourse and the foundations of its legitimation in contemporary society are thus explored as a lens to understand contestation and conformity in Spanish women's lives.

Verbal, visual, fictional, or historical discourse all form cultural representations of women.[10] Religion, science, medicine, politics, art, language, literature, media, or history are among the many cultural constructs used to develop collective imagery of women. The discourses that give meaning to cultural representations of women and gender identity take many forms and are grounded in social and cultural sources. Their exploration can help reveal the complex workings of gender and women's agency in society. The cultural representation of women is highly functional in the creation of gender roles and models. Gender identities are, to a large extent, consolidated and disseminated through images of women. These models of femininity become decisive manifestations of informal social control and help channel women into historically constructed gendered relationships.[11] It is quite clear that images and representations do not mirror the complex world of women. Gender discourse does not necessarily reflect reality. In fact, its normative framework may blur contestation or dissonance in the historical experience of women or obscure their renegotiation of gender contracts and relationships. Furthermore, the prevalence of archetypes of gender identity may, in fact, eclipse the existence of identities that are not shared but rather act in competition, thus reinforcing the monolithic dominance of a set of models of femininity.[12] Nonetheless, gender discourse can give us a clue to the system of ideas against which women had to measure their behavior and to the meanings of their challenges or compliance.

Domesticity and the Cultural Representation of Women

The ideology of domesticity provided the foundation of traditional gender discourse in late nineteenth-century Spain. As in Europe and North America, this model of good mothering and housewifery—the product of male thought—generated the notion that women's ambitions had to be exclusively limited to home and family.[13] Motherhood figured as the maximum horizon for women's self fulfillment and social role. Women's cultural identity was shaped through marriage and motherhood to the exclusion of any other social or professional undertakings. It is true that as late as 1910 the Catalan feminist Carme Karr still had to forcefully denounce life as a nun in a convent as an inadmissible option for women.[14] However, by the turn of the century conventual life no longer constituted a valid model of femininity. By then, the biological function of reproduction had already become the key component in structuring women's cultural identity.

The notion that women were inferior to men tended to prevail in the collective mentality of this period. Patterns of this gender discourse are quite clear in this representative text by Federal Republican Pompeyo Gener, published in one of the major newspapers, *La Vanguardia* in 1889, which also openly viewed women through the lens of biological essentialism:

> In herself, a woman, unlike a man, is not a complete being; she is only the instrument of reproduction, destined to perpetuate the species; while man is charged with making it progress, he is the generator of intelligence, at the same time creator . . . of the social world.[15]

Writing later, in 1916, he also claimed psychological differences that specifically characterized Mediterranean women: "women, and especially Greco-Latin women, are highly sensitive, and act more on impressions and suggestions than on real reflection."[16] This line of thought claimed that female psychology was at odds with rationality by linking women directly with nature, in accordance with the traditional dualism of Western thought that associated rationality with men and nature with women. In Gener's text, women's natural biological distinction became transposed to a differentiating cultural category that effectively assigned women a specific gender role with an inferior social status. Through the naturalization of sexual difference and its transference to a sociocultural category, biosocial thought decreed that the biological destiny of reproduction and differential psychological traits determined women's commitment in society.

In the late nineteenth century the *Angel del Hogar*, the "Angel of the House," a familiar trope in Western culture, became the dominant cultural representation of Spanish women. Defined in 1877 as "an angel of love, consolation to our afflictions, defender of our merits, patient sufferer of our faults, faithful guardian of our secrets, and jealous depository of our honor,"[17] she was also evoked as mother, spouse, or daughter: "as a mother she is the life and sweetness of the family, as a wife the vale of tears of her husband, as a daughter, an angel who keeps watch and prays for the lovingness and peace of the home."[18] Values and beliefs about femininity continued to evoke the model of domesticity initially formulated in the still popular sixteenth-century tract by Fray Luis de León, *La Perfecta Casada*, the "Perfect Married Lady," which assigned women the sacred mission of efficient management of the home.[19] In 1861 the eminent doctor and hygiene reformer, Pedro Felipe Monlau, underlined that household chores and home management were unquestionable female attributes:

> The government of a home naturally corresponds to women, to the housewife, the mother of the family and in many cases and due to various circumstances, to the eldest daughter. Without a mother, daughter, housewife or housekeeper, a family cannot prosper, be it poor, of medium resources or opulent. Thus it has been said that women are those who make or ruin a home.[20]

The importance of women's role in the family economy was commonly acknowledged in the nineteenth century when mothers and housewives were attributed an important social status and a role of significant consequence in the family.[21] At the turn of the century, however, the modernization of the discourse of domesticity generated a less approving view of the housewife, whose status declined over the decades.

Traditional gender discourse on domesticity implied that domestic responsibilities were women's exclusive duty. In this way, the cultural identity of women was not formulated through paid work but through the assumption of services inherent to the figure of a wife and mother. By establishing a cultural identity as mothers and wives the discourse of domesticity legitimated a negative attitude towards women's right to employment in the labor market, even among the working classes.[22] Another significant long term consequence was the redefinition of housework as nonwork and services, thus leading to its invisibility, lack of monetary value and ultimately, its low social status. In addition, it was also decisive in upholding an interclass definition of femininity that denied women's identities as workers while legitimating women's discrimination in the labor market. Although paid work was central to many women's lives and also to their sense of identity, as is illuminated in the second section of this volume, women had to contest dominant gender models of femininity to integrate a work identity into their sense of self.[23] The recognition of women´s work identity and their claims to the recognition of their right to waged work and professional training were priority demands in the agenda of early twentieth-century Spanish feminism.[24]

The public and private divide implied by this discrimination became a significant feature of gender discourse in modern Spain. The connections and changing boundaries of public and private are a crucial aspect of gender discourse and provide clues to the changing dynamics of gender relations. The public/private interaction also has a crucial impact on key issues such as citizenship, feminism, and female identity politics.[25] The ideology of domesticity established separate spheres assigning men a role in the public arena of production, politics and culture while constricting women to the private domain of home and family. Despite the historical reality of women's ongoing presence in the public arena,[26] the gendered distribution of space in the model of domesticity implied that women were only to occupy the domestic realm. *Flora o la educación de una niña*, a popular educational tract for girls initially published in 1888 by the educator Pilar de Sanjuán, reaffirmed in its 1918 edition the canon of women's confinement to the home:

> Women, especially, are destined by Providence to live secluded in the modest home, perfuming it with the essence of their ignored virtue, making it beautiful with their simple grace; so that those who have received from Heaven manly values, privileged talent and other gifts, have been the most wretched of their sex.[27]

The notion of the "natural" was constantly evoked to justify the separation of public and private spaces. By attributing certain "natural" traits to women, it determined their aptitude for motherhood in the home while contending that men's natural biological and psychological capacities geared them towards activities in the public arena. Almost a decade later, in 1922, dominant cultural views concerning women still espoused the notion of separate spheres as a natural divide between public and private.

> The value of man is active, that of a woman is passive. . . . Man is reflexive, analytical; woman, imaginative. The first is characterized princi-

pally by reason, consciousness, the second by sentiment, affection. The first is exceptionally apt for public life, for a life of relationships, for social commerce; the second is, by essence, *the angel of the hearth.*[28]

Furthermore, what is at stake in these messages of domesticity is the notion that any woman who did not conform to her natural or divine destiny of a secluded life in the home in unselfish service to her family provoked misfortune by her transgression of the norms of gender behavior. The naturalization of social thought meant that any challenge to gender roles implied defying nature.[29] The force of the discourse of domesticity as a mechanism of social control resided precisely in its link with nature. Any woman who contravened the norms of nature by adopting transgressive gender conduct was implicitly threatened with disaster. The pressure of this symbolic violence can thus explain the practice of consent by women and the sustenance of traditional norms of gender conduct.[30] Transgression in this symbolical vision opened up fearful threats of chaos, disorder, and unhappiness. As one author expressed in the early 1920s, any transgression by women threatened not only men but also the established social order:

> And, woe to Humanity! and woe to women! if one day the angel [of the Hearth] lets her fine wings be burnt by the destructive fire of pride and abandons the secluded and loving shelter in which she always lived, to launch herself madly in the wild whirlpool of public life in which man has to wage the most violent and terrible battles.[31]

The invasion of the public arena was perceived as a threat to the established gender order and incompatible with the ideology of respectable femininity. By taking on a male role in the public arena, women inevitably became "the most wretched of their sex."[32]

Through its symbolic violence and forceful normative tone, male-dominated gender discourse was effective in dissuading women from openly claiming a place in politics. The ideology of domesticity reinforced the notion of the lack of political subjectivity of Spanish women and the identification of the political sphere as male. This notion was further reinforced by the political culture of Spanish politics up to the 1930s. It is important to underscore that until the development of political reform under the democratic Second Republic, the social legitimization of individual political rights was not central to the Spanish liberal and democratic tradition. Predominant political culture did not associate progress with political rights. In this context, it is not surprising to find that Spanish feminists did not focus on political rights either. I have argued elsewhere that predominant political and gender culture led most Spanish women to legitimate their claims for women's rights on the grounds of gender difference rather than in the paradigm of equality.[33] In common with other Mediterranean countries such as France or Italy, the Spanish women's movement developed a strand of social feminism oriented to civil society.[34] Thus, the agenda of Spanish and Catalan feminists in the early twentieth century did not focus on political rights and suffrage but on sociocultural demands that entailed the defense of their social and civil rights, access to quality education and professional training, integration into the labor market and a voice on social issues. The combination of the political culture of Restoration Spain and the prevalent gender discourse of domesticity formed a significant sociocultural apprenticeship that shaped women's political subjectivity and favored the development of a social rather than political definition of Spanish feminism.[35]

Despite the negation of political agency to women, Spanish feminists were politicized and mobilized in collective action to achieve a feminist agenda that challenged the core of traditional gender discourse by claiming the public arena for women.[36] Political identities were also crucial in the formation of female identities through women's mobilization and experience of identity politics in nationalist, labor, and educational movements.[37] Although political enfranchisement was not a significant feature in the definition of Spanish feminism in this period, women were actively engaged in diverse forms of political action, as is illustrated in the third section of this book.

The Modernization of Gender Discourse

The growing modernization of Spanish society in the early twentieth century entailed significant modifications in economic, social, and demographic structures. This brought about changes in social structures and the transformation of cultural modes and values which, in turn, generated modifications in the ideological discourse on women. The traditional cultural representation of women as the *Angel del Hogar* was challenged by a new gender discourse based on the *Nueva Mujer Moderna*, the "New Modern Woman"—an "ideal" woman already in vogue in many European countries and in North America.[38] In the 1910s and 1920s, this new gender model was developed more systematically in highly industrialized Catalonia.[39] However, the notion of the modern woman was prevalent in many publications of the time and defended enthusiastically by women such as the feminist and socialist, Carmen de Burgos, in her book *La mujer moderna y sus derechos (The Modern Woman and Her Rights)*.[40]

Although not as widely accepted as the traditional *Angel del Hogar*, this new cultural representation became incorporated into social values and collective imagery about gender norms. This redefinition of women in terms of modernity was an effective symbolic device for adapting women to new social, political, economic, and demographic contexts. The shift from the old traditional model of femininity to the innovative *Nueva Mujer Moderna* allowed women to adjust to the process of modernity. It accommodated more restrictive gender roles toward the new needs of the labor market and society. This readjustment was, in fact, a very functional mechanism which allowed women access to specific areas of public activity such as education, culture, social welfare, and new sectors of the labor market. It thus responded to the new socioeconomic needs of society and, in this way, became part of hegemonical discourse on women.

Nonetheless, changes in the models of femininity and gender roles also responded to contestation by women. In this sense, the gender model of the "New Modern Woman" was liberating for many Spanish women. It was intentionally used by them in their struggle for emancipation to legitimate their claims to public spaces, to new experiences and to freedom. The importance of the notion of modernity in the subjective construction of a new gender identity by women can be seen in *La Victoria*, the first novel published by anarchist leader Federica Montseny in 1925. In the subtitle she presented her book as a narrative of "the problems of a moral order that are presented to women with modern ideas." Montseny claimed that her novel was subversive because it addressed the problem of the freedom and dignity of women and thus confronted all "the millenarian prejudices of masculinity. . . . "[41]

The model of the "New Modern Woman" challenged women's restriction to the home and contested discriminatory practices toward women. This modernized version of domesticity facilitated the adaptation of gender roles to the new social and labor demands of society. Nonetheless, it also enhanced women's personal and professional options and their subjective experience as women. Women used this new gender model as active social agents in their claim for the recognition of a work identity for women. Despite its modernizing effect, however, it must be stressed that it also maintained the core of traditional gender identity by redefining women as essentially mothers and childbearers, albeit in a new way.

Motherhood, Medical Discourse and the Construction of Modern Gender Identity

In the nineteenth century the discourse on domesticity was based on Roman Catholic ideals of women and also on scientific theories of the day. This article argues that one of the characteristics of the modern redefinition of gender discourse was the transfer from a religious legitimation to a medical and scientific foundation as had occurred in previous decades in other European countries.[42] By the early twentieth century Spanish society had initiated an ongoing process of modernization which implied, amongst other features, an increasing secularization of cultural values. In this context some professional groups, and especially physicians, played a significant role in the formulation of lay cultural parameters founded on a scientific authority that gradually replaced traditional, cultural values and their cosmovision of religious legitimation. As doctors began to supplant clergymen as male authorities on cultural norms, gender issues also became a crucial topic in their emergence as a social group charged with the guardianship of the nation's morals. It can also be argued that the appropriation of gender discourse by doctors was an effective device in their strategy to gain political recognition of the sociocultural status of the medical profession in Spanish society.[43] In any case, during the 1920s and 1930s medical discourse was the most influential source in the formulation of cultural values that redefined women's identity through motherhood.[44]

Doctors intervened significantly in the dissemination of a modernized gender discourse based on a reconceptualization of motherhood as women's social duty.[45] In the 1920s prestigious medical forums such as the *Sociedad Ginecológica Española*, the *Academia Nacional de Medicina*, and medical publications such as *El Siglo Médico*, systematically presented a medical discourse that attempted to influence gender patterns and cultural values. As in Europe, the politics of motherhood was a key construct in the modernization of social welfare and health services in Spain.[46]

The outstanding authority on medical gender discourse was the prestigious endocrinologist, Dr. Gregorio Marañón, whose theory on the differentiation and complementarity between the sexes became the standard paradigm for gender discourse in Spain in the following decades.[47] A physician of renowned eminence and international scientific prestige, Marañón's theory represented a readjustment of the explanatory basis of traditional Spanish gender models in consonance with the trends towards egalitarian, liberal, and democratic values. The scientific authority that underpinned Marañón's discourse gave it a modern basis. Furthermore, his theory of sexual difference was significant in the modernizing of gender discourse because it was based on the premise that women were not inferior to men. His proposition openly admitted an equal social status between the sexes, thus challenging one of the implicit assumptions of the traditional ideology of domesticity. Despite his admission of the principle of equality, Marañón qualified it with the incontrovertible recognition of biological difference. Thus the individual subject was sexed and consequently predetermined as a person. For women, then, motherhood was still the defining feature of femininity. In addition, his definition of gender identity signified the assignment of distinct and complementary social commitments for women.

In his famous tract *Maternidad y feminismo: Tres ensayos sobre la vida sexual*, published in 1927, Marañón made it quite clear, in a curious mixture of scientific and religious language, that motherhood was still the inevitable destiny for women.

> Here there is marked, in the deepest life of the organism, a difference which teaches us, with the cold demonstrative exactitude of physical chemistry, which divergent paths have been traced for each sex by Destiny. Man's economy has been built for wear, that is, for struggle in the exterior environment. Woman is made for saving energy, for concentrating it in herself, not for dispersing it around her; as in her womb the child who prolongs his life has to be formed, and from her breast the food for the first period of the life of the new being has to gush forth.
>
> Therefore, for us, it is unquestionable that a woman must first of all be a mother, forgetting everything else if it were necessary; and that, by the inexcusable obligation of her sex; just as man must apply his energy to creative work through the same inexcusable law of his manly sexuality. Let us hear once again the voice of God, insistent and eternal: "You, woman will give birth; You, man, will work."[48]

Explicit in Marañón's proposal was the espousal of motherhood and the perpetuation of the species through reproduction as woman's "supreme mission" in life. Thus, sexual difference was established in the biological terrain and hence transposed to the social realm. This biological definition of sexual difference also enunciated a gendered social division based on an irreducible divine destiny: women must give birth while men must work. Marañón's discourse articulated gender identities that linked masculinity to "manly" sexuality and femininity to motherhood and childbearing. It converged with traditional nineteenth-century discourses on domesticity in that it legitimated a strict division of the spheres, the sexual division of labor and the construction of female identity through motherhood. However, it also maintained biosocial thought as the theoretical foundation for a modern, scientific, gender discourse.

By establishing the precedence of motherhood as women's unavoidable destiny, Marañón subordinated any other life options to this priority. According to this set of ideas, any activity by women had to be subordinated to their defining role as mothers. Thus waged work and other activities outside the home could be compatible only as long as they did not interfere with women's primary obligation of motherhood. Full-time dedication to children was a woman's duty and in line with the legacy of traditional domesticity, her cultural identity was still constructed through motherhood.[49] Thus, despite the attempt to modernize the discourse of domesticity, gender identity for women was still not defined through work. Marañón only admitted women's paid employment in exceptional circumstances; when they were single or widowed, unattended by male support. In other words, they could work when life circumstances did not allow them to be identified as mothers. "Manly sexuality" was the pole of Marañón's definition of masculinity, but he also based male gender identity on the traditional model of the breadwinner. Despite the crucial impact of women in the formal and irregular labor markets,[50] he still upheld the traditional view that ignored work as a feature in the construction of female gender identity.

The scientific arguments developed by Marañón and other doctors to assert women's gender identity as mothers gave them a decisive voice of authority in the legitimation of modern cultural patterns concerning women and their role in society.[51] Medical science confirming motherhood as the core of female identity appeared to be indisputable. Moreover, it gave a scientific, professional tone to ideological and cultural values, thus disguising cultural norms as objective, scientific facts. The modernization of gender discourse, embedded in the ideology of domesticity and placed in a scientific medical framework, was a very effective device of social control. Challenging the modern redefinition of gender roles meant contesting the scientific basis for modernity while also engaging with traditional religious canons. It also implied formulating a gendered reading of cultural norms within an alternative conceptual framework for modernity, a steep challenge indeed for Spanish women, who were long denied equal access to the universe of culture and education. They still lacked a voice in the medical profession because their late official access to higher education (1910) impeded the development of a peer group of women doctors.[52] In the era of modernity, women did not have an established genealogy of doctors or scientists and thus lacked legitimate "scientific" or medical authority to challenge the gender norms espoused by doctors.

The definition of the social role of women through maternalism redefined motherhood as a common good, thus transcending women's individual rights as persons. Many doctors espoused the view that women's maternal duties went beyond biological motherhood to embrace "social motherhood." Maternalism allowed women who were not mothers to develop their social mission of motherhood as a service to the community. Thus social motherhood was defined through the dedication of maternal resources and services to society. As has been argued for other Western countries, it can also be contended for Spain that maternalist politics and gender discourse established the basis for a differential gender citizenship.[53] According to this differential, men had the right to exercise political citizenship based on direct involvement in the public world of politics. In contrast, a social citizenship founded on human reproduction but also on social motherhood was the grounds for women's political integration. This powerful political framework legitimated women's access to some spaces within the public arena, while guaranteeing that others were out of bounds.[54] It goes beyond the scope of this paper to explore the development of social feminism in Spain; suffice it to recall that the mobilization of women within the canons of gender discourse accepted the proclaimed view of social motherhood and, thus, the idea of a gendered social citizenship for women. This undoubtedly legitimated their claims to be active in the public arena, but at the same time, redefined the gendered boundaries of the public.

The inauguration of the democratic regime in 1931 forced a redefinition of citizenship according to the paradigm of equality and political rights.[55] Then, as is discussed in later chapters, the suffragist lawyer Clara Campoamor clearly espoused the defense of women's suffrage on the grounds of equality, freedom and individual rights. However, as I have stressed elsewhere, a traditional reading of sexual difference still prevailed in the conceptualization of citizenship during the suffrage debate in 1931 when male politicians across a political divide of left and right still claimed a differential gender citizenship.[56]

Sex Reform, Conscious Maternity, and Birth Control

The practice of birth control represents a significant key to shifts in cultural and religious values on intimate matters such as sexuality and motherhood. Attitudes to sexuality and birth control also provide insights into the gender dimensions of changing mentality and cultural values. Shifts in the politics of motherhood and reproduction can also illuminate women´s agency and attitudes towards collective gender identity. In Spain changes in cultural values regarding sexual conduct and procreation represented a significant break with traditional Roman Catholic views that associated sexuality with conception and rejected birth control as sinful. And yet, despite the rejection of the language of sin, it is important to note that the medical discourse around sex reform and birth control never questioned women's primary maternal function, and thus was focused around the (mostly male) management of that function rather than the liberation of female sexuality.

Most doctors espoused motherhood as an inescapable biological mandate for women. As late as 1934 in the *Academia Nacional de Medicina*, the official seat of medical authority, Dr. Vital Aza restated this point of view:

> It is the duty of any healthy woman to accept the integral capacity of her intimate biological nature (with no desertions other than those imposed by accidental, unhealthy or passing circumstances), and with the only pauses which derive from the period when she is fulfilling her duties of nursing. This [dedication] must be required as a command, whose strength stems from a biological mandate.[57]

Women were not allowed (by male physicians) to renounce their biological destiny of reproduction on a voluntary basis. As the guardians of the nation's morals, doctors sought to be both moral and medical arbiters on reproductive rights and practice. They largely attempted to define birth control as a medical, hygienic question and claimed that its regulation should be in the hands of the medical profession.

With very few exceptions, Spanish women had no public voice on birth control and sexual conduct. Although intimately linked to women's life experience and personal subjectivity, women's groups rarely openly discussed birth control, abortion, and voluntary motherhood or identified these issues as part of a feminist agenda. The strong gender divide of Spanish society led, in fact, to a situation where women's reproductive rights were not necessarily addressed in public by women, much less defended by them, not even among women activists in radical anticlerical groups such as anarchists.

Some discussion of these issues occurred among progressives, such as anarchist sex reformers and some members of the reformist eugenics movement, who developed a new code of sexual ethics.[58] It is significant, nonetheless, that even as late as the 1930s birth control was still sufficiently controversial that many progressive eugenicists were reticent to defend it.[59] It is true that *conscious maternity*, that is the voluntary regulation of motherhood, was defended by some members of these minority groups. However, when addressed within the reformist eugenics movement, it was couched in the modern, scientific language of eugenics, sex reform, and social medicine, and not of women's emancipation. Among the minority who espoused birth control, eugenic justifications such as the protection of the health of mothers and children were the basic arguments that rendered its practice socially acceptable.[60] Eugenic arguments legitimizing the practice of birth control were less problematical, as they framed the question in relation to high profile public concerns such as the diffusion of hereditary diseases (especially the "social plagues" of tuberculosis and venereal diseases) and race degeneration. The reduction of infant and maternal mortality rates was also used by eugenicists in their justification of birth control. Conscious maternity was thus not necessarily associated with women's sexual freedom but rather with medical motives that prevailed quite clearly over economic, cultural, or gender arguments.[61] Women's voices and specific concerns were not publicly presented by women's groups in this discussion of the politics of reproduction and motherhood.

Reshaping female sexuality rather than liberating it was the goal of most Spanish eugenicists. In fact, only a tiny group of radical birth controllers and eugenicists sanctioned an unrestricted use of birth control. The gynecologist Dr. Francisco Haro justified birth control on the grounds of eugenics, economics, and health.[62] He was also exceptional in his open espousal of birth control as a free, unconditioned decision of the individual, and in his defense of women's choice in this matter.[63] Another singular figure was the adolescent feminist writer, Hildegart Rodriguez, a well known sex reformer and eugenicist who was the Secretary of the Spanish League for Scientifically Based Sex Reform.[64] She openly espoused women's freedom to practice conscious maternity. However, the adoption of birth control based on free will, individual choice, or women's freedom was not commonly admitted to be ethical or socially acceptable by most eugenicists.

Anarchist sex reformers, on the contrary, generally tended to espouse birth control. In fact, it was seen as the key to a new sexual ethics that established a powerful indictment of traditional moral and religious sexual values. They also proclaimed the legitimacy of an active sexual life unconditioned by procreation or religious puritanism.[65] Since the turn of the century, their publications had played a decisive role in the dissemination of sexual education.[66] Congruent with their anarchist outlook, these sex reformers advocated self-help in sexual education. Through numerous publications and translations, they provided information on hygienic, sexual, and reproductive issues as a means to achieve the development of the full potential of the integral person, an old anarchist ideal.

Despite its pathbreaking defense of a new sexual code, anarchist sex reform continued to be gendered, as sexuality tended mainly to be defined in terms of male sexuality. Even such an outstanding sexologist as Dr. Félix Martí Ibáñez had an essentialist view of an abounding male sexual drive.[67] Although he recognized women's right to sexual pleasure, he considered that female sexual eroticism was of less interest and that a woman's sexual drive disappeared at the age of 40 to 45.[68] Moreover, following a tradition established in the early anarchist sex reform movement led by Luis Bulffi at the turn of the century,[69] women's sexuality still tended to be linked to motherhood. Although no longer defined as ethereal unsexed angels, anarchists did not reformulate women's identity through the notion of sexuality. Motherhood continued to define female identity while sexuality continued to be a key component in male identity. Female emancipation was thus seen in terms of women's freedom from unwanted pregnancies, through conscious maternity.[70]

A similar logic informed the anarchist attitude towards abortion, which was exemplified during the Civil War by Félix Martí Ibáñez, then Director General of Health and Social Assistance of the Generalitat of Catalonia.[71] His initiative, significantly known as the "Eugenics Reform," endorsed traditional anarchist sex reform, including abortion. It responded to a eugenic and hygienic class rationale and was primarily a pragmatic measure designed to regulate the practice of abortion in Catalonia.[72] The eradication of clandestine abortions and infanticide and the reduction of illnesses and mortality due to abortive practices were among its proclaimed goals. It also targeted a reduction in overall abortion figures in Catalonia through the establishment of a parallel family planning service that would enable working-class mothers to avoid having recourse to abortion. This abortion reform was quite exceptional in the context of Europe at the time, where few countries had introduced such measures.[73] It was very advanced, in that it maintained quite an unrestricted policy of admittance to its service based on therapeutical, eugenic, neomalthusian, and personal grounds. It also respected women's reproductive rights, as a woman's choice was considered decisive in the resolution to have a voluntary abortion. However, despite such innovative legislation and respect for women's will, the regulation of abortion was a notable failure. Only one birth control clinic was established, and the records of the major hospitals in the Catalan health services show that abortion services were practically negligible.[74]

Despite the development of abortion reform, then, women still remained aloof from reproductive politics. Moreover, with the exception of the Female Secretariat of the *Partido Obrero de Unificación Marxista*, the minority dissident marxist party, none of the women's antifascist organizations (anarchist, communist, socialist and unitary antifascist) defended legal abortion publicly.[75] What is even more significant is that the anarchist women's organization, *Mujeres Libres*, did not address the issues of abortion or birth control. They did not support the initiatives of their fellow anarchist, Martí Ibáñez. Despite its revolutionary rhetoric, the "Eugenic Reform" of abortion was still experienced by women as an exclusively male, medical initiative. Birth control and the legalization of abortion were still not included on the agenda of the women's organizations and these issues were not seen as agents of women's liberation, not even in the context of war and revolution.

Un/Contested Identities: Women's Voices and Motherhood

Mainstream and radical feminists did not challenge the male, public monopoly of birth control and sex reform, nor did they openly incorporate the politics of reproduction into their agenda. I contend that this choice was shaped by predominant gender discourse and gender identity; i.e., gender codes made it extremely difficult for Spanish women to have a voice on these issues. In the context of a conservative society, the Roman Catholic Church was still pervasive in shaping cultural values although these were not necessarily adhered to in practice. Thus, demographic data clearly shows the widespread decline in birthrates by the early twentieth century.[76] Furthermore, modern scientific medical views had also firmly established motherhood as women's natural mandate. Thus for women to address the problem of voluntary motherhood or sexual conduct represented an inadmissible transgression of gender conventions and an implicit contestation to both modern and traditional cultural norms. The stigma attached to any discussion of reproductive issues was thus enormous, even for men. In 1934, Félix Martí Ibáñez admitted that only nonconformists and rebels were interested in promoting an alternative sexual culture and developing sexual eugenics.[77]

Modern female identity was shaped around motherhood. The definition of women's identity through motherhood was not contested in the early twentieth century, as it was still an essentially unquestioned cultural value. It can be argued that the theoretical glass ceiling of the Spanish women's movement was the inability to challenge motherhood as the nucleus of female identity. In this context, it would have been very difficult for most women to articulate a public discourse on reproductive rights that could have dissociated them from the definition of their primary role and subjectivity as mothers. Dissenting voices among women were thus very exceptional. Few contested motherhood as the key to female identity or defended sex reform or birth control as ways to achieve their emancipation. The tiny number of women who openly challenged established views were not representative of Spanish women as a whole nor even of the feminist movement. Their voices of transgression contested gender norms of female decorum by expressing public views on such taboo issues. Although unrepresentative of the collective views of Spanish women of the time, they are an expression of dissonance and nonconformity to established norms of conduct and gendered cultural values. The strength of their subversive convictions in such a hostile context provides an insight to a different reality of dissent not often openly expressed by Spanish women.

Hildegart Rodriguez, whose life biography makes her a uniquely extraordinary figure, was the most outspoken defender of feminist sex reform.[78] In the early thirties she openly addressed the taboo topics of sexuality and birth control.[79] She contested conventional gender identity by espousing a new sexual ethics that embraced sexual equality for women as well as men: "Both sexes, whose equality feminists claim, with respect to the law, with respect to public opinion, must also be equal with respect to sexual conduct, with no other limitations than those which their conscience imposes."[80] She denounced the traditional position of the Church that held sexuality to be sinful and blamed both the double sexual standard and conventional cultural values about sex for the deprivation and "sexual hunger" of Spanish women.[81] In her view, the prevalent norms of the Roman Catholic Church had led women to identify sexual activity exclusively with procreation and thus to reject most sexual activity as sinful. Purity, chastity, and lack of sexuality were the key elements to the cultural identity of femininity based on motherhood. Traditional female identity, grounded in the cultural representation of the angel of the hearth, had generated the view of women as ethereal, angelical, asexual beings. In contrast, the gender identity of masculinity was constructed on the basis of sexual virility and male honor, understood as the control of women's sexuality. Hildegart's questioning of gender sexual norms led her to contest the predominant gender discourse on women. She defended the "sexual revolution" as a key force of modern civilization and of women's emancipation. She thus contested motherhood as the core gender identity for women and, indeed, provided a new reading of female identity through women´s sexual identity.

The anarchist feminist Lucia Sánchez Saornil was another exceptional dissenting female voice in the 1930s in her questioning of mainstream gender discourse.[82] Cofounder of the anarchist organization *Mujeres Libres* in 1936, she was silent on the issues of birth control and sex reform.[83] Nonetheless, she was unique in her open challenge to Gregorio Marañón's gender discourse based on motherhood as the nucleus of female identity. In a series of articles published in *Solidaridad Obrera* in the early 1930s, she argued that gender identity could not be based on biological essentialism. In her view, the definition of women as mothers represented the subjection of women to the biological process of reproduction:

> By the theory of differentiation a woman is no more than a tyrannical womb which exercises obscure influences to the utmost folds of her brain; all the psychical life of a woman is subordinated to a biological process, and that biological process is no other than pregnancy. . . . "To be born, to give birth and to die." Here are all the horizons women have.[84]

She vindicated the human potential of a woman free of the biological conditioning of motherhood. The individual rights of a woman as a person were, thus, paramount. Sánchez Saornil claimed that motherhood could never annul a woman as an individual. Women's self-fulfillment, freedom, and development were to be achieved as individuals, not as mothers.

This subversive viewpoint was exceptional among Spanish women, including feminists and working-class leaders who tended to acknowledge their cultural identity as mothers, as was the case with anarchist leader Federica Montseny.[85] Conformity to traditional gender identity points to the force of the legacy of gender discourse and its biosocial foundation. Although motherhood was reframed around a more political reading of social motherhood, which was linked with the notion of differential citizenship in the process of modernization of Spanish society, it still revolved around a traditional, biological notion of motherhood. In this, to my understanding, lies the strength of modern Spanish gender discourse. Uncontested in its core definition of motherhood, gender identity shaped most women's experiences, choices, and social itinerary, including the construction of historical Spanish feminism and the definition of its goals.[86]

However, Spanish women did contest a significant feature of gender identity: the public and private divide. Although most feminists did not define feminism in terms of suffragism and women's individual political rights, they did claim civil and social rights in work and education and their own active role in these areas.[87] Women as diverse as Carme Karr, Catalan feminist and director of the journal *Feminal*, Margarita Nelken, socialist activist, or María Espinosa, feminist leader of the *Asociación Nacional de Mujeres Españolas*, demanded recognition of women's work, an improved social status and the right to be active in many sociocultural fields in the public arena.[88] In this way they questioned the boundaries that limited female activity to the private sphere. They did not accept the separation of the spheres and women's exclusive confinement to the home. In their lives and activities, they staked out new spaces for women within the public arena. Many Spanish women attempted to redefine the standard norms of gender relations. They contested gender codes of conduct although they did not challenge their gender identity as mothers. Motherhood as the core definition of gender discourse and female identity remained uncontested, even celebrated. However, women intentionally developed effective identity politics around the experience of motherhood to achieve female emancipation and to contest discriminatory practices. The contested/uncontested nature of the category and bonds of motherhood provided a collective identity for Spanish women that generated complex and multifaceted experiences of contestation, self-empowerment, compliance, and social control.

Notes

1. For a more recent example see: Guy Hermet, *L'Espagne au XXe siècle* (Paris: P.U.F., 1992) and a critique of this interpretation in Mary Nash, "*L'Espagne au XXe siècle*: Critique," *History of European Ideas* 21, no. 4 (July 1995).

2. Rosa María Capel Martínez, *El sufragio femenino en la Segunda República española* (Madrid: Horas y Horas Editorial, 1992); Concha Fagoaga, *La voz y el voto de las mujeres, 1877–1931* (Barcelona: Icaria, 1985); Pilar Folguera, ed., *El feminismo en España: Dos siglos de historia* (Madrid: Fundación Pablo Iglesias, 1988); Mary Nash, "Two Decades of Women's History in Spain: A Re-appraisal" in Karen Offen, Ruth Roach Pearson, and Jane Rendall, eds., *Writing Women's History: International Perspectives* (London: Macmillan, 1991); Geraldine Scanlon, *La polémica feminista en la España contemporánea, (1868–1974)* (Madrid: Akal, 1986).

3. Mary Nash, "Experiencia y aprendizaje: La formación de los feminismos en España," *Historia Social* 20 (1995) and "Political Culture, Catalan Nationalism and the Women's Movement in Early Twentieth-Century Spain," *Women's Studies International Forum* 19, nos. 1–2 (Jan.–Apr. 1996).

4. Ibid.

5. Michel Wieviorka, *El espacio del racismo* (Barcelona: Paidós, 1992). See also C. Guillaumin, *Sexe, race et pratique du pouvoir: L'idée de nature* (Paris: Côté. Femmes Editions, 1992).

6. Mark B. Adams, *The Wellborn Science: Eugenics in Germany, France, Brazil and Russia* (Oxford: Oxford University Press, 1990); F. Anthias and N. Yuval-Davis, *Racialized Boundaries: Race, Nation, Gender and Class and the Anti-racist Struggle.* (London: Routledge, 1992); Verena Stolcke, *Racismo y sexualidad en la Cuba colonial* (Madrid: Alianza, 1992); Vron Ware, *Beyond the Pale: White Women, Racism and History* (London: Verso, 1992); and Paul Weindling, *Health, Race and German Politics between National Unification and Nazism, 1870–1945* (Cambridge: Cambridge University Press, 1989).

7. C. Gallagher and Thomas Laqueur, eds., *The Making of the Modern Body: Sexuality and Society in the Nineteenth Century.* (Berkeley, CA: University of California Press, 1987); Thomas Laqueur, *Making Sex: Body and Gender from the Greeks to Freud* (Cambridge, MA: Harvard University Press, 1990); Mary Poovey, *Uneven Developments: The Ideological Work of Gender in Mid-Victorian England* (Chicago, IL: University of Chicago Press, 1988).

8. Pat Caplan, ed., *The Cultural Construction of Sexuality* (London: Routledge, 1991); Emily Martin, *The Woman in the Body: A Cultural Analysis of Reproduction* (Boston: Beacon Press, 1987); Susan Rubin Suleiman, ed., *The Female Body in Western Culture* (Cambridge, MA: Harvard Univesity Press, 1986).

9. Sandra Lipsitz Bem, *The Lenses of Gender: Transforming the Debate on Sexual Inequality* (New Haven, CT: Yale University Press, 1993).

10. Teresa de Lauretis, *Alicia ya no: Feminismo, semiótica, cine* (Madrid: Cátedra, 1992); Clifford Geertz, *La interpretación de las culturas* (México: Gedisa, 1987); Joan W. Scott, "Gender: A Useful Category of Historical Analysis," *American Historical Review* 91 (1986).

11. For examples in wartime see: Jean Bethke Elshtain, *Women and War* (Brighton: The Harvester Press, 1987); Margaret R. Higonnet, Jane Jenson, Sonya Michel, and Margaret G. Weitz, *Behind the Lines: Gender and the Two World Wars* (New Haven, CT: Yale University Press, 1987); Mary Nash, *Defying Male Civilization: Women in the Spanish Civil War* (Denver, CO: Arden Press, 1995).

12. For a discussion of the implications of cultural identities in an international perspective, see Valentine M. Moghadam, ed., *Identity Politics and Women: Cultural Reassertions and Feminisms in International Perspective* (Boulder, CO: Westview Press, 1994); and Rajeswari Sunder Rajan, *Real and Imagined Women: Gender, Culture and Postcolonialism* (London: Routledge, 1993).

13. Georges Duby and Michelle Perrot, *Historia de las mujeres en Occidente* (Madrid: Taurus, 1993) vol. 4; Paula Baker, "The Domestication of Politics: Women and American Society, 1780–1920," *American Historical Review* 89 (June 1984); G.

Matthews, *"Just a Housewife": The Rise and Fall of Domesticity in America* (Oxford: Oxford University Press, 1987).

14. Carme Karr, *Cultura femenina: Estudi y orientacions. (Conferències donades en l'Ateneu Barcelonès els dies 6, 13 y 20 d'abril de 1910)* (Barcelona: Tip. L'Avenç, 1910), p. 29.

15. Pompeyo Gener, "De la mujer y sus derechos en las sociedades modernas," *La Vanguardia*, February 26, 1889.

16. Pompeyo Gener, *La dona mediterrània: Llegendes històriques*. (Barcelona: Societat Catalana d'Edicions, 1916), p. 12.

17. Julián López Catalán, *Breves reflexiones sobre la educación doméstica: Discurso leído el día 1 de mayo de 1877 en la sesión pública que celebró la Sociedad Barcelonesa de Amigos de la Instrucción* (Barcelona: Librería de Juan y Antonio Bastinos, Editores, 1877), pp. 10–11.

18. Buenaventura Ribas y Quintana, "Prólogo: María de Centelles," in *Llamamiento a la Juventud de Señoras Cristianas dedicado a la Asociación de Madres Católicas* (Barcelona: Imp. Pablo Riera, 1869), pp. 5–6.

19. This model was initially proposed in 1583 by Fray Luis de León in *La perfecta casada*. See the 1932 edition published in Barcelona by Montaner y Simón.

20. Pedro Felipe Monlau, *Nociones de higiene doméstica y gobierno de la casa para uso de las escuelas de primera enseñanza de niñas y colegios de señoritas* (Madrid: Librería de la Viuda de Hernando, 1890), pp. 108–109.

21. Pilar Ballarín, "La construcción de un modelo educativo de 'utilidad doméstica'," in Duby and Perrot, *Historia de las mujeres en Occidente*, vol. 4.

22. Mary Nash, "Identidad de género, discurso de la domesticidad y la definición del trabajo de las mujeres en la España del siglo XIX," in Duby and Perrot, *Historia de las mujeres en Occidente*, vol. 4 (Madrid: Taurus, 1993).

23. See also Cristina Borderías, *Entre líneas: Trabajo e identidad femenina en la España contemporánea, La Compañía Telefónica, 1924–1980* (Barcelona: Icaria, 1993); Pilar Pérez-Fuentes Hernández, *Vivir y morir en las minas: Estrategias familiares y relaciones de género en la primera industrialización vizcaína, 1877–1913* (Bilbao, Spain: Servicio Editorial, Universidad del País Vasco, 1993).

24. Mary Nash, "Experiencia y aprendizaje."

25. Baker, "The Domestication of Politics"; G. Bonacchi and A. Groppi, *Il Dilemma della cittadinanza: Diritti e doveri delle Donne* (Rome: Laterza, 1993); Gisela Bock and S. James, eds., *Beyond Equality and Difference: Citizenship, Feminist Politics, Female Subjectivity* (London: Routledge, 1992); P. Levine, *Feminist Lives in Victorian England: Private Roles and Public Commitment* (Oxford: Blackwell, 1990).

26. Fagoaga, *La voz y el voto de las mujeres*; M.J. Lacalzada de Mateo, *Mentalidad y proyección social de Concepción Arenal* (Ferrol: Cámera Oficial de Comercio, Industria e Navegación, 1994); María Gloria Núñez Pérez, *Trabajadoras en la Segunda República: Un estudio sobre la actividad económica extradoméstica (1931–1936)* (Madrid: Ministerio de Trabajo y de Seguridad Social, 1989).

27. Pilar Pascual de Sanjuán, *Flora o la educación de una niña* (Barcelona: Hijos de Paluzié Editores, 1918), p. 357.

28. E. Escartín y Lartiga, *El triunfo de la anarquía: Los problemas del siglo XX* (1922). Reproduced in Mary Nash, *Mujer, familia y trabajo, 1875–1936* (Barcelona: Anthropos, 1983), p. 64.

29. Mary Nash, "Identidades, representación cultural y discurso de género en la España contemporánea," in Pedro Chalmeta, Fernando Checa Cremades, et al., *Cultura y culturas en la historia* (Salamanca, Spain: Universidad de Salamanca, 1995).

30. Danièle Bussy Genevois, "Le corps du délit," *Violence ordinaire, violence imaginaire en Espagne*. Les Cahiers de Paris VIII (Paris: Presses Universitaires de Vincennes, 1995); Roger Chartier, "De la historia social de la cultura a la historia cultural de lo social," *Historia Social* 17 (Fall, 1993).

31. Escartín y Lartiga, *El triunfo de la anarquía*, p. 65.

32. Pascual de Sanjuán, *Flora o la educación de una niña*, p. 357.

33. Nash, "Experiencia y aprendizaje."

34. A. Buttafuoco, "Tra cittadinanza politica e cittadinanza sociale: Progetti ed esperienze del movimento politico delle donne nell'Italia liberale," in Bonacchi and Groppi, *Il dilemma della cittadinanza*; Nancy Cott, "What's in a Name: The Limits of 'Social Feminism,' or Expanding the Vocabulary of Women's History," *Journal of American History* 76, no. 3 (1989); Steven C. Hause, *Women's Suffrage and Social Politics in the French Third Republic* (Princeton, NJ: Princeton University Press, 1984); Karen Offen, "Defining Feminism: A Comparative Historical Approach," *Signs* 14 (1988).

35. Nash, "Experiencia y aprendizaje" and "Political Culture, Catalan Nationalism and The Women's Movement in Early Twentieth-Century Spain."

36. Ibid.

37. Rosa M. Badillo Baena, *Feminismo y educación en Málaga: El pensamiento de Suceso Luengo de la Figuera (1892–1920)* (Málaga, Spain: Universidad de Málaga, 1992); Esther Cortada Andreu, *Escuela mixta y coeducación durante la Segunda República* (Madrid: Ministerio de Asuntos Sociales, 1988); Mary Nash, *Defying Male Civilization*, chap. 1.; Mary Nash, ed., *Més enllá del silenci: Historia de les dones a Catalunya* (Barcelona: Generalitat de Catalunya, 1988); Mercedes Ugalde Solano, *Mujeres y nacionalismo vasco: Génesis y desarrollo de Emakume Abertzale*

Batza (1906–1936) (Bilbao, Spain: Universidad del País Vasco, 1993) and "Dinámica de género y nacionalismo," *Ayer* 17 (1995).

38. Nancy Cott, "Mujer moderna, estilo norteamericano: Los años veinte," in Duby and Perrot, *Historia de las mujeres* vol. 5; Atina Grossman, *"Girkultur* or Thoroughly Rationalized Female: A New Woman in Weimar Germany?" in J. Friedlander, Blanche Wiesen Cook and Carroll Smith-Rosenberg, eds., *Women in Culture and Politics: A Century of Change* (Bloomington, IN: Indiana University Press, 1986).

39. Elisenda Macià, "L'Institut de Cultura: Un model de promoció cultural per a la dona catalana," *L'Avenç* 112 (1988); Mary Nash, "La dona moderna del segle XX: La 'nova dona' a Catalunya," *L'Avenç* 112 (1988).

40. Carmen de Burgos, *La mujer moderna y sus derechos*. (Valencia, Spain: Ed. Sempere, 1927). See Paloma Castañeda, *Carmen de Burgos: "Colombine"* (Madrid: Horas y Horas, 1994).

41. Federica Montseny, *"La Victoria": Novela en la que se narran los problemas de orden moral que se le presenten a una mujer de ideas modernas*, 3d. ed. (Barcelona: La Revista Blanca, 1930), p. 6. See also Carmen Alcalde, *Federica Montseny: Palabra en rojo y negro* (Barcelona: Argos Vergara, 1983); Mary Nash, "Federica Montseny: Dirigente anarquista, feminista y ministra," *Arenal: Revista de historia de las mujeres* 1, no. 2 (Jul.–Dec. 1994); Susanna Tavera García, "Federica Montseny y el feminismo: Unos escritos de juventud," *Arenal: Revista de historia de las mujeres* 1, no. 2 (Jul.–Dec. 1994).

42. Mary Jacobus, Evelyn Fox Keller, and Sally Shuttleworth, eds., *Body/Politics: Women and the Discourses of Science* (New York and London: Routledge, 1990); Ludmilla Jordanova, *Sexual Visions: Images of Gender in Science and Medicine between the Eighteenth and Twentieth Centuries* (London: Harvester Wheatsheaf, 1989); Thomas Laqueur, *Making Sex*; Emily Martin, *The Woman in the Body: A Cultural Analysis of Reproduction* (Boston: Beacon Press, 1987).

43. Mary Nash, "Maternidad, maternología y reforma eugénica en España," in Duby and Perrot, *Historia de las mujeres*, vol. 5.

44. Ibid.

45. Ibid.

46. Gisela Bock and Pat Thane, eds., *Maternity and Gender Policies: Women and the Rise of the European Welfare States, 1880s–1950s* (London and New York: Routledge, 1991); Seth Koven and Sonya Michel, eds., *Mothers of a New World: Maternalist Politics and the Origens of Welfare States* (London: Routledge, 1993).

47. Gregorio Marañón, *Tres ensayos sobre la vida sexual: Sexo, trabajo y deporte, maternidad y feminismo, educación sexual y diferenciación sexual* (Madrid: Biblioteca Nueva, 1927) and *Amor, conveniencias y eugenesia* (Madrid: Historia Nueva, 1929).

48. Marañón, *Tres ensayos*, pp. 82–84.

49. Marañón, *Amor, conveniencias y eugenesia*, p. 27.

50. Núñez Pérez, *Trabajadoras en la Segunda República*; Pilar Pérez-Fuentes Hernández, *Vivir y morir en las minas.*

51. Teresa Ortiz, "El discurso médico sobre las mujeres en la España del primer tercio del siglo XX," in M.T. López Beltrán, ed., *Las mujeres en Andaluciá: Actas del segundo encuentro interdisciplinario de estudios de la mujer en Andalucía* (Málaga, Spain: Diputación Provincial, 1993).

52. M.C. Alvarez Ricart, *La mujer como profesional de la medicina en la España del siglo XIX* (Barcelona: Anthropos, 1988).

53. Bock and Thane, eds., *Maternity and Gender Policies*; Bonacchi and Groppi, eds., *Il Dilemma della cittadinanza*; E. Janes Yeo, "Social Motherhood and the Sexual Communion of Labour in British Social Science, 1850–1950," *Women's History Review* 1 (1992); Seth Koven and Sonya Michel, *Mothers of a New World*; Linda Gordon, ed., *Women, the State and Welfare* (Madison, WI: The University of Wisconsin Press, 1990).

54. The politics of motherhood was also quite clear during the Civil War and the Franco period: See Mary Nash, *Defying Male Civilization*, and "Pronatalism and Motherhood in Franco's Spain" in Bock and Thane, eds., *Maternity and Gender Policies* pp. 160–177.

55. Mary Nash, "Género y ciudadanía," in Santos Juliá, ed., "Política en la Segunda República," *Ayer*, no. 20 (1995).

56. Ibid. On the suffrage debate see Capel Martínez, *El sufragio femenino en la Segunda República española*; Scanlon, *La polémica feminista en la España contemporánea*; María Gloria Núñez Pérez, *Madrid, 1931: Mujeres entre la permanencia y el cambio* (Madrid: Horas y Horas, 1993).

57. Vital Aza y Díaz, "Derechos y deberes biológicos de la mujer: Parte doctrinal del discurso leído en su recepción como miembro de número de la Academia Nacional de Medicina," in *El Siglo Médico* 24 (February 1934).

58. R. Alvarez Peláez, "Introducción al estudio de la eugenesia española (1900–1936)," *Quipu* 2, no. 1 (1985); Mary Nash, "Social Eugenics and Nationalist Race Hygiene in Early Twentieth-Century Spain," *History of European Ideas* 15, nos. 4–6 (1992), and "Riforma sessuale e 'nuova morale' nell'anarchismo spagnolo," in Giuliana Di Febo and Claudio Natoli, eds., *Spagna anni Trenta: Società, cultura, istituzioni* (Milan, Italy: Franco Angeli, 1993); P. Pérez Sanz, C. Bru Ripoll, "La sexología en la España de los añós 30," *Revista de Sexología* 30 (1987).

59. Mary Nash, "El control de la natalidad y la difusión de los medios de contracepción: El debate en el movimiento eugénico español," *Actas del I Congrès Hispano Luso Italià de Demografía Històrica* (Barcelona, 1987).

60. *Genética, eugenesia y pedagogía social: Libro de las Primeras Jornadas Eugénicas Españolas* (Madrid: Javier Morata, 1934).

61. For comparative international perspectives on eugenics and sex reform see Mark B. Adams, ed., *The Wellborn Science*; Eugenics in Germany, France, Brazil and Russia. New York: Oxford University Press, 1990). N. Leys Stepan, "Race, Gender and Nation in Argentina: The Influence of Italian Eugenics," *History of European Ideas* 15, nos. 4–6 (1992); Angus McLaren, *Birth Control in Nineteenth-Century England* (London: Croom Helm, 1978); R.A. Soloway, *Demography and Degeneration: Eugenics and the Declining Birthrate in Twentieth-Century Britain* (Chapel Hill, NC: University of North Carolina, 1990); Jeffrey Weeks, *Sex, Politics and Society: The Regulation of Sexuality since 1800* (London: Longman, 1981); Paul Weindling, *Health, Race and German Politics between National Unification and Nazism, 1870–1945* (Cambridge: Cambridge University Press, 1989).

62. Years earlier Dr. Haro had participated in a controversial debate sanctioning the practice of abortion. See Mary Nash, "Ordenamiento jurídico y realidad social del aborto en España: Una aproximación histórica," in *Ordenamiento jurídico y realidad social de las mujeres* (Madrid: Universidad Autónoma Madrid, 1986).

63. Francisco Haro, "Concepción y anticoncepción," *Genética* 1: 339.

64. R. Alvarez Peláez and R. Huertas García-Alejo, *¿Criminales o locos? Dos peritajes psiquiátricos del Dr. Gonzalo R. Lafora* (Madrid: CSIC, 1987); Eduardo de Guzmán, *Aurora de Sangre: Vida y muerte de Hildegart* (Madrid: G. del Toro, 1972); Mary Nash, "A Disreputable Sex Reformer: Hildegart, the Red Virgin," in Aránzasu Usandizaga and Elizabeth Russell, *Wayward Girls and Wicked Women: In Memoriam of Angela Carter* (Barcelona: Universitat Autónoma de Barcelona, 1995).

65. Mary Nash, "Riforma sessuale e 'nuova morale' nell'anarchismo spagnolo."

66. Mary Nash, "El neomaltusianismo anarquista y los conocimientos populares sobre el control de la natalidad," in Mary Nash, ed., *Presencia y protagonismo: Aspectos de la historia de la mujer.* (Barcelona: Serbal, 1984).

67. See prologue by Ignasi Vidal in Félix Martí Ibañez, *Consultorio psíquico-sexual* (Barcelona: Tusquets, 1975).

68. Félix Martí Ibáñez, *Higiene sexual: Fisiología e higiene de las relaciones sexuales y del anticoncepcionismo* (Valencia, Spain: Biblioteca Estudios, 1934), pp. 17, 27.

69. Mary Nash, "El neomaltusianismo anarquista."

70. Luis Bulffi, *Huelga de vientres* (Buenos Aires: Editorial la Poligráfica, s.d.), p. 2.

71. See Mary Nash, "Marginality and Social Change: Legal Abortion in Catalonia during the Spanish Civil War," in William D. Phillips and Carla R. Phillips,

eds., *Marginated Groups in Spanish and Portuguese History: Proceedings of the 17th Annual Meeting of the Society for Spanish and Portuguese Historical Studies* (Minneapolis, MN: University of Minnesota Press, 1989).

72. Félix Martí Ibáñez, *Diez meses de labor en Sanidad y Asistencia Social* (Barcelona: Ed. Tierra y Libertad, 1937), pp. 69–79. Also Domènec Bellmunt, *La revolució i l'assistència social* (Barcelona: Imp. Clarasó, 1937).

73. Malcolm Potts, Peter Diggory, and John Peel, *Abortion* (Cambridge: Cambridge University Press, 1977).

74. Mary Nash, "L'avortement legal a Catalunya: una experiència fracassada," *L'Avenç* 58 (March 1983).

75. Nash, *Defying Male Civilization.*

76. See the *Boletín de la Asociación de Demografía Histórica.*

77. Márti Ibáñez, *Higiene sexual*, p. 11.

78. Alvarez Peláez and Huertas García-Alejo, *¿Criminales o locos?*; de Guzmán, *Aurora de Sangre.*

79. Hildegart Rodriquez, *La rebeldía sexual de la juventud* (1931; reprint Madrid: Anagrama, 1977), p. 195; and *El problema sexual tratado por una mujer española* (Madrid: Javier Morata, 1931).

80. Rodriquez, *La rebeldía sexual*, p. 57.

81. Rodriquez, *La rebeldía sexual*, p. 195.

82. Nash, Mary. "Dos intelectuales anarquistas frente al problema de la mujer: Federica Montseny y Lucia Sánchez Saornil," *Convivium*, nos. 44–45 (1975).

83. On Mujeres Libres see Martha A. Ackelsberg, *Free Women of Spain: Anarchism and the Struggle for the Emancipation of Women* (Bloomington, IN: Indiana University Press, 1991); Mary Nash, *Mujeres Libres: España 1936–1939* (Barcelona: Tusquets, 1976), *Mujer y movimiento obrero en España, 1931–1939* (Barcelona: Fontamara, 1981), and *Defying Male Civilization.*

84. Lucía Sánchez Saornil, "La cuestión femenina en nuestros medios," *Solidaridad Obrera* 15 (October 1935).

85. Nash, "Dos intelectuales anarquistas frente al problema de la mujer."

86. Nash, "Experiencia y aprendizaje."

87. Ibid.

88. A.M. Aguado, et al., *Textos para la historia de las mujeres en España* (Madrid: Cátedra, 1994).

2

Shaping True Catholic Womanhood: Francoist Educational Discourse on Women

Aurora Morcillo Gómez

> Women never discover anything,
> they lack the creative talent that
> God reserved only for male intelligence.[1]
>
> —Pilar Primo de Rivera

The politics and construction of the nation remained a predominantly male endeavor in Spain, as in most European countries, until the twentieth century. The sociocultural formation of identity was shaped by the ideology of separate spheres based on different gender roles.[2] According to Victoria de Grazia, "'nationalizing the masses' largely referred to male subjects." Men were the soldiers, workers, taxpayers, consumers, and ultimately, voters of the nascent nation-states,[3] and women were excluded from the public rhetoric and process of nation-building. Under totalitarian regimes such as those of Italy or Nazi Germany, gender difference figured centrally in the political discourse that defined national and individual identities.[4] These regimes took great care to articulate women's roles and obligations as part of the national agenda.

Likewise, Franco's state viewed women as its indispensable partner in nation-building. It put in place institutions and promulgated laws to officiate women's duties as mothers and daughters of the fatherland. Both the state and the Catholic Church reinforced the separate spheres ideology. As the regime (and the Catholic Church) saw it, gender difference constituted the very essence of selfhood; it rendered stability and social order to the nation, and clarity of purpose to the individual.[5] This chapter explores gender relations under Franco's regime by focusing on the educational discourse about women. More specifically, it examines the new regime's National-Catholic agenda from a gender perspective and the elaboration of what I call "true Catholic womanhood."

From his ascendancy in 1939 to his death in 1975, Francisco Franco's dictatorial power rested on his ability to forge a popular consensus around a Catholic nationalist platform. Franco's regime looked back with nostalgia to Spain's birth as a nation, to 1492 and the Columbian discovery, to the Spanish Empire and its Catholic crusades.[6] As in the glorious past, Catholicism became the spiritual axis around which nationhood would be fashioned. The same Church that blessed the empire would bless Franco's campaign against those twentieth-century infidels—the Reds.

On both the national and the individual levels, this National-Catholic ideology lent cohesion to Franco's regime and legitimized its existence. It was the glue that bound together those diverse right-wing forces that fought during the Civil War on the self-proclaimed nationalist side against the legally-constituted Second Republic. As the term implies, National-Catholicism fused Falangist (i.e., Spanish fascist) doctrine with traditional Catholic tenets, affording Franco the political and divine sanction to govern Spain.[7] Gender ideology became, as well, crucial in defining the state, its territory, and authority. Spiritual/Catholic values, authority, and discipline were to govern an important institution: the family. Social and gender relations blended in the family, and women—as mothers—represented an essential element in the reconstruction of the fatherland.

Franco's permanence in power required a considerable degree of sustained popular support—a national consensus, of sorts—which the regime sought to forge through its system of education. The new educational system sought to dismantle the secular quest for modernization initiated in the eighteenth century and carried out by the Free Institution of Learning (F.I.L.) and later the Second Republic. Francoist recovery of tradition implied the total destruction of the Republican attempt to bring Spain closer to Europe. To focus on the Francoist educational system and the university in particular is significant because education came to serve the forces of unity and uniformity. It was the process by which the individual related to the concept of nation. Through the promotion of a singular language, history, and religion, the Francoist educational system inculcated, on a grand scale, a sense of individual duty to the National-Catholic agenda.[8] Duty, for its part, was defined differently for men and women. The official arbiters of female duties, the Catholic Church and the women's section of the Falange (the *Sección Femenina*), dictated that women were to serve the *patria* with abnegation through dedication of the self to the common good.[9] This was the central tenet of "true Catholic womanhood," rooted in principles set forth in Catholic encyclicals and treatises dating from the sixteenth century. These texts served as guideposts for women's education policy in Franco's Spain. In general terms, the educational system became the instrument by which the state perpetuated its patriarchal politics; the university, in particular, was a male realm, a site of state power, where the political elites were educated, where few women attended, and where scholarship stood inimical to femininity.

The Secular Movement and the Second Republic

The Francoist crusade to resurrect and revitalize Catholic tradition, including its influence in education, was counter to the social reforms of the Second Republic and a secular movement dating back to the Enlightenment. Enlightenment thinkers, like Gaspar Melchor de Jovellanos or Manuel José Quintana, looked to secular education to redeem the country from backwardness and religious superstition, and to bring it closer to the rest of modern Europe.[10] But lay notions of education did not go uncontested. Traditionalists, who in the nineteenth century called themselves neo-Catholics, protested any effort to diminish their influence in education, viewing reform as a threat to the Spanish heritage.

Throughout the nineteenth century, the educational system served as an ideological battlefield, in which the forces of secularization engaged the forces of tradition. Spain's secular movement gained momentum with the introduction of the ideas of Karl Christian Friedrich Krause (1781–1832), an obscure German philosopher, and the founding of the *Institución Libre de Enseñanza* (Free Institution of Learning) in 1876.[11] Krausism spread in Spain in the mid nineteenth century with Julián Sanz del Río, professor at the University of Madrid. Krausists rejected the utility of faith as the guiding norm for human knowledge, and hence, rejected the involvement of the Church in the learning process. By contrast, traditionalists—or neo-Catholics—embodied the antithesis of Krausism. Their belief in the greatness of Spanish history and religious orthodoxy constituted the main component of traditional thought. Neo-Catholics insisted that Spain's historical mission was to revitalize the Christian doctrine that had originally inspired its forging as a nation.

Toward the end of the nineteenth century, the educational debate incorporated other social forces: an active proletariat, regionalist movements (particularly in Catalonia), the development of anarchist ideals, and the emergence of the "woman question." Within the context of broader social and political debates, discussions about female education at the turn of the century (taking place at the Pedagogical Conference of 1892) revolved around two important issues: the propriety of coeducation, and the right of access to higher education and professional training for women.

The twentieth century witnessed some coeducational initiatives in Spain. The Free Institution of Learning in Madrid and the anarchist Modern School of Francisco Ferrer Guardia in Barcelona promoted coeducation in contrast to the Catholic Church prescription of sex-segregated schools. According to Catholic doctrine, coeducation was an offense to morality. The fact that it was part of the curriculum of the liberal Free Institution of Learning and the anarchist schools of Ferrer Guardia made both institutions, from the Catholic point of view, hotbeds of rebellion and anticlericalism.

Ferrer Guardia's pedagogy sought global emancipation of the individual. He developed his revolutionary program in the School of Barcelona (Escuela de Barcelona), inaugurated in 1901. Following the precepts of a rational and secular school, Ferrer Guardia proposed coeducation for the equality of the sexes. He considered coeducation the only way to make women true companions of men.[12] Meanwhile, the founders of the Free Institution of Learning emphasized secular schools, coeducation, and the instruction of women. In the public arena, women's access to higher education was encouraged by some members of the F.I.L. in such institutions as the Students' Residence and the Institute (*Instituto Escuela, Residencia de Estudiantes)*, the Female Residence (*Residencia Femenina)*, the Council of Public Instruction (*Consejo de Instrucción Pública*), and the Committee for Post-Graduate Studies (*Junta de Ampliación de Estudios*)—all in Madrid. As a result of these efforts, during the first three decades of the twentieth century women's access to higher education improved.[13]

The Second Republic sought to bring the secular ideals of the F.I.L. to a wider audience with a reform of the state educational system that would reach the proletarian masses. Article 48 of the Constitution of 1931, for example, established that education was entirely the responsibility of the state, not the Catholic Church. The touchstone of the Republican legislation was the secularization of schools, embodied in the law of June 6, 1933 which granted state institutions control over the educational system, excluding the Catholic Church from the process. Despite its introduction, the law was never effective, due to a shortage of public schools and the rise of the new conservative Coalition of the Spanish Right (Coalición Española de Derechas Autónomas, CEDA) in 1933.[14] The Republic's desire to educate the Spanish people, however, was not entirely fruitless. Republican educational policy aspired to eradicate illiteracy for both sexes. Further, women's access to, and opportunities in, higher education greatly improved during the Republican years. The presence of women at Spanish universities grew slowly and, although small, this growth was indicative of the official interest in education. Such progress would abruptly come to an end with the outbreak of the Civil War in 1936 and the victory of conservative Catholic forces by 1939.

The Francoist Recovery of Tradition

From its inauguration in 1939 the Francoist regime sought to fuse Catholicism with the concept of fatherland and national identity. It aspired to restore what it considered Spanish tradition, to revive the imperial spirit of the

Catholic Monarchs five centuries earlier. José Pemartín, a Monarchist-turned-Falangist, proclaimed the nationalist movement to be founded on "sixteenth-century Spanish Catholicism, because our national identity forged itself in that historical moment, incarnating the Catholic ideal of our Military Monarchy."[15] Fragmented and demoralized after the Civil War, Spain's reconstruction consisted of achieving a national unity, but only through the restoration of her glorious "imperial Catholic past."[16]

Spain's destiny demanded the cooperation of all Spaniards, especially the younger generations. Hence, education became the new "crusade" for the forces of tradition. The Francoist educational system aspired to dismantle that of the Second Republic. Extremely hostile to secular ideals, Francoist National-Catholic pedagogy presented itself as antithetical to the F.I.L.'s anti-Christian and "anti-Spanish" postulates.[17] Against democratic materialism and disorder, the new educational system tried to restore an authentic Spanish ethos and spiritual values through authority and discipline.

Catholic values started with the family. The family represented a microcosm of social and gender relations, and so preparing women to be mothers became a bedrock of Francoist reconstruction. Thus, educating women in the preservation of Spanish feminine values was fundamental. The domestic orientation of Spanish women's training was regulated by two legal texts. The first established the Central Junta for the Professional Instruction of Women (Junta Central de Formación Profesional de la Sección de Enseñanzas Profesionales de la Mujer) on November 17, 1943, while the Decree of March 2, 1945 established the Institute for Women's Professional Training (Instituto de Enseñanzas Profesionales de la Mujer).[18] In its introduction, the March 1945 decree proclaimed the essential participation of Spanish women in the national endeavor. "The female sex," it stated, "is entrusted with the task of defending traditional family values and preserving the domestic arts, essential to maintain happiness in the home."[19] Rooted in this assumption, the regime's propaganda presented a woman's intellectual interests as dangerous to her femininity, especially to her ultimate destiny, motherhood.

The new educational system aspired to forge true Catholic womanhood by appealing to Spanish historical tradition. First, the regime sought to revive sixteenth-century devotions to saintly female figures—such as Santa Teresa de Jesús or the Virgen del Pilar—and hoped to repopularize Renaissance treatises on the character and proper education of women by Fray Luis de León and Juan Luis Vives. Second, the Francoist official discourse on women drew on the traditional doctrine of the Catholic Church as prescribed in Pius XI's encyclicals "Divini Illius Magistri" (1929) and "Casti Connubii" (1930). Finally, the decree of December 28, 1939 and the University Regulatory law of 1943 had already entrusted the Female Section of the Falange with the task of preserving Catholic values among Spanish women.

National-Catholicism and Gender Relations: The Foundations of True Catholic Womanhood

To establish role models for both men and women, the Francoist regime manipulated traditional sacred images. In particular, Giuliana di Febo has pointed to the importance of Saint James, the Virgen del Pilar,[20] and the Sacred Heart, as well as that of the figure of Saint Teresa de Jesús, one of the great mystics, reformer of the Carmelite Order, and founder of new convents throughout Spain. Teresa de Jesús was designated one of the most important role models for Spanish womanhood.[21] She was portrayed as "old Christian," noble and obedient to the Church dogma against Lutheran threats, and was later proclaimed "Santa de la Raza" (Saint of the Race), despite the fact that in 1946, the researcher Narciso Alonso Cortés found documents in Valladolid that demonstrated her Jewish origins. This discovery was conveniently ignored by the regime.[22]

In addition to manipulating the saint figures, the Francoist regime sought to revive Catholic tradition with the republication in the 1940s and 1950s of Renaissance treatises on the education of Christian women. These works included Juan Luis Vives' *La instrucción de la mujer cristiana* (1523) and Fray Luis de León *La perfecta casada* (1583).[23] For Vives, the only goal of women's education was to preserve their honesty and chastity, for their lives rotated around the protection of their physical and spiritual virginity. "When women do not know how to protect their chastity," wrote Vives, "they deserve the worst of punishments; paying with their own life is not enough."[24] Virtue was the product of education. Vives did not deny women's ability to learn, but he considered that the main goal in educating a lady was to separate wisdom from lust. The curriculum should be chosen carefully to train women's character for life in the "womanly sphere." The readings assigned included the Bible, the writings of the Church Fathers, Plato, Cicero, and Seneca. Vives considered educated women to be more virtuous and morally superior to those who did not study. Educated women were deemed better "amas de casa" and more virtuous mothers, and were more receptive to their husband's authoritative "reason."

Although chastity was the road to absolute female perfection, marriage represented the ultimate goal for the Christian woman, allowing her to achieve motherhood. In Fray Luis de León's *La perfecta casada*, the author praised the excellence of virginity over marriage but argued that each state provided its own path to the perfection of the female soul. The author used the Sacred Scriptures to define his own theory of a "woman of value" [mujer de valor]. Such value resided precisely in the fact that such women were more than rare. A "*woman of value* . . . is difficult to find, and there are very few. Therefore, the foremost compliment to the good woman is to say that she is a rare thing . . .

because a woman by nature is feebler and weaker than any other animal."[25] In the treatise, de León spelled out the virtues of the Christian married woman. Spiritual and physical chastity after marriage was inherent to female identity. Adultery represented the worst of transgressions: "A woman is not laudable for being chaste, because it would be indecent and abominable if she was not. Hence, the Holy Spirit does not ask her to be chaste, but assumes she already is. Breaking her husband's trust would be like the stars losing their light and the sky falling; it would violate the laws of her nature."[26]

In both works, female identity emanated from the objectification of women's bodies. First they emphasized the preservation of virginity, and then sacralized the female body as the receptacle of human life through motherhood after marriage. The ultimate role model prescribed for women was the Virgin Mary, in whom both virginity and motherhood coincided. In such a way, the discourse established the Catholic binary opposition within female essence: Mary/Eve; holy/evil. According to Vives and de León, Christian perfection for Catholic women was achieved through a struggle against an evil nature bent on subverting either virginity or motherhood. Such redemption was possible only through suffering: suffering for God, the fatherland, their husbands, and their children.

In addition to reclaiming sixteenth-century treatises on female education, Franco's regime looked to contemporary Church doctrine to reaffirm its agenda. In particular, it heeded two encyclicals of Pius XI: "Divini Illius Magistri" and "Casti Connubii." These documents laid the foundation for notions of Spanish femininity—notions that would remain well into the 1960s.[27] Reaching the reading public in journals such as *Razón y Fe, Ecclesia*, or *Senda*, Church doctrine stressed the biological differences between men and women.[28] This was not a negation of women's right to be educated, but the belief that they ought to be trained differently and separated from men. Men were to be the soldiers and scholars; women the wives and mothers. Educated in separate disciplines and settings, the destinies of men and women would converge in marriage and progeny, and in their service to the Church and the nation.

"Divini Illius Magistri," published in 1929, was an encyclical letter on the Christian education of youth. It proclaimed educators and students to be agents of Catholicism in Christian nations. Education was a social endeavor, to be consecrated by the Church, facilitated by the state, and carried out by the family. The Vatican assumed supremacy in questions of education, proclaiming that "only the Church possesses . . . the total moral authority, *Omnem Veritatem*, that encompasses all the particular truths."[29] Invoking its divine power, the Church presumed to regulate truth and morality in Catholic countries, insisting on its right to watch over public and private institutions of knowledge. The roles of the Church and family in Christian education superseded that of the state, explained "Divini Illius Magistri," since both "have this divine and natural right [which] is undeniable, inevitable, [and] uncompromisable."[30] The familial right to educate the children prevailed over the right of the state in matters of instruction.

For its part, the state possessed a double function in the educational process: to protect and to promote Christian education without depriving the family of its primacy in the matter. The state's laws were to secure the family's sacred duty of educating its progeny, while at the same time respecting the supernatural rights of the Church. Christian education, according to Pius XI, was not only directed to the soul but to the body as well. Individuals in their totality constituted the subjects to be educated. Because of original sin and the feeble nature of humanity, the Church thought it necessary to correct man's disorderly inclinations and cultivate his good ones from childhood on.

"Divini Illius Magistri" grounded gender differentiations in biological disparity. Physical separation of the sexes was deemed necessary to achieve biological determinism. Coeducation, therefore, was not only wrong but pernicious to Christian learning. It stemmed from a deplorable misconception of what the legitimate social order ought to be. Based upon the idea of a levelling equality, coeducating the sexes would produce a promiscuous human society. "Our Lord," reads the text, "orders and disposes that the perfect coexistence of the sexes must take place within marriage."[31] Nature had made them different not only biologically, but in inclinations and capabilities; therefore, there was no need to educate both sexes in equal terms. In this light, and in view of the androcentric character of the institution, the presence of women at university would be seen not only as strange but as a transgression of the ideal of Catholic womanhood promoted by the Church and the regime.

Gender relations were further spelled out in 1930 in an encyclical letter on the dignity of Christian marriage, "Casti Connubii." It reiterated the principles that Leo XIII had laid out fifty years earlier, in his encyclical "Arcanum." Both documents endorsed four Victorian feminine virtues: piety, purity, submissiveness, and domesticity. "Casti Connubii" ordained that women should submit their very being to men's will, following the so-called "love hierarchy" which "embraces both the supremacy of the man over the woman and children, as well as the *diligent submission of the woman and her complete obedience* [my emphasis], recommended by the apostle with the following words: 'married women ought to be subjected to their husbands, as they are subjected to the Lord; because the man is the head of the woman as Christ is the head of the Church'."[32] If education policy was to segregate the sexes, "Casti Connubii" legitimized gender relations only in marriage and family, declaring sacred the cooperation between the spouses.

It further claimed that the ultimate purpose of marriage was reproduction, and permitted sexuality only within the terms of reproduction, condemning contraception "because the man who avoids the conception of progeny, even with his own wife, acts illicitly and immodestly."[33] In promoting reproduction, self-sacrifice as well as submission should be the motto of a woman's life. Thus, Pius XI asserted that the heroism of motherhood was the pride and glory of the Christian wife, even when there was the risk of losing her own life. "Who will not admire extraordinarily, a mother who gives herself up to a certain death, with heroic strength, to preserve the life in her womb?"[34]

Any rebellion from this role condemned her to life as a sinner, and thus feminism was regarded as the most ominous threat to the female soul. "Casti Connubii" described women's efforts to achieve equality as debasing and unnatural: "There are many who dare to say, with much audacity, that the servitude of one spouse to another is an indignity, that both spouses have equal rights, defending presumptuously that . . . there ought to be a certain emancipation for the woman."[35] True freedom for the Christian woman resided within the domestic realm, at home. The Church recognized that, as a human being, she deserved the same respect as the man. But as in everything else there was to be a certain inequality and moderation, in order to preserve the welfare of the family and the proper unity and stability of the household. The state was to guarantee that changes in modern society did not alter the purity of social conventions and subvert the common good of the family. Therefore, the laws would accommodate those changes, taking into account that women were, by nature, different.[36]

Gender Relations in the Francoist University

Shortly after its victory, the Francoist regime set the stage for education reform with an agreement with the Vatican that mandated the use of Church doctrine in education—private and public—and made the ecclesiastical hierarchy the guardian of spiritual purity and social customs.[37] Only two weeks after the end of the war, the government initiated a project to reform the university.[38] It envisioned that the main goal of the Spanish university was to inculcate morality and patriotism, revitalizing the ideals of *hispanidad* along with tradition and Catholicism.[39]

This reform inspired the *Ley de Ordenación Universitaria*, (University Regulatory Law, U.R.L.) of 1943, which regulated higher education until 1970. The U.R.L. represented the clearest politicization of the university in the service of the new regime's National-Catholic precepts. While there was no explicit exclusion of women from higher learning, their presence at the university level was discouraged and not recognized during the two first decades of the regime. Probing into the legal text we learn how the regime defined the identity of the university subject, and how this identity was irreconcilable with the official discourse on Spanish femininity, i.e., of true Catholic womanhood.

The U.R.L. consisted of thirteen chapters and 101 articles and provisions. The introduction was little more than a bombastic discourse that defined the "Hispanic concept of university." The primary mission of the new university was to transmit Catholic knowledge concerning morality, spirituality, discipline and service to the fatherland and state. Thus, the U.R.L. defined the Spanish university as follows:

> The corporation to which the state entrusts its spiritual enterprise to fulfill the scientific, cultural, and educational activities of the nation, with service as the norm imposed in the current Spanish revolution. To develop this concept, the law restores to the university all its traditional functions, creating, reorganizing, and restoring the proper organs.[40]

Most importantly, the law entrusted the university with the task of creating a political elite able to fulfill the Francoist spiritual revolution and, implicitly, to lead that revolution in the broader (male) public realm.

The law's second chapter focused on the scholar/subject that the university hoped to create. Being a good scholar and a good Catholic were one and the same; the soul of a scholar was also that of a soldier; thus, in the introduction, we read: "Such flowering of the university creates a theological army which will fight against heresy."[41] The main goal was to restore the genuine Spanish identity that had been betrayed by the Free Institution of Learning and by laicization:

> We are living through times of crisis and routine in which, if intellectual education was unsettled, it had also succumbed to the hands of academic freedom. Moral and religious education, and even love for the fatherland, was hidden by ominous shame, suffocated by the foreign, secular, cold, Krausist, and masonic Free Institution of Learning.[42]

The university mission rested on its ability to restore traditional Spanish values as prescribed by God and tradition.[43]

As is clear by the military images, the U.R.L. defined the scholar in the purest male sense by *his* allegiance and devotion to the fatherland and the Catholic hierarchy. During this time of spiritual revolution, the male student had to devote himself to Spain's imperial destiny (*destino imperial*). The participation of a scholar in the national endeavor involved defending Spain's Catholic homogeneity and exporting those ideas to the world:

> When the time comes for national unity and the supreme moment of Spain arrives, our University . . . appears in its plenitude to serve the ideals of Spain's imperial destiny . . . to produce a knowledge that takes

over the world and educates and shapes men who . . . honor Spain and serve the Church.[44]

To fulfill these goals, the law established a system of normalization that regulated the university with a rigorous disciplinary structure to better exercise power and control over its population. Thus, the Spanish university may be understood as one of those intersections of knowledge and power that Foucault calls "technologies." According to Foucault, "disciplinary technologies" arise in a large number of different settings such as workshops, schools, prisons and hospitals. Their aim is to forge a "docile body that may be subjected, used, transformed, and improved."[45] Of paramount importance to the Francoist regime was to guarantee that those involved in higher learning remained faithful to the fatherland. Throughout the U.R.L., one finds an implicit and constant appeal to the university governing bodies to maintain surveillance and discipline over the university departments and population. Thus, Chapter V (article 36b) declares that the *Servicio de Protección Escolar* should "exercise surveillance over the life of the students." The same idea of surveillance appeared in articles 41g, 43a, 46a, and 48a. The last chapter is entirely dedicated to "Academic discipline" and spelled out the different degrees of violation and the pertinent punishment of faculty, students, and administrative personnel. It advised academic authorities to evaluate the degree to which the individual escaped or flouted the normalizing network of the university institution. Individuals had to be supervised and disciplined. Control of the population remained essential to the automatic functioning of power.[46]

The Spanish University Student Union (*Sindicato Español Universitario, S.E.U.*), founded in 1934 as a division of the Falangist movement, served as the organizing body to carry out the mission prescribed by the Church and state. The U.R.L. required all students, male and female, to register in the S.E.U. upon enrollment, but the organization was subdivided by gender. Thus, a separate Female Section of the Falange (*Sección Femenina*) was founded along with the S.E.U., and in 1939 it was appointed as the only women's political organization, with the task of indoctrinating Spanish women in the regime's precepts. A part of the Female Section within the S.E.U., known as the *Sección Femenina*/S.E.U., became the mediator between the state and the female population at the university level. This group was in charge of keeping domestic values alive among female students through mandatory university social service. In contrast, male students served the country by completing their military obligations in the University Militia, founded in 1941 to foster within students a militant sense of enthusiasm toward their duties and obligations in the context of the Second World War.[47]

Gender distinction was further defined in section nine of the U.R.L. Article 70f addressed the responsibilities and rights of scholars: "performing university duties, taking into account, when necessary, the distinction of the sexes."[48] Though college women who belonged to the S.E.U. were the intellectual elite of the Falangist women, their future roles as wives and prolific mothers remained uncontested. Within an institutionalized setting in high schools and later in college, women were to learn the domestic arts of cooking and infant care through their training in Social Service, in the Domestic Schools (*Escuelas del Hogar*), and in the schools of professional training for women.

To reconcile the contradiction between scholarly and female identities, the regime demanded of the women of the *Sección Femenina*/S.E.U. that they be involved first and foremost in indoctrinating the female population with the ideological spirit of the Francoist state. Secondly, they were to enlist the support of male S.E.U. leaders, but only in the most discrete way. Pilar Primo de Rivera, the national head of the *Sección Femenina*, underlined women's subordination, a principal tenet of National-Catholic discourse:

> Do not pretend to be equal to men, because far from achieving what you want, men will detest you tremendously and you will not be able to have any influence on them.[49]

Gender difference was also explicit in article 34b of the U.R.L., which established that all college women had to render a social service to the state under the direction of the female section/S.E.U. This female version of the University Militia required female students to complete six months of training in domestic duties. College women completed their service in two phases: Instruction (*Formación*), which entailed political indoctrination and home economics; and Service (*Prestación*), which normally involved working in an office, nursery, or shelter.[50] This training made it clear to the women that it was their duty to become true women by fulfilling their motherly destiny.

Paradoxically, Falangist university women took on a public role while promoting a submissive female model. They created a space of their own within a public male terrain. The regime regarded them as nonthreatening because of their constant rejection of feminism. The *Sección Femenina's* domesticated discourse on femininity was not different from that of the state and the Catholic Church, but it granted Falangist-educated women the opportunity to be agents in the national enterprise. The best contribution women could make to the construction of the new Spain was to excel in their motherly (social or private) duties. Thus, Falangist women became social mothers. They embodied the humane values of the Falange. Ultimately, accepting their "second sex" status helped them to preserve their own empowered space.[51]

Conclusion

Since the sixteenth century, Catholic tradition and Church doctrine informed the traditional discourse on Spanish identity in general, and on femininity in particular. This traditional Catholic discourse endorsed and sanctified the ideology of separate spheres that dictated different gender roles for men and women. Men and women's souls were, by nature, different.

Catholicism defined the nexus between public and private, articulating the relationship between individual, family, state, and Church. After the Civil War, Franco's permanence in power rested upon the elaboration of a National-Catholic ideology that restored such legitimizing historical tradition after its endangerment during the Second Republic. Under the Francoist regime, education became the new battlefront for the old nineteenth-century confrontation between tradition and secularization, continuity and change. Catholic education became a normalizing process, bringing the individual soul and body within the realm of both the church and the state. The Francoist state, for its part, seized the Catholic principles and canonized them into law, thereby incorporating them into its own agenda: to survive and perpetuate its authority.

It was through the school system and the family that the regime would attempt to shape the Spanish soul and the Spaniards' souls.[52] The university in particular, as we have seen in this article, represented a site of the regime's power by means of preparing the political elite. The University Regulatory Law issued in 1943 echoed the separate spheres ideology that both Church and state prescribed, and delineated different identities for female and male scholars. The responsibility of a male scholar was to his fatherland, and his cooperation in spreading Catholic spirituality and knowledge to the world would lead to the fulfillment of the spiritual revolution launched in 1936. By contrast, women's mission meant the realization of true Catholic womanhood, rooted in the Church doctrine as prescribed in the encyclicals of Pius XI and the Renaissance treatises by Juan Luis Vives and Fray Luis de León. Like de León's "woman of value," a university-educated woman was a *rara avis*. The *Sección Femenina*/S.E.U. sought to keep domestic values alive in college women through the mandatory Social Service. To be a *real* woman (*mujer muy mujer*) entailed the self-negation of the scholar identity: to be a scholar and a woman was cast as a contradiction in terms. Catholic womanhood remained the norm until the end of the regime, keeping Spanish women's bodies and minds imprisoned in the iron ring of their motherly soul.[53]

Notes

1. "Las mujeres nunca descubren nada; les falta el talento creador, reservado por Dios a las inteligencias masculinas." Pilar Primo de Rivera, quoted in Daniel Sueiro

and Bernardo Diaz Nosty, *Historia del Franquismo* (Madrid: Ediciones Sedmay, 1978), p. 222.

2. I understand separate spheres as a rhetorical construction, or a metaphor, to explain historically the complex power relations between men and women in social and economic contexts. For a critical analysis of the "separate spheres" as historical paradigm within the American context see: Linda K. Kerber, "Separate Spheres, Female Worlds, Woman's Place: The Rhetoric of Women's History," *Journal of American History* 75, no. 1 (June 1988): 9–39; and Rosalind Rosenberg, *Beyond Separate Spheres: Intellectual Roots of Modern Feminism* (New Haven, CN: Yale University Press, 1982).

3. "At least until the second half of the nineteenth century, most of the Europeans remained marginal to the political process, even those in societies with liberal constitutions. Excluded from the formal political system, they were nonetheless socialized through the civil culture to fulfill their duty to the state." Victoria de Grazia, *How Fascism Ruled Women: Italy 1922–1945* (Berkeley, CA: University of California Press, 1992), p. 6.

4. George Mosse, *Nationalism and Sexuality: Respectability and Abnormal Sexuality in Modern Europe* (New York: Howard Fertig, 1985); Andrew Parker et al., eds., *Nationalisms and Sexualities* (New York: Routledge, 1992); Claudia Koonz, *Mothers in the Fatherland: Women, the Family, and Nazi Politics* (New York: St. Martin's Press, 1987).

5. For more on gender difference and biological determinism, see the chapter by Mary Nash in this volume.

6. For more on this subject, see María A. Escudero, "The Image of Latin America Disseminated in Spain by the Franco Regime: Repercussions in the Configuration of a National Identity" (Ph.D. diss., University of California, San Diego, 1994).

7. Spanish fascism, a latecomer to the European scene, took form on October 29, 1933, when José Antonio Primo de Rivera and others constituted a new party, the Falange Española. Four months later they merged with another ultraconservative group, Juventudes Ofensivas Nacional-Sindicalistas, or JONS, (dating from 1931) to form the Falange Española Tradicionalista y de las JONS. Initially, the Falange did not have substantial support because Catholic conservatism occupied the same ideological domain. Unlike many of its European counterparts, Spanish fascism was deeply Catholic. The Civil War, however, offered the Falange the opportunity to play a greater role; thus it provided both the ideological cloak and the umbrella party apparatus for Franco's military dictatorship. On the Falange, see Stanley Payne, *Falange: A History of Spanish Fascism* (Stanford, CA: Stanford University Press, 1965) and Sheilagh Ellwood, *Spanish Fascism in the Franco Era: Falange Española y de las JONS, 1936–76* (Basingstoke: Macmillan, 1987.)

8. On National-Catholicism and education see Gregorio Cámara Villar, *Nacional-Catolicismo y escuela: La socialización política del Franquismo*

(1936–1951) (Madrid: Editorial Hesperia, 1984); Clotilde Navarro García, *La educación y el Nacional-Catolicismo* (Spain: Universidad de Castilla la Mancha, 1993); and Andrés Sopeña Monsalve, *El Florido Pensil: Memoria de la escuela nacional-católica* (Barcelona: Crítica, 1994).

9. Victoria Enders, "Nationalism and Feminism: The *Sección Femenina* de Falange," in *History of European Ideas* 15, no. 4–6, (1992): 673–680; Rosario Sánchez López, *Mujer española: Una sombra de destino en lo universal* (Murcia: Universidad de Murcia, 1990); and María Teresa Gallego Méndez, *Mujer, Falange y Franquismo* (Madrid: Taurus, 1983); Luis Suárez Fernández, *Crónica de la "Sección Femenina" y su tiempo* (Madrid: Asociación Nueva Andadura, 1993).

10. Men like Gaspar Melchor de Jovellanos (1744–1811) believed in the power of education to successfully regenerate the country. In 1809, during the War of Independence, Jovellanos presented to the Junta Central his report on "Bases para la formación de un Plan General de Instrucción Pública." He pointed out the obligation of the state to provide education for all citizens. Later, during the constituent Cortes de Cádiz, Manuel José Quintana presented another report (1813) for educational reform that revisited Jovellanos' ideals: education for all citizens, respect of religious creeds, academic freedom, and the limitation of the Catholic Church's influence in the learning process.

11. Andrés Ollero Tassara, *Universidad y política: Tradición y secularización en el siglo XIX español* (Madrid: Instituto de Estudios Políticos, 1972).

12. On October 12, 1909, Ferrer Guardia was shot in the trenches of the Montjuich Fortress at Barcelona. A Military Council had found him guilty of being "head of the insurrection" which had, a few months before, lit the flame of civil war in the city during the so called "Tragic Week." See: Francisco Ferrer y Guardia, *The Origin and Ideals of the Modern School* (London: Watts & Co., 1913); Buenaventura Delgado, *La Escuela Moderna de Ferrer i Guardia* (Barcelona: Ediciones CEAC, 1979).

13. Esther Cortada Andreu, *Escuela mixta y coeducación en Cataluña durante la II República* (Madrid: Instituto de la Mujer, 1988); Rosa María Capel Martínez, *El trabajo y la educación de la mujer en España (1900–1930)* (Madrid: Ministerio de Cultura, 1986); Joan Connelly Ullman, "La enseñanza superior de la mujer en España: Relaciones entre universitarias españolas y estadounidenses (1877–1980)," in *Nuevas perspectivas sobre la mujer: Actas de las Primeras Jornadas de Investigación Interdisciplinaria* (Madrid: Universidad Autónoma de Madrid, 1982), pp. 196–205; María Carmen García Nieto and Esperanza Yllán, "La educación de la mujer," in *Historia de España (1808–1978)* (Barcelona: Crítica, 1989); Geraldine Scanlon, "La mujer y la instrucción pública: De la Ley Moyano a la Segunda República," in *Historia de la Educación* 6 (1987): pp. 193–208; María Luisa Barrera Peña and Ana López Peña, *Sociología de la mujer en la universidad: Análisis histórico-comparativo Galicia-España, 1900–1981* (Santiago de Compostela, Spain: Universidad de Santiago de Compostela, 1984).

14. Antonio Molero Pintado divides the Republican period into three stages of educational reform: the first biennium of creation; the second of revision; and the third of dissolution. *La reforma educativa en la Segunda República española* (Madrid: Aula XXI. Educación Abierta/Santillana, 1977), p. 16.

15. José Pemartín, *Qué es "lo nuevo": Consideraciones sobre el momento español actual* (Sevilla: Tip. Alvarez y Zambrano, 1937) quoted in Alejandro Mayordomo Pérez, *Nacional-Catolicismo y educación en la España de la posguerra* (Madrid: Ministerio de Educación y Ciencia, Secretaría General Técnica, 1990), pp. 22–23.

16. Ibid., p. 23.

17. The regime published two works against the spirit of F.I.L.: E. Suñer, *Los intelectuales y la tragedia española* (San Sebastián: Biblioteca España Nueva, 1937); and a collective book under the title *Una poderosa fuerza secreta: La Institución Libre de Enseñanza* (San Sebastián: Editorial Española, 1940).

18. Alicia Alted Vigil, "La mujer en las coordenadas educativas del régimen franquista," in *Ordenamiento jurídico y realidad social de las mujeres, siglos XII a XX: IV Jornadas de Investigación Interdisciplinaria Seminario de Estudios de la Mujer* (Madrid: Universidad Autónoma de Madrid, 1986).

19. Decree of March 2, 1945, "Creación del Instituto de Enseñanzas Profesionales de la Mujer," *Boletín Oficial del Estado*, March 17, 1945.

20. Giuliana di Febo, *La santa de la raza* (Barcelona: Icaria, 1988), pp. 37–38.

21. One of her biographers, Father Silverio de Santa Teresa, wrote *Santa Teresa modelo de feminismo cristiano* (Burgos, Spain: Topografía del Monte Carmelo, 1931). This book popularized a so-called Christian feminism incarnated in Saint Teresa. Such Christian feminism was more desirable and genuinely Spanish than the so-called lay feminism represented by the progressive and left-wing parties of the Second Republic.

22. Rosa Rossi, "Teresa de Jesús: La mujer y la Iglesia," *Mientras Tanto* 14 (1982): 63–79; and "Teresa de Jesús: La mujer y la palabra," *Mientras Tanto* 15 (1983): 29–47.

23. Juan Luis Vives, *La instrucción de la mujer cristiana* (Buenos Aires: Editorial Espasa Calpe, 1940); Felix García, *Obras completas de Fray Luis de León* (Madrid: Biblioteca de Autores Españoles, 1944).

24. ". . . las mujeres, cuando no saben guardar su castidad, merecen tanto mal, que no es bastante el precio de la vida para pagarlo." Juan Luis Vives, *La instrucción de la mujer cristiana* (Buenos Aires: Espasa Calpe, 1940), p. 56.

25. "*Mujer de valor* ¿Quién la hallará? . . . que es dificultoso el hallarla, y que son pocas las tales. Y así la primera loa que da a la buena mujer es decir de ella que es cosa rara . . . porque como la mujer sea de su natural flaca y deleznable más que ningún

otro animal." Fray Luis de León *La perfecta casada* in Felix García, *Obras completas de Fray Luis de León*, pp. 219–220.

26. ". . . Así la mujer no es tan loable por ser honesta, cuando es torpe y abominable si no lo es. De manera que el Espíritu Santo en este lugar no dice a la mujer que sea honesta, sino presupone que ya lo es . . . . Entendiendo que el quebrar la mujer a su marido la fe es perder las estrellas su luz y caerse los cielos, y quebrantar las leyes su naturaleza." Ibid., pp. 226–227.

27. The legal status of Spanish women was revised with the reform of the civil code by the law of April 1958, and in 1961 when the government promulgated the "Ley de Derechos políticos, profesionales y del trabajo de la mujer" [Women's Political and Civil Rights Act]. These laws redefined the rights of Spanish women, but sustained domesticity as a precious female trait.

28. Both encyclicals are founded on the writings of Leo XIII, in particular his encyclical "Rerum Novarum" (1891); Mayordomo Pérez, *Nacional-Catolicismo y educación*, p. 47.

29. ". . . ella sola posee originaria e inadmisiblemente la verdad moral toda entera [*Omnem Veritatem*] en la cual todas las verdades particulares de la moral están comprendidas." "'Divini Illius Magistri': Carta Encíclica de Su Santidad Pio XI sobre la educación cristiana de la juventud," in *El Papa habla a los padres de familia.* (Madrid: Confederación Católica de Padres de Familia, 1941), p. 103.

30. "La misión de la educación toca, ante todo y sobre todo, en primer lugar a la Iglesia y a la familia, y que les toca por derecho natural y divino, y, por tanto, de manera inderogable, ineluctable, insubrogable." Ibid., p. 108.

31. "Nuestro Señor ordena y dispone que la perfecta coexistencia de los sexos ha de tener lugar dentro del matrimonio." Ibid., p. 122.

32. ". . . abraza tanto la primacía del varón sobre la mujer y los hijos, como *la diligente sumisión de la mujer y su rendida obediencia*, recomendada por el apostle con estas palabras: 'las casadas estén sujetas a sus maridos, como al Señor; por cuanto el hombre es cabeza de la mujer, así como Cristo es cabeza de la Iglesia." "'Casti Connubii': Carta encíclica de su Santidad Pio XI sobre la dignidad del matrimonio" in *El Papa habla a los padres de familia*, p. 25.

33. "Porque ilícitamente e impúdicamente yace, aún con su legítima mujer, el que evita la concepción de la prole." Ibid., p. 40.

34. "¿Quién no se admirará extraordinariamente al contemplar a una madre entregándose a una muerte segura, con fortaleza heroica, para conservar la vida del fruto de sus entrañas?" Ibid., p. 42.

35. ". . . y muchos se atreven a decir, con mayor audacia, que es una indignidad la servidumbre de un cónyuge al otro; que son iguales los derechos de ambos cónyuges; defendiendo presuntuosamente que, . . . se debe llegar a conseguir una cierta 'emancipación de la mujer.'" Ibid., p. 50.

36. Ibid., p. 53.

37. In 1941, Franco entered into an agreement with the Vatican that ratified the Concordat of 1851, which established the official role of the Church in public and private education.

38. Order of April 25, 1939, "Proyecto de Ley de Reforma Universitaria," *Boletín Oficial del Estado*, April 27, 1939. By the end of 1939 university faculty purges were well under way and the *Centro de Investigaciones Científicas* (C.S.I.C.) was erected to preserve the purity of knowledge.

39. I use "hispanidad" here as a synonym of "authentic" Spanish national identity or character. According to María Escudero, "the myth of Hispanidad promoted the idea that there were various links—language, religion, culture—with roots in the colonial era, and which made possible a Hispanic community of nations." See María Escudero, "The Image of Latin America Disseminated in Spain by the Franco Regime," 11. See also Escudero's article in this anthology.

40. "Corporación a la que el estado confía su empresa espiritual la de realizar y orientar las actividades científicas, culturales y educativas de la nación con la norma de servicio que impone la actual revolución española. Para desarrollar este concepto la ley devuelve a la universidad la plenitud de sus funciones tradicionales, restaurando, reorganizando o creando los órganos adecuados." *Boletín Oficial del Estado* 7408, July 31, 1943.

41. "Tal florecimiento universitario es el creador de un ejército teológico que se apresta contra la herejía." *Boletín Oficial del Estado* 7407, July 31, 1943.

42. "Vivimos momentos de crisis y de rutina en que si la educación intelectual estaba desquiciada, había sucumbido también en manos de la libertad de cátedra, la educación moral y religiosa y hasta el amor a la Patria se sentía con ominoso pudor, ahogado por la corriente extranjerizante, laica, fría, krausista y masónica de la Institución Libre de Enseñanza." *Boletín Oficial del Estado* 7407, July 31, 1943.

43. Article 3 of the U.R.L. declared the Catholic nature of the University and its commitment to the teaching of Catholic dogma and morality, and articles 31 and 32 established the Dirección de Formación Religiosa Universitaria [Secretary of Religious University Formation].

44. "Cuando adviene la unidad nacional y suena la hora universal de España, nuestra universidad . . . aparece en la plenitud de su concepto para servir los ideales de su destino imperial . . . . produce una ciencia que se enseñorea en el mundo y educa y forma hombres que . . . honren a España y sirvan a la Iglesia." *Boletín Oficial del Estado* 7406, July 31, 1943.

45. Michel Foucault, *Discipline and Punish* (New York: Vintage Books, 1975), p. 198, quoted in Paul Rabinow, ed., *The Foucault Reader* (New York: Pantheon Books, 1984), p. 125.

46. Michel Foucault defines bio-power as the disciplinary control of a population. Normative, serialized order is an essential component of bio-power in which surveillance is the key to achieving the desired control. Franco's regime articulated a system of normalization to sustain its grip over power structures. This system clearly delineated what was marginal, or in other words that which is outside the center and the norm. Paul Rabinow defines Foucaldian normalization as "a system finely arranged in measurable intervals in which individuals can be distributed around a norm: a norm which both organizes and is the result of this controlled distribution." Paul Rabinow, Introduction to *The Foucault Reader*, p. 20. See Michel Foucault, *The History of Sexuality*, vol. 1 (New York: Pantheon Books, 1978); and Colin Gordon, ed., *Power/Knowledge* (New York: Pantheon Books, 1980).

47. Conscription was mandatory for young Spanish men. By the Order of June 28, 1941, a voluntary legion was created to help Hitler in Russia, the so-called Blue Division, whose officers were mainly professionals. The head of S.E.U., Agustín Aznar, joined this division. Through the university militia, the country drew professional officers and young men rendered their patriotic services in better conditions than those experienced by the regular troops. Manuel Tuñón de Lara, *Historia de España: España bajo la dictadura franquista* (Barcelona: Labor, 1980), pp. 174–179.

48. "Prestar los servicios universitarios, atendida, cuando la naturaleza de los mismos lo exija, la *diversidad de los sexos*" (my emphasis) *Boletín Oficial del Estado* 7424, July 31, 1943.

49. "No pretendais poneros de igual a igual, porque entonces, lejos de conseguir lo que pretendeis, os tendrán los hombres un desprecio infinito y jamás podreis influir sobre ellos." Pilar Primo de Rivera, *Discursos, Circulares, Escritos* (Madrid: n.d.), pp. 172–173.

50. The instruction was delivered in two periods: the so called winter course [*Curso de Invierno*] and a School-retreat [*Albergue-Escuela*].

51. See Koonz, *Mothers in the Fatherland.*

52. I use the word "soul" in a metaphoric manner here, to refer to the essence or identities shaped by the official discourse.

53. María Antonietta Macciocchi, "Female Sexuality in Fascist Ideology," *Feminist Review* 1 (1979): 67–77.

3

"Cortes and Marina": Gender and the Reconquest of America Under the Franco Regime

María A. Escudero

In the last two decades, the development of gender studies has transformed the field of women's history. Traditional political historians have been slower to acknowledge the relevance of gender categories in the construction and maintenance of male-dominated formal power structures. However, in recent years, it has become increasingly difficult to maintain this distance. As Geoff Eley has pointed out, "an accumulating tradition of feminist critique has shown how far modern political thought is highly gendered in its basic structures."[1] Thus, in Joan Scott's words, even when women themselves are excluded from formal politics, "gender is a primary way of signifying relationships of power."[2]

This chapter is another attempt to demonstrate how "seemingly gender-neutral categories encode gender assumptions and tacitly embody gendered images" that ultimately intend to legitimate power.[3] More specifically, it analyzes the legitimating function assigned to gender in the political discourse of international relations and national identity formation. Ann Stoler has shown how in colonial regimes subtle relationships between the categories of gender, race, and class are constructed as a means to naturalize inequality.[4] The analysis I present here explores the symbiotic relation between gender, race and the concept of colonization itself, in a regime's attempt—in this case the Franco regime (1939–1975)—to re-imagine its colonial past.

As suggested by Puertolas' and Morcillo's chapters, one of the mechanisms utilized by the Francoist state to consolidate its power was to reinforce the existence of two separate gender spheres, based on a specific image of female identity rooted in the concept of "maternity." As Mary Nash argued for the early twentieth century, such images permeated Spanish society at large, promoted by institutions such as local governments, the University, and, as I will demonstrate in this chapter, primary schools.

In particular, this study describes how school textbooks adopted during the Francoist dictatorship used gender metaphors in their reinterpretation of the conquest of America as a way to prove the existence of "natural" differences between nations. As Joan Scott has argued, since gender hierarchy was seen as "natural," gender metaphors could be employed to communicate hierarchy in other kinds of relationships without directly referring to hierarchy.[5] In this case, Francoist authors established a gendered correlation between the relationship of indigenous women, the American territory, and the Spanish conquistadors, as Spain's representatives. By establishing a clear gender hierarchy between the indigenous women and the conquistadors and then using this relationship as a metaphor in the analysis of the relation the conquistadors had with the territory itself, Francoist authors attempted to justify "naturally" the leading role they imagined for the Spanish government in its present-day relations with the Latin American republics. This role was crucial, not only for the regime's sense of international prestige, but in its internal development of a "Spanish" national identity.

History and National Identity in Francoist Spain

The Spanish Civil War (1936–1939) was ultimately the confrontation between two different visions of what Spain was and should be. Once the war was over, in spite of its military victory the Franco regime was still in a very delicate position because half of Spain and several foreign governments still questioned both its legitimacy and its future. Consequently, two aims of the new government were to guarantee foreign support and recognition of the regime, and to unite the country and expand the regime's internal support through the creation of a Francoist Spanish national identity. In order to impose their particular concept of national identity, the Francoists resorted both to direct repression and persuasion/indoctrination. It was in this process of indoctrination that the authors of history textbooks during the Franco regime resorted to the use of gender metaphors.

From the Francoist perspective, Spaniards had to recuperate the coherent sense of national identity that had been lost during the nineteenth and the beginning of the twentieth centuries. Francoist ideologues interpreted national identity as a broad concept that included a genetically derived national character, as well as cultural trademarks developed through a supposedly shared, unified history. These ideologues were convinced that they could create a particular national identity in the coming generations through the utilization-manipulation of history. In other words, the re-creation of the past would be used as the base for the configuration of national identity in the present. Consequently, the teaching of history became an important tool in achieving the ideological targets set by the regime.[6] History became the example and origin of the traits it attempted to instill in children from an early age. Thus, what Boyd has called "the crusade to create a new elite committed to traditional 'Spanish' values" was initiated.[7]

To do this, historians isolated and selected those parts of history that supported the image they wished to paint of Spain and the Spaniards, and promulgated this portion of history as "the authentic" version. In particular, they focused on the period of the so-called Catholic monarchs in the late fifteenth and early sixteenth centuries, and also on the process of conquest and colonization of America.[8] By establishing an identification between the reign of the Catholic monarchs and the Franco regime, Francoists opened the possibility of an imperial future for Spain. According to Francoist ideologues, if in the twentieth century Spaniards managed to achieve unity in the name of God, God would once again reward Spaniards by opening for them the possibility of territorial greatness.

This time unity would come not in the form of an empire but rather through the Hispanic community, or *Hispanidad*, of which Franco's Spain would be the leader. The myth of *Hispanidad* promoted the idea that there were various links—language, religion, culture—with roots in the colonial era, that would make possible the creation of a Hispanic Community of Nations. This myth served the Franco regime a double purpose, first as a means of external legitimation,[9] and second as an integral part of the regime's efforts to legitimate itself within Spain. In the propaganda campaign aimed at securing the regime's domestic legitimation, the myth of *Hispanidad* played a fundamental role for two reasons. First, it offered an image of a glorious past, and second the regime could use this past as a model for predicating a prosperous future. In this way Francoist ideologues furnished the regime with a goal that would ostensibly unite the longings of all Spaniards and overcome their international isolation.

In order to justify Spain's right to lead the Hispanic Community of Nations, Francoist authors of school textbooks employed a gendered discourse of the Spanish conquest and colonization of America. Although Spanish women rarely appear in the narrative of the conquest and colonization of America, much less indigenous women, the narrative itself is gendered. The gendering of Spain and Latin America as male and female, respectively, was a subtle mechanism that allowed these Francoist authors to present and justify their vision of the origins and characteristics of an idealized relationship between Spain and the Latin American republics. In this manner, they managed to avoid explicit reference to Spain's superiority, which would have insulted the national pride of the governments of the Latin American republics. To make the gender metaphor work according to their objectives, Francoist authors first had to define the hierarchical characteristics of the relationship between the conquistadors and the indigenous women in terms that everyone could understand. Indigenous women played a distinctive role in the Francoist discourse, very different from that assigned to indigenous men, proving that there was a separate gender component not subsumed under race. Once the relationship between the indigenous women and the conquistadors was well defined, it would set the foundation for the hierarchical mating of Spain and Latin America.

In order to present the different layers that compounded this gender metaphor, I initially describe the characteristics of the relationship between conquistadors and Native American women as they appear in the textbooks. I continue with the analysis of a special relationship, that between Cortes and Marina, as it was portrayed in a fictional comic strip narrative. Finally, I show how the composite narrative gendered the relationship between the conquistadors and the American territory in order to promote the idea of the superiority of Spain in the international arena.

There are two reasons why I chose history textbooks as the primary sources for this study. First, schoolbooks were considered of paramount importance in the formation of ideology in fascist—or semi-fascist—regimes. These governments paid special attention to the education of the youth and specifically to the teaching of history as a way to create an "elite" capable of carrying out the national transformation desired by the regime.[10] Secondly, neither schoolbooks nor comic strips appeared outside of Spain, as did other types of propaganda, such as periodicals, radio or movies. Consequently, aspects that might have been offensive to other nations could be expressed more openly in internal media.[11] I consider the analysis of a comic strip as a counterpart to schoolbooks appropriate and illustrative because Francoist authors established remarkable similarities between history and fiction.[12]

The textbooks analyzed here were intended for children in their last years of primary school. The Franco regime did not impose a single official history textbook, but all the textbooks published had to pass through government, ecclesiastical, and editorial censorship. Due to this selection process, the content of the majority of the texts was very similar, sometimes to the extent that they appeared to be copies of one another.[13] However, for the analysis of the period 1939–1960, four books seem particularly relevant, both in terms of the political significance of their authors,[14] and their wide distribution in time and space.[15] These books were José María Pemán's *La historia de España contada con sencillez*, Luis Ortiz Muñoz's *Glorias imperiales*, Agustín Serrano de Haro's *España es asi* and *Guirnaldas de la Historia*.[16] These four books were, according to a survey done by Francisca Montilla in 1954, among the most popular books with teachers.[17] They were first published in Madrid in the years immediately after the Civil War, and they were all approved both by the Ministry of Education and the ecclesiastical authority.[18] Although there was no single official history textbook, all four of these received some sort of official recognition.[19]

Indigenous Women and Conquistadors

The treatment of indigenous women in the conquest and colonization of America was probably one of the more difficult issues that the narratives, intended for children and youth, confronted. On the one hand, the fact that in Francoist terms the indigenous woman was doubly inferior, due to both gender and race, immediately excluded her from playing any kind of central role in the narrative. At the same time, however, the indigenous women—as the "mothers" of the new Latin-American nations—were critical to the process of *mestizaje*[20] which, according to the Francoists, supported the idea that, even in the present, there existed a Hispanic Community of Nations. The importance given to the end result of this racial mixture, and the need to counteract the so-called Black Legend,[21] made it impossible to ignore the *mestizaje* process itself. It had to be dealt with, even though taking racial mixture into account meant having to confront matters like abuse, rape, and interracial consensual sex, issues that, in the view of Francoist authors, were difficult and not exemplary or edifying for children.

In order to avoid the direct analysis of these issues, Francoist textbook authors resorted to several strategies. The most common was to avoid any specific reference to physical contact—whether sexual or not—between the conquistadors and the indigenous women. The authors of these textbooks ultimately placed the emphasis on the final result of the sexual relationship: the mixture of bloods. To make the mixing process even more indirect and independent from human contact, the textbooks presented Spain, not the conquistadors, as the donor of the blood. A good example is the following quote, in which Spain acted both as the "promoter" of the "fusion" between indigenous people and Spaniards, and as the donor of the blood and education that transformed the indigenous people into a new race:

> Instead of *exterminating* the Indians, as other nations have done with the inhabitants of dominated countries, Spain *fused* Indians and Spaniards together to constitute a new race, young and strong, a race that is the daughter of Spain, because Spain has given it her blood and education.[22]

Thus, according to these textbooks, the so-called mixture of bloods was not the result of an exchange, but of a one-way transfusion.[23] Spain—the conquistador—was the donor, and the Americans the recipients. In this "altruistic" transaction, the Spanish blood did not get polluted. Furthermore, in those few cases in which the textbooks referred specifically to the mixture of blood between individuals, these were the conquistadors and the "indigenous nobility." By not mixing their blood with the rest of the indigenous people, the Spaniards avoided "contamination" and maintained their superior status.[24]

Another strategy used in the school textbooks to avoid referring to sexual relations between the conquistadors and the indigenous women, and more specifically to deny the accusation of rape on the part of the conquistadors, was to allude to the gratitude of indigenous women towards the conquistadors for having "liberated" them from the oppressiveness of their previous lives.[25] As exemplars of this gratitude, the authors always referred to women who occupied a privileged position within their society, whether they were queens or daughters of the main indigenous actors in the conquest drama. Pemán's textbook, for example, alluded to the fact that:

> Charles V received the daughters of Moctezuma, sent by Hernan Cortes, as princesses in his court, and he arranged marriages for them with the principal knights of the Court, which made them feel extremely honored.[26]

According to this quote, Moctezuma's daughters felt honored by the king, and so his actions in arranging their futures and giving them as gifts to certain knights of the Spanish court were justified. The indigenous women, by choosing the white men as partners over their indigenous counterparts, legitimated the actions of the conquistadors, corroborated European masculinity, and emasculated the Native Americans. The conquistador's virility allowed him to win the indigenous woman without having to resort to rape. In this way, the indigenous woman was separated from her own race and transformed into the mother of the new Hispanic race. This metaphor legitimated the superiority of the white man and his culture. What better proof exists of his superior civilization than the judgment implicit in the actions of indigenous women? Their fidelity to the conquistadors was presented as their way of giving thanks to the Europeans for having liberated them from the oppressiveness of their previous lives.

The difference between the behavior of the Spaniards and the behavior of the indigenous people established the implicit superiority of the colonizer. According to these textbooks, indigenous men treated women as if they were things, while the conquistadors behaved towards them as gentlemen: "if the Spaniards had not been gentlemen and Christians, the poor Indian women would have been poor slaves."[27] By implication, the proof of the Spaniards' gentlemanliness lay in the conquistadors' willingness to make indigenous women their wives. Marriage was one of the ways through which the conquistadors liberated indigenous women from the sufferings of the miserable existences they lived before the Spaniards' arrival.

However, the narrators admit that this marriage was not the spontaneous result of love, but had to be encouraged. Pemán referred to specific instructions given by the Spanish kings to Nicolás Ovando, in which "it was said that Christians should be encouraged to marry indigenous women and vice versa."[28] None of the texts, however, mentioned that the encouragement was unsuccessful, and that, in fact, the conquistadors considered that in order to avoid sin it was enough to baptize the indigenous women before having sex with them.[29] Pemán's attempt to justify the sexual relations between conquistadors and indigenous women by implying the existence of matrimonies that never took place is particularly interesting. Euphemistically, Pemán called these relations "love unions" but at the same time stated that they were by no means the result of an "unscrupulous Spanish heat for love," but part of a policy of the Spanish state. In other words, the love unions were not the result of spontaneous love, but the imposition of a law:

> This policy of love unions with the conquered savage peoples, is one of the great glories of Spain. It is childish to present this mixing of races as a mere product of the greater sensuality of the Spaniards who accepted relationships with indigenous women rejected by more exquisite peoples. Without denying this, the truth is that race mixing is the daughter of an ideological concept and a Christian pattern for life that considered as equals those human beings who inhabited the discovered lands.[30]

In order to further justify these love unions, Pemán tried to downplay the role of sensuality without denying, however, the "greater sensuality of the Spaniards" compared to "more exquisite"—but obviously less virile—people. Denying the conquistadors greater sensuality would have questioned their virility, and therefore their right to conquer. Pemán's argument established a clear, if paradoxical, logic. First, it assumed the savage nature of the indigenous people and therefore their inferiority that both made possible and justified the conquest. Once the indigenous people—women—were conquered, the Spaniards married them in holy matrimony. Therefore, both partners' status was different from the beginning of the marriage. This conclusion seems to contradict Pemán's last assertion about the "ideological concept and Christian pattern for life that considered as equals those human beings who inhabited the discovered lands." However, the explanation of this apparently paradoxical argument lies precisely in the sexual difference between the conquistador and the indigenous woman. The sacrament of holy matrimony sealed this difference and justified the institutionalization and sacralization of inequality. Marriage was therefore seen as the maximum gift the conquistador could give the indigenous woman, that is, the opportunity to fulfill her natural role as wife and mother.

Cortes and Marina

While Pemán, Ortiz Muñoz, and Serrano de Haro, as well as all the other authors of school textbooks, avoided giving details about the relationships between the conquistadors and the indigenous women, fictional narratives do make specific references to particular relationships, such as that between Cortes and Marina. I have chosen to analyze one comic strip, significantly called: "Así nació América: Malinalli, historia de una india mejicana" (This is the way America was born: Malinalli, the story of a Mexican Indian woman), because it put Marina at the center of the narrative.[31] However, as I will show, the description of Marina's relationship with Cortes presented the same characteristics that abounded in the Francoist textbooks' more general description of the relationships between the conquistadors and the indigenous women. In addition, the story "Así nació América" presented the relationship between Cortes and Marina as exemplary of the relationships between indigenous women and the conquistadors during the conquest of America.

According to common accounts of Marina's life,[32] she was an indigenous woman born within the Aztec Empire in a small village called Painala. She was the only daughter of the *cacique*[33] of this village who died when she was still very young. Her mother remarried and had a son. Marina's stepfather, in order to provide his son with the *cacicato*[34] that legally belonged to Marina, sold her to some merchants and told everybody that she was dead. The merchants sold her to the king of Tabasco, who, years later, gave her to Cortes as a gift.[35] As Marina spoke both the Mayan and the Náhuatl languages, Cortes used her as his personal translator. Due to her knowledge and intelligence, she was a great help to the Spaniards during the conquest of Mexico. Following common practice during the conquest, Cortes arranged for Marina to become a slave for one of his soldiers, Hernández de Portocarrero. Soon after, Cortes sent Puertocarrero back to Spain to present a letter to the king, and in his absence, made Marina his lover. As the result of this relationship they had a son called, like Cortes' father, Martín. Upon Portocarrero's death Cortes forced one of his subordinates, Juan Jaramillo, to marry Marina and separated her from their son, Martín.

However, the narrative in "Así nació" presented a different story: Malinalli was happily living with her father, Puerta Florida, a kind and protective father who adored his daughter and feared that one day other Indian enemies might capture her. On a day that an enemy king demanded Puerta Florida's people to surrender and give to him, as war trophy, all the young women of the village, Puerta Florida gave Malinalli to a group of merchants to look after her until he could rescue her. The rescue never occurred and, years later, Malinalli was given to Cortes as a gift.[36] Although Marina's life before she met Cortes is not the subject of this study, the narrative's deviation from the standard interpretation serves as an example of the inaccuracy that characterized the whole work.

According to this narrative, once Malinalli met Cortes, her life changed, starting from her own name. It was changed to Marina and she received the title "doña" as a way of emphasizing the high regard in which she was supposedly held. This regard derived from her special relation with Cortes, but the narrative reduced Marina's role to that of a translator, and never mentioned either her sexual relation with him or the son they had together. In emphasizing her secondary role as a translator, the narrative portrayed her as a person who did not have a voice of her own, thus omitting those moments when Marina took the initiative in favor of the conquistadors during their negotiations with indigenous groups.[37]

> From that moment on, Malinalli, or Doña Marina, became Cortes's great help in the conquest of Mexico. She learned the Castillian language quickly, and not a single conversation or treaty took place that was not mediated by her translation.[38]

The focus on her submissiveness over and above her ability to take action emphasized the "utilization" of the indigenous woman by the conquistador. Hence, according to the narrative, the indigenous woman acquired an identity as a person and as a woman—she got a name, a title and a role within Spanish society—only by "letting herself be used" by the white man. However, while the narrative did not provide specifics about this utilization, it did establish that the conquistadors' treatment of Marina was not only respectful and considerate, but even praiseworthy.

To support this argument it is worth including with the text one of the drawings that accompanied it in the narrative. The importance of the analysis of images, especially when dealing with works intended for children, has already been established.[39] As Geertz pointed out long ago, images should be read and interpreted as "text."[40] The following image can be viewed as an ideologically constructed text bearing political meaning. Generally, in Francoist fictional narratives intended for children, the drawing's main function was to summarize the most relevant issues presented in the narrative, trying above all to catch the children's attention. This function is clear in the following drawing and accompanying caption (See Figure 3.1):

> She always rode on a white horse, her head covered by the shawl Indian women use, next to Hernan Cortes and Father Luque, the Spanish army chaplain who had baptized her. The soldiers respected and loved this hard-working young woman, intelligent and simple, and the Mexicans

admired her because it was not customary for women among them to behave like she did.[41]

FIGURE 3.1

"Así nació América: Malinalli, historia de una india mejicana" (This is the way America was born: Malinalli, the story of a Mexican Indian woman).

In the description and drawing, Marina is portrayed as fully integrated into the world of the conquistadors. In the quote, Marina's incorporation into the culture of the conquistadors was symbolized by her baptism. According to the narrative, once given a Christian identity, Marina occupied a position of privilege that was guaranteed by the symbols of Spanish power: the Army and the Church, represented by Cortes and Father Luque. Visually, this privileged position was emphasized by her being astride a white horse. The horse, the symbol of the conquistadors' contributions to America, was the proof, par excellence, of Spanish superiority. The depiction of her riding this symbolic animal, towering over even the Spanish soldiers and other Native Americans—who are almost never granted this privilege—underscored her distinction and the consideration given to her because of her decision to support the Spaniards. Her incorporation into the cultural world of the conquistador immediately elevated her social status, allowing her to transcend the barriers of gender within her own race.

Although Marina still kept some of the traits that distinguished her as a Native American, such as her shawl, her transition to the cultural world of the conqueror had begun, and as the following quote reflects, it continued throughout the narrative:

> Time passed and, when peace reigned over Mexico, Doña Marina married one of Hernan Cortes's pages, named Juan de Xaramillo, and Emperor Charles V bestowed upon her the title of Marquise. She had become a noble lady in the style of Castille, and her wardrobe was exactly like those of Spanish ladies. She was soon widowed and retired to her lands, where she lovingly protected the poor Indians. Although she was far away from the palaces and the wars, she never forgot her life next to the great Spanish caudillo who conquered, with a handful of men, the most powerful empire in America.[42]

The narrative presented Marina as a cultural version of the later genetic process of *mestizaje.* According to this interpretation, Marina's assimilation was completed, from her manner of dress to her practice of Christian teachings like charity. Above all, however, the author incorporated Marina into the world of the conquistador by giving her a position within the socioeconomic structure: as a noble landowner. Marina's complete separation from her original environment once again proved the indigenous woman's acceptance of the conquistadors' cultural superiority. The narrative presented an image of Marina who, despite having been used, discarded, and passed on to a subordinate, remained faithful to Cortes, whom she continued to admire even after he had left. Marina's faithfulness toward the conquistador reached such a degree that she followed him into battle against her own people.[43]

Marina was not only the witness to the conquistadors' actions; she was also their justification. This justification encompassed two fundamental aspects of the conquest. On the one hand, the texts presented the indigenous woman as the judge who confirmed the objective superiority of the conquistadors. On the other hand, given that she saw, judged, and chose what she thought was best, her union with the conquistador was in no way a rape, but rather the result of a personal decision based on the evaluation of the conquistador's virility.

The fact that, in many ways, Marina's personal traits and behavior made her unique, does not keep her from being displayed as representative of the whole of the indigenous female population. Nor does it keep her from being used as an example of indigenous female (as well as male) cooperation with the conquest.

> Doña Marina, that little Malinalli that one day had to escape from her home, is like the symbol of what Spain did in America, the marvelous conquest of [a people] through blood and love to incorporate them into Christian civilization.[44]

The ambiguity of the term *blood* is rather significant, especially followed by the term *love*. The word blood could either refer to the transfusion of blood already mentioned and therefore represent the process of *mestizaje*, or it could be interpreted as the representation of the killing. In either case, the word love smoothed the aggressive connotations, justifying the conquistadors' actions.

The American Territory and the Conquistadors: A Gendered Metaphor

The discourse of the Francoist textbooks analyzed here established a parallelism between the process of appropriation of indigenous women and that of the American territory. From the Francoist perspective, the land and the individual were analogous because both had a body and a soul, although the land, whether Spain or America, was always portrayed as female.[45] Therefore, both Spain and America, as women, could be seduced, dominated, fertilized, and could give birth. But as metaphorical constructions, their sexuality, especially in terms of the relationship between America and the conquistadors, could be explored more freely. Thus, in contrast to actual indigenous women, who were rarely mentioned, the texts present numerous references to this relationship, including aspects and vocabulary that the narrators carefully avoided when talking about the relationship between the conquistadors and the indigenous women. They stated, for instance, that the conquistadors were "dazzled" by the lands' beauty, and pointed out how this beauty intensified the conquistadors' desire and anxiety to conquer, dominate, and possess the lands.[46] The intensity of this anxiety could be compared with the "passionate" feeling that, according to Pemán, the conquistadors felt towards the indigenous women.

One sees the comparison between sexual and territorial conquest in a description of the conquistadors as "heroes whose *intrepidity* needed entire worlds to be satiated."[47] The conquistadors satiated their desire to dominate and possess the virgin lands by fertilizing them.

Conversely, the continuous reference in the textbooks to the virginity of the lands[48] denied the indigenous men's power to dominate and fertilize the lands—that is, denied their virility. Pemán implied this lack of virility by stating that before the arrival of the conquistadors, the American lands were never "tamed by a man."[49] The same conclusion could be inferred from Ortiz's sensual definition of America as the "land yet untouched by human caress,"[50] and from his reference to the "sterility" of the American lands until they met "Spain's fecundity."[51] Thus, the process of fertilization, which was avoided in discussions of individuals, could be approached on this metaphorical level.

According to the textbooks, fertilization was provided by several subjects. First were the conquistadors, who transported to America a variety of goods.[52] Although the texts did not explain in detail how the conquistadors fertilized the lands, they nevertheless pointed out that, as they had done with the indigenous women, the leaders distributed the lands among the Spanish soldiers so that they could cultivate, that is fertilize, them.[53] However, in order to provide a greater justification of the conquistadors' actions and at the same time emphasize that they were God's representatives, the narrators often put the fertilization of the lands in the hands of the missionaries. They emphasized how the action of the missionaries fertilized and therefore transformed the appearance of the lands, incorporating them into the culture of the conquistadors. As happened to Marina, the action of the conquistadors gave the lands power, wealth, and access to Christianity and civilization. As Serrano de Haro stated it, "The nations of America today belong to the faith, are civilized, powerful, and wealthy, because they have harvested the robust seeds that our missionaries spread throughout those immense, virgin and fertile lands."[54] As we can see in this excerpt, the missionaries were able to fertilize the American lands without having them lose their virginity or be raped. The contact took place abstractly, distanced from the reality of the relationship between conquistadors and indigenous women.

However, just as we saw with the indigenous women, the contact with the white men—fertilization—gave them a defined identity. In fact, according to Ortiz Muñoz, the fertilization process gave the lands their mere existence. As he pointed out, "From North to South, America came to be, thanks to the civilizing and colonizing fecundity of the Spanish friars."[55] In the same way that their relation with the conquistadors allowed indigenous women to enter into the culture of the white men, the conquistadors' spiritual and material fertilization of the New World offered the land something priceless: entry into civilization. Pemán particularly emphasized the marvelous "speed with which those lands of America altered their appearance and entered into civilization."[56] According to the narrators, the change in the external appearance of the land was essential—as it was when talking about women—to prove their belonging to the civilized world. In other words, the change is the proof of the lands' previous lack of civilization, which is of course a code word for western European culture.[57]

According to the authors, an essential part of this civilization was Christianity, and consequently the process of civilizing the lands included the Christianization of the territory, a process that was consolidated, as was the case with the indigenous women, through baptism.[58] The process of baptism was greatly symbolic and finalized the separation of the land from its original owners, the Native Americans. Baptism meant the death of the past: all the territory that had been owned by the original inhabitants died and was reborn as a part of the Christian world controlled by the white men. Consequently, outside of this world these territories had no identity or reason for being. The process of baptism had a double implication: it consecrated the lands and gave them an identity on the world stage. In other words, according to the Francoist narrative in the textbooks, the republics of Latin America acquired their identity as nations, not with their independence from Spain, but during the conquest, despite the fact that they did not yet exist as nations.

But the texts recognized that the process of fertilization was simultaneously a process of domination, in which the lands had to be submitted, in some cases against their volition, to the conquistadors' will.[59] Sometimes, as Ortiz pointed out, the lands rebelled against the Spaniards, showing their pride and "indomitable ferocity."[60] The authors attributed to the American lands all the characteristics traditionally assigned to women by western European culture, such as the identification with nature and irrationality, as opposed to the rationality and civilization attributed to men.[61] However, the narrators remarked that in spite of the opposition, the conquistadors always behaved like gentlemen, going to the extreme, when necessary, of risking their lives to perform their higher mission.[62] Ortiz, for example, explained in sadistic detail how the Araucanians severed Valdivia's arms with seashells and ate them in a "horrendous banquet."

Valdivia's suffering, however, was not in vain. Its clear objective was "that Chile could become a civilized nation in concert with the contemporary world."[63] In this way the author established a distinction between the irrational and uncivilized Native Americans who were torturing Valdivia and the future nation, quasi-person and woman, for whom he was suffering the maximum sacrifice: giving his life. Apparently, these proofs of gentlemanliness were not always necessary to obtain the lands' consent. The American lands often not only accepted the action of the conquistadors, but offered themselves to the Spaniards' will and asked "for civilization and conquest."[64] Once the domination of the conquistadors was consolidated, the American lands enjoyed their new life and lived "happily under the rule of Spain."[65] As if it were a fairy tale, the protagonists—the American lands and the conquistadors—got together by mutual agreement and lived happily ever after. Although the authors did not explicitly use the word "matrimony" to refer to the culmination of the relationship between the conquistadors and the American lands—as they did when referring to the indigenous women—it was obviously implicit. Pemán gave us a fine example when explaining the ceremony that consolidated the Spanish domination of the lands:

> For Spain the colonization was a state enterprise, an enterprise of the Kings that thought that the Pope gave them those lands to convert and civilize them. As soon as the Spaniards arrived in a new land, when they possessed her, they always solemnly remembered this: that she [the land] was occupied in the name of the King and by authorization of the pope. This was publicly announced in the presence of a public notary.[66]

Pemán's description significantly resembled the ceremony of marriage. The Pope—God's representative—gave the American lands to the Spanish kings so that they could convert them to Christianity and civilize and possess them. According to the quote, the conquistadors, when possessing the lands, were fulfilling a duty, following orders that came from God himself, through his representative, the Pope. To legalize the union between the conquistadors and the lands, a representative of the Spanish law—presented by the author as universal law—was always present. Thus, a legal contract sealed the relationship. Once the symbolic marriage was consolidated, the fertilization process took place, and America gave birth to the fruits of this fertilization. These fruits were both the products of the land, such as precious metals or crops, and the lands themselves as they became nations within the international arena.[67] The conquistadors as fathers—males—played in these texts the role of donors, while the lands played the female role of receptors. In this symbolic marriage, the conquistador, as donor, had the right to share the fruits of the land, and as father had the right to guide his children's lives. In this way the authors justified both the Spanish appropriation of America's wealth in the past, and the plans for Spain's leadership of the Hispanic Community in the future. In these future plans, indigenous people, both women and men, were marginalized.

According to the narrative that emerges, the indigenous people had not given the lands proper treatment, because they were not sufficiently strong, able, or civilized, and certainly not masculine enough, to dominate and civilize the space. The conquistador, however, had all of the power and masculinity needed to do so. Nothing is more illustrative of this point than the cover of Ortiz Muñoz's history, *Glorias Imperiales* (see Figure 3.2). The conquistador

FIGURE 3.2

"Glorias Imperiales" (Imperial Glories).

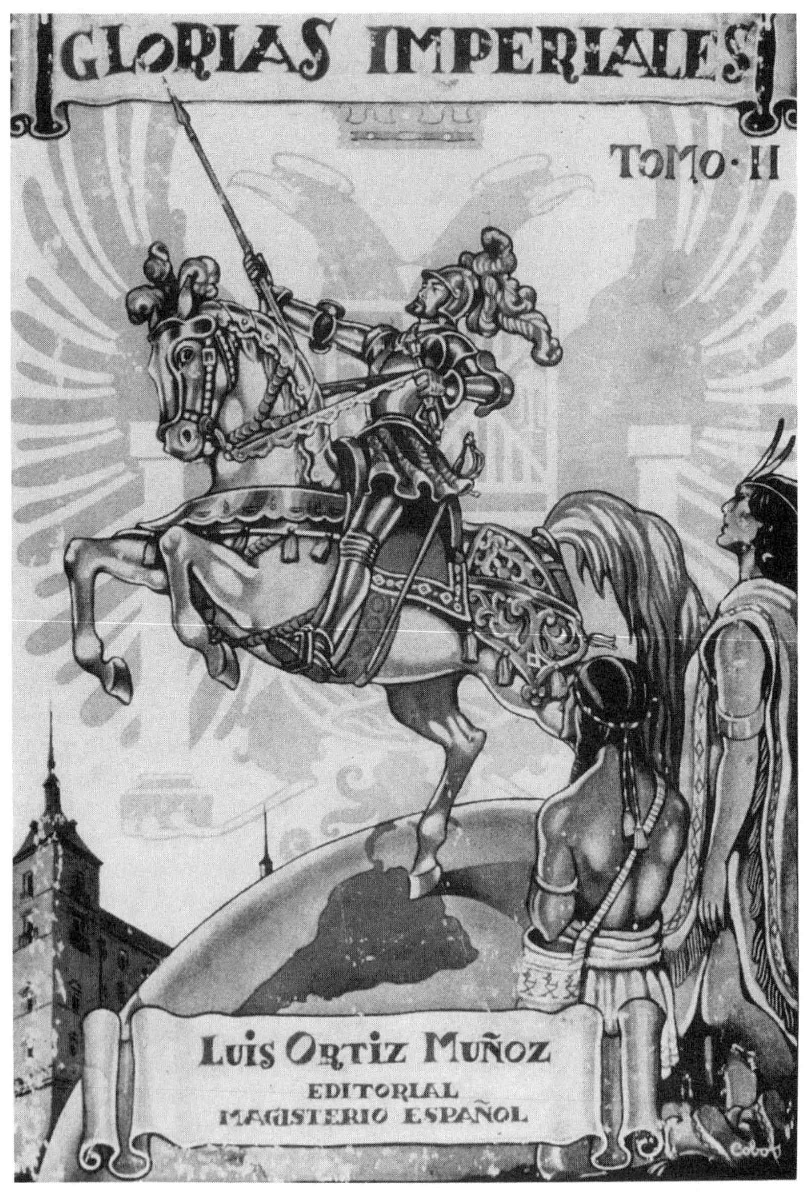

appeared in the center of the drawing, occupying most of the space from a height that is enhanced by the fact that he is on horseback. His mount elevated his torso and the horse's front legs. The horse, considered by Spanish tradition to symbolize manliness and nobility, along with the knight's armor and military decorations, emphasized the masculinity, nobility, and power of the conquistador. The horse, indispensable to the conquest because, among other things, of the fear it inspired among the Native Americans, reinforced the conquistadors' superiority over them. The conquistador, therefore, had the right to dominate the territory not only because of what he was—a man—but also because of what he represented: a civilized, Spanish, and Christian society. That is, this man did not act out of his own initiative but rather as the representative of God and of his fatherland, with which he maintained contact through the horse's left leg, thus bridging the continents. The discovery and conquest therefore not only permitted the linking of Europe and America, but also consolidated man's control and dominion over the land, with the man—in this case the conquistador—becoming the center of the universe. The lands' submission and domination was not harmful, however, because it turned a savage landscape into a civilized one by means of elements introduced by the conquerors and colonizers—notably, in this case, the horse.

In this process of transformation, however, the lands are separated from their owners. The image described here showed the Native Americans looking at the conquistador from a corner, one of them kneeling in submission and respect, both separated from their lands—their women. The drawing showed the lands already belonging to the conquistador, and the usurpation is legitimated by the imperial laws of white men, represented by the two-headed eagle that, carrying the imperial coat of arms and Hercules' columns, covers the background of the scene. American territory was tied to the representation of Spain's power, the crown, which as God's representative on Earth, delegates its power over the lands to the conquistadors.

The relationship between the conquistadors and the land was thus sealed, marginalizing the Native Americans. Nevertheless, when the Spaniards left America, they "passed" the lands, as Cortes did with Marina, to the Native American descendants to look after them. The admiration and gratitude of the lands towards the Spaniards would remain and, consequently, within this logic, so would the ascendancy of Spain over the Latin American republics.

As demonstrated in this chapter, the authors of history school textbooks during the Franco regime used gender metaphors extensively in their attempt to indoctrinate children and youth. These gender metaphors, which naturalized and assigned value to difference, were crucial in the regime's effort to justify hierarchy in its relations with the Latin American republics, both in the past and, more subtly, in the present. Gender metaphors could be easily appropriated for this purpose because no one would question the principle of a "natural" gendered social order in the 1940s and 1950s. In contrast, the more direct imperialist discourse of hierarchy was coming under increasing attack as, internationally, the colonial world demanded independence and self-determination. Thus, gender remained the most acceptable signifier of difference and hierarchy.

By using a gendered metaphor, Francoist discourse portrayed the American lands themselves—in the guise of women—as the ones that chose and consented to domination. The notion that the conquered consented to conquest makes sense only within a gendered order in which virgin females require male protection and authority, as well as fertilization, to achieve their full potential. The land's female qualities further allowed the narrators to establish a direct, personal link between the conquistadors and the space being occupied, without the mediation of Native Americans. The indigenous woman appears briefly as a key figure through her act of choosing the white man over the emasculated Native as her protector and savior, thus confirming the conquistadors' superiority and legitimating the conquest. Once she performs this role, which establishes her as the mother of the new Latin American race, she, too, is marginalized. In this way, the narrative guaranteed the existence of permanent ties between Spaniards and the American territories that the inhabitants of the land themselves could not sever. The indigenous people were then relegated the servile task of caring for the land that no longer belonged to them. Such simple and yet sophisticated gender arguments could then be processed by children and youth alike in such a way that rape was exonerated, the conquistadors' superiority was legitimated, and the relationship between Latin Americans and Spaniards was reinforced, thereby providing the Franco regime its much-needed unifying national identity and international status.

Notes

1. Geoff Eley, "Nations, Publics and Political Cultures: Placing Habermas in the Nineteenth Century," in Nicholas B. Dirks, Geoff Eley and Sherry B. Ortner, eds., *Culture/Power/History: A Reader in Contemporary Social Theory*, (Princeton: Princeton University Press, 1994), p. 311.

2. Joan W. Scott, *Gender and the Politics of History* (New York: Columbia University Press, 1988), p. 42.

3. Dirks et al., *Culture/Power/History*, p. 33.

4. Ann Stoler, "Rethinking Colonial Categories: European Communities and the Boundaries of Rule," in *Comparative Studies in Society and History* no. 31, 1 (1989): 134–161.

5. Scott, *Gender and the Politics of History*, pp. 48–49.

6. Gregorio Camara Villar, *Nacional-Catolicismo y escuela: La socialización política del Franquismo (1936–1951)* (Jaen, Spain: Hesperia, 1984); Carolyn P. Boyd, "History in the Schools and the Problem of Spanish Identity," in Richard Herr, and John H.R. Polt, eds., *Iberian Identity. Essays on the Nature of Identity in Portugal and Spain.* (Berkeley, CA: University of California, Institute of International Studies, 1989); Gonzalo Pasamar Alzuria, *Historiografía e ideología en la posguerra española: La ruptura de la tradición liberal* (Zaragoza, Spain: Universidad de Zaragoza, 1991).

7. Boyd, "History in the Schools and the Problem of Spanish Identity," pp. 186–187.

8. Francoist authors were not the first ones in using this period as the model for the "regeneration" of Spain. See Raul Morodo, *Los origenes ideológicos del franquismo: Acción Española* (Madrid: Alianza, 1985).

9. According to Francoists, Spain's importance at the international level did not rest on what Spain was at that time—devastated by the Civil War and desperately poor—but in what the Latin American nations were and what they might become. In the 1940s, the Francoists viewed these countries as underdeveloped nations with immense potential. In other words, unable to seek international recognition based on the importance of Spain in and of itself, Francoists exploited the concept of a Hispanic Community by presenting Spain as its leader before the United States and Europe.

10. L. Minio-Paluello, *Education in Fascist Italy* (London: Oxford University Press, 1946); Gilmer W. Blackburn, *Education in the Third Reich: A Study of Race and History in Nazi Textbooks* (Albany: State University of New York Press, 1985); John Godwin Caiger, "Education, Values and Japan's National Identity: A Study of the Aims and Content of Courses in Japanese History, 1872–1963." (Ph.D. diss., Australian National University, 1967). For the Spanish case see María A. Escudero, "The Image of Latin America Disseminated in Spain by the Franco Regime: Repercussions in the Configuration of a National Identity." (Ph.D. diss., University of California, San Diego, 1994.) See also Camara Villar, *Nacional-Catolicismo y Escuela*; Clementina García Crespo, *Léxico e ideología en los libros de lectura de la Escuela Primaria (1940-1975)* (Salamanca, Spain: Ediciones Universidad de Salamanca, 1983); Ramón Navarro Sandalinas, *La enseñanza primaria durante el franquismo (1936–1975)* (Barcelona: PPU, 1990); Richard Anthony Nuccio, "The Socialization of Political Values: The Content of Official Education in Spain." (Ph.D. diss., University of Massachusetts, 1977); José Antonio Rodriguez Alarcón, "La visión de América en los textos escolares españoles (1930-1960): Una doble imagen," in M. Huguet, A. Niño, and P. Pérez, eds., *La formación de la imagen de América Latina en España, 1898–1989* (Madrid: OEI, 1992), pp. 389–399.

11. While since 1941 the Francoist foreign office and the Instituto de Cultura Hispánica paid special attention to censoring imperialistic remarks towards the Latin American republics in newspapers and books, I did not find any evidence of that kind of censorship in school textbooks until the mid-sixties, when an internal report of the Instituto de Cultura Hispánica suggested cutting out a sentence from one of Serrano de

Haro's books called *Yo soy español.* For further details see María A. Escudero, *El Instituto de Cultura Hispánica* (Madrid: Ed. Maphre, 1994), pp. 63–68, 148.

12. It is not uncommon to find textbooks full of euphemistic statements such as "it seems like a fairy tale," "how tradition tells it," or "it is said," as well as vague and incorrect references to historical sources. Furthermore, parallels between textbook narration and fictional accounts suffused the latter with a sense of truthfulness. See Escudero, "The Image of Latin America Disseminated in Spain by the Franco Regime," pp. 17–18.

13. Ibid., pp. 22–24.

14. Luis Ortiz Muñoz was *vocal* of the Consejo Nacional de Educación between 1941-1944; he was also Catedrático de Latin de Enseñanza Media; Director General de Enseñanza Media, Secretario Central del Servicio Español del Profesorado de Enseñanza Media de la Delegación de Educación Nacional de FET y de las JONS, Subsecretario de Educación Popular in 1946, and subsequently Subsecretario de Información under the rule of Gabriel Arias-Salgado. José María Pemán was one of the most prominent intellectual figures of the Franco Regime, with extensive literary and journalistic work. During the Civil War he was President of the Comisión Depuradora de Cultura y Enseñanza created on the seventh of December of 1936, and director of the Real Academia Española until 1947. After the Civil War he was member of the Consejo Nacional de FET y de las Jons. Agustín Serrano de Haro was chief inspector of primary education and probably the most prolific author of school textbooks of the Franco regime. Among his works were *Hemos visto al Señor* (Jaén, 1941), *Cristo es la Verdad* (Madrid, 1941), *Yo soy español* (Madrid, 1945), *Guirnaldas de la Historia* (Madrid, 1947), and *España es así* (Madrid, 1942).

15. These textbooks were extensively published until the mid-sixties. As an example, *España es así* reached a twenty-third edition in 1964, and *Guirnaldas de la Historia*, an eleventh edition in 1962.

16. Luis Ortiz Muñoz, *Glorias Imperiales*, 2 vols. (Madrid: Ed. Magisterio Español, 1957); José María Pemán, *La Historia de España contada con sencillez: Para los niños . . . y para muchos que no lo son* 2 vols. (Madrid: Escelier, S.A., 1958); Agustín Serrano de Haro, *España es así* (Madrid: Ed. Escuela Española, 1964) and *Guirnaldas de la Historia. Historia de la cultura española contada a las niñas* (Madrid: Ed. Escuela Española, 1962).

17. This survey queried national teachers and inspectors "with the aim of determining educators' preferences with respect to the numerous reading books, encyclopedias and texts on the market." The results of this survey are compiled in Francisca Montilla, *Selección de libros escolares de lectura* (Madrid: C.S.I.C., 1954).

18. Pemán's first edition was in 1939; Ortiz Muñoz's, in 1940; Serrano's *España es así* in 1947, and *Guirnaldas* in 1947.

19. The Francoist Ministry of Education commissioned Pemán to write his *Historia* and then declared it of "compulsory use" in schools (Orden Ministerial of

April 11, 1938). The Ministry also declared both the Muñoz and Serrano de Haro's *Guirnaldas* books of "public utility" for the schools, and the Academy of History selected *España es así* for a national award.

20. Francoist authors understood *mestizaje* as the result of the physical and cultural union (exchange) of two races: the white race represented by the Spaniards, and the Amerindian race represented by Native Americans. The result, according to Francoist authors, was the creation of a new race of *mestizos*. These individuals shared not only the physical characteristics of both races, but also their cultural features.

21. The Black Legend, originally developed in England, labeled the Spaniards as decadent, authoritarian, corrupt, cruel, and intolerant, as demonstrated by the atrocities they perpetrated against the Native Americans in their zeal to spread Roman Catholicism and in their merciless exploitation of the defenseless indigenous population throughout the colonial era. For further details see Charles Gibson, *The Black Legend: Anti-Spanish Attitudes in the Old World and the New* (New York: Knopf, 1971).

22. Serrano de Haro, *España es así*, p. 115. Boldface in original.

23. As Ortiz Muñoz stated: "Spain went to the New World—to transfuse to them her blood," Ortiz Muñoz, *Glorias Imperiales*, vol. 2, pp. 187–188.

24. "He possesses the secret to intercede quickly and efficiently—first the blood of the indigenous nobility has to be fused with that of the conquistadors." Ibid., p. 178.

25. Serrano de Haro, *Guirnaldas de la Historia*, p. 126.

26. Pemán, *La Historia de España*, 2:187–188.

27. Serrano de Haro, *Guirnaldas de la Historia*, p. 126.

28. Pemán, *La Historia de España*, 2:187.

29. Ricardo Herren, *Doña Marina, La Malinche* (Barcelona: Planeta, 1992), p. 26.

30. Pemán, *La Historia de España*, 2:187.

31. This narrative appeared in 1953 in *Bazar*, a comic strip intended for girls, published weekly in Madrid since 1945 by the *Sección Femenina* de FET y de las JONS, and directed by Elisa de Lara. The fact that it was a publication intended for girls explains the attention given to Marina. No publication intended for boys would, at the time, have made an indigenous woman the focus of their attention. Marina, however, presented a great example of submissiveness and fidelity, characteristics that Francoist educators wanted to impose on girls.

32. Marina's original name is controversial. Some authors believe that her original name was Malinalli—a name that corresponded to the Aztec name of the day she was born, the twelfth day of the Aztec calendar—and that this name became Malintzin, a name that other Native Americans used to call her, by the addition of the suffix *tzin*

that in the Náhuatl language was the equivalent to the Spanish *doña*. Other authors are of the opinion that the difficulty for the Náhuatl-speaking indigenous people in pronouncing the Castillian *r* resulted in the name Doña Marina evolving to that of Malintzin. Malinche is the popular name by which she is commonly known, and is a deformation of the word Malintzine, a name the indigenous people gave to Cortes (due to the addition of the final *e*, which is the Náhuatl possessive, this word meant "Marina's owner"). Herren, *Doña Marina*, pp. 34–36.

33. In the language of the natives of Santo Domingo, this meant chief.

34. Territory controlled by the *cacique*.

35. According to Ricardo Herren, this version of Marina's early years is probably a mystification created both by indigenous people and Spaniards, in which there are many of the elements characteristic of the lives of fictional heroes. However, it has been commonly accepted because it is yet impossible to establish the veracity of the events of Marina's life before she was given to Cortes. See Herren, *Doña Marina*, pp. 28–36.

36. "Así nació América: Malinalli," in *Bazar*, May, 1953.

37. Todorov points out that there were many occasions in which Marina acted independently in favor of the conquistadors and against the indigenous people. Tzvetan Todorov, *La conquista de América: El problema del otro* (México: Siglo XXI, 1989), pp. 108–109.

38. "Así nació América: Malinalli," in *Bazar*, June, 1953.

39. See Dorothy M. Broderick, *Image of Black in Children's Fiction* (New York: R.R. Bowker, 1973).

40. Clifford Geertz: *The Theater State in Nineteenth-Century Bali*. (Princeton, NJ: Princeton University Press, 1980).

41. "Así nació América: Malinalli," in *Bazar*, June, 1953.

42. Ibid.

43. Ibid.

44. Ibid.

45. In the textbooks, both individuals and nations are historical subjects. Nations are presented either implicitly or explicitly as quasi-persons. Borrowed from the Francoist philosopher García Morente, this term implies that nations possess a body and a soul that can be defined and represented symbolically. Manuel García Morente, *Ideas para una filosofía de la historia de España* (Madrid: Universidad de Madrid, Servicio de Publicaciones, 1943).

46. Serrano de Haro, *España es así*, pp. 108, 109, 119. Ortiz Muñoz, *Glorias Imperiales*, 2:119. In all texts there are continuous references to the conquistadors' desire to conquer, dominate, and possess the American lands.

47. Serrano de Haro, *España es así*, p. 105. Boldface in original.

48. See as an example Ortiz Muñoz, *Glorias Imperiales*, pp. 105, 115, 123–124.

49. Pemán, *La Historia de España*, p. 216.

50. Ortiz Muñoz, *Glorias Imperiales*, 1:258.

51. Ortiz Muñoz, *Glorias Imperiales*, 2:182.

52. Serrano de Haro, *España es así*, p. 91.

53. Ortiz Muñoz, *Glorias Imperiales*, 2:124.

54. Serrano de Haro, *Guirnaldas de la Historia*, p. 122. See also Ortiz Muñoz, *Glorias Imperiales*, 2:182.

55. Ortiz Muñoz, *Glorias Imperiales*, 2:184.

56. Pemán, *La Historia de España*, 2:225.

57. Pemán, *La Historia de España*, 2:187, 188.

58. Pemán, *La Historia de España*, 2:225.

59. Serrano de Haro, *España es así*, p. 106; Pemán, *La Historia de España*, 2:216, 220.

60. Ortiz Muñoz, *Glorias Imperiales*, 2:109, 132.

61. Cynthia E. Russett, *Sexual Science. The Victorian Construction of Womanhood* (Cambridge, MA: Harvard University Press, 1989).

62. For example, Ortiz pointed out how Pedro de Mendoza risked his life to save Argentina. Ortiz Muñoz, *Glorias Imperiales*, 2:127.

63. Ibid.

64. Ibid., pp. 104 and 128. See also 2:108.

65. Ibid., p. 178.

66. Pemán, *La Historia de España*, 2:223–224.

67. Ibid., 216, 227; Ortiz Muñoz, *Glorias Imperiales*, 2:99, 113; Serrano de Haro, *España es así*, p. 115.

4

Masculinity Versus Femininity: The Sanfermines: 1939–1978

Clotilde Puertolas

When in 1978 a group of women interrupted an event of Pamplona's annual fiestas honoring the local patron saint, *San Fermín*,[1] the audience was bewildered. Dating from the twelfth century,[2] the Sanfermines was among the most famous festivities in Spain[3] and the best known outside its borders.[4] Although citizens of the provincial capital of Navarre were accustomed to political and social protest during the fiesta, especially in the 1970s, previous demonstrations had focused on political issues and had been executed almost exclusively by men.[5] In addition, women's participation in boycotts or other actions during the July fiestas had always been in a secondary or supporting role. Never before had women collectively raised their voices during the Sanfermines. Consequently, the feminist protest took Pamplona's citizens by surprise.

The space selected to dramatize this collective action was chosen for two main reasons. First, the space was symbolically masculine, a taurine spectacle sponsored by the *peñas* (exclusively male recreational associations) and a highly visible element of the festival. Second, it took place in a bullring with a large seating capacity. Thus, in the middle of the *peñas* event, several women in the audience stood up and unfurled an *ikurriña* (the Basque flag) and a banner which read, "*Madrinas Kampora*" (which in the Basque language means "No More Godmothers")[6] while chanting this slogan until the event was fully disrupted. The *madrinas*, selected by each *peña* as their official representatives during the fiesta,[7] sat still during the protest. The members of the *peñas* also remained quiet and the taurine spectacle subsequently resumed. Yet, the women achieved what they had sought: the full attention of the almost 20,000 spectators and complete disruption of the event.

By specifically attacking the role of the *madrinas*, the protestors were criticizing the use of gender double standards during the fiestas. The feminist group strongly believed that the institutionalization of the *madrinas* perpetuated the most traditional and narrow concept of femininity. Since the festival was mainly a masculine affair, men could participate in nearly all of the rituals and could violate social norms, whereas women were granted none of these liberties. "The Sanfermines is a planned, permitted and institutionalized orgy," the feminists later stated, "but these excesses are exclusively arranged for men."[8] In a press conference defending themselves from the feminist attack, the *madrinas* asserted that they also supported the women's liberation movement and increased participation of Pamplonese women in the festival.[9] The *madrinas* argued that they had evolved politically since the end of the Franco regime, substituting the Basque flag for the traditional Spanish *mantilla*, a radical change of image.[10] They claimed that they did not consider themselves to be "objects," as the feminists had suggested, because they were not competing in a beauty pageant. Furthermore, the *madrinas* emphasized that by representing the *peñas*, they were not only actively participating in the fiesta, but they were cultivating the image of the Sanfermines, and maintaining its essence, spirit, and tradition as well.

This story exemplifies not only the tension and inequality that existed between the genders during the festival but also the difference of opinion among women about their identity and the extent of their participation. Both *madrinas* and feminists, in their attempt to define their image and identity, had distinct interpretations of how changes in cultural norms regarding women should be incorporated into the festival and into the public sphere. Both groups challenged tradition, the *madrinas* by substituting the *ikurriña* for the *mantilla*, and the feminists by openly protesting women's discrimination. Nevertheless, both groups accepted the masculine essence of the fiesta's rituals to a certain extent, thus demonstrating the power of the event's constructed gender categories.

Femininity in the Sanfermines from 1939 to 1978 was defined and controlled by the local government, the media, and the *peñas*. This chapter argues that the concepts of masculinity, femininity, and tradition were fabricated and manipulated by these entities to maintain a status quo that effectively preserved divisions between the genders and male hierarchy. The period studied begins with the end of the Civil War, and includes the Franco regime (1939–1975) and the initial years of the democratic transition and installation of a parliamentary monarchy (1975–1978). These years are particularly interesting due to the profound social, economic, political, and ideological changes as well as the transformations in the role of women that took place in Spanish society in general and Pamplonese society in particular.[11] Pamplona itself underwent rapid urban expansion, industrialization, and population growth. The number of residents nearly tripled from 61,000 inhabitants in 1940 to 176,000 in 1978. New social classes developed, and novel social attitudes emerged. In addition, sharp ideological divisions polarized the city on the issue of the integration of Navarre within the Basque Country.

This chapter demonstrates that although political ideology and social attitudes underwent significant transformations, the imposition of the concepts of masculinity, femininity, and tradition by the local government, media, and the *peñas*, as seen through the Sanfermines, remained unaltered. Moreover, the construction of these concepts became reinforced with the passage of time, illustrating that the web of norms, values and customs that dictated "proper" gender related behavior and that defined "true" feminine identity was deeply rooted within the community, transcending the political transition that occurred during the years from 1939 to 1978. This phenomenon confirms that changes in collective attitudes towards cultural issues like gender roles, are not necessarily correlated with, or do not follow automatically from, political and social change.

The Pamplonese Fiesta: Meaning and Functions

Festivals, in their many forms, are directly linked to their environment and their context. Every society and historical period creates its own celebrations.[12] As with other public rituals, the Sanfermines evolved since its creation in the twelfth century. And like every previous government, the Francoist regime imprinted its principles and values on the fiesta. Thus, under Franco, the Pamplonese festival became a tool to stress its achievements and notions of masculinity, femininity, and tradition.[13] It is not a coincidence that in 1965, one year after its celebration of twenty-five years in power, the Francoist government labeled the Sanfermines a "Fiesta of Interest to Tourists" in order to market abroad the image of a traditional local festival in a peaceful and orderly Spain. Even after 1975, however, as the nation slowly opened to new trends in thought and behavior, there was no attempt by the Pamplonese municipality, the media, or masculine associations to alter the masculine and feminine images or identities during the fiesta. On the contrary, the classic definitions of masculinity, femininity, and tradition were strengthened. Consequently, masculine and feminine identities were strongly reinforced and deeply rooted in the community.

Like other festivals, the Sanfermines was participatory. Public rituals are collective manifestations when members of a community actively participate, sharing its content, symbols, and rites.[14] Scholars of cultural performances, however, disagree on the significance of this participation. Some consider the festival a moment of total communion among all social groups and classes. The festival unifies its participants, defining a community and distinguishing it from others.[15] Other scholars argue that because every group interprets, celebrates and participates in the festival differently, cultural performances are far from being celebrations of unity, solidarity, and wholeness. These authors argue that festivals may intensify class cohesion, generating confrontation, aggression and tension.[16] Following this dual nature of celebrations, festivities have two main functions.[17] On the one hand, festivals can be a total transgression of quotidian life, potentially inducing social conflict. The festival can become a permissive period when the established order is temporarily suspended, values are reversed, rules disobeyed, and excess accepted.[18] On the other hand, festivals can be a reflection of societal values that reproduce the established structure.[19]

The Sanfermines was characterized by both extremes. The fiesta embodied inversion, transgression, disobedience, and excess, and at the same time it ratified the established system. Role reversal rites occurred as well as rituals applauding the status quo. There were moments of total transgression and excess and occasions of order and discipline. The Sanfermines also combined both solidarity and division. It united the city's inhabitants regardless of their gender in a singular way, but it also divided them. All community members shared the codes, content, language, and argument[20] of the festival, but they interpreted and lived them differently depending on their level of participation and role within the community. Consequently, both genders experienced the fiesta and took part in a distinct manner. While men were the protagonists of the rituals and were allowed to invert, transgress, and disobey, women were relegated to a more passive secondary position.

This chapter analyzes the Sanfermines as a vivid document, as a text, facilitating a more complete understanding of the internal structure of the community and the dynamics among its members. Although the community was diverse and its collective manifestation was far from homogeneous, the fiesta operated as a global symbolic display of the rules, values, attitudes, norms, and ideas about the collectivity, the community as a whole.[21] As the "very soul" and "core" of Pamplona,[22] the fiesta exemplified the collective consciousness of its inhabitants, and served as a social commentary on the city itself.

Men, Women, and the Fiesta

In 1939, when the fiesta was still a provincial celebration, as in 1978, when it had become internationally known, the Sanfermines was the main event of Pamplona's life. The fiesta made Pamplona unique. Like public rituals in other communities, the arrival of the festival on July 6 was eagerly anticipated. Time was measured by the annual celebration. The city prepared for this special occasion by decorating its gardens and cleaning its downtown buildings and streets, a symbolic decontamination of the festive space.[23] All Pamplonese readied their red neckerchiefs, symbol of the Sanfermines, for the days of the festival.

Once the fiesta began, participation was clearly differentiated in terms of gender. The festival was basically a masculine affair, as it had been in previous years. From 1939 to 1978 the central rituals were culturally reserved for males. Both the opening and closing events were fundamentally gatherings of men. The *Chupinazo* (Firecracker) on July 6, and the *Pobre de Mí* (Pity Me) on July 14, congregated a considerable number of men in the city hall square to joyfully greet and bid the fiesta farewell. Only men were permitted to run in front of the bulls through the streets, the so called *encierro*, to demonstrate their bravery. Only men could belong to the *peñas*.[24] Only men sat in the sunny section of the bullring, where they sang, drank, and chanted refrains about the matador and the bullfight or the current political situation, while the rest of the audience occupied the shaded bleachers and observed this unique dual spectacle. Only men marched in the *Riau-Riau*, the role reversal ritual in which citizens blocked the official entourage of the City Council from the City Hall to the Chapel of Saint Fermín on its way to honor the saint in the liturgical ceremony of *Vísperas*.[25] Only men belonged to the *Comparsa de Gigantes y Cabezudos* (Retinue of Giants and Big-Heads) and controlled the huge papier-maché figures of Giants, Big-Heads, and *Kilikis* (Men-horses) that danced through the streets. Only men carried and guarded the figure of Saint Fermin in the procession. Men were the sole members of the official escort of mace bearers, kettle drummers, and trumpeters who accompanied almost every ritual of the fiesta.

In addition, the men were permitted to transgress, disobey, and "exceed," and were expected to break regular social boundaries and norms. Men were allowed to behave boisterously, get drunk, overeat, and flirt openly with other women. For example, it was common for married men to disappear from home for several days without notifying their families,[26] and for engaged men to break up with their fiancées to freely enjoy the celebration.[27]

Although by 1978 Pamplonese women behaved more freely than in 1939, spending part or the whole night out partying, and drinking openly, their role in the festival had not changed tremendously. Women were still excluded from membership in the *peñas* and from participation in the main rituals, although they could attend the religious ceremonies, the public dances, the fireworks, and other spectacles and entertainment. Women's participation was restricted by social boundaries, public opinion and the collective conceptualization of femininity, masculinity, the family, and family values. Women were expected not only to avoid excess in any form but also to stoically tolerate masculine excesses. It was commonly considered that the feminine role, and even the patriotic duty of a good and pure Navarrese woman, a *castiza*,[28] was to accept and even encourage men's festive behavior because it was typical, traditional, and genuinely virile.[29]

Thus, the feminist protest in 1978 was a general complaint against the continued application of the traditional norms to women. It targeted both discrimination and double standards in the festival. The demonstrators' goals were to expose the social boundaries by which women's lives were limited and to pressure for a change. By unifying their feminist perspective with their Basque nationalist ideology (by displaying the Basque flag and shouting all their slogans in the Basque language), these women demonstrated that Pamplonese women were directly involved in the political process, having not only the right to vote but also the license to publicly display their opinion and protest. The feminist demonstration was the first outspoken demand for a redefinition of women's role within the festival and the accompanying search for a new female identity.

The Ideal Masculine Figure

During the period from 1939 to 1978, historiography about the annual Sanfermines was defined in terms of masculine values. Both local and foreign historiography, written almost exclusively by men, described the fiesta in terms of bravery, virility, courage, controlled misbehavior, gaiety, and comradeship: all qualities attributed to men. Fictional and historical works promoted the concept that the festival was mainly a series of events where men tested themselves; they essentially ignored the role of women. The process of defining masculinity in Pamplona's fiesta began long before 1939,[30] but it was even more strongly delineated after the triumph of General Franco.

The festival of 1939, the first celebrated after three years of Civil War,[31] turned into a tribute to the Pamplonese *mozo*, or young men, who had been among the first to support the military uprising against the Second Republic in 1936. The local press emphasized that the bravery and courage demonstrated by Pamplonese men during the festival and during the war came from the same source: the particular endurance of the Navarrese race. As one journalist pointed out, the *mozo* manifested the same valor facing death while defending "the trenches of God and Spain" as when he was eluding the bulls' horns.[32]

The 1939 Sanfermines set the tone for the exaltation of masculine values. In the following decades, the municipal government, media, and fellow citizens continued glorifying the *mozo*, especially if he belonged to a *peña.* The *peñas* were one of the most visible elements of the fiestas. They participated actively in all of the rituals, sitting in the sunny section of the bullring, and organizing daily parades through the streets with their musical instruments and *pancartas*, which were banners that displayed the *peñas*' names as well as satirical drawings targeting local, national and international topics related to political, cultural, and economic issues. Local newspapers praised the *peñas*' participation in the festive rituals, and pronounced the masculine associations to be emblems of virility and manhood. Running in the *encierro* became synonymous with bravery, virility, and nobility, while the manliness of those who did not run was questioned.[33] The bleachers in the sun became a "mirror in which the city's inhabitants and visitors" could observe "the nerve of the Sanfermines."[34] The emphasis on the *mozo*'s endurance prompted a journalist to claim that "whoever is not Navarrese would be exhausted within a day."[35] In one instance, the media proudly stated that the *mozo* was a man of metal;[36] and out of pride, one *peña* named itself *Los del Bronce* (Men of Bronze).[37]

The *peñas* were seen as the symbolic embodiment of the traditions and customs of the land, and as the bearers of the essence of the Navarrese race.[38] The *peña mozo*, especially the one dressed in the typical *sanferminero* outfit—white pants and shirt, red neckerchief, red scarf around the hips, and white and red shoes—became the popular symbol of the fiesta.[39] This image was highlighted in the annual official posters printed by the Municipality to promote the festival. Thirty-five of the forty posters from 1939 to 1978 showed muscular athletic men dressed in the festive uniform running in front of the bulls (See Figures 4.2–4.5).

In this atmosphere glorifying masculine ideals, it is not surprising that the number of *peñas* dramatically increased. In 1939 there were three *peñas*.[40] By 1978, the number had quadrupled to thirteen and they had become a social institution. The public considered them the "ferment, mother, yeast, catalyst, and fuse of the festival,"[41] and the local government provided them a municipal subsidy.[42] Not surprisingly, the *peñas* internalized this glorification. They claimed that their dancing, drinking, eating, and other excesses were simply displays of traditionally male festive behavior. The *peñas* argued that they were the popular political and social voices of the city, advocates of the spirit and traditions of the fiesta and representatives of its essence. Gradually, they began to define what was traditional and anti-traditional, what constituted public order, what was properly masculine and feminine conduct. The *peñas* gradually perceived themselves as the popular police of the festival.[43]

With the certainty that they symbolized popular sentiment and represented "people power,"[44] the *peñas* operated as guardians of public order and of the traditional essence of the festival. This defense of the spirit of the fiesta was formalized in 1945, when the *peñas*' presidents formed the Commission of *Peñas*, which, among its many goals, claimed "to defend and emphasize all the characteristics of human, artistic, social and historical interest that take place during our *Fiestas de San Fermín*."[45] Naturally, the definition of these characteristics was largely determined by the *peñas* themselves. The maintenance of order and tradition was not only carried out through their "exemplary" behavior but also through active and direct intervention. The *peñas* guarded the festival in all its aspects and policed those individuals who did not conform to their perception of proper and traditional conduct.

FIGURE 4.1

"Pamplona, San Fermin de 1949."

FIGURE 4.2

"Pamplona, San Fermin de 1953."

FIGURE 4.3

"San Fermin de 1960, Pamplona."

FIGURE 4.4

"Sanfermines 1969, Pamplona."

FIGURE 4.5

"Sanfermin, Pamplona, 1977."

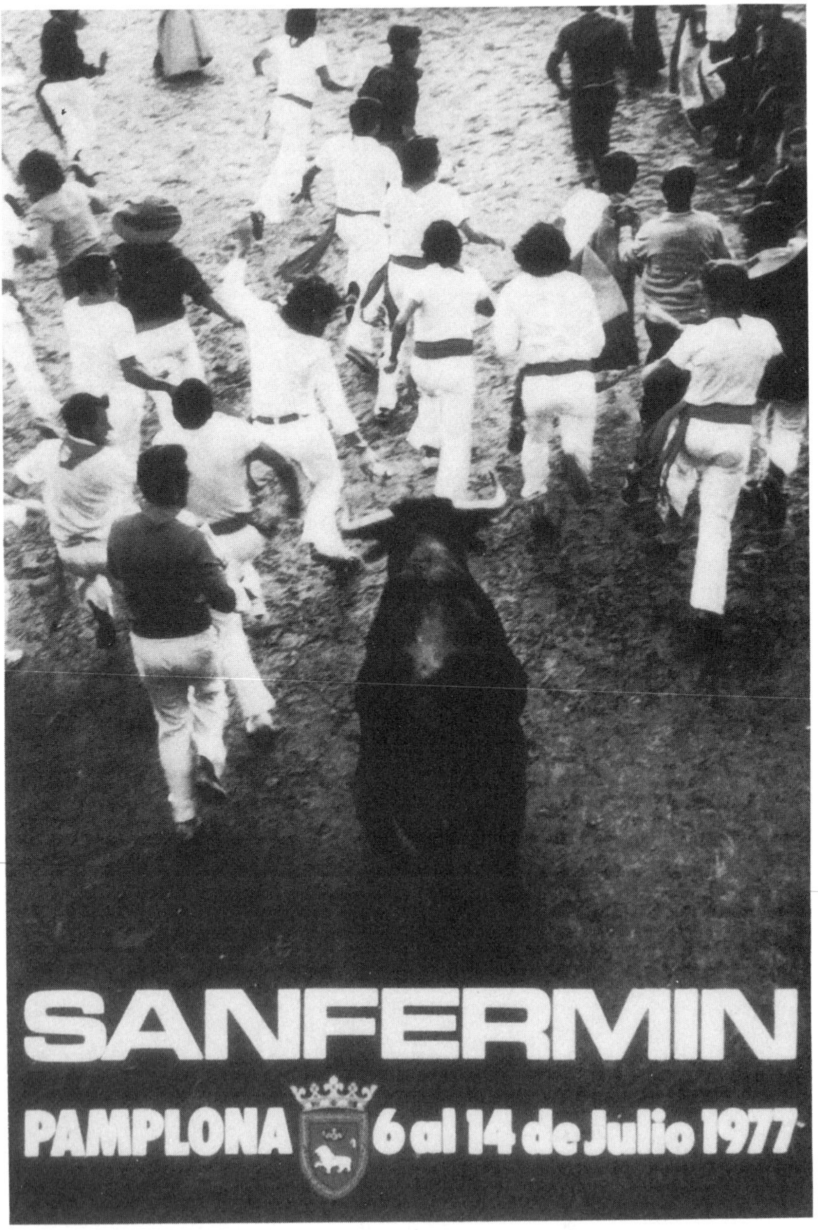

The masculine associations began their policing by controlling the festival's rituals. The *peñas* targeted those participants causing problems during the *encierro*, bullfight, or other rituals. For instance, when an individual ran "dangerously" in the *encierro* by provoking a bull or putting another runner in jeopardy, when a person jumped into the arena to fight the bull while the *matador* was performing, or when a participant behaved "improperly" (such as when a man exposed himself to the crowd during a bullfight), the *mozos* interrupted the action, expelled the individual from the ritual, and delivered the offender to the police.[46] The *peñas* intervened when "indecent" conduct had occurred, as when some *mozos* expelled a performing musical group for their "provocative" attire.[47] The masculine associations mediated when they thought that the spirit and tradition of the fiesta were in jeopardy, as they believed happened with the massive arrival of tourists, especially foreign tourists, in the 1960s and 1970s.[48] Harassment and public mocking of foreigners became common,[49] for instance in the *peñas'* use of long colorful burlap wigs parodying foreigners' long hair.[50]

The protection of tradition and order during the Sanfermines included policing women. From 1939 to 1978, the *peñas* became the guardians and controllers of traditional feminine behavior during the festival. The *peñas* claimed that women should not participate in the fiesta in the same manner as men. Thus, they did not allow women to join their ranks nor even to visit their headquarters unless accompanied by a *peña* member, and then only on special occasions. In the late 1960s, when women began to be more visible participants in the Sanfermines, spontaneously parading in the *Riau-Riau* and in the march of the peñas after the bullfight, the *peñas* decided to take action against this "vulgar" act, as the local press had described it.[51] In 1970, the *peñas* collectively issued an official proclamation "begging" the *mozas* (young women) not to participate in their march after the bullfight, arguing that the march was a masculine affair.[52] In 1974 they issued a similar proclamation referring to the *Riau-Riau.* Of the eleven presidents of the *peñas*, ten declared that the *Riau-Riau* was an exclusively male event in which women should not take part; women were not only discouraged from participating but even politely threatened.[53] The opposition to women's participation in the *Riau-Riau*, the only ritual in which citizens symbolically rebelled by blocking the city council's march, was a way of refusing the integration of women into the community's activities. Also, the *peñas* dissuaded women from sitting with them in the sunny area of the bleachers during bullfights.[54] Public discussion of—or even official proclamations about—other forms of participation, for instance women's involvement in dancing the papier-maché *Gigantes* and *Cabezudos* of the *Comparsa*, or running in the *encierro*, were considered unnecessary. If a woman, often disguised as a man, was seen running in the bulls' route, runners themselves physically removed her from the path.

The *peñas*' vision of women and masculinity were well illustrated in the anthems of the masculine associations and other popular songs. Songs reflect the soul of a community; they symbolically express the particular view that a community has about itself and its residents. The *peñas*' anthems pictured the associations' image of masculine values and feminine identity. "We love the revelry, the wine, and the beautiful girls with their grace and humor," proclaimed the lyrics from the hymn of the *peña La Jarana* (The Revelry). "We like girls a lot," the hymn of the *peña Los del Bronce* (Men of Bronze) claimed, "the prettiest the best, especially if they are Navarrese because they always have good humor." The use of the term "good humor" was referring not only to "high spirits" but mainly to the indulgent disposition towards men that was required of a woman.

The *peñas* also performed other popular songs that further expressed prevailing attitudes toward women and tradition. Masked with catchy music and humorous tones, the songs exalted heroic male values such as heavy drinking and other excesses, and were full of violent sexist remarks. Songs referred to the vagina and called upon men to maintain discipline with their wives. Such songs were sung loudly at the bullring and in the streets. All Pamplona knew the tunes and the streets were permanently filled by their sound. Music and songs were performed not only as a playful form of festive entertainment but also as a symbolic public reminder of the collective masculine attitude towards women and their role.

The *peñas* took total control in the defense of tradition during the 1978 Sanfermines. That year the festival was canceled due to riots that shook the city after a Pamplonese man was killed by police.[55] More than ever, the *peñas* projected themselves as the guardians of public and social order, tradition, and masculine values, and as the defenders of a community in grief. The Commission of *Peñas* refused to join other groups investigating the police actions and organized an independent investigation of the events.[56] The Commission even lobbied for a rescheduling of the fiestas in order to ameliorate economic damage and recapture the festive spirit. The minor fiesta of *San Fermín Chiquito* (small Saint Fermin)—normally celebrated each September in the downtown Navarrería neighborhood—functioned as a late fiesta for a frustrated Pamplona. Dressed in their *sanferminero* outfits, which they kept impeccable, *peña* members played a central role in this fiesta. They carried and escorted the figure of Saint Fermin[57] in the procession (a role not regularly played by the *peñas*), patrolled the streets, controlled political expression, keeping public and social order on their own terms, and demonstrated "exemplary" masculine behavior. In this newly created reenactment of the Sanfermines, the masculine associations reinvented their contribution to the traditions of the fiesta and reasserted the concept of their indispensability.[58]

From 1939 to 1978, Pamplonese men, especially those embodied in the *peñas*, played a fundamental role in the festival. The *peña* members not only maintained a high presence in the fiesta but they became its core, its axis. The *peñas*, supported and encouraged by municipal authorities and the local media, created an image of the perfect Pamplonese and Navarrese *mozo*: honest, noble, humorous, strong, courageous, and respectful of the traditions of the Navarrese race and land. The masculine associations helped shape and define public and social order, tradition, femininity and masculinity. Furthermore, they delineated the ideal masculine identity.

The Model Woman: The Passive and Traditional Feminine Role

Women's participation in the Sanfermines was limited. Historiography about the festival reinforced the stereotype of the passive and submissive feminine figure. According to this historiography, Pamplona's women could be divided into two categories: those who understood what the Sanfermines meant, and those who did not. The *castiza*, a woman of good Navarrese breed, was the representative of the former. She was giving, perceptive, patient, and above all loyal to her land and faithful to her traditions. Because she comprehended the essence and the implications of the festival, the *castiza* tolerated and even encouraged typical masculine festive behavior, which included drunkenness, verbal excesses, and emotional abuse. She understood and accepted her secondary role. The second category was formed by those women who were unable to understand the essence and significance of the fiesta.[59] These women were portrayed as tyrants who did not allow men to have fun and freely enjoy the festivities, as controllers of their spouses' daily lives who wanted to further regulate male behavior during the Sanfermines.[60] Women who did not fit the first category were deemed not only anti-traditional and anti-patriotic, but also anti-feminine. These women were depicted as hard and sarcastic through narrative descriptions as well as pictorial representations.[61] Local historiography defined femininity and feminine identity as a woman's capability for tolerance, acceptance, and understanding of the festive masculine universe of excess, in addition to the more general traits of passivity, silence, chastity, and fidelity.

The passive, limited, and secondary role of women was clearly exemplified in the "*Día del Marido Suelto*" (Day of the Free Husband), the so-called *DIMASU*. Established by the *peñas* in the 1950s, the *DIMASU* was an official day when *peña* members, as well as other Pamplonese men, were encouraged to spend twenty-four hours away from their families and to transgress social boundaries.[62] The *DIMASU* was indeed a male bonding celebration that ratified women's subordination to men.

A visual message of this subordination was transmitted through the official posters of the Sanfermines. Only three posters out of almost forty printed during the period included women (See Figure 4.1). The drawings portrayed women dressed in typical Navarrese outfits, *goyesco*[63] attire, or in Spanish *mantillas*, always perfectly combed, wearing red lipstick and red polished fingernails, and carrying fans and flowers. They were clean and neat, radiating inner and outer serenity. This was in contrast to the posters featuring athletic and active men, who were directly involved in the rituals. Printed in 1939, 1944, and 1949, the posters clearly depicted what one journalist had described about Pamplonese women: they were the "flower and the honor" of the Sanfermines.[64]

Certainly, the local press played a significant role in cultivating this passive and nonparticipatory image of the Pamplonese woman. Journals and newspapers applauded women who silently suffered their beloveds' excesses, proudly watched them running in the *encierro*, patiently washed and ironed their husbands' and sons' *sanferminero* outfits, and prayed to Saint Fermin on behalf of their menfolks' safety and protection during the fiesta.[65] The media led a crusade to convince the community that the spiritual and physical values of femininity needed to be emphasized during the celebration. Articles reminded women of the importance of guarding their chastity, protecting their virtue, and tempering their enjoyment during the Sanfermines.[66] Dances, which provided moments of direct interaction between members of the opposite sex, both locals and outsiders, were considered particularly risky.[67] In order to avoid danger, during the 1940s and 1950s it was common for parents, brothers, or elder sisters to chaperone girls at both public and private dances as well as in other diversions where members of the opposite sex might be present.[68] The media went even further in encouraging intervention in the preservation of the feminine ideal. For example, they strongly condemned those women who did not dress femininely enough—for example, in pants—or those who behaved out of the norm, such as those who smoked in public.[69] Thus, local newspapers operated as public forums, criticizing and scrutinizing women who did not follow the dominant paradigm of femininity.

Many Pamplonese women contributed to this feminine identity. From the 1950s through the 1970s, Francis Bartolozzi, one of the few women journalists prominent in the Pamplonese press, supported the passive and submissive role of women, stressing that their role was to allow men to enjoy the festival by themselves. She acknowledged that the beginning of the festivities meant panic and terror for a married woman; the fiesta threatened tragedy and promised matrimonial quarrels. Despite a long list of complaints, Bartolozzi recommended that women remain supportive of their men and accept the situation. In 1952, the journalist even suggested that the best solution for married women, and especially those with children, was to leave Pamplona before the start of the fiesta and not return until it was over in mid-July.[70]

This idea was publicly supported by several Pamplonese women. In a collective letter to a local newspaper, these women stated that this solution would certainly benefit Pamplona as a whole. According to them, in the absence of their families men could conduct themselves as they pleased without bothering the rest of the family and without making their spouses suffer. In addition, free from family control, demands and restrictions, men could behave more spontaneously, and consequently, their participation in the fiesta would be facilitated "for the sake of tourism, in order to preserve and foment folklore."[71] Equating men as the guardians of folklore and traditional comportment during the festivities, the letter gave Pamplonese men the responsibility for the survival and continued appeal of the essence of the Sanfermines, while claiming that women should be completely excluded from the festivities. Furthermore, the collective letter suggested that women were behaving patriotically and traditionally by leaving Pamplona, accepting masculine excesses and abuses, and sacrificing enjoyment of their annual festival. In other words, the masculine population as well as the community as a whole expected such a feminine attitude from *castiza* women. Certainly, there was a double standard regarding the behavior of women. As a Pamplonese writer acknowledged in 1963, the Sanfermines was a masculine celebration and women were reduced to the role of a chorus.[72]

After the late 1960s, the sound of the chorus became louder as female participation in the fiesta progressively increased. Women began to dance along with men in public, play musical instruments, dress in the typical *sanferminero* uniform, and even join the march of the *Riau-Riau.* In other words, women's visible participation increasingly became the norm.[73] During these activities, however, they had to be accompanied and even protected by men. Women's participation in the festival on their own terms was still unthinkable. For instance, women began to sit in the sunny part of the bleachers during the bullfight. Historically restricted to the *peñas*, it became acceptable for women to sit in this area with their male friends, who escorted and defended them from verbal attack and physical abuse from other men. If women went alone or in a group, however, they risked being the target of insults, harassment, and even physical assault. In this context, masculine consent was needed to authorize a woman's presence in the fiesta.

Despite the increase in women's visibility, the city council, local press, *peñas*, and even women themselves continued to encourage their passive role. The same female journalist who years before had implored Pamplonese women to abandon the city during the festivities asserted in 1972 that the fiesta was an occasion to be enjoyed by men alone because women had them "tied up" the rest of the year. Furthermore, she predicted that the festival would die if women actively participated in it, especially in those rituals reserved for the male population. "We should not deceive ourselves," the journalist declared. "The true fiesta that gave fame to Pamplona and attracted tourism was the fiesta performed by men."[74] Bartolozzi strongly believed that the Sanfermines was created exclusively for men and that masculine participation and behavior were the main reasons for its unique essence and international fame. Along with other journalists, the *peñas* and the municipality, Bartolozzi's interpretation represented the official perspective on gender roles in the fiesta. In this way, the traditional concept of femininity was perpetuated.

The most direct and virulent opposition towards increased participation of Pamplonese women in the Sanfermines came, not surprisingly, from the masculine associations. As mentioned previously, the *peñas* issued official proclamations criticizing woman's involvement in the *Riau-Riau* and the associations' parades, presented as monolithic masculine rituals.

When the feminists interrupted the event in 1978, they were protesting the lack of improvement in women's participation in the Sanfermines. In testimony to the local press, the protesters affirmed that, although certain external elements had changed since 1939, the same ideology dominated women's lives. They claimed that whereas women were allowed to dance in the streets and even drink publicly, the same undercurrent of traditional values that divided the genders was promoted by the municipality, the *peñas*, the media, and the community as a whole. Due to this dichotomy, the feminists saw the *madrinas* as a contradiction, even a parody. The *madrinas* symbolized the most traditional concept of femininity not only because their institutionalization had been orchestrated by the masculine associations but also because they symbolized the female passivity that the community praised. Therefore, for the feminists, the *madrinas*' elimination was the first step toward creating a new female identity.

Sanfermines as Social Commentary

The Pamplonese fiesta from 1939 to 1978 vividly documents the community's basic principles and values regarding gender roles. Through the annual fiesta, the local government, the media, and the *peñas* publicly constructed, shaped and defined the concepts of masculinity, femininity, and tradition in order to maintain a status quo that would perpetuate divisions between the genders. By imposing these definitions, these groups suppressed any movement toward equal participation of women in the festival. These actions denied women the participation that would have occurred if changes in the fiesta had reflected concurrent social transformation.

In 1939, immediately after the Civil War, and coinciding with the imposition of Francoist ideology in all sectors of society, the Pamplonese municipality, the local press, and the masculine associations conspired to define the "true" character and qualities of the perfect masculine and feminine figures. They utilized the Sanfermines as the scenario to link these attributes to the preservation of tradition. The ideal concept of masculinity was directly associated with active participation in the fiesta, whereas femininity was linked to a more passive role. Masculinity was synonymous with bravery, demonstrated by running in front of the bulls, the endurance to drink, eat, and dance endlessly, and with rough behavior and transgression of social and family restrictions. Conversely, the ideal of femininity was epitomized by tolerance, passivity, submission, and a spirit of sacrifice; qualities that were exalted as symbols of tradition and female patriotism. Although the nation and Pamplonese society were transforming politically, ideologically, and socially during the period, by 1978 the concepts of masculinity, femininity, and tradition in the fiesta had not experienced substantial change.

The Sanfermines represented different worlds for Pamplonese men and women. Although the codes and languages of the annual festival were shared, participation by the sexes was very different. For men, the fiesta brought strong bonds of communion among the masculine population. Pamplonese men shared a sense of masculine identification. The festival was an occasion for men to test themselves and transgress social boundaries. From the *encierro* to the bullfights, from the *Riau-Riau* to other rituals, from excessive drinking to lack of sleep, masculine participation was a sequence of male bonding rituals.

The sense of identification was intensified for *peña* members. In addition to sharing and participating in the fiesta like the rest of Pamplona's male population, *peña* members shared a particular sense of masculine identity.[75] Membership conferred a unique and strong bond of communion that differentiated them from others.[76] With their banners and songs, musical bands, and different colored shirts, *peña* members organized special parades and events and enjoyed distinct privileges. They received an annual municipal subsidy to maintain their expenses, occupied most of the sunny area of the bleachers during the bullfight at special prices, and were considered the bearers of the core and essence of the fiesta. In addition, the all-male associations represented a refuge from quotidian social and family ties, rules, and pressures. The concept of masculinity, and consequently the concept of femininity, was reinforced through socialization as the members ate, drank, and danced together. Because *peña* members perceived the fiesta as a series of male events, they molded the festival into an exclusively masculine expression of personal and collective freedom. Due to the protagonist role of men, they perceived themselves (and were perceived by the community) as the "natural" experts of the festival, making them its official narrators. In this sense, it is not a coincidence that historiography about the Sanfermines was monopolized by men.

While the annual festival drew Pamplonese men together, it had a different effect on women. Women were indeed familiar with the content, rituals, codes, and languages of the festival, and shared a communal bonding; but they were not able to participate in a similar fashion. Because women were not allowed to take part in the rituals, or form their own organizations for the festival, they were denied the same experience of communal bonding. It seems that the Sanfermines not only failed to unify women but also tore them apart and separated them from their community. Many women abandoned the city during the festivities while others secluded themselves at home only to go out to specific events. Certainly, not all women followed this pattern. By the end of the period, many were out in the streets participating in the fiesta more visibly. However, their role remained secondary. Women were not granted the same privileges as men, particularly regarding festive behavior.

The feminist protest in 1978 was the first of its kind during the fiesta. Never before had Pamplonese women raised their voices collectively to denounce double standards in the festival. Never before had women's role within the fiesta been challenged. It was the first time that a redefinition of women's identity was demanded. Yet the protesters did not attempt to defy the web of norms, values and customs that shaped such a traditional identity and that delineated "proper" gender related behavior. Thus, the feminists did not attempt to organize an alternative *peña* exclusively for women; nor did they call for participation in the *encierro*, to dance the papier-maché figures of the *Comparsa*, to carry the figure of Saint Fermin in the Procession, or to take part in the official parades. The power of the festival was such that many feminists, like the *madrinas*, had accepted gendered divisions in participation. This acceptance, however, did not prevent them from aspiring to alter some attitudes. Their complaints were based on more ordinary matters: they simply demanded more respect towards Pamplonese women during the annual fiesta, both symbolically and practically. And they did so through direct action, halting the Sanfermines for a brief instant. During that short moment, a new feminine identity began to emerge.

The protest was considered a rebellion against tradition. The feminists were perceived as anti-traditional and anti-feminine radicals because they were questioning the very core of the concepts of masculinity, femininity, and tradition as defined by the community. Although all of Pamplona's citizens learned about the protest, the demonstration did not have the effects that the feminists had envisioned. The community's indifference to the protest strengthened its collective consciousness regarding the traditional values of masculine and feminine identities. As social commentary, the Sanfermines expressed the symbolic resistance to altering the tapestry of values, customs, and norms that were deeply rooted in the community. The festival glorified masculine power and silenced the engraving of a new feminine identity.

Notes

1. The fiesta was born around the cult of Saint Fermin. The saint's chronology has been confusing; he has been placed in the first to the fourth centuries by various authors. Despite this basic disagreement, bibliography about the saint agrees that Ferminus (Saint Fermin) was born in Pamplona and was the son of a Roman senator. Converted to Catholicism, he became the city's first Bishop.

2. The celebration in honor of Saint Fermin began in 1186, the year his first relic was brought to Pamplona. It took place on October 10, the date when the saint entered Amiens, the French city where he was named Bishop. The two-day festivities had an exclusively religious character and focused on liturgical ceremonies. In 1591 the festival was rescheduled for July 7, so that the religious ceremonies could be combined with the commercial fairs and the taurine performances that annually took place at the end of June and beginning of July respectively. Thus, since 1591, the characteristic elements of these three distinct events were incorporated into a unique fiesta, and the Sanfermines was institutionalized. Since then, the annual festival has taken place on July 7.

3. Along with the March Fallas of Valencia and the April Ferias of Seville, the July Sanfermines is the most prominent fiesta in Spain.

4. The festival became internationally known through Ernest Hemingway's novel *The Sun Also Rises*. Dealing partially with Sanfermines in the 1920s, the novel acquired an intense popularity during the 1950s. In 1957 it was adapted into a movie starring Tyrone Power, Ava Gardner, and Errol Flynn. Although both novel and film misrepresented and distorted the atmosphere of Pamplona during the fiesta, they incited many visitors to travel from abroad to Pamplona during its festival.

5. On political protests, see Clotilde Puertolas, "A Festival in Change: A Case Study of the Fiesta de San Fermín: 1930–1978" (Ph.D. diss., University of California San Diego, 1989).

6. Literally, "Madrinas Kampora" means "Godmothers out of the Streets."

7. Each association chose a *madrina*, or godmother, to represent them. The *madrinas* never took part in the main activities of the fiesta but officially represented the masculine associations at receptions, ceremonies, and taurine spectacles. They dressed in the Spanish *mantilla* and often in an Andalusian hat. The *madrinas* were institutionalized in the 1960s, during the Francoist regime. *El Pensamiento Navarro*, July 9 and 11, 1968; *Hoja del Lunes*, June 30, 1975.

8. *Egin*, July 9, 1978.

9. *Egin*, July 2, 1978; *Expedientes de la Comisión de Relaciones y Cultura: Fiestas San Fermín*, 1978, no. 9.

10. After 1977, the *madrinas* did not wear the *mantilla* to the bullfights but instead they displayed an *ikurriña* from the balcony where they sat. *Deia*, July 8, 1977.

11. From 1939 to 1978, Spain transformed from being a basically agricultural, Catholic, and conservative country to a more industrial, modernized, and open society. Women's role also evolved. See Raymond Carr and Juan Pablo Fusi, *Spain: Dictatorship to Democracy* (London: George Allen & Unwin, 1979); Giuliana Di Febo, *Resistencia de mujeres en España*, 1936–1976 (Barcelona: Icaria, 1979); Pilar Folguera, ed., *El feminismo en España: Dos siglos de historia* (Madrid: Editorial Pablo Iglesias, 1988).

12. See Mona Ozouf, *La fête révolutionnaire* (Paris: Gallimard, 1976); Agnes Villadary, *Fête et vie quotidienne* (Paris: Les Editions Ouvrières, 1969); Michel Vovelle, *Les métamorphoses de la fête en Provence: De 1750 à 1820* (Paris: Aubier Flamarion, 1976); Susan G. Davis, *Parades and Power: Street Theater in Nineteenth Century Philadelphia* (Philadelphia, PA: Temple University Press, 1986).

13. The Francoist regime maintained an avowedly conservative ideology based on religion and a traditional social order. On Francoist gender ideology, see the article by Aurora Morcillo Gómez in this book.

14. Salvador Rodríguez Becerra, "Métodos, técnicas y fuentes para el estudio de las fiestas tradicionales populares," in Honorio de Velasco, ed., *Tiempo de Fiesta* (Madrid: Tres-Catorce-Diecisiete, 1982), p. 3.

15. Roger Callois, *Man and the Sacred* (Glencoe, IL: Free Press of Glencoe, 1959); Harvey Cox, *The Feast of Fools: A Theological Essay on Festivity and Fantasy* (Cambridge, MA: Harvard University Press, 1969); Mikhail Bakhtin, *Rabelais and His World* (Bloomington, IN: Indiana University Press, 1984); Jean Jacques Wununburger, *La fête, le jeu et le sacré* (Paris: J.P. Delarge, 1977); Carmelo Lisón Tolosana, *Antropología social y hermeneútica* (Madrid: Fondo de Cultura Económica, 1983); Victor Turner, ed., *Celebration: Studies in Festivity and Ritual* (Washington, DC: Smithsonian Institution Press, 1982).

16. David Gilmore, "Carnaval en Fuenmayor: Class Conflict and Social Cohesion in an Andalusian Town," *Journal of Anthropological Research*, 30 (1975): 331–349.

17. Public rituals have indeed many functions. Due to the diverse variety of functions and connotations of festivals, the theory of public rituals is controversial and offers multiple interpretations. See Jean Duvignaud, *Le don du rien: Essai d'anthropologie de la fête* (Paris: Editions Stock, 1977), and *Fêtes et civilizations* (Paris: Librarie Weber, 1973); Peter Stallybrass and Allon White, *The Politics and Poetics of Transgression* (Ithaca, NY: Cornell University Press, 1986); James L. Peacock, *Rites of Modernization: Symbols and Social Aspects of Indonesian Proletarian Drama* (Chicago, IL: University of Chicago Press, 1968); Barbara Babcock, ed., *The Reversible World: Symbolic Inversion in Art and Society* (Ithaca, NY: Cornell University Press, 1978); Alfred Simon, *Les signes and the songs: Essai sur le théatre et la fête* (Paris: Editions du Seuil, 1976); Edward Muir, *Civil Ritual in Renaissance Venice* (Princeton, NJ: Princeton University Press, 1981); Marianne Mesnil, *Trois essais sur la fête: Du folklore à l'ethnosémiotique* (Bruxelles: Editions de L'Université

de Bruxelles, 1974); Victor Turner, *The Ritual Process: Structure and Anti-Structure* (Ithaca, NY: Cornell University Press, 1969); Sally F. Moore and Barbara G. Myerhoff, *Secular Ritual* (The Netherlands: Van Gorcum, Asseu, 1977); Agnes Villadary, *Fête et vie quotidienne* (Paris: Les Editions Ouvrières, 1969).

18. Yves-Marie Bercé, *Fête et révolte: Des mentalités populaires du XVIe au XVIIIe Siècle* (Paris: Hachette, 1976); Natalie Z. Davis, *Society and Culture in Modern France* (Stanford, CA: Stanford University Press, 1975); Emmanuele Le Roy Ladurie, *Carnival in Romans* (New York: George Braziller, Inc., 1980); Laura Barletta, *Il Carnevale del 1742 a Napoli: Protesta e integrazione in uno spazio urbano* (Napoli, Italy: Societá Editrice Napoletana, 1981).

19. Jacques Heers, *Fêtes, jeux et joutes dans les sociétés d'Occident à la fin du Moyen Age* (Montreal: Institut d'Etudes Médiévales, 1971); Antonio Bonet Correa, "La fiesta barroca como práctica del poder," *Diwan* 5–6 (1979): 53-85; Max Gluckman, *Customs and Conflict in Africa* (Oxford: Blackwell, 1965).

20. Temma Kaplan, *Red City, Blue Period: Social Movements in Picasso's Barcelona* (Berkeley, CA: University of California Press, 1992), p. 20.

21. Clifford Geertz, *The Interpretation of Cultures* (New York: Basic Books, 1973); Alice Pomponio Logan, "The Palio of Siena: Performance and Process," *Urban Anthropology*, 7, no. 1 (1978): 045–065.

22. Alan Dundes and Alessandro Falassi, *La Terra in Piazza: An Interpretation of the Palio of Siena* (Berkeley, CA: University of California Press, 1975), p. xvi.

23. Mary Douglas, *Purity and Danger: An Analysis of Concepts of Pollution and Taboo* (London: Routledge & Kegan Paul, 1966), pp. 7–28, 135–139, and 159–161.

24. The *peñas* were formed in the middle of the nineteenth century by groups of male friends and coworkers. According to Vicente Galbete, former Municipal Archivist, in 1852 a *peña* already appeared in bullfights, seated in the bleachers in the sun. Jokintxo Ilundain reports that before the year 1900, male friends used to attend bullfights together and danced, sang, ate, and drank. The *peñas'* members wore whitish or grayish blouses, so they were generally known as the *blusas blancas* (white blouses). Each *peña* had a different name. The *peñas* did not allow women in the rank and file; while apparently the peña *La Unica* (The Only One) had some women members, their role is not clear. In the years 1933, 1934, and 1935 the number of women reduced to such a degree that *La Unica* become practically an all-male association. Luis Carrión Arguiñano and José María Rodrigo Jiménez, *Las pancartas de las peñas: (A través de los dibujos de Pedro Martín Balda)* (Pamplona: Caja de Ahorros Municipal de Pamplona, 1981); Vicente Galbete, "Loa de las Peñas Sanfermineras," *Programa de Fiestas*, 1967; Jokintxo Ilundain, "Las cuadrillas de los mozos de Pamplona," *Pregón*, 36 (1953); Jenaro Iraizoz Unzué, "Algunos ingredientes de nuestras fiestas Sanfermineras," *Pregón*, 108 (1971); Bernardo Apesteguía, "De los tendidos y sucedáneos (Hasta 1900)," *Revista Peña San Juan*, (1983): 9–10; Félix Urabayen, *El barrio maldito* (San Sebastián: Auñamendi, 1982), p. 176; José María Iribarren, *Hemingway y*

los Sanfermines (Pamplona: Gómez, 1984), pp. 79–80; Juan Zapater, "La Unica: Siempre un poco diferente," *Navarra Hoy*, June 25, 1982.

25. The parade took hours even though the distance easily could have been covered in ten minutes. The official march of the *Riau-Riau* became progressively slower over the years, increasing its duration. The march was fairly short from 1939 to 1959, averaging thirty minutes to an hour. During the 1960s, the *Riau-Riau* lasted two to three hours, and in the 1970s, four to five hours. In 1978, it took five hours and thirty minutes for the City Council to reach the Chapel of Saint Fermin. *Expedientes de la Comisión de Relaciones y Cultura: Fiestas de San Fermín*, 1978, folder 3, no. 7.

26. *El Pensamiento Navarro*, July 12, 1959; *El Español*, July 7–23, 1955; Rafael García Serrano, *Los Sanfermines* (Madrid: Espasa-Calpe, 1963), p. 48; Conversations with Ana María Villanueva; Correspondence with María Eugenia Villanueva, December 5, 1986; José Joaquín Arazuri, *Historia de los Sanfermines* (I) (Pamplona: Industrias Gráficas Casuera, 1983), p. 14.

27. Conversations with María Eugenia Villanueva.

28. *Castizo* or *castiza* is considered an individual of good and pure (Navarrese) race. It also can be described as regional ethnocentric pride.

29. José Soria Ayerra, "Sanfermines de antaño," *Pregón*, 132 (1979).

30. Puertolas, "A Festival in Change."

31. The Sanfermines of 1937 and 1938 were not officially celebrated due to the Civil War.

32. *El Pensamiento Navarro*, July 8, 1941.

33. Santiago Erice Ruiz, "Los apuros de Teodoro," *Pregón*, 76 (1963).

34. *El Pensamiento Navarro*, July 7, 1959.

35. José María Donosty, "Frenesí y dramatismo de los Sanfermines," *Pregón*, 28 (1951).

36. *Pregón*, 1 (1941).

37. Each *peña* had a particular name. Although the majority had Spanish names, a few had Basque ones.

38. Manuel Iribarren, "Visión forastera de los Sanfermines," and Plácido Argomoso, "Impresión de la fiesta única," *Pregón*, 1 (1943); *España en paz: Sanfermines en Navarra* (Madrid: Junta Interministerial para la Conmemoración del XXV Años de la Paz Española, 1964), p. 123.

39. Miguel Angel Astiz, "Los Mozos, defensores del buen tono de nuestras fiestas," *El Pensamiento Navarro*, July 12, 1952; *El Pensamiento Navarro*, July 7, 1959.

40. Information about the *peñas* in 1939 is scarce because the number of associations is not well documented. However, it seems that there were only three associations.

41. Antonio García Tabuenca, Mario Gaviria and Patxi Tuñón, *El espacio de la fiesta y la subversión: Análisis sociológico del Casco Viejo de Pamplona* (Donostia, Spain: Hordago, 1979), p. 111.

42. From the early 1950s, every *peña* received a municipal subsidy. The subsidy varied in amount every year. In 1969 the national government also began to grant money to the masculine associations. Although the aid provided by the central government stopped after General Franco's death, the local government continued to provide support.

43. Although the *peñas* were the most visible guardians of the festival, not all order-keepers belonged to a *peña.* Furthermore, it was often difficult to distinguish a non-member dressed in the *sanferminero* outfit from a *peña* member. Unless the latter wore the shirt of his particular *peña, peña* members and non-*peña* members dressed identically. Consequently, Pamplonese men unaffiliated with a masculine association also regulated the fiesta. However, to show publicly that they belonged to one thus granted them the authority to police with impunity. In this respect, the *peñas* were semi-sacred.

44. García Tabuenca, Gaviria, and Tuñon, *El espacio*, p. 113.

45. *Expedientes de la Comisión de Relaciones y Cultura: Fiestas San Fermín*, 1977, folder 1, no. 11.

46. *Diario de Navarra*, July 13, 1974; *Deia*, July 8, 1977.

47. In 1969, when the members of the well-known musical group, the Pop-Tops, appeared dressed in swimming suits and painted with pacifist symbols for their performance at a private club, a few *peña* men in the audience interfered immediately. Jumping onto the stage and interrupting the show, they threatened to throw the musicians into the swimming pool unless they returned to the stage "decently" dressed. Once the group reappeared fully robed, a *mozo* dressed in the *sanferminero* outfit welcomed its members back, shaking hands in a sign of peace and triumph in the midst of a full ovation. *Diario de Navarra*, July 15, 1969.

48. Initially, the tourists, especially foreign tourists, were not well accepted in Pamplona. The local press complained about the snobbery and conduct of the tourists, who believed that they were in an "underdeveloped country," and behaved as if Pamplona was a "free zone" and a "city without law." The main target of criticism was the tourists who had different codes of dress and behavior, such as those who wore long hair, shorts, and backpacks. Labeled as "dirty," "trouble-makers," (*gamberros*) "indecent," "immoral," and often described as a "plague of hippies," these foreigners, the press claimed, behaved in a manner which was degrading and in conflict with the essence of the festival. *El Pensamiento Navarro*, July 11, 1968; José María Vidal, "Mano dura durante las fiestas," *Diario de Navarra*, July 6, 1968. "Honestidad

Sanferminera," Diario de Navarra, July 9, 1966; Vidal, "Mano dura," *Diario de Navarra*, July 6, 1968; Ollarra, "Cara y cruz de las fiestas," *Diario de Navarra*, July 8, 1970; "Plaga de hippies en Pamplona," *Blanco y Negro*, July 1972, in *Expedientes de la Comisión de Relaciones y Cultura: Fiestas de San Fermín*, 1972, no. 7.

49. Miguel Angel Astiz, "Reacciones con gracia ante los barbudos y melenudos," *La Gazeta del Norte*, July 9, 1966.

50. *Hoja del Lunes*, July 12, 1970.

51. Andrés Briñol Echarren, "Ahora estamos a tiempo," *El Pensamiento Navarro*, July 7, 1974.

52. *El Pensamiento Navarro*, July 3, 1970.

53. Sebastián Valencia, "El Riau-Riau a examen. Contestan los presidentes de las peñas," *Hoja del Lunes*, July 1, 1974.

54. *El Pensamiento Navarro*, July 3, 1970; *Hoja del Lunes*, July 1, 1974; Andrés Briñol Echarren, "Ahora estamos a tiempo," *El Pensamiento Navarro*, July 7, 1974.

55. The cancellation of the Sanfermines occurred after the events of the July 8 bullfight. At the end of the performance, many *peña* members jumped into the arena with a huge banner demanding amnesty for political prisoners. The action generated a fight among those who supported the *peñas*' protest and those who opposed it. While this confrontation was taking place, a large number of policemen charged into the bullring with batons, tear gas, rubber bullets and live ammunition, causing numerous injuries among the spectators. Riots spread around the city during the following hours, in which a Pamplonese man was killed by police and approximately 250 civilians were wounded. The remainder of the festival was canceled. In the following days, protests occurred in the Basque Country. In addition, the Parliament opened an official investigation about the police intervention in the bullring.

56. Comisión Investigadora de los Mozos de Pamplona, *Así fué* (Pamplona, Spain: Gráficas Irujo, 1978).

57. The Procession with the *peñas* took a different route than the July Procession. The figure taken in this Procession belonged to the Church of Saint Fermin of Aldapa, located in the Navarrería neighborhood, rather than the one from the Chapel of Saint Fermin in the Church of Saint Lorenzo, which was the figure taken in the July Procession.

58. See Eric Hobsbawm and Terence Ranger, eds., *The Invention of Tradition* (Cambridge: Cambridge University Press, 1983).

59. Katontxu, "Oda al Sol o los del Tendido 5," *Pregón*, 28, (July 1951).

60. José Arteche, "Aún fué a tiempo (Humorada Sanferminera)," *Pregón*, 20 (July 1948); "Instantáneas Sanfermineras," *Pregón*, 32 (July 1952); *El Español*, July 7–23, 1955; Santiago Erice Ortiz, "La jaqueca de Ramón," *Pregón*, 56 (July 1958).

61. José María Baroga, *Eternos Sanfermines* (Pamplona: Gráficas Navasal, 1978), pp. 175–203.

62. Katontxu, "Oda al Sol o los del Tendido 5," *Pregón*, 28 (July 1951); *El Pensamiento Navarro*, July 12, 1959; *El Español*, July 7–23, 1955; José María Baroga, *La vida íntima de Pamplona (1955–1960)* (Pamplona: José María Baroga, publisher, 1976), p. 86.

63. This is a typical outfit dating from the times of the painter Francisco de Goya (1746–1828). *Goyesco* attire was commonly used for taurine performances.

64. *Pregón*, 1 (July 1943).

65. "Película de los Sanfermines," *Pregón*, 1, (July 1943); *El Español*, 7–23 July, 1955.

66. *El Pensamiento Navarro*, July 7, 1942; see also "La oración a San Fermín," *Pregón*, 28 (July 1951).

67. During these years it was commonly thought that during the fiesta women preferred to spend time with outsiders rather than with Pamplonese men. Local historiography is full of jokes and comments about this. See Iribarren, "Museo de borrachos, castizos y humoristas del Sanfermín," *Pregón*, 8 (July 1946).

68. Correspondence with María Eugenia Villanueva, December 5, 1986.

69. Alberti Landivar Aguirre, "Un ruego a la mujer pamplonesa," *Pregón*, Extra (1945); *El Pensamiento Navarro*, July 12, 1951.

70. Francis Bartolozzi, *¡Arriba España!*, July 13, 1952.

71. "Las mujeres y las Fiestas de San Fermín," *¡Arriba España!*, July 20, 1952.

72. García Serrano, *Los Sanfermines*, p. 48.

73. María Antonia Estévez "Los Sanfermines: ¿Son unas fiestas decididamente masculinas?" *Diario de Navarra*, July 6, 1966.

74. Bartolozzi, "Y de nuevo Sanfermín," *Hoja del Lunes*, July 1, 1972.

75. Henk Driessen, "Male Sociability and Rituals of Masculinity in Rural Andalusia," *Anthropological Quarterly*, 56, no. 3 (July 1983): 125–133; Javier Escalera Reyes, "Hermandades, religión oficial y poder en Andalucía," in Carlos Alvarez Santaló, María Jesús Buxó i Rey, and Salvador Rodríguez Becerra, eds., *La religiosidad popular. III. Hermandades, romerías y santuarios* (Barcelona: Anthropos, 1989), pp. 458–470; Fuensanta Plata García, "Asociacionismo masculino y rituales festivos en la Campiña Cordobesa. Una aproximación," in Santaló, Buxó i Rey, and Rodríguez Becerra, eds., *La religiosidad popular*, pp. 544–556; Domingo Munuera Rico, "El cambio de protagonismo: De la dependencia a la supremacía," in Santaló, Buxó i Rey, and Rodríguez Becerra, eds., *La religiosidad popular*, pp. 597–616; Isidoro Moreno Navarro, *La Semana Santa en Sevilla: Conformación, mixtificación y significaciones* (Sevilla, Spain: Ayuntamiento de Sevilla, 1986).

76. Rodríguez Becerra, "Las fiestas populares: Perspectivas socio-antropológicas," in *Homenaje a Julio Caro Baroja* (Madrid: Centro de Investigaciones Científicas, 1978), pp. 919–920; Lisón Tolosana, *Antropología*, pp. 60–61; Gilmore, "Carnaval."

Part II

Work Identities

Work Identities

Despite the culturally assigned role of wife and mother which placed women in an idealized private sphere, women's lives spanned many other roles. One of those roles was that of worker, even though the vast majority of women in Spain did not hold regular, full-time employment. Like men, women struggled to define and integrate their work roles into their sense of self. However, the gendered meaning of work, which has privileged wage labor, has prevented historians from exploring the full range of women's work identities. The purpose of this section is to explore the complex—and contested—relationship between work and female identity. In order to establish the context for this relationship, the introduction will provide historical background on women and work in modern Spain.

The chapters in this section argue that work was central to women's identities, whether or not they participated in regular paid employment. However, they also find that the gendered work culture created a problematic relationship between women and work. From this viewpoint, each chapter examines a specific case of female work experience and its impact on identity formation. The first two chapters explore the gendered nature of work identity for an elite group of paid women workers—the cigarette makers. The second two chapters look at the work experience of women defined by the census as unemployed, but who engaged in a number of tasks essential to the economic livelihood of the household. By bridging the distinction between formal and informal work, or between worker and homemaker, this section exposes the weakness of such oppositional pairs and illustrates the common gender themes in all forms of work identity.

This broader conception of work and work identity has special relevance in the Spanish context, since Spain's formal workforce has been even more heavily masculine than that of other Western European countries. Obviously, female employment directly contradicted all the sacred precepts of ideal womanhood and threatened to topple one of the pillars of masculine legitimacy. As elsewhere, in practice a double standard distinguished between what was acceptable for middle- and upper-class women versus women of the lower classes. However, the percentage of women of all classes who were counted in the work force remained significantly lower than in other Western European countries until the 1980s.[1] In addition to the stronger cultural prohibitions against female employment, this discrepancy was also probably partly a result of Spain's slower industrial and commercial expansion before its take-off in the 1960s. The result has been an even more exaggerated tendency to code work and worker as masculine.

For middle and upper-class women in the nineteenth century, charitable volunteerism, much of it organized through the Church, was at first the only acceptable work for a respectable lady. Getting paid for the same work was as discouraged as any other employment. Thus, for example, the prominent feminist writer Concepción Arenal was the only nineteenth-century woman to hold a visible position in public welfare; in 1865 she was appointed visitor of women's prisons in Galicia, and in 1868 was promoted to inspector.[2] By the end of the nineteenth century, a few women were breaking barriers to enter the professions, although their ability to practice faced various forms of discrimination well into the twentieth century.[3]

The first professions to open their doors to more than a handful of women were the least prestigious and those considered closest to women's maternal nature: nursing and midwifery, pharmacy (considered a "superior form of cooking"[4]), and elementary school teaching. These jobs, especially that of teacher, became the classic options for unmarried young women of the middle and lower middle classes in the late nineteenth and early twentieth centuries. By the turn of the century, 12,000 women (or sixty-four percent of all professional women) taught primary education in the state school system. However, they were very poorly paid and few woman teachers crossed into the upper levels. A few were allowed to teach in girls' secondary schools, and the first female university professor was appointed only in 1916, when the Ministry of Education forced the eminent writer Emilia Pardo Bazán on a faculty that voted against her nomination.[5]

The other more elite professions were equally inhospitable to women. The first woman doctor, Martina Castells, received her degree in 1882, after which she intended to treat children in her husband's practice, but she died at a young age during a difficult pregnancy. Critics manipulated the tragedy to underline their arguments, by insisting that her weak feminine body had been destroyed by too much intellectual work.[6] Women doctors were gradually accepted into certain fields, like gynecology and pediatrics, where it was argued that they could better preserve female patients' chastity, but their numbers were significantly lower than in the United States and other European countries.[7] Even fewer women took up law, perhaps partly because legal restrictions on their practice of the profession held firm as late as 1928. Thus, by the Second Republic, only two women lawyers had ever appeared in court.[8]

More than in the professions, middle-class women began to find increasing employment in lower paid areas of the rapidly expanding service economy, in either the private or public sector. The legal turning point came in 1882, when the state decreed that women could be hired to work in telegraph and postal service, but not until 1918 could they compete for civil service positions, and then only as assistants. As in other countries, the large-scale entry of women into these and similar jobs occurred in the 1910s and 1920s, when the female clerk became a familiar part of the commercial and public service landscape. Despite the trend toward hiring women in these jobs, the total number employed in the tertiary sector, including the liberal professions, only rose from 86,552 in 1900 to 145,583 by 1930.[9]

As always, more women from poor families entered the work force at some point during their lifetime, usually before marriage, but even among these sectors participation was low by European standards. The female industrial work force was concentrated in three areas: textiles, the sweated trades, and cigarette manufacture. Because of the location of these industries, the industrial workers were further concentrated geographically: the majority of textile workers in the region of Catalonia, the cigarette makers distributed in eleven factories in major cities around the country, and even the sweated industries (mostly clothing manufacture) were clustered in a few provinces. Altogether, these women, plus those in smaller industries, comprised 13% of the female work force in 1900 and 31.82% in 1930.[10] However, because of their concentration in a few industries and geographical locations, the female proletarian remained a marginal and shadowy entity for most Spaniards.

Like most European countries in the nineteenth century, the two sectors that employed the most women were domestic service and agriculture. In contrast to many western countries, however, Spain did not experience as massive a female transfer from these sectors to industrial and public service jobs in the early twentieth century. Thus, during the first third of the century, when the number of domestic servants was declining elsewhere, their numbers increased in Spain.[11] The number of female agricultural workers did drop dramatically, as the sector shrank, but many of these women did not reappear in other categories. Thus, the total number of women in the work force actually declined between 1877 and 1930, from 1.5 million to 1.1 million, or from 17% of all women to only 9% in 1930.[12]

Although there are no statistics for the Republican period, this decline probably continued through the Depression of the 1930s. One indication of the cultural resistance to women workers, even under the leftist Civil War administrations, was the reluctance to train women to replace men in skilled industrial jobs as the latter left to go to the front. Despite complaints by activist women's organizations like the *Mujeres Antifascistas*, it appears that few women crossed over into male jobs, even under the special demands of a wartime economy.[13]

Not surprisingly, the Franco regime encouraged the decline in female labor with a powerful campaign to convince women to stay home and raise large families. Thus, one of its earliest defining pieces of legislation, the

"Labor Charter" (1938), proclaimed the intention to "liberate married women from the workshop and the factory" at the same time that it declared labor both a right and a duty.[14] As in the nineteenth century, the regime instead tried to channel women's energies into volunteer work. Through the *Sección Feminina*, it organized a "social service," a six month stint of instruction and charity work which it required women to participate in at some point during their lives.[15]

Despite this propaganda, it proved increasingly difficult to keep women out of the paid labor force during the economic boom of the 1960s and 1970s, when an extra salary could boost families' access to the expanding goods of a consumer society. As a result, the 16% of Spanish women who worked in 1950 jumped to 29% in 1977, when the percentage finally began to approach the lower end of the European scale. By the end, the regime could no longer control the consequences of a rapidly transforming society. Nevertheless, because the ideology of women's primary domesticity persisted, women's place in the work force remained insecure. Thus, after recession hit Spain in the late 1970s, sending unemployment levels skyrocketing, women and youths were the two categories that suffered disproportionately.[16] Those who were employed remained clustered, even more than elsewhere, in a few low-paid feminine sectors.[17]

The history of women's wage labor has thus made it easy to minimize the role of work in female identity. Following a general European pattern, Spanish women's access to formal employment came only gradually, in the face of tremendous opposition. Within this pattern, however, an unusually strong degree of resistance, coupled with slower growth, translated into even lower levels of women's participation in the Spanish labor market. What the following chapters suggest, however, is that this narrative does not tell the whole story of women and work in Spain. Instead of the false dichotomy between women who worked and women who did not, the chapters ask what kind of work women did, and then the chapters try to understand how *work* figured into women's sense of identity.

Notes

1. Thus, in 1910, when the percentage of women in the European work force ranged from 38% in Sweden and Denmark to 36% in France, 32% in England, and 27% in Germany, in Spain it was only 13.5%. Rosa María Capel Martínez, *El trabajo y la educación de la mujer en España (1900–1930)* 2d ed. (Madrid: 1986), p. 48. In 1950, the percentage was still only 15.8%, finally climbing to 29% in 1977, and 32% in 1989. At that point, it was still somewhat lower than the European average of 40%, but within the general range. Instituto de la Mujer, *La Mujer en España: Situación social* (Madrid: Ministerio de Asuntos Sociales, 1990), p. 101.

2. Geraldine Scanlon, *La polémica feminista en la España contemporánea (1968–1974)* (Madrid: Siglo Veintiuno, 1976). Arenal was also the first woman to complete a law degree at a Spanish university.

3. In 1900, women working in the liberal professions constituted 1.34% of the employed female population: 18,593 women; and in 1930, 3.59%, or 39,859 women. Capel Martínez, *El trabajo y la educación*, p. 186. In 1910, the Ministry of Education finally removed most of the legal barriers to women practicing the professions in which they received degrees, although specific restrictions, like the prohibition on taking the exams for legal positions, remained. Esther Cortada and Montserrat Sebastià, "La dona i la institucionalització de l'educació," in Mary Nash, ed., *Més enllà del silenci: Les dones a la història de Catalunya* (Barcelona: Generalitat de Catalunya, 1988), p. 219.

4. Scanlon, *La polémica feminista*, p. 74.

5. Adrian Shubert, *A Social History of Spain* (London: Unwin Hyman, 1990), pp. 41–42. In addition to being an acclaimed naturalist novelist, Pardo Bazán was perhaps the first serious woman journalist in Spain, as well as an articulate defender of women's interests. Her close relationship with the novelist Galdós, and the fact that she and her husband separated because she was too immersed in her career, gave her a certain notorious reputation, much like that of the more famous nineteenth century woman of letters, Georges Sand. Scanlon, *La polémica feminista*, pp. 65–71.

6. Scanlon, *La polémica feminista*, p. 72.

7. In 1950, Spain had one of the lowest percentages of female doctors in the world: only 3%, versus 8% in the United States, 10% in Italy, 19% in England, 21% in France and 25% in Germany. Phyllis Stock, *Better than Rubies: A History of Women's Education* (New York: Putnam's Sons, 1978), p. 211.

8. They were Clara Campoamor and Victoria Kent, two of the three female deputies elected to the Parliament in 1931. Shubert, *A Social History of Spain*, p. 38.

9. Capel Martínez, *El trabajo y la educatión*, pp. 184–185, 194. This number excludes domestic service, which is included in this category on the census. To get a comparative sense, the number of white-collar female employees in Germany rose from almost 500,000 in 1907 to almost 1.5 million in 1925. In France, those employed in public service and the liberal professions were almost 300,000 in 1906 and nearly 500,000 by 1925. Bonnie Anderson and Judith Zinsser, eds., *A History of Their Own: Women in Europe from Prehistory to the Present*, vol. 2 (New York: Harper & Row, 1988), p. 467, n. 2.

10. Capel Martínez, *El trebajo y la educación*, p. 67.

11. In 1900 there were 264,000, and in 1930 340,000. In 1900, they were still the largest category of worker, but by 1930, the number of female industrial workers (350,000) just surpassed them. Capel Martínez, *El trabajo y la educación*, p. 67.

12. Shubert, *A Social History of Spain*, p. 38. However, Spain was not alone in this decline between 1900 and 1930: France, Italy, Britain, Holland, Belgium, and

Denmark also experienced a decline in the percentages of women working in non-agricultural jobs. Fewer countries, for example Germany, Sweden, and the U.S., experienced the reverse. María Gloria Nuñez Pérez, *Trabajadoras en la segunda Républica: Un estudio sobre la actividad económica extradoméstica (1931-1936)* (Madrid: Ministerio de Trabajo y Seguridad Social, 1989), p. 115, n. 17.

13. Pamela Radcliff found complaints in letters and circulars produced by the *Mujeres Antifascistas* about women's underutilized potential in the labor force of the city of Gijón in the province of Asturias. See Radcliff, *From Mobilization to Civil War: The Politics of Polarization in the Spanish City of Gijón, 1900–1937.* (Cambridge: Cambridge University Press, 1996), pp. 246–247.

14. Shubert, *A Social History of Spain*, p. 214.

15. Scanlon, *La polémica feminista*, pp. 326–327.

16. Manuel Tuñon de Lara, et al., *Historia de España: Transición y democracia (1973–1985)*, vol. 10 (Barcelona: Editorial Labor, 1991), p. 292. In fact, between 1983 and 1991, the gap between unemployed men and women widened further. In 1983, female unemployment was 20%, versus 15% among men (Instituto de la Mujer, *La situación de la mujer en España, 1983* [Madrid: Ministerio de Cultura, 1983] p. 5), while in 1991 the numbers were 23% and 13% (*El País*, October 28, 1992).

17. For employment breakdowns, see María Pilar Alcobendas, *Employment of Women in Spain* (Luxembourg: Office for Official Publications of the European Communities, 1984), pp. 21–38.

5

Life and Work in the Tobacco Factories: Female Industrial Workers in the Early Twentieth Century

Rosa María Capel Martínez

It is a generally accepted fact today, on the eve of the twenty-first century, that the feminist movement is one of the defining features of contemporary society. From its appearance in the mid-nineteenth century, we may consider the feminist movement in Western society a consequence of the revolutions of the eighteenth century. From our point of view, this struggle of women to participate in all areas of common life as citizens with full rights has had two main goals: access to an education equal in level and content to that of men, and incorporation into the world of non-domestic salaried work in increasing numbers and in non-traditional areas.

Women and Industrial Work

Women have always undertaken unpaid work in the home which should count as work, as Kelley and Rees argue in other articles in this volume. In addition to domestic tasks, women have performed essential non-domestic tasks for the family economy, such as weaving, spinning, agricultural work, etc. However, the industrial revolution introduced significant modifications in the way women participated in activities outside the household and the manner in which these activities were perceived. The replacement of the craft workshop by the factory obliged women to leave their homes in order to seek wage work where it could be found.[1] The tasks carried out in the new factories were not very different in principle from those to which women were accustomed, as these continued to be subordinate, non-mechanized posts. What was new — and indeed transcendental for women—was their dependence on an entrepreneur whom they did not know, the payment of a salary, and the discrimination on the part of male colleagues toward women since they constituted cheap labor. Earning a wage potentially enabled female workers to achieve economic independence with respect to the men of their family circle and to be sure of meeting their needs, including those of their children, without being dependent upon anyone.[2] In turn, the discrimination suffered by women in the workplace distinguished their work experience from that of their male counterparts, and served to promote both their awareness of women's rights and their association in order to defend these rights.

Historians continue to debate whether the widespread incorporation of women into industrial work facilitated the adoption of laws more favorable to them, generally improving women's situation, or whether it actually had disastrous effects for them, their households, and their families.[3] That debate aside, it is our belief that this incorporation of women was important because it facilitated both economic autonomy and the awareness of forming part of a group with its own personality and its own interests, which are two preconditions of the emancipation of any social group.

The entry of women into the world of wage work became irreversible by the end of the nineteenth century. Social opposition to female labor was significant, but not sufficient to defeat the multiplicity of economic interests which required it. Entrepreneurs drew substantial profits from hiring women, national economic development required their participation, and working- and middle-class families needed the wages of their female members in order to survive. For all those reasons, by the beginning of the twentieth century the European industrialized countries were able to count on a significant female presence among the wage-earning population.[4]

In Spain the incorporation of women into the industrial workforce was delayed until the second decade of the twentieth century.[5] The industrial female worker is thus a minority figure until the time of the First World War, when women became more involved in a new phase of industrialization.[6] As a result, while at the beginning of the present century the figure of the female worker—in industry or office—was somewhat familiar in the developed western nations, in Spain it was still making its first appearances.[7]

However, in specific industries, women's presence was already felt in the eighteenth century. Most typical were the textile industry, centered in Catalonia, and the tobacco industry. Both sectors stand out in the process of initiating Spanish women into the world of the factory. Female textile workers were noteworthy for their large numbers: 51,519 in 1900; 127,321 in 1930.[8] Figures for female tobacco workers are lower: 21,317 for 1902; 12,570 for 1930. However, women workers in tobacco factories achieved a virtual monopoly of jobs. Thus, cigarette and cigar making constituted the first all-female industry in Spain.

Their conspicuousness made the tobacco workers the most charismatic female workers at the beginning of the twentieth century. With this high profile they carved out a prominent leadership role whose power was not limited to the workplace. As workers, their high degree of awareness and militancy, often weak among other workers, gave "their presence in popular movements a great importance." As one observer stated, "their strikes are feared by the public authorities, as the populace is always on their side."[9] The deep-rooted collective identity of the female tobacco workers also left its imprint on the community in which they lived, and on their own families where they played a noteworthy role in the transmission of culture.[10] It is these tobacco workers who are the subject of the present chapter.

This chapter explores the specific characteristics of the working life of the tobacco workers, in order to better understand the world of working women in past times, to identify the extent to which it was similar to or diverged from sociological models that have been developed, and to analyze some of the real consequences of the incorporation of women into the industrial work force.

We raised these questions about tobacco workers in previous research,[11] but a visit to the Madrid tobacco factory in 1985 unearthed documentation in the company archives that shed new light on the basic conditions of women's employment in the industry. This information is contained in the "Regulations Concerning Laborers in Tobacco Factories" (Reglamento referente al personal obrero de las fábricas de tabaco). Approved by Royal Decree on December 13, 1926 and January 14, 1927, the text is signed by the Managing Director of the company licensed to produce tobacco (*Arrendataria*), a Mr. Luis de Albacete, and approved by the Chairman of the Board, the Marquis of Amurrio. It contains 47 articles plus one transitional provision and a further article divided into four main chapters. The document refers to various aspects of life within the factory: types of laborer, internal rules, disciplinary provisions, working hours, medical facilities, basis for fixing salaries, and so on. These regulations replaced an earlier set published in 1884, and therefore reflect the demands and achievements of the tobacco workers during the years separating the two sets of regulations.

In addition, the archive provides a window into the personal lives of workers in the tobacco factory. From the time of recruitment, the factory kept a personnel file on each member of the work force including full family details, home address, certificates obtained or details of activities undertaken within the factory, dates of appointment to various posts and services carried out in the various workshops or departments, prizes awarded for good work, sanctions imposed and the reasons for them, and dates and reasons for termination. As one can imagine, the wealth of information offered by these personnel files is immense; they have incalculable value in reconstructing the course of the careers of the tobacco workers and their life within the factory.[12]

Cigar and Cigarette Making: The First All-Female Industry

In 1755 a new tobacco factory was opened at Seville with a new design, "a single factory complex within a fenced off area," in an attempt to better control and safeguard output.[13] Construction of the building was warranted by increased demand for tobacco products, and the future of the industry would surpass even the most optimistic forecasts. Although this development centralized the work, the system of production remained pre-industrial until well into the nineteenth century. Thus, the work force, both male and female, consisted of individuals carrying out non-mechanized tasks in a workshop environment.[14]

Conceived from the beginning as a state monopoly, the profits earned were such that soon new factories were built throughout the Spanish peninsula. Thus a factory opened in Madrid in 1809, and by the twentieth century there were a total of eleven: in Alicante, Bilbao, Cádiz, La Coruña, Logroño, Madrid, Gijón, San Sebastián, Santander, Seville, and Valencia. In 1887 the Spanish State decided to license its monopoly on the production and sale of tobacco in Spain. A public tender was organized and the concession went to an enterprise representing the Bank of Spain: the "Compañía Arrendataria," which assumed responsibility for the management of all the factories under the supervision of the Ministry of Finance.

During the first years of production and in those establishments where the production of snuff predominated, the workers were mostly male and the presence of women was very limited. By the end of the eighteenth century, however, a rapid and irreversible process of female substitution began. There were various reasons for the change. First, sales of snuff fell significantly at the end of the century of enlightenment, while those of "smoking tobacco" or "burning tobacco," as cigars were called at the time, increased. Cigar production required skill rather than strength, and dexterity and precision rather than force, faculties which were considered more female than male. Thus, overseers increasingly protested the lack of discipline of the male workers and the significant waste of leaf tobacco. At the same time there were words of praise for the female workers for the better quality of their output and their more efficient use of raw materials. The idea of replacing men with women gained currency, assisted by a clearly determining factor: women carried out the same work for less pay.[15] Thus, female labor became a cheap substitute for male labor. However, the phenomenon also benefitted the female workers, who came to constitute a paradigm of what women workers should be and a representative par excellence of women's struggle for collective and individual work identity.

During the nineteenth century, tobacco became the first and only all-female industry, in contrast, for example, to the United States of America, where female workers never monopolized jobs in the industry. As a result, in the U.S., female tobacco workers existed within a strong hierarchical organization based on sex and race.[16] In Spain, on the other hand, the presence of male workers was reduced to minimal levels. Thus, by 1914 there were only 112 men among the total of 15,063 persons employed, and they were divided between the factories at Madrid and Oviedo. From 1925 to 1930 this disproportion was somewhat reduced as the number of male operatives increased to 1,686 while the number of female workers declined to 12,570.[17] If we examine the data more closely we will see that the increase in the one group is less than the loss recorded in the other, indicating an overall shrinkage in the workforce as a result of mechanization plans implemented by the license holder from the beginning of the century onwards.

Recruitment and Jobs Offered in the Factory. Although they occupied the same premises, were subject to the same regulations and in specific cases held similar responsibilities, there were two distinct labor forces in the factory. The gendered worlds of the factory were physically codified in the regulations by the prohibition forbidding men to enter the female workshops except to carry out their work in the presence of the foreman or overseer. Also, from the administrative viewpoint, the two were established with differentiated occupations and even special conditions for entry or promotion to higher grades.

The existence of two work forces differentiated by sex was to have important consequences. First, as a result of the jobs they held, it led to distinct personal experiences which created a greater identification of the female workers with the production of tobacco. Also, the separation led to the tobacco factories being the only ones that offered women a career in which they could ascend to the highest levels. Furthermore, the male workers were not a point of reference for determination of salaries. This gave greater freedom, even to the unions, to campaign for wage increases. In contrast, in other mixed-gender industries, competition between male and female workers for the same posts accentuated the incidence of social stigma, justifying the relegation of women to inferior posts and lower wage scales.

A woman could aspire to enter the tobacco factory from a very early age—when she had barely reached fourteen years—while the maximum entry age was thirty. Furthermore, the daughter or the grand-daughter of a male or female worker "alive or deceased" had priority in hiring, according to the provisions of the transitional article of the regulations. This priority also follows an established and cherished tradition that already existed at the beginning of the nineteenth century and which, for Baena Luque,[18] reflects the original artisanal, family character of tobacco production which survived during the preindustrial epoch. Later, this tradition became one of the acquired rights of the female workers.

Men, on the other hand, did not enjoy this privilege and could not enter the factory until they had reached twenty-one years. The reasons for this difference are perhaps related to the lower demand for male workers and the work for which they would be hired, which required greater physical strength and specialization—as will be seen. It is possible that, for the same reason, the maximum age limit in this case was thirty-five years, with the exception of machine operators and electricians, who could work until the age of forty-five; and porters, security guards or messengers who had worked elsewhere in the factory might be appointed until they turned fifty.

There are other points of divergence between the sexes with regard to requirements for entering company service. Future female workers needed "to have the approval of the person entitled to give it, in accordance with the law," that is to say the father in the case of a minor, or, in the case of a married woman, the husband. Male candidates were exempt from these requirements, which is logical in terms of civil law concerning majority and legal personality.[19] Instead they were required to be strong and robust, intelligent, and able to demonstrate through certification and examination that they had the necessary knowledge and required specialization. Curiously the tobacco workers were exempt from the examination requirement, perhaps because the traditional succession of mothers and daughters presupposed the professional capacity of the new recruits.

In addition, those who wished to enter the factories, whether male or female, needed to meet other requirements: they were required to be Spanish, be free of contagious diseases and physical defects, be vaccinated, show evidence of good conduct by a certificate from the competent authority and other references, be able to read and write, and in order to aspire to certain posts, have knowledge of arithmetic. It is worth pausing over the significance of these last mentioned requirements. For while those previously quoted do not differ from those in force in other industries, these latter may seem aimed at those who would have administrative and accounting responsibilities. Perhaps this requirement reflects the contemporary desire to improve the level of education of the Spanish population, or perhaps it reflects a desire by the company to be selective in recruiting. In any case, if the female cigar maker was required to show a minimum level of educational achievement in a country where half the female population was illiterate (and the level was higher among modest classes and in certain regions), there was no doubt that she would be or could easily become a figure of distinction among those working in industry, with a personality of her own.

And so she was. It is sufficient to recall for example the testimony that the prominent novelist Emilia Pardo Bazán leaves us of these workers in her novel *La Tribuna*. Doña Emilia, credited with introducing literary realism into Spain, gives a detailed description of the world of the Coruña tobacco factory.[20] The very title of the novel refers to the nickname by which her fellow workers knew the protagonist of the story, a nickname which she had earned through her union activity.

For those who met all the necessary requirements, the next step was appointment to a post. For the first six months the worker needed to demonstrate her ability, and subsequently she was offered a permanent post. The female work force comprised the following categories: senior, second, and registry porter, instructress, and operator. These last in turn could be overseers, forewomen or group leaders, packers, operators (as such), and apprentices. There were also sweepers, whose inclusion among the permanent staff of the tobacco factories was a relatively recent achievement of the female workers. The regulations of 1884, following tradition, had designated that when the day was over the production workers were responsible for cleaning the workshops. These workers eventually decided to pay out of pocket for other women to do this work, showing that their salaries were fairly high by the standards of the time. Concurrently, they began a campaign to persuade the licence holder (*Arrendataria*) to bear the costs of cleaning. In 1921 their request was accepted and the regulations of 1927 were drafted accordingly.

While in virtually all other industries, women's work offered scant possibilities of career development and few or no possibilities of promotion, tobacco production was a clear exception to the rule. The internal structure of the female labor force offered careers to whoever had ability, and promotion was possible on the basis of experience and training. For that reason, the entry-level posts offered to women were limited to two: sweepers or apprentices. The former would always remain in the same post; the latter would be promoted according to age and years of service, motivation, aptitude and demonstrated competence as well as arithmetic ability. In this way a female apprentice could become an operator; later, provided she had reached twenty-three years of age with two years as an operator, she could become an overseer, forewoman, or group leader. At twenty-five years old and with two years experience at the previous level she could become an instructress, and, finally, at thirty years of age and with ten years of experience in the workshop, a porter.

The male staff was divided into two categories: fixed (or part of the permanent labor force) and casual workers, from among whom new appointments were frequently made. Male posts included machine operator, foreman—with various grades and functions, porter—senior or factory, watchman—interior or exterior, machine operator, general worker, and craftsman—mechanic, electrician, carpenter, plasterer, plumber, glazier, fireman, locksmith, fitter, machinist, or smith. Unlike the female workers, male applicants could opt for any one of the remunerated posts except that of foreman, which required experience in the craft.

The options open to newly recruited male or female workers (with the exception of foremen) directly correlated with the type of work undertaken. In the case of the tobacco workers, there was only one type of job or working situation open: the manufacture of tobacco, regardless of the workshop to which she belonged, the experience she acquired, or the level she reached. Consequently, the work of the female tobacco worker maintained continuity over the years and justified promotion through the greater experience that is acquired with time. As for the male workers, job vacancies were so varied that they necessarily had to be filled individually and discretely. Nevertheless, for a job with important responsibilities and without a specific skill requirement, the company sought to recruit those who possessed "learning . . . unimpeachable conduct, command skills, ability to carry out the general tasks of the factory and physical strength." Thus, while employment in the tobacco factory signified a career for the female workers, for their male counterparts it was only a job. This distinction accounts for the differing degrees of identification of male and female workers with their work: greater in the case of the women, and of course, weaker in the case of the men.

Appointments and promotions were the responsibility of the factory managers in some cases, and of the company board in others. The board was exclusively responsible for appointing the higher categories of worker—instructor and porter—as well as some male occupations.[21] They always made their selections from a short list prepared by the factory managers and on the basis of reports from those responsible for each service. As a result, it was the factory managers who truly made decisions about the assignment of work. This procedure gave them tremendous authority over the workforce, both male and female, which could easily be abused.

Concerning the Tasks Entrusted to the Workers. Chapter II of the 1927 regulations mandated the division of labor between male and female workers: the women were responsible for all productive activity, and the men were responsible for the management and functioning of the workshops.

In practice, management posts involving more than merely administrative tasks were always occupied by men, including the factory managers with authority over all female workers. The instructresses, next on the hierarchical organization chart, passed on orders. Among the male workers, only the machine operators and general workers answered directly to the factory manager, while the others reported exclusively to their responsible chiefs.

Those workers who were considered established were responsible for a wide range of tasks in the factory: machine operators, senior electricians, and senior operators carried out all the maintenance services of the factory; watchmen were entrusted with safeguarding the factory and its machinery; senior porters and factory porters controlled the entry and exit—as well as the movement—of staff and material during the working day. These porters also supervised the work of the warehouses where the leaf tobacco, the finished tobacco product, and other materials necessary for production, such as paper and packets, were stored; porters were also responsible for their distribution to the workshops. In fact, it was another achievement of the female workers that the male operatives distributed the tobacco. Until 1920, the tobacco workers themselves had to bring the tobacco up from the warehouses to the workshops, or pay someone to do it. Union pressure resulted in the license holder agreeing to deposit the raw material on the workbenches.[22] This responsibility belonged to the general workers who, in turn, were responsible to their foremen who were scrupulous in overseeing the proper conduct and the exact salaries of the workers.

The tobacco workers were responsible for all the tasks involved in preparing the finished tobacco product, from the tobacco leaf to the finished cigar or cigarette ready to be sold. The various workshops in the factory were arranged in a certain hierarchy that was fixed according to the degree of precision and dexterity required for the work done there. This hierarchy could be seen in the physical location occupied in each workshop, in the type of worker who was entrusted with the work, and in the average salaries that they received.

The initial steps in the production process took place in the leaf and vein removal departments, generally the poorest workshops in the factory. Here the workers, who were generally the eldest or least dexterous, carefully processed the tobacco leaves to remove veins or prominent fibers from the reverse side of the leaf. They took care to separate the leaves which were large enough and clean enough to be used as the external binder of large cigars—called wrapper leaf—from those which would be used for smaller cigars and for filling the larger ones, known as "stuffing."

Next, the leaves and veins intended as filler or "mince" went to the cutting workshop, while packets of large and small wrappers—and kilos of filler—went to the cigar rooms, all perfectly cleaned and sorted. This stage of production required precision; the most skillful female workers were assigned to the cigar rooms and they occupied the workshops with the best light and ventilation. First the workers moistened and readied the tobacco branch to be fashioned later into cigars: the company placed great emphasis on the care required to ensure full use of the tobacco leaves. Next, the cigars went to the airing rooms where they were kept until they could be wrapped, packed and boxed without suffering any damage. Finally, the cigars were stored in the warehouses.

The cut tobacco followed another route through the factory: it went from the workshop where it was produced to the cigarette or cut-tobacco packing room. Workers checked the freshness of the tobacco and then, without using humidification or the admixture of any other material, they carefully prepared the cigarettes. Their weight had to correspond to the tariff and their appearance had to be satisfactory, with both ends properly finished. The cigarettes then were packaged in units "carefully cleaned and presented" and were boxed, with care taken to avoid causing even the slightest damage.

Workers in the cut-tobacco packing room put this tobacco into wrappers or pouches, once more taking care to ensure cleanliness and to prevent the glue used in closing the packet from damaging the tobacco. Once the packages were closed, workers checked their weight and placed them in cases, seeing that they did not stick to one another, again in order to avoid possible damage when they were subsequently removed.

As a result of the transformation of the industry that began around the turn of the century, by the end of the 1920s tobacco production combined manual workshops, rooted in traditional methods of production and control of work, with more modern mechanical workshops. In these, quantity control succeeded quality control. Since quality was guaranteed, supervisors turned their attention to the speed of female workers, their cleanliness and their care of the machinery.

The staff in all the workshops, whether manual or mechanical workers, were organized in a clearly hierarchical fashion. The front of the workshop was the domain of the instructress, entrusted with directing the workshop in accordance with "the factory officials and engineers of the establishment." Her responsibilities were wide and varied, covering everything that took place within the workshop. The instructress oversaw the quality of work and documented the attendance and behavior of the female workers; she accounted for "deliveries of tobacco, filler, paper, packets, miscellaneous," and other daily tasks; she conducted the payment of salaries (though not deductions from operators' bonuses or piece-working pay); and if she controlled a mechanical workshop, she also taught apprentices. In addition, she was required to report on the cleanliness of the workshop and its associated rooms, and that of the machinery.

> If on the floor there were found tobacco, cut tobacco or paper; and that clothing, shoes, baskets, food, bottles or jugs and other property of the operators were found on the working table or surfaces and worst of all on the machines, packaging tables or reception area or in the entrances or walkways of the workshops,[23]

these breaches were considered "serious neglect."

The instructress was not alone, however, in carrying out her tasks. When there were many workers in the shop, they were divided into teams, each headed by a worker with equivalent authority. Bench-housekeepers, section overseers and group leaders assumed responsibility for subdivisions of workers by bench or section. In actual practice, it was they who directed the work, monitored the operators and kept the accounts of all the workers and the machines for which they were responsible. The parity between their obligations and those of the instructresses allowed the periodic replacement of the instructress by a group leader when that was necessary. Two years' experience as a housekeeper, overseer, or group leader was required to aspire to teaching duties.

The lowest level in the female work force of the tobacco factories consisted of simple workers and apprentices. According to the regulations, their responsibilities were limited to obeying the orders of their superiors and carrying out their work while behaving irreproachably. The majority of female workers belonged to these two groups, with a certain differentiation due to seniority and work performed. The apprentices occupied the lowest level, naturally, while workers could be entrusted temporarily to replace housekeepers, overseers, and group leaders. Permanent appointments to these posts were made from among the most proficient of the workers.

In addition to manufacturing tobacco, it was also the exclusive responsibility of the female personnel to keep the factory clean. For this task, sweepers reported to the instructress, porter, or senior porter. It is the latter who really controlled them, since she determined for which part of the building each one was responsible and they reported to her any events that happened within their area. In the case of illness of one of the sweepers, it was also the senior porter who decided whether or not to accept the person that the sweeper had entrusted to replace her.

A Day at the Factory

Although the regulations do not explicitly paint a picture of daily life in the factory, the precision of the text regarding tasks, disciplinary rules and general provisions allows us to elicit such a portrait. The working day began at an hour fixed by the factory and, in accordance with current labor law, lasted eight hours. This time could be reduced in the case of elderly female workers, bearing in mind their age and allowing them "a prudent margin of time to enter the workshop."[24] The rest of the work force was required to be strictly punctual, and in certain cases, to appear from fifteen to thirty minutes early. This was the case with the weekly overseer (the worker responsible for collecting the keys of the factory before opening and closing), the senior porter (who was responsible for opening and shutting the factory), the foremen, workers, the night watchmen, porters and whichever instructresses were assigned to carry out an inspection on a rotating basis.

If the regulations provide an approximate reflection of actual practice, they indicate that in the tobacco factories all tasks were strictly fixed and planned, all the workers were rigidly controlled, and there was even a certain ritual marking the beginning and the end of the working day. Since something similar occurred in other female industries of the time,[25] one can generalize about an iron discipline in the workplace with regard to female factory workers. This is not surprising; such conditions represent the first stage of industrialization in Spain. They also reflect the preference of entrepreneurs—as social historians have shown—for well-trained, faithful, and submissive workers who guaranteed the highest profits with a minimum of conflict.[26]

A quarter of an hour before opening the gates, the senior porter was required to confirm, in the presence of the officer of the guard and the exterior night watchman, that the seal placed by the officer of the guard was "intact and in its due form." Next, the inspection squad entered and carried out its tasks behind closed doors. Once this inspection was completed, the workers began to arrive and from that moment on were subject to strict control of their personal and working lives.

Upon entering the factory, workers submitted to an inspection by senior porters (male or female for each sex of employee) who recorded the names of those who were absent. With the help of watchmen, the porters personally searched each worker to ensure that they did not introduce "prohibited effects, articles or material," such as "firearms, knives or any other arms, sticks . . . and in general anything intended for personal attack or defense"; and powder, explosives, and any material that could cause fire or destruction; and liquor, spirits, or wine, except for the half liter permitted to those who could verify that they normally drank with meals.[27] Only the following could be introduced into the factory: food, for those who did not use the factory canteen, and work clothing. Work clothing was obligatory for women who worked in the mechanized workshops and for the sweepers. (Regulations required the periodic provision of a uniform from the factory budget, except in case of premature deterioration of clothing due to ill treatment. In that case, the worker herself had to meet the costs of new work clothes).

Once inside the factory, no member of the work force could leave until the working day was over without the expressed consent of the responsible chief and without undergoing an exhaustive search. Nor could she leave her work station; thus permanent attendance in the workshops was required of women workers, except during lunch time. Similarly, during working hours no one could enter the factory unless they were visiting the manager, chiefs, or other factory officials. Movement of material and parcels was inevitable, of course; all arriving and departing material was recorded in the porter's register, required to be completed daily (with no blank spaces remaining).

The work of the male and female employees took place under the constant supervision of overseers, machinists, or senior electricians in the case of men; and of instructresses, housekeepers, overseers or group leaders in the case of women. Supervisors would pay great attention at the beginning of the working day to the personal effects that the work force might introduce so as to detect the possible existence of any prohibited items that might have escaped attention during the entry search. After that they would observe the way in which the work was carried out, placing emphasis on quality standards and correct use of materials so far as the tobacco workers were concerned, and in the correct transport, storage and distribution of the tobacco within the warehouses so far as the male workers were concerned. Maximum attention was also paid to keeping the factory as well as tools and machinery perfectly clean.

Finally, at the end of the day the work performed by each worker was noted, and especially the volume of work in the case of the women. This was an important operation, not only because it enabled the factory to keep an exact note of the productivity of the factory and its personnel, but it was also the means by which salaries were fixed. Piecework was the usual basis for appointment and the fixed rate paid per working day was substantially augmented by bonuses for achieving various production levels. If, as we have observed elsewhere, the hourly pay of the female tobacco worker in the first third of the twentieth century was situated above the rate in other industries,[28] the addition of these bonuses enhanced the privileged status of the work even though this could be achieved only by personal effort and the levels achieved were below those of male salaries.

No less strict were the general rules to which the male and female workers were subject during the working day in the factory. "Discipline and good order" were principles that all were expected to observe on their own initiative, or if for no other reason, to avoid the penalties fixed for infringement. Above all, management expected punctuality, obedience, composure in the workplace, and careful work.

Persistent unjustified lateness was considered a "minor fault," and unexcused absences of more than one day invoked a penalty. Disobedience to superiors and the factory management was classified in the catalogue of "serious faults." The seriousness of the offense varied with each increasing level in the factory hierarchy. "Due composure," another rule of worker behavior, prohibited speaking with a loud voice, or worse, quarreling with workmates or engaging in disputes, as well as using words that ". . . offended morality or the family, threatened discipline or brought into question religious, political and social ideas which could be freely professed by all but could not be the subject of discussion or propaganda within the factory."[29] Brawls were also prohibited, and above all one could not ". . . lead or direct agitation, riots or tumults . . . or take part in or be identified in such events as well as preside, form part of or contribute to groups responsible for initiating or encouraging agitation. . . ."[30] Depending on whether the disturbance was a mere quarrel or a more organized protest movement with larger repercussions, these acts were qualified on a list running from "minor fault" to "serious fault" of the highest degree when the interests of the factory were harmed. Among such acts, drunkenness was considered an intermediate fault.[31]

Finally, all workers had to exercise the greatest care to avoid the slightest damage to the finished product, raw materials, tools, implements, and fixtures. Regulations specifically prohibited workers from stealing, or concealing the theft of, tobacco or any other factory property. They were not to: pass any product to any workmate or to the instructress; smoke or light a fire in the workshops and warehouses; interrupt or abandon work without permission from a superior; or enter another department without due authorization. Also prohibited were the initiation of or participation in festivities or demonstrations which threatened order and paralyzed production, even if only temporarily. Nor were they to make purchases, offer goods for sale, hold lotteries or organize them among the staff, or fail to respect safety and hygiene rules. Willful disregard of these rules was considered a serious offense, though in some cases an offense was attributed to no more than neglect, error, negligence, or lack of interest, and was thus considered a less serious fault.

While male and female workers and apprentices were subject to strict rules, the factory management itself and those with responsibility were not exempt from discipline. They were required to show complete trustworthiness in the exercise of their responsibilities, and this included not making errors which would benefit contractors or suppliers. Such errors were considered faults, as were attitudes and external signs of the abuse of power towards their subordinates, or other failures to carry out duties with which they had been entrusted.

As one might imagine, violation of the rules of internal discipline was duly punished in accordance with the seriousness of the offense in each case. The range of punishments was quite large; it extended from a private warning to dismissal or definitive separation from company service—following appropriate proceedings—if the fault so warranted, especially if theft or attempted tobacco theft was involved. Punishment could also mean public warnings or temporary suspension without pay. The factory managers decided punishments in the case of a warning or suspension for up to eight days; the management of the license holder decided in the case of more serious penalties. The workers could appeal the penalties up to the level of managing director, and the staff member concerned was to be informed immediately of the final decision taken.

Considering everything that has been said concerning the internal rules of the tobacco factories, it is undeniable that work within them required great attention on the part of those who carried out the work and that the conditions under which work went on were frequently harsh. However, neither the conditions nor the efforts required of the male and female workers differed from those that could be found in other jobs at the same time period.

On the other hand, the tobacco workers enjoyed certain benefits which for most other Spanish female workers were only a dream. For example, female workers over the age of sixty with a disability were allowed to perform such work as they were able in the auxiliary workshops. For this work, they received a fixed salary approved by the board. Further, in the case of illness, and on presentation of a certificate signed by the company doctors, all workers would receive a half daily wage or a fixed emolument for three months. In exceptional cases this period could be prolonged until the staff member had completely recovered. In addition, female workers could earn a fixed emolument for eight days if they were obliged to take care of a parent or child who was seriously ill. Alternatively, male workers' jobs were held for them while they completed military service. Finally, free medical services and first aid were available for the permanent staff. These benefits complemented the higher salaries already mentioned, the preference for entry of daughters or granddaughters of female employees, and the concession for senior workers regarding entry time into the factory without deduction from their salary.

The negotiation of such concessions from the tobacco company cannot have been easy. They were the fruit of years of struggle and attributable to good organization, a high level of awareness, and a determined attitude toward the defense of their rights, all of which were maintained by the tobacco workers from the early years.

The closure of the working day at the factory was subject to the same controls and rituals similar to those of its opening. The workers lined up according to sex under the supervision of the overseers or the instructresses to facilitate conduct of the departure search "without hurry, disorder or precipitation." When the search was complete the senior male and female porters were required to report anything unusual to the officer of the guard, presenting to him if necessary any worker caught with tobacco or other materials. If these were workers, instructresses, or porteresses, the name was recorded and a note made of the substance discovered.

Once the factory was empty of the day's shift, the foremen of the week closed the doors. The officer of the guard then affixed the seal in the presence of the exterior night watchman who, together with the interior watchman, would be responsible for the factory until the following day. Half an hour before opening the next day, they presented themselves at the main gate and prepared to hand over the factory to the officer of the guard. The shift of the night watchman was over, and another working day had begun for the tobacco factory.

The aforegoing reconstruction of the way in which the tobacco workers carried out their work, and the rules that directed their behavior within the factory reflect the ideal model of the working day according to the license holder. In practice, obviously, there were occasions when the ideal was not achieved or was openly subverted, as when female workers mobilized in support of their demands. Indeed, the minute detail in which the regulations describe the acts not permitted by male or female employees can only convince us that such acts did occur. Through the press we have information that union propaganda was distributed in the workshops and that at times there were conflicts between members of unions with distinct ideologies that even led to physical violence.[32] Furthermore, the disciplinary files preserved in the archives show that drinks other than those permitted, above all anisette, were introduced into the factory and that tobacco was taken home in order to be processed there. This infraction was a frequent practice by which female workers found a way to increase their salary in periods of crisis.[33]

Historically, the tobacco worker can be considered a singular figure in the workplace and in the world of Spanish women at the beginning of the twentieth century. The incorporation of these women into the labor force and the monopoly they achieved in manufacturing lent them a status, which in turn gave rise to a sense of solidarity that was lacking in most other groups of workers. Their status and solidarity had ramifications well beyond the confines of the workshops where they spent most of their existence.

The tobacco workers challenge the dualistic world model created by sociologists with its categories of public/private and traditional/modern.[34] These women stood halfway between one category and the other; sometimes they appeared in both. As mothers, wives, and daughters, their lives evolved in the private sphere; as workers and citizens, they did not hesitate to occupy the public stage when necessary, as O'Connor's chapter in this volume illustrates. Their strikes and demonstrations reflected the spirit of contemporary social movements, while the evolution of their strikes sometimes brings to mind mutinies, or insurrections associated with the early stages of industrialization. The independent character of the tobacco workers (exaggerated and immortalized by "Carmen") and their resolve to defend what is just, did not prevent them from respecting the decisions of management or conforming when they saw their employment endangered. Lastly, despite the monopoly which, as we have seen, women tobacco workers held in the factory and despite their acute proletarian awareness, the management of their principal trade union—the National Federation of Cigar Makers and Tobacco Workers (FNCT)—was always in the hands of men.

We should not, in truth, be surprised by these ambiguities that make up the personality of the female cigar and cigarette makers. In the final account, they were products of the age in which they lived and of the society in which they made their living. Early twentieth-century Spain underwent a period of demographic and economic change that began to shift the inertia of traditional attitudes, maintained by the immense social weight of conservative forces. As a result, internal contradictions were accentuated. The tobacco workers reflected their particular version of this ambiguity. This double aspect makes them all the more attractive as historical figures.

Notes

1. Evelyne Sullerot, *Historia y sociología del trabajo femenino* (Barcelona: Ediciones 62, 1970).

2. The need of many women to attend to their own survival and those of their children is one of the first reasons advanced to justify recognition of women's right to remunerated work. See Mary Wollstonecraft, *Vindication of the Rights of Woman*, first published in 1792.

3. See R.M. Hartwell, *The Industrial Revolution and Economic Growth* (London: Methuen, 1971); Neil McKendrick, ed., *Historical Perspectives: Studies in English Thought and Society in Honor of J.H. Plumb* (London: Europa, 1974); Louise Tilly and Joan W. Scott, *Women, Work and Family* (New York: Holt, Rinehart, and Winston, 1987); Jane Rendall, *Women and Industrialization in England, 1750–1880* (Cambridge, MA: Basil Blackwell, 1990).

4. In 1910, females comprised 38% of the working population in Sweden and Denmark, 36% in France, 32% in England and 27% in Germany. See Claude Fohlen and François Bedarida, *La era de las revoluciones*, vol. 3 of Louis-Henri Parias, ed., *Historia General del Trabajo* (Mexico: Grijalbo, 1965), pp. 459–460.

5. On the subject of industrialization in Spain, see Bartolomé Bennassar, et al., *Orígenes del atraso español* (Barcelona: Ariel, 1985); Rafael Myro, et al., *Lecciones de economía española* (Madrid: Civitas, 1993); Jordi Nadal, *El fracaso de la revolución industrial en España* (Barcelona: Ariel, 1984); Jordi Nadal and Albert Carreras, eds., *Pautas regionales de la industrialización española (siglos XIX y XX)* (Barcelona: Ariel, 1990); Clara E. Nuñez and Gabriel Tortella, *La maldición divina: Ignorancia y atraso económico en perspectiva histórica* (Madrid: Alianza, 1993); Nicolás Sánchez-Albornoz, ed., *The Economic Modernization of Spain, 1830–1930* (New York: New York University Press, 1987); Ramón Tamames, *Estructura económica de España* 19th ed. (Madrid: Alianza, 1993); Gabriel Tortella Casares, *El desarrollo de la España contemporánea: Historia económica de los siglos XIX y XX* (Madrid: Alianza, 1994).

6. For a more detailed analysis of this point, see Rosa María Capel Martínez, *El trabajo y la educación de la mujer en España (1900–1936)*, 2d ed. (Madrid: Ministerio de Cultura, 1986).

7. For a comparative perspective on European women's work, see Georges Duby and Michelle Perrot, *Historia de las mujeres: El siglo XX* (Madrid: Taurus,

1991), pp. 465-478; Elizabeth Roberts, *Women's Work: 1840–1940* (Hampshire, MA: Macmillan, 1988); Gail Braybon, *Women Workers in the First World War: The British Experience* (Totowa, NJ: Barnes and Noble, 1981); C. Hakim, "Occupational Segregation," *Dept. of Employment Research Paper* no. 9 (1979); Pat Thane, Geoffrey Crossick, Roderick Floud, eds., *The Power of the Past: Essays for Eric Hobsbawm* (New York: Cambridge, 1984).

8. Capel Martínez, *El trabajo y la educación*, pp. 115, 138–159.

9. See Carmen de Burgos, *La mujer en España (lecture delivered at the "Italian Press Association" in Rome on April 28, 1906)* (Valencia: n.d.), pp. 26–27. The same idea can be found in this volume in the article of D.J. O'Connor.

10. See Pamela Radcliff, "Elite Women Workers and Collective Action: The Cigarette Makers of Gijón, 1890–1930," *Journal of Social History* 27, no. 1 (September 1993).

11. Capel Martínez, *El trabajo y la educación*, pp. 150–159.

12. The studies of Eloisa Baena Luque and Paloma Candela Soto concerning the Seville and Madrid factories are examples of the importance of the data contained in these files and the abundant information they provide. See E. Baena Luque, *Las cigarreras Sevillanas: Un mito en declive (1887–1923)* (Málaga, Spain: Universidad, Secretariado de Publicaciones e Intercambios científicos, 1993); Paloma Candela Soto, "Trabajo y vida en la experiencia laboral de las cigarreras madrileñas, 1888–1927," (unpublished thesis).

13. Until the end of the seventeenth century, tobacco production in Seville was carried out in scattered workshops. The hazards and health problems inherent in this basis of production led to its being transferred to a single large building at the beginning of the eighteenth century where it remained until the new factory was inaugurated. See José Manuel Rodríguez Gordillo, "La Real Fábrica de Tabacos de Sevilla" in *Sevilla y el Tabaco* (Seville, 1984); José Pérez Vidal, *España en la historia del tabaco* (Madrid: Centro de Estudios de Etnología Peninsular, 1959); Antonio Bonet Correa, "La Fábrica de Tabacos de Sevilla: Primer edificio de la arquitectura industrial en España" in *Sevilla y el Tabaco* (Seville, 1984); L. Alonso Alvarez, "De la manufactura a la industria: La Real Fábrica de Tabacos de La Coruña (1804–1857)," *Historia Económica* 3 (1984).

14. In the Seville factory the female workers had to bring "their chairs, scissors, baskets, cloths to cover and protect the leaf tobacco, etc." Up to 1883 they were even charged the cost of the paper seals. See Baena Luque, *Las cigarreras sevillanas*, p. 37.

15. José Manuel Rodríguez Gordillo, "El personal obrero en la Real Fábrica de Tabacos" in *Sevilla y el Tabaco* (Seville, 1984).

16. See Radcliff, "Elite Women Workers and Collective Action."

17. Ministerio de Trabajo, Comercio e Industria, *Estadística de salarios y jornadas de trabajo referida al período 1914–1930* (Madrid: Ministerio de Trabajo, Comercio e Industria, 1930).

18. Baena Luque, *Las cigarreras sevillanas*, pp. 36–37.

19. In Spain at the beginning of the twentieth century the age of majority was twenty-three years. However, emancipation from paternal custody only affected a woman's private life, while professional activities continued to be subject to legislation in force. On the other hand, capacities acquired at majority were lost upon a woman's marriage, at which time she came under the authority of the husband. Article 61 of the Spanish Civil Code barred wives from any professional activity without the authorization of their respective husbands. That being the case, it is not surprising that most Spanish women passed from paternal tutelage to the tutelage of the husband without a break. This situation contrasts with that which existed in other countries such as England, the United States, and Switzerland, where towards the end of the nineteenth century and in the first years of the twentieth century, the married woman was recognized as having full legal capacity for all civil acts and could furthermore freely dispose of earnings from employment.

20. Emilia Pardo Bazán, *La Tribuna* (1882) vol. 2 in *Obras completas* (Madrid: Aguilar, 1956), pp. 101–196.

21. The male posts designated by the factory management were machine operator, senior electrician, foremen, porter, and office messenger.

22. Baena Luque, *Las cigarreras sevillanas*, pp. 48–49.

23. *Regulations*, chap. 2, art. 23.

24. Ibid., chap. 4, art. 40.

25. The same rigour in the rules governing the activity of the female worker within the factory can be found within the textile industry as has been shown in our research. See: Rosa María Capel Martínez, "El trabajo industrial femenino a comienzos de siglo en un medio rural: La fábrica de seda de Ugíjar (Granada)," *Anuario de Historia Moderna y Contemporánea*, no. 4–5, (1978): 177–195.

26. See among other publications the article of E.P. Thompson, "Time, Work-Discipline and Industrial Capitalism," *Past and Present* 38 (December 1967).

27. *Regulations*, chap. 3, art. 30, 31.

28. Consider that, according to the *Estadística de salarios 1914–1930*, in 1914 the hourly rate for a female worker in the textile industry was 0.23 pesetas, in the clothing industry, 0.17, and in the tobacco industry, 0.28. For 1930 the difference is still more noteworthy, the levels being 0.42, 0.41, and 0.84 respectively.

29. *Regulations*, chapt. 3, art. 31.

30. Ibid.

31. Ibid.

32. This happened in a labor dispute at the Madrid Factory in July 1920 between "red" and "yellow" union members. The former belonged to the Federacion Nacional de Cigarreras y Tabaqueros, affiliated to the U.G.T. (General Workers' Union), the socialist union; the latter, to Catholic Trades Unions created to serve the interests of managements and to break down worker solidarity. See Capel Martínez, *El trabajo y la educación*, pp. 254–257.

33. Baena Luque, *Las cigarreras sevillanas*, p. 45.

34. See Radcliff, "Elite Women Workers and Collective Action."

6

Representations of Women Workers: Tobacco Strikers in the 1890s

D.J. O'Connor

Two events in early 1896 drew public attention to female tobacco workers (*cigarreras*). In Seville at the end of January, over 5,000 *cigarreras* smashed up their working quarters at the tobacco factory demanding that the director be replaced. After two days of rioting, the Prime Minister, Antonio Cánovas del Castillo, and the Minister of the Hacienda, Navarro Reverter, in consultation with the president and the director of the state-owned tobacco monopoly, decided to close the factory.[1] The factory remained shut down for nearly two weeks as the management sought assurances from the *cigarreras* that there would be no further disturbances. Some 8,000 families in Seville connected to the women were directly affected. Widespread sympathy for the *cigarreras* who took to the streets to explain their grievances led civic authorities to fear public shows of support, including solidarity strikes.[2]

Meanwhile, in Madrid on February 7, 1896, shortly after the Seville factory reopened, a procession was held to honor General Martínez Campos who only days before had been relieved of his command in Cuba. A young fishmonger, Tomás Carrera, whistled disrespectfully at the general and was shot dead by a civil guardsman when he tried to flee the scene. The young man's funeral cortege on the following day turned into a prorepublic demonstration focusing on the monarchy's repressive police measures, and on a denunciation, fueled by popular patriotic sentiment, of Martínez Campos' alleged stand in favor of autonomy for the colony.[3] A delegation of *cigarreras* from the Madrid tobacco factory marched in the vanguard and took the lead in voicing the crowd's protest.[4]

Evident public interest in issues raised by these two incidents afforded journalists ample opportunity to depict *cigarreras* in their coverage: in the first instance, as women workers who chose to riot, destroy property, and defy authority in order to make their demands heard; in the second, as working women demonstrating against police brutality and in favor of a largely uncontested state policy toward Cuba. Representations of working women in the late nineteenth-century Spanish press were, in fact, rather rare. Women were most likely to be mentioned in the press if they were members of royal families, artistes, criminals, or the victims of crimes. But while women workers in general were invisible and undefined in the nineties, female tobacco workers were already stereotyped when they became the focus of press attention in 1896.[5]

The *cigarrera*'s principal characteristics had been unforgettably defined by Prosper Mérimée's *Carmen.* The French author's 1845 novella, based on a Spanish story, and Georges Bizet's operatic version of Mérimée's work, produced in 1875, furnished key texts for the creation of a public persona for the *cigarreras*—especially, of course, the Seville *cigarreras*.[6] Popular literature in the 1890s, particularly the intensely topical musical theatre (*zarzuela*) and one-act plays (*sainetes*) which were attended by all classes, elaborated the image of the *cigarrera* as Carmen. In due course, public awareness of the Seville strike and the Madrid demonstrations contributed to contemporary stage depictions of *cigarreras*, a type long familiar to audiences in plays purporting to reflect life in Madrid's lower-class neighborhoods.

Press and Stage Stereotypes of *Cigarreras*

Representations of the *cigarreras* on stage and in the press reveal that, different as they may have appeared when compared to other women workers, they were still subject to the prevalent gender discourse in *fin de siglo* Spain. How their female sexuality was defined in accord with that discourse and, specifically, how it was defined in relation to each of the two 1896 incidents in which *cigarreras* participated took on primary importance as reporters and writers sought both to form and to accommodate the ideological expectations of theatergoers and mostly middle-class readers of the high-circulation papers.

When circumstances permitted, and when it suited their purposes, journalists and dramatists alike interpreted signs of a mature, self-assertive, and potentially powerful female sexuality in such a way as to channel it toward the promotion of patriotic fervor. So, in 1896, at a time when the mainstream press assiduously avoided criticism of official policy concerning Cuba, reporters appropriated what they perceived to be the distinctively female wrath and passion—which the Madrid *cigarreras* expressed in their denunciations of Martínez Campos—in order to impress the women into service as advocates of continued Spanish rule on the island. In quite different circumstances, the press's attribution of immaturity to the traditionally well-dressed, flirtatious, and attractive Seville *cigarreras*, served two important purposes. Reporters clearly aimed to undermine the appearance of a mature "female consciousness" (to employ Temma Kaplan's phrase) in the women who rioted in Seville by representing them as "girls"—flighty creatures who were just as concerned with being able to buy the elegant patent leather shoes which, like spoiled children, they considered their due, as with feeding and maintaining their families.[7] By adopting this line, the press weakened women workers' traditionally accepted role of providing for their families—even if it entailed violent struggle—while at the same time, by infantilizing the *cigarreras*, they weakened any claims the *cigarreras* made to autonomy, i.e., to an ability to organize and to negotiate with the bosses.

Press and stage thus reinforced the two principal stereotypes imposed on the *cigarreras*—their image as strong mothers acting in defense of the country, and that of attractive but immature girls, incapable of serious social and political action on their own behalf. Within this context, the *Noticiero Sevillano*'s highly circumstantial accounts of the 1896 riots are notable since alternative images of the women workers unmistakably emerged from its reporter's coverage. These images in turn permitted different perceptions of their capacity for autonomy in relation to structures of power. Solidarity among *cigarreras*, for example, was most commonly associated with the charitable acts which they more or less spontaneously carried out on behalf of disabled or otherwise unfortunate sisters.[8] But in the aftermath of the 1896 riot, their understanding of a relatively sophisticated workers' solidarity aimed at achieving specific labor goals, can be deduced from the *Noticiero Sevillano*'s accounts of those events. Solidarity did not lead to practical benefits at the time; indeed, whatever the *cigarreras* gained in 1896 was won largely because of the economic impact their sheer numbers exerted on the local economy and by their exploitation of older defining images epitomized by the Carmen stereotype. Nonetheless, even random press references to actions designed to bring about solidarity opened up space for constructing new ways of viewing these women.

Teresa de Lauretis has argued that "the representation of gender *is* its construction."[9] The commercial press and theater of the 1890s clearly offered numerous representations of the *cigarreras* which attributed to them a well-defined gender role and contributed significantly to the formation of their public identity as women workers. While the accessibility of press and stage as sources and forums for public discourse at the end of the century made them powerful purveyors of the ideology favored by the oligarchy which they typically promoted, it is important to recognize that stereotypes were questioned and unorthodox views did win a hearing on occasion. *Juan José*, by Joaquín Dicenta, first presented in 1895 and considered by some literary historians to be the first socialist play produced in Spain, provides one among several contemporary examples of dramas that provoked class-based opposition for its depiction of conflict between workers and capitalists. (It carefully preserved accepted gender roles.) But despite being denounced and rejected by upper-middle-class and upper-class viewers, and despite its prohibition by some ecclesiastical authorities and civil governors, *Juan José* became a staple of workers' theatres across Spain and, more significantly, often played in 1896 before general audiences in Madrid to benefit returning soldiers from Cuba.[10] In regard to the *cigarreras*, the theater was not similarly open to new perspectives on their role as women workers. Rather it was the practice of modern journalism that in the two above-mentioned events of 1896 permitted the introduction of contestatory views—even those of the women themselves—into a public discourse from which they had been largely excluded as subjects.

The material reviewed here presents problems that women workers still confront: first, the reductive representation of women in the media designed in accord with a gender role assigned by dominant religious and political traditionalists; second, the need to establish a strategy for negotiating labor conflicts either from a position accepting of women's difference, or from one which is gender-neutral—this last, an option not avaliable to the *cigarreras*.[11] One century later the media remain reluctant to portray women workers who do not conform to traditional gender roles. Media representations still function to justify women's marginalization in a work world dominated by men.

The Seville Riots and the Madrid Demonstrations

On the afternoon of January 23, 1896, after the *cigarreras* in Seville began to wreck whatever lay at hand in their work areas, security guards were called to block the entrance to the building in order to prevent outsiders from joining forces with the rioters. The cavalry and the civil guard arrived next, followed shortly afterwards by municipal authorities, including the chief of police. Before long, all the forces that could be deployed to maintain order were positioned to quell the disturbance. Despite these precautions, the *cigarreras* rioted again on January 24. The factory was then closed and the riot—which had led to extensive property damage and minor injuries among several curious bystanders, a few *cigarreras*, and a handful of law enforcement personnel—came to an end.

The *cigarreras* had demanded that the director of the factory be dismissed. They complained that their day's work was often discounted for reasons that had more to do with inferior paper and tobacco than with poor work. They argued that their wages were too low (many workers had had their wages reduced from two pesetas per day to forty or fifty *céntimos*), that dismissals of "mothers of families" were often arbitrary, that the *maestras* (matrons in charge) spied on their conversations in order to come up with reasons for dismissal, that they were insulted by being subjected to two body searches rather than the customary one, and that menstruating women were forced to undergo searches in a drafty place at a time when they were susceptible to illness.

Finally, the women—who in Seville were paid on a monthly basis—complained that they were prohibited from borrowing money from fellow workers under threat of dismissal. Further, any worker who lent money was liable to be dismissed if she did not publicly pardon the debt.[12]

Between January 25 and February 4, when the *cigarreras* were permitted to reenter the building, the women demonstrated in the streets waving yellow and red—and occasionally black—flags and sent delegations charged with presenting their case to various authorities. Meanwhile the private persons who directed the tobacco factory, along with local authorities, the Minister of Gobernación, Cos-Gayón, the Minister of the Hacienda, Navarro Reverter, together with the Prime Minister, Antonio Cánovas del Castillo, consulted on a course of action. From their point of view, the inviolability of authority was the issue at stake in the *cigarreras*' riot. Accordingly, the women's request that the director of the factory be replaced was refused. A further indication of management's intransigence appeared in the local newspaper, *El Noticiero Sevillano*, on February 3. The journalist covering the strike advised readers that the statutes regulating the operation of the state tobacco monopoly included the proviso that no explanation or justification was required should the directors of a tobacco factory decide to relocate.

Because the *cigarreras* were paid on a monthly basis and had been without any income since the end of December, the lockout soon forced them to beg on the streets. In the end, indigence and powerlessness forced the women to capitulate to nearly all the terms set by the employers; most importantly, the continuance of the current director and *maestras* and the dismissal of nineteen ringleaders. The director did agree to pay the women every two weeks in future. He also promised to rehire the ringleaders whom he had dismissed, but later reneged on his word. As a result of immediate preventive measures taken by the police against any show of solidarity with the locked-out workers, the authorities' fears of other effective worker actions in support of the women proved to be groundless.

Authorities in Madrid similarly maintained the upper hand following the disturbances of February 7 and 8, 1896, successfully preventing further disruptions of public order. While there were no reports of detentions of *cigarreras* (several men were arrested for "attacks against authorities"), reporters emphasized the women's role in the demonstrations and, like the correspondents who covered the riots in Seville, reenforced the generally-held perception that the public comportment of women opposing authority was different from that of men.

In Spain, as elsewhere, rioting women were believed to be exceptionally ferocious. The combative nature of the *cigarreras*, in particular, was legendary.[13] Journalists covering the two incidents in 1896 characterized both groups of women as fearless and fierce. They described how the women workers in Madrid defied the civil guard, knowing well that it had no compunctions about retaliating violently. (Indeed, the women's instincts and fears would again be borne out only four months later [as reported by *El Socialista* on July 3] when the *Guardia Civil* forcibly countered a peaceful demonstration mounted by the Madrid *cigarreras* to protest a management-imposed work slowdown; the guardsmen cut several women, among them a girl of fifteen or sixteen who suffered wounds to the face.) In Seville on January 24, 1896, the reporter for *El Noticiero Sevillano* emphasized the *cigarreras*' excitement as they cried out for the director to be handed over to them so that they could devour him. He also described their destructive fury as they smashed objects and threw bricks at civil guards. What impressed him most, however, was the deafening clamor of their strident voices.

Press representations of such behavior, assumed to stem from a potentially violent female sexuality, controlled their interpretation. In general, the conservative press presented the workers as destructive women who reverted to ineffective childishness once their fury had subsided, while the republican press—*El País*, for example, in its coverage of the Madrid demonstrations—denied them genuine autonomy just as surely by casting them in the traditional role of tribunes of the people.

There is an illuminating difference between the depiction of the *cigarreras* opposing the combined forces of capitalism, government, and police authority in Seville, and that of the *cigarreras* in Madrid protesting police brutality directed at a "patriot" who protested official honors given to the "turncoat" General Martínez Campos. Reporters on the scene in Seville initially stressed the chaotic, primitive, and savage nature of the women rioters. Then, after the rioting ceased, the reporter for *El Noticiero Sevillano* described them quite differently. The same women he described as "shrieking furies" on January 23 and 24, he subsequently referred to as "girls," thereby infantilizing them at the very time when they were entering into negotiations of a sort with the director and civil authorities. Reporters in Madrid who relayed news of the Seville uprising followed his lead. On the other hand, the *cigarreras* in Madrid, whose spirited protests, although public, were not work related, emerged from the pages of the republican press as tribunes of the people, possessed by a wild but noble fury as they harangued the crowd. Their fearless leadership, their defiant actions and demands were portrayed as exemplifying an admirable virility.

The temporary transformation of these women into honorary men served an ideological function long familiar in Spanish fiction. Strong, self-assertive Spanish women who stand out in fictional public demonstrations or crises—women such as Laurencia, the heroine of Lope de Vega's seventeenth-century play, *Fuenteovejuna*—perform a strictly limited role. However firmly rooted their actions may be in wrongs they have suffered or demands they feel entitled to make, their actions are essentially designed to shock, shame, and rouse men whose own failure to act indicates that they have become feminized. At such moments of violent confrontation with authority—as in *Fuenteovejuna*—women may accuse men directly of being effeminate (*maricones*).[14] As soon as the women have recalled men to their duty, they slip back into their customary roles as wives and mothers. Males reassert their rightful dominance and the crisis is over.

Such a real life role for women became most appropriate and plausible in the nineteenth century when the crisis could be linked to a popularly endorsed patriotic cause. In February of 1896 it was uncommon to speak publicly about Cuba's separation from Spain in terms other than as a dismemberment, or the wrenching away of a child from its mother. Few voices in the press or in other public forums questioned the duty of Spaniards to maintain the integrity of the fatherland. The Madrid *cigarreras* joined other Spaniards who had been demonstrating against Martínez Campos since his return to the mainland on the grounds that he was a traitor. By taking this stand, the *cigarreras* fell in line with traditional conceptions linking them to popular democracy and to the active defense of the country. In this connection, the youthful Manuel Azaña (who three decades later would become president of the Second Republic), recalled how, having plunged into a crowd gathered to see a convoy off to Cuba, he was swept along by their emotion. "The hurrahs grew louder when the *cigarreras* arrived, granddaughters—as the newspapers assured us—of the heroines of the Second of May, hoarse like their grandmothers, although not manning cannons."[15]

The note of scepticism in Azaña's description was not misplaced. The *cigarreras* accommodated themselves—or were accommodated—perhaps too easily in his view and in the view of some others, to a puzzling variety of so-called democratic traditions. The *cigarreras* who demonstrated in Madrid in 1896 supported the Republic, but they opposed autonomy for Cuba. Shouting out imprecations directed at the Queen Regent too inflammatory to print in the newspapers, they called on their fellow demonstrators to storm the Royal Palace; yet their grandmothers had famously fought alongside the people on behalf of the captive Spanish king and against the French invasion and reform.[16]

On February 8, 1896, *El Correo*—in accord with common practice at the time—reprinted a stirring description from *El País* of the *cigarreras*' role in Carrera's funeral cortege:

> The most terrible curses, the cruellest exclamations came from the lips of those women angered, indeed infuriated, by grief. They were the first to cheer the Republic and to shout "Death!" to the man whose failures earned him no longer the name of the hero of Cuba. Throughout the

> funeral procession's long march, they followed on foot, shouting on occasion, crying off and on, furious, indignant, magnificent in their grief. It was they who obliged the agents of public order to uncover their heads before the body of Carrero [sic] when the procession arrived at the cemetery.

The reporter's description of the procession's departure from the cemetery back towards Madrid was even more dramatic:

> When the procession left the cemetery, a woman of the people who had climbed up onto a pillar, harangued the crowd, saying:
>
>> "Let us march on to Madrid to demonstrate to the tyrants, to the assassins of the people, that the people are still capable of great energy and still have a conscience. Down with the government! Death to Martínez Campos! Long live the Republic! Long live *El País!"*
>
> Those cries were repeated amidst thunderous applause. At the shouts of "To Madrid!" "To Madrid!" the imposing, threatening, and terrible multitude headed for the capital.[17]

In addition to the cries already mentioned, *El Imparcial* reported on the same day (February 8) that the women used words "offensive to the most exalted institutions."

The close relations suggested by reporters between the *cigarreras* and *El País* in the above citation and elsewhere between the women and *El Tribuno* and *El Noticiero Sevillano* in Seville were probably more opportunistic on both sides than unions forged by genuinely common interests. It is possible, for example, that the socialist paper in Seville, *El Tribuno*, encouraged the *cigarreras* to riot in January of 1896 in the hope that it would serve as a catalyst for a strike that would draw in and benefit male workers. Charges (unproved) that the paper had incited the women to riot also served to deny them agency.

Without intending to minimize the genuine passion of the *cigarreras* on the occasion of Carrera's funeral procession, or the impact they had on the crowd, it is not inappropriate to question the good faith of journalists reporting on this and similar patriotic demonstrations involving *cigarreras*—or women of any kind. References to the "virility" of the *cigarreras* were evidently meant to raise questions as to what constituted real manhood. And for this reason it was a handy stick to use for beating political opponents over the head. So, for example, according to *El Socialista* on June 25, 1897, conservative papers "continue to bemoan the state of moral 'depression' in which we live, claiming that the only men left in Spain are the *cigarreras*." When the lauded "virility" of the *cigarreras* was represented in the press, the intent was surely not so much to depict an unusual and spectacular display of manly courage and forceful tactics employed by brave women to achieve their objectives, as it was to perpetuate a familiar ritual—a tradition of political invective dramatically inserted into scenes of female riot or protest, but used for the benefit and in the interest of men.

The Madrid *cigarreras* were, in any case, depicted as mature women. In Seville, although many of them were wives and mothers, they were not presented as mature exemplars of the passionate virago type. Following his first descriptions of the rioting women, the reporter for *El Noticiero Sevillano* underscored what he viewed as childish destructiveness and the instinctive coquetry of the Seville *cigarrera.* On January 24 he wrote that the man currently designated to talk with the *cigarreras*, Lieutenant Colonel Zuleta of the Civil Guard, had dealt successfully in the past with women's riots. His strategy lay in alternating jokes, flattery, or compliments, with well-timed displays of severity. He did add that the *cigarreras* protested repeatedly against officials' attempts to string them along with "sweet talk."[18] Yet the *Noticiero*'s coverage presented them as publicly coquettish and, on several occasions, disposed to fawn on authorities. When the women marched in demonstration to the Plaza Nueva on January 26, for example, the Civil Guard, with Zuleta in charge, tried to disband them. The "girls," as the reporter termed them, called out compliments to the Lieutenant Colonel—"Long live the man with the star!" (He wore the star of San Hermenegildo on his chest.)[19] "Oh, what a precious, handsome little man!" They grabbed his goatee, kissed his hands, and threw their arms around him.

Their legendary hot blood was confirmed by reports in several Madrid papers (*El Correo, La Época* and *El Día*) on January 26. These reports stated that a group of the women who marched to the Plaza Nueva the day before, under the mistaken impression that the director of the factory had been recalled to Madrid, improvised a flamenco fiesta. "One of the women," according to *El Correo*, "began by dancing a tango, another followed with a *sevillana*, and the fiesta began in earnest; some of the women danced, others sang, and the rest clapped and urged them on. After they had shouted and danced to their hearts' content, and when the *cigarreras* were quite exhausted, the demonstration broke up." Curiously, the reporter for *El Noticiero Sevillano*—whose description of the march to the Plaza Nueva and the events that transpired there was highly detailed—omitted this account, writing only that the women standing on a platform at the Plaza had, at one time, stamped their feet. It is quite plausible that the Madrid reporters seized upon that reference in order to fabricate a familiar image of gypsy self-abandon on the part of the impulsive "girls."

Journalists covering the Madrid demonstrations and the Seville riots thus evoked images of *cigarreras* consecrated by tradition: fierce combativeness, adherence to democratic or popular tradition, spontaneity, and coquetry. Almost from the outset, however, reports appeared complicating such generally accepted depictions of the women. On January 25, the reporter for *El Noticiero Sevillano* disclosed the existence of two communications—a letter and a statement of grievances and demands—that had originated with the *cigarreras* themselves. On the previous day, as it turned out, a delegation of *cigarreras* had left the statement at the editorial office of the paper because, they said, the paper's reporter had claimed that no one knew what had motivated them to riot. In addition, an individual *cigarrera* wrote the letter, which explained the women's position on a more personal level. The paper printed most of the first item under the rubric, "A Reasonable Statement." The reporter limited himself, however, to a paraphrase of the letter, assuring readers that he could not print it in its entirety because of its excessively colorful language. The Madrid papers reported the contents of the statement, but did not elaborate on its significance as an indication of strategic planning. The fact that the Seville *cigarreras*, like their fellow workers in Madrid, understood the power of the press and knew how to make use of it may have gone unremarked, but it nonetheless revealed a sophistication in their tactics that contrasted sharply with previous descriptions of their disorganized rioting and flamboyant parading through the streets.

In what appears to have been a similar display of ignorance or reluctance to credit the women with any capacity to organize, authorities had initially warned the *cigarreras* that if they did not call a halt to their protests, their jobs might go to the tobacco workers in Cádiz or Málaga. Readers of *El Nacional* (a Madrid paper) learned on January 29 that the Seville women had been in telegraphic communication with their counterparts in Valencia as well as in the other two cities. The directors' attempt to split the workers clearly had not succeeded.

While there was little indication that anyone feared the *cigarreras*—precisely because of their supposed lack of organization—there was apprehension in Seville that male outsiders might seize the opportunity to foment labor unrest by joining women whose cause was popular with the people. Other women workers—apparently considered a negligible threat—did join the *cigarreras*. According to the *Noticiero* reporter on January 28, seamstresses and match makers marched in sympathy on that date, and the *cigarreras* planned to invite stopper makers (*taponeras*) to join them the following day. As time passed and male supporters were effectively kept away, reporters reenforced the usual perceptions of the women's supposed childishness. When they were allowed to return to the factory on February 4, the reporter for *El Noticiero Sevillano* was there. The next day's report began: "They were good little girls. They all entered the factory in an orderly fashion; happy, some of them a teensy bit worried—still, the majority walked in looking like proper children who have never broken a dish." The reporter added that the factory director bore no resentment, ". . . he looks upon his subordinates as nothing more than good mothers and dutiful daughters deserving of the most generous protection."[20]

Perceptions of the *cigarreras*'s conduct in Seville were further controlled by the fortuitous arrival in Seville on January 28 of the Archduke Eugenio, brother of the Queen Regent. The Archduke was on a tour of Andalusia, visiting its artistic monuments and acquainting himself with its picturesque traditions, customs and types. When he arrived in Seville, he found the *cigarreras* marching through the streets. "The Archduke took several photographs of the picturesque groups of women," reported *El Heraldo de Madrid* on January 28, adding that he then proceeded to the tobacco factory where he took more pictures. The next day, the *cigarreras* sent to his hotel a delegation (according to the same paper) of "very pretty and discreet *cigarreras*" who explained the workers' grievances and asked him to serve as intermediary on their behalf with his sister. Eugenio ordered his aides to distribute to the women coins worth five pesetas each—the equivalent of almost three day's wages, or, from the Archduke's point of view, the price of a dinner at the well-known Madrid restaurant, Fornos.

The Archduke granted daily interviews to the press in which he communicated his impressions of the *cigarreras*. In this way, newspaper readers learned more about the workers' grievances, but perhaps more significantly, they were at the same time invited to see the women through the eyes of a privileged member of the royal family whose remoteness from the realities of working-class life and whose appreciation of pretty women, colorful dress, and the picturesque permitted the vision of Carmen to resurface in full force.

When the Archduke returned to Madrid, he was asked what he had liked best on his tour. He ranked the *cigarreras* just after the Alhambra in Granada and the Mezquita in Córdoba. This reply, together with the visit the *cigarreras* had paid him, undoubtedly provided the inspiration for a cartoon that appeared in *El Heraldo de Madrid* on January 30, 1896 (See Figure 6.1). Its caption read: "A commission of Monuments of Seville, inspired by conciliatory proposals, resolves to visit the authorities in order to arrange the end of the conflict." The drawing depicted two *cigarreras*—part woman, part monument (the monuments recognizably represented two of Seville's most famous buildings, the *Giralda* and the *Torre de Oro*), fanning themselves and outfitted like the Carmen figures they were also meant to suggest. The full emergence of the traditional Carmen image could not be suppressed—had anyone wanted to do so—once the Archduke Eugenio appeared on the scene with his camera. And that image undoubtedly did much to obscure views of the women as workers in negotiations with their bosses.

FIGURE 6.1

"The Conflict in Seville."

"Una comisión de monumentos de Sevilla, inspirada en propósitos conciliadores, resuelve visitar á las autoridades para gestionar la terminación del conflicto" (A commission of Monuments of Seville, inspired by conciliatory proposals, resolves to visit the authorities in order to arrange the end of the conflict).

EL CONFLICTO DE SEVILLA

The representation of *cigarreras* as Carmen was the only one offered to readers in late May of 1896 when three of the *cigarreras* who had been fired in January from their jobs at the Seville factory travelled to Madrid to request an audience with the Queen Regent. They wanted her to enforce the factory director's promise, made when the women returned to work in February, to reinstate the nineteen women who had been dismissed as ringleaders of the riots. The delegation visited the office of *El Nacional*, among other papers. The tone of this paper's coverage of their visit was typical. On May 22, it printed a story about them which included their likenesses. The article noted first that it was difficult for the artist to draw the mercurial women—but how, the reporter asked archly, could anyone expect a woman from Seville to be still for even five minutes? The reporter then provided thumbnail sketches of the three women: Angela was the plumpest and the prettiest; Dolores was quite as loquacious as her friends; and pug-nosed Aurora was charming and chattier than an ex-minister of the opposition party. Thus were the dangerous ringleaders of the January riots reduced to the familiar stereotype of the charmingly picturesque Seville tobacco worker.

In addition, *El Nacional* made note of the *cigarreras*' appreciation and gratitude to the Queen Regent. The women telegraphed their comrades in Seville following their interview with the representative of monarchy—who gave them 200 pesetas—to communicate high hopes of favorable action on their plea for reinstatement. Their optimism led grateful Sevillians to buy an "infinity" of likenesses of the Regent available in the city's shops.[21] Apart from the concessions which the Seville tobacco factory director made regarding pay periods, the *cigarreras*' most tangible gains came from royal largesse. Press coverage ensured that in relation to the Regent and to the Archduke the women were perceived as picturesque supplicants deserving of charity.

The *Cigarreras* on Stage

During the period in question here, representations of *cigarreras* on the commercial stage preserved gender and class stereotypes more successfully than was the case in the press. Images of *cigarreras* in popular literature conformed in general to those purveyed by most press coverage. Attractive and colorful, their sexuality was toned down and sentimentalized, or expressed primarily as maternal solicitude and its variant, a fiercely patriotic zeal. The opera, *Carmen*, recast as a *zarzuela* in Spanish, had appeared on stage in 1890, and in this form made Bizet's version of the already well-known character even more accessible to the public.[22] In the period following the 1896 events in Seville and Madrid, two *zarzuelas* appeared which dealt with tobacco workers. In October of 1896, a *zarzuela* entitled *La Chula* was performed in Madrid.[23] Its protagonist, an ex-*cigarrera*, embodied many of the traits traditionally associated with *cigarreras*, especially in regard to their relations to men and to their characteristic ethic of female solidarity. In 1897 *Las Cigarreras* appeared on the Madrid stage.[24] This *zarzuela*, whose action begins at the tobacco factory in Madrid and, in the closing scenes, moves to Seville, connects the women somewhat more directly to their work and to problems they experience as workers.

In the world of the *zarzuela*, everyone considers the tobacco workers national treasures, worthy successors to the picturesque *manolas* of the early part of the century.[25] The *cigarreras* themselves celebrate their charm, independence, and heart—the latter quality, in particular, translating easily into the maternal image fostered by the prevailing gender ideology. One of the characters in *Las cigarreras*, piqued by a slur voiced against the women, described the Spanish *cigarrera* thus:

> Born poor, she lives a hard but honorable life—all her fortune consists in loving and being loved. A stranger to sorrow, she dances and sings unceasingly, and kills herself working in order to collect a few miserable pennies every two weeks that scarcely permit her to support her relatives. But she truly reigns; no one threatens her power, for her rule is hope and her sceptre, charity. Her goodness is beyond question: she cries when she sees another cry, consoling rich and poor alike. She aids the helpless and goes without food to help the needy. The heart in her breast is noble and true: if people treat her well, she is generous, but if they wrong her, she is a wild beast. She loves her beloved country with genuine devotion. To it she gives her money, her children and even her life. She never cheats on her man, but gives him her whole heart. And that is what Spanish *cigarreras* are like![26]

The *cigarreras* who appear in *zarzuelas* are charitable in the way Mérimée's Carmen was when she nursed José through his long recuperation. Also like Carmen they are generous with their sexual favors until they find their man. Then they take great pride in staying with him through thick and thin and, above all, in supporting him financially. The praise which the *cigarreras* garnered on stage for their sexual liberality may, to an extent, have reflected their conduct offstage. They were presented on stage, for example, as being especially beloved of poor university students. *Las Cigarreras* opens with a scene in which students and *cigarreras* express mutual satisfaction at the ties of affection that bind them. In Seville, as *El Noticiero Sevillano* reported on January 25, 1896, the demonstrating women had passed before the University in order to cheer the students—who gallantly returned the homage.

The *cigarreras*' sexuality as presented on the stage was, apparently, a glamorized, even sanitized version of the reputation they had offstage. The report filed in 1885 for the section of the survey entitled "The Moral Condition of (Female) Workers," included in a comprehensive study of conditions in contemporary Spain, remarked darkly that *cigarreras* did not enjoy a good reputation among the general population.[27] Indeed, in order to obtain work in a tobacco shop, a woman had to provide a certificate attesting to good conduct. She was closely watched subsequently. C. Bernaldo de Quirós and J.M. Aguilaniedo included a few words on the *cigarreras* in the section on tribadism of their 1901 study, *La mala vida en Madrid*. Noting that lesbianism was often found in all-female work places, they wrote that Sapphism abounded in the tobacco factories. A new cause had been advanced to explain this phenomenon, they announced—the irritation produced by the fine powder from the tobacco leaves. They also noted that the *cigarreras* frequented a tavern near the tobacco factory which might well have displayed the sign, "To the Isle of Lesbos."[28] Such intimations of an aberrant sexuality were suppressed on stage just as other threatening aspects of female sexuality were customarily interpreted by the press and channeled in different directions.

Not surprisingly, the *cigarreras*' reputation for charity and solidarity in the musicals in question formed the basis of an active concern for those who were suffering the consequences of the war in Cuba. In *La Chula*, the *cigarreras* donate money to a coworker—the wife of a conscript. When word spreads that she and her children are cold and starving, the women do not hesitate to help, and in so doing, also support the war effort. In *Las Cigarreras*, at the suggestion of one of the *maestras*, the women gladly contribute money for a *kermesse* (fair) designed to raise funds for disabled war veterans. The spontaneous solidarity of the *cigarreras* is thus presented as benefitting the country—Spain's fighting men and the women and children they left behind—in a time of crisis, while it is ignored as a potentially important factor in their conduct as workers in the factory. When, in *Las Cigarreras*, a stage Englishman appears with a plan to mechanize the process of rolling cigarettes, the women do proclaim themselves willing to die together rather than to allow modernization that would deprive them of work, but happily, the Englishman is smitten by a vivacious *cigarrera* in Seville and promptly cancels his projects. In the final scene of *Las Cigarreras* women appear on stage representing famous monuments in Seville such as the *Torre de Oro* and the *Giralda*—a tableau that undoubtedly recalled to many newspaper readers the cartoon from *El Heraldo de Madrid* described above, which had also depicted the Seville *cigarreras* as human monuments emblematic of their city. Thus did the *zarzuela* contribute to representations of *cigarreras* which promoted their identification with sources of national pride and, further, with a patriotism specifically enlisted in the cause of the Cuban war.

The Representation of *Cigarreras* and the Imperatives of Modern Journalism

On January 28, when the press was denied entry to a meeting between a delegation of *cigarreras* and management, the *Noticiero* reporter inventively turned to several *cigarreras* who were waiting for their companions and asked them for their views. He printed three of them. One of the women referred to the prevalent and, in her opinion, unjust interpretation of the *cigarreras*' actions: "[When we take to the streets] out of desperation and hunger, people say we are bad and ask for too much because of deep-seated vice in our nature."[29] Such a plea—that the comfortable classes consider the real desperation of the poor rather than speculate about their innate viciousness—was unique in the reporting of the 1896 strike.

As this passage once again suggests, the possibility existed that the high-circulation press—in contrast to the theatre—might modify its representations of the *cigarreras* because of the particular demands of modern reporting. The more detailed the narrative of real events the better; journalists whose coverage achieved the vividness of a short story or a novel, then as now, drew the most readers. The reporter for *El Noticiero Sevillano*, who had the advantage of being on the scene, acted upon these imperatives of modern journalism by providing not only a densely detailed account of events, but also close descriptions of the locales of the action and of the actors.

Despite overall conformity with the conservative orientation of his newspaper, and despite frequent references to those aspects of women's relations to paid work that were determined by their gender roles and which further served to disqualify them in the view of contemporaries from equality with male workers—their role as mothers nursing babies on the job, as cooks who return home at midday to prepare family meals, as daughters required to help parents and siblings—the *Noticiero* reporter also indicated women's capacity as workers to organize, to speak out in public and through the press, and to establish bonds of solidarity. (Their resolve to defend themselves during the outbreaks of violence in Seville, even to the extent of using babies as shields to ward off cavalry charges, civil guards, and police was not new.)

Coverage that made a dent in the mold of representational stereotypes and permitted the emergence of differing, even contrasting images of this group of working women did not become more common. Not surprisingly—given the increase in labor violence in the years following the events discussed here—the press and stage persisted in reinforcing traditional stereotypes in their representations of the *cigarreras*. Nonetheless, the 1896 strike as presented in *El Noticiero Sevillano* affords a glimpse of the press's power to modify as well as to perpetuate such representations, and of the *cigarreras*' ability to seize the opportunity to make their voices heard. In some instances the *cigarreras*, keenly aware of the press' power, manipulated it in order to benefit from whatever advantages their publicly assigned gender role accorded them. On other occasions, they used it to invite the newspaper reading public to rethink the implications of that role in relation to the real-life concerns of working women. Indeed, on those few occasions when women were permitted self-representation through letters to the editor or by being quoted, they articulated their motives and described their actions so ably as to put dominant explanations of their conduct and identity clearly in question.

Notes

1. On both January 24 and 25, 1896, *El Noticiero Sevillano* reminded readers that government authorities had no jurisdiction over the *cigarreras*' dispute with the Seville tobacco factory since the state *Tabacalera* monopoly was run with complete independence by private individuals. Nonetheless, the government did intervene immediately (on January 25) in support of the tobacco factory's director. Subsequently, the government again intervened, but only to authorize military occupation of the factory in the aid of the tobacco factory's director. Appeals for compromise, directed both to representatives of government and of the *Tabacalera*, based on the interests of local business and civil authorities who feared the consequences of a loss of buying power on the part of so many unemployed—not to mention the possibility of sympathy strikes and violence—collided with the Cánovas regime's resolve to maintain authority at any cost.

2. The most circumstantial account of the Seville riots and ensuing lockout available to me is in *El Noticiero Sevillano*. The run of the local socialist paper, *El Tribuno*, held in the newspaper archives in Seville, ends with the issue of December 28, 1895, and is also not available for the period in question in the Hemeroteca Municipal in Madrid. The other principal local paper, the conservative *La Región*, was occasionally quoted by the Madrid press. Agencia Mencheta, along with local correspondents, supplied information to Madrid papers such as *La Iberia, El Correo, La Época, El Imparcial, El País, El Heraldo de Madrid*, and *El Socialista*. The narrative account I have reconstructed in this essay is based on material selected from the sources named above. The details are drawn largely from the unsigned reports of the correspondent for *El Noticiero Sevillano*.

3. General Martínez Campos' *pronunciamiento* at Sagunto in 1874 brought Spain's First Republic to an end and ushered in a constitutional monarchy. Republicans of different stripes composed the principal political opposition to the restored monarchy. In 1896 General Weyler replaced Martínez Campos and remained in command until 1898 when the American intervention brought an end to the second Cuban War of Independence begun in 1895.

4. My account of the disturbances in Madrid on February 7 and 8, 1896, comes primarily from *El Nacional* and *El Correo*. The latter paper's coverage often included passages from *El Imparcial* and *El País*.

5. See Mary Nash's chapter in this book in which she argues that the Spanish woman's identity as constructed by traditional/religious discourse, and reinforced in the early twentieth century by eugenics reformers, generally precluded her identity as a worker. Yet within the limits discussed in the present essay, the female tobacco workers constituted an exception to Nash's argument. Further—contrary to general expectations for females, whether workers or not—they did move in the public sphere, with the consequences discussed below.

6. According to D.S. Blondheim, editor of Mérimée's *"Carmen" et autres nouvelles* (New York: D.C. Heath, 1930), p. 133, the novella was based on a story which the Countess of Montijo, mother of the Empress Eugénie of France, had told Mérimée.

7. For the formulation of what constitutes "female consciousness," see Temma Kaplan's essay, "Female Consciousness and Collective Action: The Case of Barcelona 1910–1918," *Signs* 7 (1982): 545—66. Essentially, female consciousness acknowledges "the sexual division of labor" and "assigns women the responsibility of preserving life." See also E.P. Thompson, *Customs in Common: Studies in Traditional Popular Culture* (New York: The New Press, 1993), pp. 305–336, for a discussion of current thinking about perceptions of women's roles in nineteenth-century riots.

8. On February 7, 1896, Madrid's *El Socialista* commented on the strike's significance—workers who were not unionized simply could not hope to achieve their goals. The *cigarerras* were united in a religious fellowship established to benefit members. *El Nacional* reported on February 8, 1896, that the *Hermandad de las cigarreras* (Sodality of Tobacco Workers) had celebrated its annual religious fiesta the day before in the Church of the Terceros. According to the newspaper the church was full, and the Duchess of Montpensier was in attendance. Presumably, the event also celebrated the women's return to work on February 4.

9. Teresa de Lauretis, *Technologies of Gender* (Bloomington, IN: University of Indiana Press, 1987), p. 28.

10. See J. Rubio Jiménez, *Ideología y teatro en España, 1890–1900* (Zaragoza, Spain: Libros Pórtico, 1982), p. 170. For examples of censorship aimed at representations of workers and capitalists in the commercial theater, see Lily Litvak's *Musa Libertaria* (Barcelona: Bosch, 1981), pp. 229, 236–237, 240.

11. See Eileen Boris' review of three books on women and work, "Beyond Dichotomy," in *The Nation*, October 18, 1993: 433–437, for a discussion that begins with her observation that in the U.S. "feminist jurisprudence has begun to turn away from gender neutrality [equal rights for men and women] and back toward theories of difference." But, she asks, do laws that mandate equality always generate it? And will difference always maintain inequality? One of the authors in question, Lise Vogel,

warns against a reliance on difference since it reinforces traditional notions "in a world where Pat Robertson and Phyllis Schlafly continue to define family values" (p. 435)—a warning relevant to Spanish social and cultural realities in 1896. Vogel, the reviewer points out, "understands 'woman' to be a term always under contestation and identity to be a process constantly in flux. Through the concept of multiple identities, she passes beyond an exclusive focus on gender—with its inherent dualism—to consider the full range of human heterogeneity" (p. 435). In short, she moves beyond the dichotomy referred to in the review's title.

12. In *Once a Cigar Maker: Men, Women and Work Culture in American Cigar Factories, 1900–1919* (Urbana and Chicago: University of Illinois Press, 1987), Patricia A. Cooper describes and analyzes women tobacco workers' strikes with some references to the period from 1870–1900. Strikes were generally motivated by demands for wage increases, fear of wage cuts resulting from work changes, demands concerning management policy, protests over fines, hours, work rules, stock changes, and the discharge of fellow employees. Cooper notes factors, including ethnic bonds, which favored female workers' solidarity and the emergence of a women's work culture. She also includes material on the generally hostile attitudes of unionized male workers toward striking women, who were not unionized (see pages 247–270).

13. In "Las cigarreras de la Fábrica Nacional de Tabacos de Madrid," Sergio Vallejo Fernández Cela writes that their combativity was proverbial in nineteenth-century Spain, supporting his claim first with a quotation from Benito Pérez Galdós, the author of over forty historical novels (the *Episodios Nacionales*) which chronicle the history of Spain in the last century, and then with a quotation from the conservative paper, *La Época*. See pages 146–147 of Fernández Cela's essay, included in *Madrid en la sociedad del siglo XIX*, vol. 2 (Madrid: Alfoz, 1986). There is abundant written support for this perception in the late nineteenth century.

14. Benito Pérez Galdós supports this point explicitly in two of his popular *Episodios Nacionales*. In *Zaragoza* (1874), which fictionalizes the resistance of the townspeople to the French during the two long sieges suffered in the Peninsular War, Galdós portrays women who must spur hesitant men on to fight. In *Zumalacárregui* (1898), Galdós was even more insistent on the role of women vis-à-vis men—whose passions were less primordial—in the struggle against the French: "In order to throw the mass of men into desperate combat with any confidence at all, it was necessary to kindle feelings of implacable fury in them—a fury which necessarily originated and fed on female hatreds" (chap. 5). Galdós's representation of women in combat against the invading French or in the factional battles that followed, accordingly casts them in the role of the more primitive sex which must incite men to kill and to be killed.

15. "Los vivas subieron de tono al llegar las cigarreras, nietas—averiguaron los periódicos—de las heroínas del Dos de Mayo; roncas, como sus abuelas, aunque no empujasen cañones." From *Jardín de los frailes* (Madrid: Alianza, 1982), p. 163. See John Tone's essay in this collection for a discussion of the role of women in the incidents of May 2, 1808, the famous uprising against the French forces.

16. Emilia Pardo Bazán remarked on the strange fact that the religious devotion of the anti-Carlist, pro-republic *cigarreras* who worked in a tobacco factory in Galicia in the late 1860s and early 1870s increased in intensity as their revolutionary fervor grew. See page 156 of her 1882 novel, *La Tribuna* (in *Obras completas*, vol. 2 [Madrid: Aguilar, 1956], pp. 101–196), based on first-hand investigation of the life of *cigarreras* in Galicia. The explanation for this seeming paradox may lie in the narrator's earlier surmise (p. 132), that women in general supported the Republic because it promised to abolish conscription. Pardo Bazán noted the characteristics that distinguished the *cigarreras*, but, at the same time, she attributed to them some of the conventionally agreed upon generic characteristics assigned to lower-class women. Thus, on page 142, she writes that her protagonist, the *cigarrera* Amparo, possessed the strength of the "self-abnegation and sacrifice latent in the soul of the woman of the people" (fuerzas de abnegación y sacrificio latentes en el alma de la mujer del pueblo). For a later essay on the Spanish woman ("La mujer española," *La España Moderna* 17 [1890]: 101–113), Pardo Bazán reported a conversation with the director of the tobacco factory in Madrid which nicely summarized perceptions of the *cigarreras*' fundamental incapacity, instinctive sense of justice, and ferocity: "These women . . . are at bottom unfortunate wretches; they have hearts of gold, and can be led wherever one chooses to lead them. But their sense of justice is so highly developed and vigorous, it spells woe to any administrator whom they accuse of being unjust. They are capable of tearing him to pieces in the heat of a riot" (Estas mujeres . . . son en el fondo unas infelices; tienen un corazón de oro, y por bien se las lleva adonde se quiere. Pero existe en ellas tan desarrollado y vigoroso el sentimiento de la justicia, que pobre de aquel administrador a quien acusen de injusto. Son capaces, en un momento de alboroto, de hacerle pedazos). Emilia Pardo Bazán, *La mujer española y otros artículos feministas*. Selección y prólogo de Leda Sciavo (Madrid: Editora Nacional, 1976), pp. 64–65.

17. "De labios de aquellas mujeres irritadas y hasta furiosas por el dolor, salían los más crueles apóstrofes, las más terribles invectivas. Ellas fueron las primeras en vitoriar la República y en dar mueras al héroe fracasado de Cuba. Durante todo el largo trayecto siguieron a pie al fúnebre cortejo gritando unas veces, llorando otras, furiosas, indignadas, magníficas en su dolor. Ellas fueron las que obligaron a los agentes de orden público a descubrirse ante el cadáver de Carrero [sic] al llegar la comitiva al cementerio' . . . .

> Al salir del cementerio, una mujer del pueblo, encaramada sobre un pilar, arengó a la muchedumbre, diciendo:
>
> > 'Vamos a Madrid a demostrar a los tiranos, a los asesinos del pueblo que aún tiene éste energías y vergüenza. ¡Abajo el gobierno! ¡Viva la República! ¡*Viva El País!*'
>
> Gritos que fueron repetidos entre atronadores aplausos. A las voces de '¡A Madrid!' '¡A Madrid!,' aquella imponente muchedumbre dirigióse a la capital, amenazadora y terrible.

18. The translation of "dar cobo" as "sweet talk" is inadequate. According to Constancio Bernaldo de Quirós and J.M. Llanes Aguilaniedo *La mala vida en Madrid* (Madrid: B. Rodríguez Serra, 1902), p. 242, the expression was used to refer to the "conversation of prostitutes along with other manifestations of their presence." The *Noticiero Sevillano* noted that the women complained repeatedly that authorities deliberately used such language to deceive them. The *cigarreras* used "dar cobo," in fact, as a synonym for "to deceive." It should be noted here that the Seville *cigarreras*' reported use of *caló*—the gypsy language adapted to popular speech—marked them not only as lower class, but also, potentially, as gypsies. Such an identification would have further eroded their credibility as workers, given contemporary perceptions of the gypsy way of life.

19. Fernando VII created the military Order of San Hermenegildo in 1815 to reward the military and other functionaries for constancy in service. St. Gregory the Great attributed the conversion of Arian Visigothic Spain to the merits earned by St. Hermenegildo's martyrdom at Tarragona in 585.

20. ". . . no ve en sus subordinadas sino buenas madres o hijas de familia dignas de la más generosa protección."

21. *El Nacional*, May 22, 1896. The paper also noted that the women in the Seville tobacco factory received the telegram with cheers, made plans to meet the three women on their return at the railroad station with a demonstration of gratitude to the Regent, and also announced their intention to invite the "august lady" to visit Seville in October.

22. *Carmen*. Zarzuela en 4 actos y en verso, basada en la ópera del mismo nombre. Letra de D.P. Eduardo de Bray. Música del maestro Georges Bizet (Barcelona: Tipografía de José Cunill, 1890). This work was first performed "with extraordinary success," according to the title page, in the Teatro-Circo Alegría of Barcelona on April 7, 1890. The opera, *Carmen*, was performed in Madrid in 1896 at the Teatro Real.

23. *La Chula*. Zarzuela en un acto, original libro de Alfonso Benito y Alfaro. Música de Teodoro San José (Madrid: Arregui y Aruej, Editores, 1896).

24. *Las Cigarreras*. Zarzuela cómica en un acto y siete cuadros, en verso original de Angel Munilla y Luis Ferreiro. Música del Maestro Miguel Santonja (Madrid: Florencio Fiscowich, 1897). This *zarzuela* opened in Madrid about one year after the three Seville *cigarreras* travelled to the capital seeking the intervention of the Queen Regent in their dispute with the director of the Tobacco Factory.

25. The term *manola* was used in the eighteenth century to refer to a young woman from Madrid's lower class, typified by a saucy demeanor and colorful, distinctive dress. The term *chula* replaced it in the early nineteenth century. *Chulas* were usually employed as *cigarreras*—all were subsumed in an identifiable group of women rendered picturesque in fiction and *zarzuela*. Sergio Vallejo Fernández Cela writes that in the view of the Madrid middle classes during the last third of the nineteenth century, the tobacco workers were no longer the colorful, traditional types of thirty or forty years

earlier. They were, rather, a group of noisy rebellious women inhabiting the lower-class neighborhoods of the city. Despite their preindustrial mentality and absolute lack of class consciousness, he continues, they were by no means seen as the colorful personages depicted earlier by chroniclers of popular customs. They were now viewed simply as part of the Madrid working class (Fernández Cela, "Las *cigarreras* de la Fábrica Nacional de Tabaco," p. 147). That the middle class may have viewed the *cigarreras* as ordinary though unruly members of the working class as the result of real contact with them is one thing. How the press and popular literature continued to represent and manipulate them is another. Besides appearing often in the theater, a Madrid tobacco worker served as protagonist for the popular and prolific female novelist, Faustina Sáez de Melgar. Editor of the journal directed to women, *La Guirlanda*, she published *Rosa, la cigarrera* in 1872.

26. Nacida en humilde cuna,/ vive pobre, pero honrada,/ que en amar y ser amada/ cifra toda su fortuna./ No sabe lo que son penas,/ canta y baila sin cesar,/ y se mata a trabajar/ para cobrar en las quincenas/ unos perros indecentes,/ que apenas si dan abasto/ para sufragar el gasto/ y mantener sus parientes./ Ella reina de verdá,/ y su poder nadie alcanza;/ tiene por ley, la esperanza,/ por cetro, la caridá./ De su bondá certifico:/ llora, cuando ve llorar,/ y trata de consolar/ lo mismo al pobre que al rico./ Ella ampara al desgraciado/ y se queda sin comer,/ tan sólo por socorrer/ al que está necesitado./ Su corazón, de primera;/ su pecho, noble y hermoso;/ si la miman, generoso;/ si la faltan, de una fiera./ Ama a su patria querida/ con cariño verdadero;/ por ella da su dinero,/ sus hijos, y hasta su vida./ Al hombre jamás engaña/ y le da su corazón./ ¡Ahí tienes tú quiénes son/ las *cigarreras* de España!" (pp. 23–24).

27. Santiago Castillo, ed., "Industrias explotadas por el Estado: Fábricas de tabacos," *Reformas sociales: Información oral y escrita publicada de 1889 a 1893* (Madrid: Ministerio de Trabajo y Seguridad Social, 1985), pp. 33–38.

28. See page 286.

29. When we take to the streets, "impulsadas por la desesperación, por el hambre," (people say that) "somos muy malas, unas exigentes que nos quejamos de vicio."

7

Women on the Land: Household and Work in the Southern Countryside, 1875–1939

Timothy Rees

The history of rural women remains largely unwritten even though the overwhelming majority of Spanish women lived in the countryside in the half century preceding the Civil War. While a dramatic reevaluation of the rural economy and society has taken place, overturning many previous assumptions about rural life in Spain, the experiences of rural women have as yet received little specific analysis. Moreover, women's history as it has developed in Spain has tended to focus on women in industry and the cities. This is particularly evident in the key area of female work where historical studies of the activities of urban women proliferate while those of country women and their wider significance for rural society during the modern period are still relatively rare.[1]

Within this small body of studies on rural Spanish women, few have analyzed rural women's work within a broader social context. Many existing historical studies have tended to look at women's activities from a rather narrowly defined economic perspective that ignores the wider cultural, social, and political environments within which work took place, and within which its meaning was constructed.[2] Thus, studies in rural history have too readily accepted both sweeping generalizations and dubious assumptions about female and male roles. On one extreme is the assumption of a preindustrial "peasant household economy" with no real separation of home and workplace and often a minimal gender division of labor.[3] On the other extreme is acceptance of rigidly defined separate public and private spheres, reflecting a biologically determined distinction in work roles between unpaid female domestic labor and paid male labor in the formal economy.[4] In contrast, this chapter aims to show, in the context of a particular Spanish rural society, that no universal model of women's work can be applied to all countrywomen. While not pretending to offer an exhaustive treatment of an under-researched subject, it examines the contrast between the rhetoric of gender divisions of work and the more complex reality where distinctions between male and female spheres of responsibility were shifting and blurred. A rhetorical ideal did exist, which, taken at face value, suggests a strong separation into male and female spheres. However, while this gender ideology clearly influenced patterns of rural work, the reality was more complex; the accepted ideal is not an accurate description of the wide variety of tasks actually undertaken by rural women. Thus, historians can distinguish between a normative ideology and the different reality behind it.

In addition, definitions of what constitutes women's work are themselves problematical and must be treated with care, since the value and status of diverse activities varies with circumstances. The notion of work itself is a historical construct, and must be analyzed in a broader cultural, economic, and social context. Occupational identities, for instance, are clearly not neutral economic categories but are linked to the wider roles and positions of men and women in society. This complexity is especially true for rural societies where a focus on the commonly used criteria for defining work such as paid employment frequently ignores the unpaid or casual employment of women. There is also the associated danger of emphasizing the domestic role of women thereby reproducing rather than uncovering the gendered nature and significance of work.[5]

A further difficulty of Spanish agrarian history is a tremendous degree of regional differentiation, which makes meaningful generalization very difficult. This chapter focuses on the nature and meaning of work for rural women in the southern provinces of Andalusia and Extremadura. Although this region shared some common characteristics with other areas, it had its own distinctive economic and social features which set it apart, especially compared to the northern and eastern parts of Spain.[6] Social divisions in Andalusia and Extremadura have been particularly sharp, marked by great disparities of wealth and power, as well as a finely differentiated peasantry. A focus on southern Spain allows us to view women in many different situations in a rural society where the overwhelming majority of the population was supported by the land: through agricultural and livestock production, and to a certain extent from food processing to make olive oil, wine, hams, and cheeses.[7]

In the late nineteenth and early twentieth centuries, work in the south of Spain appeared very clearly and deeply gendered, reflecting the general cultural ideal of separate masculine and feminine spheres of work. At least in theory, activities were strictly divided according to gender: men's work lay in the formal economy outside of the home, while women worked in the domestic environment. The role of men was that of producers, providing for the household. Women were responsible for consumption, child rearing and the maintenance of that household. Such notions have often been seen by historians as characteristic of urban and industrial environments, but as this chapter will demonstrate, such ideas also prevailed in the countryside of southern Spain. The development of such a deeply gendered understanding of work in the south is difficult to trace. One would assume the influence of traditional Catholicism, and indeed the Church was a strong promoter of such values across the whole of Spain. However, in an area as strongly anticlerical as the south, the presence of these ideas of work suggests that it was not simply religious sanction that embedded them in society.[8]

Contemporary records relating to work contain evidence of this ideology of separate spheres. Most explicit are the census returns, which began listing occupations from 1900 onwards and declared that the number of women working in the primary sector of the economy was insignificant. The returns processed by the census authorities listed the overwhelming majority under the category of "family members undertaking domestic labor."[9] Consequently such records are of more value for the perceptions of male and female work they reveal rather than for their documentation of gender divisions of work that actually existed. As we shall see, women also undertook a great many tasks in the rural economy of the south, albeit very rarely on the same terms as men. Work boundaries were often blurred and the area of women's domestic activities was extended flexibly to encompass a range of activities that were, to all intents and purposes, within the formal economy. Indeed, such work was a necessity to most household economies and a vital contribution to the functioning of agriculture and husbandry in general. One important consequence of the disguised level of women's work in the southern rural economy is to bring into question the reliability of statistical approaches to labor supply and productivity. However, rather than abandon attempts at calculation as impossible, economic historians of Spanish agriculture have tended to either ignore the problem by basing their calculations on reported male employment alone, or they have resorted to various uncertain estimates of the level of the female workforce.[10]

Although the existence of prevailing ideas about work cannot be taken as a strict guide to reality, they remain significant as a prescription rather than a description, as ideology rather than a strict reflection of the actual pattern of gender work roles. As in any society, work was of great significance in defining power and status. By de-legitimizing or denying the role of women in extra-domestic work while correspondingly stressing their domestic duties, dominant ideas underpinned a rigid gender hierarchy and acted as a strong constraint on female participation in the public arena. Such ideas both reflected and powerfully shaped attitudes about women by outlining an ideal in which women had no occupational identity and took their status solely from men, as fathers, husbands, or brothers, and were subordinated to them in the public affairs of society.[11]

Women in the Rural Household: Marriage, Property and the Land

Within these constraints on female activity, women undertook a great variety of tasks, with their options determined primarily by the socioeconomic level of the household they inhabited. Contrary to what might be expected, differences in the nature of women's activities did not relate to variations in the basic composition of the household, which was relatively uniform and unchanging across the whole of society in southern Spain during the modern period. In common with central Spain, nuptuality was virtually universal for all sections of society. Marriage for both men and women came early and was accompanied almost simultaneously by household formation; this practice followed the prevailing system of neolocal residence of simple, nuclear families and was summed up in the popular refrain *casado quiere casa* (a married person wants a house).[12] In contrast, a long period of celibacy followed by marriage and households formed around stem families, which were characteristic of the north, were rare. The majority of households in the south were composed of parents and children, married couples without children, or widows/widowers with their children. Even the exceptions bore out the norm, in that they usually involved the addition of a single widowed parent to the nuclear family, though this situation was itself infrequent given that widows and widowers usually lived alone rather than move in with their married offspring.[13]

For the overwhelming majority of women of all social classes, the result of this pattern was a lifecycle that was marked by movement from one household to another. As children or spinsters they resided in the parental home, until they set up their own household with marriage. The acquisition of housing was relatively easy, in part because of a concentrated pattern of settlement in large agro-towns (*pueblos*) peculiar to the south: the *pueblo* was an essentially urban environment from which the population traveled out into the surrounding open countryside to work the land.[14] Families often owned or rented a number of houses, had a plot of land on the outskirts of the *pueblo* on which to build, or could divide an existing building to accommodate a newly-married couple. The *pueblo* was divided into neighborhoods (*barrios*) according to class and social status, so that different branches of the same family could often be found living in separate households that were physically close together. Movement between houses also occurred across the lifecycle as households grew in size when children were born and then diminished as grown children married and left home.

Within households, women usually found themselves under male control as men were considered to be the Household Head (*Cabeza de la Familia*), a position of authority given legal status in the Civil Code of 1889. In the parental home, whether they had reached the age of majority (twenty-three) or not, all offspring were subject to the authority of their father. Marriage meant something quite different for men and women: males were freed from patriarchal control but women exchanged fatherly supervision for that of their husband. The social status of the household, and hence that of the women within it, correspondingly derived from that of its male head. Thus women were in the constant, constraining embrace of a family home, unable to establish their own solitary households or to migrate alone (a rarity in the south anyway), until widowhood brought some release. Even then, the benefits were marginal as widows did not really gain the legal position or societal recognition as a Household Head.[15]

What specifically differentiated the nature of households, and the nature of female labor, was the amount of rural property they controlled: at the heart of society in the south, for both men and women, was the land. This is not to view the significance of land in a completely deterministic manner, but instead to recognize that it touched on virtually every aspect of country life. As David Sabean has commented in his study of the German village, Neckarhausen, "... property is not a relationship between people and things but one between people about things."[16] This maxim was equally true for southern Spain, where land was a vital element in the formation of rural households, all of which were reliant either directly or indirectly on agriculture and livestock. The amount of property under its control made an enormous difference to a household's economy and its patterns of work. This indicator was particularly striking for southern Spain where the distribution of land was extremely uneven in comparison to other regions, giving rise to a strong hierarchy of households, which resulted in a pyramidal, stratified society of classes rather than a relatively uniform community of peasants. Broadly speaking, three categories of household can be identified in terms of their property: there were wealthy elites which owned or rented large amounts of land, often held in the form of great estates (*latifundios*); then a stratum of small to medium sized farms, held either by ownership, tenancy or a sharecropping agreement; and finally, there was a majority that had access to little or no land at all.[17]

Women were intimately linked to the complex structures of household land because they could inherit property. The position of women as property holders improved in so far as the aristocratic entails (*mayorazgos*), designed to maintain the integrity of estates and favoring primogeniture, were abolished in 1836 and liberal private property rights became fully established by the last third of the nineteenth century.[18] The Castillian laws of partible inheritance were enshrined in the Civil Code of 1889; despite considerable regional variations throughout Spain, all heirs—regardless of gender—were guaranteed to receive an equal share of any legacy and to pass it on in a will. It was theoretically possible to divide the shares of an inheritance to offset land against other assets—for instance capital, urban property, houses, cash, jewelery—to maintain rural property intact in male hands, but there is little evidence that this actually happened in practice. It was more likely that the tendency to the fragmentation of holdings, particularly where the great estates of the landed elites were involved, was checked through joint ownership (*pro indiviso*) amongst sibling heirs, a system particularly prominent in the south of Spain. Alternatively, the entire estate was kept within the family through informal agreements that legally divided property but preserved its cultivation as a unit.[19]

Unfortunately, a detailed picture of the extent of female landownership across the whole of the south before the Civil War is difficult to draw, in that the records themselves either ignored gender, as is the case with the cadastral surveys, or historians have tended not to have analyzed them in terms of gender. The impression is certainly that women were well represented as owners, though the evidence decreases as the size of the property decreases. Among the ranks of small to medium proprietors, an unscientific trawl through the registers compiled for the *cadastre* begun in 1906 for the Extremaduran province of Badajoz suggests that a significant number of women possessed land, although it is impossible to tell if this was on equal terms to men.[20] We can gain a closer insight into the position of women as great landowners through the register of expropriatable property drawn up under the Second Republic for the purposes of land reform. Again there is no systematic study, province by province, but the register for Badajoz shows that among the one-hundred largest holdings, thirty-six were held by women alone and twelve in joint ownerships.[21]

The practice of partible inheritance itself reinforced the cultural norms of early nuptuality and the formation of households composed of simple families.[22] The property that women held played a key part in marriage negotiations, and hence in the household economy that resulted. Marriage became, in many respects, a businesslike affair in which both sides sought a partner of similar standing. Often the negotiations were between the male heads of the two families involved, with the views of the prospective bride and groom often ignored or only fleetingly consulted. At stake was not just the property that each party immediately possessed, but also the future prospects of inheritance. Especially at the upper levels of society this became something of an obsession and the landed elites, particularly the nobility, connected their property through careful intermarriage. In all sectors, other material considerations also weighed strongly in the marriage balance. Access to a good tenancy or sharecrop most obviously favored the future well-being of the prospective household by giving it control of land. Similarly, for those with no land or the means to gain it, a reputation as an industrious individual from a respected family was a good asset. The end result of like roughly marrying like was to perpetuate the structure of households and landholding over time.[23]

While women could possess and transmit property, this essentially passive right was the extent of their control over land. The means by which women were excluded from exercising full property rights varied according to marital status. Marriage brought a legally enforced complete loss of rights. Until 1931, when the law was changed by the Republic, the Civil Code recognized the preexisting practice in the south whereby wives, though retaining ownership, passed all control over their property and any income derived from it to their husbands. This included the need to seek a husband's permission to buy, sell, and mortgage property or to accept an inheritance. Spinsters under the age of maturity were in a similar position to wives except that their property was administered by a male parent, relative, or guardian. However, at maturity spinsters were free to enter into contracts and gain inheritances in their own right, although with the practice of early nuptuality, this represented only a tiny proportion of women. Of greater significance, in terms of their number, the women who had reached the coveted position of widowhood enjoyed these same rights. This did not mean, though, that widows or spinsters were able to take full advantage of their rights and actually engage in the management of their property. They were still expected to put it into male hands, passing it to a son or male relative if possible. If this were not an option they would employ a male manager or agent as administrator to rent out their land. Absentee landlords were a marked feature of the south anyway, and unmarried or widowed women merely added to the list of rentiers. Their ranks ranged from wealthy dowagers, owning property across Spain and living in Madrid or Seville, to widows with a field or two, existing in genteel poverty in small *pueblos*.[24]

A consequence of this system of marriage and household formation was that while women owned and inherited property, they remained largely dispossessed of direct power within the rural economy. It was a legally recognized norm in the south that men carried out the most prestigious and influential forms of work; they directed the day-to-day operations of rural production at all levels, made decisions about land use and cultivation, and controlled the labor of others. This male predominance was reflected, for instance, in the landowners' and employers' associations which began to appear in the south at the end of the nineteenth century; these associations asserted the rights of property holders and were dominated by men. The practical effects of such male control were evident in the systems of tenancy where, though the land involved might belong to a female owner, the agreement was decided between a male administrator and a male tenant, thus excluding from this form of landholding even those women who theoretically had the legal right to make contracts. Provision of credit was also a transaction limited to solely male borrowers and lenders. Likewise, all paid positions of authority within the economic system, including estate managers, foremen, and agricultural engineers, were held by men. Furthermore, there was no general expectation in southern society that decisions about household economies should be shared between men and women, as was the case in other parts of Spain. Therefore, the degree to which women could wield economic influence depended on the nature of their relations with men, as fathers, husbands, or guardians. Certainly, public female involvement in economic matters was not condoned by men; rather the opposite pertained in that women who exhibited signs of independence—or men who were perceived to be weak—were denigrated in the south. This did not mean, of course, that men and women could not be partners in household economic affairs, but rather it depended entirely on their private and personal relationship.[25]

Women and the Household Economy

If custom and law distanced women from decisions about the land and household economy, very few were completely separated from rural production. On the upper end of the socioeconomic spectrum, only women in the landed elites came from backgrounds wealthy enough that they took no part in the productive economy. It was a sign of their high status that women in landowning, large tenant, and estate manager households—like their urban counterparts—actually fulfilled the domestic feminine ideal. Indeed, women from great landed families could even live an apparently leisured existence—sometimes in Seville or Madrid, possibly never seeing the lands that supported them.[26] In contrast, sheer economic necessity required the overwhelming majority of country women to engage in agricultural work in order to sustain their households. While women were excluded from particular tasks, they were not all excluded from the same ones, nor were rigid gender divisions of labor universally applied, in the south. In particular, biosocial factors such as the physical nature of work—whether it was heavy or light, required short or sustained effort—seldom made any difference. Nor was the position of a woman in her life cycle necessarily a fixed determinant of the work she could do, though inevitably it was a limiting factor. Instead, the range of tasks that women might undertake in the south was both wide and altered to some extent over time.

Inevitably, of greatest importance in determining the allocation of tasks between women and men was the degree to which households could support themselves from their own land or were thrust into the labor market. Control of property, or the lack of it, shaped the specific work demands and productive potential of the household in a wider rural economy that was changing in terms of the crops and livestock produced and the means used to cultivate and rear them.

By the late nineteenth century, male-directed, predominantly market-oriented southern agriculture was under increasing pressure to support a growing and more urbanized population. While there is some disagreement about the extent and pace of change in the region, between the 1890s and 1930s output grew in all the southern provinces, with those of western Andalusia leading the rest. Although this growth did not involve any dramatic shift away from staple products—cereals, olives and vines were universal, with livestock farming (mainly pigs and sheep) in some areas of Andalusia and large parts of Extremadura—increasing amounts of land were put to use and production was intensified. Fallows were reduced and increasingly sown with legumes, and winter vegetables were grown, in new rotation systems. Pasture, particularly in Extremadura, was ploughed and larger herds of livestock had their fodder supplemented by oats. Oxen were replaced by more efficient mules in order to pull more effective ploughs. The use of artificial fertilizers grew and there were campaigns to eliminate pests such as locusts.

In other important respects, however, change was more limited. Little advance was made in irrigation and the south remained a dry farming region with production limited by a low seasonal rainfall. Most significantly, though mechanization made some progress in the 1920s and 1930s, agriculture remained reliant on manual labor and handtool technology. Increases in output were achieved within an essentially traditional, labor intensive rural economy.[27] Accordingly, all rural households that worked the land participated in these changes and were affected by them, though in different ways and with different consequences for gender work roles.

Undoubtedly, small- to medium-sized family farms, or holdings worked by a group of related households, made the heaviest and most constant demands on women. Either owned, rented, or sharecropped, such farms represented only a relatively low proportion of the total land in the south though they tended to be clustered in particular districts. We know little about the specifics of their operation in comparison to similar family farms in other parts of Spain. However, it is clear that subsistence agriculture was not a realistic option by the end of the nineteenth century as market pressures to produce cash crops mounted—particularly through contractual obligations to do so made on tenants and sharecroppers by landlords. In order to generate sufficient output for survival, all family members including children were needed to provide unpaid labor in every phase of the agricultural cycle. With little capital for expensive inputs such as fertilizers or machinery, this form of peasant production served to maximize the use of scarce family labor to increase household income. Women had to be prepared therefore to carry out virtually any task, and did so.[28]

The sexes had to combine their efforts carefully in such a delicate household economy, substituting for one another in agricultural labor where necessary but with men undertaking the tasks seen as most important. Either or both sexes routinely performed a wide range of tasks: weeding, breaking clods, preparing seed beds, sowing, threshing, pruning vines, harvesting grapes, tending, picking and pressing olives, feeding and caring for livestock. Ploughing, in contrast, was regarded as the exclusive domain of men. For some other tasks complementarity was important, with men and women taking particular roles in teamwork. This was clearly evident in cereal harvesting, the highpoint of the agricultural year, where men usually cut the crop with the sickle while women and children followed behind collecting and stacking sheaves. During the crucial harvest season, families often cooperated—whether they normally worked the same farm or not—or a household with a larger holding might hire in a few male laborers to add to their efforts.

Where holdings were inadequate to support a household entirely, incomes had to be supplemented from the labor market. This could have important consequences for gendered work roles, as it was normally men who worked away from the family farm. Harvesting often became an all-female and younger-child affair as men joined the local market for hired labor in order to supplement family income with paid wages.[29] In the case of the Extremaduran *yunteros* and Andalusian *peletrines*—sharecroppers with only small parcels of land who owned a pair of draught animals and ploughs—ploughing was a source of paid income that took away men from their own plots of land. The burdens of cultivation then fell even more strongly on female members of the household.[30]

It was most probable that the amount of agricultural work for women and men was further increased on family farms in the south, as elsewhere in Spain, by the effort to raise incomes. Price fluctuations, particularly those following the depression that ended in the late 1890s and the period during and after the First World War, along with high rents, created the need for greater output in order to maintain a living income. Households responded by working harder to grow more crops and keep more animals. Improvements such as clearing land for the plough and using more intensive rotations could only be made through increased manual labor.[31] Many households had no choice but to work harder, as their landlords stipulated in their contracts what improvements they should make, and even which crops they should grow. For instance, during the 1920s *yunteros* in Extremadura, who previously had been given agricultural land to farm, faced a form of proletarianization when they were forced to clear plots merely for later cultivation. Another source of work was the introduction of new, more profitable, crops which were often labor intensive. A good example is vines, adopted by small farmers from the beginning of the twentieth century in favorable areas such as the Tierra de Barros district of

Badajoz.[32] With the incentive for men to seek paid employment away from their own holdings also growing, it is likely that women made a disproportionately greater contribution to the expanding workload needed to run a successful family farm.

The situation of women in the majority of households without land, and thus reliant on the labor market for a livelihood, could not have been more different. Rather than facing a constant surfeit of paid work, laboring families suffered from a lack of opportunities to work during most of the year. The chronic labor surplus, maintained by low migration in the south, created fierce competition for seasonal work on the estates of the landed elites, the main source of paid employment. This rationing of the amount of paid work available gave rise to a fairly rigid gender division of labor among the landless. Unlike family farmers, there were in effect two very different patterns of agricultural work—male and female—with very little substitution between the sexes.

Men's work was centered on what were perceived to be the most important tasks in the production cycles of estates. The small core of fixed positions in the estate workforce was held exclusively by men. These were the best paid and most secure jobs, usually involving specialized skills and the supervision of others. They varied according to the main products of the estate, which differed from region to region, but included carters, grooms, carpenters, blacksmiths, foremen, shepherds, charcoal makers, and tenders of vines and olives. Not surprisingly, when limited mechanization began on cereal estates after the First World War, the new posts as mechanics and operators also went to men. The remaining majority of the available male workforce was locked into a seasonal working year, enduring long periods of unemployment interspersed with relatively short bursts of activity when estates needed their labor for particular tasks. Again this varied according to the products of the estate, but the main sets of seasonal tasks marking the male year were ploughing, sowing, harvesting, and preparing fallows. In the low season, there was also intermittent work clearing land for the plough, digging ditches, mending roads, and repairing fences.[33]

Female tasks on estates were regarded as merely ancillary, though they were actually of vital importance to production. Women followed a cycle of very infrequent demand for their paid labor, working on average one third the number of days as men.[34] This differentiation became so well established as to be ritualized, with the sexes congregating separately in *pueblo* squares to await the foremen who hired labor for the estates. Thus, custom reinforced competition for work within the sexes, rather than between the sexes. When women were hired, widows with dependent children seem to have received preference while older women were largely excluded; otherwise the whim of the foremen held sway. The only tasks for which women were exclusively recruited were the monotonous and routine jobs of weeding, breaking clods, and cleaning olives and grapes. Long hours of gang labor (*enganche*) under the direction of a foreman and payment by piece work (*destajo*) was the norm for women, as it was for men. Children often accompanied the female gangs to the fields and worked alongside them, or were cared for by friends or relatives while their mothers worked.[35]

The only period when women and men worked together was during the short harvest seasons. These were the sole times when the demand for labor on estates was greater than supply and all available hands were needed. In many districts, employers took on additional male migrant Galician and Portuguese laborers to cover shortfalls and to undercut the wages paid to locals. Sometimes women were prevented from working, until all the available men were employed.[36] Otherwise, whole households, including children, were often recruited as units and worked as harvesting teams, in much the same way as family farmers. The different crops gave rise to different divisions of labor. When picking tobacco and harvesting beets, men and women worked alongside one another. In those areas of the south where they were grown, grapes and olives were picked by men and transported by women and children. Men cut cereals—the main crop in the majority of provinces—and women and children collected and stacked it, while threshing and winnowing were joint activities.[37] Harvests were the crucial points in the working year for the household economies of landless families, when they stood to gain the greater part of their annual income. This was when the bargaining power of labor, normally very low due to intense competition, was at its height.

Laboring households paid the price of rural economic growth, with real wages improving only very marginally in the fifty years before the Civil War.[38] Yet rather than seize the opportunity presented by the harvest to maximize family income, economic rationality was apparently thrown to the winds where women's wages were concerned. Even though women worked the same long hours from sunrise to sunset, and did equally backbreaking, if different, labor to men, they consistently received only one half to two-thirds of male pay. This was a strategy by employers to drive down costs. More interestingly, it showed that male laborers effectively connived with employers to pay women less. Instead of insisting on equal, if not greater, pay for women, male laborers themselves accepted that a differential should be maintained—following a widespread European tradition of the family wage. During negotiations and strikes over wages and conditions, the male-dominated Anarchist and Socialist rural trade unions, which developed in the south from the end of the nineteenth century onwards, always demanded lower payment for women workers. Even during the period of the Second Republic and the Civil War (1931–1939), when rural workers' movements were strengthened and the involvement of women increased, there was no attack on wage differentials.[39]

By maintaining this position, rural trade unions weakened their temporary hold on the labor market and undermined the very advantages that they sought for laboring households. Male laborers apparently could not even envisage the economic advantage of equal wages if it meant risking the recognition that women might be their equals.[40] Not, of course, that such crude calculations really needed to be articulated: it was simply taken as a fact of life that women's work was not as valuable as that of men.

A similar understanding, no doubt, helps to explain why employers did not take advantage of lower female wages to substitute them for men, as they might have done in the changing circumstances of rural production. To have done so would have run counter to the authority of men as heads of households and to the control that they ultimately exercised over women's activities. In this sense, women did the work that they were allowed or directed to do. The opportunities for women in laboring households to engage in agricultural work at best remained constant from the late nineteenth century onwards. Greater employment for women could only occur if men were not available, but population growth ensured that there was always more than sufficient male labor. In this situation, agricultural innovations, such as new rotations, planting winter crops and increased use of machinery, really changed only the nature of the tasks undertaken by men. Growing adaptation to market production on southern estates during the nineteenth century served to eliminate work opportunities for women. The reduction of common land and commons rights certainly removed the possibilities for activities such as collecting firewood and acorns for sale that women carried out. Probably, the concentration on a few products increased the amount of specialist work done by men, and simultaneously channeled women into a lesser number of more routine tasks.[41] Yet even if work opportunities were more restricted and gendered work boundaries remained rigid, women always played an essential role in the household economy.

Given that women's land and labor made such a vital and visible contribution to the rural economy, the extent to which it was ignored in terms of occupational identities is striking. Enquiries into records of landownership (such as the cadastral surveys and registers of expropriatable property, and surveys of the rural labor force undertaken by provincial and local authorities) revealed that women owned land and undertook agricultural work. Yet when the censuses specifically asked whether the varied titles used in southern society to describe economic and work identities (large landowner, smallholder, tenant, sharecropper, day laborer, etc.) were applied to women, the answer was in the negative. The rationale behind this seeming contradiction was that domestic activities were seen as women's essential area of work regardless of the range of activities women actually undertook outside the home. Female contributions to the household economy were seen in the context of this role as homemaker, and work outside the home, whether paid or unpaid, was seen as an extension of the domestic sphere. In short, men had an occupational identity while women's work in agriculture and husbandry was described as *ayuda familiar* (family help).[42]

This gender divide was reinforced as management of the home and domestic tasks were undertaken exclusively by women and female children—one instance where the spheres were truly separate. Moreover, the physical environment, with the concentration of housing into *pueblos*, meant that a clear physical distancing of home and the land always existed. As with work outside the home, the socioeconomic status of the household clearly made a difference to the exact nature of women's domestic activities. Washing clothes, cleaning, cooking, and child rearing were the basic minimum activities for most women. Many had other tasks as well, including maintaining a family vegetable plot, rearing chickens, or even a pig for household consumption, and gleaning from the fields after harvests. There was also cooperation between women from different, but related, households in such chores as child minding and cooking.

Domestic activities could themselves become the basis for paid work for rural women from laboring households. Sewing, making simple clothes, curing hams, and making cheeses for local sale were the only home-based paid work. By the nineteenth century, the once thriving cottage industries of weaving and spinning had largely disappeared in the south.[43] Other possible income earning activities involved undertaking quasi-domestic tasks outside the family home; such employment was confined mainly to young spinsters and older women—particularly widows—who could be spared or were unable to do agricultural work. One example was in the modern slaughterhouses that were built, particularly in Extremadura, in the 1920s to improve livestock production, which employed a few hundred young single women—not in killing animals but to butcher the carcasses.[44] Other kinds of food processing industries—brewing and distilling, olive pressing, milling flour, and baking bread—were dominated by men.

The identification of women with the private sphere of domestic tasks and men with the public sphere of work in the formal economy was clearly an ideological simplification of a far more complex reality. This picture of the nature and meaning of work was not a situation that was unique to southern Spain; it can be found in many other societies both rural and urban. However, it was deeply rooted in a society in which women's status always derived from that of men. This affected the whole nature of property relations, patterns of marriage, household formation and settlement, and the overall development of the rural economy. Consequently, many of the normally consulted sources on work have to be read more as reflections of this ideology than as neutral records of the real nature of women's activities. We can see that work in rural Spain, especially in the south, has often been misinterpreted because the varied contributions of women in both agricultural and livestock production, as well as in the home, have been disguised. In fact, in a variety of ways not encompassed by any single model, women made vital contributions to household incomes and to rural production as a whole which were simply not given the same status as the work of men in the formal economy. By recognizing and exploring this contradiction between the rhetoric of separate spheres and the reality of rural work in southern society, we are able to throw new light on the lives of rural women—a largely forgotten part of the female population in the historiography of modern Spain.

Notes

1. This gap is apparent in the interesting survey and commentary provided by Mary Nash, "Two Decades of Women's History in Spain: A Reappraisal" in Karen Offen, Ruth Roach Pierson, and Jane Rendall, eds., *Writing Women's History: International Perspectives* (Bloomington IN: Indiana University Press, 1991), especially pages 395–396. There are no specific books devoted to women's work in the countryside and very few articles. María Antonia Ferrer i Bosch and María Jesús Muiños Villaverde, "Economía y mujer campesina en la Cataluña del siglo XIX: Lectura de los protocolos notariales" and María Teresa Chicote Serna, "El trabajo de las mujeres en el ámbito rural de la provincia de Madrid, 1930–1945," in Seminario de Estudios de la Mujer, *El trabajo de las mujeres: Siglos XVI-XX* (Madrid: Universidad Autónoma de Madrid, 1987). More general books on women's work and rural labor do consider the subject, but the coverage on rural women is brief. See for instance Rosa María Capel Martínez, *El trabajo y la educación de la mujer en España (1900–1930)* 2d. ed. (Madrid: Ministerio de Cultura, Instituto de la Mujer, 1986), pp. 108–114; María Gloria Nuñez Pérez, *Trabajadoras en la Segunda República: Un estudio sobre la actividad económica extradoméstica (1931–1936)* (Madrid: Ministerio de Trabajo y Seguridad Social, 1989), pp. 331–338; and José Rodríguez Labandeira, *El trabajo rural en España (1876–1936)* (Madrid: Ministerio de Agricultura, Pesca y Alimentación, 1991). It would be a gross exaggeration to suggest that this subject has received really serious attention for other European countries in the modern period, though there has still been more work than for Spain. For instance in the introduction to a recent special issue on women and rural history in the journal *Rural History: Economy, Society, Culture* 5, no. 2 (1994): 123, the editors state that the subject ". . . represents, especially for agricultural history, an enormous breadth of historical experience that has been sadly neglected over many decades." For an idea of recent developments see Richard L. Randolph, "The European Family and Economy: Central Themes and Issues" in *Journal of Family History* 17, no. 2 (1992): 119-138.

2. There are no real equivalents, for instance, to carefully nuanced works such as Martine Segalen, *Love and Power in the Peasant Family: Rural France in the Nineteenth Century* (Oxford: Basil Blackwell, 1983) and David Sabean, *Property, Production and Family in Neckarhausen, 1700–1870* (Cambridge: Cambridge University Press, 1990).

3. The most influential peasant family model of this kind has clearly been that of the Russian sociologist Chayanov. Most variants emphasize the idea of a partnership in which men and women carry out roughly the same economic tasks or where they undertake complementary tasks together, though with women usually exclusively responsible for child rearing, cooking and cleaning. For a critique of this idea see the comments of S. Whatmore, "From Women's Roles to Gender Relations: Developing Perspectives in the Analysis of Farm Women," *Sociologia Ruralis* 28, no. 4 (1988): 239–247, on the case of the English farm. Rose Glickman, "Peasant Women and Their Work" in Beatrice Farnsworth and Lynne Viola, eds., *Russian Peasant Women* (New York: Oxford University Press, 1992), pp. 54–72, also offers a rather different treatment of Russia from that supposed by Chayanov.

4. Of course such a gender division of society has not been seen as exclusively found in the countryside, far from it. In fact the development of separate spheres and a cult of domesticity is usually associated with industrialization and is, therefore, often assumed to be a purely urban phenomenon. A recent collection of articles that interestingly discusses the concept, Dorothy O. Helly and Susan M. Reverby, eds., *Gendered Domains: Rethinking Public and Private in Women's History* (Ithaca, NY: Cornell University Press, 1992), is fairly typical in its lack of coverage of rural society. For a rural example see Donna Gabaccia, "In the Shadows of the Periphery: Italian Women in the Nineteenth Century," in Marilyn J. Boxer and Jean Quataert, eds., *Connecting Spheres: Women in the Western World from 1500 to the Present* (New York: Oxford University Press, 1987), pp. 166–176.

5. For a recent general discussion of ideas about work see the introduction to Patrick Joyce, ed., *The Historical Meanings of Work* (Cambridge: Cambridge University Press, 1987). More specifically focussed on the notion of women's work, largely in a British context, is Elizabeth Roberts, *Women's Work 1840–1940* (Hampshire, MA: Macmillan, 1988), pp. 11–28. One criticism of the pioneering study by Louise A. Tilly and Joan W. Scott, *Women, Work and Family* (New York: Holt, Rinehart and Winston, 1987) is its overly narrow definition of women's work. For a stimulating discussion of women's work in both its agricultural and industrial contexts see Pat Hudson and W.R. Lee, "Women's Work and the Family Economy in Historical Perspective" in Hudson and Lee, eds., *Women's Work and the Family Economy in Historical Perspective* (Manchester, UK: Manchester University Press, 1990), pp. 2–47. Also of interest is Jacques Revel, "Masculine and Feminine: The Historical Use of Sexual Roles" in Michelle Perrot, ed., *Writing Women's History* trans. (Oxford: Basil Blackwell, 1992), pp. 90–105, which looks particularly at rural society.

6. The most notable feature of the rural economy and society of the south was the existence of great estates (*latifundios*), while the north and center was characterized by smallholdings (*minifundios*). In reality a mixture of these landholding types existed in all regions of Spain, but with a predominance of one type over another. Thus in the south there were also smallholdings that existed alongside the estates. See José Sánchez Jiménez, "Pequeña y gran propiedad a finales del siglo XIX: Andalusia" in *Cuadernos de Historia Contemporánea* 16 (1994): 11–34, for an excellent explanation.

7. The percentage of the active population in agriculture across the ten provinces of Andalusia and Extremadura varied from 66.7 to 82.3 in 1900 to 49.0 to 65.8 in 1930 according to the censuses. These figures are too low, being based largely on economically active males. As we shall see below, the level of female activity was largely unrecorded (see note 9). See *Censo de la Población de España* 1900 and 1930. Rural society in the south also contained a rich mixture of artisans, professionals, urban workers, public officials, shopkeepers, schoolteachers, and religious. That part of society that found a livelihood from other sources, themselves usually dependant directly or indirectly on the rural economy, or which lived in the cities of the south—particularly Córdoba, Granada, Málaga, and Seville—lies outside of the scope of this article.

8. The anthropological study, undertaken in the late 1940s and early 1950s, by Julián Pitt-Rivers, *The People of the Sierra* 2d. ed. (Chicago, IL: University of Chicago, 1971) well illustrates these ideas in the south. See also Nuñez Pérez, *Trabajadoras en la Segunda República*, pp. 114, 465–473; Capel Martínez, *El trabajo*, pp. 51–56; Frances Lannon, *Privilege, Persecution and Prophecy: The Catholic Church in Spain, 1875– 1975* (Oxford: Clarendon Press, 1987), pp. 53–58. These notions were clearly very widespread in Spain, as elsewhere. An example of an exception in León province (a Catholic region), where the equality of women in rural work was emphasized despite the teachings of the Church, is provided in the marvellous study by Ruth Behar, *Santa María del Monte: The Presence of the Past in a Spanish Village* (Princeton, NJ: Princeton University Press, 1986), pp. 15–16 and passim.

9. There were no significant changes in the nature of rural society in the quarter century preceding 1900 to suggest that anything would have been any different then if the censuses had asked for occupations to be listed. The figures given for women occupied in agriculture and husbandry for the ten provinces were extraordinarily meager. The totals provided in the *Censo de la Población de España* 1900, 1910, 1920, and 1930 were 28,791, 2425, 4681, and 3399 at a time when the female population, of all ages, rose from roughly 2.2 million to 2.9 million. The variations in the figures give some indication of the erratic definitions that were used as well. For some insightful comment see Nuñez Pérez, *Trabajadoras en la Segunda República*, pp. 111–112, 120–145. In comparison the northern provinces, particularly Galicia and Asturias showed large numbers of women occupied in agriculture—indicating both very different attitudes and reflecting the important role that women took in dairy farming.

10. The difficulties of calculating labor productivity in the absence of adequate estimates of the female labor force are commented on in James Simpson, *Spanish Agriculture: The Long Siesta, 1765–1965* (Cambridge: Cambridge University Press, 1995), pp. 27, 52. A useful comparison is provided by Edward Higgs, "Occupational Censuses and the Agricultural Workforce in Victorian England and Wales," *Economic History Review* 48, no. 4 (November 1995). The broader question of whether such figures are reliable for any European country because of this general failure to report accurately female employment is commented upon in Patrick O'Brien and Leandro Prados de la Escosura, "Agricultural Productivity and European Industrialization, 1890–1980" *Economic History Review* 45, no. 3 (August, 1992): 516.

11. See Nuñez Pérez, *Trabajadoras en la Segunda República*, pp. 447–465, for an overview.

12. Quoted in Enrique Casas Gaspar, *Costumbres españolas de nacimiento, noviazgo, casamiento y muerte* (Madrid: Editorial Escelicer, 1947), p. 286. In the 1970s David G. Gilmore, *The People of the Plain: Class and Community in Lower Andalusia* (New York: Columbia University Press, 1980), pp. 155–185 and 165–166, found the same phrase in use and the same pattern of household formation. Southern society did not really distinguish between the household and the house itself, using the same word (*casa*) for both. On marriage see M. Livi Bacci, "Fertility and Nuptuality Changes in Spain from the Late Eighteenth to the Early Twentieth Century," *Population Studies* 22, no. 2 (1968): 222–224, which suggests that marriage rates particularly increased in the south to the extent that very few women remained unmarried. This pattern of marriage seems to have been very long lasting, according to David Sven Rehr, "Marriage Patterns in Spain, 1887-1930," *Journal of Family History* 16, no. 1 (1991): 7–30, which dates it back to at least the seventeenth century.

13. Some extension is noted in Isidoro Moreno Navarro, *Propiedad, clases sociales y hermandades en la Baja Andalucía* (Madrid: Siglo Veintiuno, 1972), p. 144. For similar examples from central Spain see David Sven Rehr, "Household and Family on the Castilian Meseta: The Province of Cuenca from 1750 to 1970," *Journal of Family History* 13, no. 1 (1988): 91–110, and José Miguel Martínez Carrión, "Peasant Household Formation and the Organization of Rural Labor in the Valley of Segura during the Nineteenth Century," *Journal of Family History* 13, no. 1 (1988): 91–110. A survey of regional differences is provided by Willian A. Douglas, "Iberian Family History," *Journal of Family History* 13, no. 1 (1988): 1–12.

14. Again this was very unlike northern Spain where settlement was dispersed into farmsteads, called *baserría* in the Basque Country and *casería* in Asturias and León.

15. Pitt-Rivers, *People of the Sierra*, p. 99. As a children's song from southern Spain states, women were categorized into five different states of being: child (*niña*), spinster (*soltera*), married (*casada*), widow (*viuda*) or nun (*monja*).

16. Sabean, *Property, Production and Family*, p. 18.

17. Figures for the different categories over time are notoriously difficult to calculate with precision given the limitations of the censuses and property records. This is particularly so in the case of large tenant farmers, and for family farmers whose existence has often been overshadowed by interest in the great estates. There was also considerable variation between the proportions of each type of holding to be found in different areas of the south. Edward Malefakis, *Agrarian Reform and Peasant Revolution in Spain* (New Haven, CT: Yale University Press, 1970), pp. 65–130, remains probably the best introduction. See also a study of the contemporary situation which offers some historical insights: M. García Fernando, "El trabajo de la mujer en los sistemas agrarios españoles," *El Campo* 107 (1988).

18. See J.P. Cooper, "Patterns of Inheritance and Settlement by Great Landowners from the Fifteenth to the Eighteenth Centuries" in Jack Goody, et al., eds., *Family and Inheritance: Rural Society in Western Europe, 1200–1800* (Cambridge: Cambridge University Press, 1976), pp. 233–253. On the liberal revolution in rural property see A.M. Bernal, *La lucha por la tierra en la crisis del antiguo régimen* (Madrid: Taurus, 1979), pp. 63–69, 97–123, for Andalusia and Fernando Sánchez Marroyo, *El proceso de formación du una clase dirigente: La oligarquía agraria en Extremadura a mediados del siglo XIX* (Cáceres, Spain: Universidad de Extremadura, 1991), pp. 44–48, on the end of *mayorazgo* and dissolution of the seigneurial regime in Badajoz.

19. See Julián Pitt-Rivers, ed., *Mediterranean Countrymen: Essays in the Social Anthropology of the Mediterranean* (Paris: Mouton, 1963), pp. 22–23.

20. The registers are available in the Archivo de la Delegación del Ministerio de Hacienda de Badajoz. The names of the owners of individual consolidated holdings are handwritten. Female names seem to occur regularly.

21. See the "Registro de Propiedad Expropriable del Instituto de Reforma Agraria, Provincia de Badajoz, 1933," Archivo del Instituto de Reforma y Desarrollo Agrario. See also Fernando Sánchez Marroyo, *La propiedad de la tierra en la provincia de Cáceres en los siglos XIX y XX* (Mérida: Asamblea de Extremadura, 1993), pp. 361–443, on the great landowners of Cáceres.

22. The rationale for this is neatly explained in Rehr, "Household and Family," pp. 68–69, though he uses an example from central Spain. See also, Sabean, *Property, Production and Family*, pp. 15–17, for some additional ideas on the subject.

23. Malefakis, *Agrarian Reform*, pp. 75–77, gives an example of elite intermarriage from Badajoz. The links between marriage and landholding are explored in Fernando Sánchez Marroyo, "La mujer como instrumento de perpetuación patrimonial," *Norba* 8–9 (1989): 207–213. On the impact of inheritance for Cáceres see Sánchez Marroyo, *La propiedad de la tierra*, pp. 320–330. Martínez Carrión, "Peasant Household Formation," pp. 97–98, gives a similar description for Murcia.

24. On absenteeism see Malefakis, *Agrarian Reform*, pp. 82–90. With current evidence it is impossible to know the degree to which women were able to exercise real power behind the scenes, using their male representatives as an acceptable public face.

25. The extent to which women could exercise some authority over economic decisions in the south is very hard to gauge. Some idea of the possibilities can perhaps be gained from other examples. For instance Behar (*Santa María del Monte*, pp. 116–117) suggests an almost equal partnership prevailed in León. An interesting modern study for Aragón suggests that women have only some say in decisions affecting family income. Sara Zapatero Molinero and Rafael Jiménez Majias, *La mujer en la explotación agraria familiar: Estudio de una zona aragonesa* (Zaragoza, Spain: I.N.I.A.-C.R.I.D.A., 1980).

26. The degree to which they were actually leisured needs some qualification in that they probably took an active role in running the household and were frequently involved in charitable work through the Catholic Church. Unfortunately, we know very little about this for Spain. Two excellent comparative discussions are to be found in Leonore Davidoff and Catherine Hall, *Family Fortunes: Men and Women of the English Middle Class, 1780–1850* (London: Hutchinson, 1987), and Sibylle Meyer, "The Tiresome Work of Conspicuous Leisure: On the Domestic Duties of the Wives of Civil Servants in the German Empire (1871–1918)," in Boxer and Quataert, eds., *Connecting Spheres*.

27. The literature on the rural economy is becoming fairly extensive. For an excellent recent overview of developments and debates see Simpson, *Spanish Agriculture: The Long Siesta.* Also relevant are Grupo de Estudios de Historia Rural, "Crisis y cambio en el sector agrario: Andalucía y Extremadura, 1875–1936" in Ramón Garrabou, ed., *La crisis agraria de fines del siglo XIX* (Barcelona: Editorial Crítica, 1988), pp. 161–179; Santiago Zapata Blanco, *La producción agraria de Extremadura y Andalucía Occidental, 1875–1935* 2 vols. (Madrid: Universidad Complutense de Madrid, 1986); James Simpson, "Spanish Agricultural Production and Productivity, 1890–1936," Universidad Carlos III de Madrid, *Working Papers* (Madrid, 1993), and "La elección de técnica en el cultivo triguero y el atraso de la agricultura española a finales del siglo XIX," *Revista de Historia Económica* 2 (1987): 271–299.

28. Antonio M. Calero Amor, *Historia del movimiento obrero en Granada (1909–1923)* (Madrid: Editorial Tecnos, 1973), pp. 46–47; "Share Tenancy in Spain," *International Review of Agricultural Economics* 1 (1923): 19–36; J. Martínez Alier, *Labourers and Landowners in Southern Spain* (Totowa, NJ: Rowman and Littlefield, 1971), pp. 249–254.

29. See Malefakis, *Agrarian Reform*, p. 118, on the effects of size of holding.

30. See Malefakis, *Agrarian Reform*, pp. 126–129; Alberto Merino de Torres, *El obrero del campo: Estudio social* (Badajoz, Spain: Imprenta de V. Rodríguez, 1920), pp. 17–18.

31. On rents in Badajoz see Eduardo Cerro, "Algunas datos sobre la vida en la provincia," *Revista del Centro de Estudios Extremeños* 2 (1927): 153–55. Simpson, "Spanish Agricultural Production," p. 14, offers an explanation for the northern and Mediterranean regions equally applicable to the south.

32. Malefakis, *Agrarian Reform*, p. 129; Manuel Rubio Díaz and Silvestre Gómez Zafra, *Almendralejo, 1930–1941: Doce años intensos* (Los Santos de Maimona, Spain: Autor Editorial, 1987), 1–3.

33. See Rodríguez Labandeira, *El trabajo rural*, pp. 151–162.

34. Ibid., p. 296; Martínez Alier, *Labourers and Landowners*, p. 87.

35. José Antonio Alarcón Caballero, *El movimiento obrero en Granada en la Segunda República, (1931–1936)* (Granada: Diputación Provincial de Granada, 1990),

pp. 76–78; Rodríguez Labandeira, *El trabajo rural*, p. 46; Nuñez Pérez, *Trabajadoras en la Segunda República*, pp. 225–226; Pitt-Rivers, *People of the Sierra*, p. 86. Manuel Pérez Yruela, *La conflictividad campesina en la provincia de Córdoba, 1931–1936* (Madrid: Servicios Publicaciones Agrarias, D.L., 1979), p. 417, reproduces a harvest agreement allowing women to stop work to breast-feed young children.

36. Nuñez Pérez, *Trabajadoras en la Segunda República*, p. 225.

37. See Merino de Torres, *El obrero del campo*; Nuñez Pérez, *Trabajadoras en la Segunda República*, pp. 332–333; Alarcón Caballero, *El movimiento obrero en Granada*, pp. 76–78.

38. James Simpson, "Technical Change, Labor Absorption and Living Standards in Rural Andalusia, 1886–1936," *Agricultural History* 66, no. 3 (1992): 15–16.

39. The absence of rural women in the labor movement in the south is made clear in Capel Martínez, *El trabajo y la educación de la mujer*, pp. 197–297. For the Republic see Nuñez Pérez, *Trabajadoras en la Segunda República*, pp. 619–631. The findings of F. Cobo Romero, "Los partidos políticos y las mujeres en la retaguardia republicana jiennense (1936–1939)," and José Gibaja Velázquez, et al., "Las mujeres en la retaguardia durante la Guerra Civil: Un estudio comparativo de ambas zonas a través del ánalisis de dos núcleos rurales: Coca (Segovia) y Castuera (Badajoz)," in Ministerio de Asuntos Sociales/Instituto de la Mujer, *Las mujeres en la Guerra Civil Española* (Madrid: Servicio de Publicaciones del Instituto de la Mujer, 1991), pp. 67–73, 241–247, suggest that change for women during the Civil War was very limited indeed, unlike the situation in other rural regions and in the urban centers. For a comparison see Martha Ackelsberg, "Models of Revolution: Rural Women and Anarchist Collectivization in Civil War Spain," *Journal of Peasant Studies* 20, no. 3 (April 1993).

40. Pay differentials are discussed in Rodríguez Labandeira, *El trabajo rural*, pp. 289–303. See also the survey for Badajoz, Consejo Provincial de Fomento, *Estadística social agraria* (Badajoz: Servicio de Publicaciones del Consejo Provincial de Fomento, 1921), which presented the results of a survey of daily wage rates in every *pueblo*, giving an average for men of 3.09 pesetas and for women of 1.54 pesetas. The figures collected in Luis Garrido González, *Riqueza y tragedia social: Historia de la clase obrera en la provincia de Jaén (1820–1939)* vol. 1 (Jaén, Spain: Diputación Provincial de Jaén, 1990), pp. 605–660, covering the period 1914–1921, also show a consistent pattern of underpayment as does Alarcón Caballero, *El movimiento obrero en Granada*, pp. 41–43. The details of agreements negotiated by unions which laid down lower wages for women are often reproduced in provincial newspapers. Perhaps the best example is that provided by the *Anuario español de político-social: 1934–1935* (Madrid: 1935), pp. 407–1,011, which gives detailed figures. See also Pérez Yruela, *La conflictividad campesina*, p. 417.

41. Far greater work needs to be done on commons rights. Martínez Alier, *Labourers and Landowners*, pp. 87–88, offers some evidence for such attitudes towards employing women. Commons rights were often very complicated, sometimes

allowing the cultivation of the soil by the owner but retaining the use of any trees and their fruits as common property. The logic of greater specialization is suggested in Hudson and Lee, "Women's Work and the Family Economy," p. 8. For detailed comparative examples of the importance they could play see Peter King, "Customary Rights and Women's Earnings: The Importance of Gleaning to the Rural Labouring Poor, 1750–1850," *Economic History Review* 44, no. 3 (1991): 461–476, and Jane Humphries, "Enclosures, Common Rights, and Women: The Proletarianization of Families in the Late Eighteenth and Early Nineteenth Centuries," *Journal of Economic History* 50, no. 1 (1990): 17–42.

42. Capel Martínez, *El trabajo y la educación de la mujer*, p. 112.

43. Pitt-Rivers, *People of the Sierra*, pp. 85–86, notes a gender division of labor in the butchering and preparing of hams. Southern Spain was an area of agricultural specialization with no real proto-industrial rural industry by the nineteenth century. Domestic manufacturing existed but was confined to the larger cities and towns. See J.K.J. Thomson, "Proto-industrialization in Spain," in Sheilagh Ogilvie and Markus Cerman, eds., *European Proto-industrialization* (Cambridge: Cambridge University Press, 1996), pp. 85–101. For excellent discussions of the impact that rural industry could make on work see Gay Gullickson, *Spinners and Weavers of Auffay: Rural Industry and the Sexual Divison of Labor in a French Village, 1750–1850* (Cambridge: Cambridge University Press, 1986) and Pamela Sharpe, "The Women's Harvest: Straw Plaiting and the Representation of Laboring Women's Employment, c. 1793-1885," *Rural History* 5, no. 2 (1994): 129–142.

44. Capel Martínez, *El trabajo y la educación de la mujer*, p. 112.

8

Enlacing Women's Stories: Composing Womanhood in a Coastal Galician Village

Heidi Kelley

Work is the only practical consolation
for having been born.

—Miguel de Unamuno

Telling stories is a favorite pastime of women in Ezaro, a coastal village in the northwesternmost Spanish region of Galicia.[1] As an ethnographer interested in unraveling the cultural construction of womanhood and female identity in Ezaro, listening to the stories told by women became a favorite pastime of mine during the time I spent living and doing research there. I have attempted to construct an understanding of female identity in Ezaro by listening to and recording the stories that women tell about themselves and about one another. I have then pieced together strands of the stories in a fashion that renders Ezaro women understandable to my readers but that still attempts to capture as authentically as possible the way in which Ezaro women understand themselves and their world. My craft is to enlace stories in order to evoke, to paraphrase Malinowski, the hold that life has on Ezaro women.[2]

A significant hold on the lives of Ezaro women is their work. As already demonstrated in this section by Capel and O'Connor for *cigarreras* of the late nineteenth and early twentieth centuries and by Rees for the women of Badajoz in the five decades preceding the Civil War, I show that work is also pivotal to the identities of contemporary Ezaro women. As Rees did for Bajadoz, I show that women's work in Ezaro calls into question any assumption of a clear-cut division between domestic and public spheres. And, as O'Connor has illustrated how representations of *cigarreras* in the press and popular fiction were contradictory and contentious, I show that neither the reputation nor self-perceptions of women in Ezaro are simple or uncontested. To capture the complex and nuanced role of work in women's identity construction, I use the process of lace-making, a local craft tradition, as a metaphor.[3]

The metaphor of enlacing is apropos to both the ethnographic craft and the social process of identity construction itself. Making lace involves going back and forth in complicated and variant patterns between two sets of pins. So too is women's experience of everyday reality a negotiation of contradictory demands and expectations. The stories that women tell about their experience reflect the contradictory discourses that they draw upon in order to make sense of that experience. The lace-making metaphor breaks down in that neither the individual negotiating her everyday world nor (ideally at least) the ethnographer trying to make sense of that process of negotiation is working with a predetermined pattern. Rather the pattern, in both the social construction of identity and ethnographic understanding, is emergent. While the ethnographer strives to reproduce local patterns authentically in her writing, ultimately she imposes her own patterns (a product of her own culture and academic training) on what she writes. Lace-making, which was becoming a lost art in Galicia, is now being self-consciously salvaged and reconstituted as a commodified craft for sale to tourists in a market economy. Likewise, ethnography is a self-conscious retelling of people's stories, removed from their original milieu, to outsiders, whose interest in hearing the stories is very different from what motivated their telling in the first place.[4]

In the pages that follow I demonstrate ethnographically how divergent conceptualizations of ideal womanhood are enlaced in the negotiation of reputation and identity by individual women in Ezaro. Through the stories they tell about themselves and others, Ezaro women construct a sense of themselves as individuals and make meaning out of their lives. At the same time, women's stories reveal the cultural context in which they live their lives: "The culture 'speaks itself' through each individual's story."[5] Underlying the stories that women tell about themselves is a debate about their moral character and their very identity as villagers, a debate in which oppositions between their identity as "traditional" agricultural vs. "modern" coastal people and between the values of hard work vs. the enjoyment of life are intertwined and juxtaposed in a multiplicity of patterns. It is in the context of this complex interlacing of paradoxical maxims and conflicting moral evaluations that Ezaro women struggle to make sense out of their current situations and plan for their futures.

In the stories they tell about their particular experiences, Ezaro women, to borrow a metaphor from Mary Catherine Bateson, compose their lives. Bateson describes composing a life as being an "improvisatory art."[6]

> Composing a life is a little like making a Middle Eastern pastry, in which the butter must be layered in by repeated folding, or like making a samu-

rai sword, whose layers of differently tempered metal are folded over and over.[7]

In relating the life stories of several professional women in the United States, Bateson contrasts the multitude of choices that they face in the precipitous flux of modern American life with the presumed stability of traditional society.[8] While the contrast drawn by Bateson may dramatically illustrate the dilemmas of modernity, its effectiveness may depend upon an obscuring of the role played by choice and flux in the lives of traditional women such as those of Ezaro. While in many respects the lives of Ezaro women may appear to be more constrained than the lives of urban, educated American women, in fact the choices they face—for instance, how to divide up the inheritance among equally deserving children and still preserve the reputation of the household for future generations; how to maintain a balance between peaceable relations with neighbors and self-advancement; how to make most advantageous use of the household's resources—are just as compelling as the choices faced by American women in juggling what often appears a nightmarish panoply of professional and family demands. Ezaro women must also confront conflicting choices and paradoxical expectations as they go about composing their lives. In presenting Ezaro women as individuals faced with difficult decisions under demanding circumstances, I draw on Abu-Lughod's concept of "writing against culture," a strategy designed to "subvert the most problematic connotations of culture: homogeneity, coherence, and timelessness."[9] Rural Galician women, like the other women portrayed in this volume, actively construct their individual identities in contexts of shifting social constraints and fluctuating cultural expectations.

The Problematic of Female Identity

My focus in this chapter on the active negotiation of identity among Ezaro women reflects an emergent theoretical discourse in the anthropology of gender that emphasizes both the agency of female actors and the symbolic malleability of gender categories.[10] Revisionist work has questioned the utility of both the honor/shame and domestic/public paradigms which have until recently dominated anthropological theorizing about gender in Spain (and in southern Europe more widely). While both of these paradigms have produced insights into the cultural construction of gender relations in southern Europe, they have also, by focusing primarily on the perspectives of male actors, muted the significance of female agency and, through heavy reliance on etic (outsider's) concepts, obscured the nuanced character of emic (insider's) categories. Alternative paradigms have drawn our attention to the fact that women may not evaluate themselves with reference to the same set of standards used by men;[11] that, at least in some regions, work may figure more prominently than sexuality as a yardstick of female reputation;[12] that male reputation itself may involve more than the sexual pursuit and protection of women;[13] that the domestic sphere to which women are "relegated" may be a significant source of power in rural communities;[14] and that male dominance may be more "mythical" than real.[15]

The honor/shame paradigm has presented women as passive victims of machismo.[16] Women are portrayed as active only in their emically presumed roles as sexual temptresses. Furthermore, this paradigm posits female gender identity as unproblematic, emphasizing disengagement and conflict in the socialization experience of boys but stressing continuity and cohesion in the experience of girls. Imperturbable seamlessness in the mother/daughter relationship has been widely assumed in ethnographic studies of southern European families. David D. Gilmore, for instance, in describing the problematic relationship of Andalusian men to their mothers-in-law (*suegras*) argues that "Naturally the *suegra's* power is enhanced by simple residential propinquity; but even more psychologically salient is the fact that she and her daughter enjoy a moral symbiosis that the husband cannot match."[17] Such assumptions about the "natural" closeness between mother and daughter, which are in fact rather widespread in anthropological studies of kinship and gender,[18] may reflect more about our own cultural ideals of family life than those of the observed family. Gilmore has extended his argument about psychological differences in socialization experience between boys and girls in Andalusia[19] to a cross-cultural explanation of manhood as an achieved status.[20] He argues that in contrast to manhood, which is cross-culturally regarded as a problematic quality that must be tested in order to be proven, womanhood "is more often construed as a biological given that is culturally refined or augmented."[21] Gilmore's argument is that men must win various tests of cultural adeptness (ranging from courage in rigorous initiation rites to proving their abilities at activities such as hunting, war, or sexual conquest) in order that their sexual identity as men not be challenged. His assumption is that sexual identity is most integral to individual gender identity and that women's sexual status as female is less open culturally to question than is man's claim to sexual status as male. Women, he argues, may be portrayed as misusing their feminine sexuality but they are not confronted with taunts of having lost it. I question whether in assuming that female sexual identity is rarely considered problematic Gilmore is not overlooking other fundamental ways in which feminine identity might in fact be subject to challenge. As ongoing research on gender in southern Europe has already begun to demonstrate,[22] shifting our perspective from an exclusive focus on female sexuality reveals other equally, if not more, potent cultural criteria around which female identity is constructed and contested. Just as, according to Gilmore, Andalusians describe men who have successfully demonstrated their manhood as "'very much a man'(*muy hombre*), 'very virile' (*muy macho*), or 'lots of man' (*mucho hombre*),"[23] successful women in Ezaro are analogously deemed "very much a woman" (*moita muller*).

The case for the contention that the appearance of male public prestige may obscure the reality of female domestic power[24] has been cogently argued with reference to ethnographic work in a variety of southern European communities, but as Gilmore points out,[25] there has still been, with some notable exceptions,[26] relatively little work on "domestic power" in Spain. A continued focus on a presumed division between domestic and public spheres may however prevent us from seeing the ways in which constructing a public reputation may be very much a concern for female actors. It may also obscure the ways in which women's negotiation of individual identity contributes to building community identity.[27] The chapters in the following section of this volume, "Political Identities," specifically explore the various ways in which Spanish women's concerns are reflected in the *polis*, in the community.

Further, the distinction between domestic and public realms may be more an artifact of outsiders' preconceptions than an accurate reflection of emic perceptions. Michael Herzfeld, for instance, argues that in rural Greece the more pertinent emic distinction is that between "inside" and "outside."[28] It is the association of women with the "inside"—ambivalently conceptualized as both comfortingly secure and perilously vulnerable—that leads to their being viewed as dangerous, explains Herzfeld. How women perceive themselves as the appointed guardians of inside knowledge is a question that remains to be answered. I suggest that it is precisely because womanhood is so powerfully associated with the intimate core of identity as household or community (or, as Herzfeld suggests, nation) that the negotiation of female identity by individual women plays a pivotal role in the cultural construction of these wider identities.[29]

For the women of Ezaro, as is also the case for women in other parts of Galicia and northern Portugal, work is the pivot on which reputation hinges. This focus on work rather than sexuality as the primary ingredient of a woman's reputation is related to a complex of social factors: dominant roles for women in subsistence labor, female inheritance of productive resources, and an inheritance system that tends to favor daughters as primary heirs.[30] And while space is symbolically engendered in important ways in the community, women's work in Ezaro—like that of the cigarette workers discussed by Capel and O'Connor and the Extremaduran rural workers described by Rees—transcends the traditional analytic distinction between domestic and public spheres.

In the pages that follow I use the stories of Ezaro women to demonstrate how the construction of identity by individual women reverberates in the negotiation of community identity. I consider the complex ways in which gender, work and community identities intersect, with the goal of providing a more nuanced understanding of Galician womanhood than that offered by the more unidimensional perspectives of the honor/shame and domestic/public paradigms. As the women of Ezaro actively contest their womanhood in their negotiation of work roles, they also define community identity.

Composing Womanhood: ¿"Traballar" o "Disfrutar"?

Work is the key ingredient of which womanhood in Ezaro is composed. Work involves much more however than agricultural labor. Work may be understood as all the activities that women engage in to advance the success of their households—managing expenses, making inheritance decisions, organizing cooperative work groups with neighbors, protecting their fields from the suspected witchcraft of envious neighbors—and hence to advance their own individual reputations. The household (*a casa*) is the basic social unit in Ezaro. Individual names refer to household origin and individual success is ultimately measured in terms of household reputation.

In listening to stories about the reputations of both households and individual women in Ezaro it became clear to me that the characteristics that were put forward as the measure of a successful reputation involved two potentially contradictory sets of expectations. I thus came to see the construction of female identity in Ezaro as a process of negotiation between two divergent conceptualizations of ideal womanhood.[31] On the one hand, the ideal woman is a hard worker, *unha traballadora*,[32] who carefully tends her household's fields and fights to preserve her household's, and hence her own, reputation. This woman must view all others—neighbors and family members alike—as potential competitors set on undermining her reputation. She must be competitive both to ensure the productivity of her fields and to protect the daily affairs of her household from the prying eyes and malicious acts of neighbors. On the other hand, the ideal woman is one who knows how to enjoy, *disfrutar*, the fruits of her work, and who cooperates with and treats as equals family members and fellow villagers alike. This woman is not suspicious of her neighbors and is open about both personal and household matters. Generous rather than suspicious, she views life as something to be enjoyed rather than as a competitive struggle.

There are situations in which these two ideals are easily reconciled, as in that of the young mother who works hard to produce fresh foods and prepare good meals to feed to her growing children. This woman will be lauded for both her diligent productivity and her nurturant generosity. There are also many situations in which these ideals clash relentlessly, as in that of the mother of grown children, who on the one hand may feel compelled to treat all of her children equally and as well as possible (so that they each may "enjoy life") but on the other is expected to select one child as primary heir (to be awarded the house and a larger portion of the fields than his or her siblings) so as to best protect the future competitiveness of the household.[33]

A woman's reputation in the eyes of other villagers hinges on the way in which she reconciles opposing expectations in everyday situations. Reputation, however, is not awarded in any uniform or homogeneous fashion. Rather, the ambiguous tension between the two ideals allows for shifting and variant evaluations to be made of the behavior of the village women. For instance, the young mother who feeds her children "too well"—purchasing canned goods and packaged snacks—can easily be criticized for being a spendthrift and for neglecting her duty to scrimp and save for the good of her household and the future of her children. On the other hand, if this same young mother is observed buying the least expensive cuts of meat and the boniest fish, she may just as easily be taken to task for being an *egoísta* (egoist) and sacrificing the health of her children in order to advance selfishly the reputation of her household. It all depends on the vantage point of the observer and, in the telling of stories, the moral point the teller wishes to make. In composing a sense of identity, Ezaro women must both negotiate these conflicting expectations in constructing a public presentation of self and reconcile individual aspirations with the expectations and evaluations of others in forming a private understanding of self.

The negotiation of individual identity in Ezaro itself reflects wider cultural contradictions. The dynamic tension in cultural ideals of womanhood echoes, for instance, a dialectical orientation between mountain and coast in community identity. The geographic contrast between mountain and sea is striking in Ezaro. Craggy mountains of granite plunge abruptly into the waters of the Atlantic. This enigmatic topography is mirrored in the paradoxical way in which villagers define their community identity. On the one hand, villagers define themselves as agriculturalists (*labradores*) and view their identity as firmly rooted in the land farmed by their respective households. Agricultural work is viewed as pivotal to household reputation. While agriculture in Ezaro is primarily subsistence-oriented, a household's productivity is measured primarily in terms of the quantity of surplus sold at the weekly market in the nearby town of Cée. The expectation is that all household members will work hard and make sacrifices to ensure the continuing viability of the household. As hardworking agriculturalists, villagers identify themselves as mountain people (*xente da montaña*) in contrast to lazy coastal people. On the other hand, villagers say that they are fishermen and emigrants (*pescadores e emigrantes*), a people who travel all around the globe (*andarse para o mundo*), albeit reluctantly, in search of a living.[34] As such, they also tend to see themselves as forward-thinking coastal people (*xente da costa*), in contrast to backward mountain people.

This dialectical construction of identity also implies divergent understandings of what constitutes a good life. Is it an agricultural life in which all work hard to maintain the household's fields and reap the benefits (both material and social) of a fruitful harvest? Or is it a life fueled by cash that allows for more material comforts and less slavish commitment to work? Ought the orientation of the household be toward its continuing viability in the future or toward enjoying life in the present? While, as described below, this tension between subsistence and consumption orientations has been exacerbated by recent shifts away from subsistence toward a cash economy, the tension between the alternative ethoses of the agricultural and emigrant ways of life, as evidenced in stories villagers told me about their parents' and grandparents' generations, appears to be of long standing in the community. But in stories told about the past there was much more congruence about how a household's success should be evaluated, i.e., in terms of agricultural productivity, than there was in the ways in which villagers evaluated contemporary households.

The dichotomous identity of villagers is also reflected in the way in which villagers describe their ideal division of labor. Women are viewed as agriculturalists, men as fishermen and emigrants. Women do the majority of the agricultural work and are responsible for most agricultural decision making. Indeed, as noted above, women's high degree of involvement with agricultural work in combination with their inheritance of productive resources, i.e., land, has been associated with their high status in coastal Galicia and the culturally similar regions of northwestern Portugal.[35] Fishing, on the other hand, is viewed as a male occupation,[36] and although today women are emigrating in increasing numbers, emigration still tends to be spoken of as a masculine endeavor.[37] In the typical village household, men go off to foreign lands (*marcharse para o extraneiro*) in search of a living, while women stay home to tend the family's fields and to maintain the household.

There are many points in everyday life in which these contrasting identities, agricultural and emigrant, overlap. While the reputation of the household has been measured primarily in terms of its agricultural productivity, it is impossible to maintain a productive household without some sort of wage income. The cash earned by the emigrant (or fishermen or factory worker) can be reinvested back into the purchase of more fields and hence into the future success of the agricultural household. At the same time, the orientation of most emigrants from Ezaro has been to return to their village and to their households. Emigrants may travel far afield but still think of themselves as profoundly connected to their village and to the land of their households.

Nonetheless, with the increasing availability of cash from emigrant labor, a new model of household success has been gradually emerging in the community. In this model, cash is invested into the purchase and development of rental property and small businesses rather than being channeled into the acquisition of more fields. A handful of Ezaro emigrants have begun purchasing apartments in Galicia's capital city of Santiago de Compostela for rental to university students there. Some emigrants have even begun to open new businesses in Ezaro. For example, two new bars opened in the village in 1987, and in 1988 a sewing cooperative opened, where women can work to earn money. Meanwhile, the amount of cultivated land in the community has been decreasing; more and more village land is succumbing to brambles and thickets. At the same time, the construction of new houses, financed by emigrant income, has been increasing. Ironically, the emigrants who build these new houses can rarely afford to live in them year-round; they remain tightly shuttered and abandoned for all but one summer month when their owners return home for vacation. These gradual changes in the economic and social contours of the community have provoked intense debate among villagers about their identity, a debate in which the long-standing dichotomy between agricultural and emigrant identities has been exacerbated.

Both ideals of womanhood may be understood as conforming to the agricultural orientation in village identity. An agricultural woman is expected to be ruthlessly competitive with neighbors in order to ensure the advance of her own household. She must also be cooperative and open with neighbors to demonstrate that she is not above fellow villagers, that she is willing to enjoy what she has reaped and not jealously guard it all for herself. She is to be both relentlessly thrifty (carefully guarding household resources) and generously nurturing (demonstrating the fruitfulness of the agricultural way of life). Villagers nevertheless also associate the *traballar*/competitive ideal of womanhood with the agricultural way of life and the *disfrutar*/cooperative ideal with the wage-labor orientation. This is often done in a disparaging manner; those defending the agricultural way of life criticize the laxness of the consumption orientation; those defending wage labor criticize agriculture as obsessively competitive. As the wage-labor model gradually gains ground in villagers' actions, if not also in their moral judgements and expectations, the tension between these two opposed expectations is increased for women.

Despite pressure to change, often applied with particular energy by husbands and/or grown children, most Ezaro women continue to work as agriculturalists.[38] These women work long and hard: hauling undergrowth from the *monte* to serve as bedding for their animals and fertilizer for their fields; planting, weeding and harvesting their crops of corn, potatoes, greens, onions, and garlic; preparing food for pigs and chickens, husband and children alike. Most of the agricultural work is done by hand. Several village women own burros; the rest carry their loads piled in baskets balanced atop their heads. The pattern of land distribution in Ezaro is one of small and fragmented plots, so women spend much of their time walking between their fields. There are two tractors available for rent in the village (the tractors are owned and operated by men), suitable for some of the larger fields, but most village fields are worked by hoe.

A woman's work defines her day. But by late afternoon and early evening the workaday tempo has begun to slow. This is the time of day when routines are relaxed and family members, friends, and neighbors gather on a front stoop or around a wood stove to tell stories about *antés e hoxe* (the past and the present), about mountain people and coastal people, and about their individual trajectories as family members. It is in the stories they tell that women put the hard work they do, and the hard choices they must make with respect to that work, in meaningful context. It is through the paradoxes posed in these stories that Ezaro women compose their womanhood and negotiate their identity, both at the individual and community levels.

"Antés e Hoxe": Negotiating Community Identity

A common motif in the stories told by Ezaro women is one that contrasts the past, *antés* (before, the old days), with the present, *hoxe* (today).[39] Central to many such stories is a skeptical and ironically derisive portrayal of the present in which villagers (and particularly village women) are understood to be hopelessly divided and selfishly obsessed with individual concerns. What varies is the way in which this divisiveness is explained. Some say that this present-day divisiveness among villagers represents a contemporary decline in the moral quality of the community; others explain today's divisiveness as a product of the past.

As might be imagined, this dichotomy in viewpoints is often drawn along generational lines. Older women in particular point to the greater degree of harmony that existed in the past. They say that people today care only for the success of their own households. They opine that it is the new orientation of the community toward emigration that is responsible for its moral decline. There is too much *vicio* (waywardness) and *egoísmo* (egotism) in Ezaro today. In these stories, emigrants are painted as products of the *disfrutar* ideal gone awry.

The young women of today in particular are faulted for their lack of spirit for work. One mother of two unmarried daughters (aged 30 and 18), for instance, remarked to me about how little energy her daughters have. If they stay out late at the discotheque, she exclaimed, they have to spend all the next day in bed. When she was young, the day after a *fiesta*, she would be up and eager to go, just as on any other day. Someone would always bring a tambourine along on a work party (young women often worked in groups at agricultural labor or hauling loads) and during their breaks they would sing and dance. "I was never tired!" she exclaimed. The women of the past are held up in examples such as this one as exemplifying the perfect integration of the values of hard work and harmonious spirit.

Younger women (i.e., roughly, women in their early forties and younger) tend to draw the opposite conclusion: they see the contentious attitude of older women as responsible for the community's stagnation today. They say that older women are so single-mindedly obsessed with work and the success of their own households that they have no interest in the future of the community. These older women are portrayed as having taken the *traballar*/competitive ideal to an unneighborly extreme. Young women are especially critical of their mothers' generation, pointing to the Civil War and events transpiring in the years following the war as having fundamentally warped that generation.

Generational disparities alone do not explain all of the differing evaluations of *antés* and *hoxe* made by village women. Ana, a returned emigrant in her early forties, frequently spoke critically of the past, emphasizing the harsh differences between strong (i.e., wealthy) and poor households that existed in her village then. She described the women of strong households as being so egotistical that they would not even lend the honey and lemon, which only they produced, to sick *pobres.* If you were poor, exclaimed Ana, you would work for them for a month to pay back the honey and lemon they had given you. But, shortly after telling me this story, Ana began to complain about her own mother's current unsociable behavior, refusing to help a neighbor who had been hospitalized because of a long-standing grudge. In the past, muttered Ana, people were more interested in helping one another. Clearly, how individual women choose to characterize *antés* and *hoxe* frequently depends upon the moral point that they wish to make in a particular context.

The period before the Civil War is generally characterized as having been a time of harmony among villagers. Older women would recount to me nostalgically how they all used to gather in one another's homes for nightly get-togethers (*xuntas*). Young women would bring their embroidery or lacemaking and they would all work together while keeping up a lively conversation. Then the young men would arrive, someone would pick up a plate on which to tap out melodies and they would all dance. This period is also acknowledged to have been a time of widespread poverty and misery. The two extremes are often contrasted in one moral judgement; even though we had nothing then, we were happier and got along better. Implicit in this statement and in characterizations of today's greed is the assumption that material wealth leads to contention. Women nonetheless also may point to the greater inequality experienced within the community in the past (e. g., Ana's story about the honey and lemon) in order to show how much better they live today.

The Civil War is often remarked upon as the seminal event that began the process of decline in village harmony. There was no fighting in the area, but village men were conscripted into military service. A good number of men delayed their entry into the military by hiding out in the mountains above Ezaro. They used their knowledge of the terrain to outwit civil guards searching for them. Women would bring them food while ostensibly taking their cows to pasture or the men would return clandestinely to their homes. These men and their families had to outfox not only the civil guards but also other villagers, particularly those whose sympathies lay with the Falangist cause and those whose male family members had already been conscripted.

While villagers often describe the Civil War as a watershed event creating conflict in their community, their stories about the war nonetheless reveal prior enmities among village households. In many stories they explain that certain neighbors turned in other neighbors because of ill will between them. The Civil War has come to be used symbolically, in villagers' inventions of Ezaro's history, to stand for contention and disharmony within their community.

In the years immediately following the war, women told me, villagers experienced even greater deprivation than before. The tension caused by the political repression of the Franco years[40] was exacerbated by the high number of deaths from silicosis, contracted by village men and women working on a dam project in the area, experienced from the 1960s on.

Today, increasing emigration is presented as the primary factor responsible for a trend towards disharmony in village character. High rates of emigration are judged as responsible for the declining spirit of work in the community. Older women, in particular, would tell me how much it pained them to see abandoned fields, overgrown with weeds, because young women are too *egoístas* (greedy for material gain) to be willing to work them. They see emigration as sapping the community of its very life force, agriculture. In other stories, however, the impact of emigration on the community is presented in a more positive light. In these stories emigrants are characterized as more open and less prone to petty quarrels. They are contrasted with their peers in the Civil War generation who did not emigrate and hence are judged to be especially quarrelsome and closed. Emigrants, in this positive light, are viewed as bringing fresh, new ideas to the community and freeing it from its traditional obsession with work. Both young and old women, nonetheless, agree that emigration is bad because it forces individuals to leave their community, to which they are ideally expected to have an inalienable tie.

In all of these stories told by village women about *antés e hoxe* in Ezaro, what is most evident is the constructed nature of tradition. The past can be seen as a glowing endorsement of the values of hard work or as a biting indictment of the discord brewed in an agricultural lifestyle. In the stories they tell about their community's past, village women also contest the meaning of modernity and negotiate the contours of their own futures. It is within the outlines of the identity they compose for their community in these stories that women enlace their own individual identities. In an analogous fashion to the contrast they draw between past and present, village women also oppose mountain and coastal identity. In the stories they tell contrasting mountain and coastal character, Ezaro women further define the contours of both community and individual identity and contest the very nature of womanhood.

"¿Xente da Montaña o Xente da Costa?" Contesting Moral Character

While the increasing preponderance of emigrants in village affairs is seen by villagers as giving their community a more coastal character today, the categories of "coastal" and "mountain" nonetheless are both still actively negotiated as descriptors of village character. Both coast and mountains dominate the landscape of the community and the parish of Santa Uxía del Ezaro incorporates, officially at least, both the coastal community of Ezaro and three much smaller mountains hamlets. Although Ezaro is located on the coast, residents alternatively define themselves as coastal and mountain people depending on the particular point they wish to make about identity. Ezaro residents declare themselves to be coastal in contrast to what they identify as the ignorant and backward character of the inhabitants of nearby mountain hamlets and as mountain people in contrast to the perceived spendthrift and lazy nature of coastal people.

The mountain/coastal distinction is especially often drawn along the line of perceived differences in female character, demonstrating the interrelationship between the negotiation of womanhood and the construction of community identity. Ezaro women talk about mountain women as hopelessly ignorant workhorses, so mired in their backwards ways of thinking that they are incapable of perceiving or achieving a more comfortable way of life. A favorite story told about mountain women is that despite the ramshackle appearance of their houses and clothing they in fact have plenty of money which they keep hidden away because of their penurious nature. A common caricature is that of the mountain woman who goes into the city to do her marketing with all of her plentiful life savings surreptitiously stuffed into the various nooks and crannies of her undergarments while her skirt is held together with safety pins. In particular, mountain women are criticized for their furtive and suspicious nature, always hiding what they have out of their ignorant fear that someone will take it away from them.

Engracia, a woman who married into Ezaro from a mountain community, is frequently criticized for her stinginess, which is attributed to her mountain origins. Although Engracia and her emigrant husband are well off, the criticism goes, Engracia skimps on both food and clothing for her family.

Upon other occasions, nonetheless, Engracia may be praised for her thriftiness. Both her clever prudence and her suspicious scrimping are attributed to Engracia's mountain character.

This ambivalence with regard to mountain character is reflected in the frequency with which Ezaro women identify themselves as mountain people. This may be done to point out the failings of the community as a whole; for instance, "We are all such egotists that we cannot cooperate and accomplish anything worthwhile." A remark of this sort is often made to point out the faults of the speaker's neighbors (e. g., "all the women in this village are such spiteful gossips"), but it may also be used as a form of collective self-criticism, a recognition of certain character deficiencies that are shared by all women—indeed by all people—in Ezaro. For instance, women often expressed a painful awareness that the economic worth of agriculture in the community has declined sharply in recent years. Some contemplate the possibility of combining fragmented plots of land in order that a more profitable type of agriculture might be practiced in the village, but then snort derisively at their own plans, complaining that it would never be possible to make mountain people such as themselves give up individual plots of land in order to cooperate with their neighbors.

Ezaro women, nonetheless, also may proudly identify themselves as mountain people in order to make a moral point about the superiority of mountain qualities. This characterization of themselves as mountain people is made to distinguish themselves from coastal people in general but in particular to distinguish themselves from the women of the neighboring coastal village of O Pindo. Perhaps because O Pindo is so close (approximately one-half mile away along the coastal highway) and because the lives of the people of the two communities have become so intertwined in recent years (Ezaro children attend elementary school in O Pindo, and Ezaro and O Pindo share a parish priest who lives in O Pindo), perceived differences in the characters of the two communities have been highlighted. Villagers enjoyed calling my attention to the cultural differences they perceive between themselves and the people of O Pindo. They point to the fact that the people of O Pindo even speak differently than they do and explain these differences by the fact that until relatively recently (the 1960s construction of a bridge to connect the two communities), communication was possible only by boat. In villagers' remarks about community identity, however, a geographical obstacle is turned into a veritable cultural chasm.

Physically, the community of O Pindo does look different from Ezaro. O Pindo has significantly less land available for agricultural work and emigrant income has been much more conspicuously invested in small businesses, especially in upbeat bars where young people—both male and female—from the surrounding area like to socialize and sample popular new drinks like Irish coffee. Ezaro bars, in contrast, tend to be neighborhood bars, usually set up in the corner of a grocery store, itself consisting of nothing more than a tiny cramped room. These bars are the exclusive province of men. A woman may joke and banter with the men standing at the bar while she makes her purchases in the grocery store, but she never lingers to prolong the conversation or join them for a drink.

Drawing on real and perceived community differences, both Ezaro and Pindo women have woven an elaborate repertoire of critical commentary regarding one another's womanhood. The women of O Pindo characterize the mountain women of Ezaro as workhorses and drudges; the women of Ezaro think that the coastal women of O Pindo are prima donnas who refuse to dirty themselves with real work. From the perspective of Ezaro women, the women of O Pindo represent the opposite of all that they value in womanhood. One of the most remarked on offenses reputed to be characteristic of Pindo women is that they never cook at home. Pindo women are seen as immoral for putting more value on a clean kitchen than on the proper feeding of their family, for spending money on food that could be more economically cooked at home and for frequenting restaurants and bars that are not proper places for women. Women should be working at home or in their fields and should not be dawdling about in eating places. Women who are seen sitting around in cafés obviously must be lazy (and it is their presumed slothfulness rather than sexual misconduct that is emphasized in accounts like this). Equally subject to criticism are those coastal women who have two kitchens, one in the house for serving guests and one in a shed or garage for cooking. Interestingly it is the mountain woman Engracia who is the one Ezaro woman who has achieved this arrangement.

Ezaro women are critical of Pindo (and all coastal) women for spending all of their money on adorning their houses, doing no work other than housework, and refusing to engage in any activity that would dirty their houses. On the other hand, Pindo women are scornful of what they characterize as the miserliness of Ezaro women and their dilapidated and dirty living conditions. From the Pindo perspective, Ezaro women do not spend money on their houses because they do not want anyone to find out how much money they really have. They are secretive, closed and backward. In rebutting these Pindo accusations, Ezaro women defend these mountain qualities as estimable characteristics. The women of Ezaro see the women of O Pindo as flagrant and immoral conspicuous consumers. In contrasting themselves with Pindo women, Ezaro women praise in themselves the very qualities that they criticize in their mountain neighbors.

Reflected in women's debates over the nature of mountain vs. coastal character, is the ongoing negotiation of community identity, which itself is cogently symbolized in Ezaro's church and two patron saint celebrations.

Villagers are proud of their new parish church, built on the beach in the 1960s, a significant monumental marker of the ongoing transition in village identity from that of *xente da montaña* to *xenta da costa.*[41] The construction of this church marked the move of the center of the parish of Santa Uxía de Ezaro, which consists of the village of Ezaro and three mountain hamlets, from one of the mountain hamlets, Santa Uxía, to Ezaro. Ezaro residents identify Santa Uxía as their maternal community and describe their village history as a process of settlement by a few families from Santa Uxía and the gradual development of a vibrant community that combines both agriculture and fishing in its way of life. The opening of the new parish church on the beach in Ezaro in 1965, and the dedication of the new church to the Virxe do Mar (Virgin of the Sea), signaled the shifting orientation of community identity from mountain to coastal.

Along with the opening of the new church, a new celebration was institutionalized, the feast day of the *Virxe do Mar*, which is now celebrated on the same day as the feast day of *Santa Uxía*, the former patroness of the mountain parish. The character of one of Ezaro's two major saint-day celebrations has thus shifted to represent the increasingly coastal character of the village. The other saint-day celebration, nonetheless, has remained dedicated to *San Saturniño*, who is regarded by villagers as a saint of mountain people. Thus, a strong element of mountain identity is retained in village patronal celebrations, cultural performances in which community identity is acted out and reinforced both for Ezaro residents and for spectators from surrounding communities.

The coastal/mountain dichotomy is a geographical gloss for what many villagers perceive to be a diachronic shift in village identity. In alternatively identifying themselves as *xente da montaña* or as *xente da costa*, Ezaro women negotiate both village identity and their own individual identity as women. They defend community moral boundaries at the same time that they define the contours of womanhood. In recent years the mountain/coastal dichotomy has proved especially "good to think" as women debate their identity as traditional agriculturalists or modern emigrants.[42]

To further illustrate the ways in which female identity is contested in the contradictory and changing terrain of community evaluations and expectations, I turn now to the interwoven stories of two women. The conflicting but nonetheless overlapping goals expressed in the stories of this mother daughter pair capture the ambivalently oppositional character of the qualities—traditional/modern, mountain/coastal, agricultural/emigrant—described above as intrinsic to the ways in which Ezaro women define their identity both as villagers and as individuals. The mother daughter relationship evokes both the tensions among villagers engendered by recent changes and those that are intrinsic to family structure in Ezaro. While anthropologists have tended to characterize the mother daughter relationship as somehow inherently stable, the structure of many households in Ezaro, in which adult women work under and gradually inherit authority from their mothers, exacerbates power struggles between mothers and daughters.[43] Mothers and daughters struggle to reconcile oftentimes conflicting visions of household success and in doing so, because of the pivotal role household reputation plays in individual identity, combat opposed definitions of womanhood. It is in the angry, frustrated and ambivalent everyday dialogues between mothers and daughters, like those of Carmen and Mari-Carmen illustrated below, that the contours of womanhood are constantly challenged and negotiated in Ezaro.

Carmen and Mari-Carmen: Debating Womanhood.

Carmen,[44] now in her fifties, emigrated to Argentina as a young woman. After working in Buenos Aires for several years, she moved to Montevideo, Uruguay, to marry Eladio, also from Ezaro. Their only daughter, Mari-Carmen, was born there. When Mari-Carmen was four years old, Carmen received a letter from her parents in Ezaro asking her to come back to care for them in their old age. In return for this care, Carmen was designated as the principal heir of her parents' estate. Despite Eladio's reluctance—he argued that the family would have a better life in Uruguay—Carmen prevailed and they moved back to Ezaro. When I first met them, Mari-Carmen was in her late twenties and still unmarried, a state of considerable concern to her mother. She had an education degree from the university, but had been unable to acquire a teaching position. Eladio had a job at a joinery in O Pindo and Carmen worked the fields she had inherited from her parents.

Carmen is strongly committed to her agricultural work role. In this role, she commands a mixture of respect and disdain from her husband and daughter. Eladio and Mari-Carmen's ambivalence about Carmen's agricultural work has provoked (and itself is exacerbated by) enduring conflicts within the household. These disagreements strongly color the relationships among all three household members and influence Carmen's own perception of her work role.

I witnessed many impassioned arguments between Mari-Carmen and her mother. These arguments usually centered on Mari-Carmen's presumed laziness (from Carmen's perspective) and Carmen's alleged slovenliness (from Mari-Carmen's perspective). In Carmen's words, it seemed that there was little that Mari-Carmen could do right. She had failed the *oposiciones* (competitive exams for teaching positions) three times, helped with agricultural tasks under only the severest of admonishments, spent far too much time enjoying herself with her friends, and, perhaps worst of all, had yet to succeed at bringing a son-in-law to the household. Mari-Carmen, in turn, found much to criticize about her mother. Her mother never had the midday meal ready on time, nor did she keep up with housecleaning. She was far too scattered and had no sense of time (of which she spent far too much working in her fields and far too little taking care of her house).

One afternoon in particular the normally ardent arguing reached volcanic proportions. Mari-Carmen had been chatting with some neighbors, an elderly woman and her emigrant daughter who was visiting from America. The conversation with her neighbors had evolved from amiable to explosive when the question of the worth of agricultural work was raised. Mari-Carmen, still heated from defending her points (in agreement with the emigrant daughter and against the elderly mother), returned home and exclaimed to her mother, who had been working long hours—often late into the night, braiding this year's crop of onions and garlic for sale at the market—that there is no longer any value in planting these crops for sale. Carmen understood her daughter to be arguing for the complete abandonment of agriculture and scolded her vehemently, "How do you think we could buy everything from your father's wages?" She then proceeded to lambast her daughter for going out too much, always running off to spend money at the movies, the discotheque, and the dance hall. Mari-Carmen shouted back, holding her five fingers up for emphasis, that she had been to the movies five times in her life. Then she turned to me and asked me how many countries I have visited. I meekly responded that I did not know offhand and Mari-Carmen exploded to her mother, "Look at her! We're the same age, but she's been to so many different countries that she can't even remember how many!" Carmen retorted, "She's different. She's the daughter of a teacher (*filla de professor*). Here we have only your father's wages to live on."

Carmen's perception of the centrality of her agricultural work is couched in her understanding of the household as a cooperative unit. In her mind, both her husband's wage labor and her own agricultural work are essential to the success of the household. In this argument with Mari-Carmen, she expresses her anger that her daughter is not also fulfilling her cooperative role in the household.

This argument is just one instance of a festering conflict between Mari-Carmen and Carmen with regard to the definition of Mari-Carmen's work role in the household. In Carmen's eyes, Mari-Carmen, her only child, is a disappointment on three accounts. First, Mari-Carmen does not help her in her agricultural tasks to the extent to which Carmen would like. This does not bode well for the future of the house, which Carmen perceives as tied up in its agricultural productivity. From Carmen's perspective, mother and daughter should be working together in the fields to ensure the continuity of the house.

Second, Mari-Carmen has failed to pass her teaching examinations. As a child Mari-Carmen showed great promise (intelligence is generally regarded to be a native ability and children are pegged at an early age with respect to their level of intelligence), so her parents were willing to invest in her education. Instead of renovating their house (which is how many other villagers have invested money earned abroad), they supported Mari-Carmen's high school and college education. Mari-Carmen's continued failure to pass the examinations necessary to acquire a teaching position is viewed by her mother as both a loss of an investment and a blow to the reputation of the household.

Finally, Mari-Carmen's unmarried status is an irritation to her mother. At twenty-seven, Mari-Carmen's chances of marrying are seen as rapidly diminishing. One day, Carmen related to me all the things that she would do if Mari-Carmen married: finish renovating the house, buy a washing machine, perhaps even purchase an apartment in La Coruña (a Galician city). Carmen assumes that if Mari-Carmen marries, she will bring her husband to live in her house and that his wages will be another source of income to the household.

Mari-Carmen perceives her work role rather differently than her mother does. She sees herself working toward the attainment of a paying job that will allow herself to achieve economic independence from her parents. Hence Mari-Carmen divides her time between preparing for the annual examination that would qualify her for a teaching job and tutoring schoolchildren for spending money (which she nonetheless turns over to her mother whose approval she must receive for every purchase). From Carmen's perspective, Mari-Carmen does nothing all day long. She even begrudges her daughter the money she needs to register for the teaching examination. In Carmen's mind, Mari-Carmen has already attempted—and failed—that examination enough times.

According to Carmen, Mari-Carmen's work role ought to be defined in terms of the goals of the household. Carmen regards her daughter as *vaga* (lazy) because she does not work hard enough and *viciosa* (spendthrift) because she spends too much money. In Carmen's eyes, all members of the household should work hard and save every peseta possible in order to augment the position of the house. Mari-Carmen, in contrast, defines her work role in terms of individual goals. She finds her mother's demands for work excessive because she does not think it is worth the effort to grow crops for sale. Mari-Carmen believes that people ought to spend money within their means in order to enjoy themselves and work towards definite goals (in her case, that goal is a teaching position). For her, the prospect of a teaching position opens the possibility of leaving her parents' household and the village of Ezaro far behind. Mari-Carmen always cautioned me, nonetheless, not to tell her mother of her dreams of leaving home. Her mother, she said, could not stand the thought of her going away. For Carmen, the house would have no meaning without a child to continue it.

This type of generational conflict is by no means new to Ezaro. Young adults have always faced a conundrum as to whether they should invest their energies into their parents' households (with the hope of inheriting the house) or into carving out independent lives for themselves. A decision as to who will be the primary heir may not be made until the parents are quite elderly and even in those cases in which a child marries in the house with the understanding of staying to care for the parents and becoming the principal heir, the parents usually maintain authority in the house until their deaths. Individuals have thus faced an inevitable conflict between displaying initiative and striking out on their own, and demonstrating cooperation with the goals of their natal households. Today, the inheritance of a house is no longer seen to be as desirable as it once was. More parents are in the position of having to lure their offspring into taking over the house. Conflict between the generations is thus cast in a new light.

Another long-standing source of bitterness in Carmen's household has been the family's decision to move back to Ezaro from Uruguay in 1964. Upon their return to Ezaro, Eladio was faced with the prospect of unemployment; the knowledge of heating and air-conditioning systems he had acquired in Montevideo was of little use in his natal village. Immediately upon their return to Galicia, Eladio left again to work on a cargo ship. Seasickness ended his career as a mariner and other health problems undermined his subsequent try at construction work in Switzerland. He worked independently (and with little financial success) as a carpenter in Ezaro until obtaining his current job in the Pindo joinery seven years ago. Eladio now deeply regrets their decision to return to Ezaro. He feels that he could have made a better life for himself and his family if they had stayed in Uruguay.

Despite the economic setbacks and the acrid conflicts they have endured, Carmen still believes in the potential for creating a good life in Ezaro. She did inherit her house, although as a consequence of the disputes involved in coming to a settlement, her mother did not speak to her in the last years of her life (although they were living in the same house) and today Carmen does not speak to any of her siblings (four of whom live in Ezaro).[45] She works toward the day when their house (which her father, a stonecutter, built himself of granite) will be fully renovated and all of the household's fields will be cultivated once again. She still hopes that her husband can claim ownership of his share of a plot of land on the beach (inherited from his father), in time for them to take advantage of its economic potential.

Carmen also believes in the superiority of money. She treats her husband with deference because he provides the bulk of the household's cash income. But this belief sways neither her conviction that agricultural work is fundamental to the reputation of the house, nor her faith in the idea that all household members ought to cooperate in furthering the goals of the house. Neither her husband nor her daughter are in complete agreement with Carmen's vision of their household. Yet they concur enough to agree to help her, albeit reluctantly, when she has planned their cooperation in her agricultural tasks. Sentiments about the value of agricultural work are still powerful enough in Ezaro to remain strong even when confronted with the seemingly contradictory values placed on money and individual goals. One day, Mari-Carmen took me on a walk in the wooded area above her house. This area had once been completely cultivated, but now it is largely overgrown. She sadly showed me two leiras that belong to her mother there. They were both so overgrown with gorse and ferns that it was impossible to walk through them. With conviction, Mari-Carmen told me that as soon as they finished renovating their house, she would come up here with her mother and together they would clear (*limpiar*) these two *leiras*. For Mari-Carmen too these overgrown *leiras* are shameful.

The landscape of work in Ezaro has for generations been defined by the contrast between mountain and sea. Ideally, the reputation of the household has been rooted tenaciously in its land, with work in fishing, emigration and local industry providing the complementary resources necessary to keep the productive *casa* thriving. As the economic and political contours of this landscape have gradually changed and as urban and foreign ways of thinking have gradually been incorporated into village discourse through the media of both returned emigrants and the increasingly ubiquitous household television set, so too has the ideal image of the household been opened to negotiation. The inherent tension in this ideal image between land and sea has been exacerbated by these changes, as has been the same tension reflected in individual work identity. This is particularly true for women, for whom agriculture, now the focus of contention, has typically formed the core of female identity.

In the years that have passed since the completion of my original fieldwork, I have returned to Ezaro twice for short visits and have maintained contact with my closest friends in the village via letters and occasional telephone calls. In the summer of 1988 Mari-Carmen, the hopeless spinster, married the son of a shopkeeper from a nearby town. The couple moved in with Mari-Carmen's parents and in the next summer a daughter, Olga, was born to them. Mari-Carmen's husband, unemployed for years, finally passed an *oposición* (examination for government job) and obtained a position as a *bedel* (clerk) at a nearby school. He nonetheless still talks about emigrating.[46] Mari-Carmen continues to be unemployed; she has taken exams for non-teaching positions and enrolled in a course in shellfishing (*marisquería*) sponsored by the regional government (Xunta de Galicia) in Ezaro. Carmen, now a doting grandmother, appears somewhat less acerbic in her continued criticism of her daughter. Although the wealth Carmen had hoped for upon the marriage of her daughter has not yet been forthcoming, Eladio did retire from his job and has nearly completed the renovation of the house. Perhaps most importantly, Olga's birth has signaled hope for the continued vitality of the household.

Conclusion

It is upon the terrain of success at work—reflected both in women's single-minded dedication to the advancement of their households and their ability to enjoy and share the fruits of their labor—that womanhood in Ezaro is defined and defended. Womanhood is contested in the everyday stories that women tell one another as opposing measures of successful work are juxtaposed and negotiated. The stories that Ezaro women tell enlace paradoxical orientations—mountain/coast, agriculture/emigration, traditional/modern—that have been part of the cultural fabric of the community for decades, if not longer. While recent changes may have exacerbated these oppositions and added new dilemmas (e. g., the care of the elderly in changing households), villagers are hardly untutored at their negotiation. Furthermore, the categories themselves are malleable, cultural constructs subject to subtle shifts of interpretation and nuanced readings. The women of *antés* may be reviled as squabbling gossips or esteemed as exemplars of the nurturance and purity of rural life. The woman who throws her life's energy into her household's fields may be judged as working successfully for the betterment of her children's future, but so may the emigrant woman who refuses to dirty her fingernails planting potatoes but carefully saves for her children's education.

What is particularly significant is that the negotiation of individual identity by women is inseparable from their negotiation of community identity. A woman must establish whether her village is to be understood as mountain or coastal, whether its past is to be esteemed or overcome, in order to situate her own individual identity. She must also negotiate the orientation of her household—towards subsistence or consumption, towards agriculture or wage labor—but however she defines it, the success of her household is integral to her own reputation and identity. Community, household and individual identity are all enlaced of the same threads. The stories that women tell about community and household identity are also very much reflections on individual identity. Thus what for many scholars has been an integral component of the cultural definition of gender in rural Spanish communities—that is, the distinction between domestic and public spheres—is essentially erased in the construction of identity by women in Ezaro. Work is the hold that life has on women in Ezaro. Work is a thread that runs through individual, household and community identity in Ezaro and enlaces all together in variegated and always changing patterns. Working hard to build a household that will flourish in her lifetime and endure into the future is a woman's consolation for having been born and the foundation on which she builds both individual identity and her identity as a community member.

Notes

1. Ezaro is a community of some 800 residents located approximately midway along the long, undulating Galician coastline. Men tell stories in Ezaro too, but as my focus here is on the cultural negotiation of womanhood, I will look primarily at the stories told by women. I am a cultural anthropologist and have spent a total of nearly two years doing ethnographic research in Ezaro. I lived in Galicia between 1985–1987 and have returned for visits in 1988 and 1990. My research in 1985–1987 was supported by the Wenner-Gren Foundation for Anthropological Research, a Fulbright-Hays/Spanish Government Grant, the National Science Foundation, the Social Science Research Council, and the American Council of Learned Societies. I thank Kenneth Betsalel, Victoria Enders, Christine Greenway, Barbara Hendry, and Pamela Radcliff for their helpful comments on earlier drafts of this article. Most of all I thank the people of Ezaro for welcoming me into their homes and sharing their stories with me.

2. Bronislaw Malinowski, *Argonauts of the Western Pacific* (New York: E.P. Dutton, 1961), p. 25. Malinowski's phrase has been used aptly by Catherine Allen as a focal point in her ethnographic description of cultural identity among the Quechua of Peru, *The Hold Life Has: Coca and Cultural Identity in an Andean Community* (Washington, DC: Smithsonian Institution Press, 1988).

3. I studied lace-making during my first months of fieldwork in Ezaro. I arrived in Ezaro in the middle of a miserably cold and damp January. All of the villagers seemed to be securely bolted inside of their houses and, still struggling with the local version of Gallego, I barely understood a word spoken to me by the chance villager I happened upon. I took solace in a lace-making class in the nearby town of Cée. There I could sit and quietly puzzle over my lace and listen to the animated chatter in Gallego carried on by my fellow (and far more proficient) lace-makers until my ears at last became attuned to the coastal accent. Then, as the winter rains tapered off and my linguistic confidence increased, the fact that I had learned to make lace (and even had two simple products to show for my efforts) considerably improved my standing in the eyes of village women. I was no longer simply an errant tourist; I was becoming *unha de nos*.

4. As is pointed out by Lila Abu-Lughod in *Writing Women's Worlds: Bedouin Stories* (Berkeley, CA: University of California Press, 1993), p. 16.

5. George C. Rosenwald and Richard L. Ochberg, "Introduction: Life Stories, Cultural Politics, and Self-Understanding," in Rosenwald and Ochbert, eds., *Storied Lives: The Cultural Politics of Self- Understanding* (New Haven, CT: Yale University Press, 1992), p. 7.

6. Mary Catherine Bateson, *Composing a Life* (New York: Plume, 1990), p. 3.

7. Ibid., p. 214.

8. Ibid., pp. 1–2.

9. Lila Abu-Lughod, "Writing Against Culture," in Richard G. Fox, ed., *Recapturing Anthropology: Working in the Present* (Santa Fe, NM: School of American Research Press, 1991), p. 154. In this article, Abu-Lughod undertakes a feminist critique of a seminal volume in contemporary anthropology, *Writing Culture: The Poetics and Politics of Ethnography*, edited by James Clifford and George E. Marcus (Berkeley, CA: University of California Press, 1986). This feminist critique is continued in *Women Writing Culture*, edited by Ruth Behar and Deborah A. Gordon (Berkeley, CA: University of California Press, 1995).

10. For an overview of the development of feminist anthropology see Micaela di Leonardo, "Gender, Culture and Political Economy: Feminist Anthropology in Historical Perspective," in Micaela di Leonardo, ed., *Gender at the Crossroads of Knowledge: Feminist Anthropology in the Postmodern Era* (Berkeley, CA: University of California Press, 1991). See the essays in di Leonardo and in Faye Ginsburg and Anna Lownhaupt Tsing, eds., *Uncertain Terms: Negotiating Gender in American Culture* (Boston: Beacon Press, 1990) for a sampling of current feminist perspectives in anthropology. A significant portion of the recent work on gender in Europeanist anthropology has been done in Greece; see for example the essays in Jill Dubisch, ed., *Gender and Power in Rural Greece* (Princeton, NJ: Princeton University Press, 1986) and Peter Loizos and Evthymios Papataxiarchis, eds., *Contested Identities: Gender and Kinship in Modern Greece* (Princeton, NJ: Princeton University Press, 1991), as well as C. Nadia Seremetakis, *The Last Work: Women, Death, and Divination in Inner Mani* (Chicago, IL: University of Chicago Press, 1991), Michael Herzfeld, "In Defiance of Destiny: The Management of Time and Gender at a Cretan Funeral," *American Ethnologist* 20 (1992) and Jill Dubisch, "'Foreign Chickens' and Other Outsiders: Gender and Community in Greece," *American Ethnologist* 20 (1992).

11. For an important early contribution, see Ann Cornelisen, *Women of the Shadows: A Study of the Wives and Mothers of Southern Italy* (New York: Vintage Books, 1977).

12. See Caroline B. Brettell, *Men Who Migrate, Women Who Wait: Population and History in a Portuguese Parish* (Princeton, NJ: Princeton University Press, 1986), Sally Cole, *Women of the Praia: Work and Lives in a Portuguese Coastal Community* (Princeton, NJ: Princeton University Press, 1991) and Heidi Kelley, "Unwed Mothers and Household Reputation in a Spanish Galician Community," *American Ethnologist* 18 (1991).

13. See, for instance, David D. Gilmore, "Honor, Honesty, Shame: Male Status in Contemporary Andalusia," in D.D. Gilmore, ed., *Honor and Shame and the Unity of the Mediterranean* (Washington, DC: American Anthropological Association, 1987).

14. The seminal statements of this position were made by Ernestine Friedl, "The Position of Women: Appearance and Reality," *Anthropological Quarterly* 40 (1967) and Joyce Riegelhaupt, "Saloio Women: An Analysis of Informal and Formal Political and Economic Roles of Portuguese Peasant Women," *Anthropological Quarterly* 40 (1967).

15. Susan Carol Rogers, "Female Forms of Power and the Myth of Male Dominance: A Model of Female/Male Interaction in Peasant Society," *American Ethnologist* 2 (1975) and "Gender in Southwestern France: The Myth of Male Dominance Revisited," *Anthropology* 9 (1985).

16. For classic statements of the honor/shame paradigm see Jean G. Peristiany, ed., *Honour and Shame: The Values of Mediterranean Society* (London: Weidenfeld and Nicolson, 1965) and Julián Pitt- Rivers, *The Fate of Shechem, or The Politics of Sex: Essays in the Anthropology of the Mediterranean* (Cambridge: Cambridge University Press, 1977).

17. David D. Gilmore, "Men and Women in Southern Spain: 'Domestic Power' Revisited," *American Anthropologist* 92 (1990).

18. For a cogent criticism of implicit biases in the anthropological study of kinship see Sylvia Junko Yanagisako and Jane Fishburne Collier, "Toward a Unified Analysis of Gender and Kinship," in Collier and Yanagisako, eds., *Gender and Kinship: Essays Toward a Unified Analysis* (Stanford, CA: Stanford University Press, 1987).

19. David D. Gilmore, "Sexual Ideology in Andalusian Oral Literature: A Comparative View of a Mediterranean Complex," *Ethnology* 22 (1983), and "Mother-Son Intimacy and the Dual View of Woman in Andalusia: Analysis Through Oral Poetry," *Ethos* 14 (1986), and Margaret M. Gilmore and David D. Gilmore, "'Machismo': A Psychodynamic Approach (Spain)," *Journal of Psychoanalytic Anthropology* 2 (1979).

20. David D. Gilmore, *Manhood in the Making: Cultural Concepts of Masculinity* (New Haven, CT: Yale University Press, 1990).

21. Ibid., p. 12.

22. See, for example, Sarah Uhl, "Special Friends: The Organization of Intersex Friendship in Escalona (Andalusia), Spain," *Anthropology* 9 (1985), "Making the Bed: Creating the Home in Escalona, Andalusia," *Ethnology* 28 (1989) and "Forbidden Friends: Cultural Veils of Female Friendship in Andalusia," *American Ethnologist* 18 (1991).

23. Gilmore, *Manhood in the Making*, p. 32.

24. A phrasing that I borrow from Friedl, "The Position of Women: Appearance and Reality."

25. Gilmore, "Men And Women in Southern Spain."

26. Jane Fishburne Collier, "From Mary to Modern Woman: The Material Basis of Marianismo and its Transformation in a Spanish Village," *American Ethnologist* 13 (1986); Susan Harding, "Women and Words in a Spanish Village," in Rayna Reiter, ed., *Toward an Anthropology of Women* (New York: Monthly Review Press, 1975);

Jenny Masur, "Women's Work in Rural Andalusia," *Ethnology* 23 (1984), and Sarah Uhl, "Special Friends," "Making the Bed," and "Forbidden Friends."

27. In "Forbidden Friends," Uhl argues that female friendships need to be investigated more closely for the role they may play in community organization in rural southern Europe. Previous studies have tended to focus only on the integrative functions of male friendships.

28. Michael Herzfeld, "Within and Without: The Category of 'Female' in the Ethnography of Modern Greece," in Dubisch, *Gender and Power in Rural Greece.*

29. For a related argument, see Heidi Kelley, "The Myth of Matriarchy: Symbols of Womanhood in Galician Regional Identity," *Anthropological Quarterly* 67 (1994).

30. This complex in some respects extends across northern Spain (John Tone, in the third part of this book, describes a comparable case from northern Navarre) and may be associated with a long-standing focus on hoe agriculture. See Julio Caro Baroja, *Los Pueblos de España*, vols. 1 and 2 (Madrid: Ediciones Istmo, 1964). For discussions of women and work in other parts of Galicia and in northwestern Portugal, see Brettell, *Men Who Migrate*, and *We Have Already Cried Many Tears: The Stories of Three Portuguese Migrant Women* (Prospect Heights, IL: Waveland Press, 1995); Hans C. Buechler and Judith-María Buechler, *Carmen: The Autobiography of a Spanish Galician Woman* (Rochester, VT: Schenkman Books, 1981); Cole, *Women of the Praia*; Susana de la Gala González, *Muller e Cambio Social* (Tesis de Licenciatura, Universidade de Santiago de Compostela, Facultade de Filosofía e Ciencias da Educación, 1990); Carmelo Lisón Tolosana, *Antropología cultural de Galicia* (Madrid: Akal Editor, 1979); Lourdes Méndez, *"Cousas de Mulleres": Campesinas, Poder y Vida Cotidiana (Lugo 1940–1980)* (Barcelona: Anthropos, 1988); and Paz Sofía Moreno Feliú, "Mujer," in *Gran Enciclopedia Gallega* (Santiago: Silverio Cañada, 1974). For a discussion of fluid notions of sex and marriage in Galicia in the sixteenth and seventeenth centuries see Allyson Poska, "It's Not a Sin: Gallegan Women and Extramarital Sexuality" (paper delivered at the twenty-seventh annual meeting of the Society for Spanish and Portuguese Historical Studies, Tucson, AZ, 1996).

31. Jane Collier, in "From Mary to Modern Woman," describes a transition in ideals of womanhood—from a preoccupation with female chastity to a concern with personal capabilities and preferences—in an Andalusian village. She correlates this transition with a wider change in the organization of inequality in the community, from focusing on inheritance to centering on salaried jobs. While I will demonstrate, like Collier, that recent changes in Ezaro have exacerbated the dichotomy between the ideals of womanhood there, I also argue that this opposition is of long standing in the community, reflecting a persistent dichotomy in community definitions of household reputation and success.

32. These and other emic terms are in Gallego, the language spoken in Ezaro.

33. Inheritance in Ezaro is characterized by a tension between partible and impartible values. In practice, parents usually elect to award one of their children with a *millora*, a larger share (from one- to two-thirds) of the inheritance, with the remainder divided equally among all heirs. Both sons and daughters are treated equally, but there does seem to be a recent trend toward favoring daughters with the *millora*. For further description of inheritance practices in Ezaro see Heidi Kelley, "Competition vs. Cooperation: Female Self-Image in a Coastal Galician Community" (Ph.D. diss., University of Washington, 1988). On inheritance in other parts of Galicia see Rainer Lutz Bauer, "Inheritance and Inequality in a Spanish Galician Community, 1840–1935," *Ethnohistory* 34 (1987) and Carmelo Lisón Tolosana, "The Ethics of Inheritance" in J.G. Peristiany, ed., *Mediterranean Family Structures* (Cambridge: Cambridge University Press, 1976).

34. Fishing has waned considerably in economic importance in Ezaro over the last twenty years. In defining themselves as *pescadores e emigrantes*, villagers today focus on wage labor as a common denominator in this identification. Local sources of wage labor are few: a small sawmill and a hydroelectric plant in Ezaro and a metallic-carbides factory in nearby Brens. Perhaps most important is the construction trade in Ezaro; it is kept bustling with orders from emigrants who want to build houses in their natal village. The primary destinations of emigrants from Ezaro today are London, Switzerland, and Bayone, New Jersey. In addition, some village men have acquired lucrative jobs on cargo ships; they are considered *emigrantes* too.

35. See Brettell, *Men Who Migrate*, Kelley, "Unwed Mothers," and Lisón Tolosana, *Antropología Cultural*. In *Women of the Praia*, Cole describes a northern coastal Portuguese community where women's involvement in maritime work is associated with a high degree of female autonomy and power.

36. There is the occasional woman whose husband has taken her along fishing once or twice, but most village women have never set foot on a fishing boat. Women are nonetheless very involved in the support activities associated with fishing. In the past, sardines were salted and as such, formed a staple of the diet year-round. Women also sold fish on foot, balancing heavy baskets of fish on their heads, to mountain villages. Today, in the few remaining households in which fishing constitutes a primary economic activity, women sell the fish door-to-door in Ezaro or at the daily market in nearby Cée.

37. The character of emigration from Galicia has evolved considerably from 1860, when emigration from the region first took off, to the present day. In the second half of the nineteenth century, according to Ramón Villares Paz in *Historia de Galicia* (Madrid: Alhambra, 1980), 70% of the emigrants did not return to Galicia. In this period few women and even fewer families participated in the exodus. From 1900 on emigration began to change markedly as women increasingly joined the ranks and the number of returnees jumped up as well. Prior to the 1930s the principal foreign destination of Galician emigrants was Latin America (primarily Cuba, Argentina, Uruguay, Brazil, and Venezuela). The world crisis of 1929 stopped the current of emigration to South America and while emigration would later resume to this area, it never again

attained its prior magnitude. From the 1940s on, and particularly in the 1960s, the tide of Galician emigration turned towards northern Europe (particularly Germany and Switzerland) and North America in response to both the increasing demand for immigrant labor from the countries of these regions and Spain's 1962 emigration law which facilitated legal emigration (in contrast to the earlier, more restrictive years of the Franco regime). After 1940, female participation in emigration increased substantially; between 1946 and 1964, 44% of Galicia's emigrants were women. See *Situación actual y perspectivas de desarrollo de Galicia*, vol. 3 (Confederación Española de Cajas de Ahorros, 1975) for emigration statistics.

38. While I have observed that some younger women are less devoted to agriculture than their mothers, most still own and tend fields, or, for those who have not yet inherited fields, help their mothers in their agricultural tasks. The opening of the sewing cooperative in 1988 has drawn a small, but significant, number of women whom I had previously observed to be highly committed to agriculture into full-time wage work. In 1990, nonetheless, these women continued to do agricultural work in the evenings and weekends.

39. In these stories, Ezaro women are actively constructing and contesting their notions of the past. On the cultural processes by which tradition and memory are invented and authenticated see, for example, Richard Handler, *Nationalism and the Politics of Culture in Quebec* (Madison, WI: University of Wisconsin Press, 1988); Eric Hobsbawm and Terence Ranger, eds., *The Invention of Tradition* (Cambridge: Cambridge University Press, 1983); Joyce S. Linnekin, "Defining Tradition: Variations on the Hawaiian Identity," *American Ethnologist* 10 (1983); and Joanne Rappaport, *The Politics of Memory: Native Historical Interpretation in the Colombian Andes* (Cambridge: Cambridge University Press, 1990). See also Rainer Lutz Bauer, "Changing Representations of Place, Community, and Character in the Spanish Sierra del Caurel," *American Ethnologist* 19 (1992) for an analysis of how interpretations of the past merge with constructions of place in Galician villagers' representations of themselves as marginalized.

40. Along with the pair of civil guards stationed in the village, local priests were considered to have been agents of Franco. Anticlericalism appears to be an attitude of long standing in the village, with historical roots in relationships of economic dependence to the Church, exacerbated by the Church's association with the Franco regime. Villagers may be both fervently anticlerical, reflecting disdain for the institutional trappings of the Church, and profoundly religious, attending mass regularly and leaving offerings for the saints. For extended discussions of anticlericalism and popular religiosity in contemporary Europe see the volume edited by Ellen Badone, *Religious Orthodoxy and Popular Faith in European Society* (Princeton, NJ: Princeton University Press, 1990) as well as Susan Tax Freeman, "Religious Aspects of the Social Organization of a Castilian Village," *American Anthropologist* 70 (1968); João de Pina-Cabral, *Sons of Adam, Daughters of Eve: The Peasant Worldview of Alto Minho* (Oxford: Clarendon Press, 1986) and Joyce Riegelhaupt, "Popular Anti-Clericalism and Religiosity in Pre-1974 Portugal," in Eric R. Wolf, ed., *Religion, Power, and*

Protest in Local Communities: The Northern Shore of the Mediterranean (Berlin: Mouton, 1984).

41. See Richard Maddox, *El Castillo: The Politics of Tradition in an Andalusian Town* (Urbana, and Chicago, IL: University of Illinois Press, 1993) for a discussion of the negotiation of the symbolic meanings of monuments in the construction of community identity in an Andalusian town.

42. See Cole, *Women of the Praia*, for a description of the construction of a new *dona de casa* (housewife) ideal of womanhood in a coastal Portuguese community. In Ezaro, women use stories about Pindo women as a backdrop against which to debate the validity of a newly emergent housewife ideal in their own community.

43. Although power struggles may be particularly acute when mother and daughter are living in, and contesting the definition of, the same household, they also flourish between mothers and daughters living separately. For an example, see Heidi Kelley, "The Invention of Motherhood: Family and Regional Histories in Galicia" (paper delivered at the ninety-first annual meeting of the American Anthropological Association, San Francisco, 1992).

44. The names used in this section are all pseudonyms.

45. Disputes such as this one among siblings are quite common in Ezaro, exacerbated by the tension between impartible and partible tendencies in inheritance practice.

46. In 1996 Mari-Carmen informed me that her husband had found a job in England. He now emigrates to England while Mari-Carmen, still living with her parents, works on contract and takes care of Olga.

Part III

Political Identities

Introduction

In the separate spheres theoretical model, politics, like work, was gendered male. This gendering of the political sphere was codified by the Constitutional exclusion of women from the universal principles of citizenship espoused by nineteenth century liberal regimes. What set Spain apart within this European pattern was the extension of this exclusion into the 1970s. With the exception of the brief period of the Second Republic (1931–1936), and then after the end of the Franco dictatorship in 1975, women were denied formal citizenship and the political rights that accompany them. Even when women gained formal rights, their participation rarely conformed to the expected categories of political behavior. Thus, women in modern Spain have been consistently marginalized from the formal political sphere. The result, as this introductory essay will demonstrate, is that women have played a very small role in the conventional political life of the nation.

Nevertheless, as the chapters in this section demonstrate, the relationship between women, gender, and politics was much more complex. Instead of an exclusionary opposition between the private female sphere and the male political sphere, the boundaries between the two were more porous. Not only did some women enter the male political sphere to defend their perceived interests, but private sphere masculine concerns shaped policy in the public realm. Thus, even though most women were barred from participation in the formal political sphere, that sphere and its activities were nevertheless profoundly gendered, and not universal in principle. Finally, women excluded from the formal political realm often pursued other avenues of political action that bypassed the channels closed to them. The question these chapters ask is not whether or not women were political, but what different forms did women's politics take, and what were the ways in which politics itself was gendered?

The first chapter by White focuses on the power of gendered metaphors in political discourse. The next three chapters look for women's politics outside the narrow boundaries of the formal political sphere—in the resistance to Napoleon, in miners' wives campaigns for social justice, and in consumer riots. The following two chapters address the role of women in the formal political sphere during the two exceptional periods when women participated as citizens in liberal democratic regimes. The final chapter focuses on another marginalized political group of women, in this case Francoist women struggling to assert their identity in the new democratic regime. From differing perspectives, all of the chapters point both to the centrality of gender in political life and to the centrality of politics in women's lives. Thus, the chapters in this section provide an alternative vision of politics, in which women and gender figure prominently.

Women's participation in formal institutional politics was almost nonexistent until the democratic transition. Until the Second Republic, women could neither vote nor run for office, whether at the national or the municipal level.[1] In 1931, in the first elections of the new Republic, women could run as candidates, but only after the establishment of the new constitution were women also granted the suffrage. In the 1931 election, three women were elected as deputies to the Cortes, and their number was increased to five in both the subsequent major elections of 1933 and 1936. Another political barrier was broken during the Civil War, when Federica Montseny became the first female—and the first anarchist—cabinet minister—and only the second in Europe, after Alexandra Kollantai.[2] However, these breakthroughs were more exceptions than the start of a new trend toward greater female participation in formal political institutions.

The Republic did mobilize some women for auxiliary political support, especially during the Civil War. Through organizations like the *Mujeres Libres*, associated with the anarchosyndicalist CNT, and the *Mujeres Antifascistas*, linked to the Communist party, thousands of women contributed to the Republican cause by doing everything from sewing bandages to taking over "male" jobs.[3] On the other side, Catholic and other right wing political organizations mobilized women's auxiliaries against the anticlerical policies of the Republic and in defense of "traditional" Spain.[4] Of these right wing women's organizations, the *Sección Femenina* of the fascist Falange party (formed in 1934), gained a prominent place in the post civil war political order. Under the authoritarian Franco regime, they embodied, like the Nazi women under Hitler and the Fascist women under Mussolini, the paradox of public functionaries who indoctrinated the rest of their countrywomen in the virtues of domesticity. Like these other rightist women they did not view their activities as formally political, and accepted that politics was men's work. Other than these few groups of women, the formal political arena fulfilled the prescription of separate spheres by remaining a male bastion. Only after 1975 did women begin to enter formal politics in numbers still low, but comparable to those in other European countries.[5]

This apparent lack of political presence was echoed in the shape of the organized women's movement, both during the epoch of so-called first wave feminism (late 19th–early 20th centuries), and more recently during the "second wave" (1960s–1970s). As in many European countries, Spain's "first wave" feminist movement was small and had little impact on the formal political sphere.[6] Moreover, most of the feminist groups were more interested in pursuing civil and social rights for women than political rights. Thus, even feminist women were not primarily agitating for more political participation by women. There were many reasons for this subordination of political rights, including the general distrust of liberal politics in a country where manipulated elections blunted the impact of suffrage.[7] As a result, the feminist movement did not act as a major bridge to propel women into formal politics.

The constituency of the first wave feminist movement was, as in most other countries, largely middle class and reformist, or even conservative. British feminism—with its famous images of radical feminists chaining themselves to the doors of Parliament—was the exception, not the rule, in European feminist movements, most of which were filled by quite proper bourgeois ladies who took care not to transgress contemporary standards of female behavior. Thus, Spanish feminists, like their French counterparts, rarely took to the streets or engaged in confrontational public actions. Furthermore, Spanish feminists, like most of their counterparts in Catholic Europe, did not try to contest women's central role in the family, but to claim rights based on their vital function in a relational social order.[8]

These qualities certainly applied to the most important of Spain's feminist organizations, the National Association of Spanish Women (ANME). Politically conservative, the ANME promoted better education for women, the opening of more professions, the suppression of legalized prostitution and some protective institutions for poor women. Although it was not explicitly included in the program, the organization also favored women's suffrage, because of its moralizing impact on politics.[9] In addition to the ANME, there were several other middle class groups dedicated to improving the legal and economic status of Spanish women, the most famous of which was the Lyceum Club, comprising a few hundred prominent Madrid women, like the future parliamentary deputies Victoria Kent and Clara Campoamor.

Although the profile of Spain's feminist movement is similar to those in other Catholic European countries, it was also one of the weakest. The slower growth of an urban, professional middle class delayed the development of an associational culture that could spawn a large women's movement. In fact, Spain's first national women's organization, the ANME, was formed only in 1918, when the "first wave" movements in other countries had achieved many of their basic programs and had begun to lose momentum. When, only thirteen years later, the Second Republic granted most of the standard feminist demands, from legal equality to the suffrage, "from above" and not as the result of feminist pressure, the movement had few victories for which it could take credit. Finally, the potential impact of the movement was further hindered by the dramatic political turmoil of the 1930s, when independent women's movements found it difficult to claim a space between a polarizing left and right.

The mainstream left and right did try to organize women for their own agendas, but even the left parties and trade unions that theoretically supported women's rights did not actively pursue women's issues. A few individuals within these movements, such as the Socialist deputies Margarita Nelken and María Lejarraga y García, did speak out for greater attention to the "woman question."[10] On the other hand, many of the other prominent women on the revolutionary left, like the Communist Dolores Ibarruri, "La Pasionaria," followed the party line that the "woman question" was irrelevant until after class liberation. The only institutional attempt to pursue a socialist feminist agenda was the anarchist-affiliated *Mujeres Libres*, which tried during the Civil War and in the face of serious resistance, to carve out an independent space within the anarchosyndicalist movement for pursuing women's issues.[11]

The nationalist victory in the Civil War brought an end to all of these women's movements, when the *Sección Femenina* became the only officially recognized women's organization for the next forty years. The death of the dictator and the political transition that followed in the mid-1970s provided the context for a "second wave" feminist movement. In contrast to the "second wave" movements elsewhere in Europe and the U.S., which rose out of the protests and countercultural movements of the late 1960s, Spanish feminism was clearly shaped by the specific political context of building a new democratic regime.[12] However, like similar movements elsewhere, Spanish feminism emerged out of the broader oppositional movements demanding the greater democratization of state and society. This context situated the Spanish feminists firmly on the left, many of them linked to the Communist and Socialist parties.

As in other countries, the relationship between feminism and the left was a troubled one. While the left parties paid lip service to women's rights, many men argued, as they had in the 1930s, that women's rights were secondary to the monumental political transition Spain was undergoing. This reluctance helped split the feminist movement between the political feminists, so-called because they argued the necessity of working with the political parties, and the anti-political feminists, who insisted that women should pursue their own independent agenda. Despite the divisions, many of the groups shared a similar vision of the future, based on a radical transformation of the capitalist, patriarchal structure of society.

But, of course, no such transformation took place, and in fact the establishment of the democratic regime was carried out within the framework of the existing capitalist and patriarchal system and without significant feminist input. Like other groups on the left, the feminists found their language of revolutionary transformation out of sync with the dominant theme of "pacts" and compromises. In addition, the feminists failed to reach the majority of Spanish women, who had grown up inside the Francoist education system. Without a mass popular base, isolated in the political discourse and fragmented into competing interests, Spain's feminist movement has remained on the margin of contemporary institutional politics.

As this brief narrative illustrates, formal politics in modern Spain was predominantly masculine. In order to transcend the simplistic conclusion that women and politics stood in opposing categories, we have suggested that politics is a broader and more complex phenomenon. From this perspective, the following chapters explore the varied relationships between politics, gender and women.

Notes

1. In 1924, during the dictatorship of Primo de Rivera (1923–1929), women were granted the right to vote in municipal elections, but none were held.

2. And, as Joan Connelly Ullman points out, she was given one of the weakest departments, the Ministry of Health. "La protagonista ausente: La mujer como objeto y sujeto de la historia de España," in María Angeles Durán, ed., *La mujer en el mundo contemporáneo* (Madrid: Universidad Autónoma de Madrid, 1981), p. 43.

3. Mary Nash estimates that *Mujeres Libres* attracted about 20,000 women at its height during the Civil War, while the *Mujeres Antifascistas* claimed 50,000 even before the war broke out, after which they established groups in 255 localities. See Nash, *Mujer y movimiento obrero en España, 1931–1939* (Barcelona: Editorial Fontamara, 1981), pp. 87, 244.

4. On the political mobilization of Catholic women, see Mary Vincent, "The Politicization of Catholic Women in Salamanca, 1931–1936," in Paul Preston and Frances Lannon, eds., *Elites and Power in Twentieth Century Spain* (Oxford: Oxford University Press, 1990).

5. From 1977 to 1993, the percentage of women deputies in the Spanish parliament has hovered around 14%. Percentages for other European countries in 1993 were: Denmark, 33%; Holland, 24%; Germany, 21%; and less than 10% in Britain, Italy, and France. *El Pais*, March 4, 1993.

6. On first wave feminism in Spain, see Concha Fagoaga, *La voz y el voto de las mujeres: El sufragismo en España, 1870–1931* (Barcelona: Icaria, 1985), and Geraldine Scanlon, *La polémica feminista en la España contemporánea, 1868–1974* (Madrid: Akal, 1986).

7. Mary Nash makes this point in *Defying Male Civilization: Women in the Spanish Civil War* (Denver, CO: Arden Press, 1995), p. 35.

8. Karen Offen distinguished between what she called "relational feminism" from the individual rights tradition of the Anglo Saxon countries. "Defining Feminism: A Comparative Historical Approach," *Signs* 14, no. 1 (1988).

9. Geraldine Scanlon, *La polémica feminista*, pp. 203–212.

10. Joan Connelly Ullman, "La protagonista ausente," pp. 42–43.

11. For a feminist reading of the *Mujeres Libres*' agenda, see Martha Ackelsberg, *Free Women of Spain* (Urbana, IL: University of Illinois Press, 1991).

12. On the "second wave" feminist movement, see Mónica Threlfall, "The Women's Movement in Spain," *New Left Review* 151 (May–June 1985): 47.

9

Liberty, Honor, Order: Gender and Political Discourse in Nineteenth-Century Spain

Sarah L. White

The chaste Christian mother—anchor of society—and the subversive sexual siren delimit the spheres of female identity in much of Spanish history. Empirical investigations of women's lives clearly reveal a more complex reality. Even more compelling is the complexity, on closer examination, of a seemingly static and rigidly binary construction of gender in public discourse. Exploring the protean imagery of feminine virtue points up the peculiar frangibility of traditionalist Spain: repressive gender constructs legitimated radical political change.

The partisans of competing political platforms in nineteenth-century Spain manipulated popular images of women to further their particular material and ideological interests. Reinforcing a traditionally masculine moral order at the same time as they struggled to construct a modern state, radical democrats, conservative republicans, and constitutional monarchists constructed feminine political allegories to represent both the virtues of their own agendas and the moral inferiority of their opponents. The monarchy, the republic, the very idea of liberty, were all portrayed as women—mythic female figures charged with the task of nurturing the nation, the family of subjects or citizens.[1] At critical moments of political transition, the proponents of revolution—or reaction—depicted such women as irrational, diseased, promiscuous, a threat to the integrity of the nation. A political enemy thus became a sexual threat, embodied in the form of the rogue female.[2]

A female out of control was not only disorderly; she was dishonorable. And the protection of honor was, in Spain, central to the quest for an appropriate marriage of liberty and order—two classic nineteenth-century ideals that defined the struggle to forge a liberal state everywhere in modern Europe.

Throughout the century, an intensely moralizing language of honor pervaded the often violent disputes over the appropriate civil, political and economic organization of the nation. And on the masculinist horizon of Spanish politics—particularly in the Mediterranean culture of Andalusia, which drew an intimate connection between physical and moral integrity[3]—honor was a matter of gender, conceptually inextricable from normative notions of sexual power, chastity, and perversity.

The gendering of political discourse translated ideological debates on the nature of legitimate government into a metaphorical vernacular immediately accessible to all levels of society. Indeed, cultural practice—in this case, the construction of female political symbols—acts as both reflection and agent of political change. By examining the production of a moral lexicon of gendered political symbology in the years preceding the Glorious Revolution of 1868 and during the six-year democratic experiment that followed, this chapter demonstrates how Spanish society imagined itself in gendered ways, and how traditional notions of the feminine shaped political attitudes and actions.

The Revolution of 1868

Like many of its neighbors north of the Pyrenees, Spain in the nineteenth century struggled to construct a liberal polity unhindered by the prerogatives of capricious monarchs and the control of oligarchic interests. The apogee of this struggle was the *Gloriosa*—the "glorious" democratic revolution that began in September 1868 with a *pronunciamiento*,[4] dethroned the reigning queen, Isabel II, carried Spain through a new constitutional monarchy and a republic, and ended with the Bourbon restoration in 1874.[5] In addition to a civil war with the reactionary Catholic Carlists[6] in the north and a colonial war in Cuba, the defenders of the *Gloriosa* faced the more devastating threat of opposition within their own ranks—federalist insurgency[7] in the south and political factionalism in Madrid.

The internal crises of the September Revolution sprang from the divergent intentions of those who forged it. To the generals who deposed Isabel II, Spain's honor was at stake; they sought to establish a legitimate constitutional monarchy free from the "profligacy" and "caprice of power" that sullied the peninsula during the last years of Isabel's rule.[8] To the provincial republicans of Andalusia, the *Gloriosa*—as the culmination of a "titanic struggle between the people and the throne"—represented a far more serious challenge to the established order.[9] Agitating for a federal and democratic republic, they claimed that a monarchy of any sort would hinder "the glorious march of the September Revolution."[10] Finally, to the mass of rural workers in southern Spain, who had little interest in the political vicissitudes of bourgeois liberalism, the *Gloriosa* brought the promise of *reparto*—the division of the land among those who worked it. And in Andalusia, where the land was monopolized by a politically powerful rural oligarchy, the call for *reparto* was a call for social revolution.

The *Gloriosa*, then, was not one revolution, but several. As the various strands of political and social radicalism intertwined and clashed during the *sexenio democrático*,[11] one of the most dramatic battlegrounds—ideological and military—was Andalusia. This notoriously recalcitrant region, comprising the eight southernmost provinces of Spain, was the springboard for numerous nineteenth century *pronunciamientos*, the home of many of the century's liberal intellectuals, the heart of republican insurrection, and the earliest theatre of rural anarchism.[12]

Out of this political volcano emerged a steady flow of ideological venom and approbation: igneous allegories of female power and corruption ruled southern political discourse. By describing the body politic as a female body, and linking the public life of the nation with the private life of the queen, Andalusian democrats created the political space for an unprecedented attack on the monarchy in 1868.

Honor and the Monarchy

Before 1868, the primary repository of national honor was the monarch. Isabel II began her reign (1833–1868) as the "innocent little queen" who rescued Spain from the threat of Carlist reaction and thus became, if by default, a symbol of liberal constitutionalism.[13]

Women attached to the throne, however, were not inherently inviolable. The queen-mother, Maria Cristina of Naples—variously demonized as thief, harlot, and bad mother—suffered sordid rumors of scandal throughout her regency. And the black legend of Isabel's grandmother, Maria Luisa of Parma, is famous in the history of Spain.[14] But these two reviled predecessors of Isabel married Spanish kings; because they did not themselves inherit the crown, their political enemies could attack them in spiteful narratives of royal impropriety without attacking monarchy itself. The infamy of such women lay precisely in manipulating or betraying a legitimate ruler who honorably headed the body politic: Maria Luisa turned the ascetic, reforming court of the eighteenth century Bourbons—symbolized by her father-in-law, Charles III—into a cradle of luxury and deceit; Maria Cristina abused the good name of her infant daughter, Isabel II, to win political power and personal financial gain.

To deride Isabel would be to defame the institution and the nation she represented. Indeed, despite her aberrant behavior—most notably, an unconstrained sexual life punctuated by remorseful periods of superstitious religiosity—Isabel was popularly perceived as a good Catholic queen and a chaste mother to the nation.

She inherited this role as an adolescent, after the political tumult of two regencies—those of Maria Cristina (1833–1840) and General Espartero (1840–1843)—prompted the Cortes to declare Isabel of age in 1843. Six years later she married an effeminate cousin, the Infante Francisco de Asis, widely rumored to be a homosexual. Frustrated with the unhappy union, the young queen turned her romantic attentions to a series of prominent officers—military heroes who had defended her throne from the Carlists. British and American observers at the Bourbon court recounted endless tales of distasteful spectacles, such as Isabel's untoward attentions to General Serrano at La Granja, where

> Her Majesty had thrown aside even the semblance of reserve . . . no care was taken to conceal her relations with Serrano from ordinary observation—in short, her passion for him had destroyed all regard for her own reputation, the dignity of her station, and the welfare of her people; and could charitably be attributed only to mental madness or physical disease.[15]

Aristocrats in Isabel's social milieux saw her not as a wayward woman, but a willful, hysterical child, given to tantrums and sentimental religious fervor. Whether excoriated by foreign diplomats or infantalized by her peers, disapproval was essentially limited to the narrow circle of the court; popular acclaim for the young queen persisted in the provinces until the political crisis at the end of her reign.

During Isabel's tour of Andalusia in 1862, for example, provincial witnesses reported effusive demonstrations of popular adoration. In Málaga, crowds of fervent well-wishers chanting the "magic name of Isabel II" filled the fields and roads demarcating the royal itinerary, and in the capital, all quarters were illuminated, all balconies adorned.[16] This atmosphere of public festivity cannot provide an intimate portrait of political sentiment; the visit of any monarch possesses spectacle value, a celebrity appeal that galvanizes communities of varied ideology and identity. Encomiastic civic celebrations, however, are not insignificant. Less than a decade later these same olive groves and highways would be lined with armed volunteers marching against royal troops, these same quarters of the capital filled with flaming portraits of a reviled queen, these balconies draped in black following the disarming of popular militias.[17]

Isabel was not the muscular monarchical symbol of a heroic nation; she did not appeal to an abstract patriotism that could summon emotional demonstrations from an otherwise oppressed populace. On the contrary, in the imagination of Andalusia, her virtues were essentially feminine. Official chronicles say nothing of her ability to rule, claiming instead to "respect her as a queen, praise her as a lady, applaud her as a mother, and salute her as a noble and loving woman."[18] Isabel reinforced this image in carefully orchestrated public appearances as a nurturing benefactress of the *pueblo*, distributing clothing, money, and food to widows and orphans, visiting working girls in local factories, and touring schools and hospitals.[19] It is not of course uncommon for a monarch in any country to be somehow above the political fray, playing a parental role and serving as the figurative embodiment of national virtue. Indeed, it is precisely the symbolic status of the queen, however traditional, which matters here, and the ways in which that representational role could be altered. For Isabel *qua* queen was, in the course of the Revolution, not unmasked but recloaked.

The popular construction of competing mythic narratives—usually juxtaposing sexual deviance and Christian beneficence—for the historical exploits of Spanish rulers has been documented by cultural anthropologists.[20] These national legends, told and retold for generations, demonstrate how the scapegoating or deification of a single protagonist reflects and legitimizes the psychological needs of the inhabitants of a particular political epoch.

The legend of Isabel was reinvented not over the course of centuries, but in a brief moment of political struggle during the *Gloriosa.* Inheriting the mantle of a namesake glorified by the gothic lore of nineteenth-century romanticism as the virtuous warrior-queen who drove the Infidel from Spain, Isabel II was designated at birth a symbol for all the nation could and should be. The hapless Bourbon was cast as a latter-day Hapsburg, a mother-figure who could shepherd a languishing Spain into a new golden age.[21] Such mythic hopes were inscribed on the triumphal arches erected to honor Isabel II as she entered the province of Málaga in 1862; opposing panels presented the majestic fifteenth-century triumphs of Isabel I alongside prayers that the current queen would "raise Spain from her prostration and make her grand again."[22]

It was an impossible demand, given the dramatic socioeconomic disparities and entrenched political interests that paralyzed Spain in the nineteenth century. That Isabel—raised in a conservative court whose absolutist traditions belied its declared ideals of constitutionalism, called to rule when she was only thirteen, and subsequently surrounded by influential clerics and generals—was entirely unsuited for the task of modernizing Spain, is not of primary import. History lurches about through perception as much as actuality, driven by the stories and representations that individuals employ to make sense of their particular universe. Thus Isabel, ill-starred hope for national resurrection, became a focal point for national frustration when the political and economic tensions of the 1860s generated a new iconography of civic honor.

Prelude to Revolution

The final years of Isabel's rule were those of Spanish economic catastrophe. Beginning in 1861, public debt increased exponentially, accompanied by a precipitous drop in exports as the Civil War across the Atlantic paralyzed the cotton market and the Catalan textile industry foundered. In 1864 it became clear that the railway system, built during the previous decade with massive support from French capital and state subsidized credit institutions, could not produce expected revenues, and construction halted. The railroad failure bankrupted the country at the same time as a European recession and financial panic in 1866 dried up the flow of foreign capital. Catastrophic harvest failures in 1867–1868 transformed Spain from a net exporter of wheat to an importer of over 400,000 tons. Thus a contracting economy with high unemployment faced the highest grain prices of the century.[23] Economic crisis engendered political vertigo as Democrats agitated for support among the restless workers of Barcelona and the agrarian poor of Andalusia, and as the demands of the liberal bourgeoisie for monetary and tariff reform became increasingly shrill.

To these bourgeois malcontents, economic disaster seemed to be a direct consequence of absolutism. Isabel's increasingly despotic rule—exercised through a government of conservative, neo-Catholic Moderados who disregarded the dictates of constitutional rule and exiled many of the liberal generals and political leaders that challenged them—united all liberal parties in opposition.[24] While liberal generals plotted revolution, southern pundits initiated a heated anti-Bourbon campaign, which, gathering force in the mid-1860s, contrasted sharply with the effusive approbation that surrounded the royal tour of Andalusia in 1862. Democratic pamphleteers, laying the ground for the myth of the bad queen that would triumph in 1868, castigated the "effete" and "theocratic" Bourbons; focusing on Isabel's *camarilla*, their tracts mocked "Paquita," her deviant husband, now seen as yet another malignant facet of the queen's anomalous sexual life, and Sor Patrocino, Isabel's clerical confidante, who claimed to have the stigmata and who symbolized a superstitious female religiosity inappropriate to the affairs of state.[25] While increasing press censorship precluded overt vilification, Andalusian journalists critiqued Isabel's impropriety through extensive commentaries on the virtuous attributes of the indisputably "civilized" Queen Victoria, and the ostensibly ruinous habits of Marie Antoinette.[26] And in a direct slight to Isabel, the Progressive city councils of Andalusia refused to support the Cortes when the Deputies decided, in 1865, to formally thank the queen for turning over to the state a large percentage of the lands belonging to the crown.[27]

When the national crisis became linked to the person of the monarch, the private life of the queen became an eminently public issue; monarchical misbehavior led to national disrepair.

Redressing National Grievances

On September 18, 1868, Generals Prim and Serrano, together with Admiral Topete, landed at Cádiz, intent on rescuing Spain from tyranny and disrepute. The rebel officers raised the ideological banner of the revolution in their manifesto of September 19, 1868, *Spain with Honor*, which explicitly attacked Isabel as the "irreconcilable enemy" of the constitution and implicitly denounced her personal indiscretions (though among these could be counted her affairs with two of the three "glorious" leaders, Serrano and Topete).[28] The revolutionary juntas that controlled the provincial capitals in the south after the *pronunciamiento* published their own manifestos, demanding not only a new and virtuous political order, but a set of very specific liberties: a free press, freedom of religion, universal suffrage, the rights of association, the abolition of conscription, and relief from commodities taxes.[29] At the same time, Andalusia saw scattered risings and land occupations by rural workers to whom the overthrow of Isabel seemed an augury of the partition of latifundia and the return of common lands.[30] According to the federalist leader Paul y Angulo, the *pronunciamiento*'s success had depended on the enthusiastic support of Andalusia's laboring masses, who "cheered on" the insurrection with a fervor that surpassed the exaltation generated by the queen's visit six years before, and without whom Serrano's decisive battle at Alcolea—where the rebel forces defeated Isabel's regular army—would have been lost.[31]

Clearly, three divergent currents of revolutionism emerged even within the first weeks of the *Gloriosa.* Each embodied a unique vision of the social and political order the revolution should construct, and the nature of liberties won. These competing paradigms—consistently represented in the language of national honor—shaped the political battles of the *sexenio.* The next six years saw the increasing estrangement of revolutionary forces as monarchists fell out with republicans, and moderate republicans with intransigent federalists. In addition, with new liberties of association granted to the working classes, the International gathered force and added its own acrimonious commentary to the already dizzying rhetoric of revolution whirling through the southern capitals and countryside.[32]

In the early days of the *sexenio*, these potentially conflictive forces of revolution stood united in opposition to the queen. Signaling the triumph of the anti-Bourbon campaign and its imagery of the errant monarch, portraits of Isabel burned in the public squares of Andalusia. In a dramatic reconfiguration of the traditional veneration of royal portraits, crowds in Málaga saluted the likeness of General Prim.[33] Prim, head of the provisional government in 1868 and favored hero of the *Gloriosa*, appeared in contemporary portraiture as a virile young officer majestically seated on a magnificent black horse. The martial leaders who peopled the triumphal art of revolutionary Spain represented a return to political virtue and sexual order. Symbols of masculine power, the generals rescued the nation by conquering the queen. Their triumph freed Spain from the stain of a scandalously tenacious old regime and its most potent symbol: the feminine debauchery of a corrupt dynasty.

Indeed, after the September Revolution, Isabel was portrayed as something more ignoble than the incompetent or inappropriately capricious ruler of a constitutional nation: the queen was a traitor to the honorable history of glorious Spain. The history of Isabel's reign was reconstructed not as that of a good girl gone bad, but of one who was bad all along. A verse typical of many circulating in the revolutionary fall of 1868 described the early "Life and Miracles of Isabel of Bourbon":

> Isabel was born / fat as a melon / before she learned to speak / she was already thinking of assassination / before she was seven / she fell in love with a soldier / her father, seeing her so eager / went and left her the crown.[34]

Isabel was irremediable. She had harbored since birth, it seemed, all the vices that purportedly made her unfit to rule—unfit, that is, to be a virtuous woman: her physical unattractiveness, her insensitivity bordering on brutality, and her amorous proclivities.

The September Revolution was thus legitimate; it could honorably dethrone the dishonorable. At the conclusion of her classic essay on gender, power, and historical analysis, Joan Scott suggests that while dramatic political changes may fundamentally alter the constellation of gender, "they may not; old notions of gender have also served to validate new regimes."[35] This was the case in modern Spain, where traditional notions of honor—defined in the nexus of female chastity and masculine power—legitimated a democratic revolution.

Indeed, if the generals who initiated the revolution demanded "Spain with Honor," the locus of dishonor—as the prolific pamphleteers of the *Gloriosa* emphasized repeatedly—was the queen, and, more generally, the monster of feminine misrule. The most scathing and direct indictments of Isabel emerged from the satiric verse that flooded Andalusia in 1868. One broadsheet entitled "Government Unmasked," for example, suggested that a populace "devoured by poverty" had been enslaved by a despotic royal family "composed of prostitutes and emasculated men." The queen's sexual transgressions were directly associated with a tyrannical abuse of political power: while the people suffer,

> the queen prostitutes herself in filthy bacchanalia, never satiated by the obscene caresses of the many lovers who surround her infamous throne. . . . Down with the immodest harlot! Down with privilege! Down with dishonorable government![36]

The relentless denunciations of the queen as "immodest" often presented in contrast the honorable nation, which, in its just judgment, preferred to see Isabel's "head without a crown, rather than her body without a head."[37] If the *pueblo* was honorable, it was not reverent, and found irresistible the irony of the queen's downfall at the hands of the military men she had so shamelessly seduced. One "admirer" made the point succinctly in a public letter to his "beloved Isabel": "the cannon of Topete / has ruined you."[38]

The language of sexual trespass was quickly translated into a broader political discourse which invoked stock perceptions of the liberal polity and the old regime in a gendered vernacular. A degenerate Isabel represented the triad of feminine vices that had undermined the resuscitation of Spain: superstition, caprice, and ignorance. In their place, the revolutionaries championed the masculine virtues of reason, law, enlightenment, and the political formula which guaranteed them: popular sovereignty.[39]

The National Revolutionary Committee described the nation's rejection of Isabel as the first *moral* act of the revolution. "Adulterous," "superstitious," "fanatical," and "cruel," the libidinous queen was not simply a feckless ruler, but a degenerate criminal. In her "corruption of society and prostitution of the family," Isabel "annulled the Virtue of Law."[40] Ferdinand's "shameless" daughter had violated the enduring moral code that governed traditional Spain, as well as the newly formulated virtues of the modern state Spanish liberals hoped to create. She would not be tried for particular constitutional crimes; rather, the Bourbon monarchy itself would fall, collapsing under the pressure of popular censure.

Although Isabel fled the country at the end of September, 1868, the imagery of the exiled queen conditioned subsequent debates over the construction of a new regime. No national consensus existed on the question of whether to institute a republic or a monarchy, or, in either case, on the complex problem of deciding what sort of constitutional framework could best produce a workable and representative system of parliamentary rule. If the men of September could not agree on what they wanted, they shared an uncompromising vision of what they did not: the corruption and illiberalism symbolized by a decadent Bourbon Queen.

The New Moral Order

In the Spanish version of enlightened revolution, the language of progress linked Reason and Honor—two things "eclipsed by Bourbon rule."[41] The *Gloriosa* represented the victory of a "modern spirit of intelligence": the triumph of reason, right and law over the obscure passions of a capricious monarchy.[42] More than expanded suffrage, democracy entailed "the application of reason to political questions previously resolved by fear or convenience." In sum, the great mission of the revolution was to replace "the evil, the defective, and the old with the rational, the pure, and the modern."[43]

Like most revolutionary upheavals in Spain and elsewhere in Europe during the eighteenth and nineteenth centuries, the *Gloriosa* did not fundamentally restructure the socioeconomic order of the nation. For all the material grievances it voiced and all the variations of regional radicalism it contained, the revolution was an essentially political struggle over the nature of individual liberty. It was about subjects becoming citizens. In Spain, however, this familiar historical metamorphosis—at least in its nineteenth-century incarnation—was constructed in terms not of right but of honor.

Absolutism was not inequitable but immoral. "Dance, laugh, rejoice," chided the revolutionaries, "but know, Heart of Stone, that the sound of your trampling feet echoes in the cemeteries."[44] In a travesty of her former role as the "loyal Catholic queen, mother of Spain," a faux-repentant Isabel "cried on her knees before superstitious priests to pardon her obscene secrets, as if they could remove the indelible stains of her impurity."[45] The *pueblo* alone, carrying the weighty standard of enlightenment and honor, could "cleanse the shame that tarnishes a sorrowful epoch."[46] Thus a new monarch rose "over the ruins of the putrefied Bourbon throne: the *Pueblo-Rey*."[47] The queen soiled the office; legitimate political power now emanated from the nation. The people were sovereign—not because they possessed a natural right to govern themselves, but because they were the new repository of the nation's virtue.

Substituting the people for the queen inverted the standard picture of virtue and social hierarchy. Honor, expressed in terms of feminine sexuality, was in many ways a class issue. In nineteenth-century Europe and America, bourgeois social and political discourse constructed working-class women as promiscuous creatures ruled by physical passions.[48] The respectable women of the middle and upper classes, in contrast, by following moral prescriptions for the proper behavior of daughters, wives, and mothers, protected the modern polity from the demons of disorder; in an era of unsettling social and economic transformation, their perceived acceptance of conventional roles provided a reassuring representation of orderly civilization.[49] During the *Gloriosa*, in a complex reversal of these class and gender assumptions, the dangerous queen displaced the dangerous classes as the fulcrum of sexualized political threat.[50] This realignment involved more than simply redefining the source of danger. It seemed, in fact, that the queen and the people had literally switched places; the sovereign *pueblo* was now the virtuous and reasonable ruler of the nation, while the queen, governed by irrational passions, behaved like "the fishmongering market women of Málaga."[51]

In this gendered inversion of ruler and ruled, the people represented order and integrity. Republicans immediately grasped the political power of such imagery. Investing the *pueblo* with quasi-mystical powers of redemption and regeneration, they reproached the provisional government for its attempt to resuscitate the corpse of monarchical Spain:

> The times of Lazarus are distant from us. The government of today, like the government of tomorrow, can organize society, but cannot grant it life. The people, and only the people, in their good judgment, by their steadfastness, can give life to the nation and convert to order that which was disorder.[52]

The *pueblo* possessed precisely those virtues Isabel lacked—prudence, constancy, and order. But this was not a masculinist rebuttal to feminine misrule; on the contrary, the republican language of generation feminized the *pueblo*; the ability to "give life"—in a century that defined women by their reproductive capacity—was a symbol of feminine power. By appropriating the imagery of female virtue, republicans at once rejected the feminine vices of the old regime and created an alternative to the masculine monarchists of the Revolution—the constitutionalist generals, like Prim, who advocated the importation of a new king.

While republican rhetoric paid eloquent homage to the redemptive power of the *pueblo*, these more conservative partisans of the September Revolution tried to segregate the concept of monarchy from the dishonor of one particular Bourbon. Thus Isabel, the seditious symbol of sexual disorder, was transformed into an innocuous object of ridicule; semaphore became cartoon. Increasingly portrayed as a dowdy fat lady, the former queen appeared in the popular press as a crown-chasing, hen-pecking has-been. Caricatures depict a corpulent shrew towering over her effeminate consort, greedily elbowing aside other unworthy throne-seekers.[53] A flagrant emphasis on her physical unattractiveness further diminished the former seductress. In one interpretation of her unlamented departure, for example, Isabel—getting her due—is swallowed by an enormous serpent. Observing the flailing legs of the disappearing queen, a horrified prince begs his amused companion to rescue her: "What will become of the Spanish without their beloved queen?" "Leave me, child," the frock-coated gentleman replies, "to contemplate for the last time the extraordinary obesity of her calves!"[54]

With the monarch so unceremoniously dispatched, debates about the moral order of the nation turned from the disorders of despotism to the nature of liberty. And as the revolutionary coalition unraveled, gendered images of salvation and misrule multiplied.

In democratic discourse, the idea of political liberty was represented by another woman: the Republic. This new mythogenic motor of revolution was peculiarly androgynous.[55] To distinguish her from the female allegory of the old regime, and enable her to compete with the heroic generals of the *Gloriosa*, democrats invested the republic with masculine attributes. The republic was at once regal and rational; her cold features offered no hint of sentimental religiosity, anathema to secular liberalism; her majestic robes cloaked any suggestion of female sexuality, antithetical to an orderly state. But despite her pointed rejection of the threatening and unenlightened aspects of femininity, she was never a man, because liberty—embodied by the republic—was transcendental, and thus, in the eye of the nineteenth century, essentially female. Associated biologically with the virtuous order of nature, the female figure was timeless, eternally legitimate; a perfect counterpoint to the grubby material world of men and the demoralizing political factionalism of the *Gloriosa*.[56]

Never a coquette, the Republic was virile, desexed, a muscular revolutionary in a phrygian cap. A creature of the enlightenment, she possessed the masculine virtue of reason: "The Republic is liberty, and liberty is enlightenment. The Republic is democracy, and democracy is reason."[57] A stern professor of mathematics in the flowing drapery of a classical goddess, she calculated the national debt—legacy of Bourbon excess—for a class of hand-wringing priests, feminized enemies of the liberal revolution. She was, most commonly, a broad-shouldered allegory of honor, an idealized female bearing the sword of liberty and the scales of justice.

Justice demanded order. The Bourbons clearly represented the wrong sort of order: one which sacrificed liberty in a "holocaust of authority." And in Isabel's "satanic regime,"—an "orgy of drunkenness, prostitution and tyranny"—Disorder ruled.[58] The Republic of Virtue, then, was a Republic of Order. To remain politically palatable, Liberty had to be chaste. The revolution, which—despite its feminine allegories and populist rhetoric— was essentially bourgeois and fundamentally masculine, sought to protect her from disorder looming on two fronts.[59] First, collective violence threatened public order. Second, and most important, rapid and tumultuous political change invited serious challenges to a social order based on sacred hierarchies of class and gender.

A Disorderly Nation

The new regime faced threats of misrule from various radical readings of liberty: the levelling gospel of anarchism, the romantic recalcitrance of provincial federalists, and the ominous imagery of the Paris Commune.

The provisional government under Prim accepted the democratic program demanded by the revolutionary juntas in 1868, only to annul these concessions to southern republicans once the Revolution seemed secure. During the fall and winter of 1868–1869, the reinstitution of military conscription and unpopular taxes, combined with Prim's call for the dissolution of the democratic juntas and the disarming of popular militias, provoked violent revolts in the republican strongholds of Andalusia and Valencia. Denouncing the ruling factions in Madrid as *continuista*, federalist leaders claimed that the ideas of Prim and Serrano were diametrically opposed to the "revolution that the people would have carried out."[60] Barricades went up in towns throughout Andalusia as the Volunteers of Liberty (civil militias), who had ushered in the revolution only three months before, faced a regular army in defense of the same. Federalists fighting for the right to remained armed and autonomous found support in the urban lower and middle classes; they resented the continued control of national affairs by Andalusian landowners, who cared little about stimulating trade and who were therefore held responsible for the economic decay of the south.[61] Rural workers, too, supported the republican struggle, embittered by the state's sale of common lands, and beleaguered by renewed taxation at the same time that crops failed and unemployment soared.

These provincial revolts, quelled by the "Machiavellian coalition" in Madrid,[62] initiated a pattern of southern insurrection that persisted throughout the *sexenio*. In the spring of 1869, when Prim ordered a new round of conscription to sustain the colonial war in Cuba, militant republicans organized strikes in Málaga and Seville. Francisco Pi y Margall, the century's preeminent federalist ideologue, denounced Prim for destroying the "sweet illusions" of Spanish mothers.[63] Once again employing feminine imagery to counter the agenda of the *Gloriosa*'s martial leaders, federal republicans invoked the distraught mother, weeping for sons lost, to castigate the conservative revolution.

The strikes crushed, provincial federalists gravitated leftward. And when an impotent republican minority failed to prevent the Cortes from declaring for a constitutional monarchy in the summer of 1869, they abandoned parliamentary struggle for armed insurrection.

Leading the battle for "social reform—for the true revolution"[64]—Andalusian federalists raised "the countryside to arms in defense of the republic."[65] Enthusiastic peasant and working-class support could not make up for the superior military might of the central government, and the rebel forces capitulated in the autumn of 1869. The International accused republican leaders of treason, insisting that they had abandoned workers for the dishonorable company of "frock-coated thieves."[66] Radical republicans, denouncing Prim's government as a new version of the old regime, offered a different explanation for the rebellion's failure: overcome by the brute force of monarchist arms, the heroic federalists were legitimate "martyrs of social revolution" devoured by that black-winged fury, the "monster of despotism."[67]

After 1869, the republicans were divided: moderate parliamentarians counseled constitutional patience and gradual social reform; provincial extremists promoted a radical and insurrectionary program for municipal rights and agrarian reform. Inflamed federalist rhetoric, along with the millenial language of anarchism that was rapidly capturing the imagination of Andalusia's rural poor, seemed a harbinger of disorder. Urban demonstrations alarmed the industrial magnates of Málaga, while intensified agrarian unrest—incendiarism, land occupations, and attacks on civil guard posts—periodically forced landowners to retreat to the cities in fear.[68] Monarchists insisted that a federalist "plague" tormented the south of Spain, and that republican influence was making the "entire nation a theatre of crime, robbery and assassination."[69] Even moderate republicans lurched to the right, pushed by the perceived power of the International, and, after 1871, the revolutionary implications of the Paris Commune.

Containment involved the invention of a new language of democratic order. After popular revolts rocked Andalusia in 1869, the liberal ideologues of the *Gloriosa* tempered their galvanizing cry for liberty with a new slogan: "True republicans conserve order!"[70] And in the wake of the Commune, republican propagandists initiated a vociferous campaign of philosophical damage control. To distance Spain from Gallic disorder while defending their own democratic aspirations, republicans conjured the demons of Isabeline corruption:

> Some think the Republic is liberty unchained. It is not. Our new redemption offers more respect for honor, family, and property than any Bourbon ever demonstrated.[71]

The republic thus betrothed liberty to order, vowing to honor and uphold the traditional hierarchies of gender (family) and class (property).

The strength of this proposed union would soon be tested, as the new monarchical regime collapsed into a Republic. At the same time that republican and peasant agitation stirred the south, Amadeo of Savoy, who had accepted the Spanish crown in 1870, faced warring factions of Unionists, Progressives and Radicals in Madrid, and renewed Carlist agitation in the north. Claiming that he was "in a cage of madmen," Amadeo abandoned the throne in 1873, thus becoming—in Engels' ironic words—the "first king ever to go on strike."[72]

Out of bedlam emerged the First Republic, declared on February 11, 1873, not in a surge of revolutionary enthusiasm, but rather by default. Political transition in Madrid again inspired widespread attacks on property in Andalusia. The conservative press decried the persistent pathology of the south, where "agitated masses armed with sticks and farm implements" marched on various estates, destroyed the houses and outbuildings, and "divided up the conquered lands."[73] While Andalusian republicans agitated for the immediate institution of a federal regime, olive groves and granaries went up in flames, and landowners took refuge in the provincial capitals.[74] Republican leaders in Madrid, alarmed by their apparent inauguration of disorder, sent the Civil Guard to contain peasant and federalist unrest.

The federalists, disillusioned and impatient, refused to wait for constitutional reform. July 1873 found Andalusia "completely in arms" as the federal republicans formed new revolutionary juntas and, beginning with Málaga, all southern provinces declared themselves independent cantons.[75]

Popular excess invalidated the Republic's promised marriage of liberty and order. The rogue cantons reinforced a key conviction of Spanish monarchism: democracy represented disorder. Fear of social radicalism and political upheaval prompted the last of the *Gloriosa*'s symbolic transpositions. Employing the very language of sexual trespass used to unseat Isabel five years before, legitimists recast the *pueblo*—that mythic monolith of honor—as an uncontrollable body. The pathology of federalist insurrection demonstrated that the people were ruled by physical passions and thus incapable of governing themselves. Their insatiable and unreasonable demands for radical democratization evoked the most threatening aspects of femininity—lust, irrationality, and imprudence. The positive female imagery of the early revolution was thus transformed into its negative counterpart—the people were not giving life to the nation, but devouring it. Having reversed the republican inversion of queen and people, the generals could, with honor, vanquish the Republic as they had Isabel.

The Republic was disrobed, and liberty exposed as perversity. Scandalized by the nation's honor lost, the conservative press argued that

> the rebellious and corrupt *pueblo*, lacking respect and obedience, seeks liberty in vain; tyrannized by their own vices, the people have forgotten their own virtue.[76]

The traditionalist paladins of Bourbon restoration conjured all the familiar villains of moral license, representing the *sexenio revolucionario* as popular bacchanalia. The democratic "cult of immodesty" violated the nation and her honorable history; and yet, they lamented, in the "perverse political orgy" of the Republic, "no one weeps." We hear instead the "laughter of the lunatic, the criminal and the whore." Drinking, singing, and dancing, the *pueblo* carried Spain to her dishonor.[77]

In an attempt to restore republican virtue, Salmerón, President of the Republic, called on the military to crush federalist insurgency in Andalusia. General Pavía y Rodríguez pacified the south in a matter of weeks, claiming to rescue "civilization" from the depredations of the people—no longer the virtuous *pueblo*, but the voracious masses who rose from the fields and streets of Andalusia to "commit atrocities against property and the upper classes."[78]

Five months later, Pavía staged a coup d'état, invading the Cortes in January 1874 to disband the deputies and establish a martial order. The enervated Republic limped on until December, when the military pronounced for Alfonso XII, Isabel's son.

The Restoration was legitimated through the demonization of popular sovereignty. Without conceding this representational reversal, liberal protagonists of the *Gloriosa* offered a symbolic capitulation. A print from the closing moments of the democratic experiment documents their version of the revolutionary narrative. Distant gibbets provide the old regime backdrop for Isabel, a screaming hag with her hand at the throat of the revolution. On the sides of this central drama, death salutes a host of kneeling generals as headless politicians stumble toward the precipice. In the foreground, the lion of justice weeps and the flag of the pueblo lies on the ground. The nation is exhausted; Spain, her dress torn, looks out blankly from a festival of political disorder.[79]

Conclusion

It is possible, then, to offer a gendered reading of the revolutionary paradigm shift—what Daniel T. Rodgers and Sean Wilentz, analyzing the constitutional discourse of the American Revolution, describe as a transition from languages of dominance to languages of common right[80]—embodied in the liberal revolutions that heralded the modern era in Europe and America. In Spain this entailed a transfer of the nation's moral heart from the corrupt body of the queen to the virtuous corpus of the body politic: the birth of the *Pueblo-Rey*. The midwives were many, and they operated on several levels. While the generals who dethroned Isabel II in September 1868 translated the political corruption, economic incompetence, and romantic indiscretions of her reign into a notion of sexual dishonor, the philosophers of liberal revolution constructed, during the *sexenio democrático*, a political vernacular in which a masculine order of reason, representing modernity and progress, triumphed over a debauched absolutism characterized by feminine caprice.

But if the sexual demonization of the queen created the political space for an attack on absolutism, the language of honor which pervaded the *sexenio* was not limited to a critique of the monarchy. Liberty, too, was a woman. And once on the barricades, fighting in the service of popular revolutionary movements throughout the South, she became a libertine in the eyes of local elites and gradualist revolutionaries in Madrid. The conflation of liberty with libertinage heralded an extreme political reaction. Once again, Spain's honor was at stake; recovering it involved the restoration of Order. Out of the lore of revolution and reaction, in 1874 as in 1868, rides a heroic, romanticized general, a masculine leader who can rescue Spain, conquering disorder and dishonor. Thus Pavía and Prim, standing at either end of the Glorious Revolution, each triumph over the threat of feminine misrule.

Notes

1. The feminine allegorization of political regimes, ideals, and institutions is a common feature of European and American history. For an introduction to gendered political symbols in comparative context, see Lynn Hunt, ed., *Eroticism and the Body Politic* (Baltimore, MD: Johns Hopkins University Press, 1991); and Marina Warner, *Monuments and Maidens: The Allegory of the Female Form* (New York: Atheneum, 1985).

2. For a comparative discussion of this phenomenon, see Gay Gullickson, "La Petroleuse: Representing Revolution," *Feminist Studies* 17, no. 2 (1991): 240–265; and Neil Hertz, "Medusa's Head: Male Hysteria under Political Pressure," *Representations* 4 (Fall 1983): 27–54.

3. In nineteenth-century Europe, the idea of honor involved both old regime conceptions of nobility, station, and family, and bourgeois tenets of middle-class respectability. Honor was a fluid notion that found voice at many levels of society, speaking simultaneously to civic, political, and economic affairs. Its unambiguous roots, however, lie in the cultural construction of sexual relationships. Comparative studies reveal that many different societies—around the world, across classes, and throughout history—share a similar ideology of honor in which the perceived purity of a woman reflects directly on the status of her family. Sherry Ortner examines the ways this ideology is enforced through social and state control, and reviews the scholarly debate on the subject, in "The Virgin and the State," in Caroline B. Brettell and Carolyn F. Sargent, eds., *Gender in Cross-Cultural Perspective* (Englewood Cliffs, NJ: Prentice Hall, 1993), pp. 257–268.

The literature on the integration of honor, gender, and sexuality in Mediterranean moral systems is voluminous. Useful texts include: Stanley Brandes, *Metaphors of Masculinity: Sex and Status in Andalusian Folklore* (Philadelphia, PA: University of Pennsylvania Press, 1980); David Gilmore, ed., *Honor and Shame and the Unity of the Mediterranean* (Washington, DC: American Anthropological Association, 1987); Julián Pitt-Rivers, *Antropología del honor o política de los sexos:*

Ensayos de antropología mediterránea (Barcelona: Grijalbo, 1979); Eric Wolf, ed., *Religion, Power and Protest in Local Communities: The Northern Shore of the Mediterranean* (Berlin: Mouton, 1984).

4. The *pronunciamiento*—a rising of military officers—was the classic formula for liberal revolution in nineteenth-century Spain. The officer corps, defining itself as the repository of national will whenever the reigning regime appeared to compromise the national interest, used the highly ritualized coup d'état to effect political change throughout the century.

5. The House of Bourbon ruled Spain—with notable interruptions during the Napoleonic occupation and the Revolution of 1868—from the death of the last Hapsburg in 1700 to the declaration of the Second Republic in 1931.

6. Carlism was a popular counterrevolutionary movement that initiated a series of civil wars when the brother of Ferdinand VII, Don Carlos, refused to recognize the succession of his niece Isabel in 1833. More than a dynastic quarrel, Carlism was a social movement in defense of the old regime against the intrusions of a liberalizing state that represented secularism, capitalism, and modernization.

7. European federalism involved an ideology of decentralized political power and a movement for provincial and municipal liberties. Spanish opposition to state centralization during the nineteenth century grew out of the junta tradition of urban radicals (Carlism being its counterpart on the right). Beginning with the War of Independence, periodic revolutionary upheaval on the peninsula precipitated the establishment of municipal juntas which, in the lore of radical democracy, included "intellectuals, men of the middle classes, students and artisans, who by living in contact with the people feel as the people do." (See Miguel Morayta, *Las constituyentes de la República española* [Paris: Sociedad de Ediciones Literarias y Artísticas, 1907]). Francisco Pi y Margall, the architect of Spanish federal republicanism, linked this idea of organic democracy with radical notions of individual liberty. During the *Gloriosa*, the writings of Pi and the legacy of de facto federalism inspired provincial republicans—in Aragón, Catalonia, Valencia, and Andalusia—to agitate for a revolution *abajo-arriba* (from the bottom up), thus setting them at loggerheads with the centrist republicans in Madrid.

8. John Hay, *Castillian Days* (Boston: Houghton Mifflin, 1887), p. 316.

9. Manuel Fernández Herrero, *Historia de las germanías de Valencia, y breve reseña del levantamiento republicano de 1869* (Madrid: Imprenta de La Viuda y Hijos de M. Alvarez, 1870), p. 253.

10. Rafael Pérez del Alamo, *Apuntes sobre dos revoluciones andaluzas* (Algorta [Vizcaya], Spain: Zero, 1971), p. 53.

11. The Revolution of 1868 has many names. Commonly referred to as the September Revolution or the *Gloriosa*, it is also described as a *sexenio*—a six-year political epoch—with any variety of epithets, e.g., the *sexenio democrático* or the *sexenio revolucionario.*

12. Much of the research for this article was conducted in the Andalusian province of Málaga. At the forefront of a long century of insurrection—from the struggles against Napoleon to those against Franco—Málaga was one of the first provinces to "pronounce" in 1868, and, after declaring itself an independent revolutionary canton during the provincial insurrections five years later, one of the last to fall to the army of General Pavía, sent south to pacify Andalusia in the summer of 1873.

13. The uneasy liaison between Isabel and liberal Spain was a function of historical fortuity. In the dynastic dispute that inspired a civil war at Ferdinand's death (see n. 6), all those who did not share the feudal dreams of Don Carlos—that is, the industrial and mercantile communities, together with large segments of the military and civil bureaucracy—chose Isabel as a foil for Carlist absolutism. María Cristina, regent for the three-year-old Isabel, garnered support where she could. Thus, in a sharp departure from the ultraconservative regime of Isabel's reactionary father, María Cristina and the Isabeline generals rallied Spain under the liberal standard of constitutional monarchy.

14. The salacious stories of María Luisa's treachery—a litany of infidelity, peculation, and political manipulation popularized by her enemies at court and recited uncritically by historians of modern Spain—have been analyzed by María Ruth Pérez Antelo, in "María Luisa de Parma: Una iconografía maldita," in *Las mujeres en Andalucía*, vol. 3 (Málaga, Spain: Diputación Provincial, 1994), pp. 225–245.

15. T.C. Reynolds to Buchanan, August 19, 1847, cited by John Edwin Fagg, "Isabel II and Constitutional Monarchy," in Richard Herr and Harold T. Parker, eds., *Ideas in History* (Durham, NC: Duke University Press, 1965), p. 248. For an excellent analysis of the medicalization of female sexuality in nineteenth-century America, which linked feminine desire with disease, depravity, and mental imbalance, see: Carol Groneman, "Nymphomania: The Historical Construction of Female Sexuality," in *Signs* 19, no. 2 (Winter 1994): 337–367. Fagg accepts contemporary commentary on Isabel's intemperate sexuality at face value, quoting at length from the private correspondence of foreign diplomats and presenting uncritically their vision of a perverse and hysterical queen. Pérez Antelo, arguing that historians employ a gendered double-standard when analyzing the political practice of male and female monarchs, suggests that much of Spanish historiography—by accepting without question the negative narratives of feminine power constructed by a regime's political opponents—is marred by such myopia.

16. *El Avisador Malagueño*, October 16, 1862.

17. Archivo Diaz de Escovar [ADE], Málaga, 305/48.

18. *Crónica del viaje de SSMM y AARR a Málaga* (Málaga: Diputación Provincial y Ayuntamiento de Málaga, 1862).

19. Ibid., n. 23.

20. For a discussion of this phenomenon, see Timothy Mitchell, *Violence and Piety in Spanish Folklore* (Philadelphia, PA: University of Pennsylvania Press, 1988).

21. The economic and political malaise of nineteenth-century Spain seemed particularly lamentable—both to contemporaries and to a number of subsequent historians—when compared to the glorious legends of Spanish Empire. Measuring national performance against the golden age of imperial Spain, the nineteenth century found its heroes in Ferdinand and Isabella, who had driven out the Moors and conquered the "new world," thus constructing the wealthy, virtuous and indomitable nation of legend. Their grandson, Charles V, was the first Spanish Hapsburg; governing Christendom as Holy Roman Emperor, he led Spain to European preeminence in the sixteenth century.

22. *Crónica*, pp. 85, 100.

23. Gabriel Tortella Casares, "La economía española, 1830–1900," in Manuel Tuñón de Lara, ed., *Revolución burguesa, oligarquía y constitucionalismo, 1834–1923*, 2d ed. (Barcelona: Editorial Labor, 1985), p. 43.

24. A number of failed military revolts and civil protests in the years preceding the *Gloriosa* pointedly voiced the general perception of political corruption. And in response to Isabel's refusal to institute a Progressive ministry, Progressives used the *retraimiento*—a traditional form of political protest involving systematic electoral abstention—from 1863 to 1868.

The liberal parties whose dynastic loyalty withered in the 1860s included Progressives, Democrats and Liberal Unionists (a coalition of conservative Progressives and liberal Moderados formed in the previous decade). Their constitutional doctrine and social power base distinguished them from the hegemonic Moderados, a conservative political party that governed Spain for most of the century. An oligarchical coalition supported by the upper classes, the Moderados had no truck with democratic theories of popular sovereignty and the revolutionary legitimacy of the *pronunciamiento*; their platform included a high property franchise, a strong executive with extensive royal prerogative, and a crown-appointed senate. The Progressives, in contrast, represented the urban middle and lower classes. Demanding a broader franchise and greater municipal liberties, they challenged Moderado plutocracy with the rhetoric of meritocracy. The more left-leaning Democrats—whose essentially conspiratorial agenda took shape in southern secret societies during the 1850s and 1860s, and whose ideals ranged from utopian socialism to moderate republicanism—were, until 1868, politically marginal.

25. Archivo Municipal de Málaga (AMM), 3/56/42.

26. The analysis of foreign monarchs—past and present—was a familiar topic in, e.g., *El Avisador Malagueño* and *El Correo de Andalucía*.

27. AMM, *Anales Malagueños*, 1865. The snub was particularly dramatic, given that such disentailment—wresting productive land from the "dead hands" of the Crown, the Church, and the absentee landlords who controlled vast portions of Southern property—was central to the liberal agenda in the nineteenth century.

28. AMM, 3/58/1.

29. Valeriano Bozal Fernández, *Juntas revolucionarias: Manifiestos y programas de 1868* (Madrid: Editorial Cuadernos para el Diálogo, 1968), pp. 91–105.

30. An excellent explanation of the socioeconomic background to rural radicalism in Andalusia—the historical development of inequitable land tenure patterns and the deleterious impact of liberal disentailment—can be found in Edward Malefakis, *Agrarian Reform and Peasant Revolution in Spain: Origins of the Civil War* (New Haven, CT: Yale University Press, 1970).

31. J. Paúl y Angulo, *Verdades revolucionarias*, reprinted in Manuel Ruiz Lagos, *Ensayos de la revolución: Andalucía en llamas, 1868–1875* (Madrid: Editora Nacional, 1977), p. 52. The battle took place on September 28, 1868; Isabel left for exile in France two days later.

32. The First International, founded in 1864, attempted to unite European working-class groups and parties across national boundaries; of the various radical ideologies competing for dominance, anarchism shaped the International's Spanish wing. It is not in the scope of this essay to analyze the development of the International in Spain or the dissemination of anarchist ideology in Andalusia. What is significant here is that peasant radicalism, or the perception of it, contributed to the rhetoric of disorder that conservatives employed to delegitimize the Revolution. Of the voluminous literature on popular radicalism in Andalusia, the briefest introductory survey is Antonio M. Calero's *Movimientos sociales en Andalucía, 1820–1936* (Madrid: Siglo Veintiuno, 1976); for a more recent and comprehensive study, see Jacques Maurice, *El anarquismo andaluz: Campesinos y sindicalistas, 1868–1936* (Barcelona: Editorial Crítica, 1990).

33. *Anales malagueños*, 1868. Royal portraiture had tremendous iconic value in Spanish history. More than a flag or anthem, portraits indicated the actual presence of a monarch, and, as such, received military and civic honors in local celebrations. Disrespect for royal symbols was not unprecedented; during the Revolution of 1854, for example, crowds in Málaga rejected the Queen and carried instead portraits of the immensely popular Progressive leader, General Espartero. Even sympathetic observers, however, were shocked by this insult to Isabel. And, more significantly, there was no desecration of the queen's portrait. The encomium was not a substitution. Espartero was the favored head of government, not of nation; the monarchy remained sacrosanct.

34. ADE, 303/135.

35. Joan Wallach Scott, "Gender: A Useful Category of Historical Analysis," in *Gender and the Politics of History* (New York: Columbia University Press, 1988), p. 49.

36. AMM, 3/58/23.

37. AMM, 3/58/26.

38. ADE, 303/1/113.

39. This was a classic revolutionary formulation of the transition from old regime to modern state. Rehearsing the European liturgy of liberal revolution, Isabel's opponents called on the *Gloriosa* to "substitute the government of caste and family with the government of all; the government of privilege with the government of right." Vicente Blasco Ibáñez, *Historia de la revolución española*, vol. 3 (Barcelona: La Enciclopedia Democrática, 1892), p. 709.

40. AMM, 3/58/25. Central to constitutional liberalism and revolutionary legitimacy in modern Europe, "The Rule of Law" was the absolute principle that replaced the absolute monarch. Law articulated the equality of citizens and defended their rights against arbitrary prerogative and privilege. At the same time, it represented institutional order in an age of democratic uncertainty; the rule of law, unlike the rule of men, guaranteed stability. The *Gloriosa*'s formulaic appeal to the rule of law, however, had a gendered twist: beyond liberty and order, law represented virtue. Isabel was thus a moral outlaw, her political illiberalism indicted with the imagery of virtue lost.

41. ADE, 303/1/81.

42. AMM, 3/58/48.

43. *Eco Revolucionario*, October 15, 1868.

44. AMM, 3/58/22. The revolutionary narrative of the queen's reign described an egregious contrast between the luxury of the Isabeline court and the poverty of the masses, and popular tales of Isabel's privileged life in exile portrayed her as a hypocritical penitent. The imagery of Isabel's sepulchral tapdance refers to the Moroccan campaign of 1859–1860, which saw a shocking mortality rate among Spanish forces. Supported with patriotic fervor in 1860, when Isabel's triumph over the "infidel" evoked celebratory images of the Reconquest and its promise of national regeneration, the colonial war was recast after 1868 as a symbol of Isabeline misrule. The plight of conscripts became a rallying point during the revolution (See n. 63).

45. AMM, 3/58/22.

46. AMM, 3/58/25.The *pueblo*—the people—served as an abstraction for the nation, the citizenry. In the more radical and romantic imagery of revolution, the *pueblo*—signifying the peasantry and the working classes—constituted the industrious backbone and virtuous heart of the body politic. The term, however, was essentially inclusive: the *pueblo*, when invoked in contrast to the monarch, referred to the common people, indicating both middle-class men of democratic sympathies and the laboring classes that constituted the bulk of the nation's population.

47. ADE, 303/1/118. The "People-King" (*Pueblo-Rey*) describes democratization in the language of monarchical power. If sovereignty rests in the nation, the sovereign is the collective body of citizens. Using the image of a *Pueblo-Rey* to illustrate the idea of popular sovereignty made an abstract notion of political legitimacy concrete and universally accessible. And the symbolism of virtuous kingship spoke directly to the Isabeline imagery of feminine misrule.

48. At the same time that essentialist biology lumped women together, cultural constructions of female sexuality segregated women by race and class. See Cynthia Eagle Russet, *Sexual Science: The Victorian Construction of Womanhood* (Cambridge, MA: Harvard University Press, 1989); and Sander L. Gilman, *Difference and Pathology: Stereotypes of Sexuality, Race and Madness* (Ithaca, NY: Cornell University Press, 1985).

49. On nineteenth-century social and scientific theories of gender, which, by positing the control of female sexuality as the basis for social order, established the moral parameters of female virtue, see Nancy Armstrong and Leonard Tennenhouse, eds., *The Ideology of Conduct: Essays on Literature and the History of Sexuality* (New York: Methuen, 1987); Thomas Laqueur and Catherine Gallagher, eds., *The Making of the Modern Body: Sexuality and Society in the Nineteenth Century* (Berkeley, CA: University of California Press, 1987); Carroll Smith-Rosenberg, *Disorderly Conduct: Visions of Gender in Victorian America* (New York: Knopf, 1985).

50. The inversion was reversed on the eve of the Restoration when monarchists recast the *pueblo* as a passion-driven and promiscuous ruler (see n. 76). The traditional link between dangerous women and the political menace of economically or culturally marginal populations is explored in Anne J. Cruz and Mary Elizabeth Perry, eds., *Culture and Control in Counter-Reformation Spain* (Minneapolis, MN: University of Minnesota Press, 1992); and Mary Elizabeth Perry, *Gender and Disorder in Early Modern Spain* (Princeton, NJ: Princeton University Press, 1990).

51. AMM 3/58/74. The queen's transgressions, then, were also constructed in the language of class: she disregarded the moral obligations of her social station. But the issue is more complicated, because the aristocracy in Europe, which had its own normative descriptions of acceptable behavior, operated outside of middle-class moral standards. Isabel, however, was not just an aristocrat; she was a monarch. As sovereign, she represented the nation, and thus was not allowed (in the discourse of the Revolution) the moral license of her peers. Moreover, the official image she projected during her reign was identical to the image of respectable womanhood defined by middle class mores: the chaste Christian mother. For a discussion of class and female sexual behavior in Spain, see María Helena Sánchez Ortega, *La mujer y la sexualidad en el Antiguo Régimen* (Madrid: AKAL, 1992).

52. Santiago Arcos, *A los electores de diputados para las próximos Cortes constituyentes* (Madrid, 1868), p. 6.

53. Such lampoons proliferate in newspapers of the period. An excellent series of political illustrations from *La Flaca* is reprinted in José Baena Reigal, "Los sucesos revolucionarios de 1868 en Málaga," *Jabega*, 42 (1983): 53–62.

54. *El Zurriago*, September 24, 1869.

55. A similar ambiguity appeared in gendered representations of the First Republic in France, where the political limitations of feminine civic allegory demanded the development of a more masculine republican iconography. Lynn Hunt examines

this dynamic in "Hercules and the Radical Image of the French Revolution," *Representations* 1, no. 2 (1983): 95–117.

56. The idea of women's moral superiority, and its link to representations of female passionlessness, is explored in Nancy Cott, "Passionlessness: An Interpretation of Victorian Sexual Ideology," *Signs* 4, no. 2 (1978): 219–236; Anne Digby, "Women's Biological Straitjacket," in Susan Mendus and Jane Rendall, eds., *Sexuality and Subordination: Interdisciplinary Studies of Gender in the Nineteenth Century* (London: Routledge, 1989); Thomas Laqueur, *Making Sex: Body and Gender from the Greeks to Freud* (Cambridge, MA: Harvard University Press, 1990); and Smith-Rosenberg, *Disorderly Conduct.*

57. Luis Calvo Revilla, "La ilustración es la república," in *Anuario Republicano Federal* (1871), p. 809. On the philosophical and allegorical gendering of reason in revolutionary France, see Michelle Vovelle, "The Adventures of Reason, or From Reason to the Supreme Being," in Colin Lucas, ed., *Rewriting the French Revolution* (Oxford: Clarendon Press, 1991), pp. 132–150.

58. Francisco Cordova y López, "Quienes son los defensores de la institución monárquica?" in *Anuario Republicano Federal* (1871), p. 150.

59. The labyrinthine discourse of threat and protection contained competing images of femininity—dissonant representations of women as threatened and threatening. While female sexuality threatened disorder, a good woman—a chaste, nonsexual woman—had to be defended. Thus the people had to be protected from their own passions, kept modest, orderly; at the same time, Liberty—the Republic—had to be protected from the dishonoring depradations of conservative predators.

60. Paúl y Angulo, *Memorias íntimas de un pronunciamiento.*

61. The social and political contours of republican radicalism in southern Spain took shape in the aspirations of a provincial bourgeoisie frustrated by a political order that confined patronage to Madrid and supported a fiscal program disadvantageous to the provinces. Federalism thus found power as an urban phenomenon in provincial cities where middle-class economic and political grievances bred regionalist resentment toward the dominant metropolitan center. Such movements employed the language of rural populism to mobilize mass support. But federal republicanism, while able to mobilize the working classes with popular crusades against conscription and taxation, remained a predominantly middle-class and petty bourgeois movement defined by issues of municipal autonomy and economic reform.

62. *El Republicano Federal*, January 12, 1869.

63. Francisco Pi y Margall, *El reinado de Amadeo de Saboya y la República de 1873* (Madrid: Seminarios y Ediciones, 1970), p. 85.

64. Paúl y Angulo, *hoja suelta*, cited by Ruiz Lagos, *Ensayos de la revolución*, p. 91.

65. Juan Díaz del Moral, *Historia de las agitaciones campesinas andaluzas-Córdoba* (Madrid: Alianza Editorial, 1967), p. 78.

66. Antoni Jutglar, *Ideologías y clases en la España contemporánea: Aproximación a la historia social de las ideas*, vol 1., 3d ed. (Madrid: Editorial Cuadernos para el Diálogo, 1972), p. 245.

67. Fernández Herrero, *Historia de las germanías de Valencia*, p. 238.

68. Julián Zugaste, *El bandolerismo: Estudio social y memorias históricas*, 10 vols. (Madrid: Imprenta de T. Fortanet, 1876), 1: 112-113; ADE, Correspondencia de Jorge Loring.

69. Salvador Bernández, Marqués de Lema, *De la Revolución a la restauración*, vol. 1 (Madrid, 1880), p. 518.

70. Antonio Porredon Ros de Eroles, *Reseña histórica de los acontecimientos de Málaga en los dias 29, 30, 31 de diciembre de 1868 y 1 y 2 de enero de 1869* (Malaga, 1869), p. 11.

71. Roque Barcia, *Quieres Ir, Pueblo*? (Madrid, 1872).

72. Frederick Engels, *The Bakuninists at Work: Review of the Uprising in Spain in the Summer of 1873* (Moscow: Progress Publishers, 1976), p. 7.

73. Josep Termes, *Anarquismo y sindicalismo en España: La primera internacional, 1864–1881* (Barcelona: Ediciones Ariel, 1972), p. 180.

74. Díaz del Moral, *Historia de las agitaciones*, p. 113.

75. Manuel Pavía y Rodríguez, *La pacificación de Andalucía* (Madrid: Minuesa de los Rios, 1878), p. 19.

76. *La defensa de la sociedad*, May 10, 1873.

77. Ibid., November 20, 1873.

78. Pavía, *La Pacificación*, pp. 70, 79.

79. *El Florete*, November 1, 1874.

80. Daniel T. Rodgers and Sean Wilentz, "Languages of Power in the United States," in Penelope J. Corfield, ed., *Language, History and Class* (Oxford: Basil Blackwell, 1991).

10

Spanish Women in the Resistance to Napoleon, 1808–1814

John Lawrence Tone

Early in May 1808 Napoleon's man in Madrid, Joachim Murat, decided his troops needed a parade. The French occupation had just been bloodied in the *dos de Mayo*, the uprising that inaugurated six years of devastating warfare in Spain. Murat's parade, like all such military displays, was intended to reinstill pride in his soldiers, who were recovering from the business of shooting civilians and who needed desperately to forget their individual atrocities in collective pomp. The careful atmosphere established by Murat was spoiled, however, by the actions of a handful of Madrileñas. According to the account of Father José de Salvador, a group of "beautiful young women" arrived, sat astride the cannons being paraded by the French artillerymen, and taunted them, saying, "Your dinky pistols do not frighten those of our regiment." Armed with scorn and humor, these women symbolically castrated the victors of May 2, making the day that much less satisfying to the men of the French occupation.[1]

This suggestive story highlights the central concern of this chapter: to rediscover the contributions of Spanish women to the defeat of Napoleon. In the past twenty years, the subject of women and warfare has inspired a large body of scholarship.[2] While it seems clear that women have never served in combat equally with men, they have been deeply implicated in warfare.[3] Women have taught their sons that it is glorious to die in patriotic battle. They have aided the wounded, shamed the cowardly, spied on the enemy, and produced and distributed weapons. Recent works on women and warfare focus on these and other aspects of women's mobilization. They eschew the battlefield narratives traditionally privileged in military histories, redefining warfare more broadly and looking behind the lines for much, if not all, of their stories.[4]

The Spanish war against Napoleon was one of sieges, guerrilla attacks, reprisals, and exemplary violence against both soldiers and civilians. There were no front lines in Spain, or rather, the front lines ran through bedrooms, kitchens, stables, and churches. As a result, women often found themselves placed directly in the line of fire, and sometimes they fired back. More often, women performed noncombat tasks that contributed in decisive but overlooked ways to the defeat of France. Women supplied intelligence, food, weapons, comfort, and encouragement to the partisans and denied all of these things to the occupation. The primary goal of this chapter is to examine these forms of women's resistance and in doing so to discover the conditions under which women were able to participate in the political life of Spain during the years of the Napoleonic occupation.

The architecture of my enquiry is straightforward. I will begin by looking at images of bellicose women in armed resistance to Napoleon, contrasting those images with what we know about the scant participation of women in combat. Second, I will examine the contributions made by women outside of armed struggle to the defeat of France. The central concern here will be to learn how women resisted and whether their resistance transported them across gender boundaries or whether it took place within spheres traditionally defined as feminine. Finally, and armed with the answers to these questions, I will attempt to explain why warfare in the context of early nineteenth-century Spain had no power to transform the place of women in Spanish society.

Amazons in the Resistance

From 1808 to 1814, Napoleon lost a war to guerrillas and Spanish, British, and Portuguese regular forces in the Iberian Peninsula. Despite the importance of this war in the defeat of Napoleon, however, there has been little attempt to reconstruct the identities of the Spaniards who fought.[5] In particular, historians have ignored the role of women. In the absence of research, an image inherited from the nineteenth century has served: the heroic Amazon, standing in for male combatants at certain decisive moments during the war. This image has a basis in reality, but it was exaggerated during the war and after for propaganda purposes. As a result, it has come to distort our understanding of women in the Spanish resistance, whose contributions were generally less dramatic than stories of Amazons suggest.

The revolutionary juntas resisting Napoleon claimed that Spaniards were fighting unanimously against the occupation. According to the propaganda, even women had taken up arms in defense of king, religion, and the nation.[6] Contemporary accounts and illustrations of the *dos de Mayo* presented women in the thick of combat, cutting down enemy troops, gutting the horses of the French cavalry as they galloped through the Puerta del Sol, and pouring tiles and boiling water down from their balconies and windows upon the French.[7] Tradition tells us that the greatest heroine on May 2 was a young working-class woman in Madrid named Manuela Malasaña, who died during the uprising. French troops shot the legendary Manuela as she carried cartridges to the men fighting around the artillery park of Monteleón, the focal point of the *dos de Mayo*. Manuela had access to munitions at Monteleón, because she was, according to one version of the legend, the fiancée of Pedro Velarde, an artillery officer leading the resistance. This story made an appearance in early works describing the *dos de Mayo* and quickly became part of street culture in Madrid.[8] Manuela Malasaña's name now stands for a street and a neighborhood in Madrid, as well as for heroism during war. (See Figure 10.1.)

Reality on May 2, 1808, was rather different for Manuela Malasaña. The fifteen-year-old Manuela had no relationship to Velarde and took no part in the uprising. She had the misfortune, however, to live near the artillery park of Monteleón. Manuela was surprised by French troops on May 2 as she returned from her work as an embroiderer, work which required her to use shears, which she wore hanging from her belt. The French were shooting civilians carrying anything resembling a weapon, and it was Manuela's fate to be shot down in the street by French troops. The image of Manuela Malasaña has been of a heroic member of the Spanish resistance. The reality was that she was a random victim of French excess.[9]

The contradiction between the legend of Manuela and the dismal reality of her murder is emblematic of the tension between the popular image of women in combat and the reality of their lives during the war with France. Certainly, some women took part in the resistance of May 2. Three women were among the five individuals who sparked the uprising in front of the Royal Palace by stopping the French coach designated to transport the last Spanish Bourbons into exile. Women also took part in the fighting around the Puerta de Toledo on the western outskirts of Madrid. Of the 409 individuals killed by the French, fifty-seven were women.[10] Nevertheless, the image of widespread involvement by the women of Madrid seems contradicted by the evidence on French casualties. The French commander, General Grouchy, reported the loss of just fourteen killed and 150 total casualties among his troops. Most of the deaths and injuries occurred in fighting with regular Spanish troops in the artillery park, while the action of the mob in the streets was not terribly devastating. In particular, the legendary horror of women pouring boiling water and tiles down upon French troops resulted in only one superficial injury.[11] Thus, while it is clear that some women fought on May 2, 1808, Amazons were neither typical nor especially effective.

In the summer of 1808 revolutionaries seized power in most major cities not occupied by French troops and declared war on the emperor. The revolution in the city of Zaragoza proved particularly important. In late May 1808 a junta took control of Zaragoza, raised an army, and withstood two sieges

FIGURE 10.1

"Dia dos de mayo."

before the city finally succumbed to the French in February 1809. No one who witnessed the carnage in Zaragoza had ever seen anything like it, each house becoming a fortress that had to be taken in hand-to-hand combat or pounded into dust. The city did not surrender until some 50,000 Spaniards had perished.[12]

Because so many men died in the siege and because the fighting took place in homes, women engaged directly in combat and became national heroines. The Condesa de Bureta nursed the wounded, supplied provisions to the front, and rallied men to defend the city by her example. Casta Alvarez helped to fight off a French assault on a key battery and received a pension and a medal after the war in recognition of her efforts. María Agustín was wounded carrying ammunition to the front lines and likewise received a pension and a medal.

The most famous amazon of Zaragoza was Agustina of Aragon, *La Artillera*. On July 4, 1808, after killing all of the soldiers manning the Portillo battery, the French stormed the position. At that moment, Agustina advanced to the breech, seized a match from the dead hand of one of the soldiers, and fired the twenty-four pounder guarding the position. Agustina's brave action, according to eyewitnesses, saved the day, and she later received a medal, an officer's commission, and a pension.

Many artists have represented Agustina. Juan Gálvez had her sit for a portrait in 1808. His sketch showed a young woman in traditional dress, with her hair pulled back by a kerchief to show off her earrings. In contrast, later works portrayed her as a *mujer varonil*, in masculine costume and in more heroic poses.[13] She appeared in the seventh of Goya's eighty aquatint plates known as "The Disasters of the War." In the etching of Agustina, captioned with the phrase "What courage!" Goya portrayed a towering, allegorical figure in gown and slippers standing upon a heap of dead men, in the act of touching match to cannon. (See Figures 10.2–10.4.)

Agustina became the archetypical heroine of the Spanish resistance, literally substituting for men in the defense of Spain. She also became an instant celebrity. She relocated to Madrid in 1809 after the fall of Zaragoza. Goya likely met her there, as did Lord Byron, who celebrated her in *Childe Harold*. The story of Agustina quickly entered the popular imagination and colored interpretations of the meaning of the war against France. The fact that Agustina and the other heroines of Zaragoza became so famous and received pensions, however, is a curious thing. A man stepping forward to fire a cannon would have been just another soldier. Such actions were normal for men. That Agustina and Casta Álvarez became national icons had everything to do with their sex and suggests how really rare such combat roles were for women even in besieged cities. Indeed, the image of women in urban warfare has surpassed the reality. The French found more collaborators than enemies among women (and men) in urban areas. In Barcelona, in Seville, in Granada, in almost all of Spain's cities, the French did not meet much resistance. In fact, the occupation achieved a certain stability and acceptance in most urban areas after 1809, including even Zaragoza.[14] Thus, the opportunity for combat presented to women in Zaragoza was rarely repeated.

The countryside of Spain, in contrast to the cities, held very little comfort for French troops.[15] Even the women appeared to be armed. In Galicia, for example, the French thought they were "fighting the entire population; all the inhabitants, men, women, children, old folks and priests, were in arms, the villages abandoned, the defiles guarded."[16] Spanish authors also indulged their imaginations in describing female combatants in Galicia.[17] However, this perception of armed women, whether in Galicia or elsewhere, is not supported by the evidence. One Basque woman, known as *la Martina*, briefly led a force of irregulars in 1810, but her case is even more exceptional than that of Agustina.[18] In general, Spanish women did not take up soldiering. Women did

FIGURE 10.2

"Agustina de Aragón." After the first siege, Agustina sat for the artist Juan Galvez, who produced this intimate portrait of the heroine of Zaragoza.

FIGURE 10.3

"Agustina de Aragón." This anonymous oil painting done soon after the siege showed Agustina striking a suitably heroic pose and wearing the uniform and decoration she earned for her bravery.

FIGURE 10.4

"Que valor" (What courage). Goya's apotheosis of Agustina in this etching from his "Disasters of the war" elevated "La Artillera" to a national icon.

not fight with el Empecinado, el Médico, Renovales, el Cura Merino, and the other *guerrilleros* of the War of Independence. Women were absent, even as camp followers, from the most important guerrilla formation, the Division of Navarre, commanded by Francisco Espoz y Mina.[19]

The absence of Spanish women in armed formations should not come as a surprise. Even in the age of total war in the twentieth century, women have been armed only as a last resort. Why, then, did the Spanish Amazon — both in the urban and the rural setting — prove such a popular device in nineteenth century descriptions of the war in Spain?

For the French, armed women were stand-ins for the barbarism they thought characterized Spaniards generally. In wars of occupation, troops are required to fire upon civilians, a situation that can become intolerable even for hardened troops. Inevitably, colonizers rhetorically solve this problem by defining the natives as less than fully human, thus allowing the slaughter to continue without affecting troop morale. In particular, occupation forces are apt to find local women uncivilized when they do not run into the invaders' arms. Jean Albert Rocca, an officer who served under Soult, remembered feeling less threatened by the male inhabitants of the mountain town of Ronda than by the women, whom he described as fierce "giants" and "wrestlers" who were "only distinguishable from the men by their dress, their greater stature, and their coarser manners."[20] The French represented the occupation of Spain as a great boon to the Spanish. The Emperor was giving his benighted neighbors modern government, more rational economic policies, superior French culture, and the Code Napoleon, in which the emperor's misogynist fantasies were codified. From the perspective of this imperial project and discourse on modernization, Spanish women bearing arms and acting like men were a sure sign that Spain needed the civilizing presence of French men to correct a topsy-turvy situation. In other words, the French used descriptions of female assassins in the countryside to justify the occupation. Where Spanish men saw heroic Amazons, the French saw unnatural giantesses. And it would be part of France's civilizing mission to remake the giantesses and wrestlers of rural Spain in the image of Parisian ladies.[21]

If the Amazon functioned for the French to justify the occupation of Spain, how did she work symbolically for Spaniards? Part of the answer may be found by looking again at Goya's series of "Disasters," for several depict women in combat. The "Disasters" were mostly based on second hand information and are, therefore, only indirect representations of the war. Still, they do link us to the images and stories of warfare to which people would have been exposed. From this perspective, Goya can tell us about the imagined roles of women in the resistance. The etchings titled "Women give courage" and "They do not want to" show women fighting off sexual assault, a recurring theme in the "Disasters." (See Figures 10.5 and 10.6.) Figure 10.5 titled "And they are wild beasts," shows women during the siege of Zaragoza fighting and dying to stop French troops. The woman in the foreground of Figure 10.5 is particularly striking. Barefoot and protecting her baby in her left arm, she uses her right arm to skewer an attacking French soldier with a pike. The women here and in other of Goya's etchings are doing more than killing French soldiers. They are describing the conditions under which women participated in the traditional male sphere of combat. Women fought, like Agustina did, when there were no men left, when they were protecting their children, and when they were defending their sexual integrity.

Further clues about the symbolic meaning of the Amazon may be extracted from a reading of the Benito Pérez Galdós novel, *Zaragoza* (1874), which recounts the events of the siege. Women, who appear frequently in this novel, serve three dramatic functions. They take up arms and shame men with the knowledge that women had to be called in to perform traditionally male

FIGURE 10.5

"Y son fieras" (And they are beasts). One of Goya's favorite subjects was the resistance of women to the French occupation. In etchings like this one women fought to protect their homes, their children, and their sexual integrity.

duties; they threaten men by promising to withhold sex and love from cowards; and they inspire men by acting as embodiments of the nation in need of defense. In one climactic scene, at a point when the men of Zaragoza have given up, Pérez Galdós has a priest harangue them into rejoining the fight. In this speech, shame and sexual blackmail motivate the men into facing death: "There will not be a single woman in Zaragoza," wrote Pérez Galdós, "who will even look at you if you do not immediately throw yourselves into these ruined houses and drive the French out of them. There is a group of women over there. Do you see them? Well, they are saying that if you do not fight, they will. Doesn't your cowardice make you ashamed?" The women, in this passage, both shame and threaten men.[22] In another scene patriotic speeches do nothing to impel the exhausted men back to the front. Neither does the flat of an officer's sword. The only thing that motivates the men to fight is seeing a

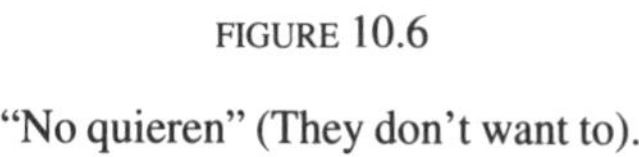

FIGURE 10.6

"No quieren" (They don't want to).

woman, Manuela Sancho, grab a rifle and enter the breach. Manuela functions explicitly as a symbol of national unity; seeing her, men experience a "heartfelt impulse" to come to the defense of Spain.[23]

Spanish patriots during the war imagined women in combat as part of a package of revolutionary propaganda that proclaimed the whole nation armed for patriotic vengeance. This image of unity became a powerful false memory precisely because Spain experienced constant civil warfare in the nineteenth century, making the dreams of past concord all the more precious to people like Pérez Galdós. Nevertheless, a unanimous and patriotic Spain never existed in 1808. In the war against Napoleon, most Spaniards tried desperately to remain neutral, and the revolutionaries' insistent carping on the unanimity of patriotic sentiment in Spain should be read as a reflection of pious wishes not reality. Thus, armed female patriots were largely mythical, but that is precisely why they could serve so well to symbolize the patriotism of the masses, which was also largely mythical.

Real Agustinas were rare, but that does not mean that women did not find other ways to resist the occupation. Their belligerency has been hidden from military historians focused on men in battle and ignored by others because it did not fit into the Amazon paradigm. Nevertheless, the resistance of Spanish women is an important part of the story of Napoleon's defeat.

Women's Resistance

A generation of writers has labored to rediscover women as political actors. By expanding the definition of politics to include such things as food riots, incidents of "popular taxation," and religious processions, scholars have revealed previously invisible women as important agents of historical change.[24] Similarly, anyone seeking to understand the participation of women in armed conflict must expand the traditional definition of warfare, for it is clear that on every battlefield we know about women have been either absent or present only in small numbers. Looking behind the lines, however, one easily discerns a pervasive female signature on military events. In the Spanish war only a small number of women participated in the fighting, but many others played active noncombat roles. Women's belligerency behind the lines was particularly important in two contexts: in the urban revolutions of 1808 and in the guerrilla warfare characteristic of northern Spain.

In Galicia women took part in the crucial revolutionary days of late May and early June 1808. Indeed, women triggered the revolution in El Ferrol, Spain's most important dockyard and one of the greatest military arsenals in the country. An early seizure of El Ferrol by the French or by French collaborators would have proved disastrous for the insurrection in Galicia. On June 1, 1808, however, the women of El Ferrol made certain that the city and its resources weighed in on the side of the revolution.

The day started with a mob of women gathered outside the mansion of the governor. They called him outside to demand that he renounce his French sympathies and proclaim Ferdinand, the Bourbon heir held prisoner by Napoleon, to be the legitimate king of Spain. The governor refused, but he did agree to meet with one of the women in his house. Once inside, she smashed one of the windows with a rock, which was a signal for everyone else to burst into the house. The governor got away by climbing out of a back window and scaling his garden wall, but the women were not finished. They broke into the armory attached to the house and seized part of the enormous arsenal of 36,000 muskets. They paraded through the streets and distributed the arms to the men they encountered. With the city armed, the governor surrendered himself, promising to abandon his French friends and to lay down his life for Ferdinand, at which point he was allowed to reoccupy his residence. Thus, women won El Ferrol for the resistance.[25]

Women's intervention in some crowds and political tumults has been characterized by Temma Kaplan as an extension of their concern with subsistence and family issues. The role of women within the family and community formed the material foundation for what she has termed "female consciousness." Women interacted with each other on a daily basis in feminized spaces like public markets and fountains. These contacts, reinforcing and channeling women's female consciousness, led to specifically feminine forms of collective action. Where living spaces and work spaces were close together and where political authorities were highly visible, female collective action became especially effective.[26]

The events in El Ferrol fit Kaplan's model to a certain extent. The military governor was visible and accessible, and his residence was located close to the port and the market where women of the popular classes worked and socialized. In this sense, the attack on the governor's house was, perhaps, not that different from traditional subsistence riots in which women played and would continue to play a leading role. On the other hand, the women of El Ferrol seem to have been motivated not by specifically female concerns but by problems of dynastic politics. The timing of the revolt in El Ferrol is explained by the fact that June 1 was the feast day of San Fernando, the namesake of the imprisoned Spanish king. There was no subsistence crisis in 1808, and the object of the crowd, the military governor, was not asked to remedy an injustice affecting the ability of women to provide for their families. The only convincing explanation for the attack by women on the military governor is that they had been mobilized, like men, by the dramatic political crisis that led to the abdication of Ferdinand and the usurpation of the Spanish throne by the Bonaparte family.

The revolt of June 1 in El Ferrol, indeed all of the urban revolutions of May and June 1808, were part of the family drama Spain was living in the form of the highly public intrigues tearing apart the Spanish Bourbons. In 1794 the weak king, Charles IV, and his queen, María Luísa, had turned power over to Manuel Godoy, a minor nobleman who owed his position in part to his amorous relations with the queen. María Luísa was thought to have betrayed both husband and son in order to further the career of her darling, Godoy. There was even talk of Godoy succeeding to the throne in place of the natural heir, Ferdinand. Finally, in March 1808, Ferdinand and his friends carried out a palace coup and deposed Godoy, Charles, and María Luísa. Justice seemed to have triumphed, when, suddenly, Napoleon lured Ferdinand to Bayonne for talks in April 1808 only to arrest and depose the young king. In the popular imagination Ferdinand was the long-suffering son betrayed by his parents and by Napoleon, an image that made him intensely popular in Spain.[27]

This family drama informed Spanish politics at every level in 1808. While most Spaniards probably did not feel the nationalism trumpeted by the patriots in the revolutionary junta, many did feel some sentimental loyalty to the royal heir, Ferdinand, especially in cities like Madrid, Zaragoza, and El Ferrol, where the details of the Bourbons' internal squabbling would have been widely known. Thus, the uprising of June 1 in El Ferrol, like other urban revolutions, is best understood as an attempt to correct an injustice and bring a satisfactory denouement to Spain's dynastic crisis. This is an important point, because it warns us against employing the notion of female consciousness in a prescriptive way, as if women could not experience any other form of consciousness. The events in el Ferrol teach us that women's consciousness, even in the early nineteenth century, was sometimes determined by the same factors that determined men's consciousness and not by gendered aspects of their lives.

The actions of the women of El Ferrol proved important in the defeat of Napoleon, since the arming of Galicia resulted in the foiling of a French invasion of Portugal in 1809. Therefore, although women did not fight with the Galician guerrillas that defeated Marshals Soult and Ney in the winter of 1808–1809, they had helped the resistance by storming the governor's house and acquiring weapons for the partisans.

Women also played an important part in the revolution in Zaragoza, triggered by a miracle that seems to have occurred on May 17, 1808. After the midday mass in the cathedral a crown appeared — some remembered it coming out of a cloud in the sky, others said it materialized above the altar inside the cathedral — bearing the unlikely inscription, "God supports Ferdinand." Female parishoners helped to spread the exciting news and participated in street demonstrations that toppled the old government and created a revolutionary junta.[28] It is likely that women also took part in initiating revolutionary tumults elsewhere, for there were dozens of urban uprisings in Spain in late May and early June 1808. Unfortunately, women have been ignored in the numerous local histories of these events.

Perhaps the most important contribution women made to the liberation of Spain was in the direct support they supplied to guerrillas. When the *guerrilleros* attempted to hold towns, women might even become involved in house-to-house fighting, as in Zaragoza.[29] More often, though, they supplied logistical support. For example, women worked as nurses and doctors, providing safe houses for *guerrilleros* who could not make it back to their own homes. Women also seem to have distinguished themselves as spies and disseminators of disinformation to the French. Within resistance movements, women can sometimes do things men cannot. Ironically, this occurs because traditional assumptions that deny women the capacity to become historical agents give women an advantage in certain kinds of subversive activities. For example, where police agents imagine a group of men discussing subversive ideas, they may see a similar group of women merely as gossips.[30] Thus, women in Spain may have been better at passing messages, reporting enemy movements, and other espionage activities than men. Most of these activities, by their very nature, go unrecorded in the historical record, but this is not always the case. The wife of the alcalde of Barbadillo helped to trick a French colonel into marching his men into a trap sprung by Merino resulting in the deaths of 465 French troops.[31] We also know that women were used to pass information into and out of Pamplona right up to the Allied siege of the city in 1813. The passing of misinformation was especially effective in Navarre, allowing the guerrillas to escape encirclement on several occasions.

Women faced arrest and deportation for these activities and for merely being related to known *guerrilleros*.[32] Unfortunately, prison records do not report the sex of inmates.[33] We know of a few individual cases of women being arrested. The mother of the Empecinado, for example, was taken prisoner in a vain attempt to force the guerrilla chieftain to lay down his arms.[34] Yet, it appears that women were relatively immune to French arrest.[35] This is significant. In propaganda, Spanish women may have been Amazons or "wrestlers," but in daily practice the French did not really think women were as dangerous as men. As a result, women could provide the indispensible auxiliary services required by the guerrilla parties better than men. At the same time women escaped repression, however, their activities also failed to register in the historical records.

The most important service women provided to the insurgents was an economic one. Women were responsible for fleeing with the household goods upon the approach of French troops. This is an essential aspect of any guerrilla campaign, for partisans must either control or destroy the food, firewood, livestock, and other resources of the countryside so that the enemy cannot benefit from them. Even more important, women broke the earth, planted seed, brought in the harvests, and carried out all of the other myriad tasks of agriculture, allowing men to spend months in the bush in the knowledge that their households were being managed by their mothers, wives, sisters, and daughters. Women were particularly effective in carrying out these tasks in northern Spain, above all in the *Montaña*, encompassing northern Navarre and parts of Upper Aragon and the Basque provinces. Indeed, one of the factors that made the Montaña, a mostly Basque-speaking territory commanded by Espoz y Mina, the very heart of guerrilla country in Spain, was the peculiar place of women in the region.

Since the time of Strabo, northern Spain has had a reputation for possessing remnants of a matriarchal society.[36] Although it is doubtful that matriarchy, if by that one means a society in which women ruled, ever existed among the Basques, we do know that people in the Montaña practiced matrilineal inheritance in recent historical times.[37] In the eleventh century, female children inherited lands and houses in preference to males. Indeed, even if a woman had no daughters, her sons might still be passed over and the land ceded to the woman's sister or another relative, thus preserving the property in the maternal line.[38] In the early nineteenth century a relaxed form of matrilineal inheritance was still practiced in the Montaña. Evidence in marriage contracts demonstrates that women in the Montaña continued to inherit lands, titles, and moveable goods equally with men right into the Napoleonic era.[39]

What impact would this inheritance pattern have had on guerrilla war? For one thing, it created a lot of young men without prospects. The Montaña was a country of small peasant proprietors, where noble entails were insignificant and where even the Church owned little land. As a result, most families had adequate landholdings. The economy was subsistence oriented, and there was almost no paid labor of any kind. In general, the peasants were very prosperous, but to remain so, and to avoid the situation of *minifundia* (tiny plots) that plagued Galicia, property had to be willed to a single heir. The heir was always the eldest child, whether male or female. A young man who did not inherit land might work within the family for his sister or brother, but often young men simply emigrated to America or to one of the cities of Castile and Aragon, where there were more opportunities for casual labor.[40] As long as these emigration outlets remained open, the Montaña was stable. However, these outlets were eliminated precisely during the Napoleonic era. The English naval blockade, followed by the French occupation, cut Spain off from its colonies, making emigration to America difficult. In addition, the economic isolation of Spain caused a crisis in the most advanced sectors of the economy, making it difficult for men to find work in cities like Madrid, Zaragoza, and Barcelona. On the eve of the Napoleonic invasion, therefore, the Montaña contained a great number of desperate young men available to the insurgency.

The most intriguing case of such a youth was the "guerrilla king" of Navarre, Francisco Espoz y Mina. In 1800, Francisco's sister, Vicenta, married. As the eldest child, she inherited the sizeable family estate, including the house in Idocín, arable land, vineyards, wine press, livestock, tools, and everything else belonging to the family. Vicenta's husband came to Idocín to live, while Francisco was relegated to the status of a laborer working for his sister and brother-in-law, a status he still suffered in 1808, when the French invasion opened up new vistas. For Francisco and for other dispossessed young men the French occupation created opportunities for booty at the same time that it gave them an outlet for asserting their masculinity in a traditional sphere of manly endeavor: warfare. Thus, matrilineal inheritance customs within an essentially subsistence economy, intersecting with a national economic and political crisis, helped create a constituency of young men for the guerrilla war.[41]

There is another way in which so-called Basque matriarchy aided the guerrillas. Women in the Montaña not only inherited land, they also worked it in the same way men did, performing precisely the same tasks as men, including tillage. In most of Europe, there was a firm gender division of labor when it came to tilling the soil, with men normally managing draft animals and the plow to the exclusion of women. However, most peasants in Basque-Navarre in 1808 did not use plows. Instead, they employed hand tools, especially the *laya*, a kind of spade, and it was the use of the *laya* instead of the plow that, in combination with other factors, helped to empower women.

The *laya* is an apparatus exclusive to the Basque people. The small size of the plots and the steep terrain made this ancient tool more practical than the plow. Another advantage of *layas* was their low cost. Anyone could own a set, and equal access to this basic tool of production worked to reinforce egalitarian tendencies in the Montaña. The *laya* required communal labor. Two or more families worked together, first on one family's land, then on the other's. In this arrangement, women performed the same work men did.[42] The absence of men permanently or seasonally relocated in America or in the cities of Castile and Aragon was a normal condition, and it had never proved an obstacle to production. Since it was ordinary for women to take a central role in economic production, they simply continued in this role when men joined the insurgency after 1808.

It is notable that within Navarre, those areas most characterized by the use of the Basque language, egalitarian land distribution, matrilineal inheritance patterns, and a preference for the *laya* over the plow, were the same areas in which the guerrilla war was fought. In contrast, southern Navarre did not play a major role in the guerrilla resistance. This region, known as the Ribera, had a completely different social structure and economy. A few wealthy, usually noble families, together with the Church, owned most of the land, which always passed to male heirs in preference to females. The *laya* was unknown, and the mass of the population depended on wages from agricultural day labor. Interestingly, there was almost no wage work for women and children. Thus, not only were women unaccustomed to tilling the soil, they remained unemployed by the wage economy most of the time. Apparently, working women in southern Navarre already occupied quite a separate and unwaged sphere from men.[43] In the economy of the Ribera, men could not have been spared by their employers for any length of time, and they certainly could not have been spared by their families, since men were the only breadwinners. It is no surprise to find, therefore, that most of the *guerrilleros* who fought with Mina in Navarre came from the Montaña. Matriarchal Basque-Navarre could afford to make men into guerrillas, southern Navarre could not.

Women in the Montaña, because of their role in household production, were not only in a position to supply the grain, fodder, meat, and draft animals required by the guerrillas. They also provided safe houses and medical support. This is not at all surprising. One of the great tactical advantages of the guerrillas was that, fighting on home turf as they always did, they could easily disperse if overwhelmed by superior French numbers. In short, they could go home, where women took care of them. Thus, women provided the logistical support to the guerrillas that in regular armies would require a supply train, medical personnel, and thousands of other auxiliary troops. In a very real sense, therefore, women constituted the sinews of war for the guerrillas of northern Spain.

Conclusion: War and the Social Construction of Gender

The literature on gender and war has focused on two central questions. First, what has been the contribution of women to war, both in combat and behind the lines? Second, what impact does the mobilization of women have on gender roles during wartime and after the fighting stops? The answer to the first question seems to be that women have fought when their homes were invaded, and then only when forced to it as a last resort. Even in the age of total war and in moments of supreme national crisis, organized violence appears to be very much a male preserve. On the other hand, women have performed important noncombat functions, including the delivery of weapons, supplies, medical aid, and intelligence to partisans. These supporting roles have been an essential component of modern warfare.[44]

The answer to the second question is that the mobilization of women behind the lines can sometimes transform gender relations, but only under certain circumstances. Although the notion that women in the twentieth century have been able to fight, nurse, and rivet their way to political and social emancipation has been effectively challenged, the great wars of the twentieth century did produce moments when women became empowered to contest their identities.[45] The mobilization of some women in combat and the presence, however temporary, of many more women in traditionally male employments disrupted the traditional gendering of work and sociability, especially during World War Two. This disruption may have served in the long run to alter perceptions of what is appropriate behavior for women and to clear the way for permanent changes in gender relations.[46]

When Napoleon occupied Spain from 1808 to 1814, there was no real front line. All of Spain was a battlefield, and women became belligerents, in certain exceptional situations even taking part in combat. Spaniards fostered the image of women in battle to cajole men into fighting and to demonstrate to themselves and the world that all Spaniards, even women, were resisting the Bonaparte dynasty. The armed woman later became a beloved literary and artistic trope of the nineteenth century, for it proved to Spaniards that the nation belonged to everyone, a belief cherished all the more because Spain, in fact, fought half a dozen bloody civil wars between 1808 and 1939.

Because of the power of the image of the Amazon, the more mundane lives of most Spanish women during the war have been ignored. The truth is that most women, like most men, collaborated or remained neutral. This was particularly the case in urban areas and throughout southern Spain, especially in Andalusia and La Mancha. Nevertheless, in El Ferrol, Zaragoza, and probably in other cities as well women participated in the revolutionary upheavals that inaugurated the war with France. They made vital contributions to the guerrilla insurgency, protecting household goods from marauding French troops, acting as spies, couriers, and nurses, and bringing in the harvests while men fought. Yet these contributions remained unrewarded and unremembered, masked because they did not fit the Amazon paradigm and because they represented nothing new. Women in guerrilla country had always participated on an equal footing with men in the management of homes and the working of lands. It is, I believe, precisely because women resisted in ways that did not violate notions of appropriate feminine behavior that the French invasion could not induce a fundamental reordering of gender roles.

Hundreds of thousands of Spanish men, hitherto excluded from politics, were politicized, mobilized, and armed in the process of defeating Napoleon. These men continued to make claims on the political system after the war, turning the period 1808–1814 into one of the most significant moments in the nationalization of men in nineteenth-century Spain. Women's contributions to the war also constituted a significant irruption of a new group into the political life of Spain. Yet, because women's resistance did not arm them nor, for the most part, involve them in nontraditional activities, there was no pressure to modify the place of women in Spain after the war ended. Fundamental changes for women had to wait until the 1930s, and then it had nothing to do with war but with the advent of the Second Republic and its willingness to gamble that women would vote republican.

Notes

1. Juan Pérez de Guzmán y Gallo, *El dos de Mayo de 1808 en Madrid* (Madrid: Sucesores de Rivadeneyra, 1908), p. 407.

2. For example, Nancy Loring Goldman, *Female Soldiers—Combatants or Noncombatants? Historical and Contemporary Perspectives* (Westport, CT: Greenwood Press, 1982); Jean Bethke Elshtain, *Women and War* (New York: Basic Books, 1987); and Margaret Randolph Higonnet, Jane Jenson, Sonya Michel, and Margaret Collins Weitz, eds., *Behind the Lines: Gender and the Two World Wars* (New Haven, CT: Yale University Press, 1987); Catherine Clinton and Nina Silber, eds., *Divided Houses: Gender and the Civil War* (New York: Oxford University Press, 1992); and T.G. Fraser and Keith Jeffery, eds., *Men, Women and War* (Dublin: Lilliput Press, 1993).

3. Even Soviet women in World War Two constituted only a small proportion of the armed forces. Jean Cottam, "Soviet Women in Combat in World War II: The Ground Forces and the Navy," *International Journal of Women's Studies* 3, no. 14 (1980): 345–357. In the Spanish Civil War, perhaps two hundred Republican women saw combat at the front. Mary Nash, "Women in War: *Milicianas* and Armed Combat in Revolutionary Spain, 1936–39," *The International History Review* 15 (May 1993): 269–282.

4. Helen M. Cooper, Adrienne Auslander Munich, and Susan Merrill Squier, eds., *Arms and the Woman: War, Gender, and Literary Representation* (Chapel Hill, NC: University of North Carolina Press, 1989); Donna Ryan, "Ordinary Acts and Resistance: Women in Street Demonstrations and Food Riots in Vichy France," *Proceedings of the Annual Meeting of the Western Society for French History* 16 (1989): 400–407.

5. My recent book attempts to correct this situation. John Lawrence Tone, *The Fatal Knot: The Guerrilla War in Navarre and the Defeat of Napoleon in Spain* (Chapel Hill, NC: University of North Carolina Press, 1995).

6. See the collection of proclamations in the Archivo Histórico Nacional, Sección Estado, legajo 13. The insistence on unanimity responded to the need of the revolutionaries to claim a popular mandate they did not in fact have. Typical of this rhetoric was the assurance given readers by *The Semanario Patriótico* that "twelve million souls, united by the most sacred bond known to man, love of the nation," were fighting for "liberty and honor" against France.

7. See Joaquín Ezquerra del Bayo, *Guerra de la Independencia, Retratos* (Madrid, 1935); and *Madrid, el dos de Mayo de 1808: Viaje a un día en la historia de España* (Madrid, Consorcio Para la Organización de Madrid Capital Europea de la Cultura, 1992); and Pérez de Guzmán, *El dos de Mayo de 1808 en Madrid*, pp. 380, 383, 405–407.

8. García Bermejo, *Oración funebre* (Madrid, 1817).

9. Jesús María Alía y Plana, "El primer lunes de Mayo de 1808 en Madrid," in *Madrid, el dos de Mayo de 1808* (Madrid: Consorcio para la Organización de Madrid Capital Europea de la Cultura), pp. 105–141.

10. Ibid., p. 133.

11. Emmanuel de Grouchy, "Etat des officier et soldats tués ou blessés," Archives de l'Armée de Terre, Paris, C8, 6.

12. The most useful account of the siege is Augustín Alcaide Ibieca, *Historia de los dos sitios que pusieron a Zaragoza en los años de 1808 y 1809 las tropas de Napoleón* (Madrid: Impr. De D. M. de Burgos, 1830).

13. For a discussion of the *mujer varonil* see, among others, Melveena McKendrick, *Woman and Society in the Spanish Drama of the Golden Age: A Study of*

the Mujer Varonil (London: Cambridge University Press, 1974); and Mary Elizabeth Perry, "The Manly Woman: A Historical Case Study," *American Behavioral Scientist* 31 (September/October 1987): 86–100.

14. José Gómez de Arteche y Moro, *La Guerra de la Independencia* vol. 8 (Madrid: Impresa del Desposito de la Guerra, 1868), pp. 41–65, 89; Juan Mercader Riba, *Barcelona durante la ocupación francesa* (Madrid: Consejo Superior de Investigaciones Científicas, Instituto Gerónimo Zurita, 1949); Louis Gabriel Suchet, *Memoirs of the War in Spain from 1808 to 1814* vol. 1 (London: H. Colburn, 1829), pp. 40–41.

15. Marshall Soult noted that towns were easily governed, in contrast to the countryside where "the people were truly Spanish, a rude people, almost savage." Nicolás Jean Soult, *Mémoires du Maréchal Soult* (Paris: Hachette, 1955), p. 176.

16. Ibid., p. 68; see also Emmanuel Martin, *La gendarmerie française en Espagne: Campagnes de 1807 á 1814* (Paris: Leautey, 1898), p. 207.

17. For example, José María Toreno, *Historia del levantamiento, guerra, y revolución de España*, Vol. 1 (Paris: Baudry, 1851), p. 98.

18. José María Iribarren, *Espoz y Mina: El guerrillero* (Madrid: Aguilar, 1965), pp. 308–310.

19. Francisco Espoz y Mina, *Memorias*, in the *Biblioteca de autores españoles*, vols. 146–47, (Madrid: Ediciones Atlas, 1962), pp. 367, 423–144.

20. Jean Albert Rocca, *Memoirs of the War of the French in Spain* (London: J. Murray, 1815), pp. 263–302.

21. The French took the bullfight as another sign of Spain's backwardness, not because of the blood, but because in the early nineteenth century the great spectacle subversively brought together nobles, bourgeois, workers, and peasants. The French were particularly disgusted to find that Spanish women seemed to enjoy the bullfight as much as men did and thought it had snuffed out their natural docility and "all sense of humanity" in them, and had prepared them for armed struggle. J.J.E. Roy, *Les Français en Espagne: Souvenirs des guerres de la péninsule, 1808–1814* (Tours: Mame, 1872), p. 96.

22. Benito Pérez Galdós, *Zaragoza* (Madrid: Est. Tip. De la Viuda é Hijos de Tello, 1874), p. 204.

23. Ibid., pp. 85–86.

24. The argument for a broader definition of politics is made nicely in Guida West and Rhoda Lois Blumberg, *Women and Social Protest* (New York: Oxford University Press, 1990).

25. Archives de l'Armée de Terre, C8, 7.

26. Temma Kaplan, "Female Consciousness and Collective Action: The Case of Barcelona, 1910–1918," *Signs* 7 (Autumn 1982): 545–66; and "Women and Communal Strikes in the Crisis of 1917–1922," in Renate Bridenthal, Claudia Koonz, and Susan Stuard, eds., *Becoming Visible: Women in European History*, 2d ed. (Boston: Houghton Mifflin, 1987), pp. 429–449. During the French Revolution women went beyond traditional forms of female collective action to engage in "male" activities. Harriet B. Applewhite and Darline Gay Levy, "Women and Militant Citizenship in Revolutionary Paris," in Sara E. Melzer and Leslie W. Rabine, eds., *Rebel Daughters: Women and the French Revolution* (New York: Oxford University Press, 1992).

27. Richard Herr, "Good, Evil, and Spain's Rising against Napoleon," in Richard Herr and Harold T. Parker, eds., *Ideas in History: Essays Presented to Louis Gottschalk* (Durham, NC: Duke University Press, 1965), pp. 157–181.

28. Prefect J. P. Chazal to Neuchatel, June 1, 1808, and an anonymous summary of news from Spain dated June 8, 1808, Archives de l'Armée de Terre, C8, 7. On the rising in Zaragoza, see Augustín Alcaide Ibieca, *Historia de los dos sitios*. Also of interest is Mariano de Pano y Ruata, *La condesa de Bureta* (Zaragoza, 1908), an interesting though romanticized life of one of the heroines of the siege.

29. In June 1809, for example, the French battled guerrilla troops for the town of Estella. During the fighting, which was going badly for the insurgents, women poured boiling water from their windows down upon the French troops. As in Madrid, boiling water did little damage. The town was later sacked in retribution. "Relación histórica de los sucesos mas notables ocurridos en Estella durante la guerra de la Independencia," Archivo General de Navarra, Sección Guerra, legajo 21, carpeta 21.

30. These points are made by Paula Schwartz, "Partisanes and Gender Politics in Vichy France," *French Historical Studies* 16 (Spring 1989): 126–152.

31. Enrique Rodríguez-Solís, *Los guerrilleros de 1808: Historia popular de la guerra de la independencia* 2 vols. (Madrid: Imprenta de F. Cao y D. de Val, 1887), vol. 1, book 6, p. 39.

32. On French terror in Navarre see Tone, *The Fatal Knot*, 107–115.

33. "Relación auténtica que contiene las personas que fueron aprisionados en Navarra por la policia francesa durante la guerra," Archivo General de Navarra, legajo 21, carpeta 19.

34. Rodríguez-Solís, *Los guerrilleros de 1808*, vol. 1, book 5, p. 18.

35. In Navarre some towns reported the names of arrested individuals, but women were absent from the lists. Archivo General de Navarra, Sección Guerra, legajo 21, carpetas 21, p. 22.

36. A recent work supporting the idea of a Basque matriarchy is Andrés Ortiz Osés, *El matriarcalismo vasco: Reinterpretación de la cultura vasca* (Bilbao, Spain: Universidad de Deusto, 1980).

37. For interesting discussions of the myth of matriarchy see Celia Amorós, *Hacia una crítica de la razón patriarcal* (Madrid: Anthropos Editorial del Hombre, 1985), pp. 273–288, and Teresa del Valle, *Mujer vasca: Imagen y realidad* (Barcelona: Anthropos, 1985).

38. Roger Collins, *The Basques* (Oxford: Basel Blackwell, 1986), pp. 159–160, 193–194.

39. Archivo de Protocolos Notariales, Pamplona, Velaz, various legajos. Matrilineal patterns of inheritance are also discernible in other parts of northern Spain, notably in Galicia, as discussed in the article by Heidi Kelley in this volume.

40. This male emigration from the Basque region is well documented, and the surplus of women over men in the Basque country is indicated by census data from the 1780s and 1790s. Archivo General de Navarra, Sección Estadística, legajos 6, 16, 20, 25, 31, 49 (census of 1786–1787), and legajos 7–8, 16–17, 20, 25–28, 31, 49 (census of 1796–1797).

41. Archivo de Protocolos Notariales, Pamplona, Peralta, legajo 50, no. 90.

42. There is a good description of the *laya* and its use in L. Louis Lande, *Basques et Navarrais* (Paris: Librairie Académique, Didier et Cie, 1878), p. 7. A study of the *laya* was made by Telesforo de Aranzadi, "Aperos de labranza y sus aledaños testiles y pastoriles," in *Folklore y costumbres de España* (Madrid: Ediciones Merino, 1988), vol. 1. Julio Caro Baroja made much of the fact that men and women historically worked in basically the same way with the *laya*. This, according to Caro Baroja, underpinned the relative empowerment of Basque women. See *Los Pueblos de España* (Madrid: Ediciones ISTMO, 1975), and *Vecindad, familia, y técnica* (San Sebastián: Editorial Txertoa, 1974).

43. Angel García Sanz, *La respuesta a los interrogatorios de población, agricultura e industria de 1802* (Pamplona, Spain: Editorial Laser, 1983), pp. 122, 136. Teresa del Valle's already cited work, *Mujer vasca*, shows that where the subsistence economy of the Basque *caserío* remained relatively undisturbed by market influences and opportunities for wage work, women retained more power in their households and communities. When women labor on an equal footing with men, as happens in a subsistence setting, they have more power than they do in cities and fishing towns, where women's work is underremunerated relative to men's.

44. In the French resistance, for example, *partisanes* did not generally engage in combat. Margaret L. Rossiter, *Women in the Resistance* (New York: Praeger, 1986); and Paula Schwartz, "Partisanes and Gender Politics in Vichy France."

45. The constructive power of war to alter gender relations may be offset by its association with a rhetoric of virile struggle that devalues women and prepares the way for the recovery of prewar norms of conduct for men and women. The most significant adjustments to gender relations have been associated with larger economic, social, and technological changes, with warfare merely reinforcing preexisting trends. See, among

other works, Leila J. Rupp, *Mobilizing Women for War: German and American Propaganda, 1939–1945* (Princeton, NJ: Princeton University Press, 1978); Maurine Weiner Greenwald, *Women, War, and Work: The Impact of World War I on Women Workers in the United States* (Westport, CT: Greenwood Press, 1980); Jean Bethke Elshtain, *Women and War*; and Steven C. Hause, "More Minerva than Mars: The French Women's Rights Campaign and the First World War," in Margaret Randolph Higonnet, Jane Jenson, Sonya Michel, and Margaret Collins Weitz, eds., *Behind the Lines.* In the same collection, the articles by Michelle Perrot and Joan W. Scott make similar points from different perspectives.

46. See Higonnet, Jenson, Michel, and Weitz, "Introduction," in *Behind the Lines*, pp. 1–17. It is notable, however, that in China, the Soviet Union, and Yugoslavia, the three places where women were mobilized for combat as nowhere else, women were hardly emancipated.

11

Redressing the Balance: Gendered Acts of Justice around the Mining Community of Río Tinto in 1913

Temma Kaplan

The varied circumstances under which women challenge political authorities to speak for communities has been evident to me in countless ways, but never more clearly than when I was studying a copper mining strike that took place in Río Tinto in Huelva in 1913.[1] In *El Socialista*, the official Socialist Party newspaper, I came across an article that described how one day hundreds of women dressed in rags formed a human chain across the railroad tracks near the mines. The civil guard on the train, rather than assert its political power to hold its wounded prisoner, released him to the women. They then carried him by chair and burro back to town.[2]

In this and thousands of similar cases throughout the world, groups of women have periodically challenged formal political authority by confronting soldiers and police and by arguing for justice. Precisely because these women seldom belong to ongoing political organizations, they frequently appear less threatening to government officials than other women mobilizing alongside men organized into political parties or trade unions. But even those women who lack sustained political identities can nevertheless act in ways that challenge existing power relations.[3] When women of the popular classes do mobilize, they often claim not to be acting politically, but to be representing the interests of justice. Despite what women activists and most historians say, the women act politically, if only episodically.

For more than two decades, I have been trying to explain what galvanizes ordinary women to get involved in certain kinds of social movements, how they act without a collective identity, and why so many women's movements evoke theories of justice that few philosophers or political leaders uphold. In one article called "Female Consciousness and Collective Action," I tried to explain how women referring to themselves as housewives and mothers took matters into their own hands when they thought that political authorities and their own male relatives were incapable of helping them survive. Women who acceded to the division of labor by sex according to their culture and historical period frequently demanded the privileges entailed by acceptance of gender obligations. I called this practice of confronting authorities in the name of preserving families or fighting for justice, "female consciousness."[4]

Working on similar problems, British political scientist Maxine Molyneux has developed a theory of gender interests.[5] What she calls "strategic gender interests" refers to concerns that focus on women's subordination and attempts to alter sexual discrimination. These strategic interests can include campaigns against sexual harassment and spousal abuse, or for women's suffrage, female education, reproductive rights, child care, and other services that women of all classes, races, and ethnicities might need. From this perspective, feminists would belong to the group of people who are pursuing strategic gender interests which are designed to aid women in becoming full citizens and social actors. Looking at an even broader range of activities, Molyneux argues that when women act in the public realm to assure the preservation of their families, class, ethnic groups, and communities, they are pursuing different goals that she calls their "practical gender interests." In other words, they carry gendered behavior into the public realm to assure the preservation of their families and communities without regard for achieving gender equality.

Both terms, female consciousness and practical gender interests, attempt to explain why during certain crises, particular women sometimes assume authority to speak for entire communities. In fact, there are even broader implications of Molyneux's theory of practical gender interests and of my ideas about female consciousness, since neither category is as clear-cut as it first appears. For example, we both refer to processes whereby women move back and forth between specific survival needs and principled demands for general goals, such as human emancipation and justice. When the patterns of everyday life come into question because of shortages of food, housing, or heating fuel, or because of disruptions in the social order, ordinary women sometimes argue that justice requires that they intercede. By justice, they often mean more balanced behavior on the part of authorities, an end to violence, and distribution of social necessities. When women of the working classes, peasantry, or subordinated ethnic or racial groups make claims for justice, they represent their demands as selfless and their claims as universal—at least for their class and their ethnicity. With these issues of justice and social movements in mind, I've focused on certain women's activities and on gendered arguments about them in the southwestern mining community of Río Tinto in the late nineteenth and early twentieth centuries.

Historical Development of the Río Tinto Mining Community

In 1873, when the British Río Tinto Company bought the sulphur and copper mines in the southwest of Spain, near southern Portugal, the landscape consisted of desolate pasture lands, small peasant farms, and large estates. The Tinto River, running halfway between the Guadalquivir and Guadiana rivers in Huelva Province, provided a thoroughfare. The name "tinto" comes from its similarity to red wine, a color it gets by running through the rugged, copper-rich soils between the port of Huelva and the inland sulfur mines to the north, which were surrounded by the towns of Minas de Río Tinto, Nerva, Valverde del Camino, La Zarza, and Zalamea la Real. The peasants and the landless laborers of these towns found work in the cast mines, which were barely utilized until British companies purchased them in the late nineteenth century.

Beginning in 1873, English companies bought the Río Tinto, San Telmo, and Tharsis sulfur and copper mines. Within a decade, by 1883, they had transformed the landscape, introducing heavy machinery, opening pits that resembled coliseums cut into the blood-red hills, constructing vast, slow-burning heaps of ore to refine the sulfur and copper from the iron pyrites, and building railroads, tunnels, and docks to transport the ores. Although the mines constituted the largest deposits of pyrites in the world until the mine fields of Zambia (formerly Northern Rhodesia) were discovered and developed by the same British companies, the mineral content of the Spanish mines, largely copper and sulfur, were poor. The output was, however, sufficient to produce a high percentage of the sulfuric acid used by the growing European chemical industry in the 1880s.

Development of the mines launched a period of urbanization that made collective action among the women far more likely as the population surrounding the mines increased. Nerva, Río Tinto, and Zalamea, under the control of the Río Tinto Company, grew from villages to large urban mining and railroad centers. The population increased fifteen-fold between 1873 and the turn of the century due to the migration of men and some women from elsewhere in Spain. By 1887, the Río Tinto enterprises employed more than 20,000 people and the local population had grown from about 48,000 in 1860 to 66,000, and again to about 100,000 by 1913.[6] Living outside any social constraints, the new immigrants frequently included unemployed coal miners from the northern mines of Asturias. Because of their misery and fear, most of the miners were drinkers and represented a social threat both to the company, which wanted a steady labor force, and to the union movement, which was attempting to create stability and solidarity. Violence was rampant; during one six week period in 1886 there were seven murders. The Río Tinto Company even tore down the local bull ring because the management feared it as a center of vice and disorder, but this act contributed to the miners' sense of being oppressed by a company that wanted to control every moment of their lives.[7]

Although sociologists, especially the famous Clark Kerr and Alan Siegel, argued in the 1950s that the isolation of mines and textile towns from the larger society accounted for the militancy of strikes occurring in such communities, the opposite seems to have been true.[8] Subsequent studies on women and gender in mining enclaves underscore the subtle ways that the lack of separation between work and family life found in mining areas, where everyone in the working classes lives close to the sounds and smells of the mines, mutes differences between the sites of production and consumption, bringing issues of the gendered nature of class and community into relief.

Louise Tilly's pioneering article, entitled "Paths of Proletarianization: Organization of Production, Sexual Division of Labor, and Women's Collective Action,"[9] highlighted how French women attempted to intervene in coal mining strikes by positioning themselves at the entrance to the pits in order to deter strike breakers from taking their husbands' jobs. Then, in quick succession a disastrous mining accident led to a strike for better safety measures, someone dynamited a house belonging to the mine owner, and a local woman testified against the accused miners. Groups of women then marched from the mines to the train station seeking the woman they regarded as a traitor to the community. Failing to find her, they met another collection of women who had been urging the mine owners to speed up rescue efforts to save workers still trapped in the flooded mines.[10] Elsewhere in a metal working community, Tilly discovered women mobilizing to bring down the prices of supplementary food items like dairy products and eggs. A line of the song performed by the demonstrating women showed what motivated them to act. They proclaimed their commitments to female consciousness by explaining that:

If one day we are victorious
We'll show our dear husbands
That all women have fought
For the lives of their poor little ones.[11]

Thus it was not isolation but tight bonds among people whose living conditions were intricately tied up with their working conditions which accounted for solidarity.

Those bonds develop not only from contiguity, from the closeness of the sites of work and home, but also from the domestic conditions of the people living around the mines. In a brilliant article on the domestic policies of copper mine owners in Zambia, in southern Africa, George Chauncey, Jr. demonstrated that in a situation of labor shortages in the 1930s, mine owners competed to provide good housing for miners and their wives in order to attract workers.[12]

Writing about the El Teniente copper mines in Chile during the 1930s and 1940s, Thomas Klubock has shown that in hope of improving worker productivity, Chilean mine owners sought to restrain alcoholism and dependence on prostitutes by promoting marriage. To encourage domesticity—believed to contribute to the docility of the workforce—and to persuade women to stay with the mine workers, who controlled their wives' labor and sexuality, the company began building houses for the miners while subsidizing food and clothing purchases through the company store.[13] Of course, this process ultimately intensified control of the managers over every aspect of the workers' lives.

In the mines of Río Tinto in Spain, the company launched similar projects. In fact, the militancy of the working-class community forced the British company to undertake a paternalist policy designed to provide miners with certain resources of housing and health care in exchange for their docility and productivity. The development of paternalist policies toward the miners took shape primarily in the domestic sphere and had profound effects on women in the mining community.

As in Chile and Zambia later on, from the late nineteenth century the Río Tinto company encouraged legal marriage and nuclear families among workers for whom mine owners increasingly tried to provide limited housing and some social services.[14] The paternalist programs did not, however, succeed in pacifying the community. Beginning in the 1880s and lasting through the 1920s, people in the mining community protested against having to pay half a day's salary for their medical expenses and against the company's failure to provide adequate pensions and insurance against mining injuries.[15]

A coalition of people, including women, who lived in the vicinity of the mines embarked upon a campaign in 1887 and 1888 to get the company of Río Tinto to limit the open-air burning of copper sulfate, to improve pensions and health benefits, and to reduce the workday from 12 to 9 hours. They also sought to ban Portuguese contract laborers, who came without their families and received their wages only when they returned to Portugal. Since these strike breakers lived as single men in barracks apart from the working-class community, the local women lacked access to them. Unable to achieve their aims, people of all kinds in the mining community began a general strike on February 1, 1888. The general strike, really a community insurrection, lasted three days and ended in a massacre in which forty-five men, women, and children died and another seventy to a hundred people were wounded.[16]

Although the popular forces met defeat in 1888, within a few years Río Tinto and the other British companies switched from open-air burnings to the Bessemer process of refining copper in foundries, thus reducing the pollution.

The families of miners gained extensive medical benefits, but the workers still had to pay a portion of the costs. Nor did social peace descend upon the community. In 1898, for example, women around the mines at Nerva rebelled because the price of bread had risen to unreasonable heights and the wives of miners could not afford to put food on their family's table. Authorities arrested thirty-three women in connection with the uprising, but the Río Tinto Company office in England immediately lowered the price of bread in the local company stores and ordered two hundred tons of flour shipped to the Río Tinto area to prevent future demonstrations by the women.[17]

The Gendered Nature of the General Strike in 1913

As with the uprising in 1888, the general strike of 1913 transcended work at the point of production and affected the entire community and its sense of the order of things. The mines, located in a ring ranging from forty-five to ninety-eight kilometers from the port city of Huelva, were completely isolated until the company constructed a vast railroad network to carry minerals to port. Since Huelva Harbor had been too shallow to dock heavy ore boats, the company built new berths and connected them with its railroads, providing employment for large numbers of people. All of those at work in offices, docks, railroads, or mines and the women married to them came to depend on the Río Tinto company.[18]

Although the miners had first organized as anarchists and anarcho-syndicalists during the 1888 strike and its aftermath, increasingly the Socialist Party made inroads among them through its General Union of Workers (UGT). Since no ore could get to the port without the socialist railroad and dock workers, miners joined the Socialist National Railroad Federation (Federación Nacional de Ferroviaria de Huelva-Río Tinto, Sección de Río Tinto), and the Río Tinto company balked. Fearing the regional strength such a union would bring, the company fired militant workers in April 1913, forcing miners to go out on strike in solidarity with their leaders. In a series of labor disputes lasting eight months, during which the workers sought reduced work hours from the usual twelve hour days, better safety conditions, overtime wages, paid days off, and improvements in medical care and pensions, the company tried to destroy the union.[19] In 1913 Río Tinto, as in other mining struggles, women and men, whose proximity to the mines structured their behavior, participated in the movement to transform social relations to more just lines. In struggling about the quality of life, gender became a guiding issue.

As administrators of a foreign company, the managers of Río Tinto would have had to take special care to observe customs and cautiously carry out their exchanges with the people of the community in order not to incur hostility. Instead, they behaved like foreign conquerors, expropriating land near the mines, destroying half the city of Río Tinto in 1908 to open a new pit, and running their own company stores and paying in scrip, thus appropriating the trade that otherwise would have gone to small shopkeepers and merchants in the towns near the mines.[20] Feelings ran high, and many people thought the Río Tinto Company treated local people as inferiors, effectively imposing curfews by demanding that parties end by midnight and silence reign in towns like Nerva.

Antagonism had only grown worse since the 1888 uprising as the company intensified its hold on every aspect of life in the mining community, and thus directly confronted the women. The Río Tinto Company became increasingly paternalistic. It engaged in a housing program, controlled the only medical plan to which local people had access, intensified the monopoly of company stores by paying salaries in scrip rather than in money, linked life in the mines to every other social need, and blurred all boundaries between everyday life and production. By undercutting independent shopkeepers and predicating medical care on submissive behavior, the company ensured that social life was intimately tied to the mining industry. In 1913, the Río Tinto Company once again managed to unite the storekeepers, the small manufacturers, the miners, and local women against itself because of what they claimed was the injustice of the company's handling of copper production and the people engaged in it.

Since hatred for the British was widespread around the mines, it remains to explain why the women rather than the men were portrayed as making the first move to express what the journalist Juan Moro called "their spirit of opposition, a mixture of strong doses of justice, a spirit that could decline but could not be contained."[21] Here Juan Moro, one of the foremost socialist intellectuals of his generation, as well as the first historian of the socialist movement, writing for *El Socialista*, underscores a methodological problem in revealing how gender is imbedded in political rhetoric. When authorities confront groups of women demonstrating on behalf of their families, the press frequently covers the encounters, thus providing rare glimpses into the lives of ordinary women. Depending on the political slant of the newspaper, journalists portray women's behavior according to one political standard or another. In the socialist press of the early twentieth century in Spain, Germany, and England, women of the working classes generally appeared in melodramatic terms, as faceless symbols of exploitation.[22] The women's stories lacked individuality as they were subsumed under a general tale of oppression.

Documenting the motivations of such women activists remains difficult since they seldom explained themselves in words, and because commentators promoted their own programs by interpreting the meaning of women's behavior. Yet, in such an imperfect world, newspapers provide the best evidence about women's social movements, and demonstrate the ways in which gender shaped class and community identity around implicit arguments about justice. In the late nineteenth and early twentieth centuries, socialist journalists frequently wrote articles with anecdotes about working-class women's lives, seemingly to show that if capitalism wrought such havoc on defenseless women, it deserved to be overthrown. By gendering class oppression and exploitation, and pointing to authorities' injustices against women, socialists and anarchists could highlight the evils of capitalism and enhance the sense of masculinity of those who might fight to overthrow it. By portraying working women as victims, leftist journalists justified their own and the women's cause. Women's behavior, seemingly outside the realm of narrow political and labor interests, lent an aura of sanctity to the social struggles that the left supported and contributed to the justice of the workers' cause. Lacking other sources of evidence about women such as those who rescued the prisoner in Río Tinto, the following narrative of the general strike depends on the work of just such a journalist/interpreter, the socialist Juan Moro.

When Moro painted resistance in epic terms, with the women as heroes, as he did at the beginning of this essay, something more was afoot than mere poetry. As he told the story, José (Antonio) Roche, a worker who had been hurt in a mining accident, returned to work, but not to the high-paying job he had previously occupied. Between his hospital costs and his reduced salary, Roche was deeply in debt with no possibility of rising to his previous level as a relatively well paid worker. Hoping to get some understanding, he went to the manager. The manager responded rudely, insulting Roche in a mixture of English and Spanish, beating him with a cane, and bathing him in his own blood. Roche, said to have tears running down his face, drew out a knife and attacked the manager. Then the Civil Guard arrested Roche and carried him on the train toward prison.[23]

Having heard what had happened, the women of Río Tinto, Mesa de los Pinos, Taja Honga, Campillo, and Nerva, whom Moro described as appearing throughout the mountains in tragic silhouettes, set out to right the wrong. They apparently presumed that if the wounded man was taken to jail the same fate should have befallen his attacker. "In name of this principle of equity, their bodies covered in rags, they gathered on the railway tracks claiming that either both or neither ought to be jailed. 'Let them arrest the Englishman or give us our prisoner,' thousands of women and children shouted." They formed a human chain blocking the train on which Roche was being transported. Unable to move, the train stopped on its tracks. Presumably hoping to avoid spilling the blood of women, the Civil Guard handed the wounded man over to his female saviors who carried him by chair a half kilometer to Mesa de los Pinos, then by burro to Nerva.[24]

According to Juan Moro, during the four-and-a-half hours that the women's uprising lasted, the women had made "a virile, heroic, and grand gesture," in contrast to the cowardly acts of "those English who call themselves men."[25] Pamela Radcliff, writing in this volume, has pointed to another incident, a consumer rebellion in 1898 in Badajoz, in which the term *mujeres varoniles* or "masculine women" appears and underlines the threat to social order that gender reversals entail.[26] Radcliff argues that women's action to solve social problems implies a challenge to the masculinity of the authorities, who have been derelict in their duties. In the mining communities, the role reversal also challenges the masculinity of the soldiers, who place their own virility in jeopardy if they attack mere women, while possibly leaving the masculinity of the workers intact. Under conditions of crisis in 1913, women defending the community may actually have enhanced the masculinity of the miners.

Gendered Languages of Justice

The narrative about how the women rescued Roche comes entirely from Moro, but Moro himself interpreted the women's actions and their interpretation of justice. Moro carefully explained that the women did not argue that Roche was right to draw a knife on the English supervisor; only that if he were taken prisoner, the person who had initiated the fight by caning the pleading Roche should also have gone to jail. But what gave women the right to take justice into their own hands and what codes did Moro depend on to justify his representation of them?

The gendered language surrounding the conflict in 1913 Río Tinto assumed its own special qualities when the physical attack on José Antonio Roche and the local women's leap to his defense brought issues of justice into relief through a coded language. Everyone involved in the conflict spoke the language of masculinity. Moro, writing for a largely male, socialist clientele, could applaud the "virility" of the women who assumed power because, effectively, the women represented justice and community—hence, they represented the men. Stealing the prisoner back was certainly not part of socialist policy and not commended as such. Moro never speculated about what would have happened if Roche's male comrades had decided to rescue him; and Moro's praise of the women did not denigrate the men. At least in the case of the Río Tinto women, their action to uphold a certain concept of justice, and the attribution of male qualities to them for acting in this way, may in fact have said more about the concept of "women" and its ties to justice and community than to any failures of the men. While I am concerned with showing that women themselves formed a part of the mining community, I'm also curious about what role his concept of womanhood played in Moro's struggle to promote community and socialist consciousness among his readers. My own project is to understand whether actual women play a part in this construction of community solidarity, or whether the community, though identified in Moro's articles as the local women and their campaigns for justice, really pertains only to the men.

Moro never explained how the women learned about Roche's predicament, how they came together, whether Roche had any female relatives and what part they played in mobilizing their neighbors, or why men did not push the women aside and replace them in the demonstration to free Roche. For Moro, it seemed self-evident that certain gestures toward justice lay in the domain of women. Moreover, Moro's omission of any reference to female relatives among the crowd indicated that either none was present or, more importantly, that justice lay with women representing the miners' community, not with particular women. This division of labor in which anonymous women spoke with their actions for justice indicates the importance of female consciousness or practical gender interests in the extra legal realm.

The heroism of the women dressed in rags, forming a silhouette across the landscape, is structured in melodramatic language. The rags are important and to some degree establish the women's legitimacy. They are not proud women, acting strategically (in Molyneux's terms), demanding their rights; they are impoverished women of the people, fit representatives of class and community, claiming justice for all. Moro of course presumes that we, his socialist readers, would not at that time support suffragists, although article after article about the British suffragists and about Cristabel and Emily Pankhurst's exiled operation in France appeared in *El Socialista* all through 1913. The fact that we view the Río Tinto women as abject, as acting only because there is a vacuum in authority, allows us to support the women in their effort to seek justice. They need to suffer in order to win our support and to justify their entering the public arena as fighters with masculine traits.

By listing the towns from which the women came, Moro also provides a generalized identity for the anonymous women he describes. The women, unlike the men, represent no union and no party; they voice the aspirations of a community that far transcends narrow, particularistic interests. In this equation, women represent the collective; and men's collectives represent the union of a lot of individual interests, which is not the same thing. The silhouettes of the women show them to be no one in particular, shadowy figures conjured up by the mines and mountains to reestablish a mystical balance, to distribute justice where there was no justice—where even local political officials lacked the power to interfere with the British mining interests. But the women did not exhaust themselves or their heroism in defending Roche.

Another article Moro wrote several months later, in November 1913, at the end of the long general strike, reported on an uprising of seven thousand people, among whom were numerous women and children, who tried to invade the mines and foundries to carry out sabotage.[27] The advance group of the crowd consisted of three women from Nerva. This time Moro places himself in the story and tells us that

> once they saw us, they began yelling, and pretty soon we were surrounded by women and children greeting us with noisy shouts. The spectacle was highly charged. Some [women] carried their babies on their shoulders; others wrapped them in rags . . . some children remained silent, giving them the semblance of serious men; and some little wizened children, scarcely eight years old, made tremendous exertions to hold their brothers and sisters in their arms. "We are going over to persuade the scabs," [the women] told us. "In a few hours, we've caught twenty people. But the one with whom we [especially] wanted to talk escaped."

Moro goes on to explain that "the women of the mines have given this struggle the epic tones that surround it. From the beginning they have strengthened their hearts against pangs of hunger. With passionate words they have inspired their men to go on strike and then they have sustained them." Realizing that pursuing the scabs was dangerous for the men, "feminine delegations" followed scabs down the different streets and through the towns, "trying to persuade them that their conduct hurt the interests of their [own] class." The women continued their attack for twenty days, speaking with more than a hundred strikebreakers, who were "afraid of these brave women." They also put pressure on the families of the scabs, "disrupting daily life at home," defining themselves as women, speaking for an entire class, community, or system of justice, and calling on the solidarity of women married to strikebreakers—just because they were women. "[A]nd besides these [activities] the women grew red in the face telling the guilty [strikebreakers] what they thought of them." At the end of twenty days, "not a single scab remained in the mine."[28]

Later, when hungry women called on the city council of Río Tinto for food, the mayor and the civil guard jeered at them and told them to ask the union leaders. "One woman from the group answered simply, 'If they [had the power] to supply bread for our children and reduce the tyranny our husbands suffer, they would do so. But since the company is responsible for all that, they are [also] responsible for our misery. And against them we will fight to the death.'"[29]

On the same day that the article on the women's struggle appeared, *El Socialista* also reported that the company had rehired the two thousand workers they had fired during the eight-month-long strike.[30] Just two weeks later, "a group of four hundred women, with banners and musical instruments, announced their presence by playing reveille. And there with them, having been pulled violently out of bed, [were] the members of the strike commission." In Nerva, a crowd estimated at ten thousand people, mostly women, "gathered from all over the mountains, creat[ing] a fantastic spectacle, and in Peña, after an enthusiastic reception, the strike commission visited the company director in order to offer him their greetings." Later that night the crowd sang Riego's Hymn, the early nineteenth-century liberal anthem that socialists in Spain had appropriated for their own.[31]

Juan Moro clearly had a flair for the dramatic, but what purpose did his emphasis on the women serve? Surely the union, consisting almost exclusively of men, bore some share of the credit for victory in an eight-month-long strike. But the women appear as the ones who can solve problems, ultimately winning justice, while the strike committee had to be dragged from their beds for the victory march.

Without going into details of the strike and its settlement, it is possible to examine what Moro's emphasis on the women indicates. The introduction of the women dressed in rags, holding children in their arms, and leading older children made the strike into something bigger—an epic of good versus evil, right versus wrong, justice versus injustice. When Moro says of the women, "They have inspired their men to go on strike, and then they have sustained them," he seems to regard women as the guiding force of the strike and the spirit of the community. Here Moro's women and my women come together.

Conclusion

Although women themselves seldom work in mines, they participate in mining struggles to ensure the health of their families and neighbors. Sometimes they take a more central role, as in the film "Salt of the Earth" in which women in a New Mexican mining community take over the picket lines when a court injunction prohibits the men from striking. A further example of this is Domitila Barrios de Chungara, the leader of the Housewife's Association of the Siglo XXI tin mines in Bolivia, who provides testimony in *Let Me Speak* about the struggles of the entire community for social justice; this shows the importance of women calling themselves housewives and mothers. By making themselves heard, such women serve as spokespeople for mine workers' struggles despite the aura of masculinity surrounding miners.[32]

Mining strikes have been among the most militant and prolonged mass struggles short of revolution. They have often erupted into political insurrections when entire communities expressed grievances that extended from workplace demands concerning the safety and conditions in the mines, to the cost of living and sanitary conditions in miners' houses. Living around the mines, everyone in the mine workers' community breathes the polluted air from the foundries and experiences the disruptions when labor struggles ensue. Uprisings around mines invariably include women, children, and the unemployed throughout the area. Even bakers, barbers, practical nurses, cafe owners, dock workers, and truckers often adopt the struggle as their own. Their adversaries include mine owners, managers, unsympathetic governors, and foreigners, who, like the British, sometimes dominate the mines.

The focus on women in Río Tinto moved the strike from the realm of politics, in which men vied for power, to the realm of justice, in which women did what they had to in order to save their children. Two issues become clear when the jeering mayor tells the women to blame the union for their suffering. First, the miners could not go to other men, pleading for food, without becoming abject and jeopardizing their masculinity. But the women appear dignified and even heroic demanding food for their children according to female consciousness and practical gender interests. In fact, speaking in the name of children justified the women's public role in stalking strikebreakers for twenty days and harassing their wives. Only high purposes legitimated such acts. Furthermore, in any strike, people suffer and sometimes blame the union for their problems. Defending themselves, the union leaders could only appear self-serving; they needed the voices of the women, which gave the campaign the aura of something that went beyond particular grievances. Selfless, undemanding, and forthright, the women defended the struggle and raised its goals to those of demands for equity, not for themselves but for their community, according to visions of order which men and women in the mining community shared.

It seems as if the masculinity of the men as represented in the union depended for its last ounce of strength on the women. Not that the union would have called the women to action. Returning to the issue of justice and its relationship to women's collective activity, it is clear that the particular kind of justice women evoked rests with fundamental human rights—rights that no agency or government upholds. But these rights—to eat, have shelter, remain well, and live in peace—are so much a part of what every human being in every culture knows are necessary for survival that few authorities are willing to say that others ought not strive for them.

For the men, the act of portraying the women as shadowy figures who were actors in an epic of good versus evil, transferred descriptions and arguments from the realm of strategy and tactics to a higher plane. As if hiding behind the women's skirts, Moro had the women speak for the larger community, not in the language of politics but in the dialect of everyday life. By gendering justice, the struggles of the union to win benefits took on epic proportions.

In Maxine Molyneux and my preoccupations with what moves ordinary women to act in times of crisis, how ephemeral groups of women can sometimes seem to represent an entire people, and why police and soldiers or socialist leaders sometimes view women acting against the law as fulfilling appropriate gender behavior, we may have underestimated another important component of how this behavior of women is received.

The appearance of the women along the railroad tracks as saviors of the wounded miner Roche, and again in their activities disciplining strikebreakers, even exerting power over the wives of strikebreakers in order to bring their husbands into line, demonstrated that there is a category called "women," at least while the women are acting. The socialist columnist, appealing to his constituency a few months after the onset of what would be a long and drawn out strike, in which the issues and negotiations might have seemed complicated and remote, could appeal emotionally by showing that the so-called weaker sex could act resolutely in the name of justice. Since justice itself is imperceptible and might not compel people who had experienced more than their share of injustice, the image of nameless, faceless women arguing with their bodies for a goal and a system of values that no one could define might have been more persuasive than reams of articles.

When women reverse their usual style of activity to raise questions about survival, they not only disrupt everyday life, but they challenge political order. Gender relations structure all systems of authority, and changes in gender behavior destabilize all previous systems of power. The claim for justice is the wedge that does this. This is true even though the women demanding improvements in their community's condition (by couching their exhortations in the language of justice) did not necessarily want to change gender relations, let alone to reverse them.

When women pursue practical gender interests or act according to female consciousness, they can sometimes violate the prevailing system of law and the principles on which gender relations and power rest. Frequently, the women make claims about justice and human rights that are tied to issues of survival rather than to strategic interests that would improve their own lot as women or put forward a program for the people of their class, race, or ethnic group. Despite the lack of commitment to future goals emblematic of many women's groups, certain commitments to practical transformations in everyday life sometimes propel women engaging in collective action to call for justice. That form of justice has seldom been codified in political programs, but the increasing frequency with which women's groups have called for it in the twentieth century may indicate that justice as a social goal may be closer at hand than any of us had previously imagined.

Notes

1. Special thanks go to Robert Moeller, who has taken time to read this article and share his insightful comments with me. I am also grateful to Jane Loadman, the Records Manager of the Río Tinto Zinc Company Archives, who guided me through

the company files. Pamela Radcliff and Victoria Enders have been most judicious editors. Part of the research for this article was carried out with a grant from the National Endowment for the Humanities at the National Humanities Center between 1992 and 1993.

2. Juan Moro, "En las Minas de Río Tinto: Haciendo justicia y restableciendo la verdad," *El Socialista*, May 24, 1913.

3. Political philosopher Iris Marion Young has recently constructed an argument about why we can speak of "women" despite the many issues that divide and differentiate women. Hoping to reclaim some notion that women can exist without presuming a strong, universalist identity that masks differences of race, class, ethnicity, sexual orientation, or age, Young has argued that women may be a useful social category even though women do not constitute a single social group. See her article "Gender as Seriality: Thinking about Women as a Social Collective," *Signs* 19, no. 3 (1994): 713–738, 728.

4. Temma Kaplan, "Female Consciousness and Collective Action: The Case of Barcelona, 1910–1918," *Signs* 7, no. 3 (Spring 1982): 545–566.

5. Maxine Molyneux, "Mobilization Without Emancipation? Women's Interests, the State, and Revolution in Nicaragua," *Feminist Studies* 11, no. 2 (Summer 1985): 227–253, 230–235.

6. G.S. Checkland, *The Mines of Tharsis: Roman, French, and British Enterprise in Spain* (London: George Allen & Unwin, 1967); David Avery, *Not on Queen Victoria's Birthday: The Story of the Río Tinto Mines* (London: William Collins Sons, 1974); and The British Public Records Office (London) Report, September 15, 1887, on the back of page 11 (Foreign Office 185/679); see also the secret report of Audrey Gosling to Claire Ford, March 8, 1888 (FO 185/694: 236). He says that the towns of Río Tinto and Zalamea experienced growths of 150 percent and 50 percent respectively.

7. Richard West, *River of Tears: The Rise of the Rio Tinto-Zinc Mining Corporation* (London: Earth Island Ltd, 1972), p. 19.

8. Clark Kerr and Alan Siegel, "The Interindustry Propensity to Strike—an International Comparison," in Arthur Kornhauser, Robert Dubin, and Arthur M. Ross, eds., *Industrial Conflict* (New York: McGraw Hill, 1954), pp. 189–221.

9. Tilly's article appeared in *Signs: Journal of Women in Culture and Society* 7, no. 2 (1981): 400–417, 411.

10. Ibid., p. 412.

11. Ibid.

12. George Chauncey, Jr., "The Locus of Reproduction: Women's Labor in the Zambian Copperbelt, 1927–1953," *Journal of Southern African Studies* 7, no. 2 (1981): 135–164.

13. Thomas M. Klubock, "Class, Community, and Gender in the Chilean Copper Mines: The El Teniente Miners and Working-class Politics, 1904–1951," (Ph.D. dissertation, Yale University, 1993) 2 vols. (Ann Arbor: University Microfilms International, 1994), see especially 1: 115–121.

14. David Avery discusses the problem of drinking, gambling, and prostitution typical of mining communities. *Not on Queen Victoria's Birthday*, p. 242.

15. *El Socialismo*, September 16, 1887; Checkland, *The Mines of Tharsis*, p. 173.

16. FO 185/694: 86–90, 246–248, 360–362, Letters of February 5 and 6, 1888; *El Obrero*, February 10, 11, 17, and March 17, 1888; *El Socialismo*, March 2, 1888. For a full account of the 1888 general strike, see Temma Kaplan, "Consciousness and Community," *Political Power and Social Theory*, 2 (1982), pp. 21–57.

17. Riotinto Zinc Company Archives, St James Place, London. Minute Book, no. 10, May 12, 1898, pp. 35, 37, 40.

18. Spain. IRS (Instituto de Reformas Sociales): *Memoria redactada por la Comisión nombrada por el Instituto para estudiar las condiciones del Trabajo en las Minas de Río Tinto* (Madrid, 1913), p. 166. (Subsequently abbreviated as IRS: 1913.) This report, commissioned in the wake of the eight-month-long labor dispute against the Río Tinto Company, represents a nostalgic view of idealized, past social relations in Spain. Taking the line that small capital allowed for more human relations and that the Río Tinto Company was reimposing feudalism through its establishment of company towns, the report expressed great sympathy for the plight of the workers. (See pages 168–169.) At a time when the Spanish state was attempting to reduce labor conflict not just through repression, but through reform, the investigators involved with this report provided sophisticated analyses of the way the British company was provoking strife.

19. IRS: 1913, pp. 34, 122–23, 130–33, 167–68; "Movimiento sindicalista de España: Ríotinto. UGT-Federación nacional de mineros" (dated October 13, 1913), *La Voz del Obrero* (La Coruña), October 30, 1913.

20. The matter of the destruction of a third of the town of Río Tinto and the consequent destabilization of the rest of the houses, which directly abutted the new section of the mine, was widely discussed. One of the most acute analyses can be found in Juan Moro's "El Asalto al coto de Ríotinto. La situación de Ríotinto, Pueblo," *El Socialista*, July 16, 1913.

21. Juan Moro, "En las Minas de Río Tinto: Haciendo justicia y restableciendo la verdad," *El Socialista*, May 24, 1913.

22. For a pathbreaking study of the ways newspapers promoted a melodramatic reading of gender in late nineteenth-century London, see Judith M. Walkowitz, *City of Dreadful Delight: Narratives of Sexual Danger in Late-Victorian London* (Chicago, IL: University of Chicago Press, 1993). On newspaper treatment of another group of working-class women in Spain, see the article by D.J. O'Connor in this collection. In considering how visual artists portrayed working-class women in melodramatic terms in the socialist press of Germany, I have been especially influenced by Patrice Petro, *Joyless Streets: Women and Melodramatic Representation in Weimar Germany* (Princeton, NJ: Princeton University Press, 1989), especially pages 94–102, that deal with the work of Käthe Kollwitz. I am grateful to Robert Moeller for calling this work to my attention.

23. Moro, "En las Minas de Río Tinto."

24. Ibid.

25. Ibid.

26. She cites *El País* of May 8, 1898, describing a women's consumer rebellion in Badajoz, which occurred during the same week as the women's uprising at Río Tinto. Pamela Beth Radcliff, "Women's Politics: Consumer Riots in Twentieth Century Spain," n. 21 in this volume.

27. Juan Moro, "Solidaridad obrera: Cómo luchan las mujeres," *El Socialista*, November 13, 1913.

28. Ibid.

29. Ibid.

30. "El 'coco' de los agitadores: La Compañía es la que quiere suspender," *El Socialista*, November 13, 1913.

31. "En Ríotinto: Después del triunfo," *El Socialista*, November 27, 1913. Colonel Riego led the first successful liberal coup against the absolutist restoration government of Ferdinand VII in 1820; the song sung by his troops became known as "Riego's Hymn," and it was later used as a rallying cry for a variety of different political groups fighting against oppression.

32. "Salt of the Earth," (MPI Home Video Release, Oak Forest, IL 60452); Michael Wilson and Deborah Silverton Rosenfelt, *Salt of the Earth* (New York: The Feminist Press, 1978); Domitila Barrios de Chungara, with Moema Viezzer, *Let Me Speak: Testimony of Domitila, A Woman of the Bolivian Mines* (New York: Monthly Review Press, 1978); and June Nash, *We Eat the Mines and the Mines Eat Us* (New York: New York University Press, 1985), a study of a Bolivian mining community and women's involvement in it, have shaped many of my ideas about gender.

12

Women's Politics: Consumer Riots in Twentieth-Century Spain

Pamela Beth Radcliff

The association between poor women and consumer riots is well-established in the literature of popular protest, particularly within the context of the early modern "moral economy."[1] Scholars have also recognized the survival of this form of protest in the twentieth century, but it occupies only a marginal space in the conceptualization of contemporary political history. That is, it is often treated as an anachronistic form of protest out of step with the more highly developed vehicles of the strike or the electoral campaign. At the least, its appearance in the twentieth century requires a search for the special circumstances that explain its survival. Thus, the modern consumer riot is either ignored as unimportant in the larger scheme of political protest, or analyzed as a relic whose reappearance needs to be explained in reference to the past.[2] The problem with this set of assumptions is that it has the effect of marginalizing the political action of many poor women and keeping it outside mainstream accounts of twentieth-century politics. Such marginalization, in turn, reinforces the much-discussed ghettoization of women's history.[3] Either most women are not political or they are political in ways that do not matter; in both cases, they contribute little to the meat and potatoes of political history.

This chapter will contest these assumptions, using evidence gathered on consumer riots in Spain during two moments of social and political crisis: at the turn of the twentieth century, and during and after the end of the First World War. Based on this evidence, it will put forth several principal arguments. The first is that the consumer riot should be acknowledged as a major form of poor women's political action, whether they were housewives or wage workers, even after many of their male counterparts turned to strikes and electoral politics. The second is that poor women, through their use of the consumer riot, played a direct and significant political role in these two defining moments in modern Spanish history. And finally, the consumer riot remained a powerful tool because participants successfully adapted it to the new rules of twentieth-century mass politics. In other words, I argue that female rioters should be taken seriously as modern political actors.[4]

These arguments have important implications for the political history of Spain and elsewhere. On a basic level, they provide evidence that "women were there too," that they contributed to the narrative of political history.[5] In and of itself, this recognition does little to overcome women's marginalization within that narrative. But on another level, to see these women as political actors requires a transformation in our understanding of politics, which in turn forces us to reevaluate the neat categories of traditional political history.[6] Instead of a world divided into private and domestic vs. public and political, the consumer riots illustrate a more complex interaction between women taking their domestic concerns public and male authorities using public policy to reinforce their private masculine identity. Thus, by placing female consumer rioters in the arena of modern politics we do more than make women visible; we see the entire political arena in a new light. The result is a political world infused with domestic concerns and power relations, a world in which gender is an important constituent of public, not just private, behavior. When applied to the specific case of Spain in the early twentieth century, this vision exposes the full dimensions of a hegemonic crisis that penetrated the gendered social order.

Gendered Politics and Consumer Riots in Spain, 1895–1922

The history of Spain from the turn of the century until the Civil War is racked with the conflict provoked by an unravelling political order, but the two moments focused on in this paper stand out as crucial turning points.[7] The turn of the century marked an important psychological shift, when the loss of its remaining colonies through a humiliating war with the United States brought into question the capacity of the elites to lead Spain into the new century.[8] The First World War, despite Spain's official neutrality, generated the next major round of such questions. The combination of economic instability and the growing European-wide crisis of confidence sparked even more vociferous calls for political restructuring that were barely contained by the regime.[9] An important element in both these political crises was a significant disruption in the distribution and access of acceptably-priced basic consumer goods, such as bread, meat, and coal for cooking and heating. The cause of the disruption was different in each case. At the turn of the century a series of bad harvests caused shortages of wheat and sent the price of bread soaring, while during and after the war speculation and the great demand for exports created domestic shortages and price hikes.[10] In both cases the political result was similar: the government's inability to remedy the situation became an important contributing factor to the more general loss of confidence in its authority.

In each case the loss of confidence in the government's ability to supply its people with the basic necessities of life spawned widespread consumer-based protests in which poor women featured prominently. These protests, along with the actions of trade unions and political parties, helped to undermine the stability of a regime that depended for its survival on apathy and apoliticization. On a basic level, then, rioting women helped create the political climate of crisis that defines these two periods as turning points in the disintegration of the hegemonic order. Furthermore, they offered a specifically gendered reading of this crisis, employing the powerful metaphor of the (male) government as failed breadwinner. Through this discourse, they exposed the shame of a government incapable of providing for its "weaker" members and thereby questioned its masculine legitimacy to rule according to its own paternalistic terms.

But while the similarities between the two moments of crisis begin to challenge the traditional political narrative, it is the differences that expose its full limitations. In 1900, the institutional opposition to the regime was at a nadir. The trade union movement was just beginning to revive after more than a decade of virtual collapse. Moreover, the political parties that opposed the government, that is, the republicans and the Socialists, controlled only a handful of seats in the Parliament and on the city councils of a few major cities. With few institutional bases, the turn-of-the-century opposition relied more heavily on spontaneous and ad hoc organizational structures. Reflecting this context, the consumer riot, often including both men and women, was one of the main collective expressions of discontent. Further, the national press recognized it as such, and reported its frequent occurrances as serious front page news.

In contrast, by 1918 the trade union movement had not only been rebuilt, but had long surpassed its nineteenth-century limits, both in numbers and geographical strongholds, to become a formidable oppositional force.[11] Likewise, republicans and Socialists had captured dozens of local city councils and forged a vocal, if small, minority in the Cortes. As a result, in the postwar period formal trade union and party organizations played a greater role in shaping the crisis.

However, although formal institutions had a higher profile in the postwar period, they did not eclipse spontaneous and informal political participation. What changes is the gender composition of these spontaneous and informal protesters. After 1900, there is a growing gap in the working-class community between the institutionally-channelled behavior of male political actors and the informal activities of female political actors. As a result, the consumer riot became an increasingly gendered political act. Male political actors still acknowledged consumer issues, but they shifted their primary energies elsewhere, towards elections and wage struggles. Furthermore, when they took on consumption problems, they did so through the new channels opened up by their institutional affiliations.

Many poor women, on the other hand, continued to mobilize primarily around consumption, and to prefer their traditional methods of direct action. Numerous examples of such protests recorded in the archives of the Ministry of the Interior, as well as in the newspapers, provide ample evidence for this conclusion.[12] What emerges from these accounts, then, is not so much an evolution of protest along a single track, but a branching off that created parallel and gendered tracks.[13] Only at certain points of convergence did the two intersect, as in the wave of social unrest in the winter of 1918, which featured a combination of female-led consumer riots and feverish trade union strike activity.[14]

Significantly, only at these points of convergence did the national political establishment take notice of the women's protests. Although they continued to shape politics on the local level, they surfaced in national political discourse only when they became part of what were considered more modern political movements. The most striking evidence of this fact is that, after the turn of the century, the national newspapers stopped reporting consumer riots in the provinces except at moments like January 1918. Anyone who relied on the national press for information would not even know that consumer riots continued to occur on a regular basis. This silence is telling, both in terms of the marginalization of women's politics by contemporaries and in the way it set the stage for later historians to underestimate or dismiss women's political participation. The contrast between this silence and the thick files of provincial administrative reports on consumer riots helps explain the apparent paradox between women's ongoing activism and the widespread perception that they withdrew from the political sphere in the modern period.[15]

Yet demonstrating the persistance of the female consumer riot into the twentieth century still does not address the argument that it survived only as an anachronistic form of politics that deserves the marginal treatment it has received. From this perspective, one could point to the typology of the consumer riot, which seems to be frozen in time despite dramatic economic and political changes over the nineteenth century, from the articulation of national markets to the development of trade unions to the extension of political rights.

Or, one could simply argue that since, in Spain, these changes came more slowly, the survival of the consumer riot there reflects Spain's "backwardness."[16] Thus, at the outset of the twentieth century, Spain was still a country with largely local agricultural markets, a weak transportation infrastructure, and a lack of formal institutions for expressing political discontent. However, by 1918, this answer would not suffice. Given the development of new and powerful forms of opposition, like trade unions and popular political parties, as well as the decline of old-style subsistence crises, we are still forced to ask whether the consumer riot was merely a quaint relic of the past or a response to contemporary political and social realities.

A close look at riot patterns during the two moments under review provides strong evidence that consumer riots proved flexible enough to adapt to the changing world, and to continue to function as effective political weapons. Participants pursued both old and new protest strategies as long as they produced results, instead of blindly following atavistic behaviors. During the later period, female activists were clearly aware of the existence of the labor movement and its alternative protest menu, and sometimes appealed to the unions for assistance. However, they refused to have their separate interests and methods subsumed within larger trade union priorities.

Furthermore, in a world defined by the ideology of separate spheres, there were good reasons for refusing. The presence of hundreds or thousands of "domestic" women publicly demanding a just price for bread or coal created a uniquely powerful impression on local and regional authorities. With their simple demands, uncluttered by calls for political revolution, they had the unique ability to shame the government into action. Although the authorities occasionally tried to argue that consumer riots were incited by "outside agitators,"[17] there was a widespread perception that women rioted only reluctantly when they were completely fed up. Thus, their collective willingness to leave their homes to protest was interpreted as a sign of extreme duress that could not be ignored, rather than as a partisan political act that threatened the social order.

The fact that the authorities generally felt obligated to respond indicates their acceptance of the responsibility thrust upon them. In other words, it reveals an implicit relationship between these women and the government, based on the series of mutually accepted rights and duties that justified the ideology of separate spheres. The terms of that relationship rested on the acknowledgement of a gendered division of labor in which women retained primary responsibility over issues of household consumption as well as the right publicly to monitor them. Ironically, their acceptance of gendered spheres legitimated working-class women's political participation, both in their eyes and in the eyes of the (male) authorities.[18]

The result of this dynamic was a gendered recasting of the moral economy in which the government felt pressured to uphold its masculine protective duties. A newspaper cartoon printed in January 1918 perfectly illustrates this relationship. With the caption "the Weaker Sex," it showed a female protester donning male breeches before going out into the streets[19] (see Figure 12.1). In other words, when working women left their natural domestic sphere to venture into the masculine political world, it was because the men (i.e., the gov-

FIGURE 12.1

"Ex sexo debil" (The Weaker Sex). (Circa January, 1918)

ernment) were not doing their job. Another cartoon rendered the same message but in more specifically class terms (see Figure 12.2). It featured angry women standing at the front of a hungry crowd demanding bread and work, while their male class enemies, the aristocrat and the fat monk, look on indifferently.[20] Within this relationship, the failure to respond to hungry women was tantamount to emasculation.[21] Thus, the power of the female consumer riot lay, not in its contestation of male authority, but in its questioning of that authority's ability to live up to its own self-image.

For the female protagonists of these riots, integration into a male trade union framework would have destroyed their special gendered relationship with the government. From this perspective, working class women's obvious reluctance to throw in their lot with the union movement may have had less to

FIGURE 12.2

"Tením fám" (We Are Hungry). *La Campana de Gracia*, March 19, 1898.

do with their lack of political awareness or their atavism than with their informed commitment to an alternative politics. Far from being anachronistic, this form of politics was attuned to a gendered social and ideological context that created different possibilities and limitations for men and women. The ideology of separate spheres did not keep women out of politics, but it did influence the shape of women's politics, as it influenced those of men.

Rather than recognize this fluid line between private and public, theoretical practice has, until recently, accepted the strict division between the two spheres in the modern period.[22] In this division of the world, consumer issues and the protests that emerge from them have been relegated to the private sphere. Thus even when it is recognized that poor women remained advocates of consumer issues, this activism has not qualified as political behavior defined in modern terms. This binary vision has both impoverished our view of politics and tautologically dismissed many female concerns as nonpolitical.

To overcome these limitations, it is necessary to transcend the narrow definition of politics and the public sphere and to recognize a much broader realm of political discourse and the public.[23] When women took to the streets to protest high prices or shortages, they crossed the line from private consumer to political actor; they mobilized collective resources, they occupied public spaces, they tried to influence government policy, and they often succeeded in doing so. Whatever the nature of their concerns or their methods, their voice was a political one and should be defined as such.

If we apply a more inclusive model of politics, we see that these women constituted one voice in the noisy din of public discourse, not always easy to hear but located inside and not outside the perimeter. Once we acknowledge their location inside the political arena, it is possible to integrate them into the main themes of twentieth-century politics, and in the Spanish case, to recognize their role in undermining the legitimacy of the Restoration monarchy. Furthermore, the consumer protests and their special engagement of the authorities throw light on a different, gendered angle of Spain's political crisis, one in which masculine as well as class or religious authority was being questioned. And although it is beyond the scope of this chapter, there is enough anecdotal evidence to suggest that this pattern was repeated outside Spain and that it is time to develop a more systematic understanding of the role of female consumer-based protests in twentieth-century politics.[24]

A Typology of Consumer Riots

To pursue this goal, the remainder of the article will delineate a typology of consumer protests in early twentieth-century Spain, and then analyze how riot patterns adapted over the twenty-five year period in response to the evolving political context. As many scholars have pointed out, these protests were not random, impulsive gestures, but constituted a well-defined genre of collective action that operated according to a strict and limited protocol.[25] Although not every riot unfolded in exactly the same way, this protocol created a circumscribed "repertoire of contention."[26] Thus, despite its irregular and spontaneous eruption, the consumer riot carved out a regular and trackable space in the political landscape.

What sparked the riots was a range of predictable events, from a sudden price hike, to a new tax levied (particularly the *consumo* taxes on foods[27]), to any concrete event that exposed the gap between people's expectations and their satisfaction.[28] The issues were all loosely related to consumption in the sense that they affected what people had to pay out of pocket for goods and services, rather than what they earned. Premeditation was rare, and any planning that took place followed rather than preceded the initial outburst. For example, after the first assault in one of Madrid's neighborhoods in 1897, rioters broke down into small groups to discuss what to do next.[29] If protests lasted for several days, informal organizational networks and leaders emerged, with plans passed by word of mouth, usually by groups of rioters traveling the streets.

Because specific transitions usually stimulated the riots, they typically began at the moment when women, often shoppers, first experienced the impact of a new tax or a higher price. Following this logic, they often erupted at the same "hot spots," like the marketplace, the docks, the bakery, or the coal outlet, all places where women engaged in their daily routines were likely to discover a potential spark. Thus, in Alicante in 1918 one riot began among women who were waiting in line to buy bread and grumbling about its scarcity when one of them shouted that they should do something about it.[30] Again, in Toledo in 1921, a riot broke out at a coal dispensary when those waiting were told that there was no more to be sold.[31] In another case, female dock workers in La Coruña initiated a riot when they discovered sacks of potatoes being loaded for export.[32]

Participants included some combination of men and women, depending on the context, but women usually figured prominently. In the majority of cases, reports identified rioters as either exclusively or mainly women and children, or as initially women who were later joined by men. A significant minority of the riots were led by "the people," usually defined as *el vecindario*, or residents, clearly implying a mix of men and women. This term, which conjured the image of the entire town rising up, most often appeared in accounts of small town riots in remote areas. In only two cases were men credited with starting a consumer riot on their own.[33] Whether they acted alone or in concert with men, then, women's participation was a central feature of the consumer protest throughout the period.

Poor women's identification with consumer riots applied regardless of their employment status. During the turn-of-the-century cycle of riots, the average female participant (like the average working-class woman) was a housewife, with the occasional appearance of women wage workers.[34] However, these cases set a precedent that continued as more women entered the work force. That is, participants assumed that all poor women maintained a primary interest in consumer issues, regardless of their formal relationship to the workforce. Following this logic, the instigators of a riot often recruited directly from local factories and workshops. For example, when a group of housewives in Seville launched their demonstration, one of their first acts was to march to all of the factories with female employees and convince them to leave work in solidarity.[35] In other cases, reporters noted more generally that groups of female rioters "forced" or "invited" all women whose path they crossed to join them.[36] Whether all women accepted the responsibility thrust on them at these moments, at least the activist participants were convinced that women's shared domestic duties both united them and gave them a moral obligation to protest.

Once the protest began, the repertoire included several possible modes of attack, depending on certain factors, including the responsiveness of the authorities. In broad terms, the consumer protest contained a spectrum of tactics that ran from peaceful demonstrations to attacks on persons and property.[37] The existence of this spectrum, recognized by authorities and participants alike, meant that behind every nonviolent demonstration lurked the potential for a full-blown riot. A demonstration, which consisted of a vocal crowd of protesters marching up and down the streets and shouting their demands, acted as a first warning, an articulation of grievances that had reached a critical point. The civil governors' reports of these incidents demonstrate that they understood this. When describing a peaceful consumer protest, they always qualified their report with fears of impending violence and escalation of tactics. From the other side, participants at times explicitly articulated the implicit threat, as in the town of Baracaldo in 1919 when protesters announced that they would pursue "more violent acts" if they received no acceptable response within five days.[38] Thus, the peaceful demonstration constituted part of the larger repertoire of consumer protest that could, but did not always, lead to violence.

In the transition from peaceful to violent demonstration, the government often but not always played a central role, regardless of the immediate villain.[39] At some point during the protest, participants invariably made an appeal to the local authorities, whether delivered through a commission or simply by the presence of the crowd shouting its demands outside the city hall. When the authorities refused to listen to this appeal, or insisted on their impotence, the crowd inevitably moved on to more violent direct tactics. But even when the government was conciliatory and promised results, the protesters seldom dispersed until they felt the impact of concrete steps. Since a breakdown of confidence in the government lay at the heart of these protests, the resolution of the conflict depended in part on its success in winning back that trust through a dramatic and effective gesture, such as revoking its own tax or reining in hoarders and speculators.

If the protest did escalate into violence, it was a highly ritualized violence that targeted a limited number of symbols and institutions.[40] Violent direct action could be used either to block an offensive action, to punish and warn transgressors, or to forcibly execute the protesters' goals.[41] A clear case of prevention was the common tactic of destroying goods before they were sold or disrupting their export. Thus, in Badajoz in 1915, groups of women protesting high wheat prices went to the train station and destroyed sacks of wheat waiting to be loaded for export.[42] Likewise, in Alicante in 1918, protesters headed for the docks, where they threw sacks of flour and onions into the sea.[43]

In part to prevent the sale of high-priced or taxed goods, and in part to punish store owners who did so, many riots also included forcible closure of stores or market stalls. Patrolling groups of protesters enforced closure by breaking the windows or inflicting further damage on those foolish enough to refuse. Protesters also sometimes punished those who bought forbidden goods. In Zamora in 1895, for example, women denouncing the high price of bread not only tried to prevent its sale, but also confiscated it from anyone found carrying it home.[44]

When the local government itself played the role of villain, for example after imposing a new tax, protesters could target the city hall or the mayor's house, as occurred in Cádiz in 1905.[45] More commonly, rioters zeroed in on the institutions responsible for the collection and administration of such taxes, particularly the hated *consumo* tax. Numerous inspectors' posts were raided and torched, often culminating in an assault on the central administrative offices. In the most dramatic instances, as in Almódovar del Campo in 1898, rioters brought all the records into the public square and burned them in a secular version of an auto da fé.[46] Raids like this one served both to chastize the government and to forcibly disrupt tax collection.

In addition to disrupting collection, protesters used other strategies to elicit the immediate acceptance of their demands. For example, they attempted to compel businessmen to sell goods at what they considered a fair price, which, in the inflationary postwar period, often meant a return to 1914 levels. Thus, in Barcelona in 1918, groups of women entered several stores requesting goods at prewar prices. If owners agreed to the terms of sale, they left peacefully, but if not, they took the article by force.[47]

As part of the protocol of confiscation, protesters usually distributed goods taken from warehouses, train stations, docks, or stores, either without charge or at the "fair" price. One of the most elaborate examples of this ritual practice occurred in Málaga in 1918, when women took forty boxes of fish from the train station to the beach where they sold it for ten pesetas a box and then delivered the money to the civil governor.[48] With this act, the rioters made an implicit distinction between confiscation and stealing, which bolstered the "moral" strength of their position. At times this distinction was explicitly made, as in Logroño in 1898, when women who broke into and emptied foodstuffs from a number of stores scolded one woman who filled her skirts with booty and explained that they were not there to take what did not belong to them.[49] On the other hand, there were cases when this distinction broke down, and rioters simply divided the goods among themselves, making sure only that all shared equally.

The length and intensity of a consumer protest varied from a couple of hours to several days, but in almost every case a cessation of hostilities required government action. Significantly, action usually took the form of acquiescence or surrender rather than repression, since authorities were reluctant to use force against women and children. Thus, the civil governor of Zaragoza reported that "since the protesters were mostly women, I did not think it opportune to give harsh orders."[50] In the few cases when significant force was ordered against female protesters, it only succeeded in fanning the flames of discontent in the rest of the population and often mobilized the men behind their women. The image of a bullying government shooting defenseless women had the power to unite the town against it. In the town of Cieza in 1904, when a child died during a clash with police, the entire population accompanied his casket to the cemetary in solidarity against local officials. [51] In Málaga in 1918, when a police cavalry charge left two women rioters dead and several wounded, the trade unions launched a five day general strike, republican newspapers called for the resignation of the civil governor, and even the Merchants' Association protested to the central government about the local authorities' "ill-considered repression carried out against women, unaccompanied by any men."[52] The motives for such diverse male groups defending unaccompanied women must have been complicated and in some cases opportunistic, but the point is that, within the paternalistic language of separate spheres, employing violence against those defined as members of the weaker sex was bad politics.

Since repression was a politically and morally unattractive alternative, and protesters could rarely be "sweet-talked" into dispersing through vague promises, real concessions were often the only viable option. For this reason, consumer riots were an extraordinarily effective method of achieving limited political demands. The most common termination of a cycle of protest was for local or regional authorities to suspend a hated tax, impose a fixed price for certain goods (*tasa*), forbid the export of scarce goods, requisition them or enforce an existing *tasa*. In fact, no other method of protest, whether in 1895 or 1922, produced such consistent results on consumer issues. Editorials written in republican newspapers or rallies organized by trade union federations did not have the power to transform policy overnight. As one reporter commented after two days of protests in Barcelona had convinced the mayor to requisition meat to supply the population, more had been accomplished in three days than in the previous three years of lobbying and formal complaints.[53] The fact that a comment like this could be made in 1918 in Barcelona, the most politically organized city in the country, demonstrates that the consumer riot remained an effective weapon even after the development of formal avenues of mass politics.

The Evolution of Consumer Riots in Post-War Spain

Nevertheless, while the consumer riot survived the articulation of modern forms of mass politics, the changing political landscape did have an impact on consumer riot patterns. Thus, the contrast between riots in the two periods under scrutiny reveals significant adaptations in the general typology. The most obvious difference was the gender composition of the riots. While some mixture of men and women continued to participate in consumer riots, they were more frequently identified as female than male. The exceptions to this point only prove the rule. In cases where reports associated riots with both men and women, as in the image of the village rising up, they erupted in rural areas where a trade union movement was conspicuously absent.[54]

Otherwise, the consumer riot became an increasingly female-defined event, differentiated from what were becoming the prevalent forms of working-class male political activity, in particular trade union strikes and demonstrations. This distinction created the basis for a growing gender gap in political behavior. The gap was most obvious in the range of activities aimed at reducing the cost of living, an issue of mounting concern to most people almost as soon as the war broke out. While concern crossed gender lines, methods of attacking the problem did so less often. Thus, for example, on the day that the civil governor of Palencia received a written request from the Workers' Federation to hold a subsistence rally, he received visits from various groups of women protesting the high cost of living. He was afraid to approve the rally for fear that the women would join in.[55]

In other words, he recognized two separate tracks of subsistence protest that he hoped to prevent from combining. The male track comprised the written demands, submitted to the local authorities, and a request to hold a rally in the *Casa del Pueblo*, or Workers' Center.[56] Significantly, their demands usually mixed consumer issues with others, such as wage hikes or the release of political prisoners.[57] Women, on the other hand, almost never submitted written demands, and never asked permission for demonstrations, which they held in the streets rather than in the workers' centers. Most importantly, trade union subsistence rallies never escalated into violent direct action, while women's demonstrations were fully capable of doing so. For trade unions, escalation meant calling a general strike, not staging a riot. Thus, on the same day that women took to the streets in Barcelona to demonstrate against high prices, the trade unions debated whether to call a general strike (which they never did).[58]

The growing gender gap in working-class political behavior did not mean that consumer riots were encased in a separate and atavistic political world. While aware of the trade unions and the areas in which their interests overlapped, female rioters seemed to realize that they could operate in spaces the unions could not penetrate. As a result, they adopted a complex attitude towards the labor movement that balanced careful distance with occasional reliance on its strength.

Maintaining independence benefitted the rioters by keeping the focus on their consumption concerns, and by exploiting the gendered relationship with the authorities. If consumer riots folded into the broader revolutionary demands of the labor movement, the rioters would lose their special "above politics" status and be subject to the same repression suffered by the trade unions. Moreover, their specific demands could be dismissed as part of a seditious movement seeking to overthrow the political order.

The rioters' understanding of these political realities emerges in the frequent instances when female protagonists in the post-war period refused to allow men, or more specifically workers, to join them, insisting they were not needed. The subtext of this refusal was the recognition that association with workers would transform the event. Significantly, such instances of enforced gender segregation were rare during the earlier period, when authorities did not automatically identify workers with subversive political movements. Thus, consumer rioters evaluated the new political context and decided that their traditional methods of direct action and limited demands, combined with the moral suasion of their gender, justified an independent space for their form of politics. The fact that this form of politics continued to produce results must have clinched the case for independence.

At the same time, however, female rioters could use the existence of the labor movement to their advantage. Thus, the specter of calling in the workers could be summoned to spur on a reluctant government, as in Barcelona in 1918, when, after four days of rioting, a commission of women warned the civil governor that they were about to ask the workers for help.[59] Even if they were not asked, the trade unions were likely to step in if the government violently repressed rioting women, as occurred in Málaga and Alicante in 1918, when unions declared general strikes to denounce the resulting deaths.[60] In both cases, the existence of the trade unions had altered the context in which the consumer riot took place, but did not supplant it.[61]

The relationship between the gendered tracks of politics is nicely demonstrated in the unfolding of events over a several week period in 1917 in the city of Gijón (Asturias).[62] During the course of the war, tension over availability of coal for domestic use had been rising, with the police called in at various points to maintain order. The fact that Gijón was the major coal port for the province made it easy to draw an explicit connection between speculative exports and domestic shortages.[63] By the fall of 1917, tensions had reached a boiling point. Women complained that half the coal outlets in the city had shut down, and that they waited all day in lines for coal that never appeared. In early November, a delegation of working women turned to the local trade union federation for help. They requested that it present a series of demands to the mayor—primarily that he requisition sufficient coal from the mine owners whether they wanted to sell it to the locals or not. The federation agreed, but after ten days and no results, the women escalated their protest to the next level. A crowd of 2,000 women and children marched through the streets denouncing the shortages and carrying kettles and pieces of flint to dramatize the desperate situation.

Yet another week later, the coal had still not arrived, and while the union federation printed its protest, the women took matters into their own hands. After several hours of waiting in lines again, their impatience erupted into shouts. They discussed whether they should go to the city hall, but this time they decided to requisition the coal themselves. The women headed for the docks, and began looting wagons waiting to be unloaded. When the police arrived, the crowd simply dispersed and reappeared on another dock. Smaller groups broke into private storehouses, which kept coal of a higher quality for industrial use. Finally, by midnight, the exhausted looters returned home. By a remarkable coincidence, the very next day a large shipment of coal arrived, and the crisis temporarily subsided.

The unfolding of the consumer protest demonstrates its adaptation to the contemporary political dynamic. The women turned first to the trade union federation, pressing it to make a formal claim to the local authorities. However, although they saw themselves as aligned with the unions, they never relinquished their separate identity. Thus, when the formal protest failed to produce results, the women turned to their traditional repertoire of direct action, which they did without either trade union approval or participation. The outcome of the protest only could have reinforced the success of their methods and the necessity to keep their interests independent of trade union control.

Beyond this immediate context, the consumer riot of November 1917 formed part of a wider political dynamic with local, regional and national implications. Just months before, the city and province had been brought to the brink of revolution by the dramatic (generally male) general strike of August 1917, which captured national attention.[64] The women's consumer movement that followed the defeat of the strike provides a more complete picture of the depths of discontent, of the degree of disillusionment with the government, and of the complexity of popular opposition to an unpopular regime.

Moreover, within the diversity of oppositional voices, the female protesters offered a uniquely gendered critique. Every time poor women entered the public sphere to protest living conditions, they challenged the government's claim to uphold its basic masculine responsibility to protect and secure the welfare of its dependents. In a regime defined by a paternalistic gender (and class) hierarchy, this challenge constituted a devastating blow to its authority. In simple terms, consumer rioters accused the government of failing to live up to its own standards of legitimacy.

By itself, this challenge would not topple the government and was not designed to do so, but it did help create the space in which an ideological alternative to the existing regime seemed necessary. In other words, by demonstrating the sterility of the existing system, even on its own terms, the women's consumer protests opened the door for the new trade union movements and republican parties to propose alternatives to that system. It was this two-pronged challenge, rather than the actions of the latter groups alone, that marked the transcendence of the post-war political crisis in Spain. Within this new gendered framework, female consumer rioters can take their rightful place as modern political actors in a complex drama in which the future of the regime was at stake.

More importantly, this framework helps transform our understanding of this political drama. Instead of a world cut off from the domestic realm, as described and prescribed by the reigning separate spheres ideology, the political sphere existed in a complex and fluid relationship with the private. Consumer rioters justified their political behavior by appealing to their domestic obligations, and the authorities responded within the gendered metaphor of masculine paternalism. Ironically, then, the ideology of separate spheres created political opportunities for women even as it denied their identity as political actors. By pulling aside the veil of binary opposition, we can begin to see the complexity and richness of the interaction between public/political and private/domestic, and, in the process, to uncover hidden forms of women's political agency.

Notes

1. The classic article is, of course, E.P. Thompson, "The Moral Economy of the English Crowd," *Past and Present* 50 (1971). See also E.P. Thompson's "The Moral Economy Reviewed" in *Customs in Common* (London: The Merlin Press, 1991), pp. 305–336; Louise Tilly, "The Food Riot as a Form of Political Conflict," *Journal of Interdisciplinary History* 2 (1971); John Bohstadt, "Gender, Household and Community Politics," *Past and Present* 120 (1988); Alan Booth, "Food Riots in the North-West of England, 1790–1801," *Past and Present* 77 (1977); and Malcolm I. Thomis and Jennifer Grimmett, *Women in Protest, 1800–1850* (London: Croom and Helm, 1982), chap. 2.

2. Although each of these studies takes a different approach, they all in some way fit this school of thought: Paul R. Hanson, "The *Vie Chère* Riots of 1911: Traditional Protests in Modern Garb," *The Journal of Social History* 21 (1988); William Friedburger, "War Prosperity and Hunger: The New York Food Riots of 1917," *Labor History* 25 (1984); María Luz Arriero, "Los motines de subsistencias en España, 1895–1905," *Estudios de Historia Social* 30 (1984); Rafael Vallejo Pousada, "Pervivencia de las formas tradicionales de protesta: Los motines de 1892," *Historia Social* 8 (1990); Carlos Serrano, *La tour du peuple: Crise nationale, mouvements populaires et populisme en Espagne, 1890–1910* (Madrid: Casa de Velázquez, 1987); David Arnold, "Looting, Grain Riots and Government Policy in South India, 1918," *Past and Present* 84 (August 1979).

Exceptions to this rule are: Dana Frank, "Housewives, Socialists and the Politics of Food: The 1917 New York Cost-of-Living Protests," *Feminist Studies* 11 (1985); Temma Kaplan, "Women and Communal Strikes in the Crisis of 1917-1922" in

Bridenthal and Koonz, eds., *Becoming Visible: Women in European History* (Boston: Houghton Mifflin, 1988) and "Female Consciousness and Collective Action," *Signs* 7 (1982). All of these articles treat consumer riots as a serious form of female political action in the industrial era.

3. On the problems of marginalization, see the now classic essays by Joan Scott in *Gender and the Politics of History* (New York: Columbia University Press, 1988), and Louise Tilly's "Gender, Women's History, and Social History," *Social Science History* 13, no. 4 (Winter 1989). On women in labor history, see Ava Baron, "Gender and Labor History: Learning from the Past, Looking to the Future," in Ava Baron, ed., *Work Engendered: Toward a New History of American Labor*, (Ithaca, NY: Cornell University Press, 1991). On the dangers of crude mainstreaming, see Gisela Bock, "Challenging Dichotomies: Perspectives on Women's History," in Karen Offen, Ruth Roach Pierson and Jane Rendall, eds., *Writing Women's History* (Bloomington, IN: Indiana University Press, 1991).

4. The idea of a developmental model of protest, in which the nineteenth century witnessed a transition from pre-modern to modern political forms, has dominated the history of social movements. In this model, consumer riots are defined as either "primitive" or "pre-modern." See George Rudé, *Protest and Punishment* (New York: Oxford University Press, 1978); Charles Tilly, "European Violence and Collective Action since 1700," *Social Research* 53, no. 1 (1986); and, as applied to women, Malcolm I. Thomis and Jennifer Grimmett, *Women in Protest, 1800–1850*. Implicitly following this model, most of the history of women's politics in the late nineteenth and twentieth centuries has focused on women's participation in "modern" political forms like elections (or suffrage campaigns) for middle-class women or trade unions for working class women.

5. In 1975, Gerda Lerner defined this "adding on" of women as "contribution" history; that is, describing women's contribution to a male-defined world. She and other historians in the mid-1970s argued that women's history had to move beyond this male-defined conception of women's place in history. See Lerner, "Placing Women in History: Definitions and Challenges," in *The Majority Finds its Past* (New York: Oxford University Press, 1981).

6. As Cecile Dauphin, et al., put it in "Women's Culture and Women's Power: Issues in French Women's History": "The political arena has been built around the decision to refuse making political subjects of women," in Offen, et al., eds., *Writing Women's History*, p. 126.

7. The unravelling political system was a constitutional monarchy reestablished in 1875 after a tumultuous republican interval. For the first twenty years, political elites successfully manipulated the system without much organized opposition. But as mass political parties and organizations began to develop after the turn of the century, the regime found it increasingly difficult to hold back the tide of popular pressure.

8. On 1898 as a hegemonic turning point, see Carlos Serrano, "1900?" in C. Serrano and Serge Salaun, eds., *1900 en España* (Madrid: Espasa Calpe, 1991), and

Manuel Tuñón de Lara, "La Guerra Civil Española, Medio Siglo Después," in Manuel Tuñón de Lara, et al., *La Guerra Civil Española: 50 años después* (Barcelona: Editorial Labor, 1985).

9. The eventual upshot of the postwar crisis in Spain was the collapse of the parliamentary monarchy and the establishment of a temporary dictatorship in 1923. On the postwar crisis in Spain, see Gerald Meaker, *The Revolutionary Left in Spain, 1914–1923* (Stanford, CA: Stanford University Press, 1974). On the broader European crisis, see Charles Maier, *Recasting Bourgeois Europe: Stabilization in France, Germany and Italy in the Decade after World War I* (Princeton, NJ: Princeton University Press, 1975).

10. On the context of the economic crises, see: Benjamin Martin, *The Agony of Modernization: Labor and Industrialization in Spain* (Ithaca, NY: I.L.R. Press, 1990), chap. 7, and Santiago Roldan and José Luis García Delgado, *La formación de sociedad capitalista, 1914–1920*, 2 vol. (Madrid: CEIC, 1973) for the postwar, and María Luz Arriero, "Los motines de subsistencia en España, 1895–1905," for the early period.

11. The trade union movement emerged during the mid-nineteenth century, flowering briefly during the revolutionary period between 1868 and 1874. As a result of repression, internal divisions between Bakuninists (anarchists) and Marxists (socialists) and a wave of terrorist actions, the movement had virtually collapsed by the 1890s. When the First World War began, the labor movement experienced its second and most dramatic period of growth. At its height at the end of 1918, the largest trade union, the anarcosyndicalist CNT, claimed 800,000 members. Antonio Bar, *La CNT en los años rojos: Del sindicalismo revolucionario al anarcosindicalismo, 1910–1926* (Madrid: Akal Editor, 1981), p. 492. The smaller Socialist UGT claimed 200,000 members in 1919.

12. The files consist of telegrams from the provincial governors to the central government reporting the incidence of consumer riots and protests over the course of the twentieth century up to the Civil War. They are obviously not complete records, and some years are missing entirely, but at least they provide a window into this type of protest. They are found at the Archivo Histórico Nacional, in the Sección de Gobernación, Serie A, Legajo 15A, 16A, 59A, 41A. They will be cited by Legajo and Expediente: i.e., Legajo 15A, #22.

13. Some women did join the trade union movement, but, as in other European countries, women had a much lower rate of unionization than did their male colleagues and there was always debate on the question of why women did not organize. On women and trade unions in Spain, see Rosa María Capel Martínez, *El trabajo y la educación de la mujer en España, 1900–1930* (Madrid: Ministerio de Cultura, 1986), chap. 5. On obstacles to female union militancy in France, see Pat Hilden, *Working Women and Socialist Politics in France, 1880–1914* (London: Oxford University Press, 1986).

14. For details of the local events surrounding the January 1918 protests, see María Dolores Ramos, "Realidad social y conciencia de la realidad en la mujer: Obreras malagueñas frente a la crisis de subsistencias (1918)," in María Carmen García

Nieto, ed., *Ordenamiento jurídico y realidad social de las mujeres* (Madrid: Seminario de Estudios de la Mujer, 1986) and Temma Kaplan, "Female Consciousness and Collective Action" and *Red City, Blue Period: Social Movements in Picasso's Barcelona* (Berkeley, CA: University of California Press, 1992), chap. 5.

15. For a greater elaboration of this issue, see Pamela Radcliff, "Elite Women Workers and Collective Action: The Cigarette Makers of Gijón, 1890–1930," *Journal of Social History* 27: 1 (Fall 1993).

16. Focusing on the state's intervention into food policy, Charles Tilly articulates a version of this argument in "Food Supply and Public Order in Modern Europe," in Charles Tilly, ed., *The Formation of Nation States in Western Europe* (Princeton, NJ: Princeton University Press, 1975), pp. 450–452.

17. The government newspaper *La Epoca* was most likely to use this strategy. For example, an editorial on a consumer riot in Cádiz blamed "foreign elements" who acted like a "yeast of disorder" among those with a "natural inclination towards violence." January 5, 1905.

18. Women's internalization of this responsibility has been defined as "female consciousness," the obligation to gather and distribute resources among their family members. See Temma Kaplan's classic article, "Female Consciousness and Collective Action: The Case of Barcelona, 1910–1918," *Signs* 7 (1982). When women entered the public sphere through unacceptable channels, they were often conflated with social disorder, as Gay Gullickson demonstrates in "The Unruly Women of the Paris Commune," in Dorothy O. Helly and Susan M. Reverby, eds., *Gendered Domains: Rethinking Public and Private in Women's History* (Ithaca, NY: Cornell University Press, 1991), or, in a different context, Judith Walkowitz, *Prostitution and Victorian Society: Women, Class and the State* (Cambridge: Cambridge University Press, 1980).

19. From a Barcelona newspaper during the consumer riots of January 1918, reproduced in Lester Golden, "Les dones com avantguarda: El rebombori del pa del gener de 1918," *L'Avenç*, December 1981.

20. The other figures, both male as well, refer to the context of the Cuban rebellion and the war with the United States. *La Campana de Gracia*, March 19,1898.

21. In several cases the newspapers called protesting women *mujeres varoniles*, or masculine men, to underline this threat. For example, *El País*, May 8, 1898, used this expression to entitle an article about a demonstration in Badajoz.

22. This practice also applied in feminist women's history, which tended to accept the existence of the categories while condemning them. Thus, historians focused either on women in the private sphere, valorizing their lives there, or looked for their rare appearance in male-defined politics. For a discussion of the use of separate spheres in women's history, see Linda Kerber, "Separate Spheres, Female Worlds, Woman's Place: The Rhetoric of Women's History," *Journal of American History* 75 (June

1988), and Susan Reverby and Dorothy Helly, "Converging on History," in *Gendered Domains: Rethinking Public and Private in Women's History.*

23. Two essays that discuss the reconceptualization of the public sphere from a gendered perspective are Mary Ryan, "Gender and Public Access: Women's Politics in Nineteenth-Century America," and Nancy Fraser, "Rethinking the Public Sphere: A Contribution to the Critique of Actually Existing Democracy," in Craig Calhoun, ed., *Habermas and the Public Sphere*, (Cambridge, MA: M.I.T. Press, 1992), p. 270. In Fraser's words, "The view that women were excluded from the public sphere turns out to be ideological; it rests on a class and gender-biased notion of publicity, one which accepts at face value the bourgeois public's claim to be the public" (page 116).

From different perspectives, all of the chapters in this section on women's politics point to this kind of reconceptualization.

24. The anecdotal references to consumer riots in the twentieth century are numerous, especially during the First and Second World Wars, when shortages and price increases were particularly dramatic and sustained. Their most recognized role was in Russia, where female-led food riots launched the February revolution. In Italy, several books mention them during both world wars: for example, Donald Bell, *Sesto San Giovanni: Workers, Culture and Politics in an Italian Town* (New Brunswick, NJ: Rutgers University Press, 1986), 93 and 191, and Paolo Spriano, *Storia de Torino operaia e socialista: Da De Amicis a Gramsci* (Turin, Italy: G. Einaudi, 1972), p. 413. For Spain, they are directly addressed in the articles cited above, and mentioned in Enric Ucelay da Cal, *La Catalunya populista: Imatge, cultura i política en l'etapa republicana (1931–1939)* (Barcelona: La Magrana 1982), pp. 309–323, and Ronald Fraser, *Blood of Spain: An Oral History of the Spanish Civil War* (N.Y.: Pantheon Books, 1979), pp. 452–453 (for the Republican and Civil War period). The articles referred to in n. 3 discuss consumer riots in France in 1911, in New York, Chicago and Boston in 1917, and in England in 1917. In a different context, Jane S. Jaquette, ed., *The Women's Movement in Latin America: Feminism and the Transition to Democracy* (Boston, MA: Unwin Hyman, 1989), looks at female consumer protests in Latin America in the 1980s.

25. On the protocol of food riots, see John Bohstedt, *Riots and Community Politics in England and Wales, 1790–1810* (Cambridge: Harvard University Press, 1983), p. 27. On well-defined forms vs. impulsive reactions, see Charles Tilly, "Food Supply and Public Order in Modern Europe," p. 386.

26. In Charles Tilly's words, "a whole set of means . . . for making claims of different kinds on different groups or individuals." *The Contentious French* (Cambridge: Harvard University Press, 1986), p. 4.

27. The *consumo* taxes were first instituted in 1845, lifted in 1868 after the "Glorious Revolution," then reimposed in 1874. Since they were levied on basic food items like bread, milk, fish, meat and so on, they were one of the most regressive forms of indirect taxation possible. For this reason, they were widely despised and often became targets of rage during times of high prices. However, local governments relied

heavily on them and found it hard to dispense with them; according to Adrian Shubert, between 1876 and 1905 they provided between 87% and 100% of all local government revenues. See Shubert, *A Social History of Modern Spain* (London: Unwin Hyman, 1990), p. 172.

28. Variations on this theme were rumors of expensive or scarce goods being exported, shop owners refusing to sell goods at a price fixed by the government, a temporary shortage of a particular item, or a change in the way certain taxes were collected.

29. *El Liberal*, August 3, 1897.

30. *El Liberal*, January 20, 1918

31. Toledo, January 16, 1921. Legajo 15A, #21.

32. *El Liberal*, January 19, 1918. Rioters targeted the export of goods when the same goods could not be found at home, or could only be purchased at high prices.

33. Alicante, *El País*, May 7, 1898, and Cieza (Murcia), *El Liberal*, April 28, 1904.

34. Interestingly, the women workers identified in these few cases were almost always cigarette makers, one of the few categories of factory women at the turn of the century. In Gijón in 1898 (*El Noroeste*, May3–4), in Cádiz in 1905 (*El Liberal*, January 10) and in Madrid in 1897 (*El Liberal*, August 3), rioters went to the tobacco factory to ask the *cigarreras* to join in. On the numbers of women in the work force, see Rosa Capel's article in this collection.

35. *El Liberal*, January 30, 1918. The logic of mobilization seemed to run from housewives to wage workers, probably because the former could monitor daily conditions at the markets and stores more easily. The few exceptions seem to prove the rule, as in the case of the female dock workers rioting when they discovered the shipment of potatoes destined for export.

36. For example, in descriptions of the Alicante riot, *La Publicidad* (January 21, 1918) used the word *obligar* while *El Liberal* (January 20, 1918) used the word *invitar*. An intriguing version of this assumption of female bonding over consumption issues was in the few cases where *señoras*, or wealthy women, were forced to join demonstrations. There were reports of this type of coercion in Málaga, Barcelona, and Alicante in January 1918. It is not clear whether poor women were trying to shame their wealthy counterparts or further taunt the government.

37. On conceptualizing the whole range of tactics as a continuous spectrum, see Craig Jenkins, "Sociopolitical Movements," in Samuel Long, ed., *The Handbook of Political Behavior* (New York: Plenum Press, 1981), p. 139: "The inclination of most analysts has been to emphasize the disjuncture between violent and non-violent actions, frequently categorizing non-violent protest actions as persuasive, rather than as congruent with coercive or bargaining strategies."

38. *El Liberal*, April 8, 1919.

39. The immediate villain could be the government if the issue were a tax, but more often it was a merchant or shopkeeper.

40. In John Bohstedt's phrase, "orderly disorder." *Riots and Community Politics*, p. 27.

41. These categories closely correspond to Charles Tilly's three categories of actions: 1) retributive action directly attacking a person or the property of a profiteer, 2) price riot, in which goods are sold at a price set by the crowd, and 3) blockage of shipments. "Food Supply and Public Order in Modern Europe," p. 386.

42. Legajo 15A, #20, Badajoz, June 11, 1915.

43. *El Liberal*, January 19, 1918.

44. *El Liberal*, July 14, 1895.

45. *El Liberal*, January 10, 1905. The local government was targeted both because it was the most accessible and because it had a degree of autonomy in deciding how to raise tax money. The national government assigned block amounts for the provinces to collect, and these did the same with localities, which had the ultimate responsibility to levy and collect taxes from individuals. Partly as a result, local elites could pressure against raising business and property taxes, leaving indirect consumer taxes as the cornerstone of local government revenues.

46. *El Liberal*, May 9, 1898. An auto-da-fé was the public ceremony in which the Inquisition pronounced judgment and sentenced heretics.

47. *El Liberal*, January 17, 1918. On the tradition of requesting a "just price," see Louise Tilly, "The Food Riot as a Form of Political Conflict."

48. *El Liberal*, January 14, 1918.

49. *El Liberal*, May 12, 1898.

50. September 13, 1920. Legajo 41A, #25a.

51. In the province of Murcia. *El Liberal*, April 28 & 30, 1904.

52. *El Liberal*, January 16 & 22, 1918.

53. *El Liberal*, January 12, 1918.

54. This is not explicitly stated but implied by the contrast with the way riots were reported elsewhere; for example, in these cases, participants were never identified as *obreros* or workers, but only as *vecinos* or residents. For example, in Aroche (Huelva), *El Liberal*, February 4, 1918, "se amotinó el vecindario," and in Fuente Cantos (Badajoz), *El Liberal*, May 19, 1918, "grupos de vecinos."

55. Legajo 41A, #21, February 1, 1918.

56. Some of these requests are contained in Legajo 15A, #20.

57. For example, Orense, January 27, 1918, Legajo 41A, #20.

58. The case of Barcelona in 1918 was the one instance in which a women's consumer protest included a strike, in addition to the other more traditional forms of direct action. However, it was a strike that built gradually and informally over several days and at its height included most of the city's women workers (about 29,000) and almost none of the men (2,000). Thus, it followed a completely different trajectory from the usual union-organized strikes.

59. *El Liberal*, January 15, 1918.

60. *El Liberal*, January 16, 19, 21, 1918.

61. However, while the consumer riot made room for the labor movement, the latter did not usually reciprocate. Unions usually dismissed consumer riots as disorganized, reactive, and primitive, and as a result made few efforts to link political energies. One might argue that the unions' own limited understanding of politics led them to miss opportunities to expand their appeal.

62. This account is taken from the local newspaper, *El Noroeste*, which is why I could piece together a richer narrative of the riot. I gathered this information during the course of dissertation research on the city of Gijón, when I spent many months poring over the local newspaper. Otherwise, almost no local newspapers for this period exist in the national newspaper archive—the Hemeroteca Municipal—and most runs of local newspapers begin in the mid-1920s or 1930s. Thus, to get a full picture of consumer riots nationwide, one would have to travel to provincial and regional archives around the country.

63. As mentioned earlier, the cause of shortages and high prices was the opening up of foreign markets as the result of war in the rest of Europe. With demand for goods abroad pushing prices and profits sky high, there was little incentive for producers to supply the domestic market, and the government made no systematic attempt to force them to do so.

64. The August 1917 general strike was part of a nationwide attack on the political system, but in Asturias, an alliance of CNT and UGT unions and republican politicians gave it a greater transcendence. As a result, the strike lasted three weeks longer in Asturias than anywhere else in the country.

13

"Into the Clear Air of the Plaza": Spanish Women Achieve the Vote in 1931

Judith Keene

On October 1, 1931 the Spanish parliament passed Article 36 of the new constitution spelling out the specific guarantees of equal voting rights for men and women over the age of twenty-three.[1] The proceedings in the Chamber carried over into the early hours of the morning and were followed closely from the public gallery by a small but vocal group of women. Some had accompanied a delegation from the National Association of Spanish Women to lobby the support of the president of the Chamber while others worked the corridors of the Cortes buttonholing deputies and distributing a flyer that urged support for the equality of the sexes. Their leaflet warned that a vote against women's suffrage would mean that the new Spanish constitution would be "stained with the inequality of privilege."[2]

During the often heated debates, women in the gallery heckled deputies who opposed women's suffrage and loudly cheered those in favor. When the announcement was made that an amendment to postpone the immediate enfranchisement of women had been defeated by 161 to 121, the public gallery erupted in noisy clapping and loud *vivas*, forcing the president of the Chamber to ring his bell repeatedly and call for order.[3] The exuberance of the female onlookers probably reflected their relief that Article 36 had finally passed. It also underlined the fact that up until the very last vote the inclusion of women's suffrage in the new constitution had not been assured.

In according full citizenship to Spanish women, the Second Spanish Republic was following the example of more than two dozen nations between World War One and World War Two that had extended the suffrage to adult females. The particular way it took place in Spain reveals a good deal about the general process of women's political emancipation between the wars and provides a rereading through the prism of gender of an important part of the political history of the Republic.

Until very recently women's suffrage movements have been a "curiously understudied phenomenon."[4] When not overlooked altogether, their histories have been analyzed as though the events took place outside politics in general. In marked contrast with the struggles for male suffrage, long seen as central to national politics and in many cases providing the defining political issue, the achievement of the women's vote has been treated as an historical nonevent. Similarly in Spain, the history of how women achieved the vote has been largely ignored in political histories of the Second Republic, which mention it in a passing sentence, if at all.[5] Yet questions about women's citizenship and political participation in Spain were deeply embedded within broader political struggles over the form of the new Spanish Republic and how a democratic state should be constructed. Contemporaries in 1931 viewed as profoundly important questions about the political nature of women, what place they should occupy in the new republic and what political and social effect they might have as full citizens. Partisans for and against positioned themselves within the particular national context of Spanish politics and according to conceptions about the structure and formation of democracy based on the experience of the new democratic states that had been created after World War One.

In light of this it is not surprising that arguments about women's suffrage were important in political debate during the first year of the Second Spanish Republic. The enfranchisement of women not only doubled the size of the Spanish electorate but in addition it plugged directly into long-standing and bitter divisions within Spain over the place of the Catholic Church in politics and society. Votes for women impacted directly on these broad general matters and in turn were influenced by them.

This chapter examines the connections between women achieving suffrage in Spain in 1931 and the interplay of political forces that provided the context within which suffrage reform took place. In the process it becomes clear that when the factor of gender is added to the analysis, a very different picture of the formation of the Second Republic emerges. It suggests, perhaps predictably, that many ardent democratic reformers held complex and often contradictory positions when it came time to enshrine within the new constitution the rights of women as citizens.

The analysis takes place in three steps. The first focuses on the general history of women's suffrage between the wars and suggests that the ways in which women achieved citizenship can be grouped into three broad configurations. I argue that these provide different models of reform which I have characterized as the Feminist model, the New States model, and the Latin model. Examples of individual nations that reformed suffrage can be assigned to each model according to the source that provided the impetus for reform. An examination of the way in which the three models operated suggests that women's suffrage in Spain contained elements of the New States and the Latin model and that those concerned with the issue shifted from one model to the other as they argued the case for and against the legal rights of Spanish women.

The second step of the analysis examines the role of the three women deputies in the first republican Cortes in 1931. Each took a radically different stance on the political question of enfranchising Spanish women. Only one, Clara Campoamor, was in favor of women's immediate suffrage, and although the other two shared an opposition to it, they did so from different political positions. The backgrounds and careers of the three shed light on the political choices they made, and also highlight the skills and drive needed by women who chose to enter the public arena in order to survive in the male preserve of the national legislature.

The third section of the chapter brings the features identified in the first two parts to bear on an examination of the debates in the Spanish Cortes towards the end of 1931 as deputies argued the case for and against women obtaining the vote. The manner in which the debate was framed sheds much light on the different ways that interwar suffrage reform was articulated within and outside Spain. More than anything else, perhaps, the debates forcefully dramatize the limitations of the democratic vision of many liberal reformers when the issue was the rights of women as citizens.

Models of Women's Suffrage Reform

Between World War One and World War Two more than twenty-five nations added women to the franchise. The reforms were clustered in two distinct periods. The first, comprising the greatest number, occurred between the very last years of the war and the end of 1922. The second group took place between 1929 and 1935.[6] When seen as part of the overall history of democracy, these interwar suffrage reforms are remarkable. They more than doubled the basis of political representation, drawing in the half of the population that had previously been excluded. In doing so these reforms created at least the potential for a diverse population of women to have an impact on national politics through the ballot box. In this sense, Ellen Du Bois is correct in her bracing reminder that "the cause of women's suffrage has been one of the great democratic forces in human history."[7]

The fact that very few women took up the challenges offered by their new status as citizens has tended to overshadow the significance of the process by which it was achieved. In general, women used their vote, or disregarded it, in ways that were unanticipated when the suffrage reforms were taking place. In turn, this has left a legacy of untested popular conceptions about the electoral proclivities of women voters in general.[8] That women were not immediately transformed into citizens participating in the public arena is a function of the male mores and ethos of public institutions and political parties. Equally important, as Carole Pateman has shown, the citizen and the civil state, key entities in the evolution of modern liberal democracies, are gender specific, and strictly hedged by an ascription of maleness.[9] Females, in contrast, were embedded within an interlocking web of social and cultural factors which tended to tie their identity to home and the private realm. The historical forms in which this identity formation took place and how it changed for Spanish women in the last two centuries provide the subjects of a number of the essays in this volume.

Although historical circumstances and the particular political configuration of parties and groups that existed in each country determined the character of women's suffrage reforms, it is possible to discern three broad patterns across the interwar period. For analytical purposes these reforms have been treated as a whole, rather than adopting the convention that separates western Europe and the United States from countries on the periphery. A methodology that links national movements has the advantage of more closely approaching the view that interwar suffrage reformers had of themselves. Even in countries where the achievement of women's suffrage was unlikely, or the feminist movement was small, activists felt themselves part of an international network. They frequently corresponded with each other, were aware of efforts at reform elsewhere, and took heart at the successes achieved by women in other countries.[10]

In the Feminist model are those nations in which there existed a significant feminist movement working for women's suffrage in the decades before women actually achieved the vote. These movements, which are well documented, include Britain, where women were partially enfranchised in 1918, the United States (1920), Brazil (1932), and Cuba, where female citizenship was instituted in 1934. In all four places, feminists had begun working in pressure groups for moral reform, and later turned their attention to the struggle for women's suffrage.

While arguing that the four examples have common modes by which they successfully achieved their objective, the philosophical bases of their struggles differed, illustrating Karen Offen's distinction between "relational" and "individualist" feminism.[11] The former, in the predominantly Catholic cultures of Brazil and Cuba, based the demand for women's rights on the special nature of women as mothers. The latter, in the Anglo-Saxon countries of Britain and the United States, drew the legitimacy of the cause from the rights of women to citizenship as individuals regardless of their gender.

Whether relational or individualist, leaders and participants in the feminist movements grouped in the Feminist model were upper class and upper middle class. Their aim was not to expand the suffrage to all members of society but rather to ensure that women were included in it on the same terms as men. All four movements could mobilize large demonstrations and garner wide publicity for their actions. Although the quintessential image in popular imagination is the fiery suffragette breaking windows or chained to the railings of parliament, it was only in Britain that there was a significant level of violence. In other places feminist militancy was manifested in more sedate, though no less effective, forms.

Whether Emmeline Pankhurst of the Women's Social and Political Union in Britain, Carrie Chapman Catt of the National American Woman Suffrage Alliance, Bertha Lutz of the Brazilian Alliance for Women's Suffrage, or María Luísa Dolz in the National Feminist Alliance in Cuba, leaders had access to the national (male) political elite. Although the four movements had ebbed from the high point of their power, leaders were able to push their demands to advantage when there was a disjuncture in the political development of their respective nations. Whether caused by war, revolution, or the change of political leadership, the new configuration emerged from the old political groupings that had strongly resisted female citizenship, and gave way with surprisingly little opposition.[12]

The second group, comprising the New States model, includes the greatest number of examples but has been given the least scholarly attention. It consists of those countries where a woman's right to vote came as part of a parcel of reforms that aimed at constructing representative institutions more appropriate to democratic forms of government. These examples hark back to the nineteenth-century suffrage reforms in New Zealand, Australia, and in the western frontier states of the U.S. in which women were given the vote as part of movements of moral reform to promote the cause of provincial progressives and nativism. Although there were women's groups working for suffrage in a number of these new states, the impetus that carried through the reform came from the broad push for democratic change.

The new states created out of the collapse of the German, the Austro-Hungarian, and the Russian empires after World War One epitomize the group. Universal suffrage (i.e., for men and women) was the centerpiece of the new constitution of the German Weimar Republic, as it was in the constitutions of Poland, Latvia, Lithuania, Estonia, Czechoslovakia, and the separated states of Austria and Hungary. These "professorial constitutions" as they were often called, demonstrated technical elegance in their drafting and the erudition of the academic and legal scholars who drew them up.[13] More ominously, they also reflected the tension inherent in their ambiguous origins. In an altruistic fashion, the Versailles settlement aimed to establish a new world order based on national self-determination and the political participation of all people, women included. At the same time, however, the major powers wanted to create a stable political system that would serve as a bulwark against Bolshevism. These two objectives were often at cross purposes.

Another case that fits the New States model is the Second Spanish Republic, created in 1931. Like the others it had come into being after the abrupt collapse of the old regime. The Spanish monarchy had been propped up for almost a decade by the military dictatorship of General Primo de Rivera. By the time it failed, a broad consensus had emerged among Spaniards that the time had come for a democratic republic that would initiate social and political changes to bring the country in line with the rest of western Europe.

Imbued with the optimistic spirit of "New Europe," the architects of the Second Republic were highly conscious of the symbolic importance of the undertaking. The first session of the Cortes opened on Bastille Day and discussion within and outside the Chamber was replete with references to other republican precedents and how Spain was similar to or different from them.[14] The female figure embodying the new Republic was represented in the form of Delacroix's "Liberty Leading the People," with one hand holding the torch of freedom aloft. Popularly referred to as *la niña bonita*—the beautiful young girl—she symbolized a new epoch and a fresh start for the nation.

The republican constitution was also very much a "professorial constitution" drawn up by two succeeding commissions of academics and legal scholars headed by distinguished professors of law at the University of Madrid.[15] They believed that they were creating the blueprint for a new Spanish society and that by adapting the most progressive parts of other models the Spanish republican constitution would stand as an example to progressive nations everywhere.[16] Those who supported equal political rights for the sexes were at pains to emphasize that liberal democracies elsewhere had already adopted this reform and that it was an essential feature of any progressive democracy.

By 1939 all of the carefully crafted constitutions and elaborate representative systems of the new democracies had been subverted and political control had passed into the hands of authoritarian leaders. In Spain, similarly, the Republic had been defeated in a civil war and General Franco's dictatorship suppressed universal suffrage and women's rights for the next thirty-six years.

The third model of suffrage reform applied predominantly to Latin countries where the struggle between the Catholic Church and those promoting secularism provided a central element of the national political culture. Between the wars the most prominent political proponents of secularism were to be found within the ranks of the Radical and republican parties and subscribed to the doctrine of liberalism.

Latin-style liberalism comprised two central elements that dated from the French Revolution. The first was the standard liberal belief that the legitimacy of the modern state must rest on the consent of the governed. As a consequence, liberals were committed to expanding the basis of citizenship to incorporate certain previously excluded groups, which in theory included women. The other element, perhaps the hallmark of nineteenth-century Latin liberalism, was a deeply ingrained anticlericalism. On the basis of their real, lived experience, liberals viewed the Catholic Church as an entrenched obstacle to social, political, and educational reform. In a choice of action in which the two elements of liberalism were at odds, as they were in the case of the vote on women's suffrage, the strength of liberal anticlericalism usually overrode any commitment to expanding the electoral bases of the state. As a consequence, liberals more often than not blocked female access to political and civil equality because it was assumed that female religiosity and proclericalism posed a threat to the secular state. This assumption was reinforced by the profound gendering of the cultures of clericalism and anticlericalism that had taken place during the nineteenth century. According to Michela De Giorgio, as the century proceeded the construction of the discourse of liberalism became increasingly masculine, leaving to women the discourse of Catholicism, the ritual and ethics of which became more and more feminized.[17]

There are numerous examples between the wars of the Latin model operating to block women's suffrage. In France in 1919, 1925, 1932, and 1935, bills granting the vote to women passed the chamber of deputies only to be defeated in the senate by Radicals who feared that French women would vote at the dictate of their priests.[18] The same combination defeated women's suffrage in Belgium.[19] In Uruguay, women's right of citizenship was recognized in the socialist-inspired constitution of 1917, but fear of female religiosity by anticlericals in the dominant Batillista faction headed off the women's vote until 1932.[20] Similarly in Mexico, where there was a theoretical commitment to reform the electoral basis of government and a great many feminists and women activists had been stalwart supporters of the national revolution, the fear that the church would exercise undue influence over Mexican women defeated every effort at female suffrage before 1953.

In Spain the conflict between anticlericals and clericals worked in a complex fashion. By 1931 Catholic action groups had come to accept the anticlerical assessment that women would vote for Catholic parties against the republican alternatives. As a consequence, in 1931 most Spanish Catholic parties, unlike their correligionists in the Latin model already discussed, voted for female suffrage. On the other hand liberals were caught in the tension between an impulse for democratic reform and a fear of female clericalism. The idealism of a "new state" mentality heightened the former while the habits of an existing anticlerical mind-set strengthened the latter. With powerful arguments on both sides, the contradictions of Latin liberalism were dramatically illustrated in the debates over women's suffrage in the 1931 Cortes. Adding to the drama was the fact that each of the two strands of Latin liberalism was separately represented by the female deputies in parliament. As a consequence, their interchange on the floor of the Cortes was one of the most remarkable events in the first year of the Republic.

Spain's Three Female Deputies

The election of three female deputies highlighted the paradox of the political situation of Spanish women in 1931. Although women were not able to vote in the first republican elections in June 1931, there were three women among the 470 deputies elected. The lawyers Clara Campoamor Rodríguez and Victoria Kent Siano represented Madrid seats for the Radical and Radical Socialist parties respectively, and Margarita Nelken y Mansbergen, a journalist and art critic, was returned on a Socialist ticket for Badajoz, the provincial capital of Extremadura. As Nelken did not enter the Cortes until November 18 and stood aside from the parliamentary debates, her position is discussed only briefly below.

By an electoral reform of May 8, 1931, the Provisional Government had widened the franchise to include males over twenty-three years of age and had lifted the legal impediment to women, priests, and public employees offering themselves as candidates for the Cortes. Seven years previously, in April 1924, Primo de Rivera had given municipal voting rights to single women but, like Mussolini's municipal electoral enfranchisement of Italian women in 1926, they had been accompanied by no municipal elections in which women could exercise their rights.

The May electoral reform also implemented a complicated system of proportional representation that ensured that minority groups in each province were represented.[21] The system was modeled on the progressive elements of the Weimar Republic. In the operation of the latter, Claudia Koonz has argued that the electoral system had a profoundly limiting effect on the activities of Weimar women deputies.[22] The fact that individuals needed the support of the party machine to be placed high on the electoral lists militated against women having any real power or being able to raise women's issues.

In Spain the system similarly worked against women's participation in political parties. Women's formal political participation was further hampered by high levels of illiteracy and clear cultural boundaries setting off the male sphere of public politics from the private female domain.[23] This does not mean that women were not politically active; rather, their militancy was expressed outside formal institutions and was triggered by issues that related to their identities as workers, consumers, or mothers.[24]

In the world of formal politics, however, the three women deputies in the first Republican Cortes in 1931 were exceptional by any standards. Highly educated and articulate, they were also well respected in male-dominated professions.[25] Campoamor and Kent were the only women lawyers at the Madrid bar, and Nelken was an outstanding journalist and art critic. Their career success brought entrée into elite male circles which in turn intersected with the leadership networks of the political parties. In 1930 these parties were inchoate and in the process of reforming after seven years of dictatorship. This situation probably favored a few outstanding women achieving party nomination.[26] Perhaps as importantly, Campoamor and Kent were versed in the skills of public speaking, polemical argument, and self-conscious display; hallmarks of courtroom style and equally prized on the parliamentary floor, these are not attributes usually cultivated in the upbringing of females.

The three deputies were also dominant figures in the small circle of politically active, well-educated women in Madrid. Of the three, Clara Campoamor was the unequivocal feminist. Attributing her determination to the need to make her own way in the world, Campoamor described herself as "a single woman without financial support or family backing."[27] Her considerable achievements were won by her own intelligence, independence, and singular hard work. Born in 1888 in Madrid into the respectable but impecunious petite bourgeoisie, she began work at the age of thirteen to help her widowed mother. Later she became a stenographer, one of the new occupations opening up to women, and eventually taught shorthand and typing to adult women in night school. At the same time she studied part time, finally graduating at the age of thirty-six from the faculty of law at the University of Madrid. The success of her first legal cases drew much attention in the city and the Madrid press.[28]

From the time of her admission to the bar Campoamor was active in professional associations at the University and within the legal fraternity in Madrid. These groups provided her with contacts and experience that would later carry over into party politics. She made valuable political contacts as well within the Ateneo, the men's literary and debating club in Madrid. Throughout the twenties she was active in its women's section and, albeit briefly from March to May 1930, was elected the first woman on the club's management committee. It is worth noting that at least seven of her ten fellow committee members became parliamentary deputies in liberal and left parties in the first Republican Cortes.[29]

When the lists were being drawn up for the first elections in mid 1931, Campoamor was sufficiently well versed in the ways of party preselection to switch her membership from the Alianza Republicana to the Radical party. The former had entered into coalition with the Socialist party and therefore had fewer electoral places to offer. Those that were available were highly sought after by men with far more political experience than had Campoamor.[30] The Radicals on the other hand were glad to welcome a woman with considerable professional cachet and guaranteed her a safe parliamentary seat on a Madrid list. Once elected, Campoamor was appointed to the constitutional commission headed by her old professor and fellow Ateneist, Luis Jiménez de Asúa.

They were charged with drawing up the draft of a new constitution to serve as the blueprint for the Second Republic.

At forty-three, Campoamor was a key figure in Madrid at the center of several Spanish and international feminist and reform organizations. She spoke and wrote extensively about the inequality of married women under Spanish law, on the significance for women of the legal definitions of nationality and paternity, and the legal protection of women and children. All of these matters she took up as a member of the new Republic's constitutional commission, and, until 1933, as a deputy in the Cortes.

Campoamor's fellow deputy, Victoria Kent, a lawyer and correspondent, was thirty-three years of age when elected on the Radical Socialist party ticket.[31] Her pattern of public involvement in feminist and professional women's associations was similar to Campoamor's, but her youth and high profile gave her a considerable public following.[32] From a wealthy Málaga family of English origin, she graduated in law from the University of Madrid and was admitted to practice in 1924.

A turning point in Victoria Kent's career had come when she defended Alvaro de Albornoz, a member of the republican revolutionary committee arrested at the end of December 1930 during the last days of the monarchy. The revolutionaries and their counsel, with Kent the only female among them, became public celebrities cheered by crowds as they came and went each day from the model prison to the courts martial.[33] Through her contact with Alvaro de Albornoz, Kent became part of the inner circle of reformers overseeing the transition from monarchy to republic. The provisional government recognized her loyalty and her ability in April 1931 by appointing her the director general of Spanish prisons, the first woman to hold such a senior position in a Spanish government. Her mentor, Albornoz, became the first republican minister of public works and later, when he moved to the justice department, was Kent's direct superior overseeing prisons as part of his portfolio.

Kent began at the department of prisons with energy and high hopes of prison reform.[34] Sadly, perhaps even predictably, they were not fulfilled. Prison reform is an intractable business at the best of times, let alone in a period of immense social turmoil and scarce finances. There were warders' strikes over pay and several highly publicized escapes associated with Kent's newly introduced periodic release scheme. Opposition to her increased within the cabinet and, after initially protecting her, Albornoz was finally overcome by his colleagues and in June 1932 she was replaced.[35]

The third female deputy was Margarita Nelken, the highly talented daughter of a Jewish German father and a French mother. Born in Madrid in 1896 and educated in Paris and Berlin, she excelled in music and art.[36] As a young woman she wrote extensively on art criticism and cultural matters in Spanish, French, Italian, English, and German periodicals and for several years gave painting classes at the Prado. During the Republic she was appointed to the board of the Madrid Museum of Modern Art.

In 1919 Nelken had set up a school in Madrid for poor children but it was closed under pressure from religious groups opposed to the school's laic policies. In the twenties she joined the Socialist Party and in 1931 was elected with a very large majority on the socialist ticket for Badajoz.

Nelken was a radical supporter of working women who was outspoken in detailing their misery; however, like most socialists, she eschewed feminism as an ideology suited only to bourgeois women. Socialists saw class as the real source of female oppression, and class struggle as the solution to it.[37] Although she became the chairman of the Socialist Party's Committee on Women's Affairs in 1931 she vehemently rejected the party's policy of supporting immediate votes for women because there was not "a single practicing Catholic woman in Spain who had not been interrogated by her confessor about her political ideas and inclinations."[38] In light of this, Nelken argued that it would be better for Spain to follow the example of Uruguay where the constitution, "the most advanced in existence," recognized equal rights of citizenship between the sexes but had postponed female suffrage.[39]

Despite the fact that these three deputies shared much in common in that they were independent, politically active, and in favor of broad democratic reform, they held different assessments of the political impact of providing Spanish women with full citizenship. The variation in their views provides a useful reminder of the complexity of the motives of those who supported and opposed the women's suffrage movement between the wars. There is no doubt that they were influential in the way that the debate was framed in Spain. Kent and Campoamor epitomized two dominant strands of the debate within the Cortes and within Spanish liberalism as a whole.

The Suffrage Debates in the Cortes

The first task that confronted the new government in 1931 was to construct a constitution that embodied the democratic principles of the new Republic. From early May, two succeeding commissions researched other constitutional models and drew up a draft document that was tabled at the end of August. After almost continuous debate over amendments and alterations the new constitution, comprising 101 articles, was passed on December 9.

The issue of votes for Spanish women arose in debate several times before the final document was signed. In September Victoria Kent and Clara Campoamor clashed over the wording of the constitutional article which gave all Spaniards equality before the law.[40] During the debate a group of Radicals proposed an amendment that would have given women the vote by parliamentary law, rather than constitutional right, thus leaving open the possibility of reversal if women voted for anti-republican parties.[41] Article 36 embodying women's suffrage was passed on October 1 by forty votes; however, two months later on December 1 a recision amendment was put forward by Victoria Kent that would have required women to serve an apprenticeship in two municipal elections before they could vote on national matters. By this time the Catholic parties that had voted for Article 36 in October had withdrawn from the Cortes, so that the amendment was defeated only by a very narrow margin of four votes. In order to provide coherence and brevity in the discussion below the parliamentary debates have been gathered together according to argument.

Within the Cortes, support or opposition for female suffrage fell into distinct party groupings, with some notable individuals breaking party ranks. Broadly, the liberal parties and their factions with the exception of the small but prestigious Group for the Support of the Republic[42] opposed votes for women while the Socialists and many within the Catholic parties favored it. Whatever their party's position, deputies who disagreed could absent themselves from the Chamber or simply abstain when the time came to vote. A great many deputies, 189 out of a total of 470, chose this option. For example Manuel Azaña, leader of the highly influential coalition Accíon Republicana, who claimed in his diary that it was "atrocious" to deny women the vote and that Clara Campoamor was right in defending it, left the chamber when the vote was taken.[43]

The only party officially to support women's enfranchisement in the Cortes was the Spanish Socialist party. It is worth adding, though, that both Julián Besteiro, the president of the Chamber, and Indalecio Prieto, a leading figure within the party, indicated their opposition to women's votes by absenting themselves from the Chamber when the vote was taken.[44] Since the end of the nineteenth century European socialists had included female suffrage in the party platform. The view was consistent with an ideology in which the working class was the source of social change and women workers carried the same oppression and the same revolutionary potential as their class brothers. It should be said though that along with a theoretical commitment to sexual equality ran a deep ambivalence to the notion that women could be the equal of men.[45] The latter probably reflected two concerns broadly shared within the socialist movement as a whole. The first was a belief in a correct gender order in which men were engaged in paid work and women raised the family at home, and the second was a fear that working women would take jobs from men.

Probably the best statement of the Socialist position came from Andrés Ovejero, who, to the cheers of his party, declared that the spirit of the new Republic was encapsulated in the first words of the constitution, that "Spain is a Republic of workers," including working women. Socialist men, he stated, did not demean their women with "bourgeois gallantries" but treated them as *compañeras* engaged in the same struggle for "equal work, equal pay, equal duties and equal rights."[46] In an eloquent defense of Article 36 on December 1, the socialist José Antonio Balbontín claimed it was "stupid, barbarous and reflecting the atavism of troglodytes" to put in doubt the equality of women with men "simply because the caprice of Nature had provided women with a different physique." He concluded that "biology held no weight against fundamental principles" and that in exercising their political rights Spanish women would be drawn "out of the shadow of the clerics and into the clear air of the plaza."[47]

In an ironical piece in the daily *El Sol*, Miguel de Unamuno, part of the Group for the Support of the Republic, also dismissed out of hand the connection between the women's vote and religion. This "legend," as he called it, had arisen out of "Don Juan's male jealousy and the confusion of free thinkers who mistook religiousness for clericalism."[48]

Catholic and conservative parties, such as the Agrarians, the Basques, and the Navarrese, carefully remained silent during the debates, but when the vote was called were counted in favor. They presumably had come to share the liberal assumption that Spanish women would vote "to a single priest" and that therefore the parties on their side of parliament would be the beneficiaries.[49] This conclusion is supported by their behavior in the succeeding election campaigns in 1933 and 1936. Catholic Action militants were energetic in courting the female vote; however, their approach was highly instrumental. Their intention was not to sponsor women into the party hierarchy or to formulate policy for the special needs of females, but rather to get out the Catholic women's vote in large numbers.[50]

The Radicals, the Radical Socialists, and the republican groups that gathered under the umbrella of Acción Republicana were outspoken opponents of votes for women.[51] These liberals frequently began with a perfunctory reference to their belief in the general principle of equality, and then railed against the uneducated religiosity of Spanish women kept under the thumb of their confessors. In many cases an unrestrained misogyny went with violent anticlericalism as in the intervention by Roberto Nóvoa Santo of the Galician Republican Federation. He decried as a "backward step" any move to include women in the suffrage because female nature is "all emotion and passion and lacks the critical spirit or the mental capacity with which to be able to weigh matters up." In enshrining female enfranchisement the new constitution would "turn hysteria into law" and expose Spanish men to "the danger of being governed by a matrilineal regime."[52]

While rejecting such biological arguments, Victoria Kent reached the same conclusion in a speech that provided a classic exposition of the fear of the anticlerical liberal that women would use their vote for reactionary parties. It was "for the survival of the republic" that she had "renounced her womanly ideals" and would vote against the suffrage. In doing so, she claimed, no injustice would be committed because "women must have time to become imbued with an ideal." They do not "throw themselves into questions they do not understand clearly" and therefore some years of living with the Republic were necessary for them to realize that it was better than the monarchy. It was not that women did not have "the capacity to vote"; it was a matter of providing the "opportunity" for the Republic to be established. When she saw women demonstrating for schools for their children, or forbidding their sons to serve with the army in Morocco, Kent would be convinced that Spanish women were ready. This happy state, however, would come to pass only after the Republic had constructed schools, universities, and popular cultural centers in which Spanish females could learn the values of citizenship. Kent reminded her colleagues not to judge all Spanish women by the standards of university students or working women and, in all conscience, fervently urged them to recognize the danger to the Republic if Article 36 was retained in its present form in the constitution.[53]

Clara Campoamor answered Victoria Kent. The spokesperson for the constitutional commission defending Article 36 of the constitution, and in contrast to her party colleagues, an ardent believer in suffrage for Spanish women, Campoamor presented her case with great skill. She earned the admiration of the Prime Minister and the Speaker, the latter describing her as "a great polemicist," though neither was moved sufficiently to remain in the House for the final vote.[54] She claimed that "it was not so much feminism" that conditioned her beliefs but "the idea of humanism and citizenship."[55]

Her powerful defense of female citizenship drew on the optimistic elements of the New States model and the democratizing strand of liberalism within the Latin model. Over and over she emphasized that Spain provided a shining example of the best of the new democracies: it had a fine constitution based on the latest precepts of international law and must maintain its progressive lead by giving Spanish women legal access to the political system.

All constitutions, Campoamor pointed out, were about redressing the past and laying out the direction of the future. Of the many constitutions created since World War One only four, and those in the most backward countries of Rumania, Yugoslavia, Greece, and Turkey, had denied women the vote. The constitution that the commission had presented to the parliament was the "most free, the most advanced and the best that now exists in the world." Spain's was "the first chamber in a Latin country to have raised the women's voice," and she urged them not to let this "ornament of the liberation of women [be] abandoned, because if it were it would surely be seized by another Latin country." If Spain were a democratic republic, all its powers must emanate from the people. If women were not accorded all the rights of men it would mean that "Spain is a republican aristocracy of male privilege and all rights emanate exclusively from men."[56] The suffrage, she argued, was the cornerstone of democracy, a universal right for men and women and not to be given or taken away by the vote of parliamentarians. In light of this, it would be "ungenerous and insupportable" to give the vote only to those who were supporters.

There were no fundamental differences, Campoamor claimed, between men and women. The only distinction between "one half of the human world" and the other was that women "bring life into the world" but their children, "future republicans" as she reminded them, were born equally of a father and a mother and "receive the same gifts from nature."[57] In answer to Victoria Kent's claims that Spanish women were politically apathetic, Campoamor pointed out that they had participated in the great days of the republican calendar, engendering the "great patriotic spirit of Zaragoza" in the War of Independence (against the French in 1809) and demonstrating in their numbers against the Disaster of Annual.[58] They now wished to participate in the new Republic.

Except for a brief reference on December 1, Campoamor eschewed entirely the question of whether Spanish women were captives of their confessors. Instead, the anticlerical card she played attacked the Church's opposition to divorce, likening traditional Catholic marriage to a life sentence where each spouse was inescapably "shackled" to the other.[59] By beating a favorite anticlerical drum, that in favor of civil marriage and divorce, she maneuvered liberal deputies into her camp. In agreeing with her on the need for sexual equality in divorce and civil marriage, it was more difficult to deny it in other areas of civic life.

The parliamentary record of Clara Campoamor's speeches suggest that she was not fazed by the robust, often antagonistic heckling she received, even when the Speaker seemed unable to control the House. Above the disorder Campoamor steadfastly insisted that her colleagues listen to what she had to say.[60] This calm public demeanor, however, was cultivated at considerable cost. Writing six years later about her campaign—what she ironically termed her "mortal sin"—Campoamor recalled that during the 1931 suffrage debates she was frequently overwhelmed by "moral fatigue" and worn down by a continuous barrage of hostility. The virulence of the attacks upon her "in the corridors, on the parliamentary benches, in political assemblies and at public and private meetings" was "astonishing" and she was outraged by constant taunts that in standing up for the enfranchisement of women she was placing the Republic in mortal danger. She attributed this acrimony to "masculine hysteria and fear" and a "real phobia" amongst men against "the dignification of women" and against herself as "a champion of women's rights."[61] The rebuff by her erstwhile liberal colleagues was the most egregious. Having given no prior indication that they would oppose votes for women in the Republic and having raised no objections within the constitutional commissions, they had set about blocking Article 36 once it was placed on the agenda in the Cortes. Campoamor reserved her most scathing words for the "men of advanced ideas" and the liberal and republican "loudmouths" (*laringeos*) from her own side of the House whose democratic rhetoric was never matched by any real action to promote democracy. Their "liberal outer clothing hid the troglodyte within."[62]

Despite the strain that she may have suffered from her colleagues' attacks, one is struck, reading her constitutional speeches almost sixty years after the event, by the clear intelligence of her analysis and the sharpness of the political acumen she displayed in parliamentary performance. By avoiding clericalism and the confessors as much as possible she kept the vote of the Catholic parties and the right. But also, evidently aware of the competing strands within liberalism, she constantly defended female citizenship in terms of universal rights. By downplaying the anticlerical, she attempted to outmaneuver her liberal colleagues who feared that the women's vote would increase the power of those clerical forces opposed to the Republic. Without such a strategy and Campoamor's sterling performance on the floor of the House it is very likely that women's suffrage would not have been included in the Republican Constitution in 1931.

Conclusion

Several conclusions can be drawn from this examination of female enfranchisement in Spain in 1931. From the point of view of the three models of interwar suffrage outlined in the first section, suffrage reform in Spain contains elements of the New State and the Latin model, while adding a uniquely Spanish quality to both. At the time, many deputies believed in the need for democracy in Spain and were proud that the Second Republic would stand as a model to other aspiring democracies. In comparison with other nations that fit the New States model there was probably a broader and more deeply rooted consensus for democracy in Spain in 1931 than in the other new states. Among many of the latter the impulse for democracy was weaker than the push for nationalism and self-determination, or the commitment to defeating the left. In Spain, however, when there was an opportunity to double popular democratic access to the political system by including women's citizenship in the constitution of the Second Spanish Republic, many deputies slipped back into the grooves of thought and behavior that had been laid down during the preceding century of conflict between clericals and anticlericals.

The shift back and forth between the elements of the New State model and the competing strands of the Latin model provided the texture and substance of the debate. Those deputies who wanted to expand the suffrage with women emphasized the altruism and democratic potential of new state creation while those wishing to postpone the suffrage underlined female clerical propensities. For most liberal deputies, female enfranchisement cut across a far more pressing agenda, which was aimed at containing the power of the church.

The particular configuration of support for women's votes in Spain in 1931 also demonstrates a different version of the Latin model. Many Spanish Catholic deputies by this time had come around to accept the liberal assessment of the reactionary proclivities of Spanish women at the ballot box and therefore voted for female suffrage. In doing this they were joined in an awkward coalition with the Socialist Party and the independent progressives. This combination proved powerful enough to carry reform in Spain at a time when in other Latin countries similar political alliances served always to block votes for women.

The passage of the women's vote ended the rather curious situation in Spain in 1931 whereby women could stand for parliament yet not vote. The issue impacted differently on the careers of the three deputies who had been elected. Margarita Nelken kept her seat in both succeeding elections. Victoria Kent was tipped out in the swing to the right in 1933 but managed to maintain the support of her party so that she was preselected and elected on a combined Popular Front list in 1936.

Clara Campoamor faced a different future. As a result of her outspoken support of the women's vote and the subsequent perception of her Radical and republican colleagues in 1933 that women had voted against the Republic, Campoamor's political career was at an end. After 1931 she was never again in the position of being one of the very few women privy to the party elite. In the 1933 elections Campoamor was denied preselection by the Radical party, and an application to join the Left Republican party in 1935 was ignominiously defeated, despite her nomination having been proposed by a leader of the faction. In the preparations for the February 1936 elections her request for the inclusion of her Women's Republican Union on the electoral lists for the Popular Front coalition was rejected. Embittered by her treatment, Campoamor left Spain during the elections in February 1936 and went into exile in France and then Argentina soon after the Civil War began.

Her political demise mirrored an erosion of the optimism associated with the early days of the Second Republic and a decline in the democratizing elements within the new states created after World War One. Probably because Campoamor's claim for women's rights drew on the inclusive strand of liberalism and the expansive element of the new democracies, she was able to outmaneuver her opponents. The hostility that her success engendered, however, highlights the narrowness of the conceptions of democracy of many Spanish republicans who remained unconvinced of the need to promote the full participation of Spanish women in national politics. Their stance, perhaps, is not surprising. It has long been a standard assertion, and not just in Spain, that citizenship encompasses only male players in the public realm. This view has remained unchallenged almost until the present day.

Notes

1. I am grateful to the Hoover Institution at Stanford University for the use of their facilities while a visiting scholar for six months in 1994 and for the expertise of Helen Solanum and Linda Wheeler in the Hoover Library. At the same time I was glad of a welcome at the Institute for Research on Women and Gender at Stanford University. The interlibrary loan staff at Fisher Library of the University of Sydney were helpful in borrowing material. Barbara Caine and Karen Offen generously offered comments on an earlier version of this essay.

2. *El Sol*, October 2, 1931; W. Fernández Flórez, *Acotaciones de un Oyente* (Madrid, 1931), p. 106.

3. Ibid.

4. Ellen Carole Du Bois, "Woman Suffrage around the World: Three Phases of Suffragist Internationalism," in Melanie Nolan and Caroline Daley, eds., *Suffrage and Beyond: International Feminist Perspectives* (University of Auckland and Pluto Press, 1994), p. 252. See also in the same volume Carole Pateman, "Three Questions about Womanhood Suffrage," pp. 331–348.

5. A good example is provided in Miguel M. Cuadrado, *Políticos de España (1868–1931): Elecciones y partidos* (Madrid: Taurus, 1969) which repeatedly refers to "universal suffrage" from 1890 when he is describing male suffrage. There are several specialized studies of the Spanish suffrage movement that focus on women's suffrage as part of the history of the women's movement in Spain. See Geraldine M. Scanlon, *La polémica feminista en la España contemporánea, 1868–1974* (Madrid: Siglo Veintiuno Editores, 1976); Concha Fagoaga, *La voz y el voto de las mujeres: El sufragismo en España, 1877–1931* (Barcelona: Icaria, 1985); Rosa María Capel Martínez, *El sufragio femenino en la Segunda República española* (Madrid: Horas y Horas, 1992).

6. The first group included the Netherlands, Canada, and the Soviet Union, 1917; Britain, Austria, Czechoslovakia, Poland, and Sweden, 1918; Germany and Luxembourg, 1919; the United States and Estonia, 1920; Hungary and Poland, 1921; and Latvia and Lithuania, 1922. In the second were Ecuador, 1929; South Africa, 1930; Brazil and Thailand, 1932; Ceylon, Cuba, Turkey, and Uruguay, 1934; and Burma and Rumania, 1935. For a useful table that indicates when women achieved the vote as well as when they first entered parliament, see *Las mujeres y el poder político: Encuesta realizada en los 150 parlamentos nacionales existentes al 31 de Octubre de 1991* (Madrid: Union Interparlamentaria Grupo Español), 1992, pp. 17–20. I am grateful to Helen Solanum for drawing this to my attention.

7. Ellen Carol Du Bois, "Woman Suffrage and the Left: An International Socialist-Feminist Perspective," *New Left Review* 186 (March/April 1991): 20.

8. In this volume Gerard Alexander attempts to remedy the situation for Spanish women in the twentieth century by contrasting the popular misconceptions about how they voted with the available electoral evidence.

9. See Carole Pateman, *The Disorder of Women: Democracy, Feminism and Political Theory* (Stanford, CA: Stanford University Press, 1989); and the essays in Gisela Bock and Susan James, eds., *Beyond Equality and Difference: Citizenship, Feminist Politics and Female Subjectivity* (London: Routledge, 1992).

10. For a superb study that presents the detail of national movements in Latin America within the context of strong interregional and international contacts through pan-American organizations, see Francesca Miller, *Latin American Women and the Search for Social Justice* (Hanover, NH: University Press of New England, 1991). On the efforts to construct a collectivist internationalist identity and the challenges to it, see Leila Rupp, "Constructing Internationalism: The Case of Transnational Women's Organizations, 1881–1945," *American Historical Review*, 99 (December 5, 1994): 1571–1600.

11. Karen Offen, "Defining Feminism: A Comparative Historical Approach," *Signs*, 14, no. 1 (Autumn 1988): 119–157; and in Gisela Bock and Susan James, eds., *Beyond Equality and Difference*, pp. 69-88.

12. See Richard J. Evans, *The Feminists: Women's Emancipation Movements in Europe, America and Australasia 1840–1920* (London: Croom Helm, 1977); Franoise Thébaud, "The Great War and the Triumph of Sexual Division," and Anne-Marie Sohn, "Between the Wars in France and England," in Françoise Thébaud, ed., *A History of Women in the West,* vol. 5, *Towards a Cultural Identity in the Twentieth Century* (Cambridge, MA: Harvard University Press, The Belknap Press, 1994); Miller, *Latin American Women*, Chap. 4; and K. Lynn Stoner, *From the House to the Streets: The Cuban Women's Movement for Legal Change, 1898–1940* (Durham, NC: Duke University Press, 1991).

13. See B. Mirkine-Guetzévitch, *Les constitutions de l'Europe nouvelle: Avec les textes constitutionnels* (Paris: Librairie Delagrave). The ten editions between 1928 and 1938 trace the constitutions of the new states and the alterations to them. The "Essai synthétique" that precedes each volume catalogues the author's growing despair at the failure of these democratic experiments. "Professorial constitutions" is Mirkine-Guetzévitch's term; see the 10th edition (1938), p. 9.

14. For references to France, the Weimar Republic, and Uruguay among others, see *El Sol*, July 16, 1931, "Noticias Políticas"; July 28, 1931; 2 August 28, 1931; *Diario de sesiones de Cortes Constituyentes de la República española* (DSCC) no. 28, (August 27, 1931), pp. 642–648.

15. See Luis Jiménez de Asúa, *Proceso histórico de la constitución de la República española* (Madrid, 1932); and Angel Ossorio y Gallardo, *Mis Memorias* (Buenos Aires: Editorial Losada, 1946).

16. See Fernando de los Ríos in *El Sol*, September 4, 1931.

17. "The Catholic Model," in Geneviève Fraissse and Michelle Perrot, eds., *A History of Women in the West*, vol. 4, *Emerging Feminism from Revolution to World War* (Cambridge, MA: Harvard University Press, The Belknap Press, 1993), pp. 166–197.

18. Karen Offen, "Women, Citizenship and Suffrage with a French Twist, 1789–1993," in Nolan and Daley, eds., *Suffrage and Beyond*, pp. 151–170; Steven C. Hause with Anne R. Kenney, *Women's Suffrage and Social Politics in the French Third Republic* (Princeton, NJ: Princeton University Press, 1984); James F. Macmillan, "Clericals, Anticlericals and the Women's Movement in France under the Third Republic," *Historical Journal* 24, no. 2 (1981): 361–376.

19. Evans, *The Feminists*, pp. 124–137.

20. Silvia Rodriguez Villamiel and Graciela Sapriza, "Feminism and Politics: Women and the Vote in Uruguay," in S. Jay Kleinberg, ed., *Retrieving Women's History: Changing Perceptions of the Role of Women in Politics and Society* (Paris: Berg/Unesco, 1988), pp. 278–297.

21. B. Mirkine-Guetzévitch and Egido Reale, *Espagne* (Paris: Librarie Delagrave. Bibliothque d'Histoire et de Politique: Documents de Politique Contemporaine, 1933), p. 33.

22. Claudia Koonz, "Conflicting Allegiances: Political Ideology and Women Legislators in Weimar Germany," *Signs* 1, no. 3, pt. 1 (1976): 663–683.

23. By 1930 with regional variations, 38% of women were illiterate and only one in eight high school students were women; see Adrian Shubert, *A Social History of Modern Spain* (London: Unwin Hyman, 1990), pp. 37. Similarly, of 12.11 million women in Spain, 935,805 were educated to primary level and only 3.8% above; see Capel, *El sufragio femenino*, 104–105.

24. See the chapters by Pamela Radcliff, Temma Kaplan, Rosa María Capel Martínez, and John Tone in this volume.

25. Adrian Shubert points out that women in law school comprised 4% of the student body in 1927–1928, and were prohibited from taking the *oposiciones*, state entrance exams for government employment; see *A Social History of Modern Spain*, p. 38.

26. Marian Sawer and Marian Simms argue that where political parties are not well established or are being formed, women have more chance of gaining party preselection; see *A Woman's Place: Women and Politics in Australia* (Sydney: Allen and Unwin, 1993), p. 17.

27. Concha Fagoaga and Paloma Saavedra, "Introducción" to Clara Campoamor, *Mi pecado mortal: El voto femenino y yo* (Barcelona: Lasal, 1981; 1936), p. 293.

28. For biographical information see her own memoir, *Mi pecado mortal*, and Concha Fagoaga and Paloma Saavedra, *Clara Campoamor: La sufragista española*, 2d ed. (Madrid: Ministerio de Cultura, Instituto de la Mujer, 1986).

29. Antonio Ruiz Salvador, *Ateneo, dictadura y república* (Valencia: F. Torres, 1976), p. 268.

30. In *La Révolution espagnole vue par une républicaine* (Paris: Plon, 1937), p. 201, Campoamor argues that the Republicans weakened the party by sharing their lists with Socialists. Her grievances with the radicals are listed in her letter of resignation to Alejandro Lerroux in February 1935 in *Mi pecado mortal*, 282–287.

31. *El Sol*, September 3, 1931, Don Cristóbal Kent.

32. See Frank L. Kluckhorn's comments in *The New York Times*, September 20, 1931, p. 3 and *El Sol*, May 6, 1931.

33. Angel Ossorio y Gallardo, *Mis memorias* (Buenos Aires: Editorial Losada, 1946), pp. 173–174.

34. Victoria Kent, "Una experiencia penitenciaria," *Tiempo de historia* no. 17 (April 1976), 4–10.

35. Manuel Azaña indicates that the cabinet agreed on Kent's removal on May 20, 1932, *Obras Completas* (Oaxaca, Mexico: Ediciones oasis, 1968) vol. 4: p. 383; and Joaquín de Arrarás states that she was replaced on June 5, in *Historia de la Segunda República Española*, 2d ed. (Madrid: Editora Nacional, 1968), 1:331.

36. *DSCC*, no. 76 (November 18, 1931), pp. 2443–2455; María Gloria Núñez Pérez, "Margarita Nelken: Una apuesta entre la continuidad y el cambio," in *Las mujeres y la guerra civil española. III. Jornadas de Estudios Monográficos, Salamanca, octubre 1989* (Madrid: Ministerio de Asuntos Sociales, Instituto de La Mujer, 1991), pp. 165–171; and Robert Kern, "Margarita Nelken: Women and the Crisis of Spanish Politics," in Jane Slaughter and Robert Kern, eds., *European Women on the Left: Socialism, Feminism and the Problems Faced by Political Women, 1880 to the Present* (Westport, CT: Greenwood Press, 1981), pp. 147–162. Kern mistakenly presents Kent and Nelken as supporting women's suffrage and Campoamor opposing it.

37. Nelken's book, *La condición social de la mujer en España* (Barcelona: Editorial Minerva, 1922) catalogues the problem of Spanish women and the solution. *La mujer ante las cortes constituyentes* (Madrid: Publicaciones Editorial Castro, 1931) discusses the political choices facing women in 1931 and why their vote should be postponed.

38. Nelken, *La mujer ante las cortes*, p. 21.

39. Nelken, *La mujer ante las cortes*, pp. 11–12.

40. *DSCC* no. 46 (29 September 1931), p. 1288.

41. *DSCC* no. 47 (30 September 1931), pp. 1336–1344.

42. The Group for the Support of the Republic comprised a small number of prominent intellectuals, including José Ortega y Gasset and Miguel de Unamuno, whose opinions were highly influential in the first year of the Republic.

43. *Obras Completas* vol. 4, p. 159; Diego Martínez Barrio, *Memorias: La Segunda República Española vista por uno de sus principales protagonistas* (Barcelona: Planeta, 1983), p. 84.

44. Martínez Barrio, *Memorias*, p. 84.

45. For a discussion of women and socialism in Spain see Mary Nash, *Mujer y movimiento obrero en España* (Barcelona: Editorial Fontamara, 1981), pp. 137–173; for European movements, Richard Evans, *Comrades and Sisters: Feminism, Socialism and Pacifism in Europe 1870–1945* (New York: St. Martin's Press, 1987) and Du Bois, "Woman Suffrage and the Left."

46. *DSCC*, no. 48 (October 1, 1931), p. 1356.

47. *DSCC* no. 83 (December 1, 1931), pp. 2744–2745.

48. "El confesionario y las mujeres de España," *El Sol*, October 4, 1931.

49. Karen Offen has pointed out that by the end of 1919 the Vatican had softened its opposition to women's suffrage, in "Women, Citizenship and Suffrage," p. 161. This change of heart perhaps was a function of the fact that with the successful Mexican and Russian revolutions, the Vatican perceived that atheism everywhere was gaining the upper hand and that armed with the vote women could be encouraged to swell the ranks of clerical supporters. It was a similar political calculation aimed at defeating the left that prompted the Vatican to embrace Mussolini a few years later.

50. See Pilar García Jordan's discussion of the instrumentalism of the right in Catalonia, in "Voto femenino: Repercusiones de su concesión y canalización del mismo por los sectores conservadores catalanes, 1931–1936," *Actas de las IV Jornadas de Investigación Interdisciplinaria 4, 1984; Ordenamiento jurídico y realidad social de las mujeres Siglos XVI a XX* (Madrid: Universidad Autónoma de Madrid. Seminario de Estudios de la Mujer, 1986), pp. 391–403. Mary Vincent's conclusions are similar in "The Politicization of Catholic Women in Salamanca," in Frances Lannon and Paul Preston, eds., *Elites and Power in Twentieth-Century Spain: Essays in Honour of Sir Raymond Carr* (Oxford: Clarendon, 1990), pp. 107–126.

51. The difference between the groups was based on style and historic orientation rather than ideology. The Radical party was a product of nineteenth-century politics, and was much tainted by scandals and political deals. Radical socialists and

republican factions of liberalism date from the 1920s and optimistically favored a new deal in Spanish politics with clean hands and a clean slate.

52. *DSCC* no. 31 (September 2, 1931), pp. 728–729.

53. *DSCC* no. 48 (October 1, 1931), pp. 1351–1352.

54. *El Sol*, September 2, 1931, "En los pasillos."

55. *DSCC* no. 46 (September 29, 1931), p. 1287; no. 48 (October 1, 1931), pp. 1352–1354.

56. *DSCC* no. 30 (September 1, 1931), pp. 698–701; *El Sol*, September 2, 1931.

57. *El Sol*, September 30, 1931.

58. The humiliating defeat of the Spanish Army at Annual in 1921 discredited the government, creating the conditions that led to Primo de Rivera's military dictatorship in 1923. For the role of Spanish women at Zaragoza see John Tone's essay in this volume.

59. *DSCC* no. 47 (September 30, 1931), pp. 1339-1340.

60. For particularly robust interruptions see *DSCC* no. 47 (September 30, 1931), p. 1337; no. 48 (October 1, 1931), pp. 1351–1354.

61. *Mi pecado mortal*, pp. 8–9. There is an intimation of this acrimony in José de Medina y Togores's accusation that Campoamor as a spinster should not speak about family, marriage, and divorce as these were things about which she knew nothing, in *Un año de cortes constituyentes; Impresiones parlamentarias* (Madrid: Editorial Ibérica, September 1932), p. 61.

62. *Mi pecado mortal*, pp. 141, 215, 232.

14

Women and Men at the Ballot Box: Voting in Spain's Two Democracies

Gerard Alexander

Historians and sociologists who study Spain have echoed their counterparts studying other European countries, in routinely asserting and assuming that Spanish women in the twentieth century were and still are politically more to the Right than Spanish men. This idea is based on the understanding that they vote more often for right-wing parties and less for Socialists and Communists than men do, and since this stereotype about the genders rests on electoral behavior, it is applied most often to the two periods in this century when Spaniards voted in free elections—during the Second Republic (1931–1936) and since the death of the dictator Francisco Franco in 1975.

The subject of gender and political preference in the Spanish case is not simply an exercise in value-neutral historical curiosity, because for many scholars making the claim, the Spanish right has emerged from the crucial events of the past sixty years with a distinctly negative historical image. Thus to say that women disproportionately supported the Spanish right is to place upon them a significant historical responsibility: it suggests that Spanish women disproportionately rejected the first, reform-minded government of the Republic; that they contributed heavily to the rise of the conservative Catholic party (the CEDA); and that women thereby helped—more than men—to propel Spain into polarization and the Civil War (1936–1939). Moreover, the stereotype suggests that after the death of Franco, Spanish women continued to support a former Francoist, Prime Minister Adolfo Suárez, long after Spanish men had already shifted their support to the Socialists under Felipe González, who governed Spain from 1982 to 1996. The unspoken stereotype suggests that more Spanish men supported the "modernizing" side that has emerged victorious and virtuous in a large part of the Spanish historiographical mind, while Spanish women championed the "traditionalists," who would support Franco in the Civil War and serve loyally under him after it.

To this first historical responsibility is typically added a second: it is usually argued that Spanish women did not even vote to the right out of genuine conservative conviction—which would at least have constituted an active political contribution—but instead because they were manipulated into voting that way by rightist men, particularly Catholic priests and charismatic conservative politicians. Women's support for the right, in other words, is not understood by most historians and sociologists as the product of independent decision-making, but as an illustration of the limited historical agency that has often been assumed to characterize women's actions in the public sphere. Following the separate sphere model of gender roles, observers assumed that women lacked the true qualities of political citizenship, even after they were granted all of its rights. Ruled by their emotions and weak in reasoning capacity, they were generally presumed to surrender their vote to the better judgment of others. This image of women was not limited to Spain, and was found in contemporary debates over female political participation and suffrage in Britain, France, Germany, and Austria. At the center of these debates, and thus the present investigation, stands the question of women's political agency.

These stereotypes and arguments concerning women as voters are enduring and quite common in the literature on modern Spain, despite the fact that almost no detailed analysis has been done to test the claims on which the theories are based. It thus comes as a surprise that, upon closer investigation, most of the claims do not stand up to the evidence available from Spain for either the 1930s or the 1970s. This obvious discrepancy between data and assumptions illustrates the power of gender ideology to shape public perceptions about female identity. On the other hand, the evidence of women's voting behavior suggests that most women entered the voting booth with the same variety of concerns and considerations that men did. In other words, despite stereotypes, female citizens shaped their own identities as independent political actors.

Women's Suffrage and The Second Republic (1931–1936)

In 1931, the Spanish monarchy collapsed in the face of strong opposition from large portions of the political class and the populace, after having stably ruled Spain for half a century. The main parties of this opposition swiftly declared the founding of the Second Republic, which, like the founders of the Weimar Republic in Germany, they intended to be a sharp and progressive departure from the political traditions of their national past. The Republican era became the first sustained period of democratic governance in Spanish history, with competitive elections and accountable governments as the norm. This era also produced what remain the strongest claims about men's and women's voting patterns in Spain: almost every historian of the Republic recites the argument that women were more to the right than men.[1] It is important to note that these claims were made despite the fact that we have no remotely reliable data on how men and women voted in this period. For this reason, such claims are necessarily based on impressionistic evidence, as they were elsewhere in Europe during the same period.

No hard evidence on how men and women voted was or is available for the Republic: the results of elections tell us only how people living in different electoral districts voted, and do not reveal how people of different religions, language-groups, sexes, or other characteristics cast their ballots. The only relatively accurate way to determine the preferences of members of different groups is effective public opinion surveys, and these did not yet exist. Historians and political scientists have developed the device of "ecological" analysis for making educated guesses about voting patterns in periods prior to survey research, but because males and females are spread almost equally across all areas of human residence, gender is perhaps the only major social characteristic that cannot be studied this way.[2] Because of this, all generalizations about gender and political preference during the Second Republic are based purely on the impressions that some people had at the time: there are simply no reliable local facts, either to support the stereotype about Spanish women and the right or to refute it.

These stereotypes about women on the right originated not in history books, but in the minds of observers of, and participants in, European (as well as Latin American) politics in the late nineteenth and early twentieth centuries. Before women were granted suffrage, debates were centrally concerned with the probable destination of women's votes—which parties women were likely to vote for. Views on this subject were largely determined by the analysis of the origin of women's votes—where women's political preferences came from. Many of those who opposed female suffrage—including in Spain—believed that at least in political matters, women's preferences were largely manipulated by other people (i.e., men), and especially by churchmen and charismatic rightist political leaders. That is to say, they believed that women were characterized by a lesser degree of agency and autonomy than men.[3]

In particular, European (and Latin American) secularists believed that women's religiosity made their political views more affected by clergymen and church teachings, which in the late nineteenth and early twentieth centuries were largely favorable to the political right and hostile to atheistic socialism. Secularists thus feared that in societies that were in many ways still traditional, women would "take their orders from the confessional" and vote against progressive social reforms and in favor of rightist parties opposed to change.[4] This stereotype gained considerable currency in Catholic countries and regions because of the Church's strong and coordinated role in political life in predominantly Catholic areas.[5] Interwar (and postwar) opponents of female suffrage also argued that women voters would be disproportionately attracted to rightist parties because of their psychological attraction to the powerful male role played by many conservative, nationalist, and fascist leaders.[6] As a result, "it was precisely on the left that many of the most serious doubts about the value of the vote for women arose."[7]

These political claims and gender images were mirrored in the arguments of the critics of female suffrage in Spain. When the self-avowedly progressive Second Republic was founded in 1931, a heated debate quickly broke out over the subject.[8] Many on the Spanish left opposed extending the vote to women, out of fear that many would vote as their conservative religious leaders instructed them.[9] Thus, Margarita Nelken, a leading Socialist activist, and soon to become the only female Socialist deputy in Parliament,[10] wrote in 1931 that only a symbolic few Spanish women were sufficiently educated to have freed themselves from the conservative influence of the Catholic Church, and that the majority would vote for parties that would retard long-term reform, including for women. The imagery she employed left no doubt that she viewed the majority of women as less than mature and sufficient decision-makers: "one cannot put dangerous weapons in the hands of children, on the assumption that after a few years they will know how to use them properly." She therefore argued that "Spanish women who truly love liberty must be the first to postpone their own gain, in favor of the progress of Spain."[11] Luis Jiménez de Asúa, a leading Socialist deputy, described women in equally dependent terms as "the prisoners of religion."[12] The other large left movement, the anarchosyndicalists, opposed the electoral system as a whole, but also believed that women's political views were largely the product of indoctrination and manipulation by others.[13]

The fight against suffrage was led, however, by the moderate and conservative Republican parties, especially the Radicals and the Radical-Socialists. Victoria Kent, the only female deputy of the Radical-Socialist party, expressed a common belief when she argued in parliament that freethinking middle-class men would vote for Republican parties, but that their religious wives would follow their Church in voting for the reactionary right, thereby destroying the Republic.[14] Kent insisted that "those who feel the Republican spirit, the democratic and liberal Republican spirit, must stand up here to say: women's suffrage must be postponed."[15]

In this debate, Kent, Nelken, and other critics of the extension of the suffrage were opposed by the champions of the immediate concession of the vote to women. The reasons for their position are not as explicit as those of suffrage's critics. Conservatives, particularly religious parties, may have agreed that women would vote disproportionately to the right: as early as 1919, a flagship newspaper of the Spanish right, *El Debate*, called for women's suffrage and pointed out that women's votes "have helped create Catholic governments and parties incorporating Catholics" elsewhere in Europe.[16] These rightists, in other words, may have supported female suffrage for the same reason that many on the left opposed it.[17]

Others, including numerous women's groups, both Republican and Catholic, explicitly favored extension because they believed that Spanish women were as capable as Spanish men of serving as independent voters. Several proponents of the extension of the suffrage, including Clara Campoamor, implicitly argued that the feared passivity could best be undone precisely by granting women the vote and the responsibilities of choice that came with it. Campoamor, a Radical deputy who broke with her party on the subject of women's suffrage, did not address the question of how Spanish women might vote, arguing that it was undemocratic to deny anyone the vote based on their political preferences. Regional parties also actively called for the extension of the vote to women.[18]

This debate was crucial to the later interpretation of women's voting behavior, once female suffrage was finally achieved after the first elections of the Republic, in June 1931. When there was a massive swing from left to right, from the April 1931 male electorate to the November 1933 mixed electorate, it only confirmed what many people already believed—that it was women's conservative votes that defeated the left, thereby sharply polarizing the Republic. Most historians have invariably used the swing from 1931 to 1933 as the best evidence for that claim. The problem with this interpretation is that a detailed examination of the elections of the Republic does not support such sweeping conclusions. To refer to the most obvious anomaly in the voting data: the historians who believe that Spanish women threw the 1933 elections to the right typically do not mention that when women again voted in the 1936 elections, the left won. Clearly, voting patterns were more complex than the stereotypes suggest.

While we never will know exactly how men and women voted during the Republic, we can come closer to having a reliable idea by analyzing in more detail the five major elections of the Republic. In each case, we attempt to show that the stereotype about women and the right does not adequately explain electoral results, including the swing to the right in 1933; and in fact, those results are better explained by a model that assumes that voters of both genders were responding to substantive events and issues. To argue this case, we present each electoral result in conjunction with a description of political trends and debates at the time.

The 1931 National Elections

The provisional government of the Republic, headed by an alliance of Republicans and Socialists, conducted the first truly democratic (among all-male voters) elections in Spanish history, in June, 1931. The big winners were members of the founding coalition itself: the Socialists, the moderate left-Republicans, and the centrist Radicals. All three were non-religious parties, representing a variety of views on economic issues ranging from support for mass nationalizations (the Socialists), to more moderate but significant reform (the left-Republicans), to general fiscal conservatism (the Radicals). The traditional Catholic right won only 11 percent of the vote, and played an ambiguous role in the first Republican parliament: they were isolated in their support for Catholic issues, but often joined the Radicals and other conservative Republicans on economic and law-and-order issues.[19]

The center-left government that emerged from these elections, headed by Manuel Azaña, was noted at the time for three fundamental achievements. First, it passed a model democratic constitution that included granting women the vote. Second, it abolished the status of Catholicism as the official religion of Spain, and secularized public life and the state. And third, the Azaña government made significant changes in the economy that were intended to favor workers, including an agrarian reform aimed at redistributing property to the landless. But these changes were also accompanied by increasing economic problems, including unemployment and an enormous rise in social conflict, especially labor strikes and violence in the countryside. The most famous early incidents of violence were the May, 1931, burnings of a number of churches and convents, which the government seemed to do little to stop. Azaña's government had enacted much of its legislative agenda, but the new laws seemed at once inadequate to some and excessive to others.

Significant political opposition therefore began to appear on both the left and right. Conservative middle-class and Catholic Spaniards were alienated by the economic deterioration, violence, and secularization associated with the Azaña government. The large Radical party left the coalition cabinet in December 1931 to become the main opposition party. It still supported the government's program against the Catholic Church (hence earning them the enduring enmity of Catholics), but consistently criticized the government on economics and law-and-order issues.

Outside of parliament, large portions of the Catholic right were reorganizing themselves into an immense political party, the CEDA. Throughout 1932 and 1933, these various conservative opposition groups gained in popularity, as unemployment rose and violence accelerated. At the same time that it had to endure this onslaught from the right, the Azaña government also had to confront a deep disillusionment on the left, as workers and landless laborers hoping for swift social change found the government's reformist legislation to be tepid and cautious. Under the pressure of worker militancy, the Socialist party radicalized leftward, and the governing coalition between Socialists and left-Republicans deteriorated.

The April 1933 Local Elections

In the April 1933 local elections, Spanish women voted for the first time. Because these elections were local, and were held only in some areas of the country, they are not routinely studied by scholars.[20] The conservative opposition won more than half the seats, and the Radicals were the biggest single winners. The results were explained in a variety of ways: Azaña attributed the conservatives' success to the nature of the rural "rotten boroughs" in which many of the partial elections were held. Many other observers on the left believed that their fears had been right all along: the fact that women's first opportunity to vote coincided with a victory by Radicals and Catholics "proved" that women voted for "the right." In fact, the left-Republican Federals in Barcelona demanded that women's right to vote be taken away before the next national elections, for fear that women voters would turn parliament over to the right.[21] But the lack of reliable evidence was clear even at the time: the same day that the Federals leveled their charge, a left-Republican newspaper in Cáceres claimed that women had in fact voted for the left, against the right.[22]

There are two persuasive reasons to believe that the stereotype of women on the right is exaggerated, and that women's votes were not the reason the government lost the local elections of 1933. First, the governing parties of the center-left had suffered substantial losses in confidence and support by the spring of 1933, and much of the swing away from the governing parties must be ascribed to general discontent with economic and other conditions; in Caro Cancela's words, the elections "demonstrated a notable shift in public opinion."[23] Second, a major winner in the local elections was the Radical party, not the Catholic CEDA, as the stereotype about gender and religious manipulation would suggest. If women had voted for Catholic candidates supported by the Church, the Radicals, which churchmen denounced for their secularizing policies, should not have gained.

The success of both the Radicals as well as the CEDA strongly suggests that generalizations concerning the electoral results should be rephrased: the local elections were won not by parties of "the right," but by parties, both Catholic and secular, that opposed the economic and social policies of the Azaña government. The Radicals—as the main force of opposition to Azaña's government on issues of economic policy and social violence—fit this description, as did the Catholic CEDA. Based on these election results, there is no reason to believe that women and men voted significantly differently from each other.

After the April 1933 elections, the governing coalition of Socialists and left-Republicans suffered further deterioration. The largest left-Republican group, the Radical-Socialists, broke up into three tiny parties. Azaña's own small party was badly tarnished by its association with the country's problems, and the Socialists assumed increasingly militant positions, criticizing the government from the left. The tensions within the governing coalition climaxed in the summer and early fall of 1933, when the alliance fell apart.

The September 1933 Supreme Court Elections

The 1931 Constitution established that the Spanish Supreme Court would be elected by electorates made up of elected local officials, members of the Academies of Lawyers, and the faculties of law universities. This was not a normal election by any means, but it is very useful for our investigation of gender and voting, because its political and professional electorate was overwhelmingly male. The two rounds of balloting produced an avalanche for conservatives, both secular and Catholic: judicial candidates of the Radicals and CEDA led in both the first round of voting among local council members and then a week later among lawyers and universitarians. Historians have generated few well-developed explanations for this result: the Supreme Court election remains the least-studied balloting of the Republic.[24]

We can consider several explanatory possibilities. First is the stereotype regarding women and the right, which would suggest that the overwhelmingly male Supreme Court electorate should have thrown more support to the Socialists and left-Republicans than the mixed-gender electorate did in the local elections four months earlier. This was not the case: the government parties suffered a worse defeat in September than they had in April. A second possible explanation is our alternative to the gender-based theory: by the fall of 1933, many Spaniards, regardless of gender, had been alienated from the parties of government for policy reasons. This theory would predict that even the mostly male electorates of the Supreme Court balloting might vote heavily for the parties of the conservative opposition, which is in fact what they did. Another interpretation of these results could be that the Supreme Court electorates were characterized by a conservatism typical of their professional class origins. This objection may have applied to the second round electorate of lawyers, but does not explain the results of the first round of voting. That first round was made up of elected local officials, such as city council members, many of whom were members of the center-left founding coalition of the Republic. Even among the latter, disciplined voting for the governmental candidates was dubious.

This election result reflected significant levels of disillusionment with the failures and tribulations of the Azaña years, and suggests that the best explanation for the rise of the conservative opposition in 1933 was widespread frustration with those experiences, and not the entry of Spanish women into the electorate. The results of the Supreme Court balloting strongly suggest that even if the national Spanish electorate had remained all male, conservatives would have won that year. Prime Minister Azaña himself accepted that the results of the first round of the Supreme Court elections expressed a serious and extensive repudiation of his government, and the ensuing crisis led the President to dissolve the Parliament and convene the second national elections of the Republic—the first national ones in which Spanish women would take part.

The November 1933 National Elections

In the November 1933 elections, all major parties campaigned for women's votes: the Socialist party called particularly for support from working-class women, and Catholic newspapers issued appeals to the faithful.[25] More women ran for Parliament than in 1931, and more were elected.[26] The Catholic right went into the election united, and the parties of the left often divided—an important difference under an electoral law that rewarded coalitions and punished small, single parties. The basic result was widely predicted: the opposition won, the Socialists lost seats, and the small left-Republican parties collapsed. The CEDA became the single largest party, but once again, it was not only Catholics who won: the secular Radicals remained the second-largest party in the parliament, and in fact increased their number of deputies.

The dramatic swing from the left to the right left a nearly indelible impression on observers, particularly on the left at the time, and on historians ever since, that the entry of women into the national electorate explains the rise of the right and the collapse of the left. Many rightists, too, were content to maintain the stereotype, trumpeting, in the words of the monarchist newspaper *ABC*, that "according to all the calculations, the immense majority of female votes tilted to the right."[27]

The widespread agreement on this issue compelled Clara Campoamor, the Radical deputy and a leader of the suffrage movement in 1931, to fend off accusations that women voters were uniquely responsible for the rise of the Catholic CEDA (and that thereby and once again, as one journalist put it, "the world was lost because of a woman").[28] Writing in a Republican newspaper one week after the vote, Campoamor pointed out that the situation did not allow for simplistic gender-based electoral analyses: in some districts, the Republicans and Socialists had gained in absolute numbers of votes since 1931, which means that some new women voters must have voted for those parties; and that in many other districts, the left had achieved fewer votes overall than in 1931, which meant that some of their disillusioned previous male voters must have abandoned them. Through this simple and powerful analysis of the 1933 election results, Campoamor established that women and men had voted for reasons more complex than just their gender.

Some on the right also found generalizations about women to be exaggerated or obnoxious: CEDA newspapers insisted that the right had earned a victory from both sexes because its policies were superior to those of the center-left, and did not simply inherit the unthinking vote of superstitious women.[29] Ramón Serrano Suñer, apparently the sole surviving CEDA deputy, believes that in fact many women simply did not vote at all in 1933, which would explain the rise in abstention from 1931 to 1933, and insists that the right succeeded because it had earned considerable support among male voters who had voted for the center-left two years earlier.[30] It is a sign of the analytic confusion of the 1930s—and the unreliable, impressionistic nature of the electoral evidence available to us from that period—that just as Serrano Suñer and Capel claim that women abstained heavily in 1933, Tuñón de Lara concludes that it is evident that they did not. There is no evidence for either conclusion.[31]

A closer inspection of the pattern of voting suggests instead that the problems of the Azaña government, and not gender, explain the November 1933 outcome. This is especially true if we analyze each party's share of the votes, rather than the exaggerated swing in the number of parliamentary seats.[32] The parties that did well in November of 1933, as in April and September, were those that opposed the record of the Azaña government of 1931–1933. These were not necessarily the religious parties: the fact that the secular Radicals did nearly as well as the CEDA provides evidence that religiosity did not determine the political preferences of the new female voters. The success of Azaña's opponents was not even limited to conservatives: the small but relentlessly critical Communist party saw its share of the votes more than double from 1931 to 1933. The parties that fared the worst were the left-Republicans most closely associated with the Azaña government. Even conservative Catholics who cooperated with the first *bienio* suffered at the polls; President Niceto Alcalá-Zamora and Miguel Maura lost half of the votes that they had together won in 1931.[33] In this interpretation, it is not a coincidence that the members of the governing coalition that did the best in November 1933—the Socialists—were also the ones that had broken with the left-Republicans and had begun vocally to criticize the Azaña record. As a result, the PSOE also maintained a stable vote-share despite the doubling of the electorate, strongly suggesting that women voted for the Socialists in numbers approximately commensurate with men. No hard evidence exists to sustain this claim, but the stable Socialist share of the vote gives us little reason to assume that the entry of women into the electorate provoked a sharp drift to the right among the electorate as a whole.

After the 1933 elections, the Radicals presided over a series of coalition governments, eventually including the CEDA itself. The style of government was quite different from 1931–1933: the conservatives reversed several economic reforms and adopted a much stricter policy toward labor strikes and social conflict. Conservatives were largely supportive of these changes, and the economy even grew slightly. But many on the left referred to the period

1933–1935 as the "two black years," and their discontent culminated in the 1934 revolutionary uprising, which the government suppressed with much bloodshed. The events of 1934 dramatically accelerated the bitterness between left and right and the nation's political polarization. In brief, the two years of conservative rule had much more mixed effects on political dynamics than Azaña's two; policy outcomes under Azaña mobilized rightist opponents but also sowed discord within the center-left coalition itself. In contrast, the record of the conservative government between 1933 and 1935 alienated the left but maintained broad support among conservatives. As a result, the 1936 elections were held under very different political conditions; both sides went into the 1936 elections unified and with their bases of voters solid.

The 1936 National Elections

In 1936, the right retained much of its share of the vote, but the left was able to unite its support and pull ahead to win a slight overall majority of votes and a larger majority of seats.[34] An electorate that was more than half female had handed victory to a left alliance that included a Communist party that was even larger than in 1933. Most historiographical texts that emphasize the role of gender in voting in 1933 do not discuss this theme regarding the 1936 elections.[35]

The traditional theory that Spanish women were heavily biased against voting for the left does not appear to hold up in the light of the Popular Front victory of 1936. Instead, the 1936 results are better explained by the notion that the preferences of Spanish voters, male and female, were guided by the performance of the governing parties weighed against the political alternatives. In 1933, the monumental problems of the center-left Azaña government had led to massive defections by voters, both male and female, toward conservatives; now, in 1936, the mixed record of the conservative government led to mixed results: a close race.

In the absence of reliable survey data, the argument that Spanish women stood considerably to the right of their male counterparts has been sustained largely by the fact that the entry of women into the Spanish electorate in 1933 coincided with a swing to the right. This chapter has argued that developments in the Second Republic's policy arenas and party system also coincide with the swing in votes between 1931 and 1933, thus providing an equally plausible alternative explanation for the electoral results. But the alternative is more than equally plausible; in fact, it is persuasive. The best evidence is the interspersed nature of the Republic's electorates, which were made up mostly of men in 1931 and in the 1933 Supreme Court votes, and of both sexes in the 1933 local and then 1933 and 1936 national elections. Each of these elections undermines the credibility of the traditional stereotype and allows us to consider the elections in policy-related and party-system terms. The elections of the Spanish Second Republic suggest that political preferences were, by and large, gender-neutral (with some undoubted variation, although of what kind is not clear), and suggest as well that the votes of both Spanish men and women were the products not of religious inculcation or ignorance, but of political events and political experience. When we speak of the Spanish voters of the 1930s, then, we are describing a category of actors in which the degree of historical agency did not appear to vary radically by gender.

The New Democracy (1977–1986)

The elections held in Spain after 1977 provide us with even clearer evidence that a substantial gap exists between persistent stereotypes about Spanish women's political beliefs and reality. In 1939, General Francisco Franco suppressed free political parties, ended competitive elections, and consolidated an authoritarian regime that lasted until his death in 1975. His record presents us with paradoxes: Franco was determined to maintain social traditions, but also liberalized the economy, beginning a process of far-reaching social change that was anything but traditional. In the ensuing boom, Spain became a heavily industrial country, there was a huge exodus of people from the countryside to the cities, and incomes and educational levels rose dramatically. The role of women under Franco was similarly riven with ambiguities: women retained the legal equality associated with the right to vote (in one-party elections) and the right to seek employment, but the regime also encouraged homemaking as a woman's priority, and many officially promoted roles for women were distinctly traditional. Spanish women nonetheless entered the workforce in considerable numbers, and as in other countries undergoing such social changes, the rate of religious practice in Spain fell sharply in these years, despite campaigns by the regime to encourage the Catholic faith.

A large number of parties emerged after Franco's death in 1975. Four were particularly relevant: conservative reformists within the regime formed the right-wing Popular Alliance (AP), led by the combative Manuel Fraga. More moderate figures within the regime formed an alliance with centrist Christian Democrats and Social Democrats; together, they organized into the Union of the Democratic Center (UCD), led by the first Prime Minister, Adolfo Suárez. And two left parties, the Communists and the Socialists, had survived clandestinely. The Socialists in particular revived in the early 1970s, under Felipe González.[36]

Suárez and the UCD won the first two elections, in 1977 and 1979, handling the transition to democracy with great skill, but were overwhelmed by problems with economic and social policy. Suárez grew increasingly debilitated and withdrawn, and after a series of severe losses in local elections, the fractured UCD lost power to the Socialists in 1982. The standard historical interpretation, propounded by Ortiz Corulla, Preston, and Threlfall, among others, is that Spanish women continued their conservative tradition, disproportionately supported the conservative UCD and AP, and stood by Suárez and the UCD even when their failures were obvious, and at a time when Spanish men had already switched most of their support to González and the PSOE.[37] Thus, it is claimed, Spanish women once again manifested their aversion to Socialist and Communist parties, and their devotion to rightist parties with religious roots. The old stereotypes appeared to be confirmed. Spanish women even seemed to be defying an international trend in which western European women in particular were voting in increasing numbers for left parties elsewhere in other countries, resulting, for instance, in the rough harmonizing of the gender bases of support of Socialist and Labor parties in Britain, western Germany, and elsewhere.[38]

These authors explain women's apparently enduring rightist political preferences by reference to factors by now familiar to us: Preston refers to women's religiosity and willingness to support a handsome leader like Suárez, while Ortiz Corulla emphasizes the lower levels of education and workforce experience characteristic of many Spanish women when compared to their male counterparts.[39] Each of these notions—of women as superstitious devotees, as whimsical decision-makers, or as inexperienced homemakers—alludes to the imagery common to anti-suffrage arguments made during the interwar period, which conceived of women as less autonomous historical agents than the men around them.

As with the Second Republic, the generalizations and stereotypes regarding gender and voting in this period are best tested by an examination of the elections held after the transition to the new democracy. For this examination, however, we are in possession of advanced research tools—reliable data from national surveys—which we lacked for the 1930s. Thus, the Center for Sociological Research (CIS) surveyed large numbers of Spaniards on their views on a wide variety of political, economic, and social questions. Their numerous pre- and post-election surveys on Spaniards' party preferences are typically cross-referenced by gender, and these reliable data have served as the basis of most scholarly analyses of the political preferences of men and women in Spain after Franco, including that of Ortiz Corulla.[40] These survey results allow us to detect much finer distinctions in patterns of voting behavior. With this data, we are able to conclude—with an even greater degree of certainty than was the case in our analysis of the Second Republic—that in most important ways, women's and men's patterns of voting in the 1970s and 1980s refute the traditional claims about women, the right, and limited female agency. Given the large amounts of survey data generated since the 1970s, we will discuss the major rounds of elections from the period 1977–1986 in turn, and follow with an analysis of the results.

The 1977 and 1979 National Elections

Suárez became prime minister in 1976, and swiftly began the negotiations with other political groups that were maintained throughout the peaceful transition to democracy. After skillfully persuading both the old Francoist elite and a majority of the electorate to support his leadership of the transition, Suárez held and won elections in 1977 and again in 1979. In both, Suárez and his UCD effectively supervised the transition process and positioned themselves as the moderate center of the political scene, leaving the conservative AP to their right. In both of these campaigns, the Communists and Socialists retained many doctrinaire features that their western European counterparts had shed during the postwar period. As a result, González's effort to portray the PSOE as centrist was undermined in both of these initial elections by the frequent failure of the PSOE leadership to maintain "a consistently moderate public posture," by the ideological "rhetoric and occasionally rancorous behavior of some [Socialist] party members," and by Suárez's willingness to sharply criticize the officially Marxist nature of the PSOE.[41] In 1977, these four largest parties attracted most of the national vote (the 1979 results were similar):

9%	29%	34%	8%
Communists	PSOE (González)	UCD (Suárez)	AP (Fraga)

We are not in possession of accurate data concerning each party's level of support among men and women for the 1977 elections, during which the CIS was not yet conducting its large and reputable surveys. Some smaller polls taken at the time suggested that while both men and women preferred Suárez's UCD, men voted somewhat more heavily for the Socialists than women did. The clearest pattern was very weak support among women for the Communist party. Gender bases of support for the very conservative AP in the early years of the new democracy remain unclear: some polls suggest that women supported it more than men; others suggest the opposite.[42] Intriguingly, the coalition of extreme-right, neo-fascist parties received disproportionate support from men, not women.[43]

The 1979 balloting represents the first Spanish elections for which we have reliable data about gender and political preference. The CIS surveys concerning voting by women and men in 1979 do not reveal a clear-cut national pattern, and in that sense do not confirm the old generalizations.[44] Indeed, they tend to reveal a complex pattern of gender-based support for different parties: men tended to vote more heavily for the Socialists than women, who directed more of their support to the UCD. But the real conservative voice in Spain, the AP, received roughly equal support from women and men. As in 1977, the clearest pattern of gender-based differences in voting was for parties at the extremes: both the neo-fascist extreme-right and the Communist party received far more votes from men than from women.[45] Patterns of voting in Spain's historic regions of Catalonia, the Basque Country, and Galicia also showed that women tended to vote for moderate parties, and men voted more for radical ones.[46]

Two successive electoral defeats plunged the Socialist party into a crisis of self-examination in the fall of 1979, which ended up dramatically pushing the party toward the political center. González argued that if the Socialists wished to compete for moderate voters, they would have to drop their doctrinaire posture and Marxist terminology, and present themselves as moderate social-democrats. Gunther, Sani, and Shabad observe that the PSOE was making the transition from a mass mobilization party, emphasizing socialist ideology and its working-class base, to a catch-all party of moderation and wider appeal to more social groups. For these scholars, the PSOE from 1977 to 1980 was "uneasily straddling two party models."[47] The 1979 crisis involved four months of organizational chaos, but resulted in a more moderate party firmly ruled by González.

The UCD followed the opposite trajectory: from unity to disaster. After the 1979 elections, Suárez formed the second government of the new democracy. Suárez's arena of specialty, the transition process, was largely complete, and political attention soon focused on the UCD's main weak points: the sagging national economy and rising unemployment. The second oil shock added to the deterioration of the economy, and the government seemed to respond only with indecision and drift. The UCD suffered a prolonged series of internal disputes, which eventually split the group apart.

The 1980–1982 Local Elections

Elections were held in the autonomous regions of Catalonia and the Basque Country (1980), Galicia (1981), and Andalucía (1982). The ruling UCD increasingly performed below expectations, and the party broke apart at the national level. At the beginning of 1981, Suárez himself resigned and eventually headed a small breakaway party with a centrist, social-democratic orientation. Two parties, the PSOE and the AP, moved to fill the political space created by the UCD's implosion, moderating their messages in order to do so.

If we continue to control for estimated abstention, surveys reveal a pattern quite different from the traditional stereotype. In three out of four of these regional elections, women voted more for the Socialists than men did. In the Andalusian elections of May, 1982, women disproportionately supported the PSOE, and more men backed the AP. Women maintained their lead in support for moderate regional parties, while men voted more for radical regional parties. As in 1979, the margin of difference in almost all of these cases was at most a few percentage points. These regional elections marked the rise of the

PSOE and the AP as the two large contenders for power. The AP moderated but retained its right-wing image, while the PSOE was able to seize the center-ground of Spanish politics.

The 1982 National Elections

In 1982, the Socialists were swept into power with an absolute majority of seats in Parliament, and as the leading party among both women and men. The AP became the main opposition party, with a quarter of the vote. Women voted somewhat more than men for the AP and the remaining portion of the UCD, while more men than women voted for the Socialists. In all these cases, the differences were slight. As usual, the gender gap was most severe for the Communist party. In Galicia, the Basque Country, and Catalonia, consistent with the emerging pattern already noted, men voted more for radical parties, and women more for moderates.

The 1986 National Elections

Four years later, González and the Socialists were re-elected for another term. Voting for the PSOE was nearly harmonized between men and women, while men voted more for Fraga's rightist AP. Women's votes, once again, were more concentrated near the center of the political spectrum, in Suárez's Social and Democratic center (CDS), the Basque PNV, and the Catalan Convergence and Union (CiU), while men voted more for radical parties, including the Communists and the Basque separatist Herri Batasuna (HB).

This voluminous evidence from the late 1970s and 1980s reveals a more complex pattern of voting by men and women than was predicted by the traditional stereotype about women, and permits us to come to a number of tentative conclusions about gender and voting in post-Franco Spain. Above all, we have little reason to believe that Spanish women voted much to the right of Spanish men between 1977 and 1986, any more than we did for the interwar years. The claim that Spanish women were located on the right after the death of Franco rests on disproportionate female support for the UCD in the 1977 and 1979 elections. But this argument rests on a problematic assumption: the Union of the Democratic Center is not clearly a party of the right. Suárez, its leader until 1981, was very much a centrist; certainly the new party he launched in 1982, the CDS, has never been considered conservative. Moreover, many rightists loudly argued that the UCD (a "catch-all party par excellence"[48]) enacted policies that any social-democratic party might have passed.[49] Disproportionate female support for the UCD only underscores the fact that the main party of the post-Franco right in the late 1970s, Fraga's AP, attracted little support from either women or men for most of the early post-transition years, and tended to attract roughly equal support from the two genders. Even more dramatically, candidacies of the extreme-right consistently attracted substantially more men than women voters.

In other words, the traditional argument that Spanish women vote to the right of men comes up against a variety of facts: women did not flock to the rightist AP, but rather voted for the centrist UCD; men tended to vote for the extreme-right more often than women and for the AP just as often as them, and in fact in 1986, it was men who supported the AP more heavily. Ostensibly, these facts should make it difficult for electoral analysts to maintain the traditional claim about gender and voting. In fact, after reviewing the evidence that women heavily favored the UCD but not the AP, Ortiz Corulla is only able to argue that Spanish women remained on the right by insisting that "conservatism lies at the center of the Spanish political spectrum."[50] This complicated semantic position reveals a strong determination to maintain the stereotype about women and the right. The overarching fact is that from 1977 until sometime in 1981, the preferred party of Spanish women was not located on the right but was rather the UCD, a party "of the center or the moderate center-right, depending on who is judging it."[51]

There is a way to reformulate the Spanish voting experience of the 1970s and 1980s that better captures the complexity of the data. Instead of crudely dividing the political spectrum between left and right (a division that results only in the muddled picture described above), we might consider it instead in three dimensions: left, center, and right. If there is a discernible trend for the period under study it is this: compared to men, women in Spain tended in the 1970s and 1980s to avoid extremist parties at both ends of the political spectrum: the neo-fascist extreme-right, radical parties in regions such as Catalonia, Galicia, and the Basque Country; the Communist party, and also the PSOE so long as it retained its historically doctrinaire posture and language. Women supported those parties that officially defined themselves as the center of the political spectrum: Suárez's Union of the Democratic Center, and later his Social and Democratic Center (CDS). When the PSOE, at González's insistence, abandoned Marxism in 1979 and moved decisively to compete with the UCD for the political center, women voted for it not only as much as men did, but in many regions more heavily. This pattern of disproportionate women's support for parties closer to the center also held in Spain's regions, where they provided support for the PNV and CiU.

The overall distribution of female and male votes, at both the national level and in the regions, supports this thesis. A substantial majority of Spaniards voted for the two largest national parties—the PSOE and the UCD in the late 1970s, and the PSOE and the AP since then.[52] Men who did not vote for these parties tended to vote more than women for parties lying *outside* them on the political spectrum, particularly the Communist party, and also the extreme-right and radical regional parties. In contrast, women who did not vote for the two largest parties tended to vote more than men for parties lying between them, including the centrist CDS and moderate regional parties, not parties to their right. The 1986 general elections exemplified this left-center-right pattern perfectly: men provided more support for both the Communists and Socialists on the left and the AP on the right, while women threw more votes to centrist parties: the CiU, the PNV, and the CDS.

It would appear that this three-fold pattern, which places women closer to the center of the political spectrum and men closer to both extremes, coincides with voting in other western European countries. As was noted above, it has been claimed that women have voted further to the right than men in France, Germany, Britain, and elsewhere. Survey and electoral evidence from across western Europe instead suggests that more women than men have consistently voted for parties located at the center and center-right of the political spectrum, while more men than women have cast ballots for parties at both extremes. This is true for most of the period after World War II and even for the one case for which we have reliable data from the interwar years: Weimar Germany. Women, for instance, voted most disproportionately for the interwar German Zentrum (center) party, and the postwar Italian, German, and French Christian Democrats.

Men, in contrast, voted more heavily than women for Socialists and Communists. They also—and this is more important, given the enduring nature of the claim that women are located to the right of men—voted much more heavily than women for extreme-right parties, beginning with the Nazi party in Weimar Germany, continuing after 1945 with the Italian MSI and the National Democratic party in West Germany, and including all significant extreme-right parties in Europe in the 1980s and 1990s, such as the MSI, the French Front National, and the German Republicans.[53] The close parallels in these cases of greater male support for extreme-right parties strongly suggests that they are a consistent and predictable pattern.

This broader western European pattern of disproportionate male support for parties located at both extremes and women's support for parties located closer to the center, coincides with the distribution of men's and women's votes in Spain's new democracy in the 1970s and 1980s. The fact that this three-fold left-center-right model extended back into the interwar era, in the form of electoral data from Weimar Germany, suggests that a similar pattern may have existed in the Spanish Republic. The data from the two Spanish cases alone serve to refute the traditional claim that Spanish women have been located to the right of men; the evidence from France, Germany, and Italy serves as the basis for a more encompassing refutation of such claims made across Europe or at the theoretical or analytic level.[54]

Conclusion

In both of Spain's two democratic experiments in this century, we have every historical and comparative reason to believe that women and men voted as they did for a wide variety of reasons—political, familial, economic, religious, and cultural. The surveys on gender and political preferences taken since Franco's death and the transition to democracy tell us that women and men in Spain do not vote exactly alike. We should probably assume that they also voted slightly differently during the Republic. However, the most important result of a close analysis of the electoral data from the 1930s and the 1970s and 1980s is the lack of any strong evidence to support the claim that Spanish women voted significantly to the right of men, for religious or any other reasons. Instead, the election returns from the 1930s suggest, quite persuasively, that women and men shifted political ground roughly in sync, as governmental performance and political alternatives seemed to justify. The data from the 1970s and 1980s similarly rejects the traditional stereotype, and reveals one further and fully compatible trend of note: if anything, women in Spain tended to cluster their votes closer to the political center, with men at the political fringes, both left and right. In doing this, Spanish men and women voters manifest a pattern visible throughout modern Europe. Quite simply, the traditional model of women on the right does not stand up to the evidence and must be replaced by some other formulation. This chapter proposed a three-fold model of voting that would reflect these important realities in gender-based voting better than the crude left-right dichotomy relied upon in many historiographical analyses.

But perhaps the most powerful fact that emerges when the Spanish (and European) evidence is considered in terms of broader themes than simply the narrow question of women and the right, is how strikingly similar male and female voting has been. The voting differences we analyzed, particularly for the period after Franco's death, were intriguing and deserve to be explained; they were also typically measured by a few percentage points. This fact appears, initially, surprising: throughout their lives, Spanish women and men in this century were, and in many ways still are, sharply distinguished from one another in terms of their upbringing, their social roles, their access to education, their opportunities to work outside the home, and by life choices and life chances of many types. And yet their broad political perceptions appear to have coincided, with some variation surely, but with a profound consistency. Compared to this bigger picture, the differences we have observed between how women and men voted in Spain are noteworthy, but not notable.

The implications of this similarity in voting patterns for understanding the process of female identity formation are significant. What they suggest is that, despite a web of institutions, ideologies and cultural practices that dictated a monolithic female identity and denied women agency in the public sphere, ordinary women quietly demonstrated their capacity to handle the burdens of citizenship and to make the independent decisions that defined their individual political identities in the democratic state. By acknowledging this simple reality, we can thus restore political agency to the millions of anonymous women who participate in this most basic act of democratic citizenship.

Notes

1. Among the many authors who present this interpretation are Rosa María Capel Martínez, who writes that most women cast their ballots for the right. *El sufragio femenino en la Segunda República* (Granada, Spain: Universidad de Granada, 1975), pp. 245–246, 255, 271; Gerald Brenan, *The Spanish Labyrinth* (Cambridge: Cambridge University Press, 2d ed., 1950), p. 266; Hugh Thomas, who writes in *The Spanish Civil War* that "the introduction of votes for women for the first time in Spain, as usual, profited the right" (London: Penguin Books, 3d ed., 1979), p. 107; Manuel Tuñón de Lara, *La Segunda República*, vol. 2 (Madrid: Siglo Veintiuno Editores, 1976), p. 12, says that women "seguramente" [certainly] voted more for the right than men; Jean Bécarud, *La Deuxième République Espagnole, 1931–1936* (Paris: Fondation Nationale des Sciences Politiques, 1962), p. 50; Ricardo de la Cierva, *Historia de la Guerra Civil española*, vol. 1 (Madrid: Libreria Editorial San Martín, 1969), p. 245, asserts that women's suffrage "weighed heavily in the right's favor." More recently, see Mariano García Andreu, *Alicante en las elecciones republicanas, 1931–1936* (Alicante, Spain: Universidad de Alicante, 1985), p. 120; José A. Sancho Calatrava, *Elecciones en la Segunda República: Ciudad Real (1931–1936)* (Ciudad Real, Spain: Diputación of Ciudad Real, 1989), pp. 207–208; and Catherine Matsell, "Spain," in Joni Lovenduski and Jill Hills, eds., *The Politics of the Second Electorate* (London: Routledge and Kegan Paul, 1981), p. 137. Paul Preston ascribes the claim to "many observers," and does not critique it, in *The Coming of the Spanish Civil War* (London: Methuen, 1978), p. 90.

2. For example, certain parts of Barcelona or Paris were predominantly (if not entirely) middle-class or working-class neighborhoods; voting in those districts strongly suggests how members of those classes voted at the time. No district in Spain was made up of either gender disproportionately enough to be able to produce estimates as to whether women and men voted differently from each other or not.

3. This belief was widespread across Europe. British antisuffragists, for instance, feared that women voters would be swayed by personalities more than issues, and Cromer joined many Liberals in fearing that women would largely support the Conservatives for religious reasons: Brian Harrison, *Separate Spheres: The Opposition to Women's Suffrage in Britain* (London: Croom Helm, 1978), pp. 33, 41. On the British debate over suffrage, see also Jane Lewis, ed., *Before the Vote Was Won:*

Arguments for and Against Women's Suffrage (New York: Routledge and Kegan Paul, 1987).

4. Leon Richer, cited in Steven C. Hause and Anne R. Kenney, *Women's Suffrage and Social Politics in the French Third Republic* (Princeton, NJ: Princeton University Press, 1984), p. 17.

5. Evans finds that few leaders opposed to female suffrage were harbored by the Socialist parties he examined, but these were largely restricted to predominantly Protestant northern Europe. His own analysis treats France as an exception to the pattern, and Spain and Italy are not discussed in the text at all. Richard J. Evans, *Comrades and Sisters: Feminism, Socialism, and Pacifism in Europe, 1870–1945* (Sussex, UK: Wheatshaft Books, 1987), pp. 66–92. Peterson concludes that gender gaps in voting were smaller in Protestant than in Catholic regions of Weimar Germany: Brian Peterson, "The Politics of Working-Class Women in the Weimar Republic," *Central European History* 10 (1977): 102. See also the discussion of religion in Hause and Kenney, *Women's Suffrage*, pp. 254–258, and Judith Keene's article in this volume for a discussion of the centrality of anticlericalism in southern European liberalism.

6. Maurice Duverger maintained this interpretation into the postwar period, to explain disproportionate female support for de Gaulle, in *The Political Role of Women* (Paris: UNESCO, 1955), pp. 70–71. By the 1980s, this claim was turned on its head by Pascal Perrineau, who argues that women voters were repelled by the "virile" and combative style of Jean-Marie Le Pen in France, in "Le Front National: Un électorat autoritaire," *Revue Politique et Parlementaire* 918 (1985): 26.

7. Evans, *Comrades and Sisters*, p. 90; Evans argues that few Socialists opposed female suffrage in principle, but reports that many were concerned about extension in practice, because of the predicted rightist nature of female voters; pp. 83–84. In 1891 the German Social Democrats became one of the first socialist groupings to officially call for female suffrage; see Renate Pore, *A Conflict of Interest: Women in German Social Democracy, 1919–1933* (Westport, CT: Greenwood Press, 1981), p. xiii.

8. For a greater discussion of this debate, see Keene's article in this volume.

9. The main parties of the Republic are described below in the discussion of the 1931 elections.

10. Women could run for office beginning in 1931 even though they could not vote until 1933. On the female deputies of the Second Republic, see Esperanza García, *La actuación de la mujer en las cortes de la Segunda República* (Madrid: Ministerio de Cultura, 1979).

11. Margarita Nelken, *La mujer ante las cortes constituyentes: El divorcio, el voto, la cuestión religiosa, la ley del trabajo* (Madrid: Editorial Castro, 1931), pp. 24–36.

12. Jiménez de Asúa, *Al servicio de la nueva generación* (Madrid: Ediciones Morata, 1930), pp. 110–117. The PSOE eventually decided to support women's suffrage after much internal debate; see Mary Nash, *Mujer y movimiento obrero en España, 1931–1939* (Barcelona: Editorial Fontamara, 1981).

13. Even before the collapse of the monarchy, one anarchosyndicalist newspaper, *Solidaridad Obrera* (the La Coruña edition), argued that a special effort would have to be made to free women from reactionary religion and superstition (April 11, 1931), p. 2. On the eve of the 1933 elections, the anarchosyndicalist newspaper in Soria expressed concern that because of their religious indoctrination, "women are afraid of the word revolution" *Trabajo* (November 12 ,1933), p. 2.

14. It is an interesting aspect of this debate—and a pattern ever since Michelet—that critics of women's suffrage assumed and argued that the men who had the power to influence women's votes were not their husbands, but rather priests and church leaders.

15. *Diario de Sesiones de las Cortes Constituyentes* no. 48 (hereafter *DSCC*) (October 1, 1931), pp. 1351–1352. This theme was repeated by Ruiz Funes in *El Sol*, October 29, 1932, p. 8; and by Brenan, *The Spanish Labyrinth*, p. 266; and Bécarud reports that it was widespread at the time, *La Deuxième République*, p. 50. During the course of the debate, most Republican parties supported amendments delaying or diluting women's suffrage, and it is safe to say that only the PSOE and the right supported extension throughout the debates.

16. *El Debate*, November 10, 1919, p. 1.

17. European conservatives were not united on this subject; the British Tories joined many Liberals in opposing female suffrage, as did many German conservatives; Evans, *Comrades and Sisters*, pp. 85–86; Harrison, *Separate Spheres*, p. 33.

18. Among Campoamor's speeches on the subject, see *DSCC* no. 47 (September 30, 1931), pp. 1339–1340, and no. 48 (October 1, 1931), pp. 1352–1354. She recounts the debate and aftermath in *Mi pecado mortal: El voto femenino y yo* (Madrid: Librería Beltrán, 1936). The Women's Republican Association, the National Association of Spanish Women, and the National Association of Women Doctors of Spain were among the groups that petitioned the Parliament to extend the vote to women. *DSCC* no. 48 (October 1, 1931), p. 1376.

19. Extreme Left, 2%; Socialists, 20%; Left-Republicans, 31%; Conservative Republicans, 26%; Catholic Right, 11%.

Three women deputies were elected in 1931: Clara Campoamor as a Radical and Victoria Kent as a Radical-Socialist, both from Madrid province; and Margarita Nelken was elected as a Socialist in a by-election in Badajoz in November of the same year.

20. Most authors omit to mention or do not address in detail the local or Supreme Court elections, including Salvador de Madariaga, *Spain: A Modern History* (New York: Praeger, 1958); Raymond Carr, *Spain, 1808–1939* (Oxford: Clarendon

Press, 1966); Thomas, *The Spanish Civil War*; Capel, *Sufragio femenino*. Both are succinctly described by Gabriel Jackson, *The Spanish Republic and the Civil War* (Princeton, NJ: Princeton University Press, 1965), pp. 104, 115; and Stanley Payne, *Spain's First Democracy* (Madison, WI: University of Wisconsin Press, 1993), pp. 135, 145.

21. Such as *El Diluvio* (Barcelona), April 25, 1933, the page 1 editorial, appearing the day after the initial municipal election results had been published.

22. *Región* (Cáceres), April 25, 1933, the page 1 editorial. The paper was a Radical-Socialist organ.

23. Diego Caro Cancela, *La Segunda República en Cádiz: Elecciones y partidos políticos* (Cádiz: Diputación de Cádiz, 1987), p. 159.

24. See note 20 above. One of the few detailed treatments of these complex elections is José Ramón Montero, *La CEDA* (Madrid: Ediciones de la Revista de Trabajo, 1977), pp. 285–289.

25. For the PSOE, see *El Socialista* and *El Obrero de la Tierra* throughout November 1933; one interesting CEDA campaign is that of the *Diario de Valencia*, October 20–November 18, 1933.

26. Apparently, 39 women ran in 43 districts: 17 ran with extreme left parties; 10 with the PSOE; 5 as left Republicans; and 7 on the right. Five of the 39 female candidates were elected: 4 Socialists and 1 *Cedista*. Nelken was reelected, but Kent and Campoamor were defeated.

27. *ABC* (Seville), November 21, 1933, p. 19. The editorialists did not make clear on what evidence these calculations were based.

28. Campoamor in *Heraldo de Madrid*, November 26, 1933, p. 16. She was responding, in part, to a column by Juan García Morales, "The World was Lost Because of a Woman," in *Heraldo de Madrid*, November 24, 1933, p. 16. *El Liberal* (Seville) also defended its support for female suffrage against criticism, December 1, 1933, p. 1.

29. For instance in a column by Luis Romera de Neydos, who wrote that claims about women and the right were "already sophistries and over-exploited," in *La Verdad* (Murcia), November 24, 1933, p. 8.

30. In an interview with the author in Madrid, June, 1993. Capel joins in this belief, *Sufragio femenino*, p. 245.

31. Tuñón de Lara, *La Segunda República*, p. 12. Abstention rose between 1931 and 1933, but there is no evidence as to who the abstainers were.

32. The Republic's electoral system granted up to 80% of the votes in a district to the leading slate of allied candidates, with the remainder going to the next slate. Even a slight shift in votes could radically swing the number of seats won by each electoral alliance.

33. The Radicals retained their vote share from 1931 to 1933 at just over 15%. The Socialists remained stable at 20%. Azaña's party lost over half of its support, falling to 1.8%. The various Radical-Socialist factions collapsed from nearly 11% to a combined total of under 3%. Catholic Republicans went from a joint 7% to a total of 3.7%.

34. Javier Tusell, *Las elecciones del frente popular* (Madrid: Edicusa, 1971).

35. For example, Jackson and Sancho Calatrava. Capel makes one of the few claims concerning gender and voting in 1936, concluding that women disproportionately abstained or voted for the right that year (*Sufragio femenino*, pp. 255, 271). As with the other elections of the 1930s, there is no direct evidence for this.

36. On the emergence of these forces, see Richard Gunther, Giacomo Sani, and Goldie Shabad, *Spain after Franco: The Making of a Competitive Party System* (Berkeley, CA: University of California Press, 1988). For a useful study of one party, Eusebio Mujal-León, *Communism and Political Change in Spain* (Bloomington, IN: Indiana University Press, 1983).

37. For example, Mónica Threlfall, "El Socialismo y el Electorado Femenino," *Sistema* 32 (September 1979) and "Women and Political Participation," in Christopher Abel and Nissa Torrents, eds., *Spain: Conditional Democracy* (London: Croom Helm, 1984), p. 140; Preston, *The Triumph of Democracy in Spain* (London: Methuen, 1986), p. 119; Carmen Ortiz Corulla, *La participación de las mujeres en la democracia (1979–1986)* (Madrid: Instituto de la Mujer, 1987); and Edward Moxon-Browne, *Political Change in Spain* (London: Routledge and Kegan Paul, 1989), p. 70.

38. See, for example, Ivor Crewe, "How to Win a Landslide Without Really Trying," in Austin Ranney, ed., *Britain at the Polls, 1983* (Washington, DC: American Enterprise Institute, 1985), p. 167; Vicky Randall, *Women and Politics* (London: Macmillan Education, 2d ed., 1987), pp. 70–71; and David P. Conradt, "The Electorate, 1980–83," in Karl H. Cerny, ed., *Germany at the Polls: The Bundestag Elections of the 1980s* (Durham, NC: Duke University Press, 1990), pp. 46–47.

39. Preston, *Triumph of Democracy*, p. 119; Ortiz Corulla, *Participación*, pp. 45–52.

40. A description and catalogue of CIS surveys can be found in the CIS's *Catálogo del Banco de Datos* (Madrid: CIS, 1993).

41. Gunther, Sani, and Shabad, *Spain After Franco*, p. 167.

42. Respectively, Threlfall, "Women and Political Participation," p. 144; and the SOFEMASA poll for *El País*, published May 25, 1977, cited in José Ignacio Cases, Lourdes López Nieto, Miguel Angel Ruiz de Azúa, and Francisco J. Vanaclocha's study of the 1977 elections, *Mujer y . . . 15 de Junio* (Madrid: Dirección General de Desarrollo Comunitario, 1978), pp. 152–53. Threlfall's "Electorado femenino" relies on opinion polls carried out for the PSOE, which suggest more accentuated concentrations of gender based voting than are indicated in the larger CIS surveys.

43. Ibid., pp. 152–153. In 1977, the Alianza Nacional was a coalition of Fuerza Nueva and Fernández Cuesta's sector of the Falange. This survey indicated that over 80% of the A.N.'s support was male.

44. The full data are available from the CIS, and portions have been published in Ortiz Corulla, *Participación*, pp. 167–190. Surveys suggest a higher abstention rate for women than men, but in this interpretation, abstention is controlled for, or recalculated to be equal between women and men. One reason for doing this is that Spanish women consistently respond to surveys less willingly than men; much of what is recorded as abstention may in fact represent an attempt to maintain the privacy of political preferences.

45. Ortíz Corulla does not present data on the extreme right—represented in 1979 by Blas Piñar's Unión Nacional. The records of the CIS's largest voting preference surveys conducted in 1979 (the UN's peak year) are technically defective, and cannot be read to cross tabulate party support with gender. The only reliable evidence concerning the UN is a postelectoral CIS-sponsored survey conducted in June–July, 1979, which shows that a minority of the UN's supporters were women (CIS Study no. 1192). See also note 44 above.

46. The category of "moderate regional parties" includes the Basque National Party (PNV) and Convergència i Unió (CiU) in Catalonia, while more radical ones would include Herri Batasuna (HB), affiliated with the Basque ETA terrorists, the separatist ERC in Catalonia, and Galician radicals.

47. Gunther, Sani, and Shabad, *Spain After Franco*, pp. 165–170.

48. Ibid., p. 183.

49. Carlos Ferrer, the leader of the employers' association in the UCD years, made this claim at the time and repeated it in an interview in Barcelona, 1993. Preston concludes that "Suárez had taken the UCD into social democrat territory felt by many PSOE leaders more properly to correspond to the Socialists," in *The Triumph of Democracy*, p. 155. Prominent UCD Ministers, including Rafael Calvo Ortega, Manuel Jiménez de Parga, Enrique Fuentes Quintana, and Francisco Fernánez Ordóñez, emphasized their progressive credentials. Jiménez de Parga, for instance, told *Cambio 16* (August 24, 1977) that "we all have something Marxist to us."

50. Ortiz Corulla, *Participación*, p. 57.

51. Cases, López Nieto, et al., *Mujer y . . . 15 de junio*, p. 156.

52. The AP is now the Partido Popular (PP).

53. See Duverger, *Political Role of Women*, pp. 54–61; Richard Hamilton, *Who Voted for Hitler*? (Princeton, NJ: Princeton University Press, 1982), p. 91; John David Nagle, *The National Democratic Party: Right Radicalism in the Federal Republic of Germany* (Berkeley, CA: University of California Press, 1970), p. 132; Perrineau, "Le Front National," p. 25; Mónica Charlot, "L'émergence du Front National," *Revue*

Française de Science Politique 36 (1986): 40; Subrata Mitra,"The National Front in France: A Single-Issue Movement?" *West European Politics* 11 (1988): 53; Forschungsgruppe Wahlen, *Bundestagwahl 1990* (Mannheim, Germany: Institut für Wahlanalysen, 1990), pp. 30–37; Douglas Wertman, "The Christian Democrats," in Howard R. Penniman, ed., *Italy at the Polls, 1979* (Washington, DC: AEI, 1981), p. 75; K. Robert Nilsson, "The Italian Socialist Party," in Howard R. Penniman, ed., *Italy at the Polls, 1983* (Durham, NC: Duke University Press, 1987), p. 83. On a comparable pattern in the UK, see Martin Harrop, Judith England, and Christopher T. Husbands, "The Bases of National Front Support," *Political Studies* 28 (1980): 274.

54. This case is made by the author in "Gender Differences in Voting: Left, Right, and Center in France, Germany, Italy, and Spain," presented to the 1994 Annual Meeting of the American Political Science Association.

15

Problematic Portraits: The Ambiguous Historical Role of the *Sección Femenina* of the Falange

Victoria Lorée Enders

> Highlighting divisions of opinion within the cultures in question . . .
> thereby becomes important,
> and it may be wise to remind ourselves as well as our readers
> that understanding why and how something happened
> is not the same as accepting it uncritically.
> Understanding does not necessarily imply agreement.[2]
>
> —Ida Blom

The remarkable growth and development of women's history in the last two decades became manifest with the founding in April of 1987 of the International Federation for Research in Women's History.[1] Dedicated to establishing dialogues between scholars, building international networks, and sharing knowledge, the Federation is part of an expanding effort towards a global women's history. Comparative studies have begun to explore, in the words of its president, Ida Blom, "whether Euro-American theories explaining gender inequalities may apply to all cultures, whether theories generated within other cultures may be applied to Euro-American history, or whether specific culturally determined theories are needed."[3]

In the present study I pose Blom's questions to the specific historical case of the *Sección Femenina* (Women's Section) of the Spanish Falange (Spain's fascist party), and examine two mutually contradictory characterizations of this women's auxiliary organization. I address the negative depiction by various historians of the nature and contribution of the *Sección Femenina*, and consider antithetical claims of the *Sección Femenina* itself that they have been misrepresented and that "history has betrayed them." By contrasting the voices of the women who "lived the experience" of the *Sección Femenina* with the "official version" of their history, I pursue questions about Spanish women's history. Drawing on the wider discourse in global women's history and feminist theory, I explore whether the particularities of Spanish history require a new (or at least reevaluated) set of analytical categories in the study of Spanish women's history; I also propose that insights gained from the Spanish case can inform the wider discourse of women's—or better, gender—history.

In 1934, Pilar Primo de Rivera organized six other young women into the *Sección Femenina* at the behest of her brother, José Antonio, who had founded the Falange in 1933.[4] José Antonio did not survive the Civil War, but his sister Pilar led the *Sección Femenina* from its origin through the Civil War and the duration of the Franco regime. After the victory of the Nationalist forces under General Franco in 1939, the *Sección Femenina* was incorporated into the regime and given authority over Spanish women, a position it maintained for the next thirty-six years. In its official capacity as the sole state organization for women charged with the formation of Spanish womanhood, the *Sección Femenina* purveyed an amalgam of traditional Catholic and Falangist values to several generations of Spanish females.

Pilar Primo de Rivera loyally adhered to the ideology bequeathed by her brother, and the members of the Women's Section styled themselves the purest of the Falangists. José Antonio had founded the Falange against the perceived threat of social revolution in Spain, a threat he attributed to the class conflicts and unconstrained individualism of modern parliamentary politics. As an alternative to social and political life based on competition and conflict, the Falange proposed a new state composed of natural and complementary—not conflicting—social units: the family, the community and the *patria.* His proposed Falangist state—based on cooperation—promised to heal the rift between men and women, between boss and laborer, between social classes—all the disaggregating effects of the French and Industrial revolutions—and restore Christian Spain to its historical destiny as the leader of the Hispanic world.

Because the Falange embraced traditional Catholicism, the *Sección Femenina* necessarily endorsed the Church's assessment of women's nature and place. In this canon, woman was to complement her husband; her sacred duty was to be a mother. The rhetoric of Pilar Primo de Rivera reiterated that woman was by nature submissive; that she realized herself most fully through self-abnegation. Never was woman to compete with man, or to attempt to replace him; she was to act in a well-defined and restricted world appropriate to her "natural" qualities. On both counts, Catholic and Falangist, the world of woman in the Falangist New State would be the domestic world.

After Franco's death and the establishment of a democratic regime in 1977, the new government officially disbanded the *Sección Femenina* as part of its desire to regenerate Spain. By 1981 the new State had completely dismantled the extensive women's organization that had permeated the educational, social, and cultural fabric of Spanish society. Thus, after forty years under the protective aegis of the Franco regime, the *Sección Femenina* confronted a newly enfranchised public—one that would shortly elect a Socialist government. In power from 1982 to 1996, the leftist government remodeled the Spain of the *Movimiento*,[5] created a network of social and cultural institutions imbued with its own reforming spirit, and fostered an efflorescence of historical and literary works that ruptured past constraints and reflected sympathy with the new political orientation. In response to forty years of official Francoist history, intellectual inquiry under the new regime primarily pursued questions that were purposely neglected during the Franco years: those exploring labor, the left, social classes, and women.

Accordingly Spanish women's history has burgeoned, dominated by the concern it shares with post-Franco historiography in general: the need to recover its own history which was suppressed under Franco.[6] Dedicated to the recovery of women's voices that were silenced through political, economic, and social oppression, historians have overwhelmingly chosen women linked to political parties of the left as their sympathetic subjects. María Dolors Calvet has explained the drawing power of this subject.

> Women in the Republic, in the civil war, with the guerillas, in exile, in jail, have been a point of reference for all the democratic and antifascist women who through all these years have denied themselves the model of the "sacrificing mother" and "long-suffering wife" that the official Church and the fascist organs imposed. That is why women have taken a leading role in the fight against the dictatorship and in favor of democracy.[7]

Enjoying institutional support and a sympathetic milieu, an impressive and growing list of Spanish scholars have been making visible and audible the contours of these previously silenced lives.[8]

Few works have inquired into women on the right, and those that have considered the *Sección Femenina* inevitably reflect the atmosphere of the post-Franco years; they critically characterize the *Sección Femenina* as having collaborated with the Francoist state, a regime that oppressed and degraded women.[9] These scholars, reflecting the cultural recovery of the left, have condemned the *Sección Femenina* for its collusion with patriarchy and capitalism. Their renderings of the women of the *Sección Femenina* have buttressed the standard depiction of rightist women: submissive, obscurantist, retrograde, and so on, while still complicit in the politics of the hated regime.

The women of the *Sección Femenina* not surprisingly repudiate this version of their historical role: they see their past as daringly progressive and their lives as dedicated to improving the condition of Spanish women. In the mental world which informed their outlook, Catholicism defied Communism, religion challenged atheism, and the family stood as the last bulwark against the license and degradation that threatened women. In their view, they prevailed because they were right; they had dedicated their lives and their unstinting labor to Spain; and they have remained firm in their beliefs and grateful for the meaning their lives have derived from those convictions. As a result, the hostility of the left towards themselves is not comprehensible to the women of the *Sección Femenina*. This chapter looks at this interchange of mutually incomprehensible realities and defines it as the setting for identity construction. Even shared historical experiences, transmuted through mutually exclusive perceptions of the world, will result in antithetical interpretations and opposing constructions.

This curious case of contested identity compels further investigation: into the strength and tenacity of the perceptions from the left, and alternatively, the intensity with which they are refuted by the members of the *Sección Femenina*. Within the prevailing discussion, criticism and self-justification center on four central facets of their identity: the ideology of the *Sección Femenina*, the implementation of its program, the political alliances employed to achieve their ends, and—most grievously—the perceived betrayal of womanhood demonstrated in their actions. In addressing the complexities in the experience of the *Sección Femenina*, this study reveals a blurring of traditional categories and verifies the need for "specific culturally determined theories" in the pursuit of women's and gender history.

History and Blame: The View from the Left

The traditionalist vision of woman endorsed by the Falange has generated unqualified disdain from its liberal and left political opponents. In the words of the Feminist Collective of Madrid,

> the *Sección Femenina* occupied itself in preserving and exacerbating the traditional sense of the Spanish woman as much as possible: the loving wife and sacrificing mother, Catholic and dissimulating, ignorant and uncultured, who in order to be included in the symbolic social order needed nothing more than the attributes of neatness, submission and silence.[10]

To the activists of the left, the Falangist "new woman" looked more like *la niña-mujer*. From their perspective, this term—the girl-woman—personified the retrograde attitude towards women underpinning both Catholic traditionalism and "fascist" *machismo*.[11]

In its function as overseer of Spanish women during the Franco regime, the *Sección Femenina* was responsible for modeling the wives and mothers of the future Falangist state. With enthusiasm, the Women's Section undertook this commission on two planes: they sought to change mentality, and they sought to reform social life. They concentrated on education and constructed an elaborate educational system to form their feminine ideal.[12] The standards and norms by which they constructed classes, school texts, and political catechisms, and by which they organized sports, holiday centers, and youth clubs—in short, the lives of female Spain—reinforced the cultural prescriptions of the Francoist state.

Critics have censured this training as repressive and detrimental to girls. "The avalanche of norms of conduct," wrote Elena Posa, "had no other object for the girl than to put an end to her spontaneity, her initiative and creativity, in order to obtain a repressed and submissive type of woman."[13] Even the step of introducing physical education for girls into the traditional school curriculum—innovative compared to Church norms of propriety for girls at the time—earned no acknowledgment of the efforts of the *Sección Femenina*. Rather, critics mistrusted the good faith behind these endeavors.

> Physical education was understood as a form of inculcating discipline and strengthening morality, never as a means of empowering all the personal capacities of women. *In reality*, the labor of the *Sección Femenina* in school sports endeavored to justify the physical inferiority of women and fostered the traditional concept of the weaker sex.[14]

In the above evaluation, the phrase "in reality" merits attention since the author offers no evidence for her claim to authority. By such assertions, critics claim an epistemic privilege—that they have a grasp on motivational causality.

The *Sección Femenina* consistently adhered to José Antonio's original principle, that the Falange stood for social justice in Spain. By "social justice" the Falangist women meant that no child born in Spain would be disadvantaged by conditions of birth. To implement social justice, the *Sección Femenina* campaigned to improve the health, sanitary, cultural, and educational standards of the poor—especially the rural poor—in Spain. They waged vaccination campaigns in rural villages; *Cátedras Ambulantes* (traveling classrooms) carried medicines and instruction, as well as entertainment, to inaccessible locations. They created a network across Spain to disseminate information, electing the most promising girls in a village, educating them and establishing them as *divulgadoras* (spreaders of information) in their native villages. These local contacts of the *Sección Femenina* then served to link rural people with town people and with the state.

In her account of the work of the *Sección Femenina* in Mallorca, Elena Posa grants that "the only effective labor that they did realize would have to be in the terrain of beneficence, [and] social assistance, such as their rural *divulgadoras*."[15] However, critics overwhelmingly assess the efforts of the *Sección Femenina* in the field of social service to be—at best—misguided, and more often, hypocritical and machiavellian. For example, Giuliana di Febo has judged reforming efforts of the *Sección Femenina* to be spurious:

> If culture, as a coming to critical consciousness, was denied to the whole of Spanish society, it was especially so for the female masses. And the *Sección Femenina* was one of the principal instruments of this policy. The social injustices, the cultural and political oppression of the country were assumed to be facts—true a-priori-in this "new" conception of the world. The high cost of living, the high index of infant mortality (the highest in Europe), unemployment, repression, all factors that weighed with particular meaning on women in those ill-fated years of the [19]40s, constituted for the female falangist the reality from which to begin an action that, far from presenting change as an objective, served *in reality* as compensation, through *pseudocompensatory* instruments (among them the campaign for hygiene and vaccination, the distribution of "little cribs") to the neediest families, and for the *false participation* and high prices paid by women in the Francoist state.[16]

In this characterization, we find not only the same claim to epistemic privilege, but in the recurrent psychological phrasing—"pseudocompensatory" and "false participation"—repeated attacks on these women at the motivational level.

Underlying the criticisms of their position on women and social reform one encounters a political judgment: the crux of the condemnation of the *Sección Femenina* was its affiliation with Franco's regime. Lidia Falcón, herself a former prisoner in the Franco jails, has summarized the political crime of fascism. She argued that

> the fascism that triumphed in Spain for forty years . . . not only crushed the male proletariat and peasants, destroyed culture, censored literature, ended theatre, and exiled the Spanish intelligentsia and the university class for two generations. In addition, and I would say above all, it savagely exploited women, oppressed and humiliated them as only fascist *machismo* can do.[17]

In the same vein, another writer concluded that it was not the "'advancement' of the Spanish woman" that motivated the *Sección Femenina*, but rather a strategy "to influence her ideologically" so she will "contribute, through her children, to the formation of a new Falangist Spain."[18] One finds, at the core of virtually all such denunciations, an uncompromising ideological rejection.

Such political censure of the Sección Femenina goes beyond condemning its affiliation with the Falange and Franco. Antagonists also have denounced them for their class loyalty, and charged them with having "defended a petit-bourgeois and urban model of culture," and promoted an elitist instead of "a participatory and popular culture."[19] Further, this petit-bourgeois mentality was to blame for the "insensitivity" of the *Sección Femenina* towards girls of modest social origins. Here the manuals of domestic economy edited and used by the *Sección Femenina* showed "inexcusable insensitivity" to how these girls might react when they perceived the "chasm between their own reality and what was presented to them by the *Sección Femenina*."[20]

Finally, liberal and radical Spanish women have denounced the *Sección Femenina* for having betrayed their sex, deeming them hopelessly retrograde because they upheld traditional gender codes. They dismiss the efforts by Pilar Primo de Rivera to reform the legal condition of Spanish women[21] as insufficient and, once again, motivated by bad faith. According to Rosario Sánchez López, the *Sección Femenina*

> adopted a Janus-like praxis, arrogantly bi-frontal, since on the one hand it developed a legislative campaign in favor of the working rights of women, and on the other hand, it questioned . . . the rule of female professional work, turning back to the ideal of the woman at home that seemed not to have been abandoned, but to have adapted to social changes. The *Sección Femenina* showed itself, with this shift, inaccessible to discouragement, fulfilling the slogan created by José Antonio, but inaccessible to coherence as well.[22]

These critics have spurned the *Sección Femenina* for its antifeminism: they have charged the *Sección Femenina* for having failed them as women. For example, they claim that any allusions to female workers in the manuals of the *Sección Femenina* overlooked them as women,

> grouping them among the enemies of the regime or of the Falange, never giving them the character of specificity. For the *Sección Femenina*, these women did not exist; nevertheless, they did exist—and from the first moment of the cruelest postwar [period].[23]

The claim is that toward the female opponents of the Franco regime, the *Sección Femenina* "maintained an absolute silence."[24] In this analysis of female antagonists located on the separate extremes of the Spanish political spectrum, women on the left charge their antagonists with gender betrayal.

As the language quoted above demonstrates, criticism of the *Sección Femenina* has stressed the issue of good faith; if they have accomplished a positive good, they have done so for the wrong reasons. Since motivation is considered so important by their critics, it is appropriate and indeed necessary to hear the voices of the *Sección Femenina* directly. The following section presents selected self-perceptions of the women of the *Sección Femenina*.

In Their Own Voices: The View from the Right

The self-characterizations of members of the *Sección Femenina* offer us an alternative interpretation of their history. Raising their voices in self-affirmation against both antagonistic portrayals of themselves and equally antagonistic silence about them, they have claimed an alternative identity. In a series of interviews that I conducted between 1989 and 1991 with former members of the *Sección Femenina*, they defended their ideology and politics, praxis and record on behalf of women.

To the women of the *Sección Femenina*, Falangist ideology had offered them a unique political alternative. As young girls in the 1930s they shared a "political discontent." They followed neither the parties of the traditional right nor those of the left. "The right seemed culpable of many things that happened in Spain. We didn't go with the left because Communist ideas didn't fit us (who in general had a Catholic concept of life, and a concept of respect for the family, for family traditions, customs.) But . . . we didn't like the concept of the very closed right."[25] Under these conditions, the Falange radiated a unique appeal for some Spaniards. "In my house," recalled Concha, a high-ranking member of the organization,

> we were all Republicans. For this reason we all took refuge in the Falange. We were not of the right, nor were we Communists. So we had to look for equilibrium, to take the good part of Communism, the sense of social program . . . and . . . the good part of the right, with its sense of the *patria*, of religion, of the family and tradition, of course. It was to unite the two things.[26]

She described the charismatic effect of José Antonio Primo de Rivera on her generation.

> His personality was something extraordinary. He was socially avant-garde, a defender of the simple and humble classes . . . . They could not understand him: many from below, because he was a *señorito* of the aristocracy; and the aristocracy repudiated him because he was socially advanced and defended the worker.[27]

And what did it mean to be socially avant-garde? Tomasa amplified this aspect of Falangist ideology. "José Antonio . . . always wanted a revolution in all the orders of Spain. Whereas Pilar Primo de Rivera saw that in order to make this revolution women had to change totally."[28] And Pilar underscored the central role of this ideology in the orientation of the *Sección Femenina.* "An ideology," she said, "yes, always the ideology, always, always . . . . Because life itself is moved by ideology."[29]

Social justice was singled out repeatedly by members of the *Sección Femenina* as the keystone of their revolutionary ideology. Lola, one of the directors of the *Sección Femenina*, explained that

> . . . social justice means that each child on being born has the same possibilities that other children have, without his birth having been privileged, or whatever, playing a part. It was José Antonio's, and it was ours: social justice before all . . . . To educate so that a child who is born can have the same rights; but if he doesn't have sufficient formation, or sufficient education, he will always be on a lower level. Thus, for us, social justice begins with education.[30]

Symbolically, they elected as their patron Saint Teresa of Avila,[31] who "in her moment, was also a revolutionary . . . in the mystical sense," explained Tomasa. "She also broke many molds in her time . . . . And of course, we chose her as an example of a courageous woman, and a woman who tried to clear away obstacles in order to attain the ends that she considered worthwhile."[32] As further evidence of their progressive past, these women differentiated themselves from their reactionary comrades on the right.

> *Acción Católica* was made up completely of very retrograde women. Next to them, [we] ended up being very progressive and very forward moving (*lanzadas*). The Acción Católica were, well, very inclined to religious types of things: spiritual formation, moral formation, etc. But the spirit of the *Sección Femenina* and the goals of the *Sección Femenina* were wider.[33]

Contrasting themselves with the women of Carlist Traditionalism,[34] the women of the *Sección Femenina* again claimed a distinctive—and progressive—identity. In their view, the Carlists, traditional Catholics too, "were conservative persons and very much to the right—too much to the right."[35]

Former members of the *Sección Femenina*, having marked out education as the arena of the battle for social justice, also remembered it as the site of successful achievements against great opposition. For example, when they introduced gymnastics for girls into the schools, it was considered very "provocative; and the mothers of the girls wouldn't let them put on bloomers. . . . Now, you hear those bloomers being laughed at, and they say, 'How ridiculous' [they were]."[36] At the time, however, these activities of the *Sección Femenina* ran counter to established Church norms. "There were bishops who did not look at us with a kind eye; they would even say to us that we were perverting the youth," Tomasa recalled. "Even I had to experience on one occasion that a priest, who had confessed me, said that if I did not leave the *Sección Femenina*, that my soul was in danger . . . . Certainly, I didn't ever return to confess with that man."[37]

The members of the *Sección Femenina* also recalled their struggle for reform in the areas of university education and professional advancement for women. One member of the organization insisted that "to us the university student was as important as the housewife. (We carried out) . . . an extraordinary labor in the university."[38] Another continued the theme.

> It's very interesting to see how the *Sección Femenina* took a great interest in impelling women to go to the university in greater proportion than they had previously. Before, women who went to the university were rare; after, women increasingly had been entering the university . . . although they didn't want to recognize it, the *Sección Femenina* had made a great promotion. And not only in the university, but in other professions.[39]

For example, argued Lula de Lara in an interview published in 1981, the 1961 Law of Political, Professional and Labor Rights for Women "opened all roads to women, until then absurdly closed to their participation, against the judgment of Pilar."[40] Pilar herself recalled, "I personally went through Ministry after Ministry so that they would erase the word *varón* (male), and girls could enter too."[41] Finally, the bill was "presented by Pilar as *Procuradora* in the Cortes (Parliament) and approved unanimously."[42] Another member of the *Sección Femenina* noted that the law of 1961 "cost more than twenty years"[43] to accomplish, yet critics have questioned its merits. This hostility to the bill has perplexed the women of the *Sección Femenina*. As another member countercharged:

> Now that they are talking so much about the rights of women—they have not made any law that has superseded this one. They speak so much now . . . because women . . . women, today, are supported by this law. After this one, the only law that they have proposed—which according to them favors women, but to me appears a stupidity—is the abortion law, and divorce law . . . But as for professional rights and labor rights and all this, they have not come out with a law that has greater amplitude than this law.[44]

Behind the concrete issue of the bill, this exchange records the clash of two mutually exclusive discourses on women's issues.

The most bitter reproaches against the *Sección Femenina* have condemned their treatment of women; to the members of this organization, these are the most incomprehensible and wounding criticisms. From their perspective, in its devotion to social services, the *Sección Femenina was* helping women. The following chronicle, offered by a former administrator, illustrates this position.

> In 1937 . . . the *Sección Femenina* realized that the role of women in Spain had to be revitalized. Women were relegated to be no more than . . . what they traditionally had been: in their homes, at their work. And the poor thing that remained single . . . ! Then the *Sección Femenina* realized that women did not participate . . . that culturally, they were very backward in relation to men; that there was much more illiteracy among women than among men; that women did not participate in sports, for example—except some select minorities, four *señoras* that played tennis, or rode horseback; that in health there were some huge problems due to the ignorance of the women of the common people, the working class women, who did not know how to care for their children; that there was a very high infant mortality rate in Spain.
>
> Once the war was over, what had been done in embryo was proposed again, but more organized, with concrete goals: working against the illiteracy that was so high, against almost non-existent health education—there were endemic diseases, in whole regions, for lack of vaccinations, for lack of hygiene, for lack of all these things. And all this is what the Sección Femenina was organizing all these years, with more or less efficiency, with more or less intensity, . . . but it has continued during all these forty years.[45]

In a more specific manner, another illustrated the impact of the *Cátedras Ambulantes* (traveling classrooms) on a rural village. In doing so, she underscored the meaning that the *Sección Femenina* had derived from their labor.

> It was a beautiful responsibility because we changed the psychology of the villages . . . even to the physical aspect of the villages. For example, once . . . in the province of Avila, the people had suffered much in the war. The houses were in very bad shape, very dirty. The people had fixed them up as well as they could. They had only one mattress, all the families together. Then the *divulgadoras* taught them to take advantage of orange crates, or whatever, to make (what they needed). Then we put on a hygiene campaign. We told them, you must clean the house . . . whitewash them. They had to plant flowers: we provided flowerpots, flowers. We brought them cleaning supplies. All this, we got free from the businesses . . . from stores. We went to them for this purpose, and they gave to us. Then we said to them (the villagers), we will return within a month. This house—cleaner, the children—cleaner, and so on. We gave them prizes. Then we gave them shoes, kitchen utensils, pots, blankets—that we also got from the stores in the capital. Then the people gained courage. The kids went to the *Frente de Juventudes*[46] and whitewashed houses; they planted the flowerpots; and when we arrived, the village had changed. A beautiful village, clean . . . and all the women made paper chains, as if it were a saint's day. All the people met us, and we—loaded with blankets and everything. And they changed; little by little, they were entering a . . . different way of living.[47]

From their point of view, members of the *Sección Femenina* had worked for decades to carry out their charge to improve the standard of living of—precisely—women and children.

After the death of Franco, Spain's new government dismantled his *Movimiento* and its *Sección Femenina*. Some of these women have since regrouped, calling themselves *La Nueva Andadura*, or the New Pace. In their view, not only has what they constructed been dismantled, but who they were has been lost to history as well. As Concha lamented,

> Now, what was ours, has not been assimilated. This generation has not yet understood it. I believe that years will have to pass before the work, our work, is seen historically. We are too close to the trees and we can't see the forest; or the forest can't see the trees.[48]

They allege that their history must be read in its proper context: that their record must be read in terms of the progressive ideals of the Falange. Further, they argue that the *Sección Femenina* must be judged in the context of the 1930s and 1940s, not of the 1980s or 1990s. Consequently, their primary orientation since regrouping has been archival and historiographical; they have been accumulating the record of their experiences (speeches, manuals, journals, etc.), in effect, stockpiling their memories. In compiling the archive of their memories, the *Sección Femenina* have given site to the transformation of individual memory into social memory. As James Fentress and Chris Wickham have suggested, one makes individual memory into social memory, "essentially by talking about it." Further, "social groups construct their own images of the world by establishing an agreed version of the past, . . ."[49] Written off, ignored, or antagonistically characterized—if noticed—the former members of the *Sección Femenina* of the Falange, by reconstituting their history, have been reconstructing—consciously and defensively—their identity.

And how have the members of the *Sección Femenina* evaluated their own role as women? Did the *Sección Femenina*, as María Teresa Gallego Méndez has argued, teach women to be closed? "No, no, no," answered one respondant. "I believe the reverse. We came to break molds."[50] And another replied that life in the women's organization had given her

> . . . (a career) very full, very full of life, that has enriched me very much in an interior way . . . . We continue all of us very united, and—I don't know—it has created in us many disquietudes, to know, to learn. And I—within what I can do—I go to courses; I go to art events . . . Always, I have an unrest to know these things.[51]

Another member argued: "One had to fight also against the mentality of a society that was closed: closed to the incorporation of women. And it was necessary to fight also against the mentality of women themselves, which was also closed."[52] Concha, in reminiscing about the past, affirmed her own life's trajectory: ". . . this epoch marked us (I feel it . . . alive inside myself—the hopes, dreams, of those times) and formed me, and gave me strength for many things . . . . I found my center in the *Sección Femenina*."[53] When recalling how they were perceived in the past, Tomasa affirmed that "They saw us as revolutionaries." And the revolution? "Simply to promote women in all areas."[54]

Explaining Oneself, Understanding Another: The Problem of Historical Agency

As we have seen, these self-perceptions of the *Sección Femenina* have not been corroborated by women on the left. Leftist women have seen antithetical qualities in the *Sección Femenina*: their submission to Catholic traditionalism and fascist *machismo*, which destroyed spontaneity and intitiative; their silence; and worse, their perceived hypocrisy and their arrogant gender betrayal. How does one explain such contrasting portraits of the identity of the *Sección Femenina*?

Former members of the *Sección Femenina* have explained these discrepancies in terms of a variety of personal, political, and philosophical factors. Lola seemed to dismiss such conflicting interpretations as inevitable.

> Nobody likes everyone .... There are always people who are antagonistic, or draw back or are suspicious of us; but, let them talk. The *Sección Femenina* was born to serve, to progress, to carry Spain forward. Therefore, anyone who says the opposite—well, he's lying, or is doing that on purpose, or is an enemy.[55]

A former Provincial Delegate from La Coruña, in Galicia, described such distortions in terms of modern egotism and present blindness to preceding values. She argued that the *Sección Femenina* had

> initiated and promoted the first female associations—the germ of all that there are today; and that is history, and there it is written, and there, by looking at the records . . . one sees who the people are that made this invention. (But) in studying the newspapers that appear—later, they want to give the impression that everything is the opposite. . . . It's a pain. I'm always irritated because it very well seems to me that people have the politics that they want, at the moment they want it. What seems horrible to me is the lack of justice, the lack of truth. I mean, to denigrate what went before is a very Spanish invention. . . . One must bury what was before, and not recognize the good that was done. It's something incredible, frightful . . . this lack of justice and of recognition of the values that there were.[56]

Tomasa put it simply in terms of winners and losers.

> They are thinking about the war over-and-over, wishing to justify the unjustifiable. I mean the losers want to justify themselves, and that what was really a defeat appears to be a victory. And besides, in the international world, it is the only time that the Communist party—directed by the Soviet Union, of course, helped, maintained and all—was smashed, almost without outside help.[57]

Behind these contending versions of the historical role of the *Sección Femenina* one discerns the bedrock of opposing political ideologies.

And at one level, a political explanation answers our inquiry. As historians we have become increasingly aware that dominion over history is the privilege of hegemonic political power; after the death of Franco and the institutionalization of democracy in Spain, that hegemonic power belonged to the left. Thus for the *Sección Femenina* the tables were turned: former losers were now winners. Former winners were now losers, and their story rested in the hands of their political enemies. But this explanation in terms of power succession is ultimately not completely satisfying, for it does not address the issue of mutual incomprehension.

We turn to women's history and feminist theory for further insights into this case of contested identity. The valuation of agency and the limits placed on its pursuit in historical inquiry are fundamental to each interpretation of the past. Mary Nash has noted that when we look for women as historical agents, we not only demonstrate our system of values but we change the content of history itself.[58] At the heart of the contested identity of the *Sección Femenina* remains the question of agency. Self-identified as progressive reformers, defiant of what they saw and experienced as a conservative norm, and as women who had realized themselves through idealism and fulfilling work, the women of the *Sección Femenina* perceive themselves as having manifested historical agency. Their antagonists deny them that agency. As we saw above, their critics have rebutted their proclaimed progressivism saying that "in reality," what they did was other. And again, through such terminology as "pseudo-compensatory instruments . . . and false participation" their interlocutors have disputed both the authenticity of the program and the self-perceptions of the *Sección Femenina.*

In other words, their critics have not been able to reconcile historical agency with a willing subscription to traditionalist and fascist values.[59] From the perspective of the left, because they subscribed to a traditional concept of women and a politics that rejected individualism, competition, and the whole Enlightenment project, the women of the *Sección Femenina* could not have played the roles they claim. Judged by the standards of Simone de Beauvoir, because they did not have "life projects of their own, because their lives have been lived as a function of male lives, . . . and because they always acted in the service of the patriarchy . . . (they) were not agents of history."[60]

This analysis demonstrates the construction or confirmation of identity through opposition and contestation. In the case of the *Sección Femenina*, we find self-affirmation in opposition to leftist models and to challenges from the left. On the other hand, the denigrators of the *Sección Femenina* have constructed their own identity in opposition to the Falangist model that they have rejected, overcome, and discredited. This case study of contested identity clearly reflects the much wider historical bifurcation of Spanish identity: revolutionary Spain locked in combat with traditional Spain. The conflict demonstrates how this deeply rooted habit of thinking in terms of oppositions—of political right and political left—has permeated Spanish culture. However, the women of the Falange are not just traditional women: habitual categories of historical analysis do not accommodate adequately the lived experience of the women of the *Sección Femenina*. There is no legitimate category that represents their lives. Thus, since they claim an agency which lacks theoretical reality in the currently dominant world view, they forfeit credence. Consequently, the incursion of a binary mode of thinking reinforces experience—the residue of enmity from the Civil War—and prevents dissident voices from being heard.

Here again we can garner insight from recent comparative work in women's history and feminist theory. In "Defining Feminism," Karen Offen has recently distinguished two strains of European feminism: individualist and relational. Relational feminism is "gender-based but egalitarian" and posits a companionate, non-hierarchical, male-female couple as the basic unit. Individualist feminism is closely associated with the Anglo-Saxon tradition and takes the individual of either sex or gender as the basic unit. These feminisms are historically rooted. The confusion within present day French feminism, according to Offen, is symptomatic of the failure among French feminists to recognize their own relational predecessors.[61]

> What feminists today must do—and are now beginning to do—is to reappropriate the relational path of our intellectual heritage, which we now know to be grounded in the very heart of Western thought on "the woman question": to reclaim the power of difference, of womanliness as women define it; to reclaim its concern for broad social goals; and to reweave it once again with the appeal to the principle of human freedom that underlies the individualist tradition. We must collapse the dichotomy that has placed these two traditions at odds historically and chart a new political course.[62]

This insight from French women's history encourages a reappraisal of the validity of the relational attitude towards women's roles in Spanish women's history. We are seeking to understand better the powerful residue of historical experience that shaped two opposing traditions: each encapsulating fundamental beliefs about woman's nature, and the nature of social and political life. Beyond superficial political loyalties, the discussions we have heard reflect the clash of opposing world views, world views which embody officially prescribed roles for women. Women on both sides of this divide have not recognized that there is in fact shared ground: a concern for Spain and for Spanish women, and a willingness to sacrifice themselves for these concerns. Divided by political categories, they have not found a common language, and each cannot understand the language of the other.

In fact, recent work by historians has disclosed evidence indicating more shared experiences among Spanish women than previously assumed. It is clear from the work of Temma Kaplan, Carmen Alcalde, and others that in fact gender relations—life as lived—on one side or the other of the Civil War lines resembled each other more than they differed. Despite rhetoric to the contrary, both men and women of the left at that time appeared to share underlying cultural assumptions about the traditional role of women.[63] Carmen Alcalde has underscored this point in her work on women in the Civil War, demonstrating that neither Communist nor Socialist men supported non-traditional roles for women. According to Alcalde, Republican women of all stripes shared with women of the right and with Catholicism a traditional attitude toward the proper role of women.[64] Temma Kaplan's study of the group *Mujeres Libres* (Free Women) confirmed that even this Anarchist organization dedicated to women's advancement "did not challenge the idea of masculine supremacy and authority in all fields."[65] Further, Kaplan has identified what she termed "female consciousness" among Spanish working women: this is the consciousness of women who accept the division of labor by sex, women's responsibility for preserving life, and also the rights that this obligation entails. In her view, this consciousness spans political identity, motivating women on the right and on the left.

Such evidence has encouraged these historians to look for possible convergences that belie categorical labels. In Kaplan's view, these shared qualities or experiences among women have opened the door to "incorporating female consciousness into feminist arguments . . . ."[66] And Mónica Threlfall has proposed a pattern in which "Catholic groups for women may serve as stepping stones to feminist consciousness."[67]

These indications of common ground in views of gender roles between feminists on the left and rightist women rooted in traditional Catholic and Falangist mores bear witness to the necessity for transcending conventional categories. In the Spanish case, in particular, they demand that automatic associations framed in political terms be put aside.

One Spanish historian has described the writing of Spanish women's history as carrying a "political and democratic baggage understandable only in function of its history."[68] And our analysis of the debate over motivations, over the actual historical role of the *Sección Femenina*, has revealed conspicuous political divisions between women on the right and women on the left that are encumbered with ideological and philosophical significance. These formulations have produced different, and mutually incompatible, vocabularies and interpretations of history; they have resulted in two antagonistic groups of Spanish women locked into mutually exclusive discourses. Perhaps the political divisions in the Spanish case are decisive in obscuring the common ground of "female consciousness." However, the Manichean terms bequeathed by the past two hundred years of Spanish history, which culminated in the Civil War, are in fact themselves a political and historical construct. In order to understand and ultimately to transcend these determining categories of thought, we need to be specific. We must look to the lived experience of all Spanish women: hear their voices, listen to their stories and heed their claims of identity. The ambiguous case of the *Sección Femenina* gives us the opportunity to do just that, and in the doing, to rethink the categories by which we have understood modern Spanish history.

Notes

1. Special thanks go to Reva Greenburg and Kit Hinsley for their careful readings of this article and for their suggestions for its development. Much of the research for this article was carried out with the support of the Organized Research Council, under the direction of Henry O. Hooper, at Northern Arizona University. I am grateful for their support. Joe Boles, as Director of Women's Studies at N.A.U., deserves recognition for his unfailing support of this and similar projects.

2. Ida Blom, "Global Women's History: Organizing Principles and Cross-Cultural Understandings," in Karen Offen, Ruth Roach Pierson and Jane Rendall, eds., *Writing Women's History: International Perspectives* (Bloomington, IN: Indiana University Press, 1991), pp. 135–149. Ida Blom presided over the IFRWH and its conference at Bellagio, Italy in July 1989 at which most of the papers in this anthology were presented.

3. Ida Blom, "Global Women's History," p. 140.

4. The Falange Española was founded in Madrid in 1933; in 1934 it fused with another small fascist group, the Juntas Ofensivas Nacionalistas, producing the Falange Española de las JONS. With the onset of civil war in July and the death of José Antonio in November of 1936, General Franco merged the Falange and the Carlist Traditionalists into the Falange Española and Tradicionalista (FET), a state party which reflected an amalgamation of Franco's nationalist forces. In 1945, as a response to shifting world events, the regime recast the FET as the Movimiento (National Movement) and rejected the fascist salute. Effectively, the regime co-opted the FET and subsequently deradicalized it. In 1958 the regime totally repudiated the Twenty-Seven Points of the Falange, completing its ideological defascistization. After the death of Franco and the accession of King Juan Carlos, the movement was officially dissolved in April 1977. Varieties of crypto-fascism and neo-fascism have appeared in Spain, but without significant numbers or strength.

5. The "*Movimiento*," or Movement, was the general designation for the amalgamated single party FET y de las JONS (Falange Española Tradicionalista y de las Juntas Ofensivas Sindicalistas) forged from his followers in 1937 by General Franco. The Movement was meant to replace the democratic system of warring political parties

with a unified organization, dedicated only to the collective good of the nation. More concretely, it served as an organizational umbrella for the diverse Nationalist forces.

6. See Martha Ackelsberg, *Free Women of Spain: Anarchism and the Struggle for the Emancipation of Women* (Bloomington, IN: Indiana University Press, 1991); Carmen Alcalde, *La mujer en la guerra civil española* (Madrid: Cambio 16, 1976); Mary Nash, *Mujeres Libres: España 1936–1939* (Barcelona: Fontamara, 1981) and *Defying Male Civilization: Women in the Spanish Civil War* (Denver, CO: Arden Press, 1995).

7. María Dolors Calvet i Puig, "Prólogo," in Giuliana de Febo, *Resistencia y movimiento de mujeres en España 1936–1976* (Barcelona: Icaria, 1979), p. 6.

8. In addition to scholarly recovery, there has been an outpouring of memoires of participants whose voices were silenced. See, for example, Tomasa Cuevas Gutiérrez, *Cárcel de mujeres (1939–1945)* 2 vols. (Barcelona: Sirocco Books, 1985) and *Mujeres de la Resistencia* (Barcelona: Sirocco, 1985); Giuliana Di Febo, *Resistencia y movimiento de mujeres en España 1936–1976* (Barcelona: Icaria, 1979); Nieves Castro Feito, *Una vida para un ideal: Recuerdos de una militante comunista* (Madrid: De la Torre, 1981); Mika Etchebehere, *Mi guerra de España* (Madrid: Plaza y Janés, 1976); Lidia Falcón O'Neill, *En el infierno: Ser mujer en las cárceles de España* (Barcelona: Ediciones Feministas, 1977); Juana López Manjon, *¿Y quién soy yo?: Memorias de la Guerra Civil en Ubeda* (Málaga, Spain: Torroy-Costa, 1986); Federica Montseny Mañé, *Cent dies de la vida de una dona* (Barcelona: Sagitario, 1977) and *Mis primeros cuarenta años* (Esplugas de Llobregat, Spain: Plaza y Janés, 1987); Dolores Ibarruri Gómez, *Memorias de Dolores Ibarruri, Pasionaria. 1939–1977* (Barcelona: Planeta, 1985).

9. For example, María Teresa Gallego Méndez's book, *Mujer, Falange y franquismo (Woman, Falange and Francoism)*, emphasized the formation of the *Sección Femenina* and its early years until 1945. María Inmaculada Pastor investigated a specific branch of their activity in *La educación femenina en la postguerra (1939–1945): El caso de Mallorca (Feminine Education in the Postwar [1939–1945]: The Case of Mallorca)* (Madrid: Ministerio de Cultura, Instituto de la Mujer, 1984). A recent work by Rosario Sánchez López, *Mujer española: Una sombra de destino en lo universal (Spanish Women: A Shadow of Destiny in the Universal)* (Murcia: Universidad de Murcia, 1990), gave an impressionistic portrait of the organization over the length of its existence.

10. Colectivo Feminista de Madrid, "El feminismo español en la década de los 70," *Tiempo de Historia* 3, no. 27 (February, 1977): 31.

11. Whether the Falange ever comprised a truly fascist party has been much debated. The official doctrine of the *Falange Española*, set out in the Twenty-Seven Points" of 1934, closely paralleled Italian fascism. Although Falangism exhibited generic fascist characteristics including hypernationalism, military appeal, an emphasis on youth, mass education, and a call for economic reform which underscored social justice, its religious conservatism distinguished the Falange from other fascist movements.

The Twenty-Fifth Point of Falangist doctrine officially affirmed Catholicism as the religiously and historically correct basis for Spain's fascist reconstruction. Additional confusion arises from the character of José Antonio, whom Stanley Payne characterized as "perhaps the most ambiguous of all European national fascist leaders" (he was "repelled by the brutality and violence" of fascism, and he dropped the term "fascist" by the end of 1934 and "totalitarian" by the end of 1935). Nevertheless, argued Payne, his humanistic qualities "do not necessarily contradict fascism." (Stanley Payne, *Fascism: Comparison and Definition.* (Madison, WI: University of Wisconsin Press, 1980), p. 150. Payne emphasized "[t]hat Falangism exhibited certain distinct characteristics of its own is undeniable, but these did not prevent it from sharing nearly all the general qualities and characteristics that would compose an inventory of generic fascism." (Payne, *Fascism*, p. 149). See also Stanley Payne, *Falange: A History of Spanish Fascism* (Stanford, CA: Stanford University Press, 1961).

12. Elena Posa, "Una educación especialmente femenina," *Cuadernos para el Pedagogía*, 3, pp. 31–32, *Supplemento* 6 (July 1977): 34.

13. Elena Posa, "Una educación especialmente femenina," p. 32.

14. Elena Posa, "Una educación especialmente femenina," p. 32. Emphasis added by author.

15. Elena Posa, "Una educación especialmente femenina," p. 34.

16. Giuliana di Febo, *Resistencia y movimiento de mujeres en España*, p. 146. All emphases added.

17. Lidia Falcón, "Spain: Women Are the Conscience of Our Country," in Robin Morgan, ed., *Sisterhood is Global*, (New York: Anchor Press/Doubleday, 1984), p. 627.

18. Elena Posa, "Una educación especialmente femenina," p. 34.

19. Rosario Sánchez López, *Mujer española*, p. 78.

20. Sánchez López, *Mujer española*, pp. 28–29.

21. The "Law of Political, Professional and Labor Rights for Women" was passed by the Cortes in 1961, promoted by Pilar Primo de Rivera as *Procuradora* (Representative) in the Cortes.

22. Sánchez López, *Mujer española*, p. 45.

23. Ibid., p. 87.

24. Ibid.

25. All the names used in this section for those interviewed by the author are pseudonyms, except for Pilar Primo de Rivera. Concha, Interview with author, Madrid, January 13, 1989.

26. Concha, Interview with author. Madrid, January 13, 1989.

27. Ibid.

28. Tomasa, Interview with author. Madrid, July 9, 1987.

29. Pilar Primo de Rivera, Interview with author. Madrid, January 9, 1989.

30. Lola, Interview with author. Madrid, June 19, 1989.

31. St. Teresa of Avila (1515–1582), spiritual reformer and founder of the Discalced Carmelite Order in Spain, was both mystic and active agent, saintly and practical. She and Isabel la Católica of Castile (1451–1504)—monarch, mother, and powerful religious leader, were chosen as patron saints by the *Sección Femenina*. See Giuliana Di Febo, *La santa de la raza: Un culto barroco en la España franquista (1937–1962)* (Barcelona: Icaria Editorial, 1987).

32. Tomasa, Interview with author. Madrid, July 9, 1987.

33. Ibid.

34. Carlist Traditionalism officially originated in 1833, and derived its name from Don Carlos, younger brother of King Ferdinand VII and unsuccessful rival of Ferdinand's daughter, Isabel II, for the Spanish throne. By World War I, Carlism had evolved into a party of the European Catholic Right, and proposed a traditionalist monarchy with paternalist and corporativist social ideals against the unrestrained liberalism, capitalism and materialist socialism of the modern world. In 1931-1932, Carlism was renamed the Traditionalist Communion and emerged as a significant force on the extreme right. Carlist paramilitary *Requetés* joined the nationalist forces. In April, 1937, Franco fused the Traditionalist Communion with the Falange, producing the *Falange Española Tradicionalista y de las JONS*, Spain's single party until 1975. See also no. 3 above.

35. Tomasa, Interview with author. Madrid, July 9, 1987.

36. Carmen, Interview with author. La Coruña, June, 1989.

37. Tomasa, Interview with author. Madrid, July 9, 1987.

38. Carmen, Interview with author. La Coruña, June, 1989.

39. Tomasa, Interview with author. Madrid, July 9, 1987.

40. Lula de Lara, as quoted in Sara Palacio, "El punto de vista de la *Sección Femenina*: 'La historia nos ha traicionado.' Entrevista con Lula de Lara," *Tiempo de Historia*, 7, no. 83 (Octubre, 1981): 20.

41. Pilar Primo de Rivera, Interview with author. *Varón* or "male": an ubiquitous designation in the list of requirements for job applicants, and for those wishing to enter *opposiciones,* or competitions for positions.

42. Lula de Lara, as quoted in Sara Palacio, "El punto de vista de la *Sección Femenina*," p. 20.

43 Tomasa, Interview with author. Madrid, July 9, 1987.

44. Ibid.

45. Ibid.

46. The *Frente de Juventudes*, or Youth Front, was the umbrella institution set up by the state in December, 1940, to oversee all juvenile organizations. The female division, separated from the male division from the beginning, came under the auspices of the *Sección Femenina*.

47. Concha, Interview with author. Madrid, January 13, 1989.

48. Ibid.

49. James Fentress and Chris Wickham, *Social Memory* (Oxford: Blackwell, 1992), pp. ix–x.

50. Tomasa, Interview with author. Madrid, July 9, 1987.

51. Concha, Interview with author. Madrid, January 13, 1989.

52. Margarita, Interview with author. Madrid, January 16, 1989.

53. Concha, Interview with author. Madrid, January 13, 1989.

54. Tomasa, Interview with author. Madrid, July 9, 1987.

55. Lola, Interview with author. Madrid, June 19, 1989.

56. Carmen, Interview with author. La Coruña, June, 1989.

57. Tomasa, Interview with author. Madrid, July 9, 1987.

58. Mary Nash, *Mujer y movimiento obrero en España, 1931–1939* (Barcelona: Fontamara, 1981), p. 11.

59. For works that explore the relations among gender or sexual politics, traditional or fascist values, and issues of agency, see: Claudia Koonz, *Mothers in the Fatherland* (New York: St. Martin's Press, 1987); Renate Bridenthal, Atina Grossmann and Marion Kaplan, eds., *When Biology Became Destiny: Women in Weimar and Nazi Germany.* (New York: Monthly Review Press, 1984); Linda Mizejewski, *Divine Decadence: Fascism, Female Spectacle, and the Makings of Sally Bowles* (Princeton, NJ: Princeton University Press, 1992); Mary Louise Roberts, *Civilization without Sexes: Reconstructing Gender in Postwar France, 1917–1927* (Chicago, IL: University of Chicago Press, 1994); Victoria De Grazia, *How Fascism Ruled Women: Italy, 1922–1945* (Berkeley, CA: University of California Press, 1992); Alison Light, *Forever England: Femininity, Literature and Conservatism between the Wars* (New York: Routledge, 1991).

60. Quoted in Mary Nash, *Mujer y movimiento obrero en España*, p. 11.

61. Karen Offen, "Defining Feminism: A Comparative Historical Approach," *Signs* 14, no. 1 (1988): 145, 147–148.

62. Ibid., p. 157.

63. For a discussion of dominant gender discourse, see Mary Nash's chapter in this volume.

64. Carmen Alcalde, *La mujer en la guerra civil*, pp. 125–126, 131, 135–136, 143–145.

65. Temma Kaplan, "Spanish Anarchism and Women's Liberation," *Journal of Contemporary History* 6, no. 2 (1971): 109.

66. Temma Kaplan, "Female Consciousness and Collective Action: The Case of Barcelona, 1910–1918," *Signs* 7 (Spring 1982): 566.

67. Mónica Threlfall, "The Women's Movement in Spain," *New Left Review*, 151 (May–June, 1985): 54.

68. Maria Dolors Calvet i Puig, "Prólogo," p. 6.

General Conclusion

At first glance, female identity in modern Spanish history seems to fall neatly into the vague but evocative category of "traditional." When placed in the context of its more rapidly changing and "modernizing" northern neighbors, Spain has often been viewed as a more traditional society resistant to change. In gender terms, this label signifies a world defined by separate spheres, a world in which female identity is equated with motherhood, marriage, and home; and male identity is linked to citizenship, work, and politics. The chapters in this volume provide abundant evidence as to the strength and persistence of these traditional gender roles, and they illustrate how difficult it was for women to openly disregard them. However, the more important contribution of this volume has been to probe beneath the surface of the traditional image and expose the greater complexity of women's roles and identities, even within a framework that apparently offered little room for their empowerment. This complexity reveals that female identity was not a static given but an arena of active construction and contestation where women themselves played a major role. It also reveals the limitations of a whole set of binary categories from traditional/modern to work/home to public/private.

Nevertheless, as many of the chapters point out, powerful cultural and political forces attempted to solidify such categories. Thus, Mary Nash introduces the dominant framework of traditional female identity as articulated in the late nineteenth and early twentieth century, a framework which forms the backdrop for nearly all the other articles, regardless of the time period or the political situation. In turn, Puertolas, Morcillo, and Escudero demonstrate the special energy devoted to maintaining and glorifying the traditional woman under the conservative dictatorship of Francisco Franco. As Morcillo points out, fascist and semi-fascist dictatorships viewed the restoration of traditional femininity as central to their revolutionary projects, and they openly pursued this goal through a variety of media, cultural practices, and institutions. What made Spain unusual in the western European context (with the exception of Portugal) was the longevity of the regime, which prevented significant public contestation of gender roles from the 1940s until the mid 1970s.

In contrast to dictatorships, liberal regimes rarely espoused an official position on such issues, but the more diffuse underlying message was similar. As White points out, even during the great liberal revolution of 1868–1874, traditional gender roles were used metaphorically to legitimize the new regime. Thus, Spain's dramatic political mutations over the course of the last two centuries did not necessarily spark corresponding changes in the "constellation of gender." Puertolas makes this point as well, when she demonstrates the gap between static festival roles and the broad political as well as social and economic changes that Spain experienced by the late 1970s.

Thus, even in the liberal political realm, the image of the traditional woman played a powerful role in defining political categories. White argues that this stereotype helped define liberal political opposition in 1868 to a queen who was dethroned as much because of her lack of feminine virtue as her incapacity to govern. The stereotype affected ordinary women as well, especially when the issue of female citizenship arose in the twentieth century. Alexander and Keene demonstrate how women were marginalized in the official political realm because the traditional woman was assumed to be incapable of upholding citizenship responsibilities. Keene reveals how reluctantly the idealistic liberals of the Second Republic granted women the vote, while Alexander shows how this grudging act did little to change perceptions of women's political abilities. The fact that women's voting behavior has been constantly demeaned allowed the old stereotypes to survive even after equal citizenship had been legally established. As a result of such marginalization, women who wanted to voice political demands were often forced to find other avenues of expression. While Kaplan, Tone, Radcliff, and Enders emphasize the way women were empowered through these alternative avenues, it is also important to acknowledge the constraints that limited their other political options.

Such constraints also affected women's relationship to the category of work. Rees, O'Connor, and Capel show how traditional gender roles shaped the perception and reality of women's work in the decades before the Civil War. Both Rees and O'Connor illustrate how women's work was rendered invisible, either through census categories or dismissive media coverage, while Capel traces the structure of the sexual division of labor in one industry. In a more contemporary study, Kelley demonstrates how community expectations about women's work provided the setting for women's choices. All of the authors make it clear, however, that traditional gender roles formed the context out of which women's work identities evolved.

While the chapters abound with examples of the constraints on women's lives, there are few women in these pages who openly rebelled against them and rejected the traditional role model. Puertolas highlights a small feminist protest against the male-dominated San Fermín festival, but it was so unprecedented that it bewildered most of the city's residents—male and female—with its strident demands. Likewise, Nash pinpoints a handful of women who advocated women's control over reproduction and injected a female perspective in a discourse largely defined by men and male concerns. Most dramatically, the three extraordinary female deputies featured in Keene's chapter broke the gender barrier of parliamentary politics even before women were granted full citizenship. Significantly, Keene emphasizes that the special circumstances that allowed these women access to the higher echelons of politics—especially their education and their connections—excluded the vast majority of women. These few voices of open rebellion stand out in dramatic contrast to the small and relatively timid feminist movement of the time and underscores their exceptional status.

The evidence thus far presented elaborates a dichotomous world filled with a mass of traditional women who seemed to live comfortably imprisoned within the domestic realm and a handful of "heroines" who openly rejected this role. Such a picture fits neatly into the binary framework of the "two Spains," traditional and modern, as well as the private/public split within the old separate spheres model. But what we have tried to argue throughout is that such dichotomies flatten the contours of women's lives and distort the more fluid reality in which identities were formed. While most women did not directly flout the reigning gender ideology, neither did they embody a monolithic and unchanging traditional woman, who rarely left the house, maintained complete submission to male authority, and left work and politics to her husband. Instead, many women incorporated autonomy, work, politics, and agency into their traditional identities as mothers and wives. In other words, women did not have to reject the framework of traditional gender roles in order to step beyond its apparent boundaries. It is this paradox that leads us to the contestation of categories and the rethinking of such oppositions as traditional and modern.

For example, several of the authors have demonstrated that a traditional sense of female identity could provide the impetus for politicization. Thus, Kaplan, Tone, Radcliff, and Enders argue that the stereotype of the traditional woman provided special avenues of political action for women willing to work within the traditional role rather than reject it. Tone, Radcliff, and Kaplan illustrate how women turned traditional expectations to their political advantage, whether it was in fighting for social justice, resisting the French invasion, or demanding lower food prices. As Kaplan emphasizes, it was often precisely because the women claimed to be non-political that their demands were so effective. Even more explicitly, Enders focuses on a group of conservative women who carved out a political identity during the Franco regime based on what we might term their "fascist renovation" of separate spheres. As Radcliff argues, however, even though these women (and the male authorities) often perceived their actions as fitting into a traditional framework, we as historians cannot take such frameworks at face value. As we try to understand their actions, we must question the prevailing definitions of *traditional* and *politics* and also question the framework that fixes them as dichotomous and mutually exclusive categories.

The chapters about women and work pose a similar challenge to the juxtaposition between traditional women and *work.* Kelley, Capel, and O'Connor demonstrate how different groups of women were able to develop strong work-based identities without transgressing the bounds of accepted female behavior. From the standpoint of anthropological theory, Kelley criticizes scholars for generally ignoring the role of work in female identity formation in traditional societies. Following the Mediterranean paradigm of honor and shame, anthropologists have often assumed that women derived their status and identity from sexual purity, but Kelley argues that, for the women in her study, their work in maintaining their households was central to their own sense of identity and their status in the community. Rees is not able to make the leap from work activity to women's sense of identity, because of the nature and limitations of his sources, but he convincingly demonstrates that these rural women are also central to the economic well-being of their households. Furthermore, he argues that it is precisely the kind of work that women engaged in that distinguished the different classes of rural women.

The strong work identity of another group of women, the cigarette makers, emerges clearly from O'Connor's and Capel's chapters. Although the media sought to portray the striking *cigarreras* as folkloric Carmen figures, another version of their identity is visible between the lines of newspaper reports. Through a combination of interview snippets, written demands, and public demonstrations, O'Connor reveals a group of women who pursued collective worker demands and who used their worker identity to make other public statements. In more general terms, Capel argues that such collective action was not an isolated incident. Through a strong national labor union and a high level of worker consciousness, the cigarette makers were able to negotiate one of the best benefit packages available to female workers. On the other hand, the cigarette makers never really threatened basic gender roles—they were loved for their public acts of motherly charity; they engaged in innocent flirtation with male authorities; and they allowed men to run their union federation. Thus, despite their unique public work identity, the cigarette makers, like most Spanish women, managed to accommodate work into an essentially traditional gender framework.

The point in all of these case studies is not to reinforce our sense of Spain's traditional gender system, but to reveal how much more flexible this system was in practice, and in so doing, to call into question the categories we use to understand women's experiences. At this point, we would like to return to our call in the introduction for a more open, unbounded reading of female identity formation that makes room for such complexities. Rather than label Spain as a traditional gender society, in contrast to its more modernized western European neighbors, we prefer to emphasize European similarities, while at the same time concentrating more on the specificities of each national case study. By focusing on both specific differences and similarities, we can break down the apparent clarity of outmoded models and be open to emergent interpretive frameworks. The result of such a resituating of Spain in the European context would contribute not only to breaking down the old Spanish model of difference, but also to challenging the monolithic nature of a narrowly-conceived European model.

This project obviously requires a new language, a vocabulary that can simultaneously incorporate differences and similarities into a more fluid framework. The chapters in this volume, while they point to ways of reconceptualizing female identity, are still struggling with avenues of expression, with navigating the uncertain waters of a post-paradigm world. These struggles situate the volume directly in the midst of current debates within feminist theory and women's history. One of the vocabularies that feminist theorists have adapted to address the new ambiguities is that of poststructuralism and the broader postmodern perspective. From this position, feminist theorists have argued that it is crucial to maintain the category *women* as an "open site of potential contest"[1] rather than an ontological entity. Such openness problematizes our understanding of subjectivity, which becomes "at once multileveled, containing multiple aspects, and having horizons or barriers to self-understanding, that work at each level."[2] At the heart of the discussion on the possibility and advisability of categorizing women lies the equality/difference debate: is the promise of liberation for women to be found in insisting on their equality with men or in emphasizing their differences from men? And in either case, how to confront the reality of differences among women? As Gisela Bock and Susan James point out, "Some feminists regard female difference as a starting point and equality a goal . . . others . . . treat equality as a means to the goal of female difference."[3]

The focus on deconstruction of categories, on the celebration of difference, has provoked some misgivings among historians who wonder whether postmodern perspectives can and do undercut the goals of feminist scholarship. Some historians have expressed concerns that "postmodern discourse may unintentionally privilege elites," and that a "focus on gender, rather than recovery, may be counterproductive in areas where women's history has yet to establish a substantial scholarship."[4] That is, there is still a need to reconstruct women as historical objects, not deconstruct them; a need to establish equality, not difference. "The desire to recover women's history, like the deconstruction of the meaning of 'difference,' is both intellectual and political" and many are concerned with finding the "appropriate relationship between feminist history and political activism."[5] Does a conceptual framework that validates diversity necessarily undercut the goals of political solidarity and women's collective agency?

In answer to these fears, we are inspired by the belief that insights from both sides of the feminist divide will benefit the work of women's historians. We agree with Nancy Fraser that "as we take up different tasks in different contexts, we need to be able to take up and discard different theoretical tools."[6] And we seek a reciprocal relationship in which "the discourse theory of knowledge advanced by postmodernism can serve as a means of correcting some of the essentialist tendencies in contemporary feminism," and that "feminists can use the discourse theory of postmodernism to increase our understanding of the constitution of gender in various societies."[7] At the same time, we agree with Ruth Rendall that "the process . . . of making visible is still of vital political importance in all attempts to challenge a masculine establishment."[8] In simple terms, we welcome the mingling of languages and multiplying of insights.

Much of the attention in the debate among feminist theorists and women's historians is focused on the nature of identities,[9] which has been the core theme of this volume. The chapters here have demonstrated that identity formation is not a fixed, permanent event; identities evolve through situations and exigencies; identities metamorphose, adding and subtracting facets as conditions unfold and disintegrate. This malleable, changeable quality of identities is an essential element in our understanding of another analytical tool: our concept of *agency.* As Judith Butler suggests, "Paradoxically, it may be by releasing the category of women from a fixed referent that something like 'agency' becomes possible."[10] Significantly, the historicization of women may be one of the best ways to achieve this goal. Feminist scholars across the disciplines acknowledge that we must inquire into specific historical contexts to uncover the substance and explain the "possibility of agency." Thus the chapters in this volume all pursue the concrete conditions under which agency becomes possible for a diverse cross-section of Spanish women over the last 200 years. In this way, agency becomes the common thread that emerges out of diversity.

We have been particularly concerned to convey the diversity of Spanish women and their experiences. In fact, we call for more work to be done on the importance of other key variables in identity formation, such as class, regional/ethnic individuality, religious, or political affiliations, etc. By presenting these studies as an open range of possibilities for identity formation and testing in the past, we encourage women—despite their differences—to discover possibilities in the world of pragmatic action, or create the "conceptual space for thinking of the possibility of agency."[11] By giving voice to many different kinds of women in many different kinds of experiences, we join that movement celebrating diversity, which is vital to both old and new democracies and particularly crucial where political and ideological divisions still run deep. Ironically, the celebration of diversity may be the best antidote for both the ideological divisions of the past and the numbing homogeneity of the present consensus.

Our present day historical and theoretical concerns are shared, we know, by many women in Spain. During the recent period of socialist governments

(1982–1996), the Women's Institute (Instituto de la Mujer) was established to further the interests of women. In its Second Plan, the Institute emphasized the "need to recognize differences and combat forms of social exclusion and marginalization."[12] To the coordinator of Madrid's women's groups, "the protagonists of 1990's feminism are the heterogeneous groups who are rejecting old oppositional activism in favor of 'a fundamental struggle . . . against stereotypical and homogenizing notions'."[13] Yet critics of the Institute discount this rhetoric. They claim that the feminist, bureaucratic state institution has failed to eradicate the "hegemonic masculine model," and that its "discourse of equality" has worked to obscure the "discourse of difference."[14] As in the more formal theoretical realm, it has proved difficult to transcend the polarities of the difference/equality contradiction, but it is important that the struggle continue.

Our work is intended to be a contribution to building a new society in which all voices may be heard. Women's history is a vehicle for the recovery of the lost voices of women—excluded from the historical narrative until so very recently—but it can also serve as a model for an inclusive history and politics. It is to this project that we dedicate this anthology, with the hope that it will spark a new dialogue about women and gender, both within Spain and across national borders.

Notes

1. Linda Nicholson, "Introduction," to Seyla Benhabib, Judith Butler, Drucilla Cornell and Nancy Fraser, *Feminist Contentions: A Philosophical Exchange* (New York: Routledge, 1995), p. 6.

2. Ann Ferguson, "Can I Choose Who I Am? And How Would That Empower Me? Gender, Race, Identities and the Self," in Ann Garry and Marilyn Pearsall, eds., *Women, Knowledge, and Reality: Explorations in Feminist Philosophy* 2d ed. (New York: Routledge, 1996), p. 112.

3. Gisela Bock and Susan James, eds., *Beyond Equality and Difference: Citizenship, Feminist Politics, Female Subjectivity* (New York: Routledge, 1992), pp. 4–5. For more on the equality/difference debate, see Marianne Hirsch and Evelyn Fox Keller, eds., *Conflicts in Feminism* N.Y.: Routledge, 1990); Ann Snitow, "A Gender Diary, "in Joan Scott, ed. *Feminism and History* (Oxford: Oxford University Press, 1996); Alessandra Tanesini, "Whose Language?" in Garry and Pearsall, eds., *Women, Knowledge and Reality*; and Joan W. Scott, "Deconstructing Equality vs. Difference: Or The Uses of Post-Structuralist Theory for Feminism," in *Feminist Studies* 14, no. 1 (Spring, 1988).

4. Ruth Rendall, as quoted in Rebecca Rogers, "Crossing Boundaries: Writing Women's History Internationally," review of, *Writing Women's History: International*

Perspectives, ed. Offen, Pierson and Rendall (Bloomington: Indiana University Press, 1991), in *Journal of Women's History* 5, no. 1 (Spring, 1991): 139. See also Elizabeth Fox-Genovese, *Feminism without Illusions: A Critique of Individualism* (Chapel Hill: The University of North Carolina Press, 1991), especially chap. 6, "The Struggle for a Feminist History."

5. Rebecca Rogers, "Crossing Boundaries," pp. 138, 141.

6. Nancy Fraser, "Pragmatism, Feminism, and the Linguistic Turn," in Benhabib, Butler, Cornell and Fraser, *Feminist Contentions*, p. 167.

7. "This theory of discourses and their mutability provides an accurate understanding of the task of feminism. Feminists have attempted to fashion new discourses about the feminine, discourses that resist the hegemony of male-domination, that utilize the contradictions in these hegemonic discourses in order to effect their transformation. In this task the perspective of postmodernism is a help rather than a hindrance. Both postmodernism and feminism are counter discourses that challenge the modem episteme at its roots. This fundamental commonality suggests that an alliance between these two movements will further the aims of both." Susan J. Hekman, *Gender and Knowledge: Elements of a Postmodern Feminism* (Boston: Northeastern University Press, 1990), pp. 189–190.

8. Ruth Rendall as quoted in Rebecca Rogers, "Crossing Boundaries," p. 139.

9. For further reading on identity issues, see Joan Wallach Scott, ed., *Feminism & History*; John Rajchman, *The Identity in Question* (N.Y.: Routledge, 1995); Bock and James, eds., *Beyond Equality and Difference*; and William E. Connolly, *Identity/Difference: Democratic Negotiations of Political Paradox* (Ithaca, NY: Cornell University Press, 1991).

10. Judith Butler, "Contingent Foundations: Feminism and the Question of 'Postmodernism'," in Benhabib, Butler, Cornell and Fraser, *Feminist Contentions*, p. 50.

11. Seyla Benhabib, "Subjectivity, Historiography, and Politics: Reflections on the 'Feminism/Postmodernism Exchange'," in Benhabib, Butler, Cornell and Fraser, *Feminist Contentions*, p. 111.

12. Anny Brooksbank Jones, "Open Forum: Spain's Institute for Women," in *The European Journal of Women's Studies*, 2 (1995): 266–267.

13. As quoted in Brooksbank Jones, "Open Forurn," p. 266.

14. Brooksbank Jones, p. 265.

Bibliography

The following bibliography is an extensive compilation of books and articles on all aspects of women in modern Spanish history. It is intended as a broad (though not exhaustive) survey of the field, as well as a point of departure for future research.

Bibliographies/General Histories

Alba, Victor. *Historia social de la mujer.* Barcelona: Plaza & Janés, 1974.

Aguado, A.M., Rosa María Capel Martínez, et al. *Textos para la historia de las mujeres en España.* Madrid: Cátedra, 1994.

Asociación de Librerías de Mujeres. *Boletín bibliográfico feminista 1990.* Madrid: Asociación de Librerías de Mujeres, 1990.

Capel Martínez, Rosa María. *El trabajo y la educación de la mujer en España (1900–1930).* Madrid: Instituto de la Mujer, 1986.

Capel Martínez, Rosa María, ed. *Mujer y sociedad en España, 1700–1975.* Madrid: Ministerio de Cultura, Instituto de la Mujer, 1986.

Díaz Sánchez, Pilar, and Pilar Domínguez Prats. "Las mujeres en la historia de España: Siglos XVII–XX." *Bibliografía comentada.* Madrid: Instituto de la Mujer, 1988.

Durán, María Angeles. *La investigación sobre la mujer en la universidad española contemporánea: Para un catálogo de tesis y memorias de licenciatura sobre la mujer.* Madrid: Ministerio de Cultura, Dirección General de Juventud y Promoción Socio-Cultural, 1982.

Folguera Crespo, Pilar, ed. *El feminismo en España: Dos siglos de historia.* Madrid: Editorial Pablo Iglesias, 1988.

Garrido, Elisa, Pilar Folguera, Margarita Ortega, and Cristina Segura. *Historia de las mujeres en España.* Madrid: Editorial Síntesis, 1997.

Gonzalez, Anabel, A. Lopez, A. Mendoza, and L. Ureña. *Los orígenes del feminismo en España.* Madrid: Zero-ZYX, 1980.

Iglesias de Ussel, Julio. *Elementos para el estudio de la mujer en la sociedad española: Análisis bibliográfico, 1939–1980.* Madrid: Instituto Universitario de Estudios de la Mujer, Universidad Autónoma de Madrid, 1982.

Instituto de la Mujer. *La mujer en la historia de España: Cuadernos bibliográficos.* 2 vols. Madrid: Ministerio de Cultura, 1988.

La femme dans la pensée espagnole: Ouvrage collectif. Paris: Editions du CNRS, 1984.

Levine, Linda G. *Spanish Women Writers: A Bio-Bibliographical Source Book.* Westport, CT: Greenwood Press, 1993.

Maquieira d'Angelo, Virginia, ed. *Mujeres y hombres en la formación del pensamiento occidental.* 2 vols. Madrid: Universidad Autónoma de Madrid, 1989.

Nash, Mary. Dos décadas de historia de las mujeres en España: Una reconsideración." *Historia Social* 9 (Winter 1991).

———. "Two Decades of Women's History in Spain: A Reappraisal." *Writing Women's History: International Perspectives.* Edited by Karen Offen, Ruth Roach Pierson, and Jane Rendall, 381–415. Bloomington, IN: University of Indiana Press, 1991.

Olmeda Gómez, Carlos. *La mujer en la bibliografía española 1984–1988. Cuadernos Bibliográficos,* no. 2. Madrid: Ministerio de Asuntos Sociales. Instituto de la Mujer, 1989.

Scanlon, Geraldine M. *La polémica feminista en la España contemporánea (1868–1974).* Madrid: Siglo Veintiuno, 1976.

Sebastià i Salat, Montserrat. *Thesaurus d'història social de la dona.* Barcelona: Generalitat de Catalunya. Departament de la Presidència. Comissió Interdepartamental de Promoció de la Dona, 1988.

Voltes, María José and Pedro Voltes. *Las mujeres en la historia de España.* Barcelona: Planeta, 1986.

Autobiographies and Memoirs.

Berenguer, Sara. *Entre el sol y la tormenta: Treinta y dos meses de guerra (1936–1939).* Barcelona: Seuba EdicioneS, 1988.

Buechler, Hans C., and Judith-Maria Buechler. *Carmen: The Autobiography of a Spanish Galician Woman.* Rochester, VT: Schenkman Books, 1981.

Campoamor, Clara. *Mi pecado mortal: El voto femenino y yo.* Barcelona: Edicions de les Dones, 1981.

———. *La révolution espagnole vue par une républicaine.* Paris: Plon, 1937.

Castro, Nieves. *Una vida para un ideal: Recuerdos de una militante comunista.* Madrid: Ediciones de la Torre, 1981.

Catalá, Neus. *De la resistencia y la deportación: 50 testimonios de mujeres españolas.* Barcelona: ISCO, 1984.

Cuevas Gutiérrez, Tomasa. *Carcel de mujeres (1939–1945).* Barcelona: Sirocco Books, 1985.

De la Mora, Constancia. *In Place of Splendor: The Autobiography of a Spanish Woman.* New York: Harcourt, Brace, 1939.

Doña Jiménez, Juana. *Desde la noche y la niebla: Mujeres en las cárceles franquistas.* 2d ed. Madrid: Ediciones de la Torre, 1978, 1993.

Etchebéhère, Mika. *Mi guerra de España.* Barcelona: Plaza & Janés, 1976.

Falcón, Lidia. *Los hijos de los vencidos, 1939–49.* Barcelona: Vindicación Feminista, 1989.

Feminismo ante el franquismo: Entrevistas con feministas de España. Miami: Ediciones Universal, 1980.

Formica, Mercedes. *Visto y vivido, 1931–1937: Pequeña historia de ayer.* Barcelona: Planeta, 1983.

García, Consuelo. *Las cárceles de Soledad Real: Una vida.* Madrid: Ediciones Alfaguara, S.A., 1983.

Herbst, Josephine. *The Starched Blue Sky of Spain.* New York: HarperCollins Publishers, 1991.

Ibárruri, Dolores. *They Shall not Pass: The Autobiography of La Pasionaria.* New York: International Publishers, 1966.

Kent, Victoria. *Quatro años de mi vida: 1940–1944.* Barcelona: Bruguera, 1978.

———. "Una experiencia penitenciaria." *Tiempo de Historia* 17 (April 1976): 4–10.

Montseny, Federica. *Mis primeros cuarenta años.* Barcelona: Plaza y Janés, 1987.

Navajo, Ymelda, ed. *Doce relatos de mujeres.* Madrid: Alianza Editorial, 1987.

Pàmies, Teresa. *Quan Érem capitans: Memòries d'aquella guerra.* Barcelona: Dopesa, 1974.

Primo de Rivera, Pilar. *Recuerdos de una vida.* Madrid: Ediciones DYRSA, 1983.

Wilkinson, Ellen. *What We Saw in Spain.* 1937.

Monographs and Articles

Ackelsberg, Martha A. *Free Women of Spain: Anarchism and the Struggle for the Emancipation of Women.* Bloomington, IN: Indiana University Press, 1991.

———. "Mujeres Libres: Individuality and Community, Organizing Women During the Spanish Civil War." *Radical America* 18, no. 4 (1984): 7–19.

———. "Separate and Equal? *Mujeres Libres* and Anarchist Strategy for Women's Emancipation." *Feminist Studies* 11, no. 1 (Spring 1985): 63–83.

Alarcón Caracuel, Manuel R. *El derecho de asociacíon obrera en España (1889–1900).* Madrid: Ediciones de la Revista de Trabajo, 1975.

Alcalde, Carmen. *Federica Montseny: Palabra en rojo y negro.* Barcelona: Editorial Argos Vergara, 1983.

———. *La mujer en la guerra civil española.* Madrid: Cambio 16, 1976.

———. *Mujeres en el franquismo: Exiliadas, nacionalistas y opositoras.* Barcelona: Flor del Viento Ediciones, 1996.

Alcobendas Tirado, María Pilar. *Datos sobre el trabajo de la mujer en España.* Madrid: Centro de Investigaciones Sociológicos, 1983.

Aldaraca, Bridget A. *El Angel del Hogar: Galdós and the Ideology of Domesticity in Spain.* Chapel Hill: University of North Carolina Press, 1991.

Aldecoa, Josefina. *Historia de una maestra.* Barcelona: Anagrama, 1990.

Alted Vigil, Alicia. "La mujer en las coordenadas educativas del régimen franquista." In *Ordenamiento jurídico y realidad social de las mujeres, siglos XII a XX*, ed. Carmen María García-Nieto Paris, pp. 425–437. Madrid: Seminario de Estudios de la Mujer. Universidad Autónoma de Madrid, 1986.

Amador, Pilar. "Pequeñas reglas de convivencia social: Una aportación al estudio de la mujer durante el régimen de Franco." In *Mujeres y hombres en la formación del pensamiento occidental*, ed. Virginia Maquieira d'Angelo, vol. 2, pp. 367–384. Actas de Las VII Jornadas de Investigación Interdisciplinaria. Madrid: Instituto Universitario de Estudios de la Mujer. Universidad Autónoma de Madrid, 1989.

Amorós, Celia. *Hacia una crítica de la razón patriarcal.* Barcelona: Anthropos, 1985.

Angeles Duran, María, ed. *La mujer en el mundo contemporáneo.* Madrid: Universidad Autónoma, 1981.

Arenas Posadas, C. "Entorno a la aristocracia obrera: El caso sevillano, 1898–1915." *Revista de Estudios de Historia Social* 3–4, no. 42–43 (1987).

Astelarra, Judith. "Feminism and Democratic Transition in Spain." *Canadian Woman Studies* (1985): 70–73.

Astelarra, Judith, ed. *Participación política de las mujeres.* Madrid: Siglo Veintiuno de España Editores, 1990.

Badillo Baena, Rosa M. *Feminismo y educación en Málaga: El pensamiento de Suceso Luengo de la Figuera (1892–1920).* Málaga: Universidad de Málaga, 1992.

Baena Luque, Eloisa. *Las cigarreras sevillanas: Un mito en declive (1887–1923).* Málaga: Universidad, Secretariado de Publicaciones e Intercambios Científicos, 1993.

Ballester, R. "Desigualdades sociales y salud en función de la ocupación y sexo: El ejemplo de la fábrica de tabacos de Alicante (1875–1936)." *Medicina social y clase obrera en España (siglos XIX–XX),* ed. Rafael Huerta and Ricardo Campos, vol. 1. Madrid: Fundación Investigaciones Marxistas, D. L., 1992.

Balcells, Albert. "La mujer obrera en la industria Catalana durante el primer cuarto del siglo XX." *Trabajo y organización obrera en la Cataluña contemporánea. 1900–1936.* Barcelona: Laia, 1974.

———. "Les dones obreres a Catalunya durant el primer quart del segle XX." *Perspectiva Social* 26 (1988): 65–74.

Balletbó, Anna. "La mujer bajo la dictadura." *Sistema* 49 (1982): 3–21.

Barrera Peña, María Luisa, and Ana López Peña. *Sociología de la mujer en la universidad: Análisis histórico-comparativo Galicia-España, 1900–1981.* Santiago de Compostela, Spain: Universidad de Santiago de Compostela, 1984.

Behar, Ruth. "The Struggle for the Church: Popular Anticlericalism and Religiosity in Post-Franco Spain." In *Religious Orthodoxy and Popular Faith in European Society*, ed. Ellen Badone. Princeton, NJ: Princeton University Press, 1990.

Beneria, Lourdes. *Mujer, economía y patriarcado durante la España franquista.* Barcelona: Anagrama, 1977.

Blasco Ruiz, Pilar. "Literatura popular en el Madrid decimónico." In *Madrid en la sociedad del siglo XIX*, ed. Luis E. Otero Carvajal and Angel Bahamonde, pp. 467–484. Madrid: Alfoz, 1986.

Boado, Emilia, "Las milicias del '36." *Historia Internacional* 1 (Abril, 1975).

Borderias-Gerena, Josette. "El discurso higiénico como conformador de la mentalidad femenina (1865–1915)." In *Mujeres y hombres en la formación del pensamiento occidental*, ed. Virginia Maquieira d'Angelo, vol. 2, pp. 299–309. Madrid: U.A.M., 1989.

Borreguero, Concha, Elena Catena, Consuelo de la Gandara, and María Salas, eds. *La mujer española de la tradición a la modernidad (1960–1980).* Madrid: Editorial Tecnos, 1986.

Botrel, Jean-François. "La littérature du peuple dans l'Espagne contemporaine." In *Clases populares, cultura, educación: Siglos XIX–XX. Coloquio hispano-francés*, ed. Jean-Louis Guereña and Alejandro Tiana, 277–299. Madrid: Casa de Velázquez, UNED, 1989.

Boyd, Carolyn P. "History in the Schools and the Problem of Spanish Identity." In *Iberian Identity: Essays on the Nature of Identity in Portugal and Spain*, ed. Richard Herr and John H. Polt. Berkeley, CA: Institute of International Studies. University of California Press, 1989.

Brandes, Stanley H. *Metaphors of Masculinity: Sex and Status in Andalusian Folklore.* Philadelphia, PA: University of Pennsylvania Press, 1980.

Bretz, Mary Lee. *Concha Espina.* Boston: Twayne, 1980.

Brooksbank Jones, Anny. "Feminisms in Contemporary Spain," *Journal of the Association for Contemporary Iberian Studies* (September 1994).

Brown, Judith L., ed. *Women Writers of Contemporary Spain: Exiles in the Homeland.* London: Associated University Presses, 1991.

Bussy Genevois, D. "El retorno de la hija pródiga: Mujeres entre lo público y lo privado (1931–1936)," in *Otras visiones de España*, ed. Pilar Folguera Crespo. Madrid: Editorial P. Iglesias, 1993.

Cabezali, E. et. al. "Myth as Suppression: Motherhood and the Historical Consciousness of the Women of Madrid, 1936–39," in *The Myths We Live By*, ed. Raphael Samuel and Paul Thompson (London: Routledge, 1990).

Cámara Villar, Gregorio. *Nacional-catolicismo y escuela. La socialización política del franquismo (1936–1951).* Madrid: Editorial Hesperia, 1984.

Capel Martínez, Rosa María. "Aspectos del mercado de trabajo femenino en España en el siglo XX." In *Estudios en homenaje al profesor Cepeda Adán*, pp. 333–357. Granada, Spain: Universidad de Granada. Servicio de Publicaciones, 1986.

———. "El modelo de mujer en España a comienzos del siglo XX." In *Mujeres y hombres en la formación del pensamiento occidental*, ed. Virginia Maquieira d'Angelo, vol. 1, pp. 311–320. Madrid: Universidad Autónoma de Madrid, 1989.

———. *El sufragio femenino en la Segunda República española.* Granada, Spain: Universidad de Granada, 1975.

———. "La mujer y el sindicalismo católico en la España de Alfonso XIII." *Revista de la Universidad Complutense.* Madrid, 1980.

Capmany, María Aurèlia. *Carta abierta al macho ibérico.* 2d. ed. Madrid: Ediciones 99, 1974.

———. *De profesión: Mujer.* Barcelona: Plaza & Janés, 1971.

———. *La dona a Catalunya: Consciència i situació.* Barcelona: Edicions 62, 1966.

Capmany, María Aurèlia, and Carmen Alcalde. *El feminismo ibérico.* Barcelona: Oikos-Tau, 1970.

Carrasco, Cristina. *El trabajo doméstico y la reproducción social.* Madrid: Ministerio de Asuntos Sociales, Instituto de la Mujer, 1991.

Carrasco, Raphael, ed. *La prostitución en Espagne de l'epoque des Rois Catholiques á la II République.* Paris: Annales Littéraires d l'Université de Besancón, 1995.

Carbonell, Montserrat, Mary Nash, and Milagros Rivera. "La storia delle donne in Spagna." *Quaderni Storici* 63 (December 1986): 996–1008.

Cases, José Ignacio. *La participación laboral de la mujer en España.* Madrid: Ministerio de Cultura, Instituto de la Mujer, 1987.

Cases, José Ignacio, Lourdes López Nieto, Miguel Angel Ruiz de Azúa, and Francisco J. Vanaclocha. *Mujer y . . . 15 de Junio.* Madrid: Dirección General de Desarrollo Comunitario, 1978.

Castellanos, Josefa. *Esclavitud y liberación de la mujer.* Bilbao, Spain: Zero, 1974.

Centro Feminista de Estudios y Documentación. *El trabajo de las mujeres a través de la historia.* Madrid: Centro Feminista de Estudios y Documentación, 1985.

Chown, Linda E. "American Critics and Spanish Women Novelists, 1942–1980." *Signs* 9, no. 1 (1983): 91–107.

Colectivo Feminista de Madrid. "El feminismo español en la década de los 70." *Tiempo de Historia* 3, no. 27 (February 1977): 29–37.

Collier, Jane F. "From Mary to Modern Woman: The Material Basis of Marianismo and Its Transformation in a Spanish Village." *American Ethnologist* 13 (1986): 100–107.

Comisión Nacional del Año Internacional de la Mujer. *Situación de la mujer en España.* Madrid: Almena, 1976.

Cortada Andreu, Esther. *Escuela mixta y coeducación en Catalunya durante la Segunda República.* Madrid: Instituto de la Mujer, 1988.

Cuevas Gutiérrez, Tomasa. *Mujeres de la resistencia.* Barcelona: Sirocco Books, 1986.

Davies, Catherine. "Feminist Writers in Spain Since 1900: From Political Strategy to Personal Inquiry." In *Textual Liberation: European Feminist Literature in the Twentieth Century*, ed. Helena Forsas-Scott. London: Routledge, 1991.

De León, Fray Luis. "La Perfecta Casada." In *Obras completas*, ed. Felix García, pp. 219–220. Madrid: Biblioteca de Autores Españolas, 1944.

Delgado, Buenaventura. *La escuela moderna de Ferrer i Guardia.* Barcelona: Ediciones CEAC, 1979.

Delibes, Miguel. *Cinco horas con Mario.* Barcelona: Ediciones Destino, 1966.

Di Febo, Giuliana. *L'altra metta della Spagna: Dalla lotta antifranchista al movimiento femminista, 1940–1977.* Napoli, Italy: Liguori, 1980.

———. *Resistencia y movimiento de mujeres en España, 1936–1976*. Barcelona: Icaria, 1979.

———. *La Santa de la Raza: Un culto barroco en la España franquista*. Barcelona: Icaria, 1987.

Di Febo, Giuliana and Marina Saba. "La condición de la mujer y el papel de la iglesia en la Italia fascista y en la España franquista: Ideologías, leyes y asociaciones femininas." In *Ordenamiento jurídico y realidad social de las mujeres, siglos XVI a XX*, ed. María Carmen García-Nieto Paris, pp. 439–452. Actas de la IV Jornadas de Investigación Interdisciplinaria. Madrid: Seminario de Estudios de la Mujer. Universidad Autónoma de Madrid, 1986.

Díaz Arnal, Isabel. "La personalidad de la asistente social." *Revista de Educación-Estudios*, 132, no. 46 (1961): 311–368.

Domínguez, Pilar, Concha Fagoaga, María Carmen García-Nieto, et al. "Interacción de pensamiento feminista e historiografía en España (1970–1986)." In *Mujeres y hombres en la formación del pensamiento occidental*, ed. Virginia Maquieira d'Angelo, pp. 367–384. Madrid: Universidad Autónoma de Madrid, 1989.

Driessen, Henk. "Male Sociability and Rituals of Masculinity in Rural Andalusia." *Anthropological Quarterly* 56, no. 2 (July 1983): 125–133.

Du Boulay, Juliet, and Rory Williams. "Amoral Familism and the Image of Limited Good: A Critique from the European Perspective." *Anthropological Quarterly* 60 (1987): 12–24.

Duch i Plana, Montserrat. "La Lliga Patriótica de Dames: Un projecte del feminisme nacional conservador." *Quaderns d'Alliberament* 6 (1981).

———. "El paper de la dona en el nacionalisme burgès." *Estudios de Historia Social* 28–29 (January–June 1984): 301–309.

Dupláa, Cristina. "La figura femenina como elemento legitimador del poder hegemónico de una cultura nacional." *Mujeres y hombres en la formación del pensamiento occidental*, ed. Virginia Maquieira d'Angelo, vol. 2, pp. 333–341. Madrid: Universidad Autónoma de Madrid, 1989.

Durán, María Angeles. *Dominación, sexo y cambio social*. Madrid: Cuadernos para el Diálogo, 1977.

Durán, María Angeles, ed. *Nuevas perspectivas sobre la mujer*. Madrid: Seminario de Estudios de la Mujer. Madrid: Universidad Autónoma de Madrid, 1982.

Duran, María Angeles and María Teresa Gallego. "The Women's Movement in Spain and the New Spanish Democracy." In *The New Women's Movement: Feminism and Political Power in Europe and the U.S.A.*, ed. Drude Dahlerup, pp. 200–216. London: Sage Publications, 1986.

Elorza, Antonio. "Feminismo y socialismo en España (1840–1868)." *Tiempos de Historia* 3 (February 1976).

"Emakumearen egoera Euskadin (Situación de la mujer en Euskadi)." Vitoria: Gobierno Vasco, Departamento de Cultura, 1982.

Enders, Victoria L. "Nationalism and Feminism: The *Sección Femenina* of the Falange." *History of European Ideas* 15, no. 4–6 (1991): 673–680.

Equipe de Philosophie Ibérique et Ibero-Americaine. *La femme dans la penseé espagnole.* Paris: C.N.R.S., 1984.

Escudero, María A. "The Image of Latin America Disseminated in Spain by the Franco Regime: Repercussions in the Configuration of a National Identity." Ph.D. dissertation, University of California, San Diego, 1994.

Espina, A. "La participación feminina en la actividad económica: El caso español." In *Familia y cambio social,* ed. Rosa Conde. Madrid: Centro de Investigaciones Sociológicas, 1982.

"Estudis sobre la dona." *Papers, Revista de Sociologia.* 13–32.

"Fábrica de tabacos de Gijón." In *Reformas sociales. Información oral y escrita publicada de 1889 a 1893*, vol. 5, pp. 472–474. Madrid: Ministerio de Trabajo y Seguridad Social, 1985.

Fagoaga, Concha. *La voz y el voto de las mujeres, 1877–1931.* Barcelona: Editorial Icaria, 1985.

Fagoaga, Concha, and Paloma Saavedra. *Clara Campoamor: La sufragista española.* 2d. ed. Madrid: Ministerio de Cultura. Instituto de la Mujer, 1986.

Fagoaga, Carmen, and Lois G. Luna. "Notas para una historia social del movimiento de las mujeres: Signos reformistas y signos radicales." In *Ordenamiento jurídico y realidad social de las mujeres: Siglos XVI a XX*, ed. María Carmen García-Nieto Paris, 453–460. Madrid: Universidad Autónoma de Madrid. Seminario de Estudios de la Mujer, 1986.

Falange E.T. y de las J.O.N.S., Delegación Nacional de la Sección Femenina. *Derechos políticos, profesionales, y de trabajo de la mujer.* 4th ed. Madrid, 1971.

———. *La Sección Femenina: Historia y organización.* Madrid, 1952.

Falcón, Lidia. *La razón feminista.* Vol. 1, *La mujer como clase social y económica: El modo de producción doméstico.* Barcelona: Editorial Fontanella, 1981.

———. *La razón feminista.* vol. 2, *La reproducción humana.* Barcelona: Editorial Fontanella, 1982.

———. *Mujer y sociedad: Análisis de un fenómeno reaccionario.* 3d. ed. Barcelona: Editorial Fontanella, 1984.

Folguera Crespo, Pilar. "City Space and the Daily Life of Women in Madrid in the 1920s," *Oral History* 13, no. 2 (1985).

———. "Notas para el estudio de la historia social de la mujer en España." In *Nuevas perspectivas sobre la mujer*, ed. María Angeles Duran, vol. 1, pp. 47–60. Madrid: Seminario de Estudios de la Mujer, Universidad Autónoma de Madrid, 1982.

———. "Política natalista y control de natalidad en España durante la década de los veinte: El caso de Madrid." In *Ordenamiento jurídico y realidad social de las mujeres: Siglos XVI a XX*, ed. María Carmen García-Nieto Paris, pp. 337–352. Actas de Las Cuartas Jornadas de Investigación Interdisciplinaria. Madrid: Seminario de Estudios de la Mujer, Universidad Autónoma de Madrid, 1986.

Folguera Crespo, Pilar, ed. *Otras visiones de España.* Madrid: Editorial P. Iglesias, 1993.

Franco Rubió, Gloria Angeles. *La incorporación de la mujer a la administración del estado, municipios y diputaciones 1918–1936.* Madrid: Dirección General de Juventud y Promoción Socio-Cultural, 1981.

Freeman, Susan Tax. "Religious Aspects of the Social Organization of a Castillian Village." *American Anthropologist* 70 (1968): 34–49.

Gallego Méndez, María Teresa. *Mujer, falange, franquismo.* Madrid: Taurus, 1983.

———. "Notas sobre el poder, la socialización politíca y la mujer (Sección Femenina de Falange)." In *Nuevas perspectivas sobre la mujer*, ed. María Angeles Durán, pp. 42–49. Madrid: Universidad Autónoma de Madrid, 1982.

García-Crespo, Clementina. *Léxico e ideología en los libros de lectura de la escuela primaria (1940–1975).* Salamanca: Ediciones Universidad de Salamanca, 1983.

García de León, María Antonia. *Las elites femeninas españolas: Una investigación sociológica.* Madrid: Queimada Ediciones, 1982.

García Ferrando, Manuel. *Mujer y sociedad rural: Un análisis sociológico sobre trabajo e ideología.* Madrid: Cuadernos para el Diálogo, 1982.

García Jordan, Pilar. "Voto femenino: Repercusiones de su concesión y canalización del mismo por los sectores conservadores catalanes, 1931–1936." In *Ordenamiento jurídico y realidad social de las mujeres: Siglos XVI a XX*, ed. María Carmen García-Nieto Paris, vol. 4, pp. 391-403. Madrid: Seminario de Estudios de la Mujer. Universidad Autónoma de Madrid, 1986.

García Méndez, Esperanza. *La actuación de la mujer en las Cortes de la Segunda República.* Madrid: Ruan, 1979.

García Nieto, María Carmen. "Movimientos sociales y nuevos espacios para las mujeres, 1931–1939." *Bulletin du Départment de Recherches Hispaniques* 29 (June 1984).

Garcia-Nieto Paris, María Carmen, ed. *Ordenamiento jurídico y realidad social de las mujeres, siglos XVI a XX.* Actas de Las IV Jornadas de Investigación Interdisciplinaria. Madrid: Seminario de Estudios de la Mujer, Universidad Autónoma de Madrid, 1986.

García Nieto, María Carmen, and Esperanza Yllán. "La educación de la mujer." *Historia de España (1808–1978).* Barcelona: Crítica, 1989.

Garrido, Luis J. *Las dos biografías de la mujer en España.* Madrid: Ministerio de Asuntos Sociales, Instituto de la Mujer, 1993.

Gilmore, David D. "Men and Women in Southern Spain: Domestic Power Revisited." *American Anthropologist* 92, no. 4 (December 1990): 953–970.

———. "Mother-Son Intimacy and the Dual View of Woman in Andalusia: Analysis Through Oral Poetry," *Ethos* 14 (1986).

Gilmore, Margaret M., and David D. Gilmore. "Machismo: A Psychodynamic Approach (Spain)." *The Journal of Psychological Anthropology* 2, no. 3 (Summer 1979): 281–299.

Golden, Lester. "Les dones com avantguarda: El rebombori del pà del gener de 1918." *L'Avenç* 45 (1981).

González Castillejo, María José. "Literatura religiosa y mentalidad femenina: El discurso de la sumisión en la Segunda República." In *Mujeres y hombres en la formación del pensamiento occidental*, ed. Virginia Maquieira d'Angelo, vol. 2, pp. 343–351. Madrid: Universidad Autónoma de Madrid, 1989.

———. *La nueva historia: Mujer, vida cotidiana y esfera pública en Málaga, 1931–1939.* Málaga, Spain: Universidad de Málaga, 1991.

González Fernández, Angeles. "Condiciones de trabajo y conflictividad laboral de la mujer trabajadora en Sevilla, 1900–1917." *Historia Social* 13 (Spring–Summer, 1993): 39–51.

González, Anabel. *El feminismo en España hoy.* Madrid: ZYX, 1979.

Graham, Helen, and Jo Labanyi, eds. *Spanish Cultural Studies: An Introduction.* Oxford: Oxford University Press, 1995.

Harding, Susan. "Women and Words in a Spanish Village," *American Ethnologist* 13 (1986).

Huston, Nancy. "Tales of War and Tears of Women." *Women's Studies International Forum* 5 (1982).

Instituto de la Mujer. *La mujer en España: Situación social.* Madrid: Ministerio de Asuntos Sociales, 1990.

Instituto de la Mujer. *Las mujeres y la guerra civil española.* III *Jornadas de estudios monográficos.* Instituto de la Mujer. Ministerio de Asuntos Sociales. Salamanca, October 1989. Madrid: Ministerio de Cultura. Dirección de los Archivos Estatales, 1991.

Jarne i Mòdol, Antonieta. *La Secció Femenina a Lleida. Els anys triomfals.* Lleida, Spain: Pagès editores, 1991.

Jiménez, Encarnación. "La mujer en el franquismo. Doctrina y acción de la Sección Femenina." *Tiempo de Historia* 83 (October 1981): 4–15.

Kaplan, Temma. "Female Consciousness and Collective Action: The Case of Barcelona." *Signs* 7 (1982): 545–566.

———. "Other Scenarios: Women and Spanish Anarchism." *In Becoming Visible: Women in European History*, ed. Claudia Koonz and Renate Bridenthal. New York: Houghton Mifflin, 1977.

———. "Politics and Culture in Women's History." *Feminist Studies*, no. 6 (Spring 1980).

———. *Red City, Blue Period: Social Movements in Picasso's Barcelona.* Berkeley, CA: University of California Press, 1992.

———. "Spanish Anarchism and Women's Liberation." *Journal of Contemporary History* 6, no. 2 (1971): 101–110.

———. "Women and Communal Strikes in the Crisis of 1917–1922." *Becoming Visible: Women in European History*, ed. Renate Bridenthal, Claudia Koonz, and Susan Stuard, 2d ed. Boston: Houghton Mifflin, 1987.

Keene, Judith. *The Last Mile to Huesca: An Australian Nurse in the Spanish Civil War.* Kensington, NSW: New South Wales University Press, 1988.

Kelley, Heidi. "The Invention of Motherhood: Family and Regional Histories in Galicia." Paper presented at the annual meeting of the American Anthropological Association, San Francisco, 1992.

———. "The Myth of Matriarchy: Symbols of Womanhood in Galician Regional Identity," *Anthropological Quarterly* 67 (1994).

———. "Unwed Mothers and Household Reputation in a Spanish Galician Community." *American Ethnologist* 18 (1991): 565–580.

Kern, Robert W. "Anarchist Principles and Spanish Reality: Emma Goldman as a Participant in the Civil War 1936–39." *Journal of Contemporary History* 11 (July 1976): 237–259.

Kirkpatrick, Susan. *"Las Románticas": Women Writers and Subjectivity in Spain: 1835-1830*. Berkeley, CA: University of California Press, 1989.

La femme dans la pensée espagnole: Ouvrage collectif. Paris: Editions du CNRS, 1984.

Lannon, Frances. "Women and Images of Women in the Spanish Civil War," *Proceedings of The Royal Historical Society*, pp. 213–228. London: The Royal Historical Society, 1991.

Lisón Tolosano, Carmelo. *Antropología cultural de Galicia*. Madrid: Akal Editor, 1979.

López-Cordón, María Victoria. "La historia inacabada." In *Mujeres y hombres en la formación del pensamiento occidental*, ed. Virginia Maquieira d'Angelo, vol. 2, pp. 103–114. Madrid: Universidad Autónoma de Madrid, 1989.

Luna, Joana. "L'esport. ¿Un miratge de l'alliberament? El club femení i d'esports, 1928–1936." *L'Avenç*, no. 112 (February 1988): 26–29.

Macià i Encarnación, Elisenda. "L'Institut de Cultura: Un model de promoció cultura per la dona catalana." *L'Avenç* 112 (February 1988): 18–21.

Maddox, Richard. *El Castillo: The Politics of Tradition in an Andalusian Town*. Chicago, IL: University of Illinois Press, 1993.

Mangini, Shirley. "Memories of Resistance: Women Activists from the Spanish Civil War." *Signs* 17 (1991): 171–187.

———. *Memories of Resistance: Women's Voices from the Spanish Civil War*. New Haven, CT: Yale University Press, 1995.

Manteiga, Roberto C., Carolyn Galerstein, and Kathleen McNerney, eds. *Feminine Concerns in Contemporary Spanish Fiction by Women*. Potomac, MD: Scripta Humanistica, 1988.

Maquieira d'Angelo, Virginia. "Antropología y movimiento de reforma sexual en las primeras décadas de siglo XX: Una redefinición de la ideología patriarcal." In *Mujeres y hombres en la formación del pensamiento occidental*, ed. Virginia Maquieira d'Angelo, vol. 2, pp. 89–99. Madrid: Universidad Autónoma de Madrid, 1989.

Martín Gaite, Carmen. *Usos amorosos de la postguerra española*. Barcelona: Editorial Anagrama, 1987.

Masur, Jenny. "Women's Work in Rural Andalusia," *Ethnology* 23 (1984).

Mayordomo Pérez, Alejandro. *Nacional-catolicismo y educación en la España de la posguerra*. Madrid: Ministerio de Educación y Ciencia. Secretaría General Técnica, 1990.

Miller, Beth. *Women in Hispanic Literature: Icons and Fallen Idols*. Berkeley, CA: University of California Press, 1983.

Ministerio de Trabajo y Seguridad Social. "Industrias explotados por el estado: Fábricas de tabacos." In *Reformas sociales: Información oral y escrita publicada de 1889 a 1893*, vol. 2, pp. 33–38. Madrid: Ministerio de Trabajo y Seguridad Social, 1985.

———. "Trabajo de las mujeres." In *Reformas sociales. Informacíon oral y escrita publicado de 1889 a 1893*, vol. 2, pp. 149–172. Madrid: Ministerio de Trabajo y Seguridad Social, 1985.

Miret Magdalena, Enrique. "La educación religiosa-moral en el franquismo." *Cuadernos de Pedagogía*. Supplement no. 63, no. 31–32 (July 1977): 4–6.

Molero Pintado, Antonio. *La reforma educativa en la Segunda República española*. Madrid: Aula XXI. Educación Abierta/Santillana, 1990.

Morange, Claude. "De 'Manola' a 'obrera' (la revuelta de las cigarreras de Madrid en 1830: Notas sobre un conflicto de trabajo." *Estudios de Historia Social* 12–13 (January–June 1980): 307–321.

Morcillo Gómez, Aurora. "Por la senda del franquismo." *Historia* 16 (May 1988): 86–90.

Moreno, Amparo. *Mujeres en lucha: El movimiento femenista en España*. Barcelona: Editorial Anagrama, 1977.

Moreno Felíu, Paz Sofia. "Mujer," in *Gran enciclopedia gallega*. Santiago, Spain: Silverio Cañada, 1974.

Mullaney, Marie Marmo. "Dolores Ibárruri, La Pasionaria, the Female Revolutionary as Symbol." In M. M. Mullaney, *Revolutionary Women: Gender and the Socialist Revolutionary Party*, pp. 191–242. New York: Praeger, 1983.

Nash, Mary. "Aproximación al movimiento eugénico español: El primer curso eúgenico y la aportación del Dr. Sebastián Recasens." *Gimbernat: Revista Catalana d'historia de la medicina i de la ciencia*, 4 (1985): 195–202.

———. *Defying Male Civilization: Women in the Spanish Civil War*. Denver, CO: Arden Press, 1995.

———. "Desde la invisibilidad a la presencia de la mujer en la historia: Corrientes historiográficas y marcos conceptuales de la nueva historia de la mujer." In *Nuevas perspectivas sobre la mujer*, ed. María Angeles Durán, vol. 1, pp. 18–37. Madrid: Seminario de Estudios de la Mujer. Universidad Autónoma de Madrid, 1982.

———. "La dona moderna del segle XX: La "Nova Dona" a Catalunya." *L'Avenç* 112 (February 1988): 7–11.

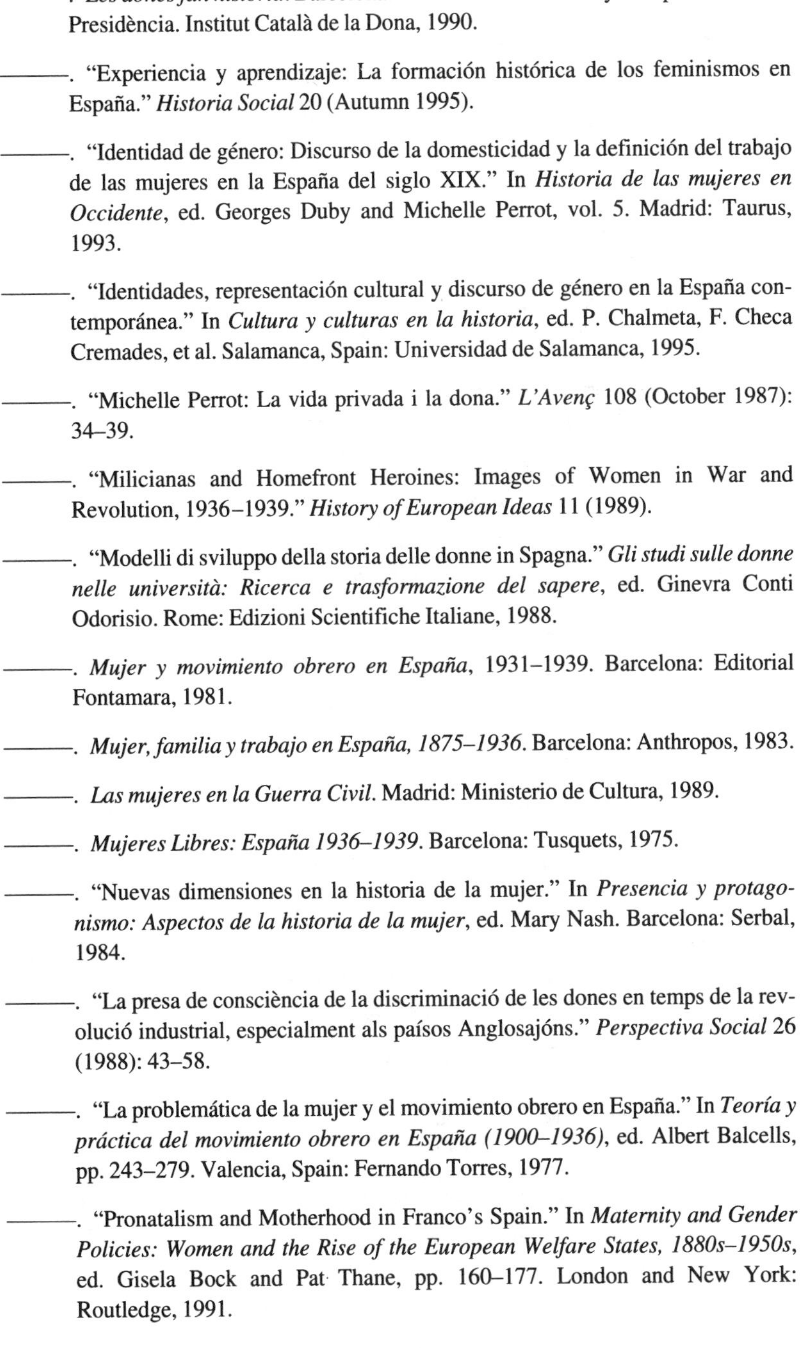

———. *Les dones fan història.* Barcelona: Generalitat de Catalunya. Department de la Presidència. Institut Català de la Dona, 1990.

———. "Experiencia y aprendizaje: La formación histórica de los feminismos en España." *Historia Social* 20 (Autumn 1995).

———. "Identidad de género: Discurso de la domesticidad y la definición del trabajo de las mujeres en la España del siglo XIX." In *Historia de las mujeres en Occidente*, ed. Georges Duby and Michelle Perrot, vol. 5. Madrid: Taurus, 1993.

———. "Identidades, representación cultural y discurso de género en la España contemporánea." In *Cultura y culturas en la historia*, ed. P. Chalmeta, F. Checa Cremades, et al. Salamanca, Spain: Universidad de Salamanca, 1995.

———. "Michelle Perrot: La vida privada i la dona." *L'Avenç* 108 (October 1987): 34–39.

———. "Milicianas and Homefront Heroines: Images of Women in War and Revolution, 1936–1939." *History of European Ideas* 11 (1989).

———. "Modelli di sviluppo della storia delle donne in Spagna." *Gli studi sulle donne nelle università: Ricerca e trasformazione del sapere*, ed. Ginevra Conti Odorisio. Rome: Edizioni Scientifiche Italiane, 1988.

———. *Mujer y movimiento obrero en España*, 1931–1939. Barcelona: Editorial Fontamara, 1981.

———. *Mujer, familia y trabajo en España, 1875–1936.* Barcelona: Anthropos, 1983.

———. *Las mujeres en la Guerra Civil.* Madrid: Ministerio de Cultura, 1989.

———. *Mujeres Libres: España 1936–1939.* Barcelona: Tusquets, 1975.

———. "Nuevas dimensiones en la historia de la mujer." In *Presencia y protagonismo: Aspectos de la historia de la mujer*, ed. Mary Nash. Barcelona: Serbal, 1984.

———. "La presa de consciència de la discriminació de les dones en temps de la revolució industrial, especialment als països Anglosajóns." *Perspectiva Social* 26 (1988): 43–58.

———. "La problemática de la mujer y el movimiento obrero en España." In *Teoría y práctica del movimiento obrero en España (1900–1936)*, ed. Albert Balcells, pp. 243–279. Valencia, Spain: Fernando Torres, 1977.

———. "Pronatalism and Motherhood in Franco's Spain." In *Maternity and Gender Policies: Women and the Rise of the European Welfare States, 1880s–1950s*, ed. Gisela Bock and Pat Thane, pp. 160–177. London and New York: Routledge, 1991.

———. Social Eugenics and Nationalist Race Hygiene in Early Twentieth Century Spain." *History of European Ideas* 15, no. 4–6 (1992).

———. "La trajectòria del moviment feminista des de finals del segle XX fins al període de les dues guerres mundials." *Perspectiva Social* 26 (1988): 43–58.

———. "Women in War: Milicianas and Armed Combat in Revolutionary Spain, 1936–1939." *International History Review* 15, no. 2 (1993): 269–.

———. ed. *Més enllà del silenci: Les dones a la història de Catalunya*. Barcelona: Generalitat de Catalunya, 1988.

———. ed. *Presencia y protagonismo: Aspectos de la historia de la mujer*. Barcelona: Serbal, 1984.

Nash, Mary, Montserrat Carbonell, and Milagros Rivera. "La storia delle donne in Spagna." *Quaderni Storici* 63, no. 3 (December 1986): 995–1008.

Nash, Mary, and Susana Tavera. *Experiencias desiguales: Conflictos sociales y respuestas colectivas (Siglo XIX)*. Madrid: Síntesis, 1994.

Navarro García, Clotilde. *La educación y el nacional-catolicismo*. Cuenca, Spain: Universidad de Castilla la Mancha, 1993.

Navarro Sandalinas, Ramón. *La enseñanza primaria durante el franquismo (1936–1975)*. Barcelona: P.P.U., 1990.

Nelken, Margarita. *La condición social de la mujer en España*. Madrid, C.V.S. Ediciones, 1975.

———. *La mujer ante las Cortes Constituyentes*. Madrid: Editorial Castro, 1931.

Nichols, Geraldine Cleary. *Des/cifrar la diferencia: Narrativa feminina de la España contemporánea*. Madrid: Siglo Veintiuno, 1992.

Núñez Orgaz, Adela. "El Instituto de Reformas Sociales en el debate sobre la función social de la mujer (1904–1924)." In *Mujeres y hombres en la formación del pensamiento occidental*, ed. Virginia Maquieira d'Angelo, pp. 321–332. Madrid: Universidad Autónoma de Madrid, 1989.

Núñez Pérez, María Gloria. "Margarita Nelken: Una apuesta entre la continuidad y el cambio." In *Las mujeres en la guerra civil española*. Instituto de la Mujer. Jornadas de Estudios Monográficos. Salamanca, October 1989. Madrid: Ministerio de Cultura. Dirección de los Archivos Estatales, 1991.

———. *Trabajadoras en la Segunda República: Un estudio sobre la actividad económica estradoméstica (1931–1936)*. Madrid: Ministerio de Trabajo, 1989.

Ollero Tassara, Andrés. *Universidad y política: Tradición y secularización en el siglo XIX español*. Madrid: Instituto de Estudios Políticos, 1972.

Ordónez, Elizabeth. *Voices of Their Own: Contemporary Spanish Narrative by Women.* Lewisburg, PA: Bucknell University Press, 1991.

Ortega, Margarita. “Casa o convento. La educación de la mujer en las edades moderna y contemporánea.” *Historia 16* 145, no. 13 (May 1988): 41–48.

Ortiz Corulla, Carmen. *La participación de las mujeres en la democracia (1979–1986).* Madrid: Instituto de la Mujer, 1987.

Ortiz Osés, Andrés. *El matriarcalismo vasco.* Bilbao, Spain: Universidad de Deusto, 1980.

Ossorio y Gallardo, Angel. “Crónica de tribunales.” In *Revista de los tribunales y legislación universal* 30, (February 8, 1896), vol. 3.

Palacio, Sara. “El punto de vista de la S. F.: La historia nos ha traicionado. Entrevista con Lula de Lara.” *Tiempo de Historia* 7, no. 83 (October 1981): 16–23.

Pasamar Alzuria, Gonzalo. *Historiografía e ideología en la posguerra española: La ruptura de la tradición liberal.* Zaragoza, Spain: Universidad de Zaragoza, 1991.

Pastor, María Inmaculada. *La educación femenina en la posguerra (1939–1945): El caso de Mallorca.* Madrid: Ministerio de Cultura. Instituto de la Mujer, 1984.

Peñalver, Carmen. “Les dones i les associaciones populars: Una prèsencia invisible.” *L'Avenç* 112 (February 1988): 22–25.

Pérez, Janet W., ed. *Contemporary Women Writers of Spain.* Boston: Twayne Publishers, 1988.

Pérez Serrano, Julio. “La mujer y la imagen de la mujer en la resistencia antifascista española: El Mono Azul (1936–1939).” In *Mujeres y hombres en la formación del pensamiento occidental,* ed. Virginia Maquieira d'Angelo, vol. 2, pp. 353–365. Madrid: Universidad Autónoma de Madrid, 1989.

Pérez-Villanueva Tovar, I. *María de Maetzu: Una mujer en el reformismo educativo español.* Madrid: UNED, 1989.

Perinat, Adolfo, and María Isabel Marrades. *Mujer, prensa y sociedad en España 1800–1939.* Madrid: Centro de Investigaciones Sociológicas, 1980.

Peristiany, Jean G. *Honor and Shame: The Values of Mediterranean Society.* London: Weidenfeld and Nicolson, 1965.

Perrot, Michelle. “La mujer en el discurso europeo del siglo XIX.” In *Mujeres y hombres en la formación del pensamiento occidental,* ed. Virginia Maquieira D'Angelo, Guadalupe Gomez-Ferrer Morant, and Margarita Ortega Lopez, pp. 115–127. Madrid: Instituto de Estudios de la Mujer. Universidad Autónoma de Madrid, 1989.

Pitt-Rivers, Julian, *The Fate of Schechem, or the Politics of Sex: Essays in the Anthropology of the Mediterranean.* Cambridge: Cambridge University Press, 1977.

Porter, David. "The Role of Women in the Spanish Revolution." In *Vision on Fire: Emma Goldman on the Spanish Revolution*, ed. David Porter, 248–260. New York: Commonground Press, 1983.

Posa, Elena. "Una dona portadora de valors eterns: La Sección Femenina 1934–1952." *Taula de Canvi* B, no. 5 (May–June 1977): 121–133.

———. "Una educación especialmente femenina." Supplement no. 6 *Mujer y Educación.* Part I. La inculcación (de como nos han deformado), vol. 3, no. 31–32. *Cuadernos de Pedagogía* (July 1977): 31–34.

Primo de Rivera, Pilar. *Discursos, circulares, escritos*. Madrid, nd.

Radcliff, Pamela Beth. *From Mobilization to Civil War: The Politics of Polarization in the Spanish City of Gijón, 1900–1937.* (Cambridge: Cambridge University Press, 1996).

———. "Elite Women Workers and Collective Action: The Cigarette Makers of Gijón." *Journal of Social History* 27 (Fall 1993): 85–108.

Ramos, María Dolores. "Belén Sárraga y la pervivencia de la idea federal en Málaga, 1889–1933." *Jábega* 53 (1986): 63–70.

———. *Mujeres e historia. Reflexiones sobre las experiencias vividas en los espacios públicos y privados.* Málaga, Spain: Universidad de Málaga, 1993.

———. "Realidad social y conciencia de la realidad en la mujer: Obreras malagueñas frente a la crisis de subsistencias (1918)." In *Ordenamiento jurídico y realidad social de las mujeres*, ed. María Carmen García Nieto. Madrid: Seminario de Estudios de la Mujer, 1986.

Remón Pérez, María Luisa. "Trabajo doméstico e ideología patriarcal: Una constante histórico." In *Nuevas perspectivas sobre la mujer*, ed. María Angeles Durán, vol. 2, pp. 201–212. Madrid: Seminario de Estudios de la Mujer. Universidad Autónoma de Madrid, 1982.

Riding, Alan. "In Spain, 'Women to the Fore!' at Last!" *The New York Times*, May 30, 1989.

Rodrigo, A. María Lejárraga. *Una mujer en la sombra*. Barcelona: Círculo de Lectores, 1992.

Roig Castellanos, Mercedes. *La mujer y la prensa: Desde el siglo XVII a nuestros días.* Madrid: Tordesillas, 1977.

Sainz Jackson, Rosario. "Los derechos de la mujer 1968." In *Temas españoles*, Madrid: Publicaciones Españolas, 1968.

Sanchez i Ferré, Pere. "Els origins del feminisme a Catalunya, 1870–1920." *Revista de Catalunya* 45 (October 1990).

Sánchez López, Rosario. *Mujer española, una sombra de destino en lo universal: Trayectoria histórica de Sección Femenina de Falange (1934–1977)*. Murcia, Spain: Universidad de Murcia, 1990.

Sánchez, Cristina, Celia Amorós, Concepción Fernández, Teresa Rodríguez de Lecea, and Maria Jesús Vara, eds. *Mujeres y hombres en la formación del pensamiento occidental*, vol. 1. Actas de Las VII Jornadas de Investigación Interdisciplinaria. Madrid: Universidad Autónoma de Madrid, 1989.

Scanlon, Geraldine M. "La mujer bajo el franquismo." *Tiempo de Historia* 27, no. 3 (February 1977): 4–28.

———. "La mujer y la instrucción pública: De la ley moyano a la Segunda República." *Historia de la Educación* 6 (1987): 193–208.

Seidman, Michael. "Women's Subversive Individualism in Barcelona in the 1930s." *International Review of History* 37 (1992): 161–176.

Serrano, Carlos. *La tour du peuple. Crise nationale, mouvements populaires et populisme en Espagne, 1890–1910*. Madrid: Casa de Velázquez, 1987.

Shubert, Adrian. *A Social History of Modern Spain*. London: Unwin Hyman, 1990.

Sopeña Monsalve, Andrés. *El florido pensil. Memoria de la escuela nacionalcatólica*. Barcelona: Ed. Crítica, 1994.

Strong, Anna Louise. *Spain in Arms*. New York: H. Holt & Co., 1937.

Suárez Fernández, Luis. *Crónica de la Sección Femenina y su tiempo*. Madrid: Asociación Nueva Andadura, 1993.

Threlfall, Mónica. "La ideología politíca de la mujer en España: Notas para una futura investigación." In *Nuevas perspectivas sobre la mujer*, ed. María Angeles Durán, vol. 2, pp. 23–35. Madrid: Seminario de Estudios de la Mujer. Universidad Autónoma de Madrid, 1982.

———. "The Women's Movement in Spain." *New Left Review* 151 (May–June 1985): 44–73.

———. "Women and Political Participation." *Spain: Conditional Democracy*, ed. Christopher Abel and Nissa Torrents, pp. 136–160. London: Croom Helm, 1984.

Tuñón, Amparo. "Carmen Alcalde: Ser mujer en España. (Entrevista recogida por Amparo Tuñón)." Part I. La inculcación (de como nos han deformado),

Supplement no. 6, vol. 3, no. 31–32. *Cuadernos de Pedagogía.* (July 1977): 23–25.

Ugarte, Michael. "The Generational Fallacy and Spanish Women Writing in Madrid at the Turn of the Century." *Siglo WW/Twentieth Century* 12 (1994).

Uhl, Sarah. "Forbidden Friends: Cultural Veils of Female Friendship in Andalusia." *American Ethnologist* 18 (1991).

———. "Making the Bed: Creating the Home in Escalona, Andalusia," *Ethnology* 28 (1989).

———. "Special Friends: The Organization of Intersex Friendship in Escalona (Andalusia), Spain." *Anthropology* 9 (1985).

Ullman, Joan Connelly. "La enseñanza superior de la mujer en España: Relaciones entre universitarias españolas y estadounidenses (1877–1980)." In *Nuevas perspectivas sobre la mujer*, ed. María Angeles Durán, vol. 1. Madrid: Seminario de Estudios de la Mujer. Universidad Autónoma de Madrid, 1982.

———. "La protagonista ausente: La mujer como objeto y sujeto de la historia de España." In *La mujer en el mundo contemporáneo*, ed. Maria Angeles Durán. Madrid: Universidad Autónoma de Madrid, 1981.

Unión Interparlamentaria Grupo Español. *Las mujeres y el poder político: Encuesta realizada en los 150 parlamentos nacionales existentes al 31 de Octubre de 1991.* Madrid: Unión Parlamentaria Grupo Español, 1992.

Valle, Teresa del. *Mujer vasca: Imagen y realidad.* Barcelona: Anthropos, 1985.

Vallejo Fernández Cela, Sergio. "Las cigarreras de la fábrica nacional de tabacos de Madrid." In *Madrid en la sociedad del siglo XIX*, vol. 2, pp. 136–149. Madrid: Alfoz, 1986.

Vilar, Pierre, ed. *La familia en la España Mediterránea: Siglos XV–XIX.* Barcelona: Editorial Crítica, 1987.

Vincent, Mary. "The Politicization of Catholic Women in Salamanca." *Elites and Power in Twentieth-century Spain: Essays in Honor of Raymond Carr*, ed. Frances Lannon and Paul Preston, pp. 107–126. Oxford: Clarendon Press, 1990.

Werner, Carmen. "Pequeñas reglas de convivencia social: Tratado de educación para las alumnas de la escuela de mandos de la Sección Femenina." Madrid: Delegación Nacional de la Sección Femenina de F.E.T. y de las J.O.N.S., 1941.

Zulueta, Carmen de. *Misioneras, feministas, educadoras.* Madrid: Editorial Castalia, 1984.

Contributors

Gerard Alexander is Assistant Professor of Government and Foreign Affairs at the University of Virginia. He has published on the role of the state in modern Britain, and is at work on his forthcoming book, *Rational Choices and Regime Change: The Consolidation of Democracy in Twentieth-Century Europe.*

Rosa María Capel Martínez is Profesora Titular de Historia Moderna at the Universidad Complutense of Madrid, Spain. A pioneer in Spanish women's history, two of her landmark books are *El trabajo y la educación de la mujer en España (1900–1936)* 2d ed. (Madrid: Ministerio de Cultura, 1986), and *El sufragio femenino en la Segunda República española* (Granada, Spain: Publicaciones de la Universidad de Granada, 1975. Rev. ed., Madrid, Horas y Horas, 1992). She continues to focus on the subject of women and work in the twentieth century.

Victoria Lorée Enders is Associate Professor of History at Northern Arizona University in Flagstaff, where she teaches in the Women's Studies Program and the New Century Honors Program. She has published on Spanish women's history, and on comparative historiography. She is currently working on an intellectual/political comparison of several women's lives in modern Spain.

María A. Escudero is Visiting Lecturer in the History Department at Royal Holloway College, University of London. She finished her Ph.D. dissertation, "The Image of Latin America Disseminated in Spain by the Franco Regime: Repercussions in the Configuration of a National Identity," at the University of California, San Diego in 1994. Her book, *El Instituto de Cultura Hispánica,* also appeared in 1994 (Madrid, Ed. Maphre). She is currently working on the analysis of children's books published in Spain to commemorate the Quincentenial of the discovery of America.

Temma Kaplan is Professor of History and Chair of the Women's Studies Program at the State University of New York at Stony Brook. Author of *Anarchists of Andalusia, 1868–1903* (Princeton University Press, 1977), *Red City, Blue Period: Social Movements in Picasso's Barcelona* (University of California Press, 1992, 1993), and *Crazy for Democracy: Women in Grassroots Movements* (Routledge, 1997), she is now finishing a study, tentatively called *Making Spectacles of Themselves: Women's Struggles for Human Rights.*

Judith Keene is Senior Lecturer in the Department of History at the University of Sydney where she teaches late modern European history and film. She completed graduate studies at the University of California at San Diego with a thesis entitled "A Very Royal Upbringing: A Study of the Influences on the Development and Education of Isabella II of Spain from 1830 to 1847." Subsequently she has published on the Spanish Republic and the Civil War, including *Last Mile to Huesca: An Australian Nurse in the Spanish Civil War* (Sydney: University of New South Wales Press, 1988) and on aspects of European film and history. Currently she is writing a book on the foreign volunteers who served with Franco during the Spanish Civil War.

Heidi Kelley is Associate Professor of Anthropology and Director of International Programs at the University of North Carolina at Asheville. She has carried out ethnographic research in Galicia since 1985 and has published and presented papers on topics including motherhood, illegitimacy, marriage, and regional identity in Galicia. She is working on a manuscript about women's lives in Ezaro, and has also begun another project which involves a dialogue between North American and Galician anthropologists studying Galician women.

Aurora Morcillo Gómez is Visiting Assistant Professor at the University of New Mexico. Her book *Gender Ideology in Modern Spain: The Education of Catholic Women under Franco*, is forthcoming from Northern Illinois University Press. She is presently working on a study of political cartoons in the Spanish press in 1898 about the Spanish American War.

Mary Nash is Professor in Contemporary History at the University of Barcelona. She is Founder President of the Spanish Association for Research in Women's History and codirector of the women's history journal *Arenal.* She has published extensively on women in contemporary Spain. Her more recent books include *Mes enllá del silenci: Les dones a la història de Catalunya* (Barcelona, 1988), *Experiencias desiguales: Conflictos sociales y respuestas colectivas* (Madrid, 1994), and *Defying Male Civilization: Women in the Spanish Civil War* (Denver, CO, 1995). Her forthcoming book is on identity politics, race and motherhood in contemporary Spain.

D.J. O'Connor is a professor of Spanish at the University of New Orleans. Her book, *Crime at El Escorial, Crime at El Escorial: The 1892 Child Murder, The Press and The Jury* appeared in 1995. She is preparing a monograph, *Representations of Race in the Spanish Press, Popular Fiction, and the Theatre, 1887–1898.*

Clotilde Puertolas is an independent scholar. She completed her Ph.D. dissertation, "A Festival in Change: A Case Study of the *Fiesta de San Fermín*: 1930–1978," at the University of California at San Diego in 1989. Currently, she is the Program Director of the Child Assault Prevention Project for the Maryland Center for Assault Prevention, and does consulting for the Library of Congress. She is a mixed media artist who has exhibited in the Washington, DC area.

Pamela Beth Radcliff is Associate Professor of History at the University of California at San Diego. She has published articles on female cigarette makers and on republicanism in Spain. Her book entitled *From Mobilization to Civil War: The Politics of Polarization in the Spanish City of Gijón, 1900–1937* (Cambridge,

1996) was awarded the Sierra Book Prize for 1997 by the Western Association of Women Historians. She is currently doing research on women's roles during the democratic transition of the 1970s.

Timothy Rees is Lecturer in History at the University of Exeter. His Ph.D. dissertation at Oxford University entitled "Agrarian Society and Politics in the Province of Badajoz under the Spanish Second Republic" will be published in 1998. He is also the author of *Franco's Spain*, and the editor of *International Communism and the Communist International, 1919–1943* and *Rethinking Revolution in Twentieth Century Europe*. He is currently working on an agrarian history of Spain.

John Lawrence Tone is Associate Professor of history at the Georgia Institute of Technology. He is the author of *The Fatal Knot: The Guerrilla War in Navarre and the Defeat of Napoleon in Spain* (Chapel Hill, 1995). An expanded and revised edition of the book will be published in Castilian by Alianza Editorial in 1998. His current project is a book titled *The Splendid Disaster: Spain's War in Cuba, 1895–1898.*

Sarah L. White chairs the Institute for Education and Social Justice, a nonprofit organization that facilitates multicultural curriculum development seminars for undergraduate faculty in the U.S. and Mexico. She is the editor of *Development TeachNet*, a global education quarterly, and is currently completing her dissertation in the Columbia University Department of History *(Liberty, Order and the "Gloriosa": Languages of Protest and the Politics of Interest in Revolutionary Spain).*

Index